A HISTORY
OF
PHILOSOPHY

A HISTORY
OF
PHILOSOPHY

VOLUME II

Medieval Philosophy

Frederick Copleston, S.J.

IMAGE BOOKS

DOUBLEDAY

New York   London   Toronto   Sydney   Auckland

AN IMAGE BOOK
PUBLISHED BY DOUBLEDAY
a division of Bantam Doubleday Dell Publishing Group, Inc.
1540 Broadway, New York, New York 10036

IMAGE, DOUBLEDAY, and the portrayal of a deer drinking from
a stream are trademarks of Doubleday, a division of Bantam
Doubleday Dell Publishing Group, Inc.

First Image Books edition of Volume II of *A History of Philosophy* published 1962
by special arrangement with The Newman Press.

This Image edition published April 1993

De Licentia Superiorum Ordinis: Martinus D'Arcy, S.J., Praep. Prov. Angliae

Nihil Obstat: T. Corbishley, S.J. Censor Deputatus

Imprimatur: Joseph, Archiepiscopus Birmingamiensis Die 24 Aprilis 1948

Library of Congress Cataloging-in-Publication Data

Copleston, Frederick Charles.
A history of philosophy / Frederick Copleston.
p. cm.
Includes bibliographical references and indexes.
Contents: v. 1. Greece and Rome—v. 2. Augustine to Scotus—v.
3. Middle Ages and early Renaissance.
1. Philosophy, Ancient. 2. Philosophy, Medieval. 3. Philosophy,
Renaissance. I. Title.
B72.C62   1993
190—dc20   92-34997
CIP

Volume II copyright 1950 by Frederick Copleston

ISBN 0-385-46844-X

3   5   7   9   8   6   4

CONTENTS

CONTENTS

PART II

THE CAROLINGIAN RENAISSANCE

PART III

THE TENTH, ELEVENTH AND TWELFTH CENTURIES

CONTENTS

PART IV

ISLAMIC AND JEWISH PHILOSOPHY TRANSLATIONS

PART V

THE THIRTEENTH CENTURY

CONTENTS

CONTENTS

CONTENTS

MEDIAEVAL PHILOSOPHY

CHAPTER I

INTRODUCTION

1. IN this second volume of my history of philosophy I had originally hoped to give an account of the development of philosophy throughout the whole period of the Middle Ages, understanding by mediaeval philosophy the philosophic thought and systems which were elaborated between the Carolingian renaissance in the last part of the eighth century A.D. (John Scotus Eriugena, the first outstanding mediaeval philosopher was born about 810) and the end of the fourteenth century. Reflection has convinced me, however, of the advisability of devoting two volumes to mediaeval philosophy. As my first volume[1] ended with an account of neo-Platonism and contained no treatment of the philosophic ideas to be found in the early Christian writers, I considered it desirable to say something of these ideas in the present volume. It is true that men like St. Gregory of Nyssa and St. Augustine belonged to the period of the Roman Empire, that their philosophic affiliations were with Platonism, understood in the widest sense, and that they cannot be termed mediaevals; but the fact remains that they were Christian thinkers and exercised a great influence on the Middle Ages. One could hardly understand St. Anselm or St. Bonaventure without knowing something of St. Augustine, nor could one understand the thought of John Scotus Eriugena without knowing something of the thought of St. Gregory of Nyssa and of the Pseudo-Dionysius. There is scarcely any need, then, to apologise for beginning a history of mediaeval philosophy with a consideration of thinkers who belong, so far as chronology is concerned, to the period of the Roman Empire.

The present volume, then, begins with the early Christian period and carries the history of mediaeval philosophy up to the end of the thirteenth century, including Duns Scotus (about 1265–1308). In my third volume I propose to treat of the philosophy of the fourteenth century, laying special emphasis on Ockhamism. In

---

[1] *A History of Philosophy*, Vol. I, Greece and Rome, London, 1946.

that volume I shall also include a treatment of the philosophies of
the Renaissance, of the fifteenth and sixteenth centuries, and of
the 'Silver Age' of Scholastic thought, even though Francis Suarez
did not die until the year 1617, twenty-one years after the birth
of Descartes. This arrangement may appear to be an arbitrary
one, and to some extent it is. But it is extremely doubtful if it is
possible to make any hard and fast dividing line between mediaeval
and modern philosophy, and a good case could be made out for
including Descartes with the later Scholastics, contrary to tradition as this would be. I do not propose, however, to adopt this
course, and if I include in the next volume, the third, some philosophers who might seem to belong properly to the 'modern period',
my reason is largely one of convenience, to clear the decks, so that
in the fourth volume I may develop in a systematic manner the
interconnection between the leading philosophical systems from
Francis Bacon in England and Descartes in France up to and
including Kant. Nevertheless, whatever method of division be
adopted, one has to remember that the compartments into which
one divides the history of philosophic thought are not watertight,
that transitions are gradual, not abrupt, that there is overlapping
and interconnection, that succeeding systems are not cut off from
one another with a hatchet.

2. There was a time when mediaeval philosophy was considered
as unworthy of serious study, when it was taken for granted that
the philosophy of the Middle Ages was so subservient to theology
that it was practically indistinguishable therefrom and that, in so
far as it was distinguishable, it amounted to little more than a
barren logic-chopping and word-play. In other words, it was taken
for granted that European philosophy contained two main periods,
the ancient period, which to all intents and purposes meant the
philosophies of Plato and Aristotle, and the modern period, when
the speculative reason once more began to enjoy freedom after the
dark night of the Middle Ages when ecclesiastical authority reigned
supreme and the human reason, chained by heavy fetters, was
compelled to confine itself to the useless and fanciful study of
theology, until a thinker like Descartes at length broke the chains
and gave reason its freedom. In the ancient period and the modern
period philosophy may be considered a free man, whereas in the
mediaeval period it was a slave.

Apart from the fact that mediaeval philosophy naturally shared
in the disesteem with which the Middle Ages in general were

commonly regarded, one factor which was partly responsible for the attitude adopted towards mediaeval thinkers was doubtless the language used concerning Scholasticism by men like Francis Bacon and René Descartes. Just as Aristotelians are prone to evaluate Platonism in terms of Aristotle's criticism, so admirers of the movement apparently initiated by Bacon and Descartes were prone to look on mediaeval philosophy through their eyes, unaware of the fact that much of what Francis Bacon, for instance, has to say against the Scholastics could not legitimately be applied to the great figures of mediaeval thought, however applicable it may have been to later and 'decadent' Scholastics, who worshipped the letter at the expense 'of the spirit. Looking on mediaeval philosophy from the very start in this light historians could perhaps scarcely be expected to seek a closer and first-hand acquaintance with it: they condemned it unseen and unheard, without knowledge either of the rich variety of mediaeval thought or of its profundity: to them it was all of a piece, an arid playing with words and a slavish dependence on theologians. Moreover, insufficiently critical, they failed to realise the fact that, if mediaeval philosophers were influenced by an external factor, theology, modern philosophers were also influenced by external factors, even if by other external factors than theology. It would have seemed to most of these historians a nonsensical proposition were one to suggest to them that Duns Scotus, for example, had a claim to be considered as a great British philosopher, at least as great as John Locke, while in their praise of the acumen of David Hume they were unaware that certain thinkers of the late Middle Ages had already anticipated a great deal of the criticism which used to be considered the peculiar contribution to philosophy of the eminent Scotsman.

I shall cite one example, the treatment accorded to mediaeval philosophy and philosophers by a man who was himself a great philosopher, Georg Wilhelm Friedrich Hegel. It is an interesting example, since Hegel's dialectical idea of the history of philosophy obviously demanded that mediaeval philosophy should be portrayed as making an essential contribution to the development of philosophic thought, while Hegel personally was no mere vulgar antagonist of mediaeval philosophy. Now, Hegel does indeed admit that mediaeval philosophy performed one useful function, that of expressing in philosophic terms the 'absolute content' of Christianity, but he insists that it is only formalistic repetition of the content of faith, in which God is represented as something 'external', and if one remembers that for Hegel faith is the mode of religious consciousness and is definitely inferior to the philosophic or speculative standpoint, the standpoint of pure reason, it is clear that in his eyes mediaeval philosophy can be philosophy only in name. Accordingly he declares that Scholastic philosophy is really theology. By this Hegel does not mean that God is not the object of philosophy as well as of theology: he means that mediaeval philosophy considered the same object as is considered by philosophy proper but that it treated that object according to the categories of theology instead of substituting for the external connections of theology (for example, the relation of the world to God as external effect to free creative Cause) the systematic, scientific, rational and necessary categories and connections of philosophy. Mediaeval philosophy was thus philosophy according to content, but theology according to form, and in Hegel's eyes the history of mediaeval philosophy is a monotonous one, in which men have tried in vain to discern any distinct stages of real progress and development of thought.

In so far as Hegel's view of mediaeval philosophy is dependent on his own particular system, on his view of the relation of religion to philosophy, of faith to reason, of immediacy to mediacy, I cannot discuss it in this volume; but I wish to point out how Hegel's treatment of mediaeval philosophy is accompanied by a very real ignorance of the course of its history. It would be possible no doubt for an Hegelian to have a real knowledge of the development of mediaeval philosophy and yet to adopt, precisely because he was an Hegelian, Hegel's general standpoint in regard to it; but there can be no shadow of doubt, even allowing for the fact that the philosopher did not himself edit and publish his lectures on the history of philosophy, that Hegel did not possess the real knowledge in question. How could one, for instance, attribute a real knowledge of mediaeval philosophy to a writer who includes Roger Bacon under the heading 'Mystics' and simply remarks 'Roger Bacon treated more especially of physics, but remained without influence. He invented gunpowder, mirrors, telescopes, and died in 1297'? The fact of the matter is that Hegel relied on authors like Tennemann and Brucker for his information concerning mediaeval philosophy, whereas the first valuable studies on mediaeval philosophy do not antedate the middle of the nineteenth century.

In adducing the instance of Hegel I am not, of course, concerned to blame the philosopher: I am rather trying to throw into relief the great change that has taken place in our knowledge of mediaeval philosophy through the work of modern scholars since about 1880. Whereas one can easily understand and pardon the misrepresentations of which a man like Hegel was unconsciously guilty, one would have little patience with similar misrepresentations to-day, after the work of scholars like Baeumker, Ehrle, Grabmann, De Wulf, Pelster, Geyer, Mandonnet, Pelzer, etc. After the light that has been thrown on mediaeval philosophy by the publication of texts and the critical editing of already published works, after the splendid volumes brought out by the Franciscan Fathers of Quaracchi, after the publications of so many numbers of the *Beiträge* series, after the production of histories like that of Maurice De Wulf, after the lucid studies of Etienne Gilson, after the patient work done by the Mediaeval Academy of America, it should no longer be possible to think that mediaeval philosophers were 'all of a piece', that mediaeval philosophy lacked richness and variety, that mediaeval thinkers were uniformly men of low stature and of mean attainments. Moreover, writers like Gilson have helped us to realise the continuity between mediaeval and modern philosophy. Gilson has shown how Cartesianism was more dependent on mediaeval thought than was formerly supposed. A good deal still remains to be done in the way of edition and interpretation of texts (one needs only to mention William of Ockham's Commentary on the *Sentences*), but it has now become possible to see the currents and development, the pattern and texture, the high lights and low lights of mediaeval philosophy with a synoptic eye.

3. But even if mediaeval philosophy was in fact richer and more varied than has been sometimes supposed, is it not true to say that it stood in such a close relation to theology that it is practically indistinguishable therefrom? Is it not, for example, a fact that the great majority of mediaeval philosophers were priests and theologians, pursuing philosophic studies in the spirit of a theologian or even an apologist?

In the first place it is necessary to point out that the relation of theology to philosophy was itself an important theme of mediaeval thought and that different thinkers adopted different attitudes in regard to this question. Starting with the endeavour to understand the data of revelation, so far as this is possible to human reason, early mediaevals, in accordance with the maxim *Credo, ut intelligam*, applied rational dialectic to the mysteries of faith in an attempt to understand them. In this way they laid the foundations of Scholastic theology, since the application of reason to theological data, in the sense of the data of revelation, is and remains theology: it does not become philosophy. Some thinkers indeed, in their enthusiastic desire to penetrate mysteries by reason to the utmost degree possible, appear at first sight to be rationalists, to be what one might call Hegelians before Hegel. Yet it is really an anachronism to regard such men as 'rationalists' in the modern sense, since when St. Anselm, for example, or Richard of St. Victor, attempted to prove the mystery of the Blessed Trinity by 'necessary reasons' they had no intention of acquiescing in any reduction of the dogma or of impairing the integrity of divine revelation. (To this subject I shall return in the course of the work.) So far they were certainly acting as theologians, but such men, who did not make, it is true, any very clear delimitation of the spheres of philosophy and theology, certainly pursued philosophical themes and developed philosophical arguments. For instance, even if St. Anselm is primarily important as one of the founders of Scholastic theology, he also contributed to the growth of Scholastic philosophy, for example, by his rational proofs of God's existence. It would be inadequate to dub Abelard a philosopher and St. Anselm a theologian without qualification. In any case in the thirteenth century we find a clear distinction made by St. Thomas Aquinas between theology, which takes as its premisses the data of revelation, and philosophy (including, of course, what we call 'natural theology'), which is the work of the human reason unaided positively by revelation. It is true that in the same century St. Bonaventure was a conscious and determined upholder of what one might call the integralist, Augustinian view; but, though the Franciscan Doctor may have believed that a purely philosophical knowledge of God is vitiated by its very incompleteness, he was perfectly well aware that there are philosophical truths which are ascertainable by reason alone. The difference between him and St. Thomas has been stated thus.[1] St. Thomas held that it would be possible, *in principle*, to excogitate a satisfactory philosophical system, which, in respect of knowledge of God for instance, would be incomplete but not false,

[1] This bald statement, however, though sponsored by M. Gilson, requires a certain modification. See pp. 245–9.

whereas St. Bonaventure maintained that this very incompleteness or inadequacy has the character of a falsification, so that, though a true natural philosophy would be possible without the light of faith, a true metaphysic would not be possible. If a philosopher, thought St. Bonaventure, proves by reason and maintains the unity of God, without at the same time knowing that God is Three Persons in One Nature, he is attributing to God a unity which is not the divine Unity.

In the second place, St. Thomas was perfectly serious when he gave philosophy its 'charter'. To a superficial observer it might appear that when St. Thomas asserted a clear distinction between dogmatic theology and philosophy, he was merely asserting a formalistic distinction, which had no influence on his thought and which he did not take seriously in practice; but such a view would be far from the truth, as can be seen by one example. St. Thomas believed that revelation teaches the creation of the world in time, the world's non-eternity; but he maintained and argued stoutly that the philosopher as such can prove neither that the world was created from eternity nor that it was created in time, although he can show that it depends on God as Creator. In holding to this point of view he was at variance with, for example, St. Bonaventure, and the fact that he maintained the point of view in question shows clearly that he seriously accepted in practice his theoretical delimitation of the provinces of philosophy and dogmatic theology.

In the third place, if it were really true to say that mediaeval philosophy was no more than theology, we should expect to find that thinkers who accepted the same faith would accept the same philosophy or that the differences between them would be confined to differences in the way in which they applied dialectic to the data of revelation. In point of fact, however, this is very far from being the case. St. Bonaventure, St. Thomas Aquinas, and Duns Scotus, Giles of Rome, and, one may pretty safely say, William of Ockham accepted the same faith, but their philosophical ideas were by no means the same on all points. Whether or not their philosophies were equally compatible with the exigencies of theology is, of course, another question (William of Ockham's philosophy could scarcely be considered as altogether compatible with these exigencies); but that question is irrelevant to the point at issue, since, whether they were all compatible with orthodox theology or not, these philosophies existed and were not the same.

The historian can trace the lines of development and divergence in mediaeval philosophy, and, if he can do this, there must clearly be such a thing as mediaeval philosophy: without existence it could not have a history.

We shall have to consider different views on the relation between philosophy and theology in the course of this work, and I do not want to dwell any more on the matter at present; but it may be as well to admit from the very start that, owing to the common background of the Christian faith, the world presented itself for interpretation to the mediaeval thinker more or less in a common light. Whether a thinker held or denied a clear distinction between the provinces of theology and philosophy, in either case he looked on the world as a Christian and could hardly avoid doing so. In his philosophic arguments he might prescind from Christian revelation, but the Christian outlook and faith were none the less there at the back of his mind. Yet that does not mean that his philosophic arguments were not philosophic arguments or that his rational proofs were not rational proofs: one would have to take each argument or proof on its own merits or demerits and not dismiss them as concealed theology on the ground that the writer was a Christian.

4. Having argued that there really was such a thing as mediaeval philosophy or at any rate that there could be such a thing, even if the great majority of mediaeval philosophers were Christians and most of them theologians into the bargain, I want finally to say something about the aim of this book (and of the succeeding volume) and the way in which it treats its subject.

I certainly do not intend to attempt the task of narrating all the known opinions of all known mediaeval philosophers. In other words, the second and third volumes of my history are not designed to constitute an encyclopaedia of mediaeval philosophy. On the other hand, it is not my intention to give simply a sketch or series of impressions of mediaeval philosophy. I have endeavoured to give an intelligible and coherent account of the development of mediaeval philosophy and of the phases through which it passed, omitting many names altogether and choosing out for consideration those thinkers who are of special importance and interest for the content of their thought or who represent and illustrate some particular type of philosophy or stage of development. To certain of these thinkers I have devoted a considerable amount of space, discussing their opinions at some length. This fact may possibly tend to obscure the general lines of connection and development, but, as I have said, it was not my intention to provide simply a sketch of mediaeval philosophy, and it is probably only through a somewhat detailed treatment of the leading philosophical systems that one can bring out the rich variety of mediaeval thought. To place in clear relief the main lines of connection and development and at the same time to develop at some length the ideas of selected philosophers is certainly not an easy task, and it would be foolish to suppose that my inclusions and omissions or proportional allotment of space will be acceptable to everybody: to miss the trees for the wood or the wood for the trees is easy enough, but to see both clearly at the same time is not so easy. However, I consider it a task worth attempting, and while I have not hesitated to consider at some length the philosophies of St. Bonaventure, St. Thomas, Duns Scotus and Ockham, I have tried to make intelligible the general development of mediaeval philosophy from its early struggles, through its splendid maturity, to its eventual decline.

If one speaks of a 'decline', it may be objected that one is speaking as philosopher and not as historian. True enough, but if one is to discern an intelligible pattern in mediaeval philosophy, one must have a principle of selection and to that extent at least one must be a philosopher. The word 'decline' has indeed a valuational colouring and flavour, so that to use such a word may seem to constitute an overstepping of the legitimate territory of the historian. Possibly it is, in a sense; but what historian of philosophy was or is *merely* an historian in the narrowest meaning of the term? No Hegelian, no Marxist, no Positivist, no Kantian writes history without a philosophic viewpoint, and is the Thomist alone to be condemned for a practice which is really necessary, unless the history of philosophy is to be rendered unintelligible by being made a mere string of opinions?

By 'decline', then, I mean decline, since I frankly regard mediaeval philosophy as falling into three main phases. First comes the preparatory phase, up to and including the twelfth century, then comes the period of constructive synthesis, the thirteenth century, and finally, in the fourteenth century, the period of destructive criticism, undermining and decline. Yet from another point of view I should not hesitate to admit that the last phase was an inevitable phase and, in the long run, may be of benefit, as stimulating Scholastic philosophers to develop and establish their principles more firmly in face of criticism and, moreover, to utilise all that subsequent philosophy may have to offer of positive value. From one point of view the Sophistic phase in ancient philosophy (using the term 'Sophist' in more or less the Platonic sense) constituted a decline, since it was characterised by, among other things, a flagging of constructive thought; but it was none the less an inevitable phase in Greek philosophy, and, in the long run, may be regarded as having produced results of positive value. No one at least who values the thought of Plato and Aristotle can regard the activity and criticism of the Sophists as an unmitigated disaster for philosophy.

The general plan of this volume and of its successor is thus the exhibition of the main phases and lines of development in mediaeval philosophy. First of all I treat briefly of the Patristic period, going on to speak of those Christian thinkers who had a real influence on the Middle Ages: Boethius, the Pseudo-Dionysius and, above all, St. Augustine of Hippo. After this more or less introductory part of the volume I proceed to the preparatory phase of mediaeval thought proper, the Carolingian renaissance, the establishment of the Schools, the controversy concerning universal concepts and the growing use of dialectic, the positive work of St. Anselm in the eleventh century, the schools of the twelfth century, particularly those of Chartres and St. Victor. It is then necessary to say something of Arabian and Jewish philosophy, not so much for its own sake, since I am primarily concerned with the philosophy of mediaeval Christendom, as for the fact that the Arabs and Jews constituted an important channel whereby the Aristotelian system in its fullness became known to the Christian West. The second phase is that of the great syntheses of the thirteenth century, the philosophies of St. Bonaventure, St. Thomas Aquinas and Duns Scotus in particular. The succeeding phase, that of the fourteenth century, contains the new directions and the destructive criticism of the Ockhamist School in a wide sense. Finally, I have given a treatment of the thought which belongs to the period of transition between mediaeval and modern philosophy. The way will then be clear to start a consideration of what is generally called 'modern philosophy' in the fourth volume of this history.

In conclusion it may be as well to mention two points. The first is that I do not conceive it to be the task of the historian of philosophy to substitute his own ideas or those of recent or contemporary philosophers for the ideas of past thinkers, as though the thinkers in question did not know what they meant. When Plato stated the doctrine of reminiscence, he was not asserting neo-Kantianism, and though St. Augustine anticipated Descartes by saying *Si fallor, sum*, it would be a great mistake to try to force his philosophy into the Cartesian mould. On the other hand, some problems which have been raised by modern philosophers were also raised in the Middle Ages, even if in a different setting, and it is legitimate to draw attention to similarity of question or answer. Again, it is not illegitimate to ask if a given mediaeval philosopher could, out of the resources of his own system, meet this or that difficulty which a later philosopher has raised. Therefore, although I have tried to avoid the multiplication of references to modern philosophy, I have on occasion permitted myself to make comparisons with later philosophies and to discuss the ability of a mediaeval system of philosophy to meet a difficulty which is likely to occur to a student of modern thought. But I have strictly rationed my indulgence in such comparisons and discussions, not only out of considerations of space but also out of regard for historical propriety.

The second point to be mentioned is this. Largely owing to the influence of Marxism there is a certain demand that an historian of philosophy should draw attention to the social and political background of his period and throw light on the influence of social and political factors on philosophic development and thought. But apart from the fact that to keep one's history within a reasonable compass one must concentrate on philosophy itself and not on social and political events and developments, it is ridiculous to suppose that all philosophies or all parts of any given philosophy are equally influenced by the social and political *milieu*. To understand a philosopher's political thought it is obviously desirable to have some knowledge of the actual political background, but in order to discuss St. Thomas's doctrine on the relation of essence to existence or Scotus's theory of the univocal character of the concept of being, there is no need at all to introduce references to the political or economic background. Moreover, philosophy is influenced by other factors as well as politics and economics. Plato was influenced by the advance of Greek mathematics; mediaeval philosophy, though distinguishable from theology, was certainly influenced by it; consideration of the development of physics is relevant to Descartes's view of the material world; biology was not without influence on Bergson, and so on. I regard it, therefore, as a great mistake to dwell so exclusively on economics and political development, and to explain the advance of other sciences ultimately by economic history, that one implies the truth of the Marxist theory of philosophy. Apart, then, from the fact that considerations of space have not permitted me to say much of the political, social and economic background of mediaeval philosophy, I have deliberately disregarded the unjustifiable demand that one should interpret the 'ideological superstructure' in terms of the economic situation. This book is a history of a certain period of mediaeval philosophy: it is not a political history nor a history of mediaeval economics.

PART I
PRE-MEDIAEVAL INFLUENCES

CHAPTER II
THE PATRISTIC PERIOD

Christianity and Greek philosophy—Greek Apologists (Aristides, St. Justin Martyr, Tatian, Athenagoras, Theophilus)—Gnosticism and writers against Gnosticism (St. Irenaeus, Hippolytus)—Latin Apologists (Minucius Felix, Tertullian, Arnobius, Lactantius)—Catechetical School of Alexandria (Clement, Origen)—Greek Fathers (St. Basil, Eusebius, St. Gregory of Nyssa)—Latin Fathers (St. Ambrose)—St. John Damascene—Summary.

1. CHRISTIANITY came into the world as a revealed religion: it was given to the world by Christ as a doctrine of redemption and salvation and love, not as an abstract and theoretical system, and He sent His Apostles to preach, not to occupy professors' chairs. Christianity was 'the Way', a road to God to be trodden in practice, not one more philosophical system added to the systems and schools of antiquity. The Apostles and their successors were bent on converting the world, not on excogitating a philosophical system. Moreover, so far as their message was directed to the Jews, the Apostles had to meet theological rather than philosophical attacks, while, in regard to the non-Jews, we are not told, apart from the account of St. Paul's famous sermon at Athens, of their being confronted with, or of their approaching, Greek philosophers in the academic sense.

However, as Christianity made fast its roots and grew, it aroused the suspicion and hostility, not merely of the Jews and the political authorities, but also of pagan intellectuals and writers. Some of the attacks levelled against Christianity were due simply to ignorance, credulous suspicion, fear of what was unknown, misrepresentation; but other attacks were delivered on the theoretical plane, on philosophical grounds, and these attacks had to be met. This meant that philosophical as well as theological arguments had to be used. There are, then, philosophical elements in the writings of early Christian apologists and Fathers; but it would obviously be idle to look for a philosophical system, since the interest of these writers was primarily theological, to defend the Faith. Yet, as Christianity became more firmly established and better known and as it became possible for Christian scholars to develop thought and learning, the philosophical element tended to become more strongly marked, especially when there was question of meeting the attacks of pagan professional philosophers.

The influence of apologetic on the growth of Christian philosophy was clearly due primarily to a cause external to Christianity, namely hostile attack; but there was also another reason for this growth which was internal, independent of attacks from outside. The more intellectual Christians naturally felt the desire to penetrate, as far as it was open to them to do so, the data of revelation and also to form a comprehensive view of the world and human life in the light of faith. This last reason operated in a systematic way perhaps later than the first and, so far as the Fathers are concerned, reached the zenith of its influence in the thought of St. Augustine; but the first reason, the desire to penetrate the dogmas of the Faith (an anticipation of the *Credo, ut intelligam* attitude), was operative in some way from the beginning. Partly through a simple desire to understand and appreciate, partly through the need of further clearer definition of dogma in face of heresy, the original data of revelation were rendered more explicit, 'developed', in the sense of the implicit being made explicit. From the beginning, for instance, Christians accepted the fact that Christ was both God and Man, but it was only in the course of time that the implications of this fact were made clear and were enshrined in theological definitions, for example, that the perfect human Nature of Christ implied His possession of a human will. Now, these definitions were of course theological, and the advance from the implicit to the explicit was an advance in theological science; but in the process of argument and definition concepts and categories were employed which were borrowed from philosophy. Moreover, as the Christians had no philosophy of their own to start with (i.e. in the academic sense of philosophy), they very naturally turned to the prevailing philosophy, which was derived from Platonism but was strongly impregnated with other elements. As a rough generalisation, therefore, one may say that the philosophic ideas of the early Christian writers were Platonic or neo-Platonic in character (with an admixture of Stoicism) and that the Platonic tradition continued for long to dominate Christian thought from the philosophic viewpoint. In saying this, however, one must remember that the Christian writers did not make any clear distinction between theology and philosophy: they aimed rather at presenting the Christian wisdom or 'philosophy' in a very wide sense, which was primarily theological, though it contained philosophical elements in the strict sense. The task of the historian of philosophy is to isolate these philosophic elements: he cannot reasonably be expected to present an adequate picture of early Christian thought, for the very good reason that he is not, *ex hypothesi*, an historian of dogmatic theology or of exegesis.

Since on the one hand pagan philosophers were inclined to attack the Church and her doctrine, while on the other hand Christian apologists and theologians were inclined to borrow the weapons of their adversaries when they thought that these weapons could serve their purpose, it is only to be expected that the Christian writers should show a divergence of attitude in regard to ancient philosophy, according as they chose to regard it as a foe and rival of Christianity or as a useful arsenal and store-house or even as a providential preparation for Christianity. Thus while in Tertullian's eyes pagan philosophy was little more than the foolishness of this world, Clement of Alexandria regarded philosophy as a gift of God, a means of educating the pagan world for Christ, as the Jews' means of education had been the Law. He thought indeed, as Justin thought before him, that Plato had borrowed his wisdom from Moses and the Prophets (a Philonic contention); but just as Philo had tried to reconcile Greek philosophy with the Old Testament, so Clement tried to reconcile Greek philosophy with the Christian religion. In the end, of course, it was the attitude of Clement, not that of Tertullian, which triumphed, since St. Augustine made abundant use of neo-Platoric ideas when presenting the Christian *Weltanschauung*.

2. As the first group of those Christian writers whose works contain philosophic elements one can count the early apologists who were particularly concerned to defend the Christian faith against pagan attack (or rather to show to the Imperial authorities that Christianity had a right to exist), men like Aristides, Justin, Melito, Tatian, Athenagoras and Theophilus of Antioch. In a brief sketch of Patristic philosophy, a sketch which is admittedly only included by way of preparation for the main theme of the book, one can treat neither of all the apologists nor of any one of them fully: my intention is rather to indicate the sort of philosophical elements which their works contain.

(i) *Marcianus Aristides*, styled a 'philosopher of Athens', wrote an Apology, which is to be dated about A.D. 140 and is addressed to the Emperor Antoninus Pius.[1] A good deal of this work is devoted to an attack on the pagan deities of Greece and Egypt, with some animadversions on the morals of the Greeks; but at the beginning Aristides declares that 'amazed at the arrangement of the world', and understanding that 'the world and all that is therein are moved by the impulse of another', and seeing that 'that which moveth is more powerful than that which is moved', he concludes that the Mover of the world 'is God of all, who made all for the sake of man'. Aristides thus gives in a very compendious form arguments drawn from the design and order in the world and from the fact of motion, and identifies the designer and mover with the Christian God, of whom he proceeds to predicate the attributes of eternity, perfection, incomprehensibility, wisdom, goodness. We have here, then, a very rudimentary natural theology presented, not for purely philosophic reasons, but in defence of the Christian religion.

(ii) A much more explicit attitude towards philosophy is to be found in the writings of *Flavius Justinus* (St. Justin Martyr), who was born at Neapolis (Nablus) of pagan parents about A.D. 100, became a Christian, and was martyred at Rome about 164. In his Dialogue with Trypho he declares that philosophy is a most precious gift of God, designed to lead man to God, though its true nature and its unity have not been recognised by most people, as is clear from the existence of so many philosophical schools.[2] As to himself, he went first for instruction to a Stoic, but, finding the Stoic doctrine of God unsatisfactory, betook himself to a Peripatetic, whose company he soon forsook, as he turned out to be a grasping fellow.[3] From the Peripatetic he went, with zeal still unabated, to a Pythagorean of repute, but his own lack of acquaintance with music, geometry and astronomy unfitted him for philosophy in his prospective teacher's eyes, and as he did not wish to spend a lot of time in acquiring knowledge of these sciences, he turned to the Platonists and was so delighted with the doctrine of the immaterial Ideas that he began to expect a clear vision of God, which, says Justin, is the aim of Plato's philosophy.[4] Shortly afterwards, however, he fell in with a Christian, who showed him the insufficiency of pagan philosophy, even of that of

---

[1] Quotations from the edition published in *Texts and Studies*, Vol. I.
[2] 2, 1.   [3] 2, 3.   [4] 2, 4-6.

Plato.[1] Justin is thus an example of the cultured convert from paganism, who, feeling his conversion as the term of a process, could not adopt a merely negative and hostile attitude to Greek philosophy.

Justin's words concerning Platonism in the *Dialogue* show clearly enough the esteem in which he held the Platonic philosophy. He prized its doctrine of the immaterial world and of the being beyond essence, which he identified with God, though he became convinced that the sure and safe and certain knowledge of God, the true 'philosophy', is to be attained only through the acceptance of revelation. In his two *Apologies* he makes frequent use of Platonic terms, as when he speaks of God as the 'Demiurge'.[2] I am not suggesting that when Justin makes use of Platonic or neo-Platonic words and phrases he is understanding the words in precisely the Platonic sense: the use of them is rather the effect of his philosophic training and of the sympathy which he retained for Platonism. Thus he does not hesitate on occasion to point out analogies between Christian and Platonic doctrine, in regard, for example, to reward and punishment after death,[3] and his admiration for Socrates is evident. When Socrates, in the power of *logos*, or as its instrument, tried to lead men away from falsehood into truth, evil men put him to death as an impious atheist: so Christians, who follow and obey the incarnate Logos itself and who denounce the false gods, are termed atheists.[4] In other words, just as the work of Socrates, which was a service of truth, was a preparation for the complete work of Christ, so the condemnation of Socrates was, as it were, a rehearsal or anticipation of the condemnation of Christ and His followers. Again, the actions of men are not determined, as the Stoics thought, but they act rightly or wrongly according to their free choice, while it is owing to the activity of the evil demons that Socrates and those like him are persecuted, while Epicurus and those like him are held in honour.[5]

Justin thus made no clear distinction between theology and philosophy in the strict sense: there is one wisdom, one 'philosophy', which is revealed fully in and through Christ, but for which the best elements in pagan philosophy, especially Platonism, were a preparation. In so far as the pagan philosophers divined the truth, they did so only in the power of *logos*: Christ, however, is the Logos itself, incarnate. This view of Greek philosophy and

---

[1] 3, 1 ff.   [2] E.g. *Apol.*, I, 8, 2.   [3] *Ibid.*, I, 8, 4.
[4] *Ibid.*, I, 5, 3 ff.   [5] *Ibid.*, II, 6 (7), 3.

of its relation to Christianity was of considerable influence on later writers.

(iii) According to Irenaeus,[1] *Tatian* was a pupil of Justin. He was of Syrian nationality, was educated in Greek literature and philosophy, and became a Christian. There is no real reason for doubting the truth of the statement that Tatian was in some sense a pupil of Justin Martyr, but it is quite clear from his *Address to the Greeks* that he did not share Justin's sympathy for Greek philosophy in its more spiritual aspects. Tatian declares that we know God from His works; he has a doctrine of the Logos, distinguishes soul (ψυχή) from spirit (πνεῦμα), teaches creation in time and insists on free-will; but all these points he could have got from the Scriptures and Christian teaching: he had little use for Greek learning and Greek thought, though he can hardly have escaped its influence altogether. He was in fact inclined to excessive rigorism, and we learn from St. Irenaeus and St. Jerome[2] that after Justin's martyrdom Tatian fell away from the Church into Valentinian Gnosticism, subsequently founding the sect of the Encratites, denouncing not only the drinking of wine and the use of ornaments by women but even marriage as such, which he said was defilement and fornication.[3]

Tatian certainly recognised the human mind's ability to prove God's existence from creatures and he made use of philosophical notions and categories in the development of theology, as when he maintains that the Word, proceeding from the simple essence of God, does not 'fall into the void', as human words do, but remains in its subsistence and is the divine instrument of creation. He thus uses the analogy of the formation of human thought and speech to illustrate the procession of the Word, and, while holding to the doctrine of creation, he uses language reminiscent of the *Timaeus* in respect of the Demiurge. But, if he made use of terms and ideas taken from pagan philosophy, he did not do so in any spirit of sympathy, but rather with the notion that the Greek philosophers had taken from the Scriptures whatever truth they possessed and that whatever they added thereto was nothing but falsity and perversion. The Stoics, for instance, perverted the doctrine of providence by the diabolic theory of fatalistic determinism. It is indeed something of an historical irony that a writer who betrayed so pronounced an hostility towards Greek thought

[1] *Against the Heresies*, I, 28.   [2] E.g. *Adv. Jovin.*, I, 3; *Comm. in Amos.*
[3] Iren., *Against the Heresies*, I, 28.

and who drew so sharp a distinction between pagan 'sophistry' and Christian wisdom should himself end in heresy.

(iv) A more tactful approach to the Greeks, and one in harmony with that of Justin Martyr, was the approach of *Athenagoras*, who addressed to the Emperors Marcus Aurelius and Commodus, 'conquerors of Armenia and Sarmatia, and above all philosophers', a *Plea for the Christians* (πρεσβεία περὶ χριστιανῶν) about the year A.D. 177. In this book the author is concerned to defend the Christians against the three accusations of atheism, cannibalistic feasts and incest, and in answering the first accusation he gives a reasoned defence of the Christian belief in one eternal and spiritual God. First of all he cites various Greek philosophers themselves, for instance Philolaus, Plato, Aristotle and the Stoics. He quotes Plato in the *Timaeus* to the effect that it is difficult to find the Maker and Father of the universe and impossible, even when He is found, to declare Him to all, and asks why Christians, believing in one God, should be called atheists, when Plato is not so called because of his doctrine of the Demiurge. The poets and philosophers, moved by a divine impulse, have striven to find God and men pay heed to their conclusions: how foolish it would be, then, to refuse to listen to the very Spirit of God, speaking through the mouths of the Prophets.

Athenagoras then goes on to show that there cannot be a multitude of material gods, that God, who forms matter, must transcend matter (though he scarcely succeeds in conceiving God without relation to space), that the Cause of perishable things must be imperishable and spiritual, and he appeals especially to the testimony of Plato. He thus adopts the same attitude as that of Justin Martyr. There is one true 'philosophy' or wisdom, which is attained adequately only through the Christian revelation, though Greek philosophers divined something of the truth. In other words, their very respect for the Greek thinkers and poets should lead thoughtful men like Marcus Aurelius to appreciate and esteem, even if not to embrace, Christianity. His primary purpose is theological and apologetic, but he utilises philosophic arguments and themes in his pursuit of that purpose. For instance, in his attempt to prove the reasonable character of the doctrine of the resurrection of the body, he makes clear his conviction, as against the Platonic view, that the body belongs to the integral man, that man is not simply a soul using a body.[1]

[1] *On the Resurrection.*

(v) A similar appeal to the intelligent pagan was made by *Theophilus of Antioch* in his *Ad Autolycum*, written about A.D. 180. After emphasising the fact that moral purity is necessary for any-one who would know God, he proceeds to speak of the divine attributes, God's incomprehensibility, power, wisdom, eternity, immutability. As the soul of man, itself invisible, is perceived through the movements of the body, so God, Himself invisible, is known through His providence and works. He is not always accurate in his account of the opinions of Greek philosophers, but he clearly had some esteem for Plato, whom he considered 'the most respectable philosopher among them',[1] though Plato erred in not teaching creation out of nothing (which Theophilus clearly affirms) and in his doctrine concerning marriage (which Theophilus does not give correctly).

3. The foregoing Apologists, who wrote in Greek, were mainly concerned with answering pagan attacks on Christianity. We can now consider briefly the great opponent of Gnosticism, St. Irenaeus, to whom we add, for the sake of convenience, Hippolytus. Both men wrote in Greek and both combated the Gnosticism which flourished in the second century A.D., though Hippolytus's work has a wider interest, containing, as it does, many references to Greek philosophy and philosophers.

Of Gnosticism suffice it to say here that, in general, it was a monstrous conflation of Scriptural and Christian, Greek and Oriental elements, which, professing to substitute knowledge (*gnosis*) for faith, offered a doctrine of God, creation, the origin of evil, salvation, to those who liked to look upon themselves as superior persons in comparison with the ordinary run of Christians. There was a Jewish Gnosticism before the 'Christian' form, and the latter itself can be looked on as a Christian heresy only in so far as the Gnostics borrowed certain specifically Christian themes: the Oriental and Hellenic elements are far too conspicuous for it to be possible to call Gnosticism a Christian heresy in the ordinary sense, although it was a real danger in the second century and seduced those Christians who were attracted by the bizarre theoso-phical speculations which the Gnostics offered as 'knowledge'. As a matter of fact, there were a number of Gnostic systems, such as those of Cerinthus, Marcion, the Ophites, Basilides, Valentinus. We know that Marcion was a Christian who suffered excommuni-cation; but the Ophites were probably of Jewish-Alexandrian

[1] *Ad Autol.*, 3, 6.

origin, while in regard to famous Gnostics like Basilides and Valentinus (second century) we do not know that they were ever Christians.

Characteristic of Gnosticism in general was a dualism between God and matter, which, though not absolute, approached that of the later Manichaean system. The resulting gulf between God and matter was filled up by the Gnostics with a series of emanations or intermediary beings in which Christ found a place. The complement of the process of emanation was the return to God by way of salvation.

In the system of Marcion, as one would expect, the Christian element was to the fore. The God of the Old Testament, the Demiurge, is inferior to the God of the New Testament, who remained unknown until He revealed Himself in Jesus Christ. In the systems of Basilides and Valentinus, however, the Christian element is less important: Christ is depicted as an inferior being (an Eon) in a fantastic hierarchy of divine and semi-divine emanations, and His mission is simply that of transmitting to man the salvific knowledge or *gnosis*. As matter is evil, it cannot be the work of the Supreme God, but it is due to the 'great Archon', who was worshipped by the Jews and who gave himself out as the one Supreme God. The Gnostic systems were thus not dualistic in the full Manichaean sense, since the Demiurge, identified with the God of the Old Testament, was not made an independent and original principle of evil (the neo-Platonic element was too prominent to admit of absolute dualism), and their main common characteristic was not so much the tendency to dualism as the insistence on *gnosis* as the means of salvation. The adoption of Christian elements was largely due to the desire to absorb Christianity, to substitute *gnosis* for faith. To enter further upon the differentiating features of the various Gnostic systems and to detail the series of emanations would be a tiresome and profitless task: it is enough to point out that the general framework was a mixture of Oriental and Greek (e.g. neo-Pythagorean and neo-Platonic) themes, with a varying dosage of Christian elements, taken both from Christianity proper and from apocryphal and spurious documents. To us to-day it is difficult to understand how Gnosticism could ever have been a danger to the Church or an attraction to any sane mind; but we have to remember that it arose at a time when a welter of philosophical schools and mystery-religions was seeking to cater for the spiritual needs of men. Moreover, esoteric and theosophical systems, surrounded with the pseudo-glamour of 'eastern wisdom', have not entirely lost their attraction for some minds even in much more recent times.

(i) *St. Irenaeus* (born about A.D. 137 or 140), writing against the Gnostics in his *Adversus Haereses*, affirms that there is one God, who made all things, Creator of heaven and earth. He appeals, for example, to the argument from design and to that from universal consent, observing that the very heathen have learnt from creation itself, by the use of reason, the existence of God as Creator.[1] God created the world freely, and not by necessity.[2] Moreover, He created the world out of nothing and not out of previously existing matter, as the Gnostics pretend relying on 'Anaxagoras, Empedocles and Plato'.[3] But, though the human mind can come to know God through reason and revelation, it cannot comprehend God, whose essence transcends the human intelligence: to pretend to know the ineffable mysteries of God and to go beyond humble faith and love, as the Gnostics do, is mere conceit and pride. The doctrine of reincarnation is false, while the revealed moral law does not abrogate, but fulfils and extends, the natural law. In fine, 'the teaching of the Apostles is the true *gnosis*'.[4]

According to Irenaeus the Gnostics borrowed most of their notions from Greek philosophers. Thus he accuses them of borrowing their morals from Epicurus and the Cynics, their doctrine of reincarnation from Plato. In this tendency to attach Gnostic theories to Greek philosophies Irenaeus was closely followed by

(ii) *Hippolytus* (died probably about A.D. 236), who was a disciple of Irenaeus, according to Photius,[5] and certainly utilised his teaching and writing. In the *Proemium* to his *Philosophumena* (now generally attributed to Hippolytus) he declares his intention, only imperfectly fulfilled, of exposing the plagiarism of the Gnostics by showing how their various opinions were taken from Greek philosophers, though they were made worse by the Gnostics, and, in order to do this more easily, he first recounts the opinions of the philosophers, relying for his information mainly, if not entirely, on the doxography of Theophrastus. The information, however, is not always accurate. His main accusation against the Greeks is that they glorified the parts of the creation with dainty phrases, but were ignorant of the Creator of all things, who made them freely out of nothing according to His wisdom and foreknowledge.

[1] 2, 9, 1.   [2] 2, 1, 1; 2, 5, 3.   [3] 2, 14, 4.   [4] 4, 33, 8.   [5] *Bibl.* cod. 121.

4. The foregoing authors wrote in Greek; but there was also a group of Latin Apologists, Minucius Felix, Tertullian, Arnobius and Lactantius, of whom the most important is Tertullian.

(i) It is uncertain whether *Minucius Felix* wrote before or after Tertullian, but in any case his attitude towards Greek philosophy, as shown in his *Octavius*, was more favourable than Tertullian's. Arguing that God's existence can be known with certainty from the order of nature and the design involved in the organism, particularly in the human body, and that the unity of God can be inferred from the unity of the cosmic order, he affirmed that Greek philosophers, too, recognised these truths. Thus Aristotle recognised one Godhead and the Stoics had a doctrine of divine providence, while Plato speaks in almost Christian terms when he talks in the *Timaeus* of the Maker and Father of the universe.

(ii) *Tertullian*, however, speaks in a rather different way of Greek philosophy. Born about A.D. 160 of pagan parents and educated as a jurist (he practised in Rome), he became a Christian, only to fall into the Montanist heresy, a form of rigorous and excessive Puritanism. He was the first outstanding Christian Latin writer, and in his works his contempt for paganism and pagan learning is made clear and explicit. What have the philosopher and the Christian in common, the disciple of Greece, the friend of error, and the pupil of heaven, the foe of error and friend of truth?[1] Even Socrates' wisdom did not amount to much, since no one can really know God apart from Christ, nor Christ apart from the Holy Spirit. Moreover, Socrates was, self-confessedly, guided by a demon![2] As to Plato, he said that it was hard to find the Maker and Father of the universe, whereas the simplest Christian has already found Him.[3] Moreover, the Greek philosophers are the patriarchs of the heretics,[4] inasmuch as Valentinus borrowed from the Platonists, Marcion from the Stoics, while the philosophers themselves borrowed ideas from the Old Testament and then distorted them and claimed them as their own.[5]

However, in spite of the antithesis he makes between Christian wisdom and Greek philosophy, Tertullian himself developed philosophical themes and was influenced by the Stoics. He affirms that the existence of God is known with certainty from His works,[6] and also that from the uncreatedness of God we can argue to His perfection (*Imperfectum non potest esse, nisi quod factum est*);[7] but he

[1] *Apol.*, 46.   [2] *De Anima*, 1.   [3] *Apol.*, 46.   [4] *De Anima*, 3.
[5] *Apol.*, 47.   [6] *De Resurrect.*, 2-3.   [7] *Herm.*, 28.

makes the astounding statement that everything, including God, is corporeal, bodily. 'Everything which exists is a bodily existence *sui generis*. Nothing lacks bodily existence but that which is non-existent':[1] 'for who will deny that God is a body, although "God is a Spirit"? For Spirit has a bodily substance of its own kind, in its own form.'[2] Many writers have concluded from these statements that Tertullian maintained a materialistic doctrine and held God to be really a material being, just as the Stoics considered God to be material: some, however, have suggested that by 'body' Tertullian often meant simply substance and that when he attributes materiality to God, he is really simply attributing substantiality to God. On this explanation, when Tertullian says that God is a *corpus sui generis*, that He is *corpus* and yet *spiritus*, he would mean that God is a spiritual substance: his language would be at fault, while his thought would be acceptable. One is certainly not entitled to exclude this explanation as impossible, but it is true that Tertullian, speaking of the human soul, says that it must be a bodily substance since it can suffer.[3] However, he speaks ambiguously even on the nature of the soul, and in his *Apology*[4] he gives as a reason for the resurrection of the bodies of the wicked that 'the soul is not capable of suffering without the solid substance, that is, the flesh'. It is probably best to say, then, that, while Tertullian's language often implies materialism of a rather crass sort, his meaning *may* not have been that which his language would often imply. When he teaches that the soul of the infant is derived from the father's seed like a kind of sprout (*surculus, tradux*),[5] he would seem to be teaching a clearly materialistic doctrine; but this 'traducianism' was adopted partly for a theological reason, to explain the transmission of original sin, and some later writers who inclined to the same view, did so for the same theological reason, without apparently realising the materialistic implications of the doctrine. This does not show, of course, that Tertullian was *not* a materialist; but it should at least lead one to hesitate before forming the conviction that his general meaning always coincided with the words he used. His assertion of the freedom of the will and of the natural immortality of the soul will scarcely fit in, from the logical viewpoint, with sheer materialism; but that again would not justify one in flatly denying that he was

---

[1] *De Carne Christi*, 11.   [2] *Adv. Prax.*, 7.   [3] *De Anima*, 7; cf. 8.
[4] 48.   [5] Cf. *De Anima*, 19.

a materialist, since he may have held a materialistic theory without realising the fact that some of the attributes he ascribed to the soul were incompatible with a fully materialist position.

One of the great services rendered by Tertullian to Christian thought was his development of theological and, to some extent, of philosophical terminology in the Latin language. Thus the technical use of the word *persona* is found for the first time in his writings: the divine Persons are distinct as *Personae*, but they are not different, divided, *substantiae*.[1] In his doctrine of the Word[2] he appeals explicitly to the Stoics, to Zeno and Cleanthes.[3] However, of Tertullian's theological developments and of his orthodoxy or unorthodoxy it is not our concern to speak.

(iii) In his *Adversus Gentes* (about 303) *Arnobius* makes some curious observations concerning the soul. Thus, although he affirms creationism, as against the Platonic doctrine of pre-existence, he makes the creating agent a being inferior to God, and he also asserts the *gratuitous* character of the soul's immortality, denying a natural immortality. One motive was evidently that of using the gratuitous character of immortality as an argument for becoming a Christian and leading a moral life. Again, while combating the Platonic theory of reminiscence, he asserts the experiential origin of all our ideas with one exception, the idea of God. He depicts a child brought up in solitude, silence and ignorance throughout his youth and declares that, as a result, he would know nothing: he would certainly not have any knowledge by 'reminiscence'. Plato's proof for his doctrine in the *Meno* is not cogent.[4]

(iv) The origin of the soul by God's direct creation, in opposition to any form of traducianism, was clearly affirmed by *Lactantius* (about 250 to about 325) in his *De opificio Dei*.[5]

5. Gnosticism, as combated by St. Irenaeus and Hippolytus, was, so far as it can reasonably be connected with Christianity, an heretical speculative system, or, more accurately, set of systems, which, in addition to Oriental and Christian elements, incorporated elements of Hellenic thought. One of its effects, therefore, was to arouse a determined opposition to Hellenic philosophy on the part of those Christian writers who exaggerated the connections between Gnosticism and Greek philosophy, which they considered to be the seed-ground of heresy; but another effect was to contribute to the effort to construct a non-heretical 'gnosis', a Christian

[1] *Adv. Prax.*, 12.   [2] *Sermo, Ratio.*   [3] *Apol.*, 21.   [4] 2, 20 ff.   [5] 19.

theologico-philosophical system. This effort was characteristic of
the Catechetical School at Alexandria, of which the two most
famous names are Clement and Origen.

(i) *Titus Flavius Clemens* (*Clement of Alexandria*) was born
about 150, perhaps at Athens, came to Alexandria in 202 or 203
and died there about 219. Animated by the attitude which was
later summed up in the formula, *Credo, ut intelligam*, he sought to
develop the systematic presentation of the Christian wisdom in a
true, as opposed to a false *gnosis*. In the process he followed the
spirit of Justin Martyr's treatment of the Greek philosophers,
looking on their work rather as a preparation for Christianity, an
education of the Hellenic world for the revealed religion, than as
a folly and delusion. The divine Logos has always illumined souls;
but whereas the Jews were enlightened by Moses and the Prophets,
the Greeks had their wise men, their philosophers, so that philosophy was to the Greeks what the Law was to the Hebrews.[1] It
is true that Clement thought, following Justin again, that the
Greeks borrowed from the Old Testament and distorted, from
vainglorious motives, what they borrowed; but he was also firmly
convinced that the light of the Logos enabled the Greek philosophers to attain many truths, and that philosophy is in reality
simply that body of truths which are not the prerogative of any
one Greek School but are found, in different measure and degree,
in different Schools, though Plato was indeed the greatest of all the
philosophers.[2]

But not only was philosophy a preparation for Christianity: it
is also an aid in understanding Christianity. Indeed, the person
who merely believes and makes no effort to understand is like a
child in comparison with a man: blind faith, passive acceptance,
is not the ideal, though science, speculation, reasoning, cannot be
true if they do not harmonise with revelation. In other words,
Clement of Alexandria, as the first Christian man of learning,
wanted to see Christianity in its relation to philosophy and to use
the speculative reason in the systematisation and development of
theology. Incidentally it is interesting to note that he rejects any
real *positive* knowledge of God: we know in truth only what God
is not, for example, that He is not a genus, not a species, that He
is beyond anything of which we have had experience or which we
can conceive. We are justified in predicating perfections of God,
but at the same time we must remember that all names we apply

to God are inadequate—and so, in another sense, inapplicable. In dependence, then, on some remarks of Plato in the *Republic* concerning the Good and in dependence on Philo Clement asserted the *via negativa*, so dear to the mystics, which reached its classical expression in the writings of the Pseudo-Dionysius.

(ii) *Origen*, foremost member of the Catechetical School at Alexandria, was born in A.D. 185 or 186. He studied the works of Greek philosophers and is said to have attended the lectures of Ammonius Saccas, teacher of Plotinus. He had to abandon the headship of the Alexandrian School because of a synodical process (231 and 232) directed against certain features of his doctrine and also against his ordination (he had, it was said, been ordained priest in Palestine in spite of his act of self-mutilation), and subsequently founded a school at Caesarea in Palestine, where St. Gregory Thaumaturge was one of his pupils. He died in 254 or 255, his death being the consequence of the torture he had had to endure in the persecution of Decius.

Origen was the most prolific and learned of all Christian writers before the Council of Nicaea, and there is no doubt that he had every intention of being and remaining an orthodox Christian; but his desire to reconcile the Platonic philosophy with Christianity and his enthusiasm for the allegorical interpretation of the Scriptures led him into some heterodox opinions. Thus, under the influence of Platonism or rather of neo-Platonism, he held that God, who is purely spiritual, the μονάς or ἑνάς[1] and who transcends truth and reason, essence and being (in his book against the pagan philosopher Celsus[2] he says, following the mind of Plato, that God is ἐπέκεινα νοῦ καὶ οὐσίας), created the world from eternity and by a necessity of His Nature. God, who is goodness, could never have been 'inactive', since goodness always tends to self-communication, self-diffusion. Moreover, if God had created the world in time, if there was ever a 'time' when the world was not, God's immutability would be impaired, which is an impossibility.[3] Both these reasons are conceived in dependence on neo-Platonism. God is indeed the creator of matter and is thus Creator in the strict and Christian sense,[4] but there is an infinity of worlds, one succeeding the other and all different from one another.[5] As evil is privation, and not something positive, God cannot be accused of being the author of evil.[6] The Logos or Word is the exemplar

---

[1] *De principiis*, 1, 1, 6.   [2] 7, 38.   [3] *De principiis*, 1, 2, 10; 3, 4, 3.
[4] *Ibid.*, 2, 1, 4.   [5] *Ibid.*, 3, 5, 3; 2, 3, 4-5.   [6] *In Joann.*, 2, 7.

of creation, the ἰδέα ἰδεῶν,[1] and by the Logos all things are created,
the Logos acting as mediator of God and creatures.[2] The final
procession within the Godhead is the Holy Spirit, and immediately below the Holy Spirit are the created spirits, who, through
the power of the Holy Spirit, are lifted up to become sons of God,
in union with the Son, and are finally participants in the divine
life of the Father.[3]

Souls were created by God exactly like to one another in quality,
but sin in a state of pre-existence led to their being clothed with
bodies, and the qualitative difference between souls is thus due to
their behaviour before their entry into this world. They enjoy
freedom of will on earth, but their acts depend not merely on their
free choice but also on the grace of God, which is apportioned
according to their conduct in the pre-embodied state. Nevertheless, all souls, and even the devil and demons, too, will at
length, through purificatory suffering, arrive at union with God.
This is the doctrine of the restoration of all things (ἐπανόρθωσις,
ἀποκατάστασις πάντων) whereby all things will return to their ultimate
principle and God will be all in all.[4] This involves, of course, a
denial of the orthodox doctrine of hell.

From even the little which has been said concerning Origen's
thought it should be clear that he attempted a fusion of Christian
doctrine with Platonic and neo-Platonic philosophy. The Son and
the Holy Ghost in the Blessed Trinity, though within the Godhead,
are spoken of in a manner which indicates the influence of the
emanationism of Philonic and neo-Platonic thought. The theory
of the Logos as 'Idea of ideas' and that of eternal and necessary
creation come from the same source, while the theory of pre-
existence is Platonic. Of course, the philosophical ideas which
Origen adopted were incorporated by him in a Christian setting
and framework, so that he may rightly be considered the first
great synthetic thinker of Christianity, but although he attached
them to Scriptural passages freely interpreted, his enthusiasm for
Greek thought led him sometimes into heterodoxy.

6. The Greek Fathers of the fourth and fifth centuries were
occupied mainly with theological questions. Thus *St. Athanasius*,
who died in 373, was the great foe of Arianism; *St. Gregory Nazianzen*, who died in 390 and was known as the Theologian, is particularly remarkable for his work on Trinitarian and Christological

---

[1] *Contra Celsum*, 6, 64.   [2] *De principiis*, 2, 6, 1.   [3] *Ibid.*, 6, 1–3.
[4] Cf. *ibid.*, 3, 6, 1 ff.; 1, 6, 3.

theology; *St. John Chrysostom* (died 406) is celebrated as one
of the greatest orators of the Church and for his work on the
Scriptures. In treating of dogmas like those of the Blessed Trinity
and the Hypostatic Union the Fathers naturally made use of
philosophical terms and expressions; but their application of
reasoning in theology does not make them philosophers in the
strict sense and we must pass them over here. One may point out,
however, that *St. Basil* (died 379) studied in the University of
Athens, together with St. Gregory Nazianzen, and that in his *Ad
Adolescentes* he recommends a study of the Greek poets, orators,
historians and philosophers, though a selection should be made
from their writings which would exclude immoral passages: Greek
literature and learning are a potent instrument of education, but
moral education is more important than literary and philosophic
formation. (St. Basil himself in his descriptions of animals
apparently depended almost entirely on the relevant works of
Aristotle.)

But, though we cannot consider here the theological speculations
of the Greek Fathers, something must be said of two eminent
figures of the period, the historian Eusebius and St. Gregory of
Nyssa.

(i) *Eusebius of Caesarea* was born in Palestine about 265, became
Bishop of Caesarea, his birthplace, in 313, and died there in 339
or 340. Best known as a great Church historian, he is also of
importance for his Christian apologetic, and under this heading
comes his attitude towards Greek philosophy, since, in general, he
regarded Greek philosophy, especially Platonism, as a preparation
of the heathen world for Christianity, though he was fully alive to
the errors of Greek philosophers and to the contradictions between
the many philosophical Schools. Yet, though he speaks sharply on
occasion, his general attitude is sympathetic and appreciative, an
attitude which comes out most clearly in his *Praeparatio evangelica*
in fifteen books. It is greatly to be regretted that we have not got
the twenty-five books of the work which Eusebius wrote in answer
to Porphyry's attack on Christianity, as his reply to the eminent
neo-Platonist and pupil of Plotinus would doubtless throw much
light on his philosophical ideas; but the *Praeparatio evangelica* is
sufficient to show, not only that Eusebius shared the general
outlook of Justin Martyr, Clement of Alexandria and Origen, but
also that he had read widely in the literature of the Greeks. He
was in fact an extremely learned man, and his work is one of the

sources for our knowledge of the philosophy of those thinkers whose works have perished.

One would probably only expect, given the attitude of his predecessors, to find Eusebius especially appreciative of Plato: in fact he devotes to Platonism three books (11–13) of the *Praeparatio*. Clement had spoken of Plato as Moses writing in Greek, and Eusebius, agreeing with Clement, considered that Plato and Moses were in agreement,[1] that Plato may be called a prophet of the economy of salvation.[2] Like Clement and Origen, and like Philo also, Eusebius thought that Plato had borrowed the truths he exposes from the Old Testament;[3] but at the same time he is willing to admit the possibility of Plato having discovered the truth for himself or of his having been enlightened by God.[4] In any case, not only does Plato agree with the sacred literature of the Hebrews in his idea of God, but he also suggests, in his Letters, the idea of the Blessed Trinity. On this point Eusebius is, of course, interpreting Plato in a neo-Platonic sense and is referring to the three principles of the One or Good, the *Nous* or Mind, and the World-Soul.[5] The Ideas are the ideas of God, of the Logos, the exemplar patterns of creation, and the picture of creation in the *Timaeus* is similar to that contained in Genesis.[6] Again, Plato agrees with the Scriptures in his doctrine of immortality,[7] while the moral teaching of the *Phaedrus* reminds Eusebius of St. Paul.[8] Even Plato's political ideal found its realisation in the Jewish theocracy.[9]

Nevertheless, it remains true that Plato did not affirm these truths without an admixture of error.[10] His doctrine of God and of creation is contaminated by his doctrine of emanation and by his acceptance of the eternity of matter, his doctrine of the soul and of immortality by his theory of pre-existence and of reincarnation, and so on. Thus Plato, even if he was a 'prophet', was no more than a prophet: he did not himself enter into the promised land of truth, though he approached near to it: it is Christianity alone which is the true philosophy. Moreover, Plato's philosophy was highly intellectualist, caviar for the multitude, whereas Christianity is for all, so that men and women, rich and poor, learned and unlearned, can be 'philosophers'.

To discuss Eusebius's interpretation of Plato would be out of place here: it is sufficient to note that he, in common with most

---

[1] 11, 28.   [2] 13,13.   [3] 10, 1; 10, 8; 10, 14.   [4] 11, 8.   [5] 11, 16; 11, 20.
[6] 11, 23; 11, 29; 11, 31.   [7] 11, 27.   [8] 12, 27.   [9] 13, 12; 12, 16.   [10] 13, 19.

other Christian Greek writers, gives the palm to Plato among Hellenic thinkers, and that, in common with all the early Christian writers, he makes no real distinction between theology in a strict sense and philosophy in a strict sense. There is one wisdom, which is found adequately and completely only in Christianity: Greek thinkers attained to true philosophy or wisdom in so far as they anticipated Christianity. Among those who anticipated the true philosophy Plato is the most outstanding; but even he stood only on the threshold of truth. Naturally the notion that Plato and other Hellenic thinkers borrowed from the Old Testament, although itself partly a consequence of their understanding of 'philosophy', helped also to confirm Christian writers like Eusebius in their very wide interpretation of 'philosophy', as including not only the result of human speculation but also the data of revelation. In fact, in spite of his very favourable judgement on Plato, the logical conclusion from Eusebius's and others' conviction that the Greek philosophers borrowed from the Old Testament would inevitably be that human speculation unaided by direct illumination from God is not of any great avail in the attainment of truth. For what are the errors with which even Plato contaminated the truth but the result of human speculation? If you say that the truth contained in Greek philosophy came from the Old Testament, that is to say, from revelation, you can hardly avoid the conclusion that the errors in Greek philosophy came from human speculation, with a consequently unfavourable judgement as to the power of that speculation. This attitude was very common among the Fathers and, in the Middle Ages, it was to be clearly expressed by St. Bonaventure in the thirteenth century, though it was not to be the view that ultimately prevailed in Scholasticism, the view of St. Thomas Aquinas and of Duns Scotus.

(ii) One of the most learned of the Greek Fathers and one of the most interesting from the philosophic standpoint was the brother of St. Basil, *St. Gregory of Nyssa*, who was born in Caesarea (in Cappadocia, not Palestine) about A.D. 335 and, after having been a teacher of rhetoric, became Bishop of Nyssa, dying about the year 395.

Gregory of Nyssa realised clearly that the data of revelation are accepted on faith and are not the result of a logical process of reasoning, that the mysteries of faith are not philosophical and scientific conclusions: if they were, then supernatural faith, as exercised by Christians, and Hellenic philosophising would be indistinguishable. On the other hand, the Faith has a rational basis, in that, logically speaking, the acceptance of mysteries on authority presupposes the ascertainability by natural reasoning of certain preliminary truths, especially the existence of God, which are capable of philosophic demonstration. Accordingly, though the superiority of faith must be maintained, it is only right to invoke the aid of philosophy. Ethics, natural philosophy, logic, mathematics, are not only ornaments in the temple of truth but may also contribute to the life of wisdom and virtue: they are, therefore, not to be despised or rejected,[1] though divine revelation must be accepted as a touchstone and criterion of truth since human reasoning must be judged by the word of God, not the word of God by human reasoning.[2] Again, it is right to employ human speculation and human reasoning in regard to dogma; but the conclusions will not be valid unless they agree with the Scriptures.[3]

The cosmic order proves the existence of God, and from the necessary perfection of God we can argue to His unity, that there is one God. Gregory went on to attempt to give reasons for the Trinity of Persons in the one Godhead.[4] For instance, God must have a Logos, a word, a reason. He cannot be less than man, who also has a reason, a word. But the divine Logos cannot be something of fleeting duration. it must be eternal, just as it must be living. The internal word in man is a fleeting accident, but in God there can be no such thing: the Logos is one in Nature with the Father, for there is but one God, the distinction between the Logos and the Father, the Word and the Speaker, being a distinction of relation. To enter into Gregory's Trinitarian doctrine as such is not our concern here; but the fact that he tries, in some sense, to 'prove' the doctrine is of interest, since it afforded a precedent for the later attempts of St. Anselm and Richard of St. Victor to deduce the Trinity, to prove it *rationibus necessariis*.

Obviously, however, St. Gregory's intention, like that of St. Anselm, was to render the mystery more intelligible by the application of dialectic, not to 'rationalise' the mystery in the sense of departing from dogmatic orthodoxy. Similarly, his theory that the word 'man' is primarily applicable to the universal and only secondarily to the individual man was an attempt to render the

---

[1] *De Vita Moysis; P.G.*, 44, 336 DG, 360 BC.
[2] Cf. *De anima et resurrectione; P.G.*, 46, 49 C.
[3] Cf. *Contra Eunom.; P.G.*, 45, 341 B.   [4] Cf. *Oratio Catechetica; P.G.*, 45.

mystery more intelligible, the application of the illustration being this, that the word 'God' refers primarily to the divine essence, which is one, and only secondarily to the divine Persons, who are Three, so that the Christian cannot be rightly accused of tritheism. But, though the illustration was introduced to defeat the charge of tritheism and make the mystery more intelligible, it was an unfortunate illustration, since it implied a hyperrealist view of universals.

St. Gregory's 'Platonism' in regard to universals comes out clearly in his *De hominis opificio*, where he distinguishes the heavenly man, the ideal man, the universal, from the earthly man, the object of experience. The former, the ideal man or rather ideal human being, exists only in the divine idea and is without sexual determination, being neither male nor female: the latter, the human being of experience, is an expression of the ideal and is sexually determined, the ideal being, as it were, 'splintered' or partially expressed in many single individuals. Thus, according to Gregory, individual creatures proceed by creation, not by emanation, from the ideal in the divine Logos. This theory clearly goes back to neo-Platonism and to Philonism, and it was adopted by the first outstanding philosopher of the Middle Ages, John Scotus Eriugena, who was much influenced by the writings of St. Gregory of Nyssa. It must be remembered, however, that Gregory never meant to imply that there was ever an historic ideal man, sexually undetermined; God's idea of man will be realised only eschatologically, when (according to St. Paul's words as interpreted by Gregory) there will be neither male nor female, since in heaven there will be no marriage

God created the world out of an abundance of goodness and love, in order that there might be creatures who could participate in the divine goodness; but though God is goodness and created the world out of goodness, He did not create the world from necessity, but freely. A share in this freedom God has given to man, and God respects this freedom, permitting man to choose evil if he so wills. Evil is the result of man's free choice, God is not responsible. It is true that God foresaw evil and that He permits it, but in spite of this foreknowledge He created man, for He knew also that He would in the end bring all men to Himself. Gregory thus accepted the Origenist theory of the 'restoration of all things': every human being, even Satan and the fallen angels, will at length turn to God, at least through the purifying sufferings of the hereafter. In a sense, then, every human being will at length return to the Ideal and be therein contained, though Gregory certainly accepted individual immortality. This notion of the return of all things to God, to the Principle from whom they sprang, and of the attainment of a state in which God is 'all in all', was also borrowed by John Scotus Eriugena from St. Gregory, and in interpreting the somewhat ambiguous language of John Scotus one should at least bear in mind the thought of St. Gregory, even while admitting the possibility of John Scotus having attached a different meaning to similar words.

But, though St. Gregory of Nyssa shared Origen's theory of the restoration of all things, he did not share Origen's acceptance of the Platonic notion of pre-existence, and in the *De hominis opificio*[1] he says that the author of the *De Principiis* was led astray by Hellenic theories. The soul, which is not confined to any one portion of the body, is 'a created essence (οὐσία γεννητή), a living essence, intellectual, with an organic and sensitive body, an essence that has the power of giving life and perceiving sensible objects, so long as the bodily instruments endure'.[2] As simple and uncompounded (ἁπλῆν καὶ ἀσύνθετον), the soul has the power of surviving the body,[3] with which, however, it will in the end be reunited. The soul is thus spiritual and incorporeal; but how is it different from body, for body, i.e. a concrete material object, is composed, according to Gregory, of qualities which in themselves are incorporeal? In the *De hominis opificio*[4] he says that the union of qualities like colour, solidity, quantity, weight, results in body, whereas their dissolution spells the perishing of the body. In the preceding chapter he has proposed a dilemma: either material things proceed from God, in which case God, as their Source, would contain matter in Himself, would be material, or, if God is not material, then material things do not proceed from Him and matter is eternal. Gregory, however, rejects both the materiality of God and dualism, and the natural conclusion of this would be that the qualities of which bodily things are composed are not material. It is true that, while asserting creation *ex nihilo*, Gregory asserts that we cannot comprehend how God creates the qualities out of nothing; but it is reasonable to suppose that in his eyes the qualities which form body are not themselves bodies: in fact they could not be, since there is no concrete body at all except in and through their *union*. Presumably he was influenced

[1] *P.G.*, 44, 229 ff.   [2] *De anima et res.*; *P.G.* 46, 29.   [3] *Ibid.*, 44.   [4] Ch. 24.

by Plato's doctrine of the qualities in the *Timaeus*. How, then, are they not spiritual? And, if they are spiritual, how does soul differ essentially from body? The reply would doubtless be that, though the qualities unite to *form* body and cannot, considered in abstraction, be called 'bodies', yet they have an essential relation to matter, since it is their function to form matter. An analogous difficulty recurs in regard to the Aristotelian-Thomistic doctrine of matter and form. Prime matter is not in itself body, but it is one of the principles of body: how, then, considered in *itself*, does it differ from the immaterial and spiritual? Thomistic philosophers answer that prime matter never *exists* by itself alone and that it has an exigency for quantity, an essential ordination to concrete body, and presumably Gregory of Nyssa would have to say something of the same sort in regard to his primary qualities. In passing, one may note that similar difficulties might be raised in regard to certain modern theories concerning the constitution of matter. Plato, one might reasonably suppose, would welcome these theories, were he alive to-day, and it is not improbable that St. Gregory of Nyssa would follow suit.

From what has been said it is clear that Gregory of Nyssa was much influenced by Platonism, neo-Platonism, and the writings of Philo (he speaks, for example, of the ὁμοίωσις θεῷ as being the purpose of man, of the 'flight of the alone to the Alone', of justice-in-itself, of *eros* and the ascent to the ideal Beauty); but it must be emphasised that, although Gregory undeniably employed Plotinian themes and expressions, as also to a less extent those of Philo, he did not by any means always understand them in a Plotinian or Philonic sense. On the contrary, he utilised expressions of Plotinus or Plato to expose and state Christian doctrines. For example, the 'likeness to God' is the work of grace, a development under the activity of God, with man's free co-operation, of the image or εἰκών of God implanted in the soul at baptism. Again, justice-in-itself is not an abstract virtue nor even an idea in *Nous*; it is the Logos indwelling in the soul, the effect of this inhabitation being the participated virtue. This Logos, moreover, is not the *Nous* of Plotinus, nor is it the Logos of Philo: it is the Second Person of the Blessed Trinity, and between God and creatures there is no intermediary procession of subordinate hypostases.

Finally, it is noteworthy that St. Gregory of Nyssa was the first real founder of systematic mystical theology. Here again he utilised Plotinian and Philonic themes, but he employed them in a Christian sense and within a Christocentric framework of thought. Naturally speaking man's mind is fitted to know sensible objects, and contemplating these objects the mind can come to know something of God and His attributes (symbolic theology, which is partly equivalent to natural theology in the modern sense). On the other hand, though man by nature has as his proper object of knowledge sensible things, these things are not fully real, they are mirage and illusion except as symbols or manifestations of immaterial reality, that reality towards which man is spiritually drawn. The consequent tension in the soul leads to a state of ἀνελπιστία or 'despair', which is the birth of mysticism, since the soul, drawn by God, leaves its natural object of knowledge, without, however, being able to see the God to whom it is drawn by love: it enters into the darkness, what the mediaeval treatise calls the Cloud of Unknowing. (To this stage corresponds the negative theology, which so influenced the Pseudo-Dionysius.) In the soul's advance there are, as it were, two movements, that of the indwelling of the Triune God and that of the soul's reaching out beyond itself, culminating in 'ecstasy'. Origen had interpreted the Philonic ecstasy intellectually, as any other form of 'ecstasy' was then suspect, owing to Montanist extravagances; but Gregory set ecstasy at the summit of the soul's endeavour, interpreting it first and foremost as ecstatic *love*.

The 'darkness' which envelops God is due primarily to the utter transcendence of the divine essence, and Gregory drew the conclusion that even in heaven the soul is always pressing forward, drawn by love, to penetrate further into God. A static condition would mean either satiety or death: spiritual life demands constant progress and the nature of the divine transcendence involves the same progress, since the human mind can never comprehend God. In a sense, then, the 'divine darkness' *always* persists, and it is true to say that Gregory gave to this knowledge in darkness a priority over intellectual knowledge, not because he despised the human intellect but because he realised the transcendence of God.

St. Gregory's scheme of the soul's ascent certainly bears some resemblance to that of Plotinus; but at the same time it is thoroughly Christocentric. The advance of the soul is the work of the Divine Logos, Christ. Moreover, his ideal is not that of a solitary union with God, but rather of a realisation of the *Pleroma* of Christ: the advance of one soul brings grace and blessing to others and the indwelling of God in the individual affects the whole Body. His mysticism is also thoroughly sacramental in character: the εἰκών is restored by Baptism, union with God is fostered by the Eucharist. In fine, the writings of St. Gregory of Nyssa are the source from which not only the Pseudo-Dionysius and mystics down to St. John of the Cross drew, directly or indirectly, much of their inspiration; but they are also the fountain-head of those Christian philosophical systems which trace out the soul's advance through different stages of knowledge and love up to the mystical life and the Beatific Vision. If a purely spiritual writer like St. John of the Cross stands in the line that goes back to Gregory, so does the mystical philosopher St. Bonaventure.

7. Of the Latin Fathers the greatest, without a shadow of doubt, is St. Augustine of Hippo; but, because of the importance of his thought for the Middle Ages, I shall consider his philosophy separately and rather more at length. In this section it is sufficient to mention very briefly *St. Ambrose* (about 333 to 397), Bishop of Milan.

St. Ambrose shared the typically Roman attitude towards philosophy, i.e. an interest in practical and ethical matters, coupled with little facility or taste for metaphysical speculation. In his dogmatic and Scriptural work he depended mainly on the Greek Fathers; but in ethics he was influenced by Cicero, and in his *De officiis ministrorum*, composed about 391 and addressed to the clergy of Milan, he provided a Christian counterpart to the *De officiis* of the great Roman orator. In his book the Saint follows Cicero closely in his divisions and treatment of the virtues, but the whole treatment is naturally infused with the Christian ethos, and the Stoic ideal of happiness, found in the possession of virtue, is complemented by the final ideal of eternal happiness in God. It is not that St. Ambrose makes any particularly new contributions to Christian ethic: the importance of his work lies rather in its influence on succeeding thought, in the use made of it by later writers on ethics.

8. The Greek Fathers, as has been seen, were mainly influenced by the Platonic tradition; but one of the factors which helped to prepare the way for the favourable reception eventually accorded to Aristotelianism in the Latin West was the work of the last of the Greek Fathers, St. John Damascene.

St. John Damascene, who died probably at the end of the year

A.D. 749, was not only a resolute opponent of the 'Iconoclasts' but also a great systematiser in the field of theology, so that he can be looked on as the Scholastic of the Orient. He explicitly says that he does not intend to give new and personal opinions, but to preserve and hand on the thoughts of holy and learned men, so that it would be useless to seek in his writings for novelty of content; yet in his systematic and ordered presentation of the ideas of his predecessors a certain originality may be ascribed to him. His chief work is the *Fount of Wisdom*, in the first part of which he gives a sketch of the Aristotelian logic and ontology, though he draws on other writers besides Aristotle, e.g. Porphyry. In this first part, the *Dialectica*, he makes clear his opinion that philosophy and profane science are the instruments or handmaids of theology, adopting the view of Clement of Alexandria and the two Gregories, a view which goes back to Philo the Alexandrian Jew and was often repeated in the Middle Ages.[1] In the second part of his great work he gives a history of heresies, using material supplied by former writers, and in the third part, the *De Fide Orthodoxa*, he gives, in four books, an orderly treatment of orthodox Patristic theology. This third part was translated into Latin by Burgundius of Pisa in 1151 and was used by, among others, Peter Lombard, St. Albert the Great and St. Thomas Aquinas. In the East, St. John Damascene enjoys almost as much esteem as St. Thomas Aquinas in the West.

9. From even the brief survey given above it is evident that one would look in vain for a systematic philosophical synthesis in the works of any of the Greek Fathers or indeed in any of the Latin Fathers save Augustine. The Greek Fathers, making no very clear distinction between the provinces of philosophy and theology, regarded Christianity as the one true wisdom or 'philosophy'. Hellenic philosophy they tended to regard as a propaedeutic to Christianity, so that their main interest in treating of it was to point out the anticipation of Christian truth which they saw therein contained and the aberrations from truth which were also clear to them. The former they frequently attributed to borrowing from the Old Testament, the latter to the weakness of human speculation and to the perverse desire of originality, the vainglory, of the philosophers themselves. When they adopted ideas from Hellenic philosophy they generally accepted them because they thought that they would help in the exposition and presentation

---

[1] *P.G.*, 94, 532 AB.

of the Christian wisdom, not in order to incorporate them in a philosophic system in the strict sense.

Nevertheless, there are, as we have seen, philosophic elements in the writings of the Fathers. For instance, they make use of rational arguments for God's existence, particularly the argument from order and design; they speculate about the origin and nature of the soul; St. Gregory of Nyssa even had some ideas which fall under the heading of philosophy of nature or cosmology. Still, since their arguments, the arguments for God's existence, for example, are not really worked out in any developed, systematic and strict manner, it may appear out of place to have considered them at all. I think, however, that this would be a mistake, as even a brief treatment of Patristic thought is sufficient to bring out one point which may tend to be forgotten by those who know little of Christian philosophic thought. Owing to the fact that St. Thomas Aquinas, who has in recent times been accorded a peculiar status among Catholic philosophers, adopted a great deal of the Aristotelian system, and owing to the fact that early thinkers of the 'modern era', e.g. Descartes and Francis Bacon, fulminate against Scholastic Aristotelianism, it is sometimes taken for granted that Christian philosophy, or at least Catholic philosophy, means Aristotelianism and nothing else. Yet, leaving out of account for the present later centuries, a survey of Patristic thought is sufficient to show that Plato, and not Aristotle, was the Greek thinker who won the greatest esteem from the Fathers of the Church. This may have been due in great part to the fact that neo-Platonism was the dominant and vigorous contemporary philosophy and to the fact that the Fathers not only saw Plato more or less in the light of neo-Platonic interpretation and development but also knew comparatively little about Aristotle, in most cases at least; but it also remains true that, whatever may have been the cause or causes, the Fathers tended to see in Plato a forerunner of Christianity and that the philosophic elements they adopted were adopted, for the most part, from the Platonic tradition. If one adds to this the further consideration that Patristic thought, especially that of Augustine, profoundly influenced, not only the early Middle Ages, not only such eminent thinkers as St. Anselm and St. Bonaventure, but even St. Thomas Aquinas himself, it will be seen that, from the historical viewpoint at least, some knowledge of Patristic thought is both desirable and valuable.

CHAPTER III

ST. AUGUSTINE—I

Life and writings—St. Augustine and Philosophy.

1. In Latin Christendom the name of Augustine stands out as that of the greatest of the Fathers both from a literary and from a theological standpoint, a name that dominated Western thought until the thirteenth century and which can never lose its lustre, notwithstanding the Aristotelianism of St. Thomas Aquinas and his School, especially as this Aristotelianism was very far from disregarding and still further from belittling the great African Doctor. Indeed, in order to understand the currents of thought in the Middle Ages, a knowledge of Augustinianism is essential. In the present work the thought of Augustine cannot be treated with the fullness which it merits, but treated it must be, even if summarily.

Born at Tagaste in the Province of Numidia on November 13th, A.D. 354, Augustine came of a pagan father, Patricius, and a Christian mother, St. Monica. His mother brought up her child as a Christian, but Augustine's baptism was deferred, in accordance with a common, if undesirable, custom of the time.[1] The child learnt the rudiments of Latin and arithmetic from a schoolmaster of Tagaste, but play, at which he wished always to be the winner, was more attractive to him than study, and Greek, which he began after a time, he hated, though he was attracted by the Homeric poems considered as a story. That Augustine knew practically no Greek is untrue; but he never learned to read the language with ease.

In about A.D. 365 Augustine went to the town of Madaura, where he laid the foundation of his knowledge of Latin literature and grammar. Madaura was still largely a pagan place, and the effect of the general atmosphere and of his study of the Latin classics was evidently to detach the boy from the faith of his mother, a detachment which his year of idleness at Tagaste (369–70) did nothing to mitigate. In 370, the year in which his father died after having become a Catholic, Augustine began the study of rhetoric at Carthage, the largest city he had yet seen. The

[1] *Conf.*, I, 11, 17.

licentious ways of the great port and centre of government, the sight of the obscene rites connected with cults imported from the East, combined with the fact that Augustine, the southerner, was already a man, with passions alive and vehement, led to his practical break with the moral ideals of Christianity and before long he took a mistress, with whom he lived for over ten years and by whom he had a son in his second year at Carthage. In spite, however, of his irregular life Augustine was a very successful student of rhetoric and by no means neglected his studies.

It was soon after reading the *Hortensius* of Cicero, which turned the youth's mind to the search for truth, that Augustine accepted the teaching of the Manichaeans,[1] which seemed to offer him a rational presentation of truth, in distinction from the barbaric ideas and illogical doctrines of Christianity. Thus Christians maintained that God created the whole world and that God is good: how, then, could they explain the existence of evil and suffering? The Manichaeans, however, maintained a dualistic theory, according to which there are two ultimate principles, a good principle, that of light, God or Ormuzd, and an evil principle, that of darkness, Ahriman. These principles are both eternal and their strife is eternal, a strife reflected in the world which is the production of the two principles in mutual conflict. In man the soul, composed of light, is the work of the good principle, while the body, composed of grosser matter, is the work of the evil principle. This system commended itself in Augustine's eyes because it seemed to explain the problem of evil and because of its fundamental materialism, for he could not yet conceive how there could be an immaterial reality, imperceptible to the senses. Conscious of his own passions and sensual desires, he felt that he could now attribute them to an evil cause outside himself. Moreover, although the Manichaeans condemned sexual intercourse and the eating of flesh-meat and prescribed ascetic practices such as fasting, these practices obliged only the elect, not the 'hearers', to which level Augustine belonged.

Augustine, now detached from Christianity both morally and intellectually, returned to Tagaste in 374 and there taught grammar and Latin literature for a year, after which he opened a school of rhetoric at Carthage in the autumn of 374. He lived with his mistress and their child, Adeodatus, and it was during this period that he won a prize for poetry (a dramatic piece, not now extant)

[1] Manichaeanism, founded by Manes or Mani in the third century, originated in Persia and was a mixture of Persian and Christian elements.

and published his first prose work, *De pulchro et apto*. The sojourn at Carthage lasted until 383 and it was shortly before Augustine's departure for Rome that an event of some importance occurred. Augustine had been troubled by difficulties and problems which the Manichaeans could not answer; for example, the problem of the source of certitude in human thought, the reason why the two principles were in eternal conflict, etc. It happened that a noted Manichaean bishop, Faustus by name, came to Carthage, and Augustine resolved to seek from him a satisfactory solution of his difficulties; but, though he found Faustus agreeable and friendly, he did not find in his words the intellectual satisfaction which he sought. It was, therefore, with his faith in Manichaeism already somewhat shaken that he set out for Rome. He made the journey partly because the students at Carthage were ill-mannered and difficult to control, whereas he had heard good reports of the students' behaviour at Rome, partly because he hoped for greater success in his career in the imperial metropolis. Arrived at Rome, Augustine opened a school in rhetoric, but, though the students were well behaved in class, they had the inconvenient habit of changing their school just before the payment of fees was due. He accordingly sought for and obtained a position at Milan as municipal professor of rhetoric in 384; but he did not leave Rome without having lost most of his belief in Manichaeanism and having been consequently attracted towards Academic scepticism, though he retained a nominal adherence to Manichaeanism and still accepted some of the Manichaean positions, for example their materialism.

At Milan, Augustine came to think a little better of Christianity owing to the sermons on the Scriptures delivered by St. Ambrose, Bishop of Milan; but though he was ready to become a catechumen again, he was not yet convinced of the truth of Christianity. Moreover, his passions were still too strong for him. His mother wished him to marry a certain girl, hoping that marriage would help to reform his life; but, being unable to wait the necessary time for the girl in question, he took another mistress in place of the mother of Adeodatus, from whom he had parted in sorrow in view of the proposed marriage. At this time Augustine read certain 'Platonic treatises in the Latin translation of Victorinus, these treatises being most probably the *Enneads* of Plotinus. The effect of neo-Platonism was to free him from the shackles of materialism and to facilitate his acceptance of the idea of immaterial reality. In addition, the Plotinian conception of evil as privation rather than as something positive showed him how the problem of evil could be met without having to have recourse to the dualism of the Manichaeans. In other words, the function of neo-Platonism at this period was to render it possible for Augustine to see the reasonableness of Christianity, and he began to read the New Testament again, particularly the writings of St. Paul. If neo-Platonism suggested to him the idea of the contemplation of spiritual things, of wisdom in the intellectual sense, the New Testament showed him that it was also necessary to lead a life in accordance with wisdom.

These impressions were confirmed by his meeting with two men, Simplicianus and Pontitianus. The former, an old priest, gave Augustine an account of the conversion of Victorinus, the neo-Platonist, to Christianity, with the result that the young man 'burned with the desire to do likewise',[1] while the latter spoke of the life of St. Anthony of Egypt, which made Augustine disgusted with his own moral state.[2] There followed that intense moral struggle, which culminated in the famous scene enacted in the garden of his house, when Augustine hearing a child's voice over a wall crying repeatedly the refrain *Tolle lege! Tolle lege!* opened the New Testament at random and lighted on the words of St. Paul in the Epistle to the Romans,[3] which sealed his moral conversion.[4] It is perfectly clear that the conversion which then took place was a moral conversion, a conversion of will, a conversion which followed the intellectual conversion. His reading of neo-Platonic works was an instrument in the intellectual conversion of Augustine, while his moral conversion, from the human viewpoint, was prepared by the sermons of Ambrose and the words of Simplicianus and Pontitianus, and confirmed and sealed by the New Testament. The agony of his second or moral conversion was intensified by the fact that he already knew what he ought to do, though on the other hand he felt himself without the power to accomplish it: to the words of St. Paul, however, which he read in the garden, he gave, under the impulse of grace, a 'real assent' and his life was changed. This conversion occurred in the summer of 386.

A lung ailment from which he was suffering gave Augustine the excuse he wanted to retire from his professorship and at Cassiciacum, through reading and reflection and discussions with friends, he endeavoured to obtain a better understanding of the Christian religion, using as an instrument concepts and themes taken from

[1] *Conf.*, 8, 5, 10.   [2] *Ibid.*, 8, 7, 16.   [3] *Rom.*, 13, 13–14.   [4] *Conf.* 8, 8–12.

neo-Platonic philosophy, his idea of Christianity being still very incomplete and tinctured, more than it was to be later, by neo-Platonism. From this period of retirement date his works *Contra Academicos*, *De Beata Vita* and *De Ordine*. Returning to Milan Augustine wrote the *De Immortalitate Animae* (the *Soliloquia* were also written about this time) and began the *De Musica*. On Holy Saturday of 387 Augustine was baptised by St. Ambrose, soon after which event he set out to return to Africa. His mother, who had come over to Italy, died at Ostia, while they were waiting for a boat. (It was at Ostia that there occurred the celebrated scene described in the *Confessions*.[1]) Augustine delayed his return to Africa and while residing at Rome wrote the *De libero arbitrio*, the *De Quantitate Animae* and the *De moribus ecc'esiae Catholicae et de moribus Manichaeorum*. In the autumn of 388 he set sail for Africa.

Back at Tagaste, Augustine established a small monastic community. From this period (388–91) date his *De Genesi contra Manichaeos*, *De Magistro* and *De Vera Religione*, while he completed the *De Musica*. It is probable that he also polished up or completed the *De moribus*, mentioned above. At Cassiciacum Augustine had resolved never to marry, but he did not apparently intend to seek ordination, for it was contrary to his own wishes that the Bishop of Hippo ordained him priest in 391, when he was on a visit to that seaport town, about a hundred and fifty miles due west of Carthage. The bishop desired Augustine's help, and the latter settled down at Hippo and established a monastery. Engaged in controversy with the Manichaeans he composed the *De utilitate credendi*, the *De duabus animabus*, the *Disputatio contra Fortunatum*, the *De Fide et Symbolo*, a lecture on the Creed delivered before a synod of African bishops, and, against the Donatists, the *Psalmus contra partem Donati*. He started a literal commentary on *Genesis*, but, as its name implies (*De Genesi ad litteram liber imperfectus*), left it unfinished. The *De diversis quaestionibus* (389–96), the *Contra Adimantum Manichaeum*, *De sermone Domini in monte*, the *De Mendacio* and *De Continentia*, as well as various Commentaries (on *Romans* and *Galatians*) also date from the early period of Augustine's priestly life.

In the year 395–6 Augustine was consecrated auxiliary Bishop of Hippo, setting up another monastic establishment within his residence very shortly after his consecration. When Valerius,

[1] 9, 10, 23–6.

Bishop of Hippo, died in 396, within a year of Augustine's consecration, he became ruling Bishop of Hippo in Valerius's place, and
remained in that post until his death. This meant that he had to
face the task of governing a diocese in which the Donatist schism
was well entrenched instead of being able to devote himself to a
life of quiet prayer and study. However, whatever his personal
inclinations, Augustine threw himself into the anti-Donatist
struggle with ardour, preaching, disputing, publishing anti-Donatist controversy. Nevertheless, in spite of this activity, he found
time for composing such works as the *De diversis quaestionibus ad
Simplicianum* (397), part of the *De Doctrina Christiana* (the fourth
book being added in 426), part of the *Confessions* (the whole work
being published by 400), and the *Annotationes in Job*. Augustine
also exchanged controversial letters with the great scholar St.
Jerome, on Scriptural matters.

In the year 400 St. Augustine started on one of his greatest
treatises, the fifteen books *De Trinitate*, which were completed in
417, and in 401 began the twelve books of the *De Genesi ad
litteram*, completed in 415. In the same year (400) appeared the
De catechizandis rudibus, the *De Consensu Evangelistarum*, the *De
Opera Monachorum*, the *Contra Faustum Manichaeum* (thirty-
three books), the first book of the *Contra litteras Petiliani* (Donatist
Bishop of Cirta), the second book dating from 401-2 and the third
from 402-3. These were followed by other anti-Donatist works,
such as the *Contra Cresconium grammaticum partis Donati* (402),
though various publications have not been preserved, and several
writings against the Manichaeans. In addition to this controversial
activity Augustine was constantly preaching and writing letters:
thus the letter to Dioscorus,[1] in which, in answer to certain
questions about Cicero, Augustine develops his views on pagan
philosophy, still showing a strong predilection for neo-Platonism,
dates from 410.

Imperial edicts were issued in the course of time against the
Donatists, and about the year 411, after the conference that then
took place, Augustine was able to turn his attention to another
set of opponents, the Pelagians. Pelagius, who exaggerated the
rôle of human volition in man's salvation and minimised that of
grace, denying original sin, visited Carthage in 410 accompanied
by Coelestius. In 411, after Pelagius had left for the East,
Coelestius was excommunicated by a Council at Carthage. Pelagius

[1] *Epist.*, 118.

had tried to use texts from Augustine's *De libero arbitrio* in support of his own heresy, but the bishop made his position quite clear in his *De peccatorum meritis et remissione, et de baptismo parvulorum, ad Marcellinum*, following it up in the same year (412) by the *De spiritu et littera*, and later by the *De fide et operibus* (413), the *De natura et gratia contra Pelagium* (415) and the *De perfectione iustitiae hominis* (415). However, not content with his anti-Pelagian polemic, Augustine began, in 413, the twenty-two books of the *De Civitate Dei* (completed in 426), one of his greatest and most famous works, written against the background of the barbarian invasion of the Empire, and prepared many of his *Enarrationes in Psalmos*. In addition he published (415) the *Ad Orosium, contra Priscillianistas et Origenistas*, a book against the heresy started by the Spanish bishop, Priscillian, and in the course of further anti-Pelagian polemic the *De Gestis Pelagii* (417) and the *De Gratia Christi et peccato originali* (418). As if all this were not enough, Augustine finished the *De Trinitate*, and wrote his *In Joannis Evangelium* (416–17) and *In Epistolas Joannis ad Parthos* (416), not to speak of numerous letters and sermons.

In 418 Pelagianism was condemned, first by a Council of African bishops, then by the Emperor Honorius, and finally by Pope Zosimus, but the controversy was not yet over, and when Augustine was accused by Julian, heretical Bishop of Eclanum, of having invented the concept of original sin, the Saint replied in the work *De nuptiis et concupiscentia* (419–20), while in 420 he addressed two books, *Contra duas epistolas Pelagianorum ad Bonifatium Papam*, to the Pope, and followed them up by his *Contra Iulianum haeresis Pelagianae defensorem* (six books) in 421. The *De anima et eius origine* (419), the *Contra mendacium ad Consentium* (420), the *Contra adversarium Legis et Prophetarum* (420), the *Enchiridion ad Laurentium, De fide, spe, caritate* (421), the *De cura pro mortuis gerenda, ad Paulinum Nolanum* (420–1), also date from this period.

In 426 Augustine, feeling that he would not live very much longer, provided for the future of his diocese by nominating his successor, the priest Eraclius, the nomination being acclaimed by the people; but the Saint's literary activity was by no means over, and in 426–7 he published the *De gratia et libero arbitrio ad Valentinum*, the *De correptione et gratia* and the two books of *Retractiones*, which contain a critical survey of his works and are of great value for establishing their chronology. All this time the situation of the Empire was going from bad to worse, and in 429

Genseric led the Vandals from Spain into Africa; but Augustine continued writing. In 427 he published the *Speculum de Scriptura Sacra*, a selection of texts from the Bible, and in 428 his *De haeresibus ad Quodvultdeum*, followed by the *De praedestinatione sanctorum ad Prosperum* and the *De dono perseverantiae ad Prosperum* in 428–9. In addition, Augustine began the *Opus imperfectum contra Julianum* in 429, a refutation of an anti-Augustinian treatise by the Pelagian Julian which had been written some time previously but had come into the Saint's hands only in 428; but he did not live to finish the work (hence its name). Augustine also came into contact with Arianism, and in 428 appeared his *Collatio cum Maximino Arianorum episcopo* and his *Contra Maximinum haereticum*.

In the late spring or early summer of 430 the Vandals laid siege to Hippo, and it was during the siege that Augustine died on August 28th, 430, as he was reciting the Penitential Psalms. Possidius remarks that he left no will, since, as one of God's paupers, he had nothing to leave. The Vandals subsequently burnt the city, though the cathedral and the library of Augustine were left intact. Possidius wrote the Life of Augustine, which is to be found in the Latin Patrology. 'Those who read what he (Augustine) has written on divine things can profit much; but I think that they would profit more were they able to hear and see him preaching in the church, and especially those who were privileged to enjoy intimate conversation with him.'[1]

2. It may perhaps seem strange that I have spoken of St. Augustine's theological controversies and listed a large number of theological treatises; but a sketch of his life and activity will suffice to make it plain that, with a few exceptions, Augustine did not compose purely philosophical works in our sense. In a book like this, one does not, of course, intend to treat of Augustine's purely theological doctrine, but, in order to elicit his philosophical teaching one has to have frequent recourse to what are primarily theological treatises. Thus, in order to obtain light on Augustine's theory of knowledge, it is necessary to consult the relevant texts of the *De Trinitate*, while the *De Genesi ad litteram* expounds the theory of *rationes seminales* and the *Confessions* contain a treatment of time. This mingling of theological and philosophical themes may appear odd and unmethodical to us to-day, used as we are to a clear distinction between the provinces of dogmatic

---

[1] *Vita S. Aug.*, 31.

theology and philosophy; but one must remember that Augustine, in common with other Fathers and early Christian writers, made no such clear distinction. It is not that Augustine failed to recognise, still less that he denied, the intellect's power of attaining truth without revelation; it is rather that he regarded the Christian wisdom as one whole, that he tried to penetrate by his understanding the Christian faith and to see the world and human life in the light of the Christian wisdom. He knew quite well that rational arguments can be adduced for God's existence, for example, but it was not so much the mere intellectual assent to God's existence that interested him as the real assent, the positive adhesion of the will to God, and he knew that in the concrete such an adhesion to God requires divine grace. In short, Augustine did not play two parts, the part of the theologian and the part of the philosopher who considers the 'natural man'; he thought rather of man as he is in the concrete, fallen and redeemed mankind, man who is able indeed to attain truth but who is constantly solicited by God's grace and who requires grace in order to appropriate the truth that saves. If there was question of convincing someone that God exists, Augustine would see the proof as a stage or as an instrument in the total process of the man's conversion and salvation: he would recognise the proof as *in itself* rational, but he would be acutely conscious, not only of the moral preparation necessary to give a real and living assent to the proof, but also of the fact that, according to God's intention for man in the concrete, recognition of God's existence is not enough, but should lead on, under the impulse of grace, to supernatural faith in God's revelation and to a life in accordance with Christ's teaching. Reason has its part to play in bringing a man to faith, and, once a man has the faith, reason has its part to play in penetrating the data of faith; but it is the total relation of the soul to God which primarily interests Augustine. Reason, as we have seen, had its part to play in the intellectual stage of his own conversion and reason had its part to play after his conversion: generalising his own experience, then, he would consider the fullness of wisdom to consist in a penetration of what is believed, though in the approach to wisdom reason helps to prepare a man for faith. 'The medicine for the soul, which is effected by the divine providence and ineffable beneficence, is perfectly beautiful in degree and distinction. For it is divided between Authority and Reason. Authority demands of us faith, and prepares man for reason. Reason leads to perception and cognition, although authority also does not leave reason wholly out of sight, when the question of who may be believed is being considered.'[1]

This attitude was characteristic of the Augustinian tradition. St. Anselm's aim is expressed in his words *Credo ut intelligam*, while St. Bonaventure, in the thirteenth century, explicitly rejected the sharp delimitation of the spheres of theology and philosophy. The Thomist distinction between the sciences of dogmatic theology and philosophy, with the accompanying distinction of the modes of procedure to be employed in the two sciences, no doubt evolved inevitably out of the earlier attitude, though, quite apart from that consideration, it obviously enjoys this very great advantage that it corresponds to an actual and real distinction between revelation and the data of the 'unaided' reason, between the supernatural and natural spheres. It is at once a safeguard of the doctrine of the supernatural and also of the powers of man in the natural order. Yet the Augustinian attitude on the other hand enjoys this advantage, that it contemplates always man *as he is*, man in the concrete, for *de facto* man has only one final end, a supernatural end, and, as far as actual existence is concerned, there is but man fallen and redeemed: there never has been, is not, and never will be a purely 'natural man' without a supernatural vocation and end. If Thomism, without of course neglecting the fact that man in the concrete has but a supernatural end, places emphasis on the distinction between the supernatural and the natural, between faith and reason, Augustinianism, without in the least neglecting the gratuitous character of supernatural faith and grace, always envisages man in the concrete and is primarily interested in his actual relation to God.

This being so, it is only natural that we should have to unravel Augustine's 'purely philosophical' ideas from the total fabric of his thought. To do this is, of course, to survey Augustinianism more or less from a Thomist viewpoint, but that does not mean that it is an illegitimate approach: it means that one is asking what ideas of Augustine are philosophical in the academic understanding of the term. It does indeed mean tearing his ideas from their full context, but in a history of philosophy, which presupposes a certain idea of what philosophy is, one can do nothing else. It must, however, be admitted that a concentration of this sort on Augustine's philosophical ideas, using the word in the Thomist

[1] *De vera relig.*, 24. 45.

sense, tends to give a rather poor idea of the Saint's intellectual achievement, at least to one who is trained in the academic and objective atmosphere of Thomism, since he never elaborated a philosophical system as such, nor did he develop, define and substantiate his philosophical ideas in the manner to which a Thomist is accustomed. The result is that it is not infrequently difficult to say precisely what Augustine meant by this or that idea or statement, how precisely he understood it: there is often an aura of vagueness, allusion, lack of definition about his ideas which leaves one dissatisfied, perplexed and curious. The rigid type of Thomist would, I suppose, maintain that Augustine's philosophy contains nothing of value which was not much better said by St. Thomas, more clearly delineated and defined; but the fact remains that the Augustinian tradition is not dead even to-day, and it may be that the very incompleteness and lack of systematisation in Augustine's thought, its very 'suggestiveness', is a positive help towards the longevity of his tradition, for the 'Augustinian' is not faced by a complete system to be accepted, rejected or mutilated: he is faced by an approach, an inspiration, certain basic ideas which are capable of considerable development, so that he can remain perfectly faithful to the Augustinian spirit even though he departs from what the historic Augustine actually said.

CHAPTER IV

ST. AUGUSTINE—II: KNOWLEDGE

Knowledge with a view to beatitude—Against scepticism—
Experiential knowledge—Nature of sensation—Divine ideas
—Illumination and Abstraction.

1. To start with the 'epistemology' of St. Augustine is perhaps to give the impression that Augustine was concerned with elaborating a theory of knowledge for its own sake or as a methodological propaedeutic to metaphysics. This would be a wrong impression, however, since Augustine never sat down, as it were, to develop a theory of knowledge and then, on the basis of a realist theory of knowledge, to construct a systematic metaphysic. If Spinoza, according to his own words,[1] aimed at developing the philosophy of God or Substance because it is only contemplation of an infinite and eternal Object which can fully satisfy mind and heart and bring happiness to the soul, far more could an analogous statement be made of Augustine, who emphasised the fact that knowledge of the truth is to be sought, not for purely academic purposes, but as bringing true happiness, true beatitude. Man feels his insufficiency, he reaches out to an object greater than himself, an object which can bring peace and happiness, and knowledge of that object is an essential condition of its attainment; but he sees knowledge in function of an end, beatitude. Only the wise man can be happy and wisdom postulates knowledge of the truth; but there is no question in Augustine's thought of speculation as an end in itself. When the young man Licentius, in the *Contra Academicos*, maintains that wisdom consists in seeking for the truth and declares, like Lessing, that happiness is to be found rather in the pursuit of truth than in the actual attainment and possession of truth, Augustine retorts that it is absurd to predicate wisdom of a man who has no knowledge of truth. In the *De Beata Vita*[2] he says that no one is happy who does not possess what he strives to possess, so that the man who is seeking for truth but has not yet found it, cannot be said to be truly happy. Augustine himself sought for truth because he felt a need for it, and looking back on his development in the light of attainment, he interpreted this as

[1] *De Intellectus Emendatione.*   [2] 2, 10 and 14; 4, 27 ff.

a search for Christ and Christian wisdom, as the attraction of the divine beauty, and this experience he universalised. This universalisation of his own experience, however, does not mean that his ideas were purely subjective: his psychological introspection enabled him to lay bare the dynamism of the human soul.

Yet to say that Augustine was not an 'intellectualist' in an academic sense and that his philosophy is eudaemonistic is not to say that he was not acutely conscious of the problem of certitude. It would, however, be a mistake to think that Augustine was preoccupied with the question, '*Can* we attain certainty?' As we shall see shortly, he did answer this question, but the question that occupied his attention in the mature period of his thought was rather this, '*How* is it that we can attain certainty?' That we do attain certainty being assumed as a datum, the problem remains: 'How does the finite, changing human mind attain certain knowledge of eternal truths, truths which rule and govern the mind and so transcend it?' After the breakdown of his faith in Manichaeism, Augustine was tempted to relapse into Academic scepticism: his victory over this temptation he expressed in the *Contra Academicos*, where he shows that we indubitably do attain certainty of some facts at least. This granted, his reading of 'Platonic works' suggested to him the problem, how it is that we are able not only to know with certainty eternal and necessary truths, but also to know them as eternal and necessary truths. Plato explained this fact by the theory of reminiscence; how was Augustine to explain it? The discussion of the problem no doubt interested him in itself, for its own sake; but he also saw in what he considered to be the right answer a clear proof of God's existence and operation. The knowledge of eternal truth should thus bring the soul, by reflection on that knowledge, to knowledge of God Himself and God's activity.

2. As I have already said, in the *Contra Academicos* Augustine is primarily concerned to show that wisdom pertains to happiness, and knowledge of truth to wisdom; but he also makes it clear that even the Sceptics are certain of some truths, for example, that of two disjunctive propositions one is true and the other false. 'I am certain that there is either one world or more than one world, and, if more than one, then that there is either a finite or an infinite number of worlds.' Similarly I know that the world either has no beginning or end or has a beginning but no end or had no beginning but will have an end or has both a beginning and an end. In other

words, I am at least certain of the principle of contradiction.[1] Again, even if I am sometimes deceived in thinking that appearance and reality always correspond, I am at least certain of my subjective impression. 'I have no complaint to make of the senses, for it is unjust to demand of them more than they can give: whatever the eyes can see they see truly. Then is that true which they see in the case of the oar in the water? Quite true. For, granted the cause why it appears in that way (i.e. bent), if the oar, when plunged into the water, appeared straight, I should rather accuse my eyes of playing me false. For they would not see what, granted the circumstances, they ought to see. . . . But I am deceived, if I give my assent, someone will say. Then don't give assent to more than the fact of appearance, and you won't be deceived. For I do not see how the sceptic can refute the man who says, "I know that this object seems white to me, I know that this sound gives me pleasure, I know this smell is pleasant to me, I know that this tastes sweet to me, I know that this feels cold to my touch." '[2] St. Augustine refers in the above passage to the Epicureans and it is clear that what he means is that the senses as such never lie or deceive us, even if we may deceive ourselves in judging that things exist objectively in the same way that they appear. The mere appearance of the bent oar is not deception, for there would be something wrong with my eyes were it to appear straight. If I go on to judge that the oar is really bent in itself, I am wrong, but as long as I simply say, 'It appears to me bent', I am speaking the truth and I know that I am speaking the truth. Similarly, if I come out of a hot room and put my hand in tepid water, it may seem to me cold, but as long as I merely say, 'This water *seems* cold to me', I am saying something the truth of which I am certain of, and no sceptic can refute me.

Again, everyone who doubts knows that he is doubting, so that he is certain of this truth at least, namely the fact that he doubts. Thus every one who doubts whether there is such a thing as truth, knows at least one truth, so that his very capacity to doubt should convince him that there is such a thing as truth.[3] We are certain, too, of mathematical truths. When anyone says that seven and three make ten, he does not say that they ought to make ten, but knows that they do make ten.[4]

[1] *C. Acad.*, 3, 10, 23.   [2] *Ibid.*, 3, 11, 26.
[3] *De vera relig.*, 39, 73.   [4] *De lib. arbit.*, 12, 34.

3. But what of real existences? Are we certain of the existence
of any real object or are we confined to certain knowledge of
abstract principles and mathematical truths? Augustine answers
that a man is at least certain of his existence. Even supposing
that he doubts of the existence of other created objects or of God,
the very fact of his doubt shows that he exists, for he could not
doubt, did he not exist. Nor is it of any use to suggest that one
might be deceived into thinking that one exists, for 'if you did not
exist, you could not be deceived in anything.'[1] In this way St.
Augustine anticipates Descartes: *Si fallor, sum.*

With existence Augustine couples life and understanding. In
the *De libero arbitrio*[2] he points out that it is clear to a man that
he exists, and that this fact would not and could not be clear,
unless he were alive. Moreover, it is clear to him that he understands both the fact of his existence and the fact that he is living.
Accordingly he is certain of three things, that he exists, that he
lives and that he understands. Similarly, in the *De Trinitate*,[3] he
observes that it is useless for the sceptic to insinuate that the man
is asleep and sees these things in his dreams, for the man is
affirming not that he is awake but that he lives: 'whether he be
asleep or awake he lives.' Even if he were mad, he would still be
alive. Again, a man is certainly conscious of what he wills. If
someone says that he wills to be happy, it is mere impudence to
suggest to him that he is deceived. Sceptical philosophers may
babble about the bodily senses and the way in which they deceive
us, but they cannot invalidate that certain knowledge which the
mind has by itself, without the intervention of the sense.[4] 'We
exist and we know that we exist and we love that fact and our
knowledge of it; in these three things which I have enumerated
no fear of deception disturbs us; for we do not attain them by any
bodily sense, as we do external objects.'[5]

Augustine thus claims certainty for what we know by inner
experience, by self-consciousness: what does he think of our knowledge of external objects, the things we know by the senses? Have
we certainty in their regard? That we can deceive ourselves in
our judgements concerning the objects of the senses Augustine
was well aware, and some of his remarks show that he was conscious of the relativity of sense-impressions, in the sense that a
judgement as to hot or cold, for example, depends to a certain
extent on the condition of the sense-organs: moreover, he did not

[1] *De lib. arbit.*, 2, 3, 7.   [2] 2, 3, 7.   [3] 15, 12, 21.   [4] *Ibid.*   [5] *De Civit. Dei*, 11, 26.

consider that the objects apprehensible by the senses constitute the proper object of the human intellect. Being chiefly interested in the soul's orientation to God, corporeal objects appeared to him as a starting-point in the mind's ascent to God, though even in this respect the soul itself is a more adequate starting-point: we should return within ourselves, where truth abides, and use the soul, the image of God, as a stepping-stone to Him.[1] Nevertheless, even if corporeal things, the objects of the senses, are essentially mutable and are far less adequate manifestations of God than is the soul, even if it is through concentration on the things of sense that the most harmful errors arise, we are dependent on the senses for a great deal of our knowledge and Augustine had no intention of maintaining a purely sceptical attitude in regard to the objects of the senses. It is one thing to admit the possibility of error in sense-knowledge and quite another to refuse any credence at all to the senses. Thus, after saying that philosophers may speak against the senses but cannot refute the consciousness of self-existence, Augustine goes on at once to say, 'far be it from us to doubt the truth of what we have learned by the bodily senses; since by them we have learned to know the heaven and the earth.' We learn much on the testimony of others, and the fact that we are sometimes deceived is no warrant for disbelieving all testimony: so the fact that we are sometimes deceived in regard to the objects of our senses is no warrant for complete scepticism. 'We must acknowledge that not only our own senses, but those of other persons too, have added very much to our knowledge.'[2] For practical life it is necessary to give credence to the senses,[3] and the man who thinks that we should never believe the senses falls into a worse error than any error he may fall into through believing them. Augustine thus says that we 'believe' the senses, that we give credence to them, as we give credence to the testimony of others, but he often uses the word 'believe' in opposition to direct inner knowledge, without meaning to imply that such 'belief' is void of adequate motive. Thus when someone tells me a fact about his own mental state, for example, that he understands or wishes this or that, I 'believe': when he says something that is true of the human mind itself, not simply of his own mind in particular, 'I recognise and give my assent, for I know by self-consciousness and introspection that what he says is true.'[4] In

[1] Cf. *De vera relig.*, 39, 72; *Serm.*, 330, 3; *Retract.*, 1, 8, 3; etc.
[2] *De Trinit.*, 15, 12, 21.   [3] *Conf.*, 6, 5, 7.   [4] *De Trinit.*, 9, 6, 9.

fine, Augustine may have anticipated Descartes by his '*Si fallor, sum*', but he was not occupied with the question whether the external world really exists or not. That it exists, he felt no doubt, though he saw clearly enough that we sometimes make erroneous judgements about it and that testimony is not always reliable, whether it be testimony of our own senses or of other people. As he was especially interested in the knowledge of eternal truths and in the relation of that knowledge to God, it would hardly occur to him to devote very much time to a consideration of our knowledge of the mutable things of sense. The fact of the matter is that his 'Platonism', coupled with his spiritual interest and outlook, led him to look on corporeal objects as not being the proper object of knowledge, owing to their mutability and to the fact that our knowledge of them is dependent on bodily organs of sense which are no more always in the same state than the objects themselves. If we have not got 'true knowledge' of sense-objects, that is due, not merely to any deficiency in the subject but also to a radical deficiency in the object. In other words, Augustine's attitude to sense-knowledge is much more Platonic than Cartesian.[1]

4. The lowest level of knowledge is, therefore, that of sense-knowledge, dependent on sensation, sensation being regarded by Augustine, in accordance with his Platonic psychology, as an act of the soul using the organs of sense as its instruments. *Sentire non est corporis sed animae per corpus*. The soul animates the whole body, but when it increases or intensifies its activity in a particular part, i.e. in a particular sense-organ, it exercises the power of sensation.[2] From this theory it would seem to follow that any deficiency in sense-knowledge must proceed from the mutability both of the instrument of sensation, the sense-organ, and of the object of sensation, and this is indeed what Augustine thought. The rational soul of man exercises true knowledge and attains true certainty when it contemplates eternal truths in and through itself: when it turns towards the material world and uses corporeal instruments it cannot attain true knowledge. Augustine assumed, with Plato, that the objects of true knowledge are unchanging, from which it necessarily follows that knowledge of changing objects is not true knowledge. It is a type of knowledge or grade of knowledge which is indispensable for practical life; but

---

[1] Scotus repeated St. Augustine's suggestion that the status of sense-knowledge may be connected with original sin.

[2] Cf. *De Musica*, 6-5, 9, 10; *De Trinit.*, 11, 2, 2-5.

the man who concentrates on the sphere of the mutable thereby neglects the sphere of the immutable, which is the correlative object of the human soul in regard to knowledge in the full sense.

Sensation in the strict sense is common, of course, to men and brutes; but men can have and do have a rational knowledge of corporeal things. In the *De Trinitate*[1] St. Augustine points out that the beasts are able to sense corporeal things and remember them and to seek after what is helpful, avoiding what is harmful, but that they cannot commit things to memory deliberately nor recall them at will nor perform any other operation which involves the use of reason; so that, in regard to knowledge of sense-objects, human knowledge is essentially superior to that of the brute. Moreover, man is able to make rational judgements concerning corporeal things and to perceive them as approximations to eternal standards. For instance, if a man judges that one object is more beautiful than another, his comparative judgement (granted the objective character of the beautiful) implies a reference to an eternal standard of beauty, while a judgement that this or that line is more or less straight, that this figure is a well-drawn circle, implies a reference to ideal straightness and the perfect geometrical circle. In other words, such comparative judgements involve a reference to 'ideas' (not to be understood as purely subjective). 'It is the part of the higher reason to judge of these corporeal things according to incorporeal and eternal considerations, which, if they were not above the human mind, would certainly not be immutable. And yet, unless something of our own were subjoined to them, we should not be able to employ them as standards by which to judge of corporeal things. . . . But that faculty of our own which is thus concerned with the treatment of corporeal and temporal things, is indeed rational, in that it is not common to us and the beasts, but is drawn, as it were, out of the rational substance of our mind, by which we depend upon and adhere to the intelligible and immutable truth and which is deputed to handle and direct the inferior things.'[2]

What St. Augustine means is this. The lowest level of knowledge, so far as it can be called knowledge, is sensation, which is common to men and brutes; and the highest level of knowledge, peculiar to man, is the contemplation of eternal things (wisdom) by the mind alone, without the intervention of sensation; but between these two levels is a kind of half-way house, in which

[1] 12, 2, 2.   [2] *Ibid.*

mind judges of corporeal objects according to eternal and incorporeal standards. This level of knowledge is a rational level, so that it is peculiar to man and is not shared by brutes; but it involves the use of the senses and concerns sensible objects, so that it is a lower level than that of direct contemplation of eternal and incorporeal objects. Moreover, this lower use of reason is directed towards action, whereas wisdom is contemplative not practical. 'The action by which we make good use of temporal things differs from the contemplation of eternal things, and the former is classed as knowledge, the latter as wisdom. . . . In this distinction it must be understood that wisdom pertains to contemplation, knowledge to action.'[1]   The ideal is that contemplative wisdom should increase, but at the same time our reason has to be partly directed to the good use of mutable and corporeal things, 'without which this life does not go on', provided that in our attention to temporal things we make it subserve the attainment of eternal things, 'passing lightly over the former, but cleaving to the latter'.[2]

This outlook is markedly Platonic in character. There is the same depreciation of sense-objects in comparison with eternal and immaterial realities, the same almost grudging admission of practical knowledge as a necessity of life, the same insistence on 'theoretic' contemplation, the same insistence on increasing purification of soul and liberation from the slavery of the senses to accompany the epistemological ascent. Yet it would be a mistake to see in Augustine's attitude a mere adoption of Platonism and nothing more. Platonic and neo-Platonic themes are certainly utilised, but Augustine's interest is always first and foremost that of the attainment of man's supernatural end, beatitude, in the possession and vision of God, and in spite of the intellectualist way of speaking which he sometimes uses and which he adopted from the Platonic tradition, in the total scheme of his thought the primacy is always given to love: *Pondus meum, amor meus*.[3]   It is true that even this has its analogy in Platonism, but it must be remembered that for Augustine the goal is the attainment, not of an impersonal Good but of a personal God. The truth of the matter is that he found in Platonism doctrines which he considered admirably adapted for the exposition of a fundamentally Christian philosophy of life.

5. The objects of sense, corporeal things, are inferior to the human intellect, which judges of them in relation to a standard in

---

[1] *De Trinit.*, 12, 14, 22.   [2] *Ibid.*, 12, 13, 21.   [3] *Conf.*, 13, 9, 10.

reference to which they fall short; but there are other objects of knowledge which are above the human mind, in the sense that they are discovered by the mind, which necessarily assents to them and does not think of amending them or judging that they should be otherwise than they are. For example, I see some work of art and I judge it to be more or less beautiful, a judgement which implies not only the existence of a standard of beauty, an objective standard, but also my knowledge of the standard, for how could I judge that this arch or that picture is imperfect, deficient in beauty, unless I had some knowledge of the standard of beauty, of beauty itself, the idea of beauty? How could my supposedly objective judgement be justified unless there were an objective standard, not mutable and imperfect, like beautiful *things*, but immutable, constant, perfect and eternal?[1] Again, the geometer considers perfect circles and lines, and judges of the approximate circles and lines according to that perfect standard. Circular things are temporal and pass away, but the nature of circularity in itself, the idea of the circle, its essence, does not change. Again, we may add seven apples and three apples and make ten apples, and the apples which we count are sensible and mutable objects, are temporal and pass away; but the numbers seven and three considered in themselves and apart from things are discerned by the arithmetician to make ten by addition, a truth which he discovers to be necessary and eternal, not dependent on the sensible world or on the human mind.[2] These eternal truths are common to all. Whereas sensations are private, in the sense that, e.g., what seems cold to one man does not necessarily seem cold to another, mathematical truths are common to all and the individual mind has to accept them and recognise their possession of an absolute truth and validity which is independent of its own reactions.

Augustine's attitude in this matter is obviously Platonic. The standards of goodness and beauty, for example, correspond to Plato's first principles or ἀρχαί the exemplary ideas, while the ideal geometrical figures correspond to Plato's mathematical objects, τὰ μαθηματικά the objects of διάνοια. The same question which could be raised in regard to the Platonic theory recurs again, therefore, in regard to the Augustinian theory, namely, 'Where are these ideas?' (Of course, one must remember, in regard to

[1] Cf. *De Trinit.*, 9, 6, 9–11.
[2] Cf. *ibid.*, 12, 14, 22–3; 12, 15, 24; *De lib. arbit.*, 2, 13, 35; 2, 8, 20–4.

both thinkers, that the 'ideas' in question are not subjective ideas but objective essences, and that the query 'where?' does not refer to locality, since the 'ideas' are *ex hypothesi* immaterial, but rather to what one might call ontological situation or status.) Neo-Platonists, seeing the difficulty in accepting a sphere of impersonal immaterial essences, i.e. the condition *apparently* at least assigned to the essences in Plato's published works, interpreted the Platonic ideas as thoughts of God and 'placed' them in *Nous*, the divine mind, which emanates from the One as the first proceeding hypostasis. (Compare Philo's theory of the ideas as contained within the Logos.) We may say that Augustine accepted this position, if we allow for the fact that he did not accept the emanation theory of neo-Platonism. The exemplar ideas and eternal truths are in God. 'The ideas are certain archetypal forms or stable and immutable essences of things, which have not themselves been formed but, existing eternally and without change, are contained in the divine intelligence.'[1] This theory must be accepted if one wishes to avoid having to say that God created the world unintelligently.[2]

6. A difficulty, however, immediately arises. If the human mind beholds the exemplar ideas and eternal truths, and if these ideas and truths are in the mind of God, does it not follow that the human mind beholds the essence of God, since the divine mind, with all that it contains, is ontologically identical with the divine essence? Some writers have believed that Augustine actually meant this. Among philosophers, Malebranche claimed the support of Augustine for his theory that the mind beholds the eternal ideas in God, and he tried to escape from the seemingly logical conclusion that in this case the human mind beholds the essence of God, by saying that the mind sees, not the divine essence as it is in itself (the supernatural vision of the blessed) but the divine essence as participable *ad extra*, as exemplar of creation. The ontologists too claim the support of Augustine for their theory of the soul's immediate intuition of God.

Now, it is impossible to deny that some texts of Augustine taken by themselves favour such an interpretation. But, granting that Augustine seems on occasion to teach ontologism, it seems clear to me that, if one takes into account the totality of his thought, such an interpretation is inadmissible. I should certainly not be so bold as to suggest that Augustine was never inconsistent, but what I do believe is that the ontologistic interpretation of

<hr>

[1] *De Ideis*, 2.   [2] Cf. *Retract.*, 1, 3, 2.

Augustine fits in so badly with his spiritual doctrine that, if there are other texts which favour a non-ontologistic interpretation (and there are such texts), one should attribute a secondary position and a subordinate value to the apparently ontologistic texts. Augustine was perfectly well aware that a man may discern eternal and necessary truths, mathematical principles, for example, without being a good man at all: such a man may not see these truths in their ultimate Ground, but he undoubtedly discerns the truths. Now, how can Augustine possibly have supposed that such a man beholds the essence of God, when in his spiritual doctrine he insists so much on the need of moral purification in order to draw near to God and is well aware that the vision of God is reserved to the saved in the next life? Again, a man who is spiritually and morally far from God can quite well appreciate the fact that Canterbury Cathedral is more beautiful than a Nissen hut, just as St. Augustine himself could discern degrees of sensible beauty before his conversion. In a famous passage of the *Confessions* he exclaims: 'Too late am I come to love Thee, O thou Beauty, so ancient and withal so new; too late am I come to love Thee . . . in a deformed manner I cast myself upon the things of Thy creation, which yet Thou hadst made fair.'[1] Similarly, in the *De quantitate animae*[2] he clearly affirms that the contemplation of Beauty comes at the end of the soul's ascent. In view of this teaching, then, it seems to me inconceivable that Augustine thought that the soul, in apprehending eternal and necessary truths, actually apprehends the very content of the divine mind. The passages which appear to show that he did so think can be explained as due to his adoption of Platonic or neo-Platonic expressions which do not, literally taken, fit in with the general direction of his thought. It does not seem possible to state exactly how Augustine conceived of the status of the eternal truths as apprehended by the human mind (the ontological side of the question he probably never worked out); but, rather than accept a purely neo-Platonic or an onto-logistic interpretation, it seems to me preferable to suppose that the eternal truths and ideas, as they are in God, perform an ideogenetic function; that it is rather that the 'light' which comes from God to the human mind enables the mind to see the characteristics of changelessness and necessity in the eternal truths.

One may add, however, a further consideration against an ontologistic interpretation of Augustine. The Saint utilised the

[1] *Conf.*, 10, 27, 38.   [2] 35, 79.

apprehension of eternal and necessary truths as a proof for the existence of God, arguing that these truths require an immutable and eternal Ground. Without going any further into this argument at the moment it is worth pointing out that, if the argument is to have any sense, it clearly presupposes the possibility of the mind's perceiving these truths without at the same time perceiving God, perhaps while doubting or even denying God's existence. If Augustine is prepared to say to a man, 'You doubt or deny God's existence, but you must admit that you recognise absolute truths, and I shall prove to you that the recognition of such truths implies God's existence,' he can scarcely have supposed that the doubter or atheist had any vision of God or of the actual contents of the divine mind. This consideration seems to me to rule out the ontologistic interpretation. But before pursuing this subject any further it is necessary to say something of Augustine's theory of illumination, as this may make it easier to understand his position, though it must be admitted that the interpretation of this theory is itself somewhat uncertain.

7. We cannot, says Augustine, perceive the immutable truth of things unless they are illuminated as by a sun.[1] This divine light, which illumines the mind, comes from God, who is the 'intelligible light', in whom and by whom and through whom all those things which are luminous to the intellect become luminous.[2] In this doctrine of light, common to the Augustinian School, Augustine makes use of a neo-Platonic theme which goes back to Plato's comparison of the Idea of the Good with the sun,[3] the Idea of the Good irradiating the subordinate intelligible objects or Ideas. For Plotinus the One or God is the sun, the transcendent light. The use of the light-metaphor, however, does not by itself tell us very clearly what Augustine meant. Happily we have to help us such texts as the passage of the *De Trinitate*[4] where the Saint says that the nature of the mind is such that, 'when directed to intelligible things in the natural order, according to the disposition of the Creator, it sees them in a certain incorporeal light which is *sui generis*, just as the corporeal eye sees adjacent objects in the corporeal light'. These words seem to show that the illumination in question is a spiritual illumination which performs the same function for the objects of the mind as the sun's light performs for the objects of the eye: in other words, as the sunlight makes corporeal things visible to the eye, so the divine illumination makes

[1] *Solil.*, 1, 8, 15.   [2] *Ibid.*, 1, 1, 3.   [3] *Rep.*, 514-18.   [4] 12, 15, 24.

the eternal truths visible to the mind. From this it would appear
to follow that it is not the illumination itself which is seen by the
mind, nor the intelligible Sun, God, but that the characteristics of
necessity and eternity in the necessary and eternal truths are made
visible to the mind by the activity of God. This is certainly not an
ontologistic theory.

But why did St. Augustine postulate such an illumination; why
did he think it necessary? Because the human mind is changeable
and temporal, so that what is unchangeable and eternal transcends
it and seems to be beyond its capacity. 'When the human mind
knows and loves itself, it does not know and love anything immutable,'[1] and if truth 'were equal to our minds, it also would be
mutable', for our minds see the truth, now more now less, and by
this very fact show themselves to be mutable. In fact, truth is
neither inferior nor equal to our minds, but 'superior and more
excellent'.[2] We need, therefore, a divine illumination, in order to
enable us to apprehend what transcends our minds, 'for no
creature, howsoever rational and intellectual, is lighted of itself,
but is lighted by participation of eternal Truth'.[3] 'God hath
created man's mind rational and intellectual, whereby he may take
in His light . . . and He so enlighteneth it of Himself, that not only
those things which are displayed by the truth, but even truth
itself may be perceived by the mind's eye.'[4] This light shines upon
the truths and renders visible to the mutable and temporal human
mind their characteristics of changelessness and eternity.

That the divine illumination is something imparted and *sui
generis* is explicitly stated by St. Augustine, as we have seen. It
hardly seems possible, therefore, to reduce the illumination-theory
to nothing more than a statement of the truth that God conserves
and creates the human intellect and that the natural light of the
intellect is a participated light. Thomists, who wish to show St.
Augustine the same reverence that St. Thomas showed him, are
naturally reluctant to admit a radical difference of opinion between
the two great theologians and philosophers and are inclined to
interpret St. Augustine in a way that would attenuate the difference between his thought and that of St. Thomas; but St.
Augustine most emphatically did not mean by 'light' the intellect
itself or its activity, even with the ordinary concurrence of God,
since it is precisely because of the deficiencies of the human

---

[1] *De Trinit.*, 9, 6, 9.   [2] *De lib. arbit.*, 2, 13, 35.
[3] *In. Ps.* 119; *Serm.*, 23, 1.   [4] *In Ps.* 118; *Serm.*, 18, 4.

intellect that he postulated the existence and activity of the divine illumination. To say that St. Augustine was wrong in postulating a special divine illumination and that St. Thomas was right in denying the necessity of such an illumination is an understandable attitude; but it seems to be carrying conciliation too far, if one attempts to maintain that both thinkers were saying the same thing, even if one affirms that St. Thomas was saying clearly and unambiguously what St. Augustine had said obscurely and with the aid of metaphor.

I have already indicated that I accept the interpretation of Augustine's thought, according to which the function of the divine illumination is to render visible to the mind the element of necessity in the eternal truths, and that I reject the ontologistic interpretation in any form. This rejection obviously involves the rejection of the view that according to Augustine the mind beholds directly the idea of beauty, for example, as it is in God; but I am also unwilling to accept the view that according to Augustine God actually infuses the idea of beauty or any other normative idea (i.e. in reference to which we make comparative judgements of degree, such as that this object is more beautiful than that, this action juster than that, etc.) ready-made into the mind. This extreme ideogenetic view would make the function of divine illumination that of a kind of separate active intellect: in fact, God would Himself be an ontologically separate active intellect which infuses ideas into the human mind without any part being played by the human sensibility or intellect other than the mind's purely passive rôle. (This reference to an active intellect is not, of course, meant to imply that Augustine thought or spoke in terms of the Aristotelian psychology.) It does not seem to me that such an interpretation, although doubtless much can be said for it,[1] is altogether satisfactory. According to St. Augustine, the activity of the divine illumination in regard to the mind is analogous to the function of the sun's light in regard to vision, and though the sunlight renders corporeal objects visible, Augustine certainly did not think of it as creating images of the objects in the human subject. Again, although the divine illumination takes the place in Augustine's thought of reminiscence in the Platonic philosophy, so that the illumination would seem to fulfil some ideogenetic function, it must be remembered that Augustine's problem is one

---

[1] See, for example, the article on Augustine by Portalié in the *Dictionnaire de théologie catholique*.

concerning *certitude*, not one concerning the content of our concepts or ideas: it concerns far more the form of the certain judgement and the form of the normative idea than the actual content of the judgement or the idea. In the *De Trinitate*[1] Augustine remarks that the mind 'gathers the knowledge of corporeal things through the senses of the body', and, so far as he deals at all with the formation of the concept, he would seem to consider that the human mind discerns the intelligible in the sensible, performing what is in some way at least equivalent to abstraction. But when it comes to discerning that a corporeal thing is, for example, more or less beautiful, to judging the object according to a changeless standard, the mind judges under the light of the regulative action of the eternal Idea, which is not itself visible to the mind. Beauty itself illuminates the mind's activity in such a way that it can discern the greater or less approximation of the object to the standard, though the mind does not behold Beauty itself directly. It is in this sense that the illumination of Augustine supplies the function of Plato's reminiscence. Again, though Augustine does not clearly indicate *how we obtain* the notions of seven and three and ten, the function of illumination is not to infuse the notions of these numbers but so to illuminate the judgement that seven and three make ten that we discern the necessity and eternity of the judgement. From a passage already referred to,[2] as from other passages,[3] it seems to follow that, while we obtain the concept of corporeal objects, a horse, for example, in dependence on the senses, and of an immaterial object like the soul through self-consciousness and interpretation, our certain judgements concerning these objects are made in the light of 'illumination' under the regulative action of the eternal Ideas. If the illumination has an ideogenetic function, as I believe it to have in Augustine's view, then this function has reference not to the content of the concept, as if it infused that content, but to the quality of our judgement concerning the concept or to our discernment of a character in the object, its relation to the norm or standard, which is not contained in the bare notion of the thing. If this is so, then the difference between St. Augustine and St. Thomas does not so much consist in their respective attitudes towards abstraction (since, whether Augustine explicitly says so or not, his view, as interpreted above, would at least *demand* abstraction in some form) as in the fact that Augustine

[1] 9, 3, 3.   [2] *Ibid.*
[3] *Solil.*, 1, 8, 15; *In Joann. Evang.*, 35, 8, 3; *De Trinit.*, 9, 15, 24; etc.

thought it necessary to postulate a special illuminative action of God, beyond His creative and conserving activity, in the mind's realisation of eternal and necessary truths, whereas St. Thomas did not.

On this view of illumination one can understand how it was that St. Augustine regarded the qualities of necessity and unchange-ability in the eternal truths as constituting a proof of God's existence, whereas it would be inexplicable on the ontologistic interpretation, since, if the mind perceives God or the divine ideas directly, it can need no proof of God's existence. That Augustine did not explain in detail how the content of the concept is formed, may be regrettable, but it is none the less understandable, since, though interested in psychological observation, he was interested therein, not from an academic motive, but rather from spiritual and religious motives: it was the soul's relation to God which concerned him primarily and, while the necessity and unchange-ability of the eternal truths (as contrasted with the contingency and changeability of the human mind) and the doctrine of illu-mination helped to set this relation in a clear light and to stimulate the soul in its Godward direction, an investigation concerning the formation of the concept as such would not have had such a clear relation to the *Noverim me, noverim Te*.

To sum up. St. Augustine asks himself the question, How is it that we attain knowledge of truths which are necessary, immutable and eternal? That we do attain such knowledge is clear to him from experience. We cannot gain such knowledge simply from sense-experience, since corporeal objects are contingent, change-able and temporal. Nor can we produce the truths from our minds, which are also contingent and changeable. Moreover, such truths rule and dominate our minds, impose themselves upon our minds, and they would not do this if they depended on us. It follows that we are enabled to perceive such truths under the action of the Being who alone is necessary, changeless and eternal, God. God is like a sun which illumines our minds or a master who teaches us. At this point the difficulty in interpretation begins. The present writer inclines to the interpretation that, while the content of our concepts of corporeal objects is derived from sense-experience and reflection thereon, the regulative in-fluence of the divine ideas (which means the influence of God) enables man to see the relation of created things to eternal super-sensible realities, of which there is no direct vision in this life, and that God's light enables the mind to discern the elements of necessity, immutability and eternity in that relation between concepts which is expressed in the necessary judgement. Owing, however, to St. Augustine's use of metaphor and to the fact that he was not primarily interested in giving a systematic and carefully defined 'scholastic' account of the process of knowledge, it does not seem possible to obtain a definitive interpretation of his thought which would adequately explain all the statements he made.

CHAPTER V

ST. AUGUSTINE—III: GOD

Proof of God from eternal truths—Proofs from creatures and from universal consent—The various proofs as stages in one process—Attributes of God—Exemplarism.

1. IT is probably true to say that the central and favourite proof of God's existence given by St. Augustine is that from thought, i.e. a proof from within. The starting-point of this proof is the mind's apprehension of necessary and changeless truths, of a truth 'which thou canst not call thine, or mine, or any man's, but which is present to all and gives itself to all alike.'[1] This truth is superior to the mind, inasmuch as the mind has to bow before it and accept it: the mind did not constitute it, nor can it amend it: the mind recognises that this truth transcends it and rules its thought rather than the other way round. If it were inferior to the mind, the mind could change it or amend it, while if it were equal to the mind, of the same character, it would itself be changeable, as the mind is changeable. The mind varies in its apprehension of truth, apprehending it now more clearly now less clearly, whereas truth remains ever the same. 'Hence if truth is neither inferior nor equal to our minds, nothing remains but that it should be superior and more excellent.'[2]

But the eternal truths must be founded on being, reflecting the Ground of all truth. Just as human imaginations reflect the imperfection and changeable character of the human mind in which they are grounded, and as the impressions of sense reflect the corporeal objects in which they are grounded, so the eternal truths reveal their Ground, Truth itself, reflecting the necessity and immutability of God. This refers to all essential standards. If we judge of an action that it is more or less just, for example, we judge of it according to an essential and invariable standard, essence or 'idea': human actions in the concrete may vary, but the standard remains the same. It is in the light of the eternal and perfect standard that we judge of concrete acts, and this standard must be grounded in the eternal and all-perfect Being. If there is an intelligible sphere of absolute truths, this cannot be conceived

[1] *De lib. arbit.,* 2, 12, 33.　　　　　　[2] *Ibid.*

without a Ground of truth, 'the Truth, in whom, and by whom, and through whom those things are true which are true in every respect'.[1]

This argument to God as the Ground of eternal and necessary truth was not only accepted by the 'Augustinian School', but reappears in the thought of several eminent philosophers, like Leibniz.

2. St. Augustine does indeed prove the existence of God from the external, corporeal world; but his words on the subject are rather of the nature of hints or reminders or summary statements than developed proofs in the academic sense: he was not so much concerned to prove to the atheist that God exists as to show how all creation proclaims the God whom the soul can experience in itself, the living God. It was the dynamic attitude of the soul towards God which interested him, not the construction of dialectical arguments with a purely theoretical conclusion. To acknowledge with a purely intellectual assent that a supreme Being exists is one thing; to bring that truth home to oneself is something more. The soul seeks happiness and many are inclined to seek it outside themselves: St. Augustine tries to show that creation cannot give the soul the perfect happiness it seeks, but points upwards to the living God who must be sought within. This basically religious and spiritual attitude must be borne in mind, if one is to avoid first looking on Augustine's proofs as dialectical proofs in a theoretic sense and then belittling them as inadequate and trifling statements of what St. Thomas was to express much better. The purposes of the two men were not precisely the same.

Thus when Augustine, commenting on Psalm 73, remarks, 'How do I know that thou art alive, whose soul I see not? How do I know? Thou wilt answer, Because I speak, because I walk, because I work. Fool! by the operations of the body I know thee to be living, canst thou not by the works of creation know the Creator?' he is indeed stating the proof of God's existence from His effects; but he is not setting out to develop the proof for its own sake, as it were: he brings it in by way of commentary in the course of his Scriptural exegesis. Similarly, when he asserts in the *De Civitate Dei*[2] that 'the very order, disposition, beauty, change and motion of the world and of all visible things silently proclaim that it could only have been made by God, the ineffably and invisibly great and the ineffably and invisibly beautiful', he is rather reminding Christians of a fact than attempting to give a systematic proof of God's existence. Again, when Augustine, commenting on Genesis,[1] states that 'the power of the Creator and His omnipotent and all-swaying strength is for each and every creature the cause of its continued existence, and if this strength were at any time to cease from directing the things which have been created, at one and the same time both their species would cease to be and their whole nature would perish . . . ', he is stating the fact and necessity of divine conservation, reminding his readers of an acknowledged fact, rather than proving it philosophically.

Augustine gives, again in very brief form, what is known as the argument from universal consent. 'Such', he says, 'is the power of true Godhead that it cannot be altogether and utterly hidden from the rational creature, once it makes use of its reason. For, with the exception of a few in whom nature is excessively depraved, the whole human race confesses God to be the author of the world.'[2] Even if a man thinks that a plurality of gods exists, he still attempts to conceive 'the one God of gods' as 'something than which nothing more excellent or more sublime exists. . . . All concur in believing God to be that which excels in dignity all other objects.'[3] No doubt St. Anselm was influenced by these words of Augustine when he took as the universal idea of God in the 'ontological argument' 'that than which no greater can be conceived'.

3. Professor Gilson, in his *Introduction à l'étude de Saint Augustin*,[4] remarks that in the thought of St. Augustine there is really one long proof of God's existence, a proof which consists of various stages.[5] Thus from the stage of initial doubt and its refutation through the *Si fallor, sum*, which is a kind of methodical preliminary to the search for truth, assuring the mind of the attainability of truth, the soul proceeds to consider the world of sense. In this world, however, it does not discover the truth which it seeks and so it turns inwards, where, after considering its own fallibility and changeableness, it discovers immutable truth which transcends the soul and does not depend on the soul. It is thus led to the apprehension of God as the Ground of all truth.

The picture of Augustine's total proof of the existence of God

---

[1] *De Gen. ad litt.*, 4, 22, 22.   [2] *In Joann. Evang.*, 106, 4.
[3] *De doct. Christ.*, 1, 7, 7.   [4] Ch. 2.
[5] Cf. also G. Grunwald: *Geschichte der Gottesbeweise im Mittelalter*, in *Beiträge*, 6, 3, p. 6.

given by M. Gilson is doubtless representative of the Saint's mind and it has the great advantage not only of bringing into prominence the proof from thought, from the eternal truths, but also of linking up the 'proof' with the soul's search for God as the source of happiness, as objective beatitude, in such a way that the proof does not remain a mere academic and theoretic string or chain of syllogisms. This picture is confirmed by a passage such as that contained in Augustine's two hundred and forty-first sermon,[1] where the Saint depicts the human soul questioning the things of sense and hearing them confess that the beauty of the visible world, of mutable things, is the creation and reflection of immutable Beauty, after which the soul proceeds inwards, discovers itself and realises the superiority of soul to body. 'Men saw these two things, pondered them, investigated both of them, and found that each is mutable in man.' The mind, therefore, finding both body and soul to be mutable goes in search of what is immutable. 'And thus they arrived at a knowledge of God the Creator by means of the things which He created.' St. Augustine, then, in no way denies what we call a 'natural' or 'rational' knowledge of God ; but this rational knowledge of God is viewed in close connection with the soul's search for beatifying Truth and is seen as itself a kind of self-revelation of God to the soul, a revelation which is completed in the full revelation through Christ and confirmed in the Christian life of prayer. Augustine would thus make no sharp dichotomy between the spheres of natural and revealed theology, not because he failed to see the distinction between reason and faith, but rather because he viewed the soul's cognition of God in close connection with its spiritual search for God as the one Object and Source of beatitude. When Harnack reproaches Augustine with not having made clear the relation of faith to science,[2] he fails to realise that the Saint is primarily concerned with the spiritual experience of God and that in his eyes faith and reason each have their part to play in an experience which is an organic unity.

4. Augustine insists that the world of creatures reflects and manifests God, even if it does so in a very inadequate manner, and that 'if any thing worthy of praise is noticed in the nature of things, whether it be judged worthy of slight praise or of great, it must be applied to the most excellent and ineffable praise of

[1] *Serm.*, 241, 2, 2 and 3, 3.
[2] *Lehrbuch der Dogmengeschichte*, 3rd edit., t. 3, p. 119.

the Creator.' Creatures tend indeed to not-being, but as long as they are, they possess some form, and this is a reflection of the Form which can neither decline nor pass away.[1] Thus the order and unity of Nature proclaims the unity of the Creator,[2] just as the goodness of creatures, their positive reality, reveals the goodness of God[3] and the order and stability of the universe manifest the wisdom of God.[4] On the other hand, God, as the self-existent, eternal and immutable Being, is infinite, and, as infinite, incomprehensible. God is His own Perfection, is 'simple', so that His wisdom and knowledge, His goodness and power, are His own essence, which is without accidents.[5] God, therefore, transcends space in virtue of His spirituality and infinity and simplicity, as He transcends time in virtue of His eternity: 'God is Himself in no interval nor extension of place, but in His immutable and pre-eminent might is both interior to everything because all things are in Him and exterior to everything because He is above all things. So too He is in no interval nor extension of time, but in His immutable eternity is older than all things because He is before all things and younger than all things because the same He is after all things.'[6]

5. From all eternity God knew all things which He was to make: He does not know them because He has made them, but rather the other way round: God first knew the things of creation though they came into being only in time. The species of created things have their ideas or *rationes* in God, and God from all eternity saw in Himself, as possible reflections of Himself, the things which He could create and would create. He knew them before creation as they are in Him, as Exemplar, but He made them as they exist, i.e. as external and finite reflections of His divine essence.[7] God did nothing without knowledge, He foresaw all that He would make, but His knowledge is not distinct acts of knowledge, but 'one eternal, immutable and ineffable vision'.[8] It is in virtue of this eternal act of knowledge, of vision, to which nothing is past or future, that God sees, 'foresees', even the free acts of men, knowing 'beforehand', for example, 'what we should ask of Him and when, and to whom He would listen or not listen, and on what subjects'.[9] An adequate discussion of this last point, which would

---

[1] *De lib. arbit.*, 2, 17, 46.   [2] *Ibid.*, 3, 23, 70.   [3] *De Trinit.*, 11, 5, 8.
[4] *De Civit. Dei*, 11, 28.
[5] *De Trinit.*, 5, 2, 3; 5, 11, 12; 6, 4, 6; 6, 10, 11; 15, 43, 22; *In Joann. Evang.*, 99, 4; etc.
[6] *De Gen. ad litt.*, 8, 26, 48.   [7] Cf. *ibid.*, 5, 15, 33; *Ad Orosium*, 8, 9.
[8] *De Trinit.*, 15, 7, 13.   [9] *Ibid.*, 15, 13, 22.

necessitate consideration of the Augustinian theory of grace, cannot be attempted here.

Contemplating His own essence from eternity God sees in Himself all possible limited essences, the finite reflections of His infinite perfection, so that the essences or *rationes* of things are present in the divine mind from all eternity as the divine ideas, though, in view of Augustine's teaching on the divine simplicity previously mentioned, this should not be taken to mean that there are 'accidents' in God, ideas which are ontologically distinct from His essence. In the *Confessions*[1] the Saint exclaims that the eternal 'reasons' of created things remain unchangeably in God, and in the *De Ideis*[2] he explains that the divine ideas are 'certain archetypal forms or stable and unchangeable reasons of things, which were not themselves formed but are contained in the divine mind eternally and are always the same. They neither arise nor pass away, but whatever arises and passes away is formed according to them.' The corollary of this is that creatures have ontological truth in so far as they embody or exemplify the model in the divine mind, and that God Himself is the standard of truth. This exemplarist doctrine was, of course, influenced by neo-Platonic theory, according to which the Platonic exemplary ideas are contained in *Nous*, though for Augustine the ideas are contained in the Word, who is not a subordinate hypostasis, like the neo-Platonic *Nous*, but the second Person of the Blessed Trinity, consubstantial with the Father.[3] From Augustine the doctrine of exemplarism passed to the Middle Ages. It may be thought of as characteristic of the Augustinian School; but it must be remembered that St. Thomas Aquinas did not deny it, though he was careful to state it in such a way as not to imply that there are ontologically separate ideas in God, a doctrine which would impair the divine simplicity, for in God there is no real distinction save that between the three divine Persons.[4] Still, though Aquinas was in this respect a follower of Augustine, it was St. Bonaventure who most insisted in the thirteenth century on the doctrine of exemplarism and on the presence of the divine Ideas in the Word of God, an insistence which contributed to his hostile attitude to Aristotle the metaphysician, who threw overboard the ideas of Plato.

[1] 1, 6, 9.   [2] 2.   [3] *De Trinit.*, 4, 1, 3.
[4] Cf. e.g. *Summa Theol.*, Ia, 15, 2 and 3.

CHAPTER VI

ST. AUGUSTINE—IV: THE WORLD

*Free creation out of nothing—Matter—*Rationes seminales—
Numbers—Soul and body—Immortality—Origin of soul.

ONE would hardly expect, once given the general attitude and complexion of Augustine's thought, to find the Saint showing very much interest in the material world for its own sake: his thought centred round the soul's relation to God; but his general philosophy involved a theory of the corporeal world, a theory consisting of elements taken from former thinkers and set in a Christian framework. It would be a mistake, however, to think that Augustine drew purely mechanically on previous thinkers for his theories: he emphasised those lines which seemed to him best calculated to underline nature's relation to and dependence on God.

1. A doctrine which was not developed by pagan thinkers, but which was held by Augustine in common with other Christian writers, was that of the creation of the world out of nothing by God's free act. In the Plotinian emanation-theory the world is depicted as proceeding in some way from God without God becoming in any way diminished or altered thereby, but for Plotinus God does not act freely (since such activity would, he thought, postulate change in God) but rather *necessitate naturae,* the Good necessarily diffusing itself. The doctrine of free creation out of nothing is not to be found in neo-Platonism, if we except one or two pagan thinkers who had most probably been influenced by Christian teaching. Augustine may have thought that Plato had taught creation out of nothing in time, but it is improbable, in spite of Aristotle's interpretation of the *Timaeus,* that Plato really meant to imply this. However, whatever Augustine may have thought about Plato's views on the matter, he himself clearly states the doctrine of free creation out of nothing and it is essential to his insistence on the utter supremacy of God and the world's entire dependence on Him. All things owe their being to God.[1]

2. But suppose that things were made out of some formless matter? Would not this formless matter be independent of God? First of all, says Augustine, are you speaking of a matter which is

---

[1] *De lib. arbit.*, 3, 15, 42.

absolutely formless or of a matter which is formless only in comparison with completely formed? If the former, then you are speaking of what is equivalent to nothingness. 'That out of which God has created all things is what possesses neither species nor form; and this is nothing other than nothing.' If, however, you are speaking of the latter, cf matter which has no completed form, but which has inchoate form, in the sense of possessing the capacity to receive form, then such matter is not altogether nothing indeed, but, as something, it has what being it has only from God. 'Wherefore, even if the universe was created out of some formless matter, this very matter was created from something which was wholly nothing.'[1] In the *Confessions*[2] Augustine identifies this matter with the mutability of bodies (which is equivalent to saying that it is the potential element) and observes that if he could call it 'nothing' or assert that it does not exist, he would do so; but if it is the capacity of receiving forms, it cannot be called absolutely nothing. Again, he remarks in the *De vera religione*[3] that not only the possession of form but even the capacity to receive form is a good, and what is a good cannot be absolute nothing. Yet this matter, which is not absolutely nothing, is itself the creation of God, not preceding formed things in time but concreated with form,[4] and he identified the 'unformed matter which God made out of nothing' with the heaven and earth mentioned in the first verse of the first chapter of Genesis as the primary creation of God.[5] In other words, St. Augustine is stating in rudimentary form the Scholastic doctrine that God created out of nothing not absolutely formless 'prime matter', apart from all form, but form and matter together, though, if we choose to think of Augustine's statements as a rudimentary expression of the more elaborate Scholastic doctrine, we should also remember that the Saint is not so concerned with developing a philosophical doctrine for its own sake as with emphasising the essential dependence of all creatures on God and the perishable nature of all corporeal creatures, even when once constituted in existence. They have their being from God, but their being is bound up with their mutability.

3. A theory which was dear to Augustine himself and to his followers, though it was rejected by St. Thomas, and which was calculated to exalt the divine agency at the expense of the causal

---

[1] Cf. *De vera relig.*, 18, 35–6.　　[2] 12, 6, 6.　　[3] *Loc. cit.*
[4] *De Gen. ad litt.*, 1, 15, 29.　　[5] *De Gen. contra Manich.*, 1, 17, 11.

activity of creatures, was that of the *rationes seminales* or 'seminal reasons', the germs of those things which were to develop in the course of time. Thus even man, as regards his body at least, to leave the origin of the soul out of account for the moment, was created in the *rationes seminales*, 'invisibly, potentially, causally, in the way that things are made which are to be but have not yet been made'.[1] The *rationes seminales* are germs of things or invisible powers or potentialities, created by God in the beginning in the humid element and developing into the objects of various species by their temporal unfolding. The idea of these germinal potentialities was to be found, and doubtless was found by Augustine, in the philosophy of Plotinus and ultimately it goes back to the *rationes seminales* or λόγοι σπερματικοί of Stoicism, but it is an idea of rather vague content. Indeed, St. Augustine never supposed that they were the object of experience, that they could be seen or touched: they are invisible, having inchoate form or a potentiality to the development of form according to the divine plan. The seminal reasons are not purely passive, but tend to self-development, though the absence of the requisite conditions and circumstances and of other external agencies may hinder or prevent their development.[2] St. Bonaventure, who maintained the theory of St. Augustine on this point, compared the *ratio seminalis* to the rosebud, which is not yet actually the rose but will develop into the rose, given the presence of the necessary positive agencies and the absence of negative or preventive agencies.

That St. Augustine asserted a rather vague theory regarding objects which are not the term of direct experience will appear less surprising if one considers *why* he asserted it. The assertion was the result of an exegetic, not a scientific problem, and the problem arose in this way. According to the book of Ecclesiasticus[3] 'He that liveth for ever created all things together', while on the other hand according to the book of Genesis the fishes and birds, for instance, appeared only on the fifth 'day' of creation, while the cattle and beasts of the earth appeared only on the sixth 'day'. (Augustine did not interpret 'day' as our day of twenty-four hours, since the sun was made only on the fourth 'day'.) How then can these two statements be reconciled, that God created all things together and that some things were made after others, that is to say, that *not* all things were created together? St. Augustine's

---

[1] *De Gen. ad litt.*, 6, 5, 8.   [2] *De Trinit.*, 3, 8, 13.   [3] 18, 1.

way of solving the problem was to say that God did indeed create all things together in the beginning, but that He did not create them all in the same condition: many things, all plants, fishes, birds, animals, and man himself, He created invisibly, latently, potentially, in germ, in their *rationes seminales*. In this way God created in the beginning all the vegetation of the earth before it was actually growing on the earth,[1] and even man himself. He would thus solve the apparent contradiction between Ecclesiasticus and Genesis by making a distinction. If you are speaking of actual formal completion, then Ecclesiasticus is not referring to this, whereas Genesis is: if you are including germinal or seminal creation, then this is what Ecclesiasticus refers to.

Why did not Augustine content himself with 'seeds' in the ordinary sense, the visible seeds of plants, the grain and so on? Because in the book of Genesis it is implied that the earth brought forth the green herb *before* its seed,[2] and the same thing is implied in regard to the other living things which reproduce their kind. He found himself compelled, therefore, to have recourse to a different kind of seed. For example, God created in the beginning the *ratio seminalis* of wheat, which, according to God's plan and activity, unfolded itself at the appointed time as actual wheat, which then contained seed in the ordinary sense.[3] Moreover, God did not create all seeds or all eggs in act at the beginning, so that they too require a *ratio seminalis*. Each species, then, with all its future developments and particular members, was created at the beginning in the appropriate seminal reason.

From what has been said it should be clear that the Saint was not considering primarily a scientific problem but rather an exegetic problem, so that it is really beside the point to adduce him either as a protagonist or as an opponent of evolution in the Lamarckian or Darwinian sense.

4. St. Augustine made use of the Platonic number-theme, which goes back to Pythagoreanism. Naturally his treatment of number sometimes appears to us as fanciful and even fantastic, as when he speaks of perfect and imperfect numbers or interprets references to numbers in the Scriptures; but, speaking generally, he looks on number as the principle of order and form, of beauty and perfection, of proportion and law. Thus the Ideas are the eternal numbers, while bodies are temporal numbers, which unfold themselves in

---

[1] *De Gen. ad litt.*, 5, 4, 7–9. [2] Gen. 1. 11.
[3] *De Gen. ad litt.*, 5, 4, 9.

time. Bodies indeed can be considered as numbers in various ways, as being wholes consisting of a number of ordered and related parts, as unfolding themselves in successive stages (the plant, for example, germinates, breaks into leaf, produces flower and fruit, seminates), or as consisting of a number of parts well disposed in space; in other words, as exemplifying intrinsic number, local or spatial number, and temporal number. The 'seminal reasons' are hidden numbers, whereas bodies are manifest numbers. Again, just as mathematical number begins from one and ends in a number which is itself an integer, so the hierarchy of beings begins with the supreme One, God, which brings into existence and is reflected in more or less perfect unities. This comparison or parallel between mathematical number and metaphysical number was derived, of course, from Plotinus, and in general Augustine's treatment of number adds nothing of substance to the treatment already accorded it in the Pythagorean-Platonic tradition.

5. The peak of the material creation is man, who consists of body and immortal soul. Augustine is quite clear about the fact that man does consist of soul and body, as when he says that 'a soul in possession of a body does not constitute two persons but one man'.[1] Why is it necessary to mention such an obvious point? Because Augustine speaks of the soul as a substance in its own right (*substantia quaedam rationis particeps, regendo corpori accomodata*)[2] and even defines man as 'a rational soul using a mortal and earthly body'.[3] This Platonic attitude towards the soul has its repercussions, as we have already seen, in Augustine's doctrine of sensation, which he represents as an activity of the soul using the body as an instrument, rather than as an activity of the total psycho-physical organism: it is, in fact, a temporary increase of intensity in the action by which the soul animates a certain part of the body. The soul, being superior to the body, cannot be acted on by the body, but it perceives the changes in the body due to an external stimulus.

6. The human soul is an immaterial principle, though, like the souls of brutes, it animates the body. A man may say or even think that his soul is composed of air, for example, but he can never know that it is composed of air. On the other hand he knows very well that he is intelligent, that he thinks, and he has no reason to suppose that air can think.[4] Moreover, the soul's

[1] *In Joann. Evang.*, 19, 5, 15.   [2] *De quant. animae*, 13, 21.
[3] *De moribus eccl.*, 1, 27, 52; *In Joann. Evang.*, 19, 5, 15.
[4] *De Gen. ad litt.*, 7, 21, 28; *De Trinit.*, 10, 10, 14.

immateriality and its substantiality assure it of immortality. On this point Augustine uses arguments which go back to Plato.[1] For example, Augustine utilises the argument of the *Phaedo* that, as the soul is the principle of life and as two contraries are incompatible, the soul cannot die. Apart from the fact that this argument is not very convincing in any case, it could not be acceptable to Augustine without modification, since it would seem to imply that the soul exists of itself or is a part of God. He adapted the argument, therefore, by saying that the soul participates in Life, holding its being and essence from a Principle which admits of no contrary, and by arguing that, as the being which the soul receives from this Principle (which admits no contrary) is precisely *life*, it cannot die. The argument, however, might clearly be taken to imply that the animal soul is immortal also, since it too is a principle of life, and so would prove too much. It must, then, be taken in conjunction with another argument, also derived from Plato, to the effect that the soul apprehends indestructible truth, which shows that it is itself indestructible. In the *De quantitate animae*[2] Augustine distinguishes the souls of beasts, which possess the power of sensation but not that of reasoning and knowing, from human souls, which possess both, so that this argument applies only to human souls. Plato had argued that the human soul, as capable of apprehending the Ideas, which are eternal and indestructible, shows itself to be akin to them, to be 'divine', that is to say, indestructible and eternal, and Augustine, without affirming pre-existence, proves the immortality of the soul in an analogous manner. In addition, he argues from the desire of beatitude, the desire for perfect happiness, and this became a favourite argument among Augustinians, with St. Bonaventure, for example.

7. Augustine clearly held that the soul is created by God,[3] but does not seem to have made up his mind as to the precise time and mode of its origin. He seems to have toyed with some form of the Platonic pre-existence theory while refusing to allow that the soul was put into the body as a punishment for faults committed in a pre-earthly condition, but the chief question for him was whether God creates each individual soul separately or created all other souls in Adam's, so that the soul is 'handed on' by the parents (Traducianism). This second opinion would appear logically to

involve a materialistic view of the soul, whereas in fact Augustine certainly did not hold any such view and insisted that the soul is not present in the body by local diffusion;[1] but it was for theological, not philosophical, reasons that he inclined towards traducianism, as he thought that in this way original sin could be explained as a transmitted stain on the soul. If original sin is looked on as something positive and not as in itself a privation, there is indeed a difficulty, even if not an insuperable difficulty, in affirming individual creation by God of each single human soul, but even apart from that it does not alter the fact that traducianism is inconsistent with a clear affirmation of the soul's spiritual and immaterial character.

[1] *Ep.*, 156.

CHAPTER VII

ST. AUGUSTINE—V: MORAL THEORY

*Happiness and God—Freedom and Obligation—Need of grace—
Evil—the two Cities.*

1. St. Augustine's ethic has this in common with what one
might call the typical Greek ethic, that it is eudaemonistic in
character, that it proposes an end for human conduct, namely
happiness; but this happiness is to be found only in God. 'The
Epicurean who places man's supreme good in the body, places his
hope in himself,'[1] but 'the rational creature . . . has been so made
that it cannot itself be the good by which it is made happy':[2] the
human being is mutable and insufficient to itself, it can find its
happiness only in the possession of what is more than itself, in the
possession of an immutable object. Not even virtue itself can be
the end: 'it is not the virtue of thy soul that maketh thee happy,
but He who hath given thee the virtue, who hath inspired thee to
will, and hath given thee the power to do.'[3] It is not the ideal
of the Epicurean that can bring happiness to man, nor even that
of the Stoic, but God Himself: 'the striving after God is, therefore,
the desire of beatitude, the attainment of God is beatitude itself.'[4]
That the human being strives after beatitude or happiness, and
that beatitude means the attainment of an object, Augustine knew
well from his own experience, even if he found confirmation of this
fact in philosophy; that this object is God, he learnt also from his
personal experience, even if he had been helped to realise the fact
by the philosophy of Plotinus. But when he said that happiness
is to be found in the attainment and possession of the eternal and
immutable Object, God, he was thinking, not of a purely philosophic and theoretic contemplation of God, but of a loving union
with and possession of God, and indeed of the supernatural union
with God held up to the Christian as the term of his grace-aided
endeavour: one cannot well separate out in Augustine's thought a
natural and a supernatural ethic, since he deals with man in the
concrete, and man in the concrete has a supernatural vocation: he
regarded the neo-Platonists as discerning something of that which

---

[1] *Serm.*, 150, 7, 8. [2] *Ep.*, 140, 23, 56.
[3] *Serm.*, 150, 8, 9. [4] *De moribus eccl.*, 1, 11, 18.

was revealed by Christ, neo-Platonism as an inadequate and partial realisation of the truth.

The ethic of Augustine is, then, primarily an ethic of love: it is by the will that man reaches out towards God and finally takes possession of and enjoys Him. 'When therefore the will, which is the intermediate good, cleaves to the immutable good . . . , man finds therein the blessed life';[1] 'for if God is man's supreme good . . . it clearly follows, since to seek the supreme good is to live well, that to live well is nothing else but to love God with all the heart, with all the soul, with all the mind.'[2] Indeed, after quoting the words of Christ, as recorded by St. Matthew,[3] 'Thou shalt love the Lord thy God with thy whole heart, and with thy whole soul, and with thy whole mind' and 'thou shalt love thy neighbour as thyself', Augustine asserts that 'Natural philosophy is here, since all the causes of all natural things are in God the Creator', and that, 'Ethics are here, since a good and honest life is not formed otherwise than by loving as they should be loved those things which we ought to love, namely, God and our neighbour.'[4] Augustine's ethic thus centres round the dynamism of the will, which is a dynamism of love (*pondus meum, amor meus*),[5] though the attainment of beatitude, 'participation in the immutable good', is not possible for man unless he be aided by grace, unless he receives 'the gratuitous mercy of the Creator'.[6]

2. The will, however, is free, and the free will is subject to moral obligation. The Greek philosophers had a conception of happiness as the end of conduct, and one cannot say that they had no idea of obligation; but owing to his clearer notion of God and of divine creation Augustine was able to give to moral obligation a firmer metaphysical basis than the Greeks had been able to give it.

The necessary basis of obligation is freedom. The will is free to turn away from the immutable Good and to attach itself to mutable goods, taking as its object either the goods of the soul, without reference to God, or the goods of the body. The will necessarily seeks happiness, satisfaction, and *de facto* this happiness can be found only in God, the immutable Good, but man has not the vision of God in this life, he can turn his attention to and cling to mutable goods in place of God, and 'this turning away and this turning to are not forced but voluntary actions'.[7]

---

[1] *De lib. arbit.*, 2, 19, 52.   [2] *De moribus eccl.*, 1, 25, 46.   [3] 22, 37–9.
[4] *Ep.*, 137, 5, 17.   [5] *Conf.*, 13, 9, 10.   [6] *Ep.*, 140, 21, 14.
[7] *De lib. arbit.*, 2, 19, 35.

The human will is, then, free to turn to God or away from God, but at the same time the human mind must recognise the truth, not only that what it seeks, happiness, can be found only in the possession of the immutable Good, God, but also that the direction of the will to that good is implanted by God and willed by God, who is the Creator. By turning away from God the will runs counter to the divine law, which is expressed in human nature, made by God for Himself. All men are conscious to some extent of moral standards and laws: 'even the ungodly . . . rightly blame and rightly praise many things in the conduct of men.' How are they enabled to do so, save by seeing the rules according to which men ought to live, even if they do not personally obey these laws in their own conduct? Where do they see these rules? Not in their own minds, since their minds are mutable, whereas the 'rules of justice' are immutable; not in their characters, since they are *ex hypothesi* unjust. They see the moral rules, says Augustine, using his customary, if obscure, manner of speaking, 'in the book of that light which is called Truth'. The eternal laws of morality are impressed in the heart of man, 'as the impression of a ring passes into the wax, yet does not leave the ring'. There are indeed some men who are more or less blind to the law, but even they are 'sometimes touched by the splendour of the omnipresent truth'.[1] Thus, just as the human mind perceives eternal theoretic truths in the light of God, so it perceives, in the same light, practical truths or principles which should direct the free will. Man is by his nature, his nature considered in the concrete, set towards God; but he can fulfil the dynamism of that nature only by observing the moral laws which reflect the eternal law of God, and which are not arbitrary rules but follow from the Nature of God and the relationship of man to God. The laws are not arbitrary caprices of God, but their observance is willed by God, for He would not have created man without willing that man should be what He meant him to be. The will is free, but it is at the same time subject to moral obligations, and to love God is a duty.

3. The relationship of man to God, however, is the relationship of a finite creature to the infinite Being, and the result is that the gulf cannot be bridged without the divine aid, without grace: grace is necessary even to begin to will to love God. 'When man tries to live justly by his own strength without the help of the liberating grace of God, he is then conquered by sins; but in free will he has

it in his power to believe in the Liberator and to receive grace.'[1] 'The law was therefore given that grace might be sought; grace was given that the law might be fulfilled.'[2] 'Our will is by the law shown to be weak, that grace may heal its infirmity.'[3] 'The law of teaching and commanding that which cannot be fulfilled without grace demonstrates to man his weakness, in order that the weakness thus proved may resort to the Saviour, by whose healing the will may be able to do what in its feebleness it found impossible.'[4]

It would be out of place here to enter on the question of Augustine's doctrine of grace and its relation to the free will, which is in any case a difficult question; but it is necessary to grasp the fact that when Augustine makes the love of God the essence of the moral law, he is referring to that union of the will with God which requires the elevation effected by grace. This is only natural, once given the fact that he is considering and treating man in the concrete, man endowed with a supernatural vocation, and it means that he supplements and completes the wisdom of philosophy with the wisdom of the Scriptures. One can, for purposes of schematism, try to separate Augustine the philosopher and Augustine the theologian; but in his own eyes the true philosopher is a man who surveys reality in the concrete, as it is, and it cannot be seen as it is without taking into account the economy of redemption and of grace.

4. If moral perfection consists in loving God, in directing the will to God and bringing all other powers, e.g. the senses, into harmony with this direction, evil will consist in turning the will away from God. But what is evil in itself, moral evil? Is it something positive? It cannot, first of all, be something positive in the sense of something created by God: the cause of moral evil is not the Creator but the created will. The cause of good things is the divine goodness, whereas the cause of evil is the created will which turns away from the immutable Good:[5] evil is a turning-away of the created will from the immutable and infinite Good.[6] But evil cannot strictly be termed a 'thing', since this word implies a positive reality, and if moral evil were a positive reality, it would have to be ascribed to the Creator, unless one were willing to attribute to the creature the power of positive creation out of nothing. Evil, then, is 'that which falls away from essence and tends to non-being. . . . It tends to make that which is cease to be.'[7]

---

[1] *Expos. quarumdam prop. ex epist. ad Rom.*, 44.   [3] *De spir. et litt.*, 19, 34.
[2] *Ibid.*, 9, 15.   [4] *Ep.*, 145, 3, 4.   [5] *Enchirid.*, 23.
[6] *De lib. arbit.*, 1, 16, 35.   [7] *De moribus eccl.*, 2, 2, 2.

Everything in which there is order and measure is to be ascribed to God, but in the will which turns away from God there is disorder. The will itself is good, but the absence of right order, or rather the privation of right order, for which the human agent is responsible, is evil. Moral evil is thus a privation of right order in the created will.

This doctrine of evil as a privation was the doctrine of Plotinus, and in it Augustine found the answer to the Manichees. For if evil is a privation and not a positive thing, one is no longer faced with the choice of either ascribing moral evil to the good Creator or of inventing an ultimate evil principle responsible for evil. This doctrine was adopted by the Scholastics generally from Augustine and finds adherents among several modern philosophers of note, Leibniz, for example.

5. If the principle of morality is love of God and the essence of evil is a falling-away from God, it follows that the human race can be divided into two great camps, that of those who love God and prefer God to self and that of those who prefer self to God: it is by the character of their wills, by the character of their dominant love, that men are ultimately marked. Augustine sees the history of the human race as the history of the dialectic of these two principles, the one in forming the City of Jerusalem, the other the City of Babylon. 'Let each one question himself as to what he loveth; and he shall find of which (city) he is a citizen.'[1] 'There are two kinds of love; . . . These two kinds of love distinguish the two cities established in the human race . . . in the so to speak commingling of which the ages are passed.'[2] 'You have heard and know that there are two cities, for the present mingled together in body, but in heart separated.'[3]

To the Christian history is necessarily of profound importance. It was in history that man fell, in history that he was redeemed: it is in history, progressively, that the Body of Christ on earth grows and develops and that God's plan is unfolded. To the Christian, history apart from the data of revelation is shorn of its significance: it is small wonder, then, that Augustine looked on history from the Christian standpoint and that his outlook was primarily spiritual and moral. If we speak of a philosophy of history in Augustine's thought, the word 'philosophy' must be understood in a wide sense as Christian wisdom. The knowledge of the facts of history may be mainly a natural knowledge, for

---

[1] *In Ps.*, 64, 2.   [2] *De Gen. ad litt.*, 11, 15, 20.   [3] *In Ps.*, 136, 1.

example, knowledge of the existence and development of the Assyrian and Babylonian empires; but the principles by which the facts are interpreted and given meaning and judged are not taken from the facts themselves. The temporal and passing is judged in the light of the eternal. That Augustine's tendency to concentrate on the aspect of Assyria under which it appeared to him as an embodiment of the City of Babylon (in the moral sense) would not commend itself to the modern historian is understandable enough; but Augustine was not concerned to play the part of an historian in the ordinary sense, but rather to give the 'philosophy' of history as he envisaged it, and the 'philosophy' of history, as he understood it, is the discernment of the spiritual and moral significance of historical phenomena and events. Indeed, so far as there can be a philosophy of history at all, the Christian at least will agree with Augustine that only a Christian philosophy of history can ever approach adequacy: to the non-Christian the position of the Jewish people, for example, is radically different from the position it occupies in the eyes of the Christian. If it were objected, as it obviously could be, that this involves a theological interpretation of history, a reading of history in the light of dogma, the objection would not cause Augustine any difficulty, since he never pretended to make that radical dichotomy between theology and philosophy which is implied in the objection.

CHAPTER VIII

ST. AUGUSTINE—VI: THE STATE

The State and the City of Babylon not identical—The pagan State does not embody true justice—Church superior to State.

1. As I have already remarked, Augustine saw in history, as he saw in the individual, the struggle between two principles of conduct, two loves, on the one hand the love of God and submission to His law, on the other hand love of self, of pleasure, of the world. It was only natural, then, that as he saw the embodiment of the heavenly city, Jerusalem, in the Catholic Church, so he should see in the State, particularly in the pagan State, the embodiment of the City of Babylon, and the result of Augustine's attitude in this matter is that one is tempted to assume that for him the City of God can be identified with the Church as a visible society and the City of Babylon with the State as such. Does he not ask, 'Without justice what are kingdoms but great bands of robbers? What is a band of robbers but a little kingdom?' And does he not approve the pirate's reply to Alexander the Great, 'Because I do it with a little ship, I am called a robber, and you, because you do it with a great fleet, are called an emperor'?[1] Assyria and pagan Rome were founded, increased and maintained by injustice, violence, rapine, oppression: is not this to affirm that the State and the City of Babylon are one and the same thing?

Undeniably Augustine thought that the most adequate historical embodiments of the City of Babylon are to be found in the pagan empires of Assyria and Rome, just as he certainly thought that the City of Jerusalem, the City of God, is manifested in the Church. None the less, the ideas of the heavenly and earthly cities are moral and spiritual ideas, the contents of which are not exactly coterminous with any actual organisation. For instance, a man may be a Christian and belong to the Church; but if the principle of his conduct is self-love and not the love of God, he belongs spiritually and morally to the City of Babylon. Again, if an official of the State is governed in his conduct by the love of God, if he pursues justice and charity, he belongs spiritually and morally to the City of Jerusalem. 'We see now a citizen of Jerusalem, a citizen of the

[1] *De Civit. Dei*, 4, 4.

kingdom of heaven, holding some office upon earth; as, for example, wearing the purple, serving as magistrate, as aedile, as proconsul, as emperor, directing the earthly republic, but he hath his heart above if he is a Christian, if he is of the faithful. . . . Let us not therefore despair of the citizens of the kingdom of heaven, when we see them engaged in the affairs of Babylon, doing something terrestrial in a terrestrial republic; nor again let us forthwith congratulate all men whom we see engaged in celestial matters, for even the sons of the pestilence sit sometimes in the seat of Moses. . . . But there will come a time of winnowing when they will be separated, the one from the other, with the greatest care. . . .'[1] Even if, then, the City of Babylon in the moral and spiritual sense tends to be identified with the State, particularly the pagan State, and the City of Jerusalem tends to be identified with the Church as a visible organisation, the identification is not complete: one cannot legitimately conclude that because a man is, for example, a Church official, he is necessarily a citizen of the spiritual City of Jerusalem, for as far as his spiritual and moral condition is concerned he may belong to the City of Babylon. Moreover, if the State were necessarily coincident with the City of Babylon, no Christian could legitimately hold office in the State, or even be a citizen, if he could help it, and St. Augustine certainly did not subscribe to any such opinion.

2. But if the State and the City of Babylon cannot simply be identified, St. Augustine certainly did not think that the State as such is founded on justice or that true justice is realised in any actual State, not at any rate in any pagan State. That there is some justice even in a pagan State is sufficiently obvious, but true justice demands that that worship should be paid to God which He requires, and pagan Rome did not pay that worship, indeed in Christian times she did her best to prevent its being paid. On the other hand pagan Rome was obviously a State. How, then, is the conclusion to be avoided that true justice must not be included within the definition of the State? For, if it is, one would be reduced to the impossible position of denying that pagan Rome was a State. Augustine accordingly defines a society as a 'multitude of rational creatures associated in a common agreement as to the things which it loves'.[2] If the things which it loves are good, it will be a good society, while, if the things which it loves are bad, it will be a bad society; but nothing is said in the definition of a

[1] *In Ps.*, 51, 6.   [2] *De Civit. Dei*, 19, 24.

people as to whether the objects of its love are good or bad, with the result that the definition will apply even to the pagan State.

This does not mean, of course, that in Augustine's eyes the State exists in a non-moral sphere: on the contrary, the same moral law holds good for States as for individuals. The point he wants to make is that the State will not embody true justice, will not be a really moral State, unless it is a Christian State: it is Christianity which makes men good citizens. The State itself, as an instrument of force, has its roots in the consequences of original sin and, given the fact of original sin and its consequences, is a necessary institution; but a just State is out of the question unless it is a Christian State. 'No State is more perfectly established and preserved than on the foundations, and by the bond, of faith and of firm concord, when the highest and truest good, namely God, is loved by all and men love each other in Him without dissimulation because they love one another for His sake.'[1] The State, in other words, is informed by love of this world, when it is left to itself; but it can be informed by higher principles, principles which it must derive from Christianity.

3. From this there follow two consequences of importance. (1) The Christian Church will try to inform civil society with its own celestial principles of conduct: it has a mission to act as the leaven of the earth. Augustine's conception of the Christian Church and her mission was essentially a dynamic and a social conception: the Church must permeate the State by her principles. (2) The Church is thus the only really perfect society and is definitely superior to the State, for, if the State must take her principles from the Church, the State cannot be above the Church nor even on a level with the Church. In maintaining this view St. Augustine stands at the head of the mediaeval exaltation of the Church vis-à-vis the State, and he was only consistent in invoking the help of the State against the Donatists, since, on his view, the Church is a superior society to which Christ has subjected the kingdoms of the world, and which has the right to make use of the powers of the world.[2] But if Augustine's view of the relation of Church to State was the one which became characteristic of western Christendom and not of Byzantium, it does not follow that his view necessarily tended to undermine the significance of civic and social life. As Christopher Dawson has pointed out,[3]

[1] *Ep.*, 137, 5, 18.   [2] Cf. *ibid.*, 105, 5, 6; 35, 3.
[3] *A Monument to St. Augustine*, pp. 76–7.

although Augustine deprived the State of its aura of divinity, he at the same time insisted on the value of the free human personality and of moral responsibility, even against the State, so that in this way he 'made possible the ideal of a social order resting upon the free personality and a common effort towards moral ends'.

CHAPTER IX

THE PSEUDO-DIONYSIUS

Writings and author—Affirmative way—Negative way—Neo-Platonic interpretation of Trinity—Ambiguous teaching on creation—Problem of evil—Orthodoxy or unorthodoxy?

1. During the Middle Ages the writings which were then ascribed to St. Paul's Athenian convert, Dionysius the Areopagite, enjoyed high esteem, not only among mystics and authors of works on mystical theology, but also among professional theologians and philosophers, such as St. Albert the Great and St. Thomas Aquinas. The reverence and respect paid to these writings were, of course, in great part due to the mistaken notion as to their authorship, a mistake which originated in the author's use of a pseudonym. 'Dionysius the Presbyter, to his fellow-presbyter Timothy.'[1] In 533 the Patriarch of Antioch, Severus, appealed to the writings of Dionysius, in support of his Monophysite doctrine, a fact which can be safely taken to mean that the writings were already regarded as possessed of authority. But, even if Severus appealed to the works in question in support of heretical doctrine, their ascription to St. Dionysius would free them from any suspicion as to their orthodoxy. In the Eastern Church they were widely circulated, being commented on by Maximus the Confessor in the seventh century and appealed to by the great Eastern Doctor, St. John Damascene, in the eighth century, though Hypatius of Ephesus attacked their authenticity.

In the West, Pope Martin I appealed to the writings as authentic at the first Lateran Council in 649, and about the year 858 John Scotus Eriugena, at the request of Charles the Bald, made a translation from the Greek text which had been presented to Louis the Fair in 827 by the Emperor Michael Balbus. John Scotus, besides translating the writings of the Pseudo-Dionysius, also commented on them, thus furnishing the first of a series of commentaries in Western Christendom. For example, Hugh of St. Victor (d. 1141) commented on the *Celestial Hierarchy*, using Eriugena's translation, while Robert Grosseteste (d. 1253) and Albert the Great (d. 1280) also commented on the writings.

---

[1] *Exordium* to the *Divine Names*.

St. Thomas Aquinas composed a commentary on the *Divine Names* about 1261. All these authors, as also, for example, Denis the Carthusian, accepted the authenticity of the writings; but in time it was bound to become clear that they embodied important elements taken from developed neo-Platonism and that they constituted in fact an attempt to reconcile neo-Platonism and Christianity, so that they would have to be attributed to an author of a much later date than the historic Dionysius the Areopagite. However, the question of the authenticity of the writings is not the same as the question of their orthodoxy from the Christian standpoint, and though in the seventeenth century, when critics began to attack the authenticity of the writings, their orthodoxy was also assailed, a recognition of their unauthentic character did not necessarily involve an admission of their incompatibility with Christian doctrine, though it was obviously no longer possible to maintain their orthodoxy on the *a priori* ground that they were composed by a personal disciple of St. Paul. Personally I consider that the writings are orthodox in regard to the rejection of monism; but that on the question of the Blessed Trinity it is highly questionable at least if they can be reconciled with orthodox Christian dogma. Whatever the intentions of the author may have been, his words, besides being obscure, as Aquinas admitted, are scarcely compatible, as they stand, with the Trinitarian teaching of Augustine and Thomas Aquinas. It may be objected that insufficient attention is paid to the dogma of the Incarnation, which is essential to Christianity, but the author clearly maintains this doctrine, and in any case to say little about one particular doctrine, even a central one, is not the same as to deny it. Taking the relevant passages of the Pseudo-Dionysius in the large, it does not seem possible to reject them as definitely unorthodox on this point, unless one is prepared also to reject as unorthodox, for example, the mystical doctrine of St. John of the Cross, who is a Doctor of the Church.

But though no one now supposes that the writings are actually the work of Dionysius the Areopagite, it has not proved possible to discover the real author. Most probably they were composed at the end of the fifth century, as they apparently embody ideas of the neo-Platonist Proclus (418–85), and it has been conjectured that the Hierotheus who figures therein was the Syrian mystic Stephen Bar Sadaili. If the writings of the Pseudo-Dionysius actually depend to any degree on the philosophy of Proclus, they cannot well have been composed before the closing decades of the fifth century, while as they were appealed to at the Council of 533, they can hardly have been composed much after 500. The ascription of about 500 as the date of their composition is, therefore, doubtless correct, while the supposition that they originated in Syria is reasonable. The author was a theologian, without doubt an ecclesiastic also; but he cannot have been Severus himself, as one or two writers have rashly supposed. In any case, though it would be interesting to know with certainty who the author was, it is probably unlikely that anything more than conjecture will ever be possible, and the chief interest of the writings is due, not to the personality of the author, but to the content and influence of the writings, these writings being the *Divine Names* (*De divinis Nominibus*), the *Mystical Theology* (*De mystica Theologia*), the *Celestial Hierarchy* (*De coelesti Hierarchia*) and the *Ecclesiastical Hierarchy* (*De ecclesiastica Hierarchia*), as well as ten letters. The works are printed in Migne's *Patrologia Graeca*, volumes 3–4; but a critical edition of the text has been begun.

2. There are two ways of approaching God, who is the centre of all speculation, a positive way (καταφατική) and a negative way (ἀποφατική). In the former way or method the mind begins 'with the most universal statements, and then through intermediate terms (proceeds) to particular titles',[1] thus beginning with 'the highest category'.[2] In the *Divine Names* the Pseudo-Dionysius pursues this affirmative method, showing how names such as Goodness, Life, Wisdom, Power, are applicable to God in a transcendental manner and how they apply to creatures only in virtue of their derivation from God and their varying degrees of participation in those qualities which are found in God not as inhering qualities but in substantial unity. Thus he begins with the idea or name of goodness, which is the most universal name, inasmuch as all things, existent or possible, share in goodness to some degree, but which at the same time expresses the Nature of God: 'None is good save one, that is, God.'[3] God, as the Good, is the overflowing source of creation and its final goal, and 'from the Good comes the light which is an image of Goodness, so that the Good is described by the name of "Light", being the archetype of that which is revealed in the image'.[4] Here the neo-Platonic light-motive is brought in, and the Pseudo-Dionysius's dependence

---

[1] *Myst. Theol.*, 2.   [2] *Ibid.*, 3.
[3] *Div. Names*, 2, 1; St. Matt. 19. 17.   [4] *Div. Names*, 4. 4.

on neo-Platonism is particularly manifest in his language when he goes on to speak of the Good as Beauty, as the 'super-essential beautiful', and uses the phrases of Plato's *Symposium*, which reappear in the *Enneads* of Plotinus. Again, when in chapter 13 of the *Divine Names*[1] the Pseudo-Dionysius speaks of 'One' as 'the most important title of all', he is clearly writing in dependence on the Plotinian doctrine of the ultimate Principle as the One.

In brief, then. the affirmative method means ascribing to God the perfections found in creatures, that is, the perfections which are compatible with the spiritual Nature of God, though not existing in Him in the same manner as they exist in creatures, since in God they exist without imperfection and, in the case of the names which are ascribed to the Divine Nature, without real differentiation. That we start, in the affirmative way, with the highest categories, is, says the author,[2] due to the fact that we should start with what is most akin to God, and it is truer to affirm that He is life and goodness than that He is air or stone. The names 'Life' and 'Goodness' refer to something which is actually in God, but He is air or stone only in a metaphorical sense or in the sense that He is the cause of these things. Yet the Pseudo-Dionysius is careful to insist that, even if certain names describe God better than others, they are very far from representing an adequate knowledge and conception of God on our part, and he expresses this conviction by speaking of God as the super-essential Essence, the super-essential Beautiful, and so on. He is not simply repeating phrases from the Platonic tradition, but he is expressing the truth that the objective reference or content of these names as actually found in God infinitely transcends the content of the names as experienced by us. For example, if we ascribe intelligence to God, we do not mean to ascribe to Him human intelligence, the only intelligence of which we have immediate experience and from which we draw the name: we mean that God is *more*, infinitely more, than what we experience as intelligence, and this fact is best expressed by speaking of God as super-Intelligence or as the super-essential Intelligence.

3. The affirmative way was mainly pursued by the Pseudo-Dionysius in the *Divine Names* and in his (lost) *Symbolical Theology* and *Outlines of Divinity*, whereas the negative way, that of the exclusion from God of the imperfections of creatures, is characteristic of the *Mystical Theology*. The distinction of the two

---

[1] 13, 1.   [2] *Myst. Theol.*, 3.

ways was dependent on Proclus, and as developed by the Pseudo-Dionysius it passed into Christian philosophy and theology, being accepted by St. Thomas Aquinas, for example; but the palm is given by the Pseudo-Dionysius to the negative way in preference to the affirmative way. In this way the mind begins by denying of God those things which are farthest removed from Him, e.g. 'drunkenness or fury,'[1] and proceeds upwards progressively denying of God the attributes and qualities of creatures, until it reaches 'the super-essential Darkness'.[2] As God is utterly transcendent, we praise Him best 'by denying or removing all things that are—just as men who, carving a statue out of marble, remove all the impediments that hinder the clear perception of the latent image and by this mere removal display the hidden statue itself in its hidden beauty'.[3] The human being is inclined to form anthropomorphic conceptions of the Deity, and it is necessary to strip away these human, all-too-human conceptions by the *via remotionis*; but the Pseudo-Dionysius does not mean that from this process there results a clear view of what God is in Himself: the comparison of the statue must not mislead us. When the mind has stripped away from its idea of God the human modes of thought and inadequate conceptions of the Deity, it enters upon the 'Darkness of Unknowing',[4] wherein it 'renounces all the apprehension of the understanding and is wrapped in that which is wholly intangible and invisible . . . united . . . to Him that is wholly unknowable';[5] this is the province of mysticism. The 'Darkness of Unknowing' is not due, however, to the unintelligibility of the Object considered in itself, but to the finiteness of the human mind, which is blinded by excess of light. This doctrine is doubtless partly influenced by neo-Platonism, but it is also to be found in the writings of Christian mystical theologians, notably St. Gregory of Nyssa, whose writings in turn, though influenced, as far as language and presentation are concerned, by neo-Platonic treatises, were also the expression of personal experience.

4. The neo-Platonic influence on the Pseudo-Dionysius comes out very strongly in his doctrine of the Blessed Trinity, for he seems to be animated by the desire to find a One behind the differentiation of Persons. He certainly allows that the differentiation of Persons is an eternal differentiation and that the Father,

---

[1] *Myst. Theol.*, 3. [2] *Ibid.*, 2. [3] *Ibid.*
[4] The author of the mediaeval mystical treatise, *The Cloud of Unknowing*, doubtless wrote in immediate or mediate dependence on the writings of the Pseudo-Dionysius. [5] *Myst. Theol.*, 1.

for example, is not the Son, and the Son not the Father, but so far as one can achieve an accurate interpretation of what he says, it appears that, in his opinion, the differentiation of Persons exists on the plane of manifestation. The manifestation in question is an eternal manifestation, and the differentiation an eternal differentiation within God, to be distinguished from the external manifestation of God in differentiated creatures; but God in Himself, beyond the plane of manifestation, is undifferentiated Unity. One can, of course, attempt to justify the language of the Pseudo-Dionysius by reference to the Nature of God which, according to orthodox Trinitarianism, is one and undivided and with which each of the divine Persons is substantially identical; but it would seem most probable, not to say certain, that the author was influenced, not only by Plotinus's doctrine of the One, but also by Proclus's doctrine of the primary Principle which transcends the attributes of Unity, Goodness, Being. The super-essential Unity would seem to represent Proclus's first Principle, and the distinction of three Persons in unity of Nature would seem to represent the neo-Platonic conception of emanation, being a stage, if an eternal stage, in the self-manifestation or revelation of the ultimate Godhead or Absolute. When we speak of the all-transcendent Godhead as a Unity and a Trinity, it is not a Unity or a Trinity such as can be known by us . . . (though) 'we apply the titles of "Trinity" and "Unity" to that which is beyond all titles, expressing under the form of Being that which is beyond being. . . . (The transcendent Godhead) hath no name, nor can it be grasped by the reason. . . . Even the title of "Goodness" we do not ascribe to it because we think such a name suitable. . . .'[1] (The Godhead) 'is not unity or goodness, nor a Spirit, not Sonship nor Fatherhood, . . . nor does it belong to the category of non-existence or to that of existence.'[2]

It is true that such phrases could be defended, as regards the intention of the author if not as regards his actual words, by pointing out that it is correct to say that the term 'Father', for instance, belongs to the first Person as Person and not to the Son, though the divine substance exists in numerical identity and without intrinsic real differentiation in each of the three divine Persons, and also by allowing that the term 'Father', as applied to the first Person, though the best term available in human language for the purpose, is borrowed from a human relationship,

---

[1] *Div. Names*, 13, 3.   [2] *Myst. Theol.*, 5.

and applied to God in an analogical sense, so that the content of the idea of 'Father' in our minds is not adequate to the reality in God. Moreover, the Pseudo-Dionysius certainly speaks of 'a differentiation in the super-essential doctrine of God', referring to the Trinity of Persons and the names applicable to each Person in particular,[1] and explicitly denies that he is 'introducing a confusion of all distinctions in the Deity',[2] affirming that, while names such as 'Super-vital' or 'Super-wise' belong to 'the entire Godhead', the 'differentiated names', the names of 'Father', 'Son' and 'Spirit', 'cannot be interchanged, nor are they held in common'.[3] Again, though there is a 'mutual abiding and indwelling' of the divine Persons 'in an utterly undifferentiated and transcendent Unity', this is 'without any confusion'.[4] Nevertheless, though much of what the Pseudo-Dionysius has to say on the subject of the Blessed Trinity can be interpreted and defended from the standpoint of theological orthodoxy, it is hardly possible not to discern a strong tendency to go behind, as it were, the distinction of Persons to a super-transcendent undifferentiated Unity. Probably the truth of the matter is that the Pseudo-Dionysius, though an orthodox Trinitarian in intention, was so much influenced by the neo-Platonic philosophy that a tension between the two elements underlies his attempt to reconcile them and makes itself apparent in his statements.

5. In regard to the relation of the world to God, the Pseudo-Dionysius speaks of the 'emanation' (πρόοδος) of God into the universe of things;[5] but he tries to combine the neo-Platonic emanation theory with the Christian doctrine of creation and is no pantheist. For example, since God bestows existence on all things that are, He is said to become manifold through bringing forth existent things from Himself; yet at the same time God remains One even in the act of 'self-multiplication' and without differentiation even in the process of emanation.[6] Proclus had insisted that the prior Principle does not become less through the process of emanation and the Pseudo-Dionysius repeats his teaching on this matter; but the influence of neo-Platonism does seem to have meant that he did not clearly realise the relation of creation to the divine will or the freedom of the act of creation, for he is inclined to speak as though creation were a natural and even a spontaneous effect of the divine goodness, even though

---

[1] *Div. Names*, 2, 5.   [2] *Ibid.*, 2.   [3] *Ibid.*, 3.   [4] *Ibid.*, 4.
[5] *Ibid.*, 5, 1.   [6] *Ibid.*, 2, 11.

God is distinct from the world. God exists indivisibly and without multiplication of Himself in all individual, separate and multiple things, and, though they participate in the goodness which springs from Him and though they may in a certain sense be thought of as an 'extension' of God, God Himself is not involved in their multiplication: the world, in short, is an outflowing of the divine goodness, but it is not God Himself. On this point of God's transcendence as well as on that of His immanence the Pseudo-Dionysius is clear; but his fondness for depicting the world as the outflowing of the over-brimming Goodness of God, as well as for drawing a kind of parallel between the internal divine Processions and the external procession in creation, lead him to speak as though creation were a spontaneous activity of God, as if God created by a necessity of nature.

That God is the transcendent Cause of all things, the Pseudo-Dionysius affirms several times, explaining in addition that God created the world through the exemplary or archetypal Ideas, the 'preordinations' (προορισμοί) which exist in Him:[1] in addition, God is the final Cause of all things, drawing all things to Himself as the Good.[2] He is, therefore, 'the Beginning and the End of all things',[3] 'the Beginning as their Cause, the End as their Final Purpose'.[4] There is, then, an outgoing from God and a return to God, a process of multiplication and a process of intercommunion and return. This idea became basic in the philosophy of the 'Areopagite's' translator, John Scotus Eriugena.

6. As the Pseudo-Dionysius insisted so much on the divine goodness, it was incumbent on him to give some attention to the existence and the consequent problem of evil, and this he gave in the *Divine Names*,[5] relying, partly at least, on Proclus's *De subsistentia mali*. In the first place he insists that, although evil would have to be referred to God as its Cause, were it something positive, it is in fact not something positive at all: precisely as evil it has no being. If it is objected that evil must be positive, since it is productive, sometimes even of good, and since debauchery, for example, which is the opposite of temperance, is something evil and positive, he answers that nothing is productive precisely as evil, but only in so far as it is good, or through the action of good: evil as such tends only to destroy and debase. That evil has no positive being of itself is clear from the fact that

---

[1] *Div. Names*, 5, 8.   [2] *Ibid.*, 4, 4 ff.   [3] *Ibid.*, 4, 35.
[4] *Ibid.*, 5, 10.   [5] 4, 18 ff.

THE PSEUDO-DIONYSIUS 99

proceeds from the Good and, as being, is good. Does this mean,
then, that evil and non-existence are precisely the same? The
Pseudo-Dionysius certainly tends to speak as if that were the
case, but his real meaning is given in his statement that 'all
creatures in so far as they have being are good and come from the
Good, and in so far as they are deprived of the Good, neither are
they good nor have they being'.[1] In other words, evil is a deprivation or privation: it consists, not simply in non-being or in the
absence of being, but rather in the absence of a good that ought
to be present. The sinner, for instance, is good in so far as he has
being, life, existence, will; the evil consists in the deprivation of
a good that ought to be there and actually is not, in the wrong
relation of his will to the rule of morality, in the absence of this
or that virtue, etc.

It follows that no creature, considered as an existent being, can
be evil. Even the devils are good in so far as they exist, for they
hold their existence from the Good, and that existence continues
to be good: they are evil, not in virtue of their existence, their
natural constitution, but 'only through a lack of angelic virtues':[2]
'they are called evil through the deprivation and the loss whereby
they have lapsed from their proper virtues.' The same is true of
bad human beings, who are called evil in virtue of 'the deficiency
of good qualities and activities and in virtue of the failure and fall
therefrom due to their own weakness'. 'Hence evil inheres not in
the devils or in us as evil, but only as a deficiency and lack of the
perfection of our proper virtues.'[3]

Physical, non-moral evil is treated in a similar manner. 'No
natural force is evil: the evil of nature lies in a thing's inability
to fulfil its natural functions.'[4] Again, 'ugliness and disease are a
deficiency in form and a want of order', and this is not wholly
evil, 'being rather a lesser good'.[5] Nor can matter as such be evil,
since 'matter too has a share in order, beauty and form':[6] matter
cannot be evil in itself, since it is produced by the Good and since
it is necessary to Nature. There is no need to have recourse to two
ultimate Principles, good and evil respectively. 'In fine, good
comes from the one universal Cause; evil from many partial
deficiencies.'[7]

If it be said that some people desire evil, so that evil, as the

---

[1] *Div. Names*, 4, 20.   [2] *Ibid.*, 23.   [3] *Ibid.*, 24.   [4] *Ibid.*, 26.
[5] *Ibid.*, 27.   [6] *Ibid.*, 28.   [7] *Ibid.*, 30.

object of desire, must be something positive, the Pseudo-Dionysius answers that all acts have the good as their object, but that they may be mistaken, since the agent may err as to what is the proper good or object of desire. In the case of sin the sinner has the power to know the true good and the right, so that his 'mistake' is morally attributable to him.[1] Moreover, the objection that Providence should lead men into virtue even against their will is foolish, for 'it is not worthy of Providence to violate nature': Providence provides for free choice and respects it.[2]

7. In conclusion one may remark that, although Ferdinand Christian Baur[3] would seem to have gone too far in saying that the Pseudo-Dionysius reduced the Christian doctrine of the Trinity to a mere formal use of the Christian terms void of the Christian content and that his system will not allow of a special Incarnation, it must be admitted that there was a tension in his thought between the neo-Platonic philosophy which he adopted and the Christian dogmas, in which, we have no real reason to deny, he believed. The Pseudo-Dionysius meant to harmonise the two elements, to express Christian theology and Christian mysticism in a neo-Platonic philosophical framework and scheme; but it can scarcely be gainsaid that, when a clash occurred, the neo-Platonic elements tended to prevail. A specific and peculiar Incarnation was one of the major points in Christianity that pagan neo-Platonists, such as Porphyry, objected to, and though, as I have said, we cannot be justified in asserting that the Pseudo-Dionysius denied the Incarnation, his acceptance of it does not well adapt itself to his philosophical system, nor does it play much part in his extant writings. One may well doubt whether his writings would have exercised the influence they did on Christian mediaeval thinkers, had the latter not taken the author's pseudonym at its face value.

---

[1] *Div. Names*, 4, 35.   [2] *Ibid.*, 33.
[3] In his *Christliche Lehre von der Dreieinigkeit und Menschwerdung Gottes*, Vol. 2, p. 42.

CHAPTER X

BOETHIUS, CASSIODORUS, ISIDORE

*Boethius's transmission of Aristotelian ideas—Natural theology
—Influence on Middle Ages—Cassiodorus on the seven liberal
arts and the spirituality of the soul—Isidore's* Etymologies *and*
Sentences.

1. IF one of the channels whereby the philosophy of the ancient
world was passed on to the Middle Ages was the writings of the
Pseudo-Dionysius, another channel, and in some respects a complementary one, was constituted by the writings of Boethius
(c. A.D. 480–524/5), a Christian who, after studying at Athens and
subsequently holding high magisterial office under the king of the
Ostrogoths, Theodoric, was finally executed on a charge of high
treason. I use the word 'complementary' since, while the Pseudo-
Dionysius helped to impregnate early mediaeval philosophy,
especially that of John Scotus Eriugena, with elements drawn
from neo-Platonic speculation, Boethius transmitted to the early
mediaevals a knowledge of at least the logic of Aristotle. His
works I have listed in my volume on Greek and Roman philosophy,[1] and I shall not repeat them here; suffice it to recall that
he translated into Latin the *Organon* of Aristotle and commented
thereon, besides commenting on the *Isagoge* of Porphyry and
composing original treatises on logic. In addition he wrote several
theological *opuscula* and while in prison his celebrated *De
Consolatione Philosophiae*.

It is uncertain whether or not Boethius translated, in accordance
with his original plan, other works of Aristotle besides the *Organon*;
but in his extant works mention is made of several salient Aristotelian doctrines. The earlier mediaeval thinkers were predominantly concerned with the discussion of the problem of universals,
taking as their starting-point certain texts of Porphyry and
Boethius, and they took little notice of the Aristotelian metaphysical doctrines to be found in Boethius's writings. The first
great speculative thinker of the Middle Ages, John Scotus Eriugena,
was more indebted to the Pseudo-Dionysius and other writers
dependent on neo-Platonism than to any Aristotelian influence,

[1] p. 485.

and it was not until the Aristotelian *corpus* had become available to the West at the close of the twelfth and the beginning of the thirteenth centuries that a synthesis on Aristotelian lines was attempted. But that does not alter the fact that Aristotelian doctrines of importance were incorporated in the writings of Boethius. For instance, in his theological work against Eutyches[1] Boethius speaks clearly of 'matter', the common substrate of bodies, which is the basis for, and renders possible, substantial change in bodies, corporeal substances, while its absence in incorporeal substances renders impossible the change of one immaterial substance into another or the change of a corporeal substance into an incorporeal substance or *vice versa*. The discussion is carried on in a theological setting and with a theological purpose, for Boethius wishes to show that in Christ the divine Nature and the human Nature are distinct and both real, against Eutyches who held that 'the union with Godhead involved the disappearance of the human nature';[2] but within that theological setting a philosophical discussion is included and the categories employed are Aristotelian in character. Similarly, in the *De Trinitate*,[3] Boethius speaks of the correlative principle to matter, namely form. For instance, earth is not earth by reason of unqualified matter, but because it is a distinctive form. (For 'unqualified matter' Boethius uses the Greek phrase ἄποια ὕλη, taking it doubtless from Alexander of Aphrodisias.[4] On the other hand, God, the Divine Substance, is Form without matter and cannot be a substrate. As pure Form, He is one.

Again, in the *De Trinitate*,[5] Boethius gives the ten Categories or *Praedicamenta* and goes on to explain that when we call God 'substance', we do not mean that He is substance in the same sense in which a created thing is substance: He is 'a substance that is super-substantial'. Similarly, if we predicate a quality of God, such as 'just' or 'great', we do not mean that He has an inhering quality, for 'with Him to be just and to be God are one and the same', and while 'man is merely great, God is greatness'. In the *Contra Eutychen*[6] occurs Boethius's famous definition of person, *naturae rationalis individua substantia*, which was accepted by St. Thomas and became classical in the Schools.

2. In his doctrine of the Blessed Trinity, Boethius relied largely on St. Augustine; but in the *De Consolatione Philosophiae* he

---

[1] *Contra Eutychen*, 6.   [2] *Ibid.*, 5.   [3] 2.
[4] Cf. the latter's *De Anima*, 17, 17, and his *De anima ibri mantissa*, 124, 7.
[5] 4.   [6] 3.

developed in outline a natural theology on Aristotelian lines, thus implicitly distinguishing between natural theology, the highest part of philosophy, and dogmatic theology which, in distinction from the former, accepts its premises from revelation. In the third book[1] he at least mentions the rational argument for the existence of God as unmoved Mover, while in the fifth book[2] he treats of the apparent difficulty in reconciling human freedom with the divine foreknowledge. 'If God beholdeth all things and cannot be deceived, that must of necessity follow which His providence foreseeth to be to come. Wherefore, if from eternity He doth foreknow not only the deeds of men, but also their counsels and wills, there can be no free-will.'[3] To answer that it is not that future events will take place because God knows them, but rather that God knows them because they will take place is not a very satisfactory answer, since it implies that temporal events and the temporal acts of creatures are the cause of the eternal foreknowledge of God. Rather should we say that God does not, strictly speaking, 'foresee' anything: God is eternal, eternity being defined in a famous phrase as *interminabilis vitae tota simul et perfecta possessio*,[4] and His knowledge is the knowledge of what is eternally present to Him, of a never-fading instant, not a foreknowledge of things which are future to God. Now, knowledge of a present event does not impose necessity on the event, so that God's knowledge of man's free acts, which from the human viewpoint are future, though from the divine viewpoint they are present, does not make those acts determined and necessary (in the sense of not-free). The eternity of God's vision, 'which is always present, concurs with the future quality of an action'.

Boethius drew not merely on Aristotle, but also on Porphyry and other neo-Platonic writers, as well as on Cicero, for example, and it may be that the division of philosophy or speculative science into Physics, Mathematics and Theology was taken directly from the *Isagoge* of Porphyry; but it must be remembered that Porphyry himself was indebted to Aristotle. In any case, in view of the predominantly neo-Platonic character of foregoing Christian philosophy, the Aristotelian element in the thought of Boethius is more remarkable and significant than the specifically neo-Platonic elements. It is true that he speaks of the divine Goodness and its overflowing in a manner reminiscent of neo-Platonism (in the *De Consol. Phil.*[5] he says that 'the substance of God consisteth in

[1] 12.   [2] 2 ff.   [3] 5, 3.   [4] 5, 6.   [5] 3, 9.

nothing else but in goodness') and that he sometimes uses such terms as *defluere* in connection with the procession of creatures from God;[1] but he is quite clear about the distinction between God and the world and about the Christian doctrine of creation. Thus he expressly affirms that God, 'without any change, by the exercise of a will known only to Himself, determined of Himself to form the world and brought it into being when it was absolutely nothing, not producing it from His own substance',[2] denying that the divine substance *in externa dilabatur*[3] or that 'all things which are, are God'.[4]

3. Boethius, then, was of very considerable importance, for he transmitted to the earlier Middle Ages a great part of the knowledge of Aristotle then available. In addition, his application of philosophical categories to theology helped towards the development of theological science, while his use of and definition of philosophical terms was of service to both theology and philosophy. Lastly we may mention the influence exercised by his composition of commentaries, for this type of writing became a favourite method of composition among the mediaevals. Even if not particularly remarkable as an original and independent philosopher, Boethius is yet of major significance as a transmitter and as a philosopher who attempted to express Christian doctrine in terms drawn, not simply from the neo-Platonists, but also from the philosopher whose thought was to become a predominant influence in the greatest philosophical synthesis of the Middle Ages.

4. *Cassiodorus* (*c.* 477–*c.* 565/70) was a pupil of Boethius and, like his master, worked for a time in the service of Theodoric, King of the Ostrogoths. In his *De artibus ac disciplinis liberalium litterarum* (which is the second book of his *Institutiones*) he treated of the seven liberal arts, i.e. the three *scientiae sermocinales* (Grammar, Dialectic and Rhetoric) and the four *scientiae reales* (Arithmetic, Geometry, Music and Astronomy). He did not aim at novelty or originality of thought, but rather at giving a synopsis of the learning he had culled from other writers,[5] and his book on the arts, like that of Martianus Capella, was much used as a text-book in the early Middle Ages. In his *De anima* Cassiodorus drew on St. Augustine and on Claudianus Mamertus (died *c.* 474) in proving the spirituality of the human soul. While the soul cannot be a part of God, since it is changeable and capable of

---

[1] Cf. *Lib. de hebdom.*, 173.   [2] *De Fide Catholica.*   [3] *De Consol. Phil.*, 3, 12.
[4] *Quomodo Substantiae.* I do not, of course mean to imply that there is any doctrine of creation in Aristotle.   [5] *De anima*, 12.

evil, it is not material and cannot be material, since it can have what is spiritual as the object of its knowledge, and only that which is itself spiritual can know the spiritual. As spiritual, the soul is wholly in the whole body and wholly in each part, being indivisible and unextended; but it operates in a given part of the body, e.g. a sense-organ, now with greater, now with less intensity.[1]

5. Cassiodorus, then, was much more a 'transmitter' than an original thinker, and the same can be said of *Isidore* (died *c.* 636), who became Archbishop of Seville in the Visigothic kingdom and whose encyclopaedia, the *Originum seu Etymologiarum libri XX*, was very popular in the early Middle Ages, being included in every monastic library of note. In this work Isidore deals with the seven liberal arts, as also with a great number of scientific or quasi-scientific facts and theories on subjects from Scripture and jurisprudence and medicine to architecture, agriculture, war, navigation, and so on. He shows his conviction about the divine origin of sovereignty and the paramount authority of morality, law and justice in civil society, even in regard to the conduct and acts of the monarch. In addition to his *Etymologies* Isidore's *Libri tres sententiarum*, a collection of theological and moral theses taken from St. Augustine and St. Gregory the Great, was also widely used. His treatise on numbers, *Liber Numerorum*, which treats of the numbers occurring in the Sacred Scriptures, is often fanciful in the extreme in the mystical meanings which it attaches to numbers.

[1] *De anima*, 4.

PART II
THE CAROLINGIAN RENAISSANCE

CHAPTER XI

THE CAROLINGIAN RENAISSANCE

Charlemagne—Alcuin and the Palatine School—Other schools, curriculum, libraries—Rhabanus Maurus.

1. IN A.D. 771 the death of Carloman left Charles (Charlemagne) sole ruler of the Frankish dominions, and his subsequent destruction of the Lombard kingdom and his general policy made him, by the close of the century, the paramount sovereign in Western Christendom. His coronation as emperor by the Pope on December 25th, 800, symbolised the success of his imperial policy and the culmination of Frankish power. The Frankish Empire was later to break up and the imperial crown was to pass to Germany, but for the moment Charlemagne was undisputed master in Western Christendom and was enabled to set on foot the work of reorganisation and reform which had become a crying need under the Merovingian dynasty. The emperor was by no means simply a soldier nor even simply soldier and political organiser combined: he had also at heart the work of raising the cultural level of his subjects by the extension and improvement of education. For this purpose he needed scholars and educational leaders, and since these were not easily obtainable in the Frankish kingdom itself, he had to introduce them from abroad. Already in the fifth century the old culture of Romanised Gaul was fast on the wane and in the sixth and seventh centuries it was at a very low point indeed; what schools there were, were teaching only reading, writing and some rudimentary knowledge of Latin, besides, of course, giving religious instruction. It was to remedy this lamentable state of learning and education that Charlemagne made use of foreign scholars like Peter of Pisa and Paul the Deacon, who were both Italians. The former appears to have been already advanced in age when he taught Latin at the Palace School of Charlemagne, while the latter (Paul Warnefrid, the Deacon), who had come to France in 782, in an attempt to obtain the freedom of his brother,

a prisoner of war, taught Greek from 782 to 786, when he retired to Monte Cassino, where he composed his *History of the Lombards.* Another Italian teacher at the Palatine School was Paulinus of Aquileia, who taught from about 777 to 787.

In addition to the group of Italian grammarians one may mention two Spaniards who came to France as refugees: Agobard, who became Archbishop of Lyons in 816, and Theodulf, who became Bishop of Orleans and died in 821. The latter was familiar with the Latin classics and was himself a Latin poet. Incidentally the oldest known mediaeval manuscript of Quintilian comes from Theodulf's private library. From the point of view of practical importance in the educational work of Charlemagne, however, the Italians and the Spaniards are overshadowed by the celebrated English scholar, Alcuin of York.

2. *Alcuin* (c. 730–804) received his early education at York. Learning had been making progress in England since the year 669, when Theodore of Tarsus, a Greek monk, arrived in the country as Archbishop of Canterbury and, together with Abbot Hadrian, developed the school of Canterbury and enriched its library. This work was carried on by men like Benedict Biscop, who founded the monasteries of Wearmouth (674) and Jarrow (682), and Aldhelm, who, after studying under Theodore and Hadrian, organised the monastery of Malmesbury in Wiltshire, of which he became abbot. A more important figure in Anglo-Saxon scholarship was, however, that of the great exegete and historian Bede (674–735), a priest and monk of Jarrow. It was due to the labours of Bede's friend and pupil Egbert, who became Archbishop of York shortly before Bede's death, that the school of York became the leading cultural and educational centre of England and noted for the richness of its library.

At York Alcuin was more particularly under the care of Aelbert, in company with whom he travelled to Rome, meeting Charles on the way, and when Aelbert succeeded Egbert as Archbishop of York in 767, the chief work in the school devolved on Alcuin. However, in 781, Alcuin was sent by Aelbert to Rome, and in Parma he met Charles for the second time, the king utilising the meeting to urge the English scholar to enter his service. After receiving the permission of his own king and his archbishop, Alcuin accepted the invitation and in 782 took over the direction of the Palatine School, which he maintained (save for a short visit to England in 786 and a longer one from 790 to

793) until 796, when he accepted the abbacy of St. Martin at Tours, where he spent the last years of his life.

Probably about the year 777 Charlemagne wrote a letter to Baugulf, Abbot of Fulda,[1] in which he exhorts the abbot and community to zeal for learning, and this is merely one of the examples of his constant solicitude in the cause of education. The school which is, however, particularly associated with the name of Charlemagne is the so-called Palace or Palatine School, which though not a new creation of the emperor, owed its development to him. Before its development under Charlemagne the school would seem to have existed for the purpose of training the royal princes and children of the higher nobility in the knightly way of life; but the emperor laid emphasis on intellectual training and, as a result of his reform, the pupils appear to have been drawn from a wider circle than the court. French writers have commonly claimed that the Palatine School was the origin of the University of Paris; but it must be remembered that the emperor's court was at Aachen or Aix-la-Chapelle, and not at Paris, though it would seem to have been later removed to Paris by Charles the Bald (d. 877). However, as the University of Paris eventually grew up out of an amalgamation of the Parisian schools, it may be said that the Palatine School was in some sense a remote ancestor of the University, even if the connection was somewhat loose.

Charlemagne's main instrument in the organisation of the Palatine School was Alcuin, from whose writings we can form some idea of the curriculum. Alcuin was certainly not an original thinker, and his educational works, written in dialogue form, rely for the most part on former authors. For example, the *De Rhetorica* makes use of Cicero, with additions from other authors, while in other treatises Alcuin draws on Donatus, Priscian, Cassiodorus, Boethius, Isidore, Bede. But, though Alcuin was unoriginal and mediocre as a writer and can hardly be held to merit the title of philosopher, he seems to have been eminent and successful as a teacher, and some of the best-known figures of the Carolingian renaissance, e.g. Rhabanus Maurus, were his pupils. When he retired to the abbey of St. Martin at Tours, he continued this work of teaching, as is clear from a celebrated letter to the emperor, in which Alcuin describes how he serves to some youths

---

[1] If, however, Baugulf became abbot only in 788, the letter cannot be dated before that year.

the honey of the Holy Scriptures, while others he tries to intoxicate with the wine of ancient literature: some are nourished on the apples of grammatical studies, while to others he displays the order of the shining orbs which adorn the azure heavens. (Charlemagne had a considerable personal interest in astronomy and the two men corresponded on this subject.)

At Tours Alcuin enriched the library with copies of manuscripts which he brought from York, the best library in western Europe. He also devoted his attention to improving the method of copying manuscripts. In a letter of 799[1] he speaks of his daily battle with the 'rusticity' of Tours, from which one may conclude that the path of reform was not always an easy one. It is certain that Alcuin also gave attention to the accurate copying and amending of the manuscripts of the Scriptures, since he speaks explicitly of this in letters to Charlemagne in 800[2] and 801;[3] but it is not certain exactly what part he took in producing the revision of the Vulgate which was ordered by the emperor, known as the 'Alcuinian revision'. However, in view of the important position occupied by the scholar in the implementation of the emperor's reforms, it would seem only reasonable to suppose that he took a leading part in this important work, which helped to arrest the progress of manuscript corruption.

3. As regards the development of other schools (i.e. other than the Palatine School and that of Tours), one may mention the schools attached to the monasteries of St. Gall, Corbie and Fulda. In the monasteries education was provided not only for those pupils who were destined to become members of the religious order, but also for other pupils, though it appears that two separate schools were maintained, the *schola claustri* for the former class of pupil, the *schola exterior* for the latter. Thus at St. Gall the *schola claustri* was within the precincts of the monastery, while the *schola exterior* was among the outer buildings. A capitulary of Louis the Pious (817) ordained that the monasteries should only possess schools for the 'oblates'; but it seems that not much notice was taken of this ordinance.

If one sets the Palatine School in a class by itself, the other schools fall, then, into two main classes, the episcopal or capitular schools and the monastic schools. As for the curriculum this consisted, apart from the study of theology and exegesis, especially in the case of those pupils who were preparing for the priesthood

[1] *Ep.*, 4, 172.   [2] *Ibid.*, 195.   [3] *Ibid.*, 205.

or the religious life, in the study of the *Trivium* (grammar, rhetoric and dialectic) and the *Quadrivium* (arithmetic, geometry, astronomy and music), comprising the seven liberal arts. There was, however, little fresh or original work done on these subjects. Thus grammar, which included literature, would be studied in the writings of Priscian and Donatus, and in the text-books of Alcuin, for example, though some commentaries were composed on the works of the ancient grammarians, by Smaragdus, for instance, on Donatus, and a few undistinguished grammatical works were written, such as the *Ars grammaticae* of Clemens Scotus, who began teaching at the Palatine School in the later years of Charlemagne. Logic too was studied in the handbooks of Alcuin or, if something more was required, in the works of the authors on whom Alcuin relied, e.g. Boethius. In geometry and astronomy little work was done in the ninth century, though the theory of music was advanced by the *Musica enchiriadis*, attributed to Hoger the Abbot of Werden (d. 902). Libraries, e.g. the library of St. Gall, received a considerable increase in the ninth century and they included, besides the theological and religious works which composed the bulk of the items listed, legal and grammatical works, as well as a certain number of classical authors; but it is clear that, as far as philosophy is concerned, logic or dialectic (which, according to Aristotle, is a propaedeutic to philosophy, not a branch of philosophy itself) was the only subject studied. There was only one real speculative philosopher in the ninth century, and that was John Scotus Eriugena. Charlemagne's renaissance aimed at a dissemination of existing learning and what it accomplished was indeed remarkable enough; but it did not lead to original thought and speculation, except in the one instance of John Scotus's system. If the Carolingian empire and civilisation had survived and continued to flourish, a period of original work would doubtless have eventuated at length; but actually it was destined to be submerged in the new Dark Ages and there would be need of another renaissance before the mediaeval period of positive, constructive and original work could be realised.

4. Because of his importance for education in Germany one must mention, in connection with the Carolingian renaissance, the name of Rhabanus Maurus, who was born about 776 and who, after having been a pupil of Alcuin, taught at the monastery of Fulda, where he became abbot in 822. In 847 he was appointed Archbishop of Mainz and continued in that post until his death

in 856. Rhabanus concerned himself with the education of the clergy, and for this purpose he composed his work *De Institutione Clericorum* in three books. In addition to a treatment of the ecclesiastical grades, the liturgy, the training of the preacher and so on, this work also deals with the seven liberal arts, but Rhabanus showed no more originality in this work than in his *De rerum naturis*, an encyclopaedia which was derived very largely from that of Isidore. In general the author depended almost entirely on former writers like Isidore, Bede and Augustine. In regard to exegesis he favoured mystical and allegorical interpretations. In other words, the *Praeceptor Germaniae* was a faithful product of the Carolingian renaissance, a scholar with a real enthusiasm for learning and a lively zeal for the intellectual formation of the clergy, but markedly unoriginal in thought.

CHAPTER XII

JOHN SCOTUS ERIUGENA—I

Life and works

ONE of the most remarkable phenomena of the ninth century is the philosophical system of John Scotus Eriugena, which stands out like a lofty rock in the midst of a plain. We have seen that there was a lively educational activity in the course of the century and, considering the standard, materials and opportunities of the time, a growing interest in learning and scholarship; but there was little original speculation. This is a fact which need cause no surprise in regard to a period of conservation and dissemination; but it is all the more remarkable that an isolated case of original speculation on the grand scale should suddenly occur, without warning and indeed without any immediate continuation. If John Scotus had confined himself to speculation on one or two particular points, we might not have been so surprised, but in point of fact he produced a system, the first great system of the Middle Ages. It may, of course, be said that he relied largely on the former speculations of St. Gregory of Nyssa, for instance, and particularly on the work of the Pseudo-Dionysius, and this is quite true; but one can scarcely avoid the impression, when reading his *De Divisione Naturae*, that one is watching a vigorous, profound and original mind struggling with the categories and modes of thought and ideas which former writers had bequeathed to him as the material on which and with which he had to work, moulding them into a system and impregnating the whole with an atmosphere, a colour and a tone peculiar to himself. It is indeed interesting, if not altogether profitable, to wonder on what lines the thought of John Scotus would have evolved, had he lived at a later and richer period of philosophical development: as it is, one is confronted with a mind of great power, hampered by the limitations of his time and by the poverty of the material at his disposal. Moreover, while it is, of course, a mistake to interpret the system of John Scotus in terms of a much later philosophy, itself conditioned by the previous development of thought and the historical circumstances of the time, for example, the Hegelian system, one is not thereby debarred from endeavouring to discern the peculiar characteristics of John's thought, which, to a certain extent, altered the meaning of the ideas and categories he borrowed from previous writers.

Of the life of John Scotus we do not know very much. He was born in Ireland about 810 and studied in an Irish monastery. 'Eriugena' means 'belonging to the people of Erin', while the term 'Scotus' need not be taken as indicating any near connection with Scotland, since in the ninth century Ireland was known as *Scotia Maior* and the Irish as *Scoti*. It was doubtless in an Irish monastery that he acquired his knowledge of the Greek language. In the ninth century the study of Greek was, speaking generally, peculiar to the Irish monasteries. Bede, it is true, attained to a working knowledge of the language, but neither Alcuin nor Rhabanus Maurus knew any Greek worth speaking of. The former used Greek phrases in his commentaries but, though he must have known at least the Greek alphabet, these *Graeca* were taken over from the writings of other authors, and, in general, it has been shown that the occurrence of Greek phrases in a manuscript points to Irish authorship or to some association with or influence from an Irish writer. The attention given to Greek at St. Gall, for instance, was due originally to Irish monks. However, even if the presence of *Graeca* in a manuscript indicates an Irish influence, direct or indirect, and even if the study of Greek in the ninth century was characteristic of the Irish monasteries, it would be extremely rash to conclude that all Irish writers who used Greek phrases, still less that all Irish monks, studied and knew Greek in any real sense. The use of a Greek phrase is, by itself, no more a proof of a real knowledge of the Greek language than the use of a phrase like *fait accompli* is, by itself, a proof of a real knowledge of French, and the number of even Irish monks who knew much more than the rudiments of Greek was doubtless small. John Scotus Eriugena at any rate was among their number, as is shown clearly by the fact that he was able, when in France, to translate from the Greek writings of St. Gregory of Nyssa and the works of the Pseudo-Dionysius, and even attempted the composition of Greek verse. It would be absurd to take John's knowledge of the language as typical of the century or even as typical of Irish monasteries: the truth of the matter is that he was, for the ninth century, an outstanding Greek scholar.

Sometime in the forties John Scotus crossed over to France. In any case he was at the court of Charles the Bald by 850 and occupied a prominent position in the Palatine School. There is no sure evidence that he was ever ordained priest; but, whether layman or not, he was induced by Hincmar, Bishop of Rheims, to intervene in a theological dispute concerning predestination and the result was his work *De praedestinatione* which pleased neither side and brought its author under suspicion of heresy. John thereupon turned his attention to philosophy and in 858 he undertook, at the request of Charles the Bald, the translation of the works of the Pseudo-Dionysius from Greek into Latin. These works had been presented to Louis the Fair in 827 by the Emperor Michael Balbus, but they had never been adequately translated. John, then, undertook not only to translate them, but also to comment on them, and in fact he published commentaries on the Pseudo-Dionysius's writings, except on the *Mystical Theology*, though Pope Nicholas I made it a subject of complaint that the publication had taken place without any reference to him. John Scotus also published translations of the *Ambigua* of Maximus the Confessor and the *De Hominis Opificio* of St. Gregory of Nyssa, and it appears that later he commented on St. John's Gospel and on Boethius's *De Consolatione Philosophiae* and theological *opuscula*.

The work for which John Scotus is celebrated, however, is the *De Divisione Naturae*, which he composed probably between 862 and 866. This work consists of five books and is written in dialogue form, a form of composition which was popular at the time and which was much used by Alcuin and others. It is not a very easy work to interpret, since the author's attempt to express Christian teaching and the philosophical doctrine of Augustine on lines suggested by the Pseudo-Dionysius and the neo-Platonic philosophy leaves room for dispute whether John Scotus was an orthodox Christian or very nearly, if not quite, a pantheist. Those scholars who maintain his orthodox intentions can point to such statements as that 'the authority of the Sacred Scriptures must be followed in all things',[1] while those who maintain that he regarded philosophy as superior to theology and anticipated the Hegelian rationalism can point, for example, to the statement[2] that 'every authority' (e.g. that of the Fathers) 'which is not confirmed by true reason seems to be weak, whereas true reason does not need to be supported by any authority'. However, one cannot profitably discuss the question of interpretation until the

[1] *De Div. Nat.*, 1, 64.   [2] *Ibid.*, 1, 69.

doctrine of the *De Divisione Naturae* has first been exposed, though it is as well to indicate beforehand the fact that there is a dispute about its correct interpretation.

John Scotus seems not to have outlived Charles the Bald, who died in 877. There are indeed various stories about his later life which are given by chroniclers, e.g. that he became Abbot of Athelney and was murdered by the monks, but there seems to be little evidence for the truth of such stories, and probably they are either legends or are due to a confusion with some other John.

CHAPTER XIII

JOHN SCOTUS ERIUGENA—II

Nature—God and creation—Knowledge of God by affirmative and negative ways; inapplicability of categories to God—How, then, can God be said to have made the world?—Divine Ideas in the Word—Creatures as participations and theophanies; creatures are in God—Man's nature—Return of all things to God—Eternal punishment in light of cosmic return—Interpretation of John Scotus's system.

1. AT the beginning of the first book of the *De Divisione Naturae* John Scotus explains through the lips of the Master, in a dialogue which takes place between a *Magister* and a *Discipulus*, what he means by 'Nature', namely the totality of the things that are and the things that are not, and he gives various ways of making this general division. For example, things which are perceived by the senses or are penetrable by the intellect are the things that are, while the objects that transcend the power of the intellect are the things that are not. Again, things which lie hid in their *semina*, which are not actualised, 'are not', while the things which have developed out of their seeds 'are'. Or again, the objects which are objects of reason alone may be said to be the things which are, while the objects which are material, subject to space and time and to dissolution, may be called the things which are not. Human nature, too, considered as alienated from God by sin may be said 'not to be', whereas when it is reconciled with God by grace, it begins to be.

The term 'Nature', then, means for John Scotus Eriugena, not only the natural world, but also God and the supernatural sphere: it denotes all Reality.[1] When, therefore, he asserts[2] that nature is divided into four species, namely Nature which creates and is not created, Nature which is created and creates, Nature which is created and does not create, and Nature which neither creates nor is created, thus apparently making God and creatures species of Nature, it might well seem that he is asserting a monistic doctrine, and indeed, if these words be taken in their literal significance, we should have to conclude that he was. Nevertheless at the beginning of Book 2, in a long and somewhat complicated period, he

[1] Cf. 3, 1.   [2] 1, 1.

makes it clear that it is not his intention to assert that creatures are actually a part of God or that God is a genus of which creatures are a species, although he retains the fourfold division of 'Nature' and says that God and creatures may be looked at as forming together a *universitas*, a 'universe' or totality. The conclusion is warranted that John Scotus did not intend to assert a doctrine of pantheistic monism or to deny the distinction between God and creatures, though his philosophic explanation or rationalisation of the egress of creatures from God and their return to God may, taken by itself, imply pantheism and a denial of the distinction.

2. 'Nature which creates and is not created' is, of course, God Himself, who is the cause of all things but is Himself without cause. He is the beginning or first principle, since all creatures proceed from Him, the 'middle' (*medium*); since it is in Him and through Him that creatures subsist and move; and the end or final cause, since He is the term of the creature's movement of self-development and perfection.[1] He is the first cause, which brought creatures into existence from a state of non-existence, out of nothing (*de nihilo*).[2] This doctrine of God is in accordance with Christian theology and contains a clear enunciation of the divine transcendence and self-existence; but John Scotus goes on to say that God may be said to be created in creatures, to be made in the things which He makes, to begin to be in the things which begin to be. It would, however, be an anachronism to suppose that he is asserting an evolutionary pantheism, and maintaining that nature, in the ordinary sense, is God-in-His-otherness, for he proceeds to explain[3] that when he says that God is made in creatures, he means that God 'appears' or manifests Himself in creatures, that creatures are a theophany. Some of the illustrations he uses are indeed somewhat unfortunate from the orthodox standpoint, as when he says that, just as the human intellect, when it proceeds into actuality in the sense of actually thinking, may be said to be made in its thoughts, so God may be said to be made in the creatures which proceed from Him, an illustration which would seem to imply that creatures are an actualisation of God; but, whatever illustrations John Scotus may use and however much he is influenced by the philosophical tradition which derived from neo-Platonism, it seems clear that his intention at least was to conserve the real distinction between God and creatures and

[1] I, II.   [2] I, 12.   [3] *Ibid.*

that God, in relation to creation, is *Natura quae creat et non creatur*. On the truth of this formula he is emphatic.

3. In attaining to some knowledge of the *Natura quae creat et non creatur* one can use the affirmative (καταφατική) and negative (ἀποφατική) ways. When using the negative method one denies that the divine essence or substance is any of those things, 'which are', i.e. which can be understood by us: when using the affirmative method one predicates of God those things 'which are', in the sense that the cause is manifested in the effect.[1] This twofold method of theology was borrowed by John Scotus from the Pseudo-Dionysius, as he himself plainly affirms,[2] and it was from the same writer that he took the idea that God should not be called, e.g. Truth or Wisdom or Essence, but rather super-Truth, super-Wisdom and super-Essence, since no names borrowed from creatures can be applied to God in their strict and proper sense: they are applied to God *metaphorice* or *translative*. Moreover, in a succeeding passage[3] John Scotus indulges in a most ingenious piece of dialectic in order to show that the use of the affirmative method does not contradict the doctrine of the ineffable and incomprehensible character of the Godhead and that the negative method is the fundamental one. For example, by the affirmative method we say that God is Wisdom, while by the negative way we say that God is not wisdom, and this appears at first sight to be a contradiction; but in reality, when we say that God is Wisdom, we are using the word 'wisdom' in a 'metaphorical' sense (an 'analogical' sense, the Scholastic would say), while when we say that God is not wisdom, we are using the word in its proper and primary sense (i.e. in the sense of human wisdom, the only wisdom of which we have direct experience). The contradiction is, there-fore, not real, but only verbal, and it is reconciled by calling God super-Wisdom. Now, as far as words go, to predicate super-Wisdom of God would seem to be an act of mind pursuing the affirmative way, but if we examine the matter more closely we shall see that, although the phrase belongs formally and verbally to the *via affirmativa*, the mind has no content, no idea, corre-sponding to the word 'super', so that in reality the phrase belongs to the *via negativa*, and the addition of the word 'super' to the word 'wisdom' is equivalent to a negation. Verbally there is no negation in the predicate 'super-Wisdom', but in regard to the mind's content there is a negation. The *via negativa* is thus

---

[1] I, 13.   [2] I, 14.   [3] *Ibid.*

fundamental, and as we do not pretend to define *what* the 'super' is in itself, the ineffability and incomprehensibility of the Godhead is unimpaired. Of course, if we say that the use of the word 'super' is *simply and solely* equivalent to a negation, the obvious objection arises (and would be raised by a Logical Positivist) that there is no meaning in our minds when we use the phrase, that the phrase is non-significant. John Scotus, however, though he does not discuss this real difficulty, provides one answer when he indicates that when we say that God is, for example, super-Wisdom, we mean that He is *more than* wisdom. If this is so, then the addition of 'super' cannot be simply equivalent to a negation, since we can say that 'a stone is not wise' and we certainly mean something different when we say 'God is not wise' and 'a stone is not wise': we mean that if 'wise' be taken to refer to human wisdom, then God is not wise, in the sense that He is *more* than human wisdom, whereas a stone is not wise, in the sense that the stone is *less* than wise. This thought would seem to be indicated by John Scotus's concluding example. '(God) is essence', an affirmation; 'He is not essence', a negation; 'He is super-essential', an affirmation and negation at the same time.[1] The thesis and the antithesis are thus reconciled dialectically in the synthesis.

If, then, God cannot be properly termed wise, for this term is not predicated of purely material things, much less can we predicate of Him any of the ten categories of Aristotle, which are found in purely material objects. For example, quantity can certainly not be predicated of God, as quantity implies dimensions, and God has no dimensions and does not occupy space.[2] Properly speaking, God is not even substance or οὐσία, for He is infinitely more than substance, though He can be called substance *translative*, inasmuch as He is the creator of all substances. The categories are founded on and apply to created things and are strictly inapplicable to God: nor is the predicate 'God' a genus or a species or an accident. Thus God transcends the *praedicamenta* and the *praedicabilia*, and on this matter John Scotus is clearly no monist but he emphasises the divine transcendence in the way that the Pseudo-Dionysius had done. The theology of the Blessed Trinity certainly teaches us that relation is found in God, but it does not follow that the relations in God fall under the category of relation. The word is used *metaphorice* or *translative* and, as applied to the divine Persons, it is not used in its proper and intelligible sense: the divine 'relations' are more than relations. In fine, though we can learn from creatures *that* God is, we cannot learn *what* He is. We learn that He is more than substance, more than wisdom and so on; but what that more is, what substance or wisdom mean as applied to God, we cannot know, for He transcends every intellect, whether of angels or of men.

4. But though the doctrine of the inapplicability of the categories to God would seem to place the transcendence of God and the clear distinction between Him and creatures beyond all doubt, consideration of the categories of *facere* and *pati* seems to lead John Scotus to a very different conclusion. In a most ingenious discussion[1] he shows, what is obvious enough, that *pati* cannot be predicated of God and at the same time argues that both *facere* and *pati* involve motion. Is it possible to attribute motion to God? No, it is not. Then neither can making be attributed to God. But, how in this case, are we to explain the Scriptural doctrine that God made all things? In the first place, we cannot suppose that God existed before He made the world, for, if that were so, God would not only be in time but also His making would be an accident accruing to Him, and both suppositions are impossible. God's making, therefore, must be co-eternal with Himself. In the second place, even if the making is eternal and identical with God, and not an accident of God, we cannot attribute motion to God, and motion is involved in the category of making. What does it mean, then, to say that God made all things? 'When we hear that God makes all things, we should understand nothing else but that God is in all things, i.e. is the essence of all things. For He alone truly is, and everything which is truly said to be in those things which are, is God alone.'[2] Such a statement would seem to come very near, to put it mildly, to pantheism, to the doctrine of Spinoza, and it is small wonder that John Scotus prefaces his discussion with some remarks on the relation of reason to authority[3] in which he says that reason is prior to authority and that true authority is simply 'the truth found by the power of reason and handed on in writing by the Fathers for the use of posterity'. The conclusion is that the words, expressions and statements of Scripture, however suited for the uneducated, have to be rationally interpreted by those capable of doing so. In other words, John Scotus does not think of himself as unorthodox or intend to be unorthodox, but his philosophic interpretation of Scripture

[1] I, 70–2.   [2] I, 72.   [3] I, 69.

sometimes seems equivalent to its rationalisation and to the setting
of reason above authority and faith. However, this point of view
should not be overstressed. For example, in spite of the pantheistic
passage quoted he goes on to reaffirm creation out of nothing, and
it is clear that when he refuses to say that God makes or made the
world, he is not intending to deny creation but rather to deny of
God making in the only sense in which we understand making,
namely as an accident, as falling under a particular category.
God's existence and essence and His act of making are ontologically one and the same,[1] and all the predicates we apply to God
really signify the one incomprehensible super-Essence.[2]

The truth of the matter seems to be that John Scotus, while
maintaining the distinction between God and creatures, wishes at
the same time to maintain the conception of God as the one all-
comprehensive Reality, at least when God is regarded *altiori
theoria*. Thus he points out[3] that the first and fourth divisions of
Nature (*Natura quae creat et non creatur* and *Natura quae nec creat
nec creatur*) are verified only in God, as first efficient cause and
final cause, while the second and third divisions (*Natura quae et
creatur et creat* and *Natura quae creatur et non creat*) are verified in
creatures alone; but he goes on to say[4] that inasmuch as every
creature is a participation of Him who alone exists of Himself, all
Nature may be reduced to the one Principle, and Creator and
creature may be regarded as one.

5. The second main division of Nature (*Natura quae et creatur
et creat*) refers to the 'primordial causes', called by the Greeks
πρωτότυπα, ἰδέαι, etc.[5] These primordial causes or *praedestinationes* are the exemplary causes of created species and exist in the
Word of God: they are in fact the divine ideas, the prototypes of
all created essences. How, then, can they be said to be 'created'?
John Scotus means that the eternal generation of the Word or
Son involves the eternal constitution of the archetypal ideas or
exemplary causes in the Word. The generation of the Word is not
a temporal but an eternal process, and so is the constitution of the
praedestinationes: the priority of the Word, considered abstractly,
to the archetypes is a logical and not a temporal priority. The
emergence of these archetypes is thus part of the eternal procession
of the Word by 'generation', and it is in this sense only that they
are said to be created.[6] However, the logical priority of the Word
to the archetypes and the dependence of the archetypes on the

---

[1] I, 77.   [2] I, 75.   [3] 2, 2.   [4] *Ibid*.   [5] *Ibid*.   [6] 2, 20.

Word mean that, although there never was a time when the Word was without the archetypes, they are not *omnino coaeternae* (*causae*) with the Word.[1]

In what sense, then, can the primordial causes be said to create? If one were to press statements such as this, that the πρωτότυπον is diffused (*diffunditur*) through all things giving them essence, or again that it penetrates all the things which it has made,[2] one would naturally incline to a pantheistic interpretation; yet John Scotus repeats[3] that the Holy Trinity 'made out of nothing all things that it made', which would imply that the prototypes are causes only in the sense of exemplary causes. Nothing is created except that which was eternally pre-ordained, and these eternal *praeordinationes* or θεῖα θηλήματα are the prototypes. All creatures 'participate' in the archetypes, e.g. human wisdom in the Wisdom-in-itself.[4] He drew copiously on the Pseudo-Dionysius and Maximus for his doctrine and it would seem that he intended to reconcile his philosophic speculation with orthodox Christian theology; but his language rather gives the impression that he is straining at the leash and that his thought, in spite of his orthodox intentions, tends towards a form of philosophic pantheism. That his intentions were orthodox seems clear enough from the frequent *cautelae* he gives.

Is there actually and ontologically a plurality of *praedestinationes* in the Word? John Scotus answers in the negative.[5] Numbers proceed from the *monas* or unit, and in their procession they are multiplied and receive an order; but, considered in their origin, in the monad, they do not form a plurality but are undivided from one another. So the primordial causes, as existing in the Word, are one and not really distinct, though in their effects, which are an ordered plurality, they are multiple. The monad does not become less or undergo change through the derivation of numbers, nor does the primordial cause undergo change or diminution through the derivation of its effects, even though, from another point of view, they are contained within it. On this point John Scotus adheres to the neo-Platonic standpoint, according to which the principle undergoes no change or diminution through the emanation of the effect, and it seems that his philosophy suffers from the same tension that is observable in neo-Platonism, i.e. between a theory of emanation and a refusal to allow that emanation or procession impairs the integrity of the principle.

[1] 2, 21.   [2] 2, 27.   [3] 2, 24, col. 580.   [4] 2, 36.   [5] Cf. 3, 1.

6. *Natura quae creatur et non creat* consists of creatures, exterior to God, forming the world of nature in the narrow sense, which was made by God out of nothing. John Scotus calls these creatures 'participations', and asserts that they participate in the primordial causes, as the latter participate immediately in God.[1] The primordial causes, therefore, look upwards towards the ultimate Principle and downwards towards their multiple effects, a doctrine which obviously smacks of the neo-Platonic emanation theory. 'Participation' means, however, derivation from, and, interpreting the Greek μετοχή or μετουσία as meaning μεταέχουσα or μεταουσία (*post-essentia* or *secunda essentia*), he says that participation is nothing else than the derivation of a second essence from a higher essence.[2] Just as the water rises in a fountain and is poured out into the river-bed, so the divine goodness, essence, life, etc., which are in the Fount of all things, flow out first of all into the primordial causes and cause them to be, and then proceed through the primordial causes into their effects.[3] This is clearly an emanation metaphor, and John Scotus concludes that God is everything which truly is, since He makes all things and is made in all things, 'as Saint Dionysius the Areopagite says'.[4] The divine goodness is progressively diffused through the universe of creation, in such a way that it 'makes all things, and is made in all things, and is all things'.[5] This sounds as if it were a purely pantheistic doctrine of the emanation type; but John Scotus equally maintains that the divine goodness created all things out of nothing, and he explains that *ex nihilo* does not imply the pre-existence of any material, whether formed or unformed, which could be called *nihil*: rather does *nihil* mean the negation and absence of all essence or substance, and indeed of all things which have been created. The Creator did not make the world *ex aliquo*, but rather *de omnino nihilo*.[6] Here again, then, John Scotus tries to combine the Christian doctrine of creation and of the relation of creatures to God with the neo-Platonic philosophy of emanation, and it is this attempt at combination which is the reason for diversity of interpretation, according as one regards the one or other element in his thought as the more fundamental.

This tension became even clearer from the following consideration. Creatures constitute, not only a 'participation' of the divine goodness, but also the divine self-manifestation or theophany. All objects of intellection or sensation are 'the appearance of the

[1] 3. 3.   [2] *Ibid.*   [3] 3. 4.   [4] *Ibid.*   [5] *Ibid.*   [6] 3. 5.

non-appearing, the manifestation of the hidden, the affirmation of the negated (a reference to the *via negativa*), the comprehension of the incomprehensible, the speaking of the ineffable, the approach of the unapproachable, the understanding of the unintelligible, the body of the incorporeal, the essence of the super-essential, the form of the formless', etc.[1] Just as the human mind, itself invisible, becomes visible or manifest in words and writing and gestures, so the invisible and incomprehensible God reveals Himself in nature, which is, therefore, a true theophany. Now, if creation is a theophany, a revelation of the divine goodness, which is itself incomprehensible, invisible and hidden, does not this suggest a new interpretation of the *nihilum* from which creation proceeds? Accordingly John Scotus explains in a later passage[2] that *nihilum* means 'the ineffable and incomprehensible and inaccessible brightness of the divine goodness', for what is incomprehensible may, *per excellentiam*, be called 'nothing', so that when God begins to appear in His theophanies, He may be said to proceed *ex nihilo in aliquid*. The divine goodness considered in itself may be said to be *omnino nihil*, though in creation it comes to be, 'since it is the essence of the whole universe'. It would indeed be an anachronism to ascribe to John Scotus a doctrine of Absolutism and to conclude that he meant that God, considered in Himself apart from the 'theophanies', is a logical abstraction; but it does seem that two distinct lines of thought are present in his teaching about creation, namely the Christian doctrine of free creation 'in time' and the neo-Platonic doctrine of a necessary diffusion of the divine goodness by way of 'emanation'. Probably he intended to maintain the Christian doctrine, but at the same time considered that he was giving a legitimate philosophic explanation of it. Such an attitude would, of course, be facilitated by the fact that there was at the time no clear distinction between theology and philosophy and their respective spheres, with the result that a thinker could, without being what we would nowadays call a rationalist, accept a revealed dogma like the Trinity, and then proceed in all good faith to 'explain' or deduce it in such a way that the explanation practically changed the dogma into something else. If we want to call John Scotus an Hegelian before Hegel, we must remember that it is extremely unlikely that he realised what he was doing.

The precise relation of the created nature to God in the philosophy of John Scotus is not an easy matter to determine. That

<hr>

[1] 3. 4.   [2] 3. 19.

the world is eternal in one sense, namely in its *rationes*, in the primordial causes, in God's will to create, occasions no difficulty, and if the author, when he maintains that the world is both eternal and created, meant simply that as foreseen and willed by God it is eternal, while as made it is temporal and outside God, there would be no cause for surprise; but he maintains that the world is not outside God and that it is both eternal and created *within* God.[1] As regards the first point, that the world is not *extra Deum*, one must understand it in terms of the theory of participation and 'assumption' (*est igitur participatio divinae essentiae assumptio*).[2] As creatures are derived from God and owe all the reality they possess to God, apart from God they are nothing, so that in this sense it can be said that there is nothing outside God: if the divine activity were withdrawn, creatures would cease to be. But we must go further.[3] God saw from eternity all that He willed to create. Now, if He saw creatures from all eternity, He also made them from all eternity, since vision and operation are one in God. Moreover, as He saw creatures in Himself, He made them in Himself. We must conclude, therefore, that God and creatures are not distinct, but one and the same (*unum et id ipsum*), the creature subsisting in God and God being created in the creature 'in a wonderful and ineffable manner'. God, then, 'contains and comprehends the nature of all sensible things in Himself, not in the sense that He contains within Himself anything beside Himself, but in the sense that He is substantially all that He contains, the substance of all visible things being created in Him'.[4] It is at this point that John Scotus gives his interpretation of the 'nothing' out of which creatures proceed as the divine goodness,[5] and he concludes that God is everything, that from the super-essentiality of His nature (*in qua dicitur non esse*) He is created by Himself in the primordial causes and then in the effects of the primordial causes, in the theophanies.[6] Finally, at the term of the natural order, God draws all things back into Himself, into the divine Nature from which they proceeded, thus being first and final Cause, *omnia in omnibus*.

The objection may be raised that first of all John Scotus says that God is *Natura quae creat et non creatur* and then goes on to identify with God the *Natura quae creatur et non creat*: how can the two positions be reconciled? If we regard the divine Nature as

---

[1] See the long discussion in 3, 5 ff.   [2] 3, 9.   [3] 3, 17.
[4] 3, 18   [5] 3, 19.   [6] 3, 10.

it is in itself, we see that it is without cause, ἄναρχος and ἀναίτιος,[1] but at the same time it is the cause of all creatures: it is, then, rightly to be called 'Nature which creates and is not created'. From another point of view, looking on God as final Cause, as *term* of the rhythm of the cosmic process, He may be called 'Nature which neither creates nor is created'. On the other hand, considered as issuing out from the hidden depths of His nature and beginning 'to appear', He appears first of all in the primordial causes or *rationes aeternae*. These are identical with the Word, which contains them, so that, in 'creating' the primordial causes or principles of essences, God appears to Himself, becomes self-conscious, and creates Himself, i.e. as generating the Word and the *rationes* contained in the Word. God is thus 'Nature which both creates and is created'. In the second stage of the divine procession or theophany God comes to be in the effects of the primordial causes, and so is 'Nature which is created', while, since these effects have a term and include together all created effects, so that there are no further effects, He is also 'Nature which does not create'.[2]

7. John Scotus's allegorical explanation of the Biblical account of the six days of creation,[3] which he explains in terms of his own philosophy, brings him, in the fourth book, to his doctrine of man. We can say of man that he is an animal, while we can also say that he is not an animal,[4] since while he shares with the animals the functions of nutrition, sensation, etc., he has also the faculty of reason, which is peculiar to him and which elevates him above all the animals. Yet there are not two souls in man, an animal soul and a rational soul: there is a rational soul which is simple and is wholly present in every part of the body, performing its various functions. John Scotus is therefore willing to accept the definition of man as *animal rationale*, understanding by *animal* the genus and by *rationale* the specific difference. On the other hand the human soul is made in the image of God, is like to God, and this likeness to God expresses the true substance and essence of man. As it exists in any actual man it is an effect: as it exists in God it is a primordial cause, though these are but two ways of looking at the same thing.[5] From this point of view man can be defined as *Notio quaedam intellectualis in mente divina aeternaliter facta.*[6] That this substance of man, the likeness to God or participation in God, exists, can be known by the human mind, just as the human mind

---

[1] 3, 23.   [2] *Ibid.*   [3] 3, 24 ff.   [4] 4, 5.   [5] 4, 7.   [6] *Ibid.*

can know *that* God exists, but *what* its substance is the human mind cannot know, just as it cannot know *what* God is. While, then, from one point of view man is definable, from another point of view he is undefinable, since the mind or reason of man is made in the image of God and the image, like God Himself, exceeds our power of understanding. In this discussion of the definition of man we can discern Aristotelian elements and also neo-Platonic and Christian elements, which give rise to different attitudes and views on the matter.

John Scotus emphasises the fact that man is the microcosm of creation, since he sums up in himself the material world and the spiritual world, sharing with the plants the powers of growth and nutrition, with the animals the powers of sensation and emotional reaction, with the angels the power of understanding: he is in fact what Poseidonius called the bond or δέσμος, the link between the material and spiritual, the visible and invisible creation. From this point of view one can say that every genus of animal is in man rather than that man is in the genus animal.[1]

8. The fourth stage of the process of Nature is that of *Natura quae nec creat nec creatur*, namely of God as the term and end of all things, God all in all. This stage is that of the return to God, the corresponding movement to the procession from God, for there is a rhythm in the life of Nature and, as the world of creatures proceeded forth from the primordial causes, so will it return into those causes. 'For the end of the whole movement is its beginning, since it is terminated by no other end than by its principle, from which its movement begins and to which it constantly desires to return, that it may attain rest therein. And this is to be understood not only of the parts of the sensible world, but also of the whole world. Its end is its beginning, which it desires, and on finding which it will cease to be, not by the perishing of its substance, but by its return to the ideas (*rationes*), from which it proceeds.'[2] The process is thus a cosmic process and affects all creation, though mutable and unspiritualised matter which John Scotus, following St. Gregory of Nyssa, represented as a complex of accidents and as appearance,[3] will perish.

Besides the cosmical process of creation as a whole, there is the specifically Christian theme (though John Scotus not infrequently does a little 'rationalising') of the return of man to God. Fallen man is led back to God by the incarnate Logos, who has assumed

---

[1] 4, 8.   [2] 5, 3.   [3] 1, 34.

human nature and redeemed all men in that human nature, and John Scotus emphasises the solidarity of mankind both in Adam's fall and in Christ's resurrection. Christ brings mankind back to God, though not all are united to God in the same degree, for, though He redeemed all human nature, 'some He restores to the former state of human nature, while others He deifies beyond human nature', yet in no one except Himself is human nature substantially united with the Godhead.[1] John Scotus thus affirms the unique character of the Incarnation and of the relation of Christ's human nature to the Deity, though, when he gives the stages of the return of human nature to God, another—and less orthodox—point of view seems to show itself. These stages are:[2] (1) the dissolution of the human body into the four elements of the sensible world; (2) the resurrection of the body; (3) the change of body into spirit; (4) the return of human nature in its totality into the eternal and unchangeable primordial causes; and (5) the return of nature and the primordial causes to God. 'For God will be all in all, where nothing will exist but God alone.' Yet if at first sight this latter viewpoint seems quite inconsistent with orthodox theology and especially with the unique position of Christ, John Scotus clearly did not mean to assert a real pantheistic absorption in God, since he goes on to state that he does not mean to imply a perishing of individual substance but its elevation. He uses the illustration of the iron made white-hot in the fire and observes that, though the iron may be said to be transmuted into fire, the substance of the iron remains. Thus when, for example, he says that the human body is changed into spirit, what he refers to is the glorification or 'spiritualisation' of the human body, not to a kind of transubstantiation. Moreover, it must be remembered that John Scotus expressly states that he is basing his teaching on the doctrine of St. Gregory of Nyssa and his commentator Maximus, and his teaching must accordingly be understood in the light of that statement. Lest it be thought, he says, that he is entirely neglecting the Latins in favour of the Greeks, he adds the testimony of St. Ambrose. Though the heavens and the earth will perish and pass away (their perishing being interpreted as a *reditus in causas*, which means the cessation of the generated material world), that does not mean that the individual souls of men, in their *reditus in causas*, will cease to exist: their *deificatio* no more means their substantial absorption in God than the

[1] 5, 25.   [2] 5, 8.

permeation of the air by light means its destruction or transub-stantiation. John Scotus is quite clear on that point.

The fact is that in the case of the cosmic 'return', as elsewhere, John Scotus tries to combine the teaching of the Scriptures and the Fathers with philosophical speculation of the neo-Platonic tradition or rather to express the Christian *Weltanschauung* in terms of such speculation. As the Christian wisdom is looked at as a totality, no clear distinction being made between revealed theology and philosophy, the application of John's speculative method necessarily means a *de facto* rationalisation on occasion, however orthodox his intentions may have been. For instance, though he insists on the fact that the return to God does not spell the annihilation or the complete absorption of the individual human being and though he expresses himself perfectly clearly on this point, yet his attitude towards matter as the term of the descending divine procession leads him to say[1] that before the Fall human beings were not sexually differentiated and that after the resurrection they will return to this state (in support of which views he appeals to St. Paul, St. Gregory and Maximus). Man, had he not fallen, would have been sexually undifferentiated and in the primordial cause human nature is sexually undifferentiated: the *reditus in causam* involves, therefore, a return to the state of human nature *in causa* and a liberation from the state consequent on the Fall. The *reditus in causam*, however, is a stage in the cosmic process of Nature, so that John Scotus has to maintain that the resurrection of the body takes place by nature, *natura et non per gratiam,*[2] though he appeals for support in this to St. Gregory of Nyssa, Maximus and St. Epiphanius. On the other hand, it is certain, theologically at least, that something is attri-butable to grace, and John Scotus accordingly attributes the *deificatio*, which is not attained by all human beings, to the free gift and disposition of God, to grace. This is an example of his attempt to combine revelation with the exigencies of his specula-tive system, an attempt for which, of course, he undoubtedly received support from the writings of earlier Christian authors. On the one hand John Scotus, owing to his Christian intentions, must attribute the resurrection in at least one aspect to God's free grace operating through Christ, while on the other hand, his philosophical doctrine of the return of all things to God means that he must make the resurrection in some degree a natural and

[1] 5, 20.   [2] 5, 23.

necessary process, not only because human nature itself has to return into its cause, but because all creation has to return into its cause and endure eternally, and this it does effectively as being contained in man, the microcosm.[1]

9. But if there is to take place a cosmic return to God in and through human nature, so that God, as St. Paul says, will be 'all in all', how is it possible to maintain the theologically orthodox doctrine of the eternal punishment of the damned? The Scriptures teach that the fallen angels and human beings who are finally impenitent will be eternally punished, while on the other hand reason teaches that evil cannot be without end, since God will be all in all and evil is diametrically opposed to God, who is goodness.[2] How can one reconcile these two positions without rejecting either authority or reason? John Scotus's answer[3] is ingenious and affords a good example of his 'rationalisation'. Nothing that God has made can be evil: the substances or natures, therefore, of the devils and evil men must be good. On this point he quotes the Pseudo-Dionysius. The demons and evil men will never, then, suffer annihilation. All that God has made will return to God and all 'nature' will be contained in God, human nature included, so that it is impossible that human nature should undergo eternal punishment. What, then, of the punishments described in the Scriptures? In the first place they cannot be corporeal or material in character, while in the second place they can only affect what God has not made and what, in this sense, is outside 'nature'. Now, God did not make the perverse will of demons or evil men, and it is this which will be punished. But, if all things are to return to God and God will be all in all, how can punishment be contained in God? Moreover, if the malice has disappeared and all impiety, what is there left to punish? The punishment must consist in the eternal prevention by God of the will's tendency to fix itself on the images, conserved in the memory, of the objects desired on earth. God, then, will be all in all, and all evil will have perished, but the wicked will be eternally punished. It is obvious, however, that from the viewpoint of orthodox theology 'wicked' and 'punished' must be placed in inverted commas, since John Scotus has rationalised the Scriptural teaching in order to satisfy the exigencies of his philosophical system.[4] All human nature, all men without exception, will rise with spiritualised bodies and the full possession of natural goods, though only the elect will enjoy 'deification'.[5]

[1] 5, 25.   [2] 5, 26-7.   [3] 5, 27-8.   [4] 5, 29-36.   [5] 5, 36.

The conclusion is, then, that the divine nature is the end and term of all things, which will return into their *rationes aeternae* and there abide, 'ceasing to be called by the name of creature', for God will be all in all, 'and every creature will be cast into the shade, i.e. changed into God, as the stars at the rising of the sun'.[1]

10. Although the *De Divisione Naturae* did not have the effect that its outstanding quality as a systematic metaphysic deserved, it was utilised by a succession of mediaeval writers from Remigius of Auxerre to Amalric of Bene, including Berengarius, Anselm of Laon, William of Malmesbury, who praised the work, though he disapproved of John Scotus's predilection for Greek authors, and Honorius of Autun, while the Pseudo-Avicenna borrowed from the work in his *De Intelligentiis*, written in the middle or later part of the twelfth century. However, the fact that the Albigensians appealed to the book, while Amalric of Bene (end of twelfth century) used the doctrine of John Scotus in a pantheistic sense, led to its condemnation in 1225 by Pope Honorius III, who ordered that the work should be burnt, though the order was by no means always fulfilled. This condemnation of the *De Divisione Naturae* and the interpretation which led to the condemnation naturally raises the question, whether John Scotus was or was not a pantheist.

That John Scotus was in intention orthodox has already been given as my opinion; but there are several points that might be mentioned by way of summary argument in support of this statement. First of all, he draws copiously on the writings and ideas of authors whom he certainly regarded as orthodox and with whose ideas he felt his own thought to be in harmony. For example, he makes extensive use of St. Gregory of Nyssa, of the Pseudo-Dionysius (whom he regarded as St. Dionysius the Areopagite), and, not to appear to neglect the Latins, quotes St. Augustine and St. Ambrose in favour of his views. Moreover, John Scotus considered his speculation to be founded on the Scriptures themselves. For instance, the theory of the fourth stage of Nature, *Deus omnia in omnibus*, has its foundation in the words of St. Paul:[2] 'And when all things shall be subdued unto him, then the Son also himself shall be subject unto him that put all things under him, that God may be all in all,' while the doctrine of the body 'becoming spirit' at the resurrection is based on the Pauline statement that the body is sown in corruption and raised in incorruption,

[1] 3, 23.   [2] 1 Cor., 15. 28.

that the risen body is a 'spiritual' body. Again, John Scotus draws from the first chapter of St. John's Gospel the conception of the Logos by whom all things were made, in his account of creation, while the theme of *deificatio* was common in the writings of the Fathers.

But, even if John Scotus wrote as though his system had a foundation in Scripture and Tradition, might it not be that he was consciously rationalising the text of Scripture, that he had, to put it crudely, 'his tongue in his cheek'? Does he not say[1] that authority proceeds from true reason and reason in no way from authority; that every authority which is not approved by true reason seems to be weak; that true reason does not need the confirmation of any authority and that authority is nothing else but the truth found by the power of reason and handed on by the Fathers in their writings for the use of posterity; and does not this indicate that he set no store by authority? It seems to me that, to judge by the context, when John Scotus speaks about 'authority' here, he is not referring to the words of Scripture but to the teaching of the Fathers and to the interpretation they had put on the words of the Scriptures. Of course, although it is true that authority must rest on reason, in the sense that the authority must have good credentials, the statement of John Scotus to the effect that authority is nothing else than the truth found by reason and handed on by the Fathers is, as it stands, unacceptable from the theological standpoint (I mean, if compared with the orthodox doctrine of Tradition); but what John Scotus apparently *means* is, not that the doctrine of the Trinity, for example, is simply a truth found by reason and not revealed, but that the attempted 'explanation' or development of the dogma by this or that Father is simply the result of the Father's rational effort and is not final. He does not mean to suggest that the bare dogma, as found in Scripture and preserved by, for example, St. Augustine, can legitimately be questioned, but rather that the intellectual development of the dogma given by St. Augustine, though worthy of respect, is the work of reason and cannot be placed on the same level as the dogma itself. His position is, therefore, this. If St. Paul says that God will be *omnia in omnibus*, this is a revealed truth, but when it comes to deciding what St. Paul meant by this statement and how precisely it is to be understood, reason is the final court of appeal. I am not trying to suggest that this attitude

[1] I, 69.

is theologically acceptable: my point is rather that, whether his actual view is acceptable or not, John Scotus is not questioning a dogma as such or claiming a right to deny it, but is claiming the right to interpret it, and that his 'rationalisation' consists in this. He has not got his tongue in his cheek when he appeals to Scripture, for he sincerely believed that the data of revelation have to be interpreted rationally and, as we would say, philosophically. This is partly due to the fact that he makes no clear-cut distinction between theology and philosophy. His system presupposes the 'Christian wisdom' (including truths discoverable by reason alone, e.g. God's existence, and truths which are revealed, but not discoverable by reason alone, e.g. the Trinity of Persons in the Godhead) and is a speculative attempt to exhibit the Christian wisdom as an organic and interconnected whole, without making any clear distinction between the spheres of philosophy and revelation, and this attempt inevitably involves some rationalisation. I repeat that I am not trying to defend John Scotus's rationalisation, but to explain his attitude, and my thesis is that it is a mistake to interpret his 'rationalisation' as if it post-dated the clear division of philosophy and theology: his attitude is not essentially different from that of later mediaeval theologians who attempted to prove the Trinity *rationibus necessariis*. If John Scotus had consciously been a 'philosopher' in the narrow sense and nothing more, we would have had to call him a rationalist in the modern sense; but he was both theologian and philosopher in combination (in confusion, if one prefers), and his rationalisation was, *psychologically*, quite compatible with a belief in revelation. Therefore, when he says[1] that he does not want to seem to resist the Apostle or the testimony *summae ac sanctae auctoritatis*, he is quite sincere. Indeed his true attitude is admirably indicated by his statement[2] that 'it is not for us to judge the opinions of the holy Fathers, but to accept them with piety and reverence, though we are not prohibited from choosing (among their opinions) that which appears to reason to agree better with the divine words'. John Scotus accepts, for instance, the doctrine of eternal punishment, because it is revealed, and he accepts it sincerely; but he does not consider that this prevents him from attempting to explain the doctrine in such a way that it will fit in with the rest of his system, a system which he regards as fundamentally based on revelation.

[1] 1, 7.   [2] 2, 16.

The discussion may seem to have strayed from the point at issue; but this is not so in reality. For instance, revelation, Christian dogma, teaches clearly that the world was made by God from nothing and that creatures are not God. Now John Scotus' general system demands that creatures should return to God and that God should be all in all. Regarding both truths as founded on divine teaching, John Scotus has to reconcile them rationally, in such a way that the *reditus in Deum* does not lead to the conclusion to which it might seem to lead, namely pantheistic absorption, and that the presentation of the distinction between God and creatures does not contradict the Pauline statement that God will be all in all. The process of reconciliation may involve him in what the Thomist theologians would call 'rationalisation', but his *cautelae*, e.g. that creatures return to God and 'become' God, not *ita ut non sint* but '*ut melius sint*', are not sops thrown to the theologians with the writer's tongue in his cheek, but they are sincere expressions of John Scotus' desire to preserve Christian teaching or what he regards, rightly or wrongly, as Christian teaching.

That a tension develops between the Christian and neo-Platonic elements in John Scotus' thought has already been pointed out, but it is as well to emphasise it again, as it has a bearing on the question of his 'rationalism'. In accordance with the neo-Platonic tradition inherited through the Pseudo-Dionysius, John Scotus maintained[1] that God in Himself, *Natura quae creat et non creatur*, is impenetrable to Himself, unknown to Himself, as being infinite and super-essential, and that He becomes luminous to Himself only in His theophanies. This is, of course, an echo of the neo-Platonic doctrine that the One, the ultimate Godhead, is beyond thought, beyond self-consciousness, since thought and self-consciousness involve a duality of subject and object. Now, that God in Himself is incomprehensible to the created mind is certainly a Christian tenet, but that He is not self-luminous is not the teaching of Christianity. John Scotus, therefore, has to reconcile the two positions somehow, if he wishes to retain them both, and he attempts to do so by making the first 'theophany' the emergence of the Logos containing the primordial causes, so that in and through the Logos God becomes (though not temporally) self-conscious, appearing to Himself. The Logos thus corresponds to the neo-Platonic *Nous*, and a rationalisation arises out of the

[1] E.g. 3, 23.

desire to preserve both the Christian doctrine and the principles of what John Scotus regards as true philosophy. The desire to preserve Christian doctrine is sincere enough, but a tension between the two elements is inevitable. If one takes a particular set of isolated statements of John Scotus one would have to say that he was either a pantheist or a theist. For example, the statement that the distinction between the second and third stages of Nature is due only to the forms of human reasoning[1] is in itself clearly pantheistic, while the statement that the substantial distinction between God and creatures is always preserved is clearly theistic. It might seem that we should opt for one or the other set in an unqualified manner, and it is this attitude which has given rise to the notion that John Scotus was a conscious pantheist who made verbal concessions to orthodoxy with his tongue in his cheek. But if one realises that he was a sincere Christian, who yet attempted to reconcile Christian teaching with a predominantly neo-Platonic philosophy or rather to express the Christian wisdom in the only framework of thought which was then at hand, which happened to be predominantly neo-Platonic, one should also be able to realise that, in spite of the tension involved and the tendency to rationalise Christian dogma, as far as the subjective standpoint of the philosopher was concerned a satisfactory reconciliation was effected. This does not, of course, alter the fact that not a few statements, if taken in isolation, affirm a pantheistic doctrine and that other statements are irreconcilable with orthodox theological teaching on such points as eternal punishment, and it was in view of such statements that the *De Divisione Naturae* was subsequently condemned by ecclesiastical authority. However, whether orthodox or not, the work bears testimony to a powerful and acute mind, the mind of a speculative philosopher who stands head and shoulders above any other thinker of his day.

[1] 2, 2.

PART III

THE TENTH, ELEVENTH AND TWELFTH CENTURIES

CHAPTER XIV

THE PROBLEM OF UNIVERSALS

Situation following death of Charlemagne—Origin of discussion in texts of Porphyry and Boethius—Importance of the problem—Exaggerated realism—Roscelin's 'nominalism'—St. Peter Damian's attitude to dialectic—William of Champeaux—Abelard—Gilbert de la Porrée and John of Salisbury—Hugh of St. Victor—St. Thomas Aquinas.

1. ONE might have expected that the revival of letters and learning under Charlemagne would lead to a gradual and progressive development of philosophy and (the retention of what was already possessed having been provided for) that thinkers would be able to extend knowledge and pursue a more speculative path, especially as western Europe had been already supplied with an example of philosophical speculation and systematising by John Scotus Eriugena. In point of fact, however, this was not the case, since historical factors outside the sphere of philosophy plunged the empire of Charlemagne into a new Dark Age, the Dark Ages of the tenth century, and belied the promise of the Carolingian renaissance.

Cultural progress depended to some extent on the maintenance of the tendency to centralisation which had been apparent during the reign of Charlemagne; but after his death the empire was divided and the division of the empire among the descendants of Charlemagne was accompanied by the growth of feudalism, that is, by decentralisation. As nobles could be rewarded practically only through gifts of land, they tended, through the acquisition of land, to become more and more independent of the monarchy: their interests diverged or conflicted. Churchmen of the higher grades became feudal lords, monastic life was degraded (for example, through the common practice of the appointment of lay-abbots), bishoprics were used as means of honouring or rewarding servants of the king. The Papacy, which might have attempted to check and to remedy the worsening conditions in France, was itself at a very low ebb of spiritual and moral prestige, and, since education and learning were mainly in the hands of monks and ecclesiastics, the inevitable result of the break-up of the empire of Charlemagne was the decay of scholarship and educational activity. Reform did not begin until the establishment of Cluny in 910, and the influence of the Cluniac reform made itself felt only gradually, of course. St. Dunstan, who had been in the Cluniac monastery of Ghent, introduced the ideals of Cluny into England.

In addition to the internal factors which prevented the fruit of the Carolingian renaissance coming to maturity (such as the political disintegration which led in the tenth century to the transference of the imperial crown from France to Germany, the decay of monastic and ecclesiastical life, and the degradation of the Papacy), there were also operative such external factors as the attacks of the Norsemen in the ninth and tenth centuries, who destroyed centres of wealth and culture and checked the development of civilisation, as also the attacks of the Saracens and the Mongols. Internal decay, combined with external dangers and attacks, rendered cultural progress impossible. To conserve, or to attempt to do so, was the only practicable course: progress in scholarship and philosophy lay again in the future. Such interest in philosophy as existed, centred largely round dialectical questions, and particularly round the problem of universals, the starting-point for the discussion being supplied by certain texts of Porphyry and Boethius.

2. Boethius, in his commentary on the *Isagoge* of Porphyry,[1] quotes Porphyry as remarking that at present he refuses to state whether genera and species are subsistent entities or whether they consist in concepts alone; if subsisting, whether they are material or immaterial and, further, whether they are separate from sensible objects or not, on the ground that such exalted matters cannot be treated in an introduction. Boethius himself, however, goes on to treat of the matter, first of all remarking on the difficulty of the question and the need of care in considering it and then pointing out that there are two ways in which an idea may be so formed that its content is not found in extramental objects precisely as it exists in the idea. For example, one may join together arbitrarily man and horse, to form the idea of a centaur, joining together objects which nature does not suffer to be joined together, and such arbitrarily constructed ideas are

[1] *P.L.*, 64, col. 82–6.

'false'. On the other hand, if we form the idea of a line, i.e. a mere line as considered by the geometer, then, although it is true that no mere line exists by itself in extramental reality, the idea is not 'false', since bodies involve lines and all we have done is to isolate the line and consider it in abstraction. Composition (as in the composition of horse and man to form the centaur) produces a false idea, whereas abstraction produces an idea which is true, even though the thing conceived does not exist extramentally in a state of abstraction or separation.

Now, the ideas of genera and species are ideas of the latter type, formed by abstraction. The likeness of humanity is abstracted from individual men, and this likeness, considered by the mind, is the idea of the species, while the idea of the genus is formed by considering the likeness of diverse species. Consequently, 'genera and species are in individuals, but, as thought, are universals'. They 'subsist in sensible things, but are understood without bodies'. Extramentally there is only one subject for both genus and species, i.e. the individual, but that no more prevents their being considered separately than the fact that it is the same line which is both convex and concave prevents our having different ideas of the convex and concave and defining them differently.

Boethius thus afforded the material for an Aristotelian solution of the problem, though he goes on to say that he has not thought it proper to decide between Plato and Aristotle, but that he has been following out the opinions of Aristotle since his book is concerned with the *Categories* of which Aristotle was the author. But, though Boethius afforded material for a solution of the problem of universals on the lines of moderate realism and though his quotations from Porphyry and his comments on them started the discussion of the problem in the early Middle Ages, the first solution of the mediaevals was not on the lines suggested by Boethius but was a rather *simpliste* form of extreme realism.

3. The thoughtless might suppose that in occupying themselves with this problem the early mediaevals were canvassing a useless topic or indulging in a profitless dialectic juggling; but a short reflection should be sufficient to show the importance of the problem, at least if its implications are considered.

Although what we see and touch are particular things, when we think these things we cannot help using general ideas and words, as when we say, 'This particular object which I see is a tree, an elm to be precise.' Such a judgement affirms of a particular object that it is of a certain kind, that it belongs to the genus tree and the species elm; but it is clear that there may be many other objects besides the actual one perceived to which the same terms may be applied, which may be covered by the same ideas. In other words, objects outside the mind are individual, whereas concepts are general, universal in character, in the sense that they apply indifferently to a multitude of individuals. But, if extramental objects are particular and human concepts universal, it is clearly of importance to discover the relation holding between them. If the fact that subsistent objects are individual and concepts general means that universal concepts have no foundation in extramental reality, if the universality of concepts means that they are mere ideas, then a rift between thought and objects is created and our knowledge, so far as it is expressed in universal concepts and judgements, is of doubtful validity at the very least. The scientist expresses his knowledge in abstract and universal terms (for example, he does not make a statement about this particular electron, but about electrons in general), and if these terms have no foundation in extramental reality, his science is an arbitrary construction, which has no relation to reality. In so far indeed as human judgements are of a universal character or involve universal concepts, as in the statement that this rose is red, the problem would extend to human knowledge in general, and if the question as to the existence of an extramental foundation of a universal concept is answered in the negative, scepticism would result.

The problem may be raised in various ways, and, historically speaking, it has taken various forms at various times. It may be raised in this form, for instance. 'What, if anything, in extramental reality corresponds to the universal concepts in the mind?' This may be called the ontological approach, and it was under this form that the early mediaevals discussed the matter. Or one may ask *how* our universal concepts are formed. This is the psychological approach and the emphasis is different from that in the first approach, though the two lines of approach are closely connected and one can scarcely treat the ontological question without answering in some way the psychological question as well. Then again, if one supposes a conceptualist solution, that universal concepts are simply conceptual constructions, one may ask how it is that scientific knowledge, which for all *practical* purposes is a fact, is *possible*. But, however the problem be raised and whatever form it takes, it is of fundamental importance. Perhaps one of the factors which may give the impression that the mediaevals were discussing a comparatively unimportant question is this, that they practically confined their attention to genera and species in the category of substance. Not that the problem, even in this restricted form, is unimportant, but if the problem is raised in regard to the other categories as well, its implications in regard to at least the greater part of human knowledge becomes more evident. It becomes clear that the problem is ultimately the epistemological problem of the relation of thought to reality.

4. The first solution to the problem given by the mediaevals was that known as 'Exaggerated Realism'. That it was chronologically the first solution is borne out by the fact that the opponents of this view were for some time known as the *moderni*, while Abelard, for instance, refers to it as the *antiqua doctrina*. According to this view, our generic and specific concepts correspond to a reality existing extramentally in objects, a subsistent reality in which individuals share. Thus the concept Man or Humanity reflects a reality, humanity or the substance of human nature, which exists extramentally in the same way as it is thought, that is, as a unitary substance in which all men share. If for Plato the concept Man reflects the ideal of human nature subsisting apart from and 'outside' individual men, an ideal which individual men embody or 'imitate' to a greater or less extent, the mediaeval realist believed that the concept reflects a unitary substance existing extramentally, in which men participate or of which they are accidental modifications. Such a view is, of course, extremely naïve, and indicates a complete misunderstanding of Boethius's treatment of the question, since it supposes that unless the object reflected by the concept exists extramentally in exactly the same way that it exists intramentally, the concept is purely subjective. In other words, it supposes that the only way of saving the objectivity of our knowledge is to maintain a naïve and exact correspondence between thought and things.

Realism is already implied in the teaching of e.g. *Fredegisius* who succeeded Alcuin as Abbot of St. Martin's Abbey at Tours and maintained that every name or term supposes a corresponding positive reality (e.g. Darkness or Nothing). It is also implied in the teaching of *John Scotus Eriugena*. We find a statement of the doctrine in the teaching of *Remigius of Auxerre* (c. 841–908), who held that the species is a *partitio substantialis* of the genus and that the species, e.g. Man, is the substantial unity of many individuals (*Homo est multorum hominum substantialis unitas*). A statement of this kind, if understood as meaning that the plurality of individual men have a common substance which is numerically one, has as its natural consequence the conclusion that individual men differ only accidentally from one another, and *Odo of Tournai* (d. 1113) of the Cathedral School of Tournai (who is also called Odo of Cambrai, from the fact that he became Bishop of Cambrai) did not hesitate to draw this conclusion, maintaining that when a child comes into being God produces a new property of an already existing substance, not a new substance. Logically this ultra-realism should result in sheer monism. For example, we have the concepts of substance and of being, and, on the principles of ultra-realism, it would follow that all objects to which we apply the term substance are modifications of one substance and, more comprehensively, that all beings are modifications of one Being. It is probable that this attitude weighed with John Scotus Eriugena, in so far as the latter can justly be called a monist.

As Professor Gilson and others have pointed out, those who maintained ultra-realism in the early Middle Ages were philosophising as logicians, in the sense that they assumed that the logical and real orders are exactly parallel and that because the meaning of, for example, 'man' in the statements 'Plato is a man' and 'Aristotle is a man' is the same, there is a substantial identity in the real order between Plato and Aristotle. But it would, I think, be a mistake to suppose that the ultra-realists were influenced simply by logical considerations: they were influenced also by theological considerations. This is clear in the case of Odo of Tournai, who used ultra-realism in order to explain the transmission of original sin. If one understands by original sin a positive infection of the human soul, one is at once faced by an apparent dilemma: either one has to say that God creates out of nothing a new human substance each time a child comes into being, with the consequence that God is responsible for the infection, or one has to deny that God creates the individual soul. What Odo of Tournai maintained was a form of traducianism, i.e. that the human nature or substance of Adam, infected by original sin, is handed on at generation and that what God creates is simply a new property of an already existing substance.

It is not always easy to assess the precise significance to be attached to the words of the early mediaevals, as we cannot always tell with certainty if a writer fully recognised the implications of his words or if he was making an emphatic point in controversy, perhaps as an *argumentum ad hominem*, without consciously wishing his statement to be understood according to its literal meaning. Thus when Roscelin said that the three Persons of the Blessed Trinity might well be called three gods, if usage permitted, on the ground that every existing being is an individual, *St. Anselm* (1033–1109) asked how he who does not understand how a multitude of men are specifically one man, can understand how several Persons, each of whom is perfect God, are one God.[1] On the strength of this statement St. Anselm has been called an ultra- or exaggerated realist, and indeed the natural interpretation of the statement, in the light of the theological dogma involved, is that, just as there is but one Substance or Nature in the Godhead, so there is but one substance or nature (i.e. numerically one) in all men. Yet it might be that St. Anselm was arguing *ad hominem* and that his question, as intended, amounts to asking how a man who does not realise the specific unity of men (supposing, rightly or wrongly, that Roscelin denied *all* reality to the universal) can possibly grasp the far greater union of the divine Persons in the one Nature, a Nature which is *numerically* one. St. Anselm may have been an ultra-realist, but the second interpretation of his question is supported by the fact that he obviously understood Roscelin to hold that universals have no reality but are mere *flatus vocis* and by the fact that in the *Dialogus de Grammatico*[2] he distinguished between primary and secondary substances, mentioning Aristotle by name.

5. If the implied principle of the ultra-realists was the exact correspondence of thought and extramental reality, the principle of the adversaries of ultra-realism was that only individuals exist. Thus *Eric* (Heiricus) *of Auxerre* (841–76) observed that if anyone tries to maintain that white or black exist absolutely and without a substance in which they adhere, he will be unable to point to any corresponding reality but will have to refer to a white man or a black horse. General names have no general or universal objects corresponding to them; their only objects are individuals. How, then, do universal concepts arise and what is their function and their relation to reality? Neither the understanding nor the memory can grasp all individuals, and so the mind gathers together (*coarctat*) the multitude of individuals and forms the idea

---

[1] *De fide Trin.*, 2.   [2] 10.

of the species, e.g. man, horse, lion. But the species of animals or plants are themselves too many to be comprehended by the mind at once, and it gathers the species together to form the genus. There are, however, many genera and the mind takes a further step in the process of *coarctatio*, forming the still wider and more extensive concept of *usia* (οὐσία). Now, at first sight this seems to be a nominalist position and to remind one of the shorthand note theory of J. S. Mill; but, in the absence of more extensive evidence, it would be rash to affirm that this actually was Eric's consciously held view. Probably he merely meant to affirm emphatically that only individuals exist, that is, to deny ultra-realism, and at the same time to give attention to the psychological explanation of our universal concepts. We have not sufficient evidence to warrant an affirmation that he denied any real foundation to the universal concept.

A similar difficulty of interpretation arises in regard to the teaching of *Roscelin* (c. 1050–1120), who, after studying at Soissons and Rheims, taught at Compiègne, his birthplace, Loches, Besançon and Tours. His writings have been lost, except for a letter to Abelard, and we have to rely on the testimony of other writers like St. Anselm, Abelard and John of Salisbury. These writers make it perfectly clear indeed that Roscelin was an opponent of ultra-realism and that he maintained that only individuals exist, but his positive teaching is not so clear. According to St. Anselm,[1] Roscelin held that the universal is a mere word (*flatus vocis*) and accordingly he is numbered by St. Anselm among the contemporary heretics in dialectic. Anselm goes on to remark that these people think that colour is nothing else but body and the wisdom of man nothing else but the soul, and the chief fault of the 'dialectical heretics' he finds in the fact that their reason is so bound up with their imagination that they cannot free themselves from images and contemplate abstract and purely intelligible objects.[2] Now, that Roscelin said that universals are words, general words, we cannot call in question, since St. Anselm's testimony is quite clear; but it is difficult to assess precisely what he meant by this. If we interpret St. Anselm as more or less an Aristotelian, i.e. as no ultra-realist, then we should have to say that he understood Roscelin's teaching as involving a denial of any kind of objectivity to the universal; whereas if we interpret Anselm as an ultra-realist we can then suppose that Roscelin was

[1] *De fide Trin.*, 2; *P.L.* 158, 265A.   [2] *De fide Trin.*, 2; *P.L.* 158, 265B.

merely denying ultra-realism in a very emphatic way. It is, of course, undeniable that the statement that the universal is a mere *flatus vocis* is, taken literally, a denial not only of ultra-realism and moderate realism but even of conceptualism and the presence of universal concepts in the mind; but we have not sufficient evidence to say what Roscelin held about the concept as such, if indeed he gave any attention to the matter: it might be that, in his determination to deny ultra-realism, the formal subsistence of universals, he simply opposed the *universale in voce* to the subsistent universal, meaning that only individuals exist and that the universal does not, as such, exist extramentally, but without meaning to say anything about the *universale in mente*, which he may have taken for granted or never have thought about. Thus it is clear from some remarks of Abelard in his letter on Roscelin to the Bishop of Paris[1] and in his *De divisione et definitione* that, according to Roscelin, a part is a mere word, in the sense that when we say that a whole substance consists of parts, the idea of a whole consisting of parts is a 'mere word', since the objective reality is a plurality of individual things or substances; but it would be rash to conclude from this that Roscelin, if called upon to define his position, would have been prepared to maintain that we have no *idea* of a whole consisting of parts. May he not have meant simply that our idea of a whole consisting of parts is purely subjective and that the only objective reality is a multiplicity of individual substances? (Similarly he appears to have denied the logical unity of the syllogism and to have dissolved it into separate propositions.) According to Abelard, Roscelin's assertion that the ideas of whole and part are mere words is on a par with his assertion that species are mere words; and if the above interpretation is tenable in regard to the whole-part relation, we could apply it also to his doctrine of genera and species and say that his identification of them with words is an affirmation of their subjectivity rather than a denial that there is such a thing as a general idea.

One has, of course, no axe to grind in interpreting Roscelin. He may indeed have been a nominalist in a naïve and complete sense, and I am certainly not prepared to say that he was not a nominalist pure and simple. John of Salisbury seems to have understood him in this sense, for he says that 'some have the idea that the words themselves are the genera and species, although this view was long

[1] *P.L.*, 178, 358B.

ago rejected and has disappeared with its author',[1] an observation which must refer to Roscelin, since the same author says in his *Metalogicus*[2] that the view which identifies species and genera with words practically disappeared with Roscelin. But though Roscelin may have been a pure nominalist and though the fragmentary testimony as to his teaching, if taken literally, certainly supports this interpretation, still it does not seem possible to assert without doubt that he paid any attention to the question whether we have *ideas* of genera or species or not, still less that he denied it, even if his actual words imply this. All we are entitled to say with certainty is that, whether nominalist or conceptualist, Roscelin was an avowed anti-realist.

6. It has been remarked earlier that Roscelin proposed a form of 'Tritheism' which excited the enmity of St. Anselm and which led to his being condemned and having to retract his theory at a Council at Soissons in 1092. It was the fact of such incursions into theology on the part of the dialecticians which was largely responsible for the hostility shown towards them by men like St. Peter Damian. The peripatetic dialecticians or sophists, laymen who came from Italy and travelled from one centre of study to another, men like Anselmus Peripateticus of Parma, who attempted to ridicule the principle of contradiction, naturally put dialectic in a rather poor light through their verbal sophistry and jugglery; but as long as they restricted themselves to verbal disputes, they were probably little more than an irritating nuisance: it was when they applied their dialectic to theology and fell into heresy, that they aroused the enmity of theologians. Thus *Berengarius of Tours* (c. 1000–88), maintaining that accidents cannot exist without their supporting substance, denied the doctrine of Transubstantiation. Berengarius was a monk and not a *Peripateticus*, but his spirit of disregard of authority seems to have been characteristic of a group of dialecticians in the eleventh century, and it was mainly this sort of attitude which led St. Peter Damian to pronounce dialectics a superfluity or Otloh of St. Emmeran (c. 1010–70) to say that certain dialecticians put more faith in Boethius than in the Scriptures.

St. Peter Damian (1007–72) had little sympathy with the liberal arts (they are useless, he said) or with dialectics, since they are not concerned with God or the salvation of the soul, though, as theologian and writer, the Saint had naturally to make use of

---

[1] *Polycraticus*, 7, 12; *P.L.*, 199, 665A. [2] 2, 17; *P.L.*, 199, 874C.

dialectic himself. He was, however, convinced that dialectic is a very inferior pursuit and that its use in theology is purely subsidiary and subordinate, not merely because dogmas are revealed truths but also in the sense that even the ultimate principles of reason may fail to apply in theology. For instance, God, according to St. Peter Damian, is not only arbiter of moral values and the moral law (he would have had some sympathy with Kierkegaard's reflections on Abraham), but can also bring it about that an historical event should be 'undone', should not have occurred, and if this seems to go counter to the principle of contradiction, then so much the worse for the principle of contradiction: it merely shows the inferiority of logic in comparison with theology. In short, the place of dialectic is that of a handmaid, *velut ancilla dominae*.[1]

The 'handmaid' idea was also employed by *Gerard of Czanad* (d. 1046), a Venetian who became Bishop of Czanad in Hungary. Gerard emphasised the superiority of the wisdom of the Apostles over that of Aristotle and Plato and declared that dialectic should be the *ancilla theologiae*. It is indeed often supposed that this is the Thomist view of the province of philosophy, but, given St. Thomas's delineation of the separate provinces of theology and philosophy, the handmaid idea does not fit in with his professed doctrine on the nature of philosophy: it was rather (as M. De Wulf remarks) the idea of a 'restricted group of theologians', men who had no use for the newfangled science. However, they could not avoid using dialectic themselves, and *Archbishop Lanfranc* (who was born about the year 1010 and died as Archbishop of Canterbury in 1089) was only talking common sense when he observed that it is not dialectic itself, but the abuse of it, which should be condemned.

7. The opposition of a saint and a rigorist theologian to dialectic is also one of the motifs in the life of Abelard, whose controversy with William of Champeaux forms the next stage in the story of the discussion on universals, though it affected only Abelard's life, not the ultimate triumph of his fight against ultra-realism.

William of Champeaux (1070–1120), after studying at Paris and Laon, studied under Roscelin at Compiègne. He adopted, however, the very opposite theory to that of Roscelin, and the doctrine he taught at the Cathedral School of Paris was that of ultra-realism. According to Abelard, who attended William's lectures at Paris

---

[1] *De div. omnip.*; *P.L.*, 145, 63.

and from whom we have to derive our knowledge of William's teaching, the latter maintained the theory that the same essential nature is wholly present at the same time in each of the individual members of the species in question, with the inevitable logical consequence that the individual members of a species differ from one another, not substantially but only accidentally.[1] If this is so, says Abelard,[2] there is the same substance in Plato in one place and in Socrates in another place, being made Plato through one set of accidents and Socrates through another set of accidents. Such a doctrine is, of course, the form of ultra-realism current in the early Middle Ages, and Abelard had no difficulty in showing the absurd consequences it involved. For example, if the human species is substantially, and therefore wholly, present in both Socrates and Plato at the same time, then Socrates must be Plato and he must be present in two places at once.[3] Furthermore, such a doctrine leads ultimately to pantheism, since God is substance and all substances will be identical with the divine substance.

Under pressure of criticism of this kind William of Champeaux changed his theory, abandoning the identity-theory for the indifference-theory and saying that two members of the same species are the same thing, not essentially (*essentialiter*), but indifferently (*indifferenter*). We have this information from Abelard,[4] who evidently treated the new theory as a mere subterfuge, as though William were now saying that Socrates and Plato are not the same, but yet are not different. However, fragments from William's *Sententiae*[5] makes his position clear. He there says that the two words 'One' and 'same' can be understood in two ways, *secundum indifferentiam et secundum identitatem eiusdem prorsus essentiae*, and goes on to explain that Peter and Paul are 'indifferently' men or possess humanity *secundum indifferentiam* in that, as Peter is rational, so is Paul, and as Peter is mortal, so is Paul, etc., whereas their humanity is not the same (he means that their essence or nature is not numerically the same) but like (*similis*), since they are two men. He adds that this mode of unity does not apply to the divine Nature, referring, of course, to the fact that the divine Nature is identical in each of the three divine Persons. This fragment, then, in spite of somewhat obscure language, is clearly opposed to ultra-realism. When William says that Peter and Paul are one and the same in humanity *secundum indifferentiam*

---

[1] *Hist. calam.*, 2; *P.L.*, 178, 119AB.   [2] *Dialectica*, edit. Geyer, p. 10.
[3] *De generibus et speciebus;* Cousin, *Ouvrages inédits d'Abélard*, p. 153.
[4] *Hist. calam.*, 2; *P.L.*, 178, 119B.   [5] Edit. Lefèvre, p. 24.

he means that their essences are alike and that this likeness is the foundation of the universal concept of man, which applies 'indifferently' to Peter or Paul or any other man. Whatever Abelard may have thought about this modified theory or under whatever interpretation he may have attacked it, it would seem to be in reality a denial of ultra-realism and not much different from Abelard's own view.

It should be mentioned that the above is somewhat of a simplification, in that the exact course of events in the dispute between Abelard and William is not clear. For instance, although it is certain that William, after being defeated by Abelard, retired to the Abbey of St. Victor and taught there, becoming subsequently Bishop of Châlons-sur-Marne, it is not certain at what point in the controversy he retired. It would seem probable that he changed his theory while teaching at Paris and then, under fresh criticism from Abelard, whether justified or not, retired from the fray to St. Victor, where he continued teaching and may have laid the foundation for the mystical tradition of the abbey; but, according to M. De Wulf, he retired to St. Victor and there taught the new form of his theory, the indifference-theory. It has also been held that William held three theories: (i) the identity-theory of ultra-realism; (ii) the indifference-theory, which was attacked by Abelard as indistinguishable from the first theory; and (iii) an anti-realist theory, in which case he would presumably have retired to St. Victor after teaching the first and second theories. This may be correct, and possibly it is supported by Abelard's interpretation and criticism of the indifference-theory; but it is questionable if Abelard's interpretation was anything more than polemical and I am inclined to agree with De Wulf that the indifference-theory involved a denial of the identity-theory, i.e. that it was not a mere verbal subterfuge. In any case the question is not one of much importance, since all are agreed that William of Champeaux eventually abandoned the ultra-realism with which he had begun.

8. The man who worsted William of Champeaux in debate, *Abelard* (1079–1142), was born at Le Pallet, Palet or Palais near Nantes, deriving thence his name of *Peripateticus Palatinus*, and studied dialectic under Roscelin and William, after which he opened a school of his own, first at Melun, then at Corbeil and subsequently at Paris, where he conducted the dispute with his former master. Later he turned his attention to theology, studied under Anselm of Laon and started teaching theology himself at

Paris in 1113. As a result of the episode with Héloise Abelard had to withdraw to the abbey of St. Denis. In 1121 his book *De Unitate et Trinitate divina* was condemned at Soissons and he then founded the school of Le Paraclet near Nogent-sur-Seine, only to abandon the school in 1125, in order to become Abbot of St. Gildas in Brittany, though he left the monastery in 1129. From 1136 to 1149 at any rate, he was teaching at Ste. Geneviève at Paris, where John of Salisbury was one of his pupils. However, St. Bernard accused him of heresy and in 1141 he was condemned at the Council of Sens. His appeal to Pope Innocent II led to his further condemnation and an injunction against lecturing, after which he retired to Cluny and remained there until his death.

Abelard was, it is clear, a man of combative disposition and unsparing of his adversaries: he ridiculed his masters in philosophy and theology, William of Champeaux and Anselm of Laon. He was also, though somewhat sentimental, egoistic and difficult to get on with: it is significant that he left both the abbey of St. Denis and that of St. Gildas because he was unable to live in peace with the other monks. He was, however, a man of great ability, an outstanding dialectician, far superior in this respect to William of Champeaux; he was no mediocrity who could be ignored, and we know that his brilliance and dialectical dexterity, also no doubt his attacks on other teachers, won him great audiences. His incursions into theology, however, especially in the case of a brilliant man of great reputation, made him seem a dangerous thinker in the eyes of those who had little natural sympathy for dialectic and intellectual cleverness, and Abelard was pursued by the unremitting hostility of St. Bernard in particular, who appears to have looked on the philosopher as an agent of Satan; he certainly did everything he could to secure Abelard's condemnation. Among other charges he accused Abelard of holding an heretical doctrine of the Blessed Trinity, a charge the truth of which Abelard stoutly denied. Probably the philosopher was no rationalist in the usual sense, so far as intentions were concerned (he did not mean to deny revelation or explain away mystery); but at the same time, in his application of dialectic to theology he does seem to have offended against theological orthodoxy, in fact if not in intention. On the other hand it was the very application of dialectic to theology which made theological progress possible and facilitated the Scholastic systematisation of theology in the thirteenth century.

Abelard had no difficulty, as we have seen, in showing the absurdities to which William of Champeaux's ultra-realism logically led; but it was incumbent on him to produce a more satisfactory theory himself. Accepting Aristotle's definition of the universal, as given by Boethius (*quod in pluribus natum est praedicari, singulare vero quod non*), he went on to state that it is not a thing which is predicated but a name, and he concludes that 'it remains to ascribe universality of this sort to words alone'.[1] This sounds like the purely nominalistic view traditionally ascribed to Roscelin (under whom Abelard had studied), but the fact that he was willing to speak of universal and particular words shows that we cannot immediately conclude that Abelard denied any reality corresponding to the universal word, for he certainly did not deny that there is reality corresponding to the particular words, the reality in this case being the individual. Moreover, Abelard proceeded (in the *Logica nostrorum petitioni sociorum*) to distinguish *vox* and *sermo* and to say, not that *Universale est vox*, but that *Universale est sermo*. Why did he make this distinction? Because *vox* signifies the word as a physical entity (*flatus vocis*), a thing, and no thing can be predicated of another thing, whereas *sermo* signifies the word according to its relation to the logical content and it is this which is predicated.

What then is the logical content, what is the *intellectus universalis* or universal idea, which is expressed by the *nomen universale*? By universal ideas the mind 'conceives a common and confused image of many things . . . When I hear *man* a certain figure arises in my mind which is so related to individual men that it is common to all and proper to none.' Such language suggests indeed that, according to Abelard, there are really no universal concepts at all, but only confused images, generic or specific according to the degree of confusion and indistinctness; but he goes on to say that universal concepts are formed by abstraction and that through these concepts we conceive what is *in* the object, though we do not conceive it *as* it is in the object. 'For, when I consider this man only in the nature of substance or of body, and not also of animal or of man or of grammarian, obviously I understand nothing except what is in that nature, but I do not consider all that it has.' He then explains that when he said that our idea of man is 'confused', he meant that by means of abstraction the nature is set free, as it were, from all individuality and is

[1] *Ingredientibus*, edit. Geyer, 16.

considered in such a way that it bears no special relation to any particular individual but can be predicated of all individual men. In fine, *that which* is conceived in specific and generic ideas is in things (the idea is not void of objective reference), but it is not in them, i.e. in individual things, *as* it is conceived. Ultra-realism, in other words, is false; but that does not mean that universals are purely subjective constructions, still less that they are mere words. When Abelard says that the universal is a *nomen* or *sermo*, what he means is that the logical unity of the universal concept affects only the predicate, that it is a *nomen* and not a *res* or individual thing. If we wish, with John of Salisbury, to call Abelard a 'nominalist', we must recognise at the same time that his 'nominalism' is simply a denial of ultra-realism and an assertion of the distinction between the logical and real orders, without involving any denial of the objective foundation of the universal concept. The Abelardian doctrine is an adumbration, in spite of some ambiguous language, of the developed theory of 'moderate realism'.

In his *Theologia Christiana* and *Theologia* Abelard follows St. Augustine, Macrobius and Priscian in placing in the mind of God *formae exemplares* or divine ideas, generic and specific, which are identical with God Himself, and he commends Plato on this point, understanding him in a neo-Platonic sense, as having placed the Ideas in the divine mind, *quam Graeci Noyn appellant.*

9. Abelard's treatment of the problem of universals was really decisive, in the sense that it gave a death-blow to ultra-realism by showing how one could deny the latter doctrine without at the same time being obliged to deny all objectivity to genera and species, and, though the School of Chartres in the twelfth century (in contradistinction to the School of St. Victor) inclined to ultra-realism, two of the most notable figures connected with Chartres, namely Gilbert de la Porrée and John of Salisbury, broke with the old tradition.

(i) *Gilbert de la Porrée* or *Gilbertus Porretanus* was born at Poitiers in 1076, became a pupil of Bernard of Chartres and himself taught at Chartres for more than twelve years. Later he taught at Paris, though he became Bishop of Poitiers in 1142. He died in 1154.

On the subject of each man having his own humanity or human nature Gilbert de la Porrée was firm;[1] but he had a peculiar view

[1] *In Boeth. de dual. nat.; P.L.,* 64, 1378.

as to the inner constitution of the individual. In the individual we must distinguish the individualised essence or substance, in which the accidents of the thing inhere, and the *formae substantiales* or *formae nativae*.[1] These native forms are common in the sense that they are alike in objects of the same species or genus, as the case may be, and they have their exemplars in God. When the mind contemplates the native forms in things, it can abstract them from the matter in which they are embodied or rendered concrete and consider them alone in abstraction: it is then attending to genus or species, which are *subsistentiae*, but not substantially existing objects.[2] For example, the genus is simply the collection (*collectio*) of *subsistentiae* obtained by comparing things which, though differing in species, are alike.[3] He means that the idea of the species is obtained by comparing the similar essential determinations or forms of similar individual objects and gathering them together into one idea, while the idea of the genus is obtained by comparing objects which differ specifically but which yet have some essential determinations or forms in common, as horse and dog have animality in common. The form, as John of Salisbury remarks apropos of Gilbert's doctrine,[4] is sensible in the sensible objects, but is conceived by the mind apart from sense, that is, immaterially, and while individual in each individual, it is yet common, or alike, in all the members of a species or genus.

His doctrines of abstraction and of comparison make it clear that Gilbert was a moderate realist and not an ultra-realist, but his curious idea of the distinction between the individual essence or substance and the common essence ('common' meaning alike in a plurality of individuals) landed him in difficulties when he came to apply it to the doctrine of the Blessed Trinity and distinguished as different things *Deus* and *Divinitas*, *Pater* and *Paternitas*, just as he would distinguish Socrates from humanity, that is, from the humanity of Socrates. He was accused of impairing the unity of God and teaching heresy, St. Bernard being one of his attackers. Condemned at the Council of Rheims in 1148, he retracted the offending propositions.

(ii) *John of Salisbury* (c. 1115–80) went to Paris in 1136 and there attended the lectures of, among others, Abelard, Gilbert de la Porrée, Adam Parvipontanus (Smallbridge) and Robert Pulleyn. He became secretary to the Archbishop of Canterbury, first to

---

[1] *In Boeth. de Trinit.*; P.L., 64, 1393. Cf. John of Salisbury, *Metalog.*, 2, 17; P.L., 64, 875–6.
[2] *P.L.*, 64, 1267.   [3] *Ibid.*, 64, 1389.   [4] *Ibid.*, 64, 875–6.

Archbishop Theobald and then to St. Thomas à Becket, being subsequently appointed Bishop of Chartres in 1176.

In discussing the problem of universals, says John, the world has grown old: more time has been taken up in this pursuit than was required by the Caesars for conquering and governing the world.[1] But anyone who looks for genera and species outside the things of sense is wasting his time:[2] ultra-realism is untrue and contradicts the teaching of Aristotle,[3] for whom John had a predilection in dialectical matters, remarking, apropos of the *Topics*, that it is of more use than almost all the books of dialectic which the moderns are accustomed to expound in the schools.[4] Genera and species are not things, but are rather the forms of things which the mind, comparing the likeness of things, abstracts and unifies in the universal concepts.[5] Universal concepts or genera and species abstractly considered are mental constructions (*figurata rationis*), since they do not exist as universals in extramental reality; but the construction in question is one of comparison of things and abstraction from things, so that universal concepts are not void of objective foundation and reference.[6]

10. It has been already mentioned that the School of St. Victor inclined to moderate realism. Thus *Hugh of St. Victor* (1096–1141) adopted more or less the position of Abelard and maintained a clear doctrine of abstraction, which he applied to mathematics and to physics. It is the province of mathematics to attend to *actus confusos inconfuse*,[7] abstracting, in the sense of attending to in isolation, the line or the plane surface, for example, although neither lines nor surfaces exist apart from bodies. In physics, too, the physicist considers in abstraction the properties of the four elements, although in concrete reality they are found only in varying combinations. Similarly the dialectician considers the forms of things in isolation or abstraction, in a unified concept, though in actual reality the forms of sensible things exist neither in isolation from matter nor as universals.

11. The foundations of the Thomist doctrine of moderate realism had thus been laid before the thirteenth century, and indeed we may say that it was Abelard who really killed ultra-realism. When St. Thomas declares that universals are not subsistent things but exist only in singular things,[8] he is re-echoing what Abelard and John of Salisbury had said before him. Humanity,

[1] *Polycrat.*, 7, 12.   [2] *Metal.*, 2, 20.   [3] *Ibid.*   [4] *Ibid.*, 3, 10.
[5] *Ibid.*, 2, 20.   [6] *Ibid.*, 3, 3.   [7] *Didasc.*, 2, 18; *P.L.*, 176, 785.
[8] *Contra Gent.*, 1, 65.

for instance, human nature, has existence only in this or that man, and the universality which attaches to humanity in the concept is a result of abstraction, and so is in a sense a subjective contribution.[1] But this does not involve the falsity of the universal concept. If we were to abstract the specific form of a thing and at the same time think that it actually existed in a state of abstraction, our idea would indeed be false, for a false judgement concerning the thing itself would be involved; but, though in the universal concept the mind conceives something in a manner different to its mode of concrete existence, our judgement about the thing itself is not erroneous; it is simply that the form, which exists in the thing in an individualised state, is abstracted, i.e. is made the object of the exclusive attention of the mind by an immaterial activity. The objective foundation of the universal specific concept is thus the objective and individual essence of the thing, which essence is by the activity of the mind set free from individualising factors, that is, according to St. Thomas, matter, and considered in abstraction. For example, the mind abstracts from the individual man the essence of humanity which is alike, but not numerically the same in the members of the human species, while the foundation of the universal generic concept is an essential determination which several species have in common, as the species of man, horse, dog, etc., have 'animality' in common.

St. Thomas thus denied both forms of ultra-realism, that of Plato and that of the early mediaevals; but, no more than Abelard was he willing to reject Platonism lock, stock and barrel, that is to say, Platonism as developed by St. Augustine. The ideas, exemplar ideas, exist in the divine mind, though not ontologically distinct from God nor really a plurality, and, as far as this truth is concerned, the Platonic theory is justified.[2] St. Thomas thus admits (i) the *universale ante rem*, while insisting that it is not a subsistent thing, either apart from things (Plato) or in things (early mediaeval ultra-realists), for it is God considered as perceiving His Essence as imitable *ad extra* in a certain type of creature; (ii) the *universale in re*, which is the concrete individual essence alike in the members of the species; and (iii) the *universale post rem*, which is the abstract universal concept.[3] Needless to say, the term *universale in re*, used in the *Commentary on the Sentences*, is to be interpreted in the light of St. Thomas's general doctrine.

---

[1] *S.T.*, Ia, 85, 1, ad 1; Ia, 85, 2, ad 2. [2] *Contra Gent.*, 3, 24.
[3] *In Sent.*, 2; *Dist.* 3, 2 ad 1.

i.e. as the *foundation* of the universal concept, the foundation being the concrete essence or *quidditas rei*.[1]

In the later Middle Ages the problem of universals was to be taken up afresh and a different solution was to be given by William of Ockham and his followers; but the principle that only individuals exist as subsistent things had come to stay: the new current in the fourteenth century was set not towards realism but away from it. The history of this movement I shall consider in the next volume.

---

[1] The distinction between *universale ante rem*, *in re* and *post rem* had been made by Avicenna.

CHAPTER XV

ST. ANSELM OF CANTERBURY

St. Anselm as philosopher—Proofs of God's existence in the Monologium—*The proof of God's existence in the* Proslogium— *Idea of truth and other Augustinian elements in St. Anselm's thought.*

1. ST. ANSELM was born at Aosta in Piedmont in 1033. After preliminary studies in Burgundy, at Avranches and afterwards at Bec he entered the Benedictine Order and later became Prior of Bec (1063), and subsequently abbot (1078). In 1093 he became Archbishop of Canterbury in succession to his former teacher, friend and religious superior Lanfranc, and in that post he died (1109).

In general the thought of St. Anselm is rightly said to belong to the Augustinian tradition. Like the great African Doctor, he devoted his chief intellectual effort to the understanding of the doctrine of the Christian faith and the statement of his attitude which is contained in the *Proslogium*[1] bears the unmistakable stamp of the Augustinian spirit. 'I do not attempt, O Lord, to penetrate Thy profundity, for I deem my intellect in no way sufficient thereunto, but I desire to understand in some degree Thy truth, which my heart believes and loves. For I do not seek to understand, in order that I may believe; but I believe, that I may understand. For I believe this too, that unless I believed, I should not understand.' This *Credo, ut intelligam* attitude is common to both Augustine and Anselm, and Anselm is in full accord with Augustine when he remarks in the *Cur Deus Homo*[2] that it is negligence if we make no attempt to understand what we believe. In practice, of course, this means for Anselm an application of dialectic or reasoning to the dogmas of faith, not in order to strip them of mystery but in order to penetrate them, develop them and discern their implications, so far as this is possible to the human mind, and the results of this process, for instance his book on the Incarnation and Redemption (*Cur Deus Homo*), make Anselm of importance in the history of theological development and speculation.

Now, the application of dialectic to the data of theology remains

---

[1] *P.L.*, 158, 227. [2] *Ibid.*, 158, 362.

theology, and St. Anselm would scarcely earn a place in the history of philosophy through his theological speculation and developments, except indeed as the application of philosophical categories to revealed dogmas necessarily involves some treatment and development of those philosophical categories. In point of fact, however, the use of the *Credo, ut intelligam* motto was not confined by Anselm, any more than by Augustine, to the understanding of those truths exclusively which have been revealed and not discovered dialectically, but was extended to truths like the existence of God, which are indeed believed but which can be reached by human reasoning. Besides, then, his work as dogmatic theologian there is also his work as natural theologian or metaphysician to be considered, and on this count alone St. Anselm deserves a place in the history of philosophy, since he contributed to the development of that branch of philosophy which is known as natural theology. Whether his arguments for the existence of God are considered valid or invalid, the fact that he elaborated these arguments systematically is of importance and gives his work a title to serious consideration by the historian of philosophy.

St. Anselm, like St. Augustine, made no clear distinction between the provinces of theology and philosophy, and his implied attitude of mind may be illustrated as follows. The Christian should try to understand and to apprehend rationally all that he believes, so far as this is possible to the human mind. Now, we believe in God's existence and in the doctrine of the Blessed Trinity. We should, therefore, apply our understanding to the understanding of both truths. From the point of view of one who, like the Thomist, makes a clear distinction between philosophy and dogmatic theology the application of reasoning to the first truth, God's existence, will fall within the province of philosophy, while the application of reasoning to the second truth, the Trinity, will fall within the province of theology, and the Thomist will hold that the first truth is demonstrable by human reasoning, while the second truth is not demonstrable by human reasoning, even though the human mind is able to make true statements about the mystery, once revealed, and to refute the objections against it which human reasoning may raise. But, if one puts oneself in the position of St. Anselm, that is, in a state of mind anterior to the clear distinction between philosophy and theology, it is easy to see how the fact that the first truth is demonstrable, coupled with the desire to understand all that we believe, the attempt to satisfy this desire being regarded as a duty, naturally leads to an attempt to demonstrate the second truth as well, and in point of fact St. Anselm speaks of demonstrating the Trinity of Persons by 'necessary reasons'[1] and of showing in the same way that it is impossible for a man to be saved without Christ.[2] If one wishes to call this 'rationalism', as has been done, one should first of all be quite clear as to what one means by rationalism. If by rationalism one means an attitude of mind which denies revelation and faith, St. Anselm was certainly no rationalist, since he accepted the primacy of faith and the fact of authority and only then went on to attempt to understand the data of faith. If, however, one is going to extend the term 'rationalism' to cover the attitude of mind which leads to the attempt to prove mysteries, not because the mysteries are not accepted by faith or would be rejected if one could not prove them, but because one desires to understand all that one believes, without having first clearly defined the ways in which different truths are accessible to us, then one might, of course, call the thought of St. Anselm 'rationalism' or an approximation to rationalism. But it would show an entire misunderstanding of Anselm's attitude, were one to suppose that he was prepared to reject the doctrine of the Trinity, for example, if he was unable to find *rationes necessariae* for it: he believed the doctrine first of all, and only then did he attempt to understand it. The dispute about Anselm's rationalism or non-rationalism is quite beside the point, unless one first grasps quite clearly the fact that he had no intention of impairing the integrity of the Christian faith: if we insist on interpreting St. Anselm as though he lived after St. Thomas and had clearly distinguished the separate provinces of theology and philosophy, we shall only be guilty of an anachronism and of a misinterpretation.

2. In the *Monologium*[3] St. Anselm develops the proof of God's existence from the degrees of perfection which are found in creatures. In the first chapter he applies the argument to goodness, and in the second chapter to 'greatness', meaning, as he tells us, not quantitative greatness, but a quality like wisdom, the more of which a subject possesses, the better, for greater quantitative size does not prove qualitative superiority. Such qualities are found in varying degrees in the objects of experience, so that the argument proceeds from the empirical observation of degrees of,

---

[1] *De fide Trin.*, 4; *P.L.*, 158, 272.   [2] *Cur Deus Homo*; *P.L.*, 158, 361.
[3] *P.L.*, 158.

for example, goodness, and is therefore an *a posteriori* argument. But judgement about different degrees of perfection (St. Anselm assumes, of course, that the judgement is objectively grounded) implies a reference to a standard of perfection, while the fact that things participate objectively in goodness in different degrees shows that the standard is itself objective, that there is, for example, an absolute goodness in which all good things participate, to which they approximate more or less nearly, as the case may be.

This type of argument is Platonic in character (though Aristotle also argued, in his Platonic phase, that where there is a better, there must be a best) and it reappears in the *Via quarta* of St. Thomas Aquinas. It is, as I have said, an *a posteriori* argument: it does not proceed from the idea of absolute goodness to the existence of absolute goodness but from observed degrees of goodness to the existence of absolute goodness and from degrees of wisdom to the existence of absolute wisdom, the absolute goodness and wisdom being then identified as God. The developed form of the argument would necessitate, of course, a demonstration both of the objectivity of the judgement concerning the differing degrees of goodness and also of the principle on which St. Anselm rests the argument, the principle, namely that if objects possess goodness in a limited degree, they must have their goodness from absolute goodness itself, which is good *per se* and not *per aliud*. It is also to be noted that the argument can be applied only to those perfections which do not *of themselves* involve limitation and finiteness: it could not be applied to quantitative size, for instance. (Whether the argument is valid and demonstrative or not, it is scarcely the province of the historian to decide.)

In the third chapter of the *Monologium* St. Anselm applies the same sort of argument to being. Whatever exists, exists either through something or through nothing. The latter supposition is absurd; so whatever exists, must exist through something. This means that all existing things exist either through one another or through themselves or through one cause of existence. But that X should exist through Y, and Y through X, is unthinkable: the choice lies between a plurality of uncaused causes or one such cause. So far indeed the argument is a simple argument from causality, but St. Anselm goes on to introduce a Platonic element when he argues that if there is a plurality of existent things which have being of themselves, i.e. are self-dependent and un-caused, there is a form of being-of-itself in which all participate, and at this point the argument becomes similar to the argument already outlined, the implication being that, when several beings possess the same form, there must be a unitary being external to them which *is* that form. There can, therefore, be but one self-existent or ultimate Being, and this must be the best and highest and greatest of all that is.

In chapters seven and eight St. Anselm considers the relation between the caused and the Cause and argues that all finite objects are made out of nothing, *ex nihilo*, not out of a preceding matter nor out of the Cause as matter. He explains carefully that to say that a thing is made *ex nihilo* is not to say that it is made out of nothing as its material: it means that something is created *non ex aliquo*, that, whereas before it had no existence outside the divine mind, it now has existence. This may seem obvious enough, but it has sometimes been maintained that to say that a creature is made *ex nihilo* is either to make nothing something or to lay oneself open to the observation that *ex nihilo nihil fit*, whereas St. Anselm makes it clear that *ex nihilo* does not mean *ex nihilo tamquam materia* but simply *non ex aliquo*.

As to the attributes of the *Ens a Se*, we can predicate of it only those qualities, to possess which is *absolutely* better than not to possess them.[1] For example, to be gold is better for gold than to be lead, but it would not be better for a man to be made of gold. To be corporeal is better than to be nothing at all, but it would not be better for a spirit to be corporeal rather than incorporeal. To be gold is better than not to be gold only *relatively*, and to be corporeal rather than non-corporeal is better only *relatively*. But it is *absolutely* better to be wise than not to be wise, living than non-living, just than not-just. We must, then, predicate wisdom, life, justice, of the supreme Being, but we cannot predicate corporeity or gold of the supreme Being. Moreover, as the supreme Being does not possess His attributes through participation, but through His own essence, He *is* Wisdom, Justice, Life, etc.,[2] and furthermore, since the supreme Being cannot be composed of elements (which would then be logically anterior, so that He would not be the supreme Being), these attributes are identical with the divine essence, which is simple.[3] Again, God must necessarily transcend space in virtue of His simplicity and spirituality, and time, in virtue of His eternity.[4] He is wholly present in everything but not locally or *determinate*, and all things

[1] Ch. 15.   [2] Ch. 16.   [3] Ch. 17.   [4] Ch. 20–4.

are present to His eternity, which is not to be conceived as endless time but as *interminabilis vita simul perfecte tota existens*.[1] We may call Him substance, if we refer to the divine essence, but not if we refer to the category of substance, since He is incapable of change or of sustaining accidents.[2] In fine, if we apply to Him any name that we also apply to creatures, *valde procul dubio intelligenda est diversa significatio*.

St. Anselm proceeds, in the *Monologium*, to give reasons for the Trinity of Persons in one Nature, without giving any clear indication that he is conscious of leaving the province of one science to enter that of another, and into this subject, interesting as it may be to the theologian, we cannot follow him. Enough has been said, however, to show that St. Anselm made a real contribution to natural theology. The Platonic element is conspicuous and, apart from remarks here and there, there is no considered treatment of analogy; but he gives *a posteriori* arguments for God's existence which are of a much more systematic character than those of St. Augustine and he also deals carefully with the divine attributes, God's immutability, eternity, etc. It is clear, then, how erroneous it is to associate his name with the 'Ontological Argument' in such a way as to imply that St. Anselm's only contribution to the development of philosophy was an argument the validity of which is at least questionable. His work may have not exercised any very considerable influence on contemporary thinkers and those who immediately followed him, because of their preoccupation with other matters (dialectical problems, reconciling the opinions of the Fathers, and so on), but looked at in the light of the general development of philosophy in the Middle Ages he must be acknowledged as one of the main contributors to Scholastic philosophy and theology, on account both of his natural theology and of his application of dialectic to dogma.

3. In the *Proslogium* St. Anselm develops the so-called 'ontological argument', which proceeds from the idea of God to God as a reality, as existent. He tells us that the requests of his brethren and consideration of the complex and various arguments of the *Monologium* led him to inquire whether he could not find an argument which would be sufficient, by itself alone, to prove all that we believe concerning the Divine Substance, so that one argument would fulfil the function of the many complementary arguments of his former *opusculum*. At length he thought that he

---

[1] Ch. 24.   [2] Ch. 26.

had discovered such an argument, which for convenience sake may be put into syllogistic form, though St. Anselm himself develops it under the form of an address to God.

God is that than which no greater can be thought:

But that than which no greater can be thought must exist, not only mentally, in idea, but also extramentally:

Therefore God exists, not only in idea, mentally, but also extramentally.

The *Major Premiss* simply gives the idea of God, the idea which a man has of God, even if he denies His existence.

The *Minor Premiss* is clear, since if that than which no greater can be thought existed only in the mind, it would not be that than which no greater can be thought. A greater could be thought, i.e. a being that existed in extramental reality as well as in idea.

This proof starts from the idea of God as that than which no greater can be conceived, i.e. as absolutely perfect: that is what is *meant* by God.

Now, if such a being had only ideal reality, existed only in our subjective idea, we could still conceive a greater being, namely a being which did not exist simply in our idea but in objective reality. It follows, then, that the idea of God as absolute perfection is necessarily the idea of an existent Being, and St. Anselm argues that in this case no one can at the same time have the idea of God and yet deny His existence. If a man thought of God as, for instance, a superman, he would be quite right to deny 'God's' existence in that sense, but he would not really be denying the objectivity of the idea of God. If, however, a man had the right idea of God, conceived the meaning of the term 'God', he could indeed deny His existence with his lips, but if he realises what the denial involves (i.e. saying that the Being which must exist of its essence, the necessary Being, does not exist) and yet asserts the denial, he is guilty of a plain contradiction: it is only the fool, the *insipiens*, who has said *in his heart*, 'there is no God.' The absolutely perfect Being is a Being the essence of which is to exist or which necessarily involves existence, since otherwise a more perfect being could be conceived; it is the necessary Being; and a necessary being which did not exist would be a contradiction in terms.

St. Anselm wanted his argument to be a demonstration of all that we believe concerning the divine Nature, and, since the argument concerns the absolutely perfect Being, the attributes of God are contained implicitly in the conclusion of the argument. We have only to ask ourselves what is implied by the idea of a Being than which no greater can be thought, in order to see that God must be omnipotent, omniscient, supremely just and so on. Moreover, when deducing these attributes in the *Proslogium*, St. Anselm gives some attention to the clarification of the notions in question. For example, God cannot lie: is not this a sign of lack of omnipotence? No, he answers, to be able to lie should be called impotence rather than power, imperfection rather than perfection. If God could act in a manner inconsistent with His essence, that would be a lack of power on His part. Of course, it might be objected that this *presupposes* that we already know what God's essence is or involves, whereas what God's essence is, is precisely the point to be shown; but St. Anselm would presumably reply that he has already established that God is all-perfect and so that He is both omnipotent and truthful: it is merely a question of showing what the omnipotence of perfection really means and of exposing the falsity of a wrong idea of omnipotence.

The argument given by St. Anselm in the *Proslogium* was attacked by the monk Gaunilo in his *Liber pro Insipiente adversus Anselmi in Proslogio ratiocinationem*, wherein he observed that the idea we have of a thing is no guarantee of its extramental existence and that St. Anselm was guilty of an illicit transition from the logical to the real order. We might as well say that the most beautiful islands which are possible must exist somewhere, because we can conceive them. The Saint, in his *Liber Apologeticus contra Gaunilonem respondentem pro Insipiente*, denied the parity, and denied it with justice, since, if the idea of God is the idea of an all-perfect Being and if absolute perfection involves existence, this idea is the idea of an existent, and necessarily existent Being, whereas the idea of even the most beautiful islands is not the idea of something which must exist: even in the purely logical order the two ideas are not on a par. If God is possible, i.e. if the idea of the all-perfect and necessary Being contains no contradiction, God must exist, since it would be absurd to speak of a *merely possible necessary Being* (it is a contradiction in terms), whereas there is no contradiction in speaking of merely possible beautiful islands. The main objection to St. Anselm's proof, which was raised against Descartes and which Leibniz tried to answer, is that we do not know *a priori* that the idea of God, the idea of infinite and absolute Perfection, is the idea of a *possible* Being. *We* may not see any contradiction in the idea, but, say the objectors, this 'negative' possibility is not the same as 'positive' possibility; it does not show that there really is no contradiction in the idea. That there is no contradiction in the idea is clear only when we have shown *a posteriori* that God exists.

The argument of the *Proslogium* aroused little immediate interest; but in the thirteenth century it was employed by St. Bonaventure, with a less logical and more psychological emphasis, while it was rejected by St. Thomas. Duns Scotus used it as an incidental aid. In the 'modern' era it has had a distinguished, if chequered career. Descartes adopted and adapted it, Leibniz defended it in a careful and ingenious manner, Kant attacked it. In the Schools it is generally rejected, though some individual thinkers have maintained its validity.

4. Among the Augustinian characteristics of St. Anselm's philosophy one may mention his theory of truth. When he is treating of truth in the judgement,[1] he follows the Aristotelian view in making it consist in this, that the judgement or proposition states what actually exists or denies what does not exist, the thing signified being the cause of the truth, the truth itself residing in the judgement (correspondence-theory); but when, after treating of truth (rectitude) in the will,[2] he goes on to speak of the truth of being or essence[3] and makes the truth of things to consist in being what they 'ought' to be, that is, in their embodiment of or correspondence to their idea in God, the supreme Truth and standard of truth, and when he concludes from the eternal truth of the judgement to the eternity of the cause of truth, God,[4] he is treading in the footsteps of Augustine. God, therefore, is the eternal and subsistent Truth, which is cause of the ontological truth of all creatures. The eternal truth is only cause and the truth of the judgement is only effect, while the ontological truth of things is at once effect (of eternal Truth) and cause (of truth in the judgement). This Augustinian conception of ontological truth, with the exemplarism it presupposes, was retained by St. Thomas in the thirteenth century, though he laid far more emphasis, of course, on the truth of the judgement. Thus, whereas St. Thomas's characteristic definition of truth is *adaequatio rei et intellectus*, that of St. Anselm is *rectitudo sola mente perceptibilis*.[5]

In his general way of speaking of the relation of soul to body and in the absence of a theory of hylomorphic composition of the

[1] *Dialogus de Veritate*, 2; *P.L.*, 158.   [2] *Dial.*, 4.   [3] *Ibid.*, 7 ff.
[4] *Ibid.*, 10.   [5] *Ibid.*, 11.

two, Anselm follows the Platonic-Augustinian tradition, though, like Augustine himself, he was perfectly well aware that soul and body form one man, and he affirms the fact. Again, his words in the *Proslogium*[1] on the divine light recall the illumination-theory of Augustine: *Quanta namque est lux illa, de qua micat omne verum, quod rationali menti lucet.*

In general perhaps one might say that though the philosophy of Anselm stands in the line of the Augustinian tradition, it is more systematically elaborated than the corresponding elements of Augustine's thought, his natural theology, that is, and that in the methodic application of dialectic it shows the mark of a later age.

[1] Ch. 14.

CHAPTER XVI

THE SCHOOL OF CHARTRES

*Universalism of Paris, and systematisation of sciences in twelfth century—Regionalism, humanism—Platonism of Chartres—Hylomorphism at Chartres—*Prima facie *pantheism—John of Salisbury's political theory.*

1. ONE of the greatest contributions made by the Middle Ages to the development of European civilisation was the university system, and the greatest of all mediaeval universities was unquestionably that of Paris. This great centre of theological and philosophical studies did not receive its definitive charter as a University in the formal sense until early in the thirteenth century; but one may speak, in an untechnical sense, of the Parisian schools as already forming a 'university' in the twelfth century. Indeed in some respects the twelfth century was more dominated by French learning than was the thirteenth century, since it was in the thirteenth century that other universities, such as Oxford, came into prominence and began to display a spirit of their own. This is true of northern Europe at least: as to the South, the University of Bologna, for instance, received its first charter in 1158, from Frederick I. But, though France was the great centre of intellectual activity in the twelfth century, a fact which led to the oft-quoted saying that 'Italy has the Papacy, Germany the Empire, and France has Knowledge', this does not mean, of course, that intellectual activity was pursued simply by Frenchmen: European culture was international, and the intellectual supremacy of France meant that students, scholars and professors came in large numbers to the French schools. From England came men like Adam Smallbridge and Alexander Neckham, twelfth-century dialecticians, Adelard of Bath and Robert Pulleyn, Richard of St. Victor (d. 1173) and John of Salisbury; from Germany, Hugh of St. Victor (d. 1141), theologian, philosopher and mystic; from Italy, Peter Lombard (c. 1100–60), author of the celebrated *Sentences*, which were made the subject of so many commentaries during the Middle Ages, by St. Thomas Aquinas and Duns Scotus, for example. Thus the University of Paris may be said to have represented the international character of mediaeval European

culture, as the Papacy represented the international, or rather supra-national, character of mediaeval religion, though the two were, of course, closely bound together, as the one religion gave a common intellectual outlook and the language of learning, the Latin tongue, was the language of the Church. These two unities, the religious and the cultural, so closely bound together, were what one might call effective and real unities, whereas the political unity of the Holy Roman Empire was rather theoretical than effective, for, though the absolute monarchies were a development of the future, nationalism was already beginning to increase, even if its growth was checked by feudalism, by the local character of mediaeval political and economic institutions and by the common language and intellectual outlook.

This growing and expanding university life naturally found an intellectual and academic expression in the attempt to classify and systematise the science, knowledge and speculation of the time, an attempt which shows itself already in the twelfth century. We may give two examples, the systematisations of Hugh of St. Victor and of Peter Lombard. The former, in his *Didascalion*,[1] more or less follows the Aristotelian classification. Thus Logic is a propaedeutic or preamble to science proper and deals with concepts, not with things. It is divided into Grammar and into the *Ratio Disserendi*, which in turn subdivides into *Demonstratio*, *Pars Probabilis* and *Pars Sophistica* (Dialectic, Rhetoric and Sophistic). Science, to which Logic is a preamble and for which it is a necessary instrument, is divided under the main headings of Theoretical Science, Practical Science and 'Mechanics'. Theoretical Science comprises Theology, Mathematics (Arithmetic, dealing with the numerical aspect of things; Music, dealing with proportion; Geometry, concerned with the extension of things; Astronomy, concerned with the movement of things), and Physics (which has as its subject-matter the inner nature or inner qualities of things, and thus penetrates farther than Mathematics). Practical Science is subdivided into Ethics, 'Economics' and Politics, while Mechanics comprises the seven 'illiberal arts' or *scientiae adulterinae*, since the craftsman borrows his form from nature. These 'illiberal arts' are Wool-making, etc., Armoury and Carpentry, Navigation or Commerce, which, according to Hugh, 'reconciles peoples, quiets wars, strengthens peace, and makes private goods to be for the common use of all', Agriculture, Hunting (including cookery),

[1] *P.L.*, 176

Medicine and Theatricals. It is clear that Hugh's classification depended, not only on Aristotle, through Boethius, but also on the encyclopaedic work of writers like Isidore of Seville.

Peter Lombard, who was educated at the School of St. Victor, taught at the Cathedral School of Paris, and ultimately became bishop of that city between 1150 and 1152, composed his *Libri Quattuor Sententiarum*, a work which, although unoriginal in respect of content, exercised a tremendous influence, in that it stimulated other writers to the work of systematic and comprehensive exposition of dogma and became itself the subject of compendia and many commentaries, up to the end of the sixteenth century. The *Sentences* of the Lombard are admittedly a text-book[1] and were designed to gather the opinions or *sententiae* of the Fathers on theological doctrines, the first book being devoted to God, the second to creatures, the third to the Incarnation and Redemption and to the virtues, the fourth to the seven Sacraments and to the last things. The greatest number of quotations and the bulk of the doctrine are taken from St. Augustine, though other Latin Fathers are quoted, and even St. John Damascene makes an appearance, though it has been shown that the Lombard had seen only a small part of Burgundius of Pisa's Latin translation of the *Fons Scientiae*. Obviously enough the *Sentences* are predominantly a theological work, but the Lombard speaks of those things which are understood by the natural reason and can be so understood before they are believed, i.e. by faith:[2] such are the existence of God, the creation of the world by God and the immortality of the soul.

2. We have seen that the developing and expanding intellectual life of the twelfth century showed itself in the growing predominance of the 'university' of Paris and in the first attempts at classification and systematisation of knowledge; but the position of Paris did not mean that regional schools were not flourishing. Indeed, vigour of local life and interests was a complementary feature in the mediaeval period to the international character of religious and intellectual life. For example, though some of the scholars who came to Paris to study remained there to teach, others returned to their own lands or provinces or became attached to local educational institutions. Indeed there was a tendency to specialisation, Bologna, for instance, being noted for its school of law and Montpellier for medicine, while mystical theology

---

[1] Cf. the Prologue. [2] 3, 24, 3.

was a prominent feature of the School of St. Victor, outside Paris.

One of the most flourishing and interesting of the local schools of the twelfth century was that of Chartres, in which certain Aristotelian doctrines, to be noted presently, began to come into prominence, associated, however, with a very strong admixture of Platonism. This school was also associated with humanistic studies. Thus *Theodoric of Chartres* (Thierry), who, after being in charge of the school in 1121, taught at Paris, only to return to Chartres in 1141, where he became chancellor in succession to Gilbert de la Porrée, was described by John of Salisbury, himself a humanist, as *artium studiosissimus investigator*. His *Heptateuchon* was concerned with the seven liberal arts and he vigorously combated the anti-humanists, the 'Cornificians', who decried study and literary form. Similarly *William of Conches* (c. 1080–1154), who studied under Bernard of Chartres, taught at Paris and became tutor to Henry Plantagenet, attacked the Cornificians and himself paid attention to grammatical studies, thereby drawing from John of Salisbury the assertion that he was the most gifted grammarian after Bernard of Chartres.[1] But it was *John of Salisbury* (1115/20–1180) who was the most gifted of the humanist philosophers associated with Chartres. Though not educated at Chartres, he became, as we have seen earlier, Bishop of Chartres in 1176. A champion of the liberal arts and acquainted with the Latin classics, with Cicero in particular, he had a detestation for barbarity in style, dubbing those persons who opposed style and rhetoric on principle 'Cornificians'. Careful of his own literary style, he represents what was best in twelfth-century philosophic humanism, as St. Bernard, though not perhaps with full intention, represents humanism by his hymns and spiritual writings. In the next century, the thirteenth, one would certainly not go to the works of the philosophers as such for Latinity, most of them being far more concerned with content than with form.

3. The School of Chartres, though its *floreat* fell in the twelfth century, had a long history, having been founded in 990 by *Fulbert*, a pupil of *Gerbert of Aurillac*. (The latter was a very distinguished figure of the tenth century, humanist and scholar, who taught at Rheims and Paris, paid several visits to the court of the German Emperor, became in turn Abbot of Bobbio, Archbishop of Rheims and Archbishop of Ravenna, and ascended the

---

[1] *Metal.*, 1, 5.

papal throne as Sylvester II, dying in 1003.) Founded in the tenth century, the School of Chartres preserved, even in the twelfth century, a certain conservative spirit and flavour, which shewed itself in its Platonist tradition, especially in its devotion to the *Timaeus* of Plato and also to the more Platonically inclined writings of Boethius. Thus *Bernard of Chartres*, who was head of the school from 1114 to 1119 and chancellor from 1119 to 1124, maintained that matter existed in a chaotic state before its information, before order was brought out of disorder. Called by John of Salisbury the 'most perfect among the Platonists of our time',[1] Bernard also represented Nature as an organism and maintained the Platonic theory of the World-Soul. In this he was followed by *Bernard of Tours (Silvestris)*, who was chancellor at Chartres about 1156 and composed a poem *De mundi universitate*, using Chalcidius's commentary on the *Timaeus* and depicting the World-Soul as animating Nature and forming natural beings out of the chaos of prime matter according to the Ideas existing in God or *Nous*. William of Conches went even further by identifying the World-Soul with the Holy Spirit, a doctrine which led to his being attacked by William of St. Theodoric. Retracting, he explained that he was a Christian and not a member of the Academy.

In conjunction with these speculations in the spirit of the *Timaeus* one may mention the inclination of the School of Chartres to ultra-realism, though, as we have seen, two of the most outstanding figures associated with Chartres, Gilbert de la Porrée and John of Salisbury, were not ultra-realists. Thus *Clarembald of Arras*, a pupil of Theodoric of Chartres, who became Provost of Arras in 1152 and Archdeacon of Arras in 1160, maintained, in his Commentary on the *De Trinitate* of Boethius, as against Gilbert de la Porrée, that there is but one and the same humanity in all men and that individual men differ only *propter accidentium varietatem*.[2]

4. In spite, however, of their fondness for the *Timaeus* of Plato, the members of the School of Chartres showed also an esteem for Aristotle. Not only did they follow Aristotle in logic, but they also introduced his hylomorphic theory: indeed it was at Chartres that this theory made its first appearance in the twelfth century. Thus, according to Bernard of Chartres, natural objects are constituted by form and matter. These forms he called *formae nativae* and he represented them as copies of the Ideas in God. This information we have from John of Salisbury, who tells us that Bernard and his

---

[1] *Metal.*, 4, 35.   [2] Ed. W. Janssen, p. 42.

disciples tried to mediate between or reconcile Plato and Aristotle.[1] For Bernard of Tours too the forms of things are copies of the Ideas in God, as we have already seen, while Clarembald of Arras represented matter as being always in a state of flux and as being the mutability or *vertibilitas* of things, the form being the perfection and integrity of the thing.[2] He thus interpreted the matter of Aristotle in the light of Plato's teaching about the mutability and evanescent character of material things. William of Conches indeed struck out on a line of his own by maintaining the atomic theory of Democritus;[3] but in general we may say that the members of the School of Chartres adopted the hylomorphic theory of Aristotle, though they interpreted it in the light of the *Timaeus*.[4]

5. The doctrine that natural objects are composed of matter and form, the form being a copy of the exemplar, the Idea in God, clearly makes a distinction between God and creatures and is non-pantheistic in character; but certain members of this School used terminology which, if taken literally and without qualification, would naturally be understood to imply pantheism. Thus Theodoric of Chartres, who was the younger brother of Bernard, maintained that 'all forms are one form; the divine form is all forms' and that the divinity is the *forma essendi* of each thing, while creation is depicted as the production of the many out of the one.[5] Again, Clarembald of Arras argued that God is the *forma essendi* of things and that, since the *forma essendi* must be present wherever a thing is, God is always and everywhere essentially present.[6] But, though these texts, taken literally and in isolation, are pantheistic or monistic in character, it does not appear that either Theodoric of Chartres or Clarembald of Arras meant to teach a monistic doctrine. For instance, immediately after saying that the divine form is all forms Theodoric observes that, though the divine form is all forms by the fact that it is the perfection and integrity of all things, one may not conclude that the divine form is humanity. It would seem that Theodoric's doctrine must be understood in the light of exemplarism, since he says expressly that the divine form cannot be embodied, and cannot, therefore, be the actual concrete form of man or horse or stone. Similarly, Clarembald of Arras's general doctrine of exemplarism and his

[1] *Metāl.*, 2, 17.   [2] Ed. W. Janssen, pp. 44 and 63.   [3] *P.L.*, 90, 1132.
[4] Gilbert de la Porrée draws attention to the hylomorphic theory when commenting on Boethius's *Contra Eutychen* or *Liber de duabus Naturis et una Persona Christi*; *P.L.*, 64, 1367.
[5] *De sex dierum operibus*, ed. W. Janssen, pp. 16, 21, 108, 109.
[6] Ed. W. Janssen, p. 59.

insistence that the forms of material things are copies, *imagines*, is incompatible with full pantheism. The phrases which seem to teach a doctrine of emanation are borrowed from Boethius, and it is probable that they no more express a literal understanding of emanation in Theodoric or Clarembald than they do in Boethius: in a sense they are stock phrases, canonised, as it were, by their antiquity, and they should not be pressed unduly.

6. Although John of Salisbury was not educated at Chartres, it is convenient to say something here of his philosophy of the State, as given in his *Polycraticus*. The quarrels between the Holy See and the Empire and the investiture controversies had naturally led to those writers who took part in the disputes having to express some view, even if only by the way, on the function of the State and its ruler. One or two writers went beyond mere asides, as it were, and gave a rude sketch of political theory. Thus *Manegold of Lautenbach* (eleventh century) even referred the power of the ruler to a pact with the people[1] and declared[2] that if the king forsakes rule by law and becomes a tyrant, he is to be considered to have broken the pact to which he owes his power and may be deposed by the people. Such ideas concerning the reign of law and justice as essential to the State and concerning the natural law, of which the civil law should be an expression, were based on texts of Cicero, the Stoics and the Roman jurists, and they reappear in the thought of John of Salisbury, who also made use of St. Augustine's *De Civitate Dei* and the *De Officiis* of St. Ambrose.

Although John of Salisbury did not put forward any compact theory after the fashion of Manegold of Lautenbach, he was insistent that the prince is not above law and declared that whatever the whitewashers of rulers might trumpet abroad to the contrary, he would never allow that the prince is free from all restrictions and all law. But what did he mean when he said that the prince is subject to law? Partly at least he had in mind (and this was indeed his main consideration) the natural law, in accordance with the Stoic doctrine that there is a natural law, to which all positive law does, or ought to, approximate. The prince, then, is not free to enact positive laws which go counter to, or are irreconcilable with, both the natural law and that *aequitas* which is *rerum convenientia, tribuens unicuique quod suum est*. The positive law defines and applies natural law and natural justice, and the attitude of the ruler on this matter shows whether he is prince

---

[1] *Liber ad Gebehardum*, 30 and 47.   [2] *Ibid.*, 47.

or tyrant. If his enactments define, apply or supplement natural law and natural justice, he is a prince; if they infringe natural law and natural justice, he is a tyrant, acting according to caprice and not fulfilling the function of his office.

Did John of Salisbury understand anything else by law, when he maintained that the prince is subject to the law? Did he maintain that the prince is in any way subject to defined law? It was certainly the common opinion that the prince was subject in some way to the customs of the land and the enactments of his ancestors, to the local systems of law or tradition which had grown up in the course of time, and, although John of Salisbury's political writing shows little concern with feudalism, since he relied so largely on writers of the Roman period, it is only reasonable to suppose that he shared the common outlook on this matter. His actual judgements on the power and office of the prince express the common outlook, though his formal approach to the subject is through the medium of Roman law, and he would certainly not have envisaged the application in an absolutist sense to the feudal monarch of the Roman Jurist's maxim, *Quod principi placuit legis habet vigorem*.

Now, since John of Salisbury praised Roman law and regarded it as one of the great civilising factors of Europe, he was faced with the necessity of interpreting the maxim quoted above, without at the same time sacrificing his convictions about the restricted power of the prince. First of all, how did Ulpian himself understand his maxim? He was a lawyer and it was his aim to justify, to explain the legality of the Emperor's enactments and *constitutiones*. According to Republican lawyers the law governed the magistrate, but it was obvious that in the time of the Empire the Emperor was himself one of the sources of positive law, and the lawyers had to explain the legality of this position. Ulpian accordingly said that, though the Emperor's legislative authority is derived from the Roman people, the people, by the *lex regia*, transfers to him and vests in him all its own power and authority, so that, once invested with his authority, the will of the Emperor has the force of law. In other words, Ulpian was simply explaining the legality of the Roman Emperor's enactments: he was not concerned to establish a political theory by maintaining that the Emperor was entitled to disregard all natural justice and the principles of morality. When John of Salisbury observed, with express reference to Ulpian's dictum, that when the prince is said to be free from the law, this is not to be understood in the sense that he may do what is unjust, but in the sense that he ought to follow equity or natural justice out of a real love of justice and not from fear of punishment, which does not apply to him, he was expressing the general tradition of feudal lawyers and at the same time was not contradicting Ulpian's maxim. When in the late Middle Ages some political theorists detached Ulpian's maxim from the person of the Emperor, and transferring it to the national monarch interpreted it in an absolutist sense, they were forsaking the general mediaeval outlook and were at the same time changing the legal maxim of Ulpian into an abstract statement of absolutist political theory.

In conclusion it may be remarked that John of Salisbury accepted the supremacy of the ecclesiastical power (*Hunc ergo gladium de manu Ecclesiae accipit princeps*),[1] while he carried his distinction between prince and tyrant to its logical conclusion by admitting tyrannicide as legitimate. Indeed, since the tyrant is opposed to the common good, tyrannicide may sometimes be obligatory,[2] though he made the curious stipulation that poison should not be employed for this purpose.

---

[1] *Polycrat.*, 4, 3.   [2] *Ibid.*, 8, 10.

CHAPTER XVII

THE SCHOOL OF ST. VICTOR

*Hugh of St. Victor; proofs of God's existence, faith, mysticism—
Richard of St. Victor; proofs of God's existence—Godfrey of St.
Victor and Walter of St. Victor.*

THE Abbey of St. Victor outside the walls of Paris belonged to the
Augustinian Canons. We have seen that William of Champeaux
was associated with the abbey, retiring there after being worsted
by Abelard, but the school is of note principally owing to the work
of two men, one a German, Hugh of St. Victor, the other a
Scotsman, Richard of St. Victor.

1. *Hugh of St. Victor* was born in Saxony in 1096 of noble
parentage, and made his early studies in the monastery of Hamers-
leben near Halberstadt. After taking the habit he went to Paris
in 1115 to continue his studies in the Abbey of St. Victor. In
1125 he started lecturing and from 1133 until his death in 1141
he was in charge of the school. One of the foremost theologians,
dogmatic and mystical, of his time, he was yet no enemy to the
cultivation of the arts, considering not only that the study of the
arts, if rightly pursued, conduces to progress in theology, but also
that all knowledge is of utility. 'Learn everything; you will see
afterwards that nothing is superfluous.'[1] His chief work, from the
philosophical viewpoint, is the *Didascalion* in seven books, in which
he treats of the liberal arts (three books), theology (three books)
and religious meditation (one book), but his writings on the
theology of the Sacraments are also important to the theologian.
He also compared exegetic and mystical works and a commentary
on the *Celestial Hierarchy* of the Pseudo-Dionysius, using the Latin
translation of John Scotus Eriugena.

Of Hugh's classification and systematisation of the sciences
mention has already been made, in connection with the systematising tendency already discernible in the twelfth century and due
partly to the application of dialectic in theology, as also of his
theory of abstraction, in connection with the discussion on universals.[2] These two points bring out the Aristotelian aspects of
his thought, whereas his psychology is distinctly Augustinian in

[1] *P.L.*, 176, 800C.   [2] See p. 153.

character. 'No one is really wise who does not see that he exists; and yet, if a man begins truly to consider what he is, he sees that he is none of all those things which are either seen in him or can be seen. For that in us which is capable of reasoning, although it is, so to speak, infused into and mingled with the flesh, is yet distinguishable by reason from the substance of the flesh and is seen to be different therefrom.'[1] In other words, consciousness and introspection bear witness, not only to the existence of the soul, but also to its spirituality and immateriality. Moreover, the soul is of itself a person, having, as a rational spirit, personality of itself and through itself, the body forming an element in human personality only in virtue of its union with the rational spirit.[2] The mode of union is one of 'apposition' rather than of composition.[3]

Hugh contributed to the systematic advance of natural theology by giving *a posteriori* arguments both from internal and external experience. As regards the first line of proof, it rests upon the experiential fact of self-consciousness, the consciousness of a self which is 'seen' in a purely rational way and cannot be material. Regarding self-consciousness as necessary to the existence of a rational being, Hugh maintains that, as the soul has not always been conscious of its existence, there was a time when it did not exist. But it could not have given itself existence: it must, then, owe its existence to another being, and this being must be a necessary and self-existent being, God.[4] This proof is somewhat compressed, involving the premises that the cause of a rational principle must itself be rational and that an infinite regress is impossible. Its 'interiority' certainly reminds one of Augustine, but it is not Augustine's proof from the soul's knowledge of eternal truths, nor does it presuppose religious, still less mystical, experience since it rests on the natural experience of the soul's self-consciousness, and it is this reliance on experience which characterises Hugh's proofs of God's existence.

The second proof, that from external experience,[5] rests on the experienced fact of change. Things are constantly coming into being and passing away, and the totality, which is composed of such changing things, must itself have had a beginning. It requires, therefore, a Cause. Nothing which lacks stability, which ceases to be, can have come into being without a Cause external to itself. The idea of such a proof is contained in the *De Fide Orthodoxa* of

---

[1] *P.L.*, 176, 825A.   [2] *Ibid.*, 176, 409.   [3] *Ibid.*
[4] *De Sacramentis*, 3, 7; *P.L.*, 176, 219.
[5] *De Sacramentis*, 3, 10; *P.L.*, 176, 219, and *Sent.* 1, 3; *P.L.*, 176, 45.

St. John Damascene;[1] but Hugh of St. Victor attempts to supply the deficiencies in St. John Damascene's procedure.

In addition to the proof from change Hugh gives a teleological proof in several parts.[2] In the world of animals we see that the senses and appetites find their satisfaction in objects: in the world in general we see a great variety of movements (the reference is to local motion), which, however, are ordered in harmony. Again, growth is a fact of experience, and growth, since it means the addition of something new, cannot be accomplished solely by the thing which grows. Hugh concludes that these three considerations exclude chance and postulate a Providence which is responsible for growth and guides all things according to law.[3] The proof is clearly somewhat unconvincing in the form given, but it is based on facts of experience, as the starting-point, and this is characteristic of Hugh's proofs in general. Hugh adopted the theory of William of Conches concerning the atomic structure of matter. These atoms are simple bodies, which are capable of increase and growth.[4]

Hugh was thus quite clear about the possibility of a natural knowledge of God's existence, but he was equally insistent on the necessity of faith. This faith is necessary, not only because the *oculus contemplationis*, whereby the soul apprehends God within herself *et ea quae in Deo erant*, has been completely darkened by sin, but also because mysteries which exceed the power of the human reason are proposed to man's beliefs. These mysteries are *supra rationem*, in that revelation and faith are required to apprehend them, but they are *secundum rationem*, not *contra rationem*: in themselves they are reasonable and can be the object of knowledge, but they cannot be the object of knowledge in the strict sense in this life, as man's mind is too weak, especially in its sin-darkened state. Knowledge, then, considered in itself, stands higher than faith, which is a certitude of the mind concerning absent things, superior to opinion but inferior to science or knowledge, since those who comprehend the object as immediately present (the *scientes*) are superior to those who believe on authority. We may say, therefore, that Hugh of St. Victor made a clear distinction between faith and knowledge and that, though he recognised the superiority of the latter, he did not thereby impugn the necessity of the former. His doctrine of the superiority of knowledge to faith is by no means equivalent to the Hegelian

---

[1] I, 3; *P.G.*, 94, 796A. [2] *P.L.*, 176, 826.
[3] Cf. *De Fide Orthodoxa*, 1, 3; *P.G.*, 94, 795B.
[4] *De Sacramentis*, 1, 6, 37; *P.L.*, 176, 286.

doctrine, since Hugh certainly did not consider that knowledge can, naturally at least, be substituted for faith in this life.

But, though the *oculus contemplationis* has been darkened by sin, the mind, under the supernatural influence of grace, can ascend by degrees to contemplation of God in Himself. Thus supernatural mysticism crowns the ascent of knowledge in this life as the beatific vision of God crowns it in heaven. To enter upon a discussion of Hugh's mystical teaching would scarcely be in place here; but it is worth pointing out that the mystical tradition of St. Victor was not simply a spiritual luxury; their mystical theology formed an integral part of their theologico-philosophical synthesis. In philosophy God's existence is proved by the natural use of reason, while in theology the mind learns about the Nature of God and applies dialectic to the data of revelation accepted on faith. But philosophical knowledge and theological (dialectical) knowledge are knowledge about God: higher still is the experience of God, the direct knowledge of God, which is attained in mystical experience, a loving knowledge or a knowing love of God. On the other hand, mystical knowledge is not full vision, and God's presence to the soul in mystical experience blinds by excess of light, so that above both knowledge about God by faith and direct mystical knowledge of God there stands the beatific vision of heaven.

2. *Richard of St. Victor* was born in Scotland but went to Paris early in life and entered the Abbey of St. Victor, where he became sub-prior about 1157 and prior in 1162. He died in 1173. The abbey passed through a difficult period during these years, as the abbot, an Englishman named Ervisius, wasted its goods and ruined its discipline, behaving in such an independent manner that Pope Alexander III called him 'another Caesar'. With some difficulty he was induced to resign in 1172, a year before the death of Richard. However, even if his abbot was a somewhat independent and high-handed individual, the prior, we are told by the abbey necrology, left behind him the memory of a good example, a holy life and beautiful writings.

Richard is an important figure in mediaeval theology, his chief work being the *De Trinitate* in six books, but he was also a philosopher, as well as being a mystical theologian who published two works on contemplation, the *Beniamin minor*, on the preparation of the soul for contemplation, and the *Beniamin maior*, on the grace of contemplation. In other words, he was a worthy successor of Hugh of St. Victor, and like him he insisted on the necessity of using the reason in the pursuit and investigation of truth. 'I have frequently read that there is only one God, that He is eternal, uncreated, immense, omnipotent and Lord of all: . . . I have read concerning my God that He is one and three, one in Substance, three in Persons: all this I have read; but I do not remember that I have read how all these things are proved.'[1] Again, 'In all these matters authorities abound, but not arguments; in all these matters *experimenta desunt*, proofs are becoming rare; so I think that I shall have done something, if I am able to help the minds of the studious a little, even if I cannot satisfy them.'

The general attitude of St. Anselm is evident in the above quotations: *Credo, ut intelligam*. The data of the Christian religion presupposed, Richard of St. Victor sets out to understand them and to prove them. Just as St. Anselm had declared his intention of trying to prove the Blessed Trinity by 'necessary reasons', so Richard declares at the beginning of his *De Trinitate*[2] that it will be his intention in that work, so far as God grants, to adduce not only probable, but also necessary reasons for the things which we believe. He points out that there must be necessary reasons for what necessarily exists; so that, as God is necessarily Three in One, there must be a necessary reason for this fact. Of course, it by no means follows from the fact that God is necessarily Triune (God is the necessary Being) that we can discern this necessity, and Richard admits indeed that we cannot fully comprehend the mysteries of Faith, particularly that of the Blessed Trinity,[3] but that does not prevent his attempting to show that a plurality of Persons in the Godhead necessarily follows from the fact that God is Love and to demonstrate the trinity of Persons in one Nature.

Richard's speculation on the Trinity had a considerable influence on later Scholastic theology; but from the philosophical viewpoint his proofs for the existence of God are of greater import. Such proofs, he insists, must rest on experience: 'We ought to begin from that class of things, of which we can have no manner of doubt, and by means of those things which we know by experience to conclude rationally what we must think concerning the objects which transcend experience.'[4] These objects of experience are contingent objects, things which begin to be and can cease to

[1] *De Trinit.*, 1, 5; *P.L.*, 196, 893BC.   [2] *P.L.*, 196, 892C.   [3] *Ibid.*, 196, 72A.
[4] *Ibid.*, 196, 894.

be. Such things we can come to know only through experience, since what comes into being and can perish cannot be necessary, so that its existence cannot be demonstrated *a priori*, but can be known only by experience.[1]

The starting-point of the argument is thus provided by the contingent objects of experience; but, in order that our reasoning on this basis may be successful, it is necessary to start from a clearly solid and, as it were, immovable foundation of truth;[2] that is, the argument needs a sure and certain principle on which it may rest. This principle is that every thing which exists or can exist has being either of itself or from another than itself, and that every thing which exists or can exist either has being from eternity or begins to be in time. This application of the principle of contradiction allows us to form a division of being. Any existent thing must be either (i) from eternity and from itself, and so self-existent, or (ii) neither from eternity nor from itself, or (iii) from eternity, but not from itself, or (iv) not from eternity but yet from itself. This logical division into four admits immediately of a reduction to a threefold division, since a thing which is not from eternity but is *a se*, is impossible, for a thing which began to be obviously cannot either have given itself being or be a necessary existent.[3] A beginning in time and aseity are thus incompatible, and it remains to refer back to the things of experience and apply the general principle. The things of experience, as we observe them in the human, animal and vegetable kingdoms, and in nature in general, are perishable and contingent: they begin to be. If, then, they begin to be, they are not from eternity. But what is not from eternity cannot be from itself, as already said. Therefore it must be from another. But ultimately there must exist a being which exists of itself, i.e. necessarily, since, if there is no such being, there would be no sufficient reason for the existence of anything: nothing would exist, whereas in point of fact something does exist, as we know by experience. If it be objected that there must indeed be an *ens a se* but that this may very well be the world itself, Richard would retort that he has already excluded this possibility by pointing out that we experience the contingent character of the things of which the world is composed.

If in this first proof Richard's procedure shows a marked change from that of St. Anselm, in his next proof he adopts a familiar

---

[1] *P.L.*, 196, 892.   [2] *Ibid.*, 196, 893.   [3] Cf. *ibid.*, 196, 893.

Anselmian position.[1] It is a fact of experience that there are different and varying degrees of goodness or perfection, the rational, for example, being higher than the irrational. From this experiential fact Richard proceeds to argue that there must be a highest, than which there is no greater or better. As the rational is superior to the irrational, this supreme substance must be intellectual, and as the higher cannot receive what it possesses from the lower, from the subordinate, it must have its being and existence from itself. This necessarily means that it is eternal. Something must be eternal and *a se*, as has been already shown, since otherwise nothing would exist, and experience teaches us that something does exist, and, if the higher cannot receive what it possesses from the lower, it must be the highest, the supreme Substance, which is the eternal and necessary Being.

In the third place Richard attempts to prove the existence of God from the idea of possibility.[2] In the whole universe nothing can exist, unless it has the possibility of being (the potentiality or power to be) from itself or receives it from another. A thing which lacks the possibility of being, which is completely impossible, is nothing at all, and in order that anything should exist, it must receive the ability to exist (*posse esse*) from the ground of possibility. (That the objects in the universe cannot receive their possibility from themselves, cannot be self-grounded, Richard here takes for granted: in his first proof he has already shown the incompatibility of aseity and temporality or beginning to be.) This ground of possibility, then, which is the source of the possibility and the existence of all things, must be self-dependent, ultimate. Every essence, every power, every wisdom, must depend on this Ground, so that the latter must itself be the supreme Essence as the ground of all essences, the supreme Power as source of all power, and supreme Wisdom as source of all wisdom, since it is impossible that a source should confer a gift greater than itself. But there can be no wisdom apart from a rational substance in which it is immanent: so there must be a rational and supreme Substance, in which supreme wisdom is immanent. The Ground of all possibility is, therefore, the supreme Substance.

These arguments are, of course, exercises of the rational, discursive intelligence, of the *oculus rationis*, superior to the *oculus imaginationis*, which views the corporeal world, but inferior to the

[1] *De Trinit.*, 1, 11; *P.L.*, 196, 895–6.   [2] *De Trinit.*, 1, 12; *P.L.*, 196, 896.

oculus intelligentiae, by which God is contemplated in Himself.[1]
On the inferior level the objects of sense are viewed immediately
as present; on the middle level the mind thinks discursively about
things not immediately visible, arguing, for example, from effect
to cause or *vice versa*; on the superior level the mind views an
invisible object, God, as immediately present.[2] The level of
contemplation is thus, as it were, the spiritual analogue of sense-
perception, being like to it in immediacy and concreteness in
contrast with discursive thought, though it differs in that it is a
purely spiritual activity, directed to a purely spiritual object.
Richard's division of the six stages of knowledge, from the perception of God's beauty in the beauty of creation to the *mentis
alienatio*, under the action of grace, influenced St. Bonaventure in
the composition of his *Itinerarium mentis in Deum*.

3. Godfrey of St. Victor (d. 1194) wrote a *Fons Philosophiae*, in
which he classifies the sciences and treats of such philosophers and
transmitters as Plato, Aristotle, Boethius and Macrobius, devoting
a special chapter to the problem of universals and the professed
solutions of the problem. *Walter of St. Victor* (died after 1180) was
the author of the celebrated diatribe *Contra Quattuor Labyrinthos
Franciae*, Abelard, Peter Lombard, Peter of Poitiers and Gilbert
de la Porrée, the representatives of dialectical theology, who,
according to Walter, were puffed up with the spirit of Aristotle,
treated with Scholastic levity of the ineffable things of the Blessed
Trinity and the Incarnation, vomited out many heresies and
bristled with errors. In other words, Walter of St. Victor was a
reactionary who does not represent the genuine spirit of St. Victor,
of Hugh the German and Richard the Scotsman, with its reasoned
combination of philosophy, dialectical theology and mysticism.
In any case the hands of the clock could not be put back, for
dialectical theology had come to stay and in the following century
it attained its triumph in the great systematic syntheses.

---

[1] *De gratia contemplationis*, 1, 3, 7; *P.L.*, 196, 66CD, 72C.
[2] *De gratia contemplationis*, 1, 3, 9; *P.L.*, 196, 110D.

CHAPTER XVIII

DUALISTS AND PANTHEISTS

Albigensians and Cathari—Amalric of Bene—David of Dinant.

1. IN the thirteenth century St. Dominic preached against the Albigensians. This sect, as well as that of the Cathari, was already widespread in southern France and in Italy during the twelfth century. The principal tenet of these sects was a dualism of the Manichaean type, which came into western Europe by way of Byzantium. There exist two ultimate Principles, the one good and the other bad, of which the former caused the soul, the latter the body and matter in general. From this hypothesis they drew the conclusion that the body is evil and has to be overcome by asceticism and also that it is wrong to marry and propagate the human race. It may seem strange that a sect whose members held such doctrines should flourish; but it must be remembered that it was considered sufficient if the comparatively few *perfecti* led this ascetic existence, while their less exalted followers could safely lead a more ordinary life, if they received the blessing of one of the 'perfect' before death. It must also be remembered, when one is considering the attention which the Albigensians and Cathari received from the ecclesiastical and civil powers, that the condemnation of procreation and of marriage as evil leads naturally to the conclusion that concubinage and marriage are on much the same footing. Moreover, the Cathari denied the legitimacy of oaths and of all war. It was, then, only natural that the sects were looked on as constituting a danger to Christian civilisation. The sect of the Waldenses, which still exists, goes back to the Catharist movement and was originally a sect of dualists, though it was absorbed by the Reformation and adopted anti-Romanism and anti-sacerdotalism as its chief tenets.[1]

2. *Amalric of Bene* was born near Chartres and died as a professor of theology at Paris about 1206/7. St. Thomas Aquinas[2] observes that 'others said that God is the formal principle of all things, and this is said to have been the opinion of the Amalricians', while Martin of Poland says of Amalric that he held God to be the

---

[1] The sources for our knowledge of the doctrine of the Albigensians are not rich, and the history of the movement is somewhat obscure.

[2] *S.T.*, Ia, 3, 8, *in corpore.*

essence of all creatures and the existence of all creatures. Apparently he interpreted in a pantheistic sense the teaching of John Scotus Eriugena, as well as the phrases used by Theodoric of Chartres and Clarembald of Arras, even going so far as to say that the Persons of the Trinity are creatures, that all three became incarnate and that every single man is as much God as was Christ. From this doctrine some of his followers seem to have drawn the conclusion that sin is an unreal concept, on the ground that, if every man is divine, there can be no question of his sinning. Whether Amalric consciously upheld real pantheism or not, he was in any case accused of heresy and had to retract, his doctrines being condemned in 1210, after his death, along with those of John Scotus Eriugená.

3. If for Amalric of Bene God is the form of all things, for *David of Dinant* He was identified with prime matter, in the sense of the potentiality of all things. Very little is known of the life of David of Dinant, or of the sources from which he derived his doctrines, or of the doctrines themselves, since his writings, condemned in 1210 and forbidden at Paris in 1215, have perished. St. Albert the Great[1] ascribes to him a *De tomis, hoc est de divisionibus*, while the documents of the Council of Paris (1210) ascribe to him a *Quaterni* or *Quaternuli*, though Geyer, for example, supposes that these two titles refer to the same work, which consisted of a number of sections or paragraphs (*quaterni*). In any case we have to rely for our knowledge of his doctrine on quotations and reports by St. Albert the Great, St. Thomas and Nicholas of Cusa.

In the *Summa Theologica*[2] St. Thomas states that David of Dinant 'very foolishly affirmed that God is prime matter'. Elsewhere[3] he says that David divided things into three classes: bodies, souls and eternal substances, bodies being constituted of *Hyle*, souls of *Nous* or mind, and the eternal substances of God. These three constituent sources are the three indivisibles, and the three indivisibles are one and the same. Thus all bodies would be modes of one indivisible being, *Hyle*, and all souls would be modes of one indivisible being, *Nous*; but these two indivisible beings are one, and were identified by David with God, who is the one Substance. 'It is manifest (according to David) that there is only one substance not only of all bodies, but also of all souls, and that this substance is nothing else but God himself. . . . It is clear, then, that God is

[1] *S.T.*, Ia, 4, 20, 2, *quaest. incidens.*   [2] Ia, 3, 8, *in corpore.*
[3] *2 Sent.*, 17, 1, 1.

the substance of all bodies and all souls, and that God and *Hyle* and *Mens* are one substance.'[1]

David of Dinant tried to prove this position dialectically. For two kinds of substances to differ from one another they must differ in virtue of a difference, and the presence of a difference implies the presence of a common element. Now, if matter differed from mind, there would have to be a *differentia* in prime matter, i.e. a form and a matter, and in this case we should go on to infinity.[2] St. Thomas puts the argument this way.[3] When things in no way differ from one another, they are the same. Now, whatever things differ from one another, differ in virtue of *differentiae*, and in this case they must be composite. But God and prime matter are altogether simple, not composite things. Therefore they cannot differ in any way from one another, and must consequently be the same. To this argument St. Thomas replies that composite things such as, for example, man and horse, do indeed differ from one another in virtue of *differentiae*, but that simple things do not: simple things should be said, strictly speaking, to be diverse (*diversa esse*), not to be different (*differre*). In other words he accuses David of playing with terms, of choosing, to express the diversity of God and matter, a term which implies composition in God and matter.

Why did St. Albert and St. Thomas think it worth while giving such attention to a pantheistic system, the theoretical support of which was more or less a dialectical quibble? Probably the reason was not so much that David of Dinant exercised an extensive influence as that they feared that the heresy of David might compromise Aristotle. The sources from which David drew his theories constitute a disputed point, but it is generally agreed that he drew on the exposition of ancient materialism given in the *Physics* and *Metaphysics*, and it is clear that he utilises the Aristotelian ideas of prime matter and form. In 1210 the same Council of Paris which condemned David's writings forbad also the public and private teaching of the natural philosophy of Aristotle in the University. Most probably, then, St. Thomas wished to show that David of Dinant's monism by no means followed from the teaching of Aristotle; and in his reply to the objection already cited he expressly refers to the *Metaphysics*.

[1] S. Alb. M., *S.T.*, IIa, t. 12, q. 72, membr. 4, a. 2, n. 4.
[2] *Ibid.*, Ia, t. 4, q. 20, membr. 2; *In Metaph.*, t. 4, c. 7.
[3] *S.T.*, Ia, 3, 8, ob. 3.

PART IV

ISLAMIC AND JEWISH PHILOSOPHY: TRANSLATIONS

CHAPTER XIX

ISLAMIC PHILOSOPHY

Reasons for discussing Islamic philosophy—Origins of Islamic philosophy—Alfarabi—Avicenna—Averroes—Dante and the Arabian philosophers.

1. To come upon a chapter on the philosophy of the Arabs in a work devoted to mediaeval thought, in the sense of the thought of mediaeval Christendom, might astonish a reader who was making his first acquaintance with the philosophy of the Middle Ages; but the influence, positive and negative, of Islamic philosophy on that of Christendom is now a matter of common knowledge among historians, and one can scarcely avoid saying something on the subject. The Arabian philosophy was one of the principal channels whereby the complete Aristotle was introduced to the West; but the great philosophers of mediaeval Islam, men like Avicenna and Averroes, were more than mere transmitters or even commentators; they changed and developed the philosophy of Aristotle, more or less according to the spirit of neo-Platonism, and several of them interpreted Aristotle on important points in a sense which, whether exegetically correct or not, was incompatible with the Christian theology and faith.[1] Aristotle, therefore, when he appeared to mediaeval Christian thinkers in the shape given him by Averroes, for example, naturally appeared as an enemy of Christian wisdom, Christian philosophy in the wide sense. This fact explains to a large extent the opposition offered to Aristotelianism in the thirteenth century by many upholders of the Christian tradition who looked on the pagan philosopher as the foe of Augustine, Anselm and the great philosophers of Christianity. The opposition varied in degree, from a rather crude dislike and fear of novelty, to the reasoned opposition of a thinker like St. Bonaventure; but it becomes easier to understand the opposition

[1] It is true, however, that some Islamic philosophers, like Avicenna, facilitated through their writings a Christian interpretation of Aristotle.

if one remembers that a Moslem philosopher such as Averroes claimed to give the right interpretation of Aristotle and that this interpretation was, on important questions, at variance with Christian belief. It explains too the attention paid to the Islamic philosophers by those (particularly, of course, St. Thomas Aquinas) who saw in the Aristotelian system not only a valuable instrument for the dialectical expression of Christian theology but also the true philosophy, for such thinkers had to show that Aristotelianism did not necessarily involve the interpretation given to it by the Moslems: they had to dissociate themselves from Averroes and to distinguish their Aristotelianism from his.

In order, then, fully to understand the polemics of St. Thomas Aquinas and others, it is necessary to know something of mediaeval Islamic philosophy; but it is also necessary for a connected reason, namely that there arose in Paris a School of philosophers who claimed to represent integral Aristotelianism, the chief figure of this School being the celebrated opponent of St. Thomas, Siger of Brabant. These 'integral' Aristotelians, the genuine Aristotelians as they thought themselves to be, meant by genuine Aristotelianism the system of Aristotle as interpreted by Averroes, the Commentator *par excellence*. In order, therefore, to understand this school and an important phase of the controversies at Paris, it is obviously necessary to be acquainted with the place of Averroes in the history of philosophy and with his doctrine.

But, though some treatment of mediaeval Islamic philosophy must be given, it does not come within the scope of this book to discuss the Islamic philosophy for its own sake. It has indeed its own peculiar interest (for example, its relations to Islamic theology, their attempted reconciliation and the tension between them, as well as the relation of Islamic thought to mysticism in the Islamic world, and of Islamic philosophy to Islamic culture in general, have their own intrinsic interest), but the reader must expect here no more than a brief sketch of Islamic philosophy in the mediaeval period, a treatment of it less for its own sake than in function of its influence on the thought of mediaeval Christendom. This perhaps rather one-sided treatment is not designed to belittle the achievements of Moslem philosophers, nor does it involve a denial of the intrinsic interest of Islamic philosophy for its own sake: it is simply dictated by the general purpose and scope of this book, as well as, of course, by considerations of space.

2. If Islamic philosophy was connected with the philosophy of

Christendom in the way just mentioned, it was also connected with Christianity in its origins, owing to the fact that it was Christian Syrians who first translated Aristotle and other ancient philosophers into Arabic. The first stage consisted of the translation of Greek works into Syriac at the school of Edessa in Mesopotamia, which was founded by St. Ephrem of Nisibis in 363 and was closed by the Emperor Zeno in 489 because of the Nestorianism which prevailed there. At Edessa some of the works of Aristotle, principally the logical works, as well as Porphyry's *Isagoge*, were translated into Syriac, and this work was continued in Persia, at Nisibis and Gandisapora, whither the scholars betook themselves on the closure of the school. Thus works of Aristotle and Plato were translated into Persian. In the sixth century works of Aristotle and Porphyry and the writings of the Pseudo-Dionysius were translated into Syriac at the Monophysite schools of Syria.

The second stage consisted in the translation of the Syriac translations into Arabic. Even before the time of Mohammed (569–632) there had been a number of Nestorian Christians who worked among the Arabs, mainly as physicians, and when the 'Abbāsid dynasty replaced that of the Ommaiades in 750, Syrian scholars were invited to the Arab court at Baghdad. Medical works were translated first of all; but after a time philosophical works were also translated, and in 832 a school of translators was established at Baghdad, an institution which produced Arabic versions of Aristotle, Alexander of Aphrodisias, Themistius, Porphyry and Ammonius. Plato's *Republic* and *Laws* were also translated, as well as (in the first half of the ninth century) the so-called *Theology of Aristotle*, which consisted of a compilation of the *Enneads* (4–6) of Plotinus, erroneously attributed to Aristotle. To this must be added the fact that the *Liber de Causis*, really the *Institutio Theologica* of Proclus, was also attributed to Aristotle. These false attributions, as well as the translation into Arabic of neo-Platonic commentators on Aristotle, helped to popularise among the Arabs a neo-Platonic interpretation of the Aristotelian system, though other influences, as well as Aristotle and the neo-Platonists, contributed to the formation of Islamic philosophy, e.g. the Islamic religion itself and the influence of Oriental religious thought, such as that of Persia.

3. The Moslem philosophers may be divided into two groups, the eastern group and the western group. In this section I shall treat briefly of three thinkers belonging to the eastern group.

(i) *Alfarabi*, who belonged to the school of Baghdad and died about 950, is a good example of a thinker upon whom the influences mentioned above made themselves felt. Thus he helped to introduce the Islamic cultured world to the logic of Aristotle, while by his classification of the departments of philosophy and theology he made philosophy self-conscious, as it were, marking it off from theology. Logic is a propaedeutic and preparation for philosophy proper, which Alfarabi divided into physics, comprising the particular sciences (psychology being included and the theory of knowledge being treated of in psychology) and metaphysics (physics and metaphysics being the two branches of theoretical philosophy) and ethics or practical philosophy. His scheme for theology included as sections (1) omnipotence and justice of God; (2) the unity and other attributes of God; (3) the doctrine of sanctions in the next life; (4) and (5) the individual's rights and the social relations of the Moslem. By making philosophy a separate province, then, Alfarabi did not mean to supplant or undermine the Islamic theology: rather did he place schematisation and logical form at the service of theology.

In addition, Alfarabi utilised Aristotelian arguments in proving the existence of God. Thus, on the supposition that the things of the world are passively moved, an idea which fitted in well with Islamic theology, he argued that they must receive their movement from a first Mover, God. Again, the things of this world are contingent, they do not exist of necessity: their essence does not involve their existence, as is shown by the fact that they come into being and pass away. From this it follows that they have received their existence, and ultimately one must admit a Being which exists essentially, necessarily, and is the Cause of the existence of all contingent beings.

On the other hand, when it comes to the general system of Alfarabi, the neo-Platonic influence is manifest. Thus the theme of emanation is employed to show how from the ultimate Deity or One there proceed the Intelligence and the World-Soul, from the thoughts or ideas of which proceeds the Cosmos, from the higher or outer spheres to the lower or inner spheres. Bodies are composed of matter and form. The intelligence of man is illuminated by the cosmic intelligence, which is the active intellect of man (the νοῦς ἐπίκτητος of Alexander of Aphrodisias). Moreover, the illumination of the human intellect is the explanation of the fact that our concepts 'fit' things, since the Ideas in God are at once the exemplar and source of the concepts in the human mind and of the forms in things.

This doctrine of illumination is connected, not only with neo-Platonism, but also with Oriental mysticism. Alfarabi himself became attached to the mystical school or sect of the Sufis, and his philosophy had a religious orientation. The highest task of man is to know God, and, just as the general process of the universe is a flowing out from God and a return to God, so should man, who proceeds from God in the emanative process and who is enlightened by God, strive after the return to and likeness with God.

(ii) The greatest Moslem philosopher of the eastern group is without a doubt *Avicenna* or *Ibn Sīnā* (980–1037), the real creator of a Scholastic system in the Islamic world.[1] A Persian by birth, born near Bokhara, he received his education in the Arab tongue, and most of his works, which were extremely numerous, were written in Arabic. A precocious boy, he learnt in succession the Koran, Arabic literature, geometry, jurisprudence, logic. Outstripping his instructors, he studied by himself theology, physics, mathematics and medicine, and at sixteen years of age he was already practising as a doctor. He then devoted a year and a half to the study of philosophy and logic, but it was only when he chanced upon a commentary by Alfarabi that he was able to understand to his satisfaction the *Metaphysics* of Aristotle, which he had read, he tells us, forty times without being able to understand it. The rest of his life was a busy and adventurous one, as he acted as Vizir to several Sultans and practised medicine, experiencing in his travels the ups and downs of life and the favour and disfavour of princes, but being always the philosopher, pursuing his studies and writings wherever he was, even in prison and on horseback. He died at Hamadan at the age of fifty-seven, after performing his ablutions, repenting of his sins, distributing abundant alms and freeing his slaves. His principal philosophical work is the *Aš-Šifā*, known in the Middle Ages as the *Sufficientiae*, which comprised logic, physics (including the natural sciences), mathematics, psychology and metaphysics. The *Najāt* was a collection of texts, taken from the first work and arranged in a different order.

Avicenna's division of philosophy in the wide sense into logic,

---

[1] The name Avicenna, by which Ibn Sīna was known to the mediaeval world, comes from the Hebrew version, Aven Sina.

the propaedeutic to philosophy, speculative philosophy (physics. mathematics and theology) and practical philosophy (ethics, economics and politics) offers no remarkable features, save that theology is divided into first theology (equivalent to ontology and natural theology) and second theology (involving Islamic themes), and this marks off Islamic theology from the Greek. But his metaphysic, in spite of its borrowing both from Aristotle and from neo-Platonism, shows features of its own, which make it plain that, however much he borrowed from former philosophers, Avicenna had thought out his system carefully and independently and had welded it into a system of a peculiar stamp. For instance, although he is at one with Aristotle in assigning the study of being as being to metaphysics, Avicenna employs an un-Aristotelian illustration to show that the mind necessarily apprehends the idea of being, though it is acquired normally through experience. Imagine a man suddenly created, who cannot see or hear, who is floating in space and whose members are so disposed that they cannot touch one another. On the supposition that he cannot exercise the senses and acquire the notion of being through sight or touch, will he thereby be unable to form the notion? No, because he will be conscious of and affirm his own existence, so that, even if he cannot acquire the notion of being through external experience, he will at least acquire it through self-consciousness.[1]

In Avicenna's eyes the notion of necessity is also a primary notion, for to him all beings are necessary. It is necessary, however, to distinguish two kinds of necessity. A particular object in the world is not necessary of itself: its essence does not involve existence necessarily, as is shown by the fact that it comes into being and passes away; but it is necessary in the sense that its existence is determined by the necessary action of an external cause. Accordingly a contingent being means, for Avicenna, a being the existence of which is due, not to the essence of the being itself, but to the necessary action of an external cause. Such beings are indeed caused and so 'contingent', but none the less the action of the cause is determined.

This leads him on to argue that the chain of causes cannot be infinite, since then there would be no reason for the existence of anything, but that there must be a first cause which is itself uncaused. This uncaused Being, the necessary Being, cannot receive its essence from another, nor can its existence form part

[1] *Šifā*, 1, 281 and 363.

of its essence, since composition of parts would involve an anterior uniting cause: essence and existence must therefore be identical in the necessary Being. This ultimate Being is necessary of itself, whereas 'contingent' beings are not necessary of themselves but necessary through another, so that the concept 'being', as applied to necessary and contingent being, has not the same sense. They are not, then, species of one genus; but rather does Being belong *par excellence*, properly and primarily, to the necessary Being and is predicated of contingent being only secondarily and analogically.

Closely allied with the distinction between the possible and the necessary is the distinction between potentiality and act. Potentiality, as Aristotle said, is the principle of change into another as other, and this principle may exist either in the agent (active potency) or in the patient (passive potency). Moreover, there are degrees of potency and act, ranging between the lower limit, pure potentiality, prime matter, and the upper limit, pure act, the necessary Being, though Avicenna does not use the phrase 'Pure Act' *quoad verbum*. From this position Avicenna proceeds to show that God is Truth, Goodness, Love and Life. For example, the Being which is always in act, without potentiality or privation, must be absolute Goodness, and since the divine attributes are ontologically indistinguishable, the divine Goodness must be identical with absolute Love.

As God is absolute Goodness, He necessarily tends to diffuse His goodness, to radiate it, and this means that He creates necessarily. As God is the necessary Being, all His attributes must be necessary: He is, therefore, necessarily Creator. This in turn involves the conclusion that creation is from eternity, for, if God is necessarily Creator and God is eternal, creation must be eternal. Moreover, if God creates by the necessity of His Nature, it follows also that there is no free choice in creation, that God could not create otherwise or create other things than He actually creates. But God can produce immediately only by a being like Himself: it is impossible for God to create material things directly. The logically first being to proceed from God is, therefore, the first Intelligence. This Intelligence is created, in the sense that it proceeds from God: it receives, then, its existence, and in this way duality begins. Whereas in the One there is no duality, in the primary Intelligence there is a duality of essence and existence, in that existence is received, while there is also a duality of knowledge, in that the primary Intelligence knows the One or God as necessary and itself as 'possible'. In this way Avicenna deduces the ten Intelligences which exhibit a growing multiplicity and so bridges the gap between the unity of God and the multiplicity of creation. The tenth Intelligence is the 'giver of forms', which are received in prime matter, pure potentiality (or rather potentiality 'deprived of' form, and so, in a sense, 'evil'), and so rendered capable of multiplication within the species. The separate Intelligences can differ from one another only specifically, in virtue of their greater or less proximity to the One and the decreasing simplicity in the process of emanation; but, as matter is the principle of individuation, the same specific form can be multiplied in a plurality of individual concrete objects, though prime matter has first to be taken out of its state of indetermination and disposed for the reception of specific form, first through the *forma corporeitatis* and then through the action of external causes which predispose matter for the reception of one particular specific form.

The tenth Intelligence has another function to perform besides that of *Dator formarum*, for it also exercises the function of the active intellect in man. In his analysis of abstraction Avicenna will not credit the human intellect as such with the final act of abstraction, the apprehension of the universal in a state of pure intelligibility, as this would mean that the intellect passes from a state of potentiality to act entirely by its own power, whereas no agent can proceed from passive potency to act except under the influence of an agent external to itself but like itself. He distinguished, therefore, the active and passive intellects, but made the active intellect a separate and unitary intelligence which illumines the human intellect or confers on it its intellectual and abstract grasp of essences (the essence or universal *post rem*, to be distinguished from the essence *ante rem* and *in re*).

Avicenna's idea of necessary creation and his denial that the One has direct knowledge of the multiplicity of concrete objects set him at variance with the theology of the Koran; but he tried, so far as he could, to reconcile his Aristotelian-neo-Platonist system with orthodox Islam. For example, he did not deny the immortality of the human soul, in spite of his doctrine concerning the separateness of the active intellect, and he maintained a doctrine of sanctions in the after life, though he interpreted this in an intellectualist manner, reward consisting in the knowledge of purely intelligible objects, punishment in the deprivation of such knowledge.[1] Again, though his analysis and explanation of creation and the relation of the world to God necessarily involved a theory of emanation and, in this respect, tended towards pantheism, he tried to safeguard himself from pantheism by affirming the distinction between essence and existence in all beings which proceed, immediately or mediately, from God. Possibly the Islamic doctrine of the divine omnipotence, when interpreted 'speculatively', tends to pantheism, and it may well be that some fundamental principles of Avicenna's system would favour pantheism; but he was certainly no pantheist by intention.

When portions of the writings of Avicenna were translated into Latin in the twelfth century, the Christian world found itself faced for the first time with a closely knit system which was bound to exercise a strong attraction on certain minds. Thus *Gundissalinus* (d. 1151) translated into Latin the Spanish translation made by Joannes Hispanus (Avendeath) and utilised the thought of Avicenna in his *De Anima*, following the Avicennian psychology (and citing the latter's allegory of the 'flying man'), though he left Avicenna for Augustine by making the active intellect, as source of illumination, identical with God. Moreover, in his *De Processione Mundi* he attempted to reconcile the cosmogony of Avicenna with Christian doctrine, though his example in this matter was not followed. Before the entire *Metaphysics* of Aristotle became available, uncertainty reigned as to which doctrines were to be attributed to Avicenna and which to Aristotle. Thus Roger Bacon thought that Avicenna must have followed Aristotle throughout, though he (Bacon) had not got books M and N of the *Metaphysics* and so could not check the truth or untruth of this supposition. The result was that *William of Auvergne* (died *c.* 1249), the first vigorous opponent of Avicenna, attributed the cosmogony of Avicenna to Aristotle himself. This cosmogony, said William, was erroneous, in that it admitted intermediaries in the process of creation, thus allowing to creatures a divine power, denied the divine freedom, asserted the eternity of the world, made matter the principle of individuation and regarded the separate active

---

[1] It should be noted that it was the Averroistic doctrine of the unicity of the passive or possible intellect which *necessarily* involved the denial of personal immortality. The doctrine of the unicity of the active intellect does not necessarily involve such a denial, whether the active intellect is identified with a subordinate Intelligence or with God in His function as illuminator. As for Aristotle, he may not have believed in personal immortality himself, but the rejection of personal immortality does not *necessarily* follow from his doctrine of the active intellect, whereas it does follow from the doctrine of Averroes. On this point the positions of Avicenna and Averroes must be clearly distinguished.

intellect as the efficient cause of human souls. None the less William himself followed Avicenna by introducing into Latin Scholasticism the distinction between essence and existence. Moreover, denying Avicenna's doctrine of the active intellect, he pretty well identified it with God. Other thinkers, such as Alexander of Hales, John of la Rochelle and St. Albert, while denying the doctrine of a separate active intellect, made use of Avicenna's theory of abstraction and of the necessity of illumination, whereas Roger Bacon and Roger Marston found Avicenna's error to consist only in not identifying the separate and illuminating active intellect with God. Without going any further into the question of Avicenna's influence, which would require a distinct monograph, one can say that he influenced Latin Scholasticism in regard to at least three themes, that of knowledge and illumination, that of the relation of essence and existence, and that of matter as the principle of individuation.[1] Criticism of Avicenna by a Latin Scholastic does not mean, of course, that the Scholastic learnt nothing from Avicenna. For instance, St. Thomas found it necessary to criticise the Moslem philosopher's treatment of possibility,[2] but that does not mean that St. Thomas did not develop his own position partly through a consideration of Avicenna's doctrine, even if it is difficult to assess the precise degree of influence exercised by the latter's writings on the greatest of the Scholastics. Scotus, however, was much more influenced by Avicenna than was St. Thomas, though he certainly could not be called with propriety a disciple of Avicenna.

(iii) *Algazel* (1058–1111), who lectured for a time at Baghdad, opposed the views of Alfarabi and Avicenna from the viewpoint of Mohammedan orthodoxy. In his *Maqāsid* or *Intentiones Philosophorum* he summed up the views of these two philosophers, and this exposition, translated into Latin by Gundissalinus, gave the impression, when taken by itself, that Algazel agreed with the opinions expressed. Thus William of Auvergne coupled together as objects of attack the 'followers of Aristotle', Alfarabi, Algazel and Avicenna, being unaware of the fact that Algazel had proceeded to criticise the systems of the philosophers in his *Destructio philosophorum*,[3] which tried to show how the philosophers contradicted themselves. This book elicited later from Averroes a

[1] On Avicenna's influence, cf. Roland-Gosselin, commentary on the *De ente et essentia*, pp. 59 and 150.
[2] Cf. *De Pot.*, 5, 3; *Contra Gent.*, 2, 30.
[3] More properly *Incoherentia philosophorum*.

Destructio destructionis philosophorum. In his *Revivification of the Religious Sciences* he gave his positive views, defending the orthodox doctrine of the creation of the world in time and out of nothing against Avicenna's ideas of emanation and of the eternity of the world. He defended also the doctrine of God's universal causality, making the connection between cause and effect to depend on the divine power, not on any causal activity on the part of creatures. The philosopher sees consequence or constant conjunction and concludes to the relation of cause and effect, whereas in truth the following of one event on another is simply due to the power and action of God. In other words he maintained an occasionalistic doctrine.

Algazel was very far from being simply a philosopher who wished to counteract the unorthodox tendencies of his Hellenising predecessors: he was also an eminent Sufi, a mystic and spiritual writer. Leaving his work at Baghdad he retired into Syria, where he lived a life of asceticism and contemplation. Sometimes indeed he emerged from his retirement and in any case he had disciples: he even founded a kind of theological college and a school of Sufism at his place of retirement, Tūs; but the major interest of his life was the revival of religion, in the sense of mysticism. Drawing not only on previous Islamic sources, but utilising neo-Platonic ideas, and even ideas from Judaism and Christianity, he built up a system of spirituality which was personalist, i.e. non-pantheistic, in character. Some of Algazel's expressions would seem at first sight to imply or involve pantheism, but his neo-Platonism was put at the service of religious mysticism rather than of speculation. It is not that he tends to identify the world with God, but rather that his fusion of the Islamic doctrines of predestination and divine omni-causality with strongly emphasised religious mysticism leads him into a kind of panentheism. The Semitic monotheism, when seen in the light of neo-Platonism and fused with mysticism, could lead him probably in no other direction. In the field of purely philosophical speculation he shows a somewhat sceptical attitude and he represents the protest of religious mysticism against rationalism as well as that of Islamic theology against Aristotelian philosophy.

4. The background of the Moslem philosophers of the West was provided by the brilliant Islamic civilisation which grew up in Spain in the tenth century and which, at that period, was so greatly superior to what western Christendom had to offer. The

first philosopher of the western group was *Ibn Masarrah* (d. 931), who adopted ideas from the Pseudo-Empedocles, while *Avempace* or *Ibn Bājja* (d. 1138) and *Abubacer* or *Ibn Tufail* (d. 1185) represented mystical tendencies; but the greatest figure of this group is undoubtedly Averroes, who occupies that prominent position in the western group which Avicenna represents in the eastern group.

Averroes or *Ibn Rušd* (the *Commentator* of the Latin Scholastics) was born at Córdoba in 1126, the son of a judge. After studying theology, jurisprudence, medicine, mathematics and philosophy, he occupied judicial posts, first at Seville and afterwards at Córdoba, becoming physician to the Caliph in 1182. Subsequently he fell into disfavour with the Caliph al-Mansūr and was banished from court. He later crossed to Morocco, dying there in 1198.

Being convinced that the genius of Aristotle was the final culmination of the human intellect, Averroes naturally devoted a great deal of energy to the composition of commentaries. These fall into three classes: (i) the lesser or 'middle' commentaries, in which Averroes gives the content of Aristotle's doctrine, adding his own explanations and developments in such a way that it is not always easy to distinguish what comes from Aristotle and what from Averroes; (ii) the greater commentaries, in which Averroes gives first a portion of the actual text of Aristotle and then adds his own commentary; and (iii) the little commentaries (paraphrases or compendia), in which he gives the conclusions arrived at by Aristotle, omitting proofs and historical references, and which were designed for students unable to go to the sources or larger commentaries. (Apparently he composed the middle commentaries and the compendia before the greater commentaries.) The entire *Organon* of Aristotle, in the lesser commentary and in the compendium, is extant, as also Latin translations of all three classes of commentary for the *Posterior Analytics*, the *Physics*, the *De Caelo*, the *De Anima* and the *Metaphysics*. In addition to these and other commentaries in Latin translations the Christian Scholastics possessed Averroes's answer to Algazel (i.e. the *Destructio destructionis philosophorum*), several logical works, a letter on the connection between the abstract intelligence and man, a work on the beatitude of the soul, etc.

The metaphysical scale reaches from pure matter as the lowest limit to pure Act, God, as the highest limit, between these limits being the objects composed of potency and act, which form *Natura*

naturata. (The phrases of the Latin translation, *Natura naturans*
and *Natura naturata*, reappear eventually in the system of
Spinoza.) Prime matter, as equivalent to non-being, as pure
potentiality and the absence of all determination, cannot be the
term of the creative act: it is, therefore, co-eternal with God. God,
however, draws or educes the forms of material things from the
potency of pure matter, and creates the Intelligences, ten in
number, connected extrinsically with the spheres, so that the
Avicennian emanation-theory is avoided and real pantheism is
excluded. The order of the creation or generation of things is,
however, determined.

Nevertheless, even if Averroes's rejection of emanation makes
him in a sense more orthodox than Avicenna, he did not follow
Avicenna in accepting personal immortality. Averroes did indeed
follow Themistius and other commentators in holding that the
intellectus materialis is the same substance as the *intellectus agens*
and that both survive death, but he followed Alexander of
Aphrodisias in holding that this substance is a separate and
unitary Intelligence. (It is the Intelligence of the moon, the
lowest sphere.) The individual passive intellect in the individual
man becomes, under the action of the active intellect, the 'acquired
intellect', which is absorbed by the active intellect in such a way
that, although it survives bodily death, it does so not as a personal,
individual existent, but as a moment in the universal and common
intelligence of the human species. There is, therefore, immortality,
but there is no personal immortality. This view was earnestly
combated by St. Thomas Aquinas and other Scholastics, though it
was maintained by the Latin Averroists as a philosophical truth.

More interesting, however, than Averroes's particular philosophical doctrine is his notion of the general relation of philosophy
to theology. Holding, as he did, that Aristotle was the completer
of human science,[1] the model of human perfection and the author of
a system which is the supreme truth, interpreting Aristotle as
holding the unicity of the active intellect and accepting the
doctrine of the eternity of matter, Averroes had necessarily to
attempt a reconciliation of his philosophical ideas with orthodox
Islamic theology, especially as those were not wanting who were
ready to accuse him of heresy because of his devotion to a pagan
thinker. He accordingly attempted this reconciliation by means
of the so-called 'double truth' theory. This does not mean that,

[1] *De Anima*, 3, 2.

according to Averroes, a proposition can be true in philosophy and false in theology or *vice versa*: his theory is that one and the same truth is understood clearly in philosophy and expressed allegorically in theology. The scientific formulation of truth is achieved only in philosophy, but the same truth is expressed in theology, only in a different manner. The picture-teaching of the Koran expresses the truth in a manner intelligible to the ordinary man, to the unlettered, whereas the philosopher strips away the allegorical husk and attains the truth 'unvarnished', free from the trappings of *Vorstellung*. Averroes's idea of the relation of philosophy to theology resembles somewhat that of Hegel, and it would be unacceptable, and was unacceptable, to the orthodox Islamic theologian; but it was not the absurd idea that one proposition can be true in philosophy and the diametrically opposite proposition true in theology. What Averroes did was to make theology subordinate to philosophy, to make the latter the judge of the former, so that it belongs to the philosopher to decide what theological doctrines need to be allegorically interpreted and in what way they should be interpreted. This view was accepted by the Latin Averroists, and it was this view, moreover, which drew upon Averroes, and upon philosophy generally, the hostility of the Islamic theologians. In regard to statements attributed to Averroes which taken literally imply that one proposition, for example, that the active intellect is numerically single, is true in philosophy and false in theology, it has been suggested that this was simply a sarcastic way of saying that the theological doctrine is nonsense. When Averroes says that some proposition is true in the fideistic theology of the conservatives, who rejected philosophy, he means that it is 'true' in the School of the enemies of science, i.e. that it is simply false. He had no use for the traditionalists as the traditionalists had no use for him, and his attitude in this matter led to the prohibition in Islamic Spain of the study of Greek philosophy and to the burning of philosophic works.

5. Of the influence of Averroes in Latin Christendom I shall speak later; but it may be of interest to add a word here on the attitude of Dante (1265–1321) towards the Arabian philosophers.[1] The question of Dante's attitude to the Arab philosophers arose when scholars began to ask themselves seriously and without prejudice why Dante, who in the *Divina Commedia* places Mohammed in hell, not only placed Averroes and Avicenna in

---

[1] For some further remarks on this subject see pp. 439–40.

Limbo, but also placed the Latin Averroist Siger of Brabant in heaven and even went so far as to put his eulogium into the mouth of St. Thomas Aquinas, who was a doughty opponent of Siger. Obviously Dante was treating these men as philosophers, and it was because of this fact that he placed the two Islamic thinkers as high in the scale as he could: as they were not Christians, he did not consider that he could release them from *Inferno* altogether, and so he placed them in Limbo. Siger on the other hand was a Christian, and so Dante placed him in heaven. That he made St. Thomas speak his praises and that he put him on the left of St. Thomas, while St. Albert the Great was on Aquinas's right, is explicable if we remember that the Thomist system presupposes a philosophy which is built up by natural reason alone and that to build up a philosophy by reason alone was precisely what Siger of Brabant professed to do: it is not necessary to suppose that Dante approved all Siger's notions, but he takes him as the symbol of 'pure philosophy'.

However, why did Dante single out Avicenna, Averroes and Siger of Brabant? Was it simply because they were philosophers or did Dante owe something himself to the Moslems? It has been shown by Bruno Nardi,[1] and the theme has been resumed by Asín Palacios,[2] that Dante owed to the systems of Alfarabi, Avicenna, Algazel and Averroes important points in his philosophy, for example, the light-doctrine of God, the theory of the Intelligences, the influence of the celestial spheres, the idea that only the intellectual part of the soul is directly and properly created, the need of illumination for intellection, etc. Some of these ideas were found in the Augustinian tradition, it is true; but it has been shown that Dante, far from being a Thomist pure and simple, owed a considerable debt to the Moslems and to Averroes in particular. This will explain why he singles out for special treatment the most eminent of the Islamic philosophers, and why he places in heaven the greatest of the Latin Averroists.

---

[1] *Intorno al tomismo di Dante e alla quistione di Sigieri* (*Giornale Dantesco*, XXII, 5).

[2] *Islam and the Divine Comedy* (abridged Engl. Transl., London, 1926).

CHAPTER XX

JEWISH PHILOSOPHY

The Cabala—Avicebron—Maimonides.

1. PHILOSOPHY among the Jews really owes its origin to inter-course with other nations and cultures. Thus in the first volume of this history I have already treated of Philo, the Alexandrian Jew (*c.* 25 B.C.–*c.* A.D. 40), who attempted a reconciliation of the Jewish Scriptural theology and Greek philosophy, producing a system in which elements of the Platonic tradition (the theory of Ideas), of Stoicism (doctrine of the Logos) and of Oriental thought (intermediary beings) were combined. In the philosophy of Philo the transcendence of God was strongly emphasised, and this insis-tence on the divine transcendence was characteristic of the doctrine of the *Cabala*, as modified by Greek, particularly by Platonic, theories. The *Cabala* consisted of two works, the *Jezirah* (creation), which was probably composed after the middle of the ninth century A.D., and the *Sohar* (brightness), which was built up from the beginning of the thirteenth century and committed to writing by a Spanish Jew about the year 1300. Additions and commentaries were subsequently made. The Cabalistic philosophy shows the influence of neo-Platonism in its doctrine of emanation and inter-mediary beings between God and the world, and one of the channels by which neo-Platonism influenced the construction of the emanationist philosophy of the *Sohar* was the thought of the Spanish Jew who was known to the Latin Scholastics as Avicebron.

2. *Salomon Ibn Gabirol* or *Avicebron* (so called by the Latin Scholastics, who thought that he was an Arab) was born at Malaga about 1021, was educated at Saragossa and died in 1069/70. He was naturally influenced by the Arabian philosophy and his chief work, the *Fons Vitae*, was originally composed in Arabic. The Arabic original is, however, no longer extant, though we possess the work in the Latin translation of Joannes Hispanus (Avendeath) and Dominicus Gundissalinus. The work consists of five books and had a considerable influence on the Christian Scholastics.

The neo-Platonic influence shows itself in the emanationist scheme of Avicebron's philosophy. The summit of the hierarchy of being and the source of all limited being is, of course, God, who is one and unknowable by the discursive reason, apprehensible only in the intuition of ecstasy. To this Avicebron added a peculiar doctrine concerning the divine will by which are created, or from which emanate, all lesser beings. The divine will, like God Himself, transcends the composition of matter and form and can be apprehended only in mystical experience; but the exact relation of the divine will to God is not easy to determine. The distinction drawn between the divine essence and the divine will would appear to make of the latter a distinct hypostasis, though on the other hand the divine will is depicted as being God Himself as active *ad extra*, as God in His appearance. In any case there is a substitution of Will for Logos. From God, *via* the divine will, whether God under one aspect or a distinct hypostasis, proceeds the cosmic spirit or World-Soul, which is inferior to God and is composed of matter and form, *materia universalis* and *forma universalis*. From the World-Soul in turn proceed pure spirits and corporeal things.

The interesting point about Avicebron's system is, however, not his emanationist scheme, but rather his doctrine of universal hylomorphic composition in all beings inferior to God, a doctrine which was derived, at least indirectly, from Plotinus and which influenced one tradition of Christian Scholasticism. Just as from the World-Soul proceed the individual forms, so from the World-Soul proceed also spiritual matter, which is present in the Intelligence and in the rational soul, and corporeal matter. Matter, then, which does not *of itself* involve corporeality, is the principle of limitation and finiteness in all creatures: it is the hylomorphic composition in creatures which marks them off from God, for in God there is no composition. This doctrine of universal hylomorphic composition in creatures was maintained by St. Bonaventure, for example, the great Franciscan contemporary of St. Thomas Aquinas. Moreover, there is a plurality of forms in every being which possesses in itself a plurality of grades of perfection, as the human being, for example, the microcosm, possesses the perfections of corporeality, vegetative life, sensitive life and intellectual life. Every corporeal being possesses the *forma corporeitatis*, but it has further to be given its determinate place in the hierarchy of being, and this is accomplished by the reception of the form or forms by which it becomes, e.g. living thing, animal, dog. It has been maintained that the doctrine of Avicebron was the real origin of the Augustinian School's theory of the plurality of forms, but, even granting this, it must also be remembered that the doctrine fitted well into the scheme of the Augustinians' philosophy, since Augustine had himself taught that the function of the lower forms is to lead on to the higher forms and that this is true also of these forms as represented in human knowledge, i.e. that contemplation of the lower stages of being should lead the mind to higher stages.

3. The most interesting of the Jewish mediaeval philosophers is, however, *Moses Maimonides*, who was born at Córdoba in 1135 and died in Cairo in 1204, having had to abandon Moorish Spain, which was no longer favourable to philosophers. In his *Guide of the Doubting* he attempted to give to theology its rational basis in philosophy, which for him meant the philosophy of Aristotle, whom he reverenced as the greatest example of human intellectual power apart from the Prophets. We must hold fast to what is given us in sense-perception and what can be strictly demonstrated by the intellect: if statements contained in the Old Testament plainly contradict what is plainly established by reason, then such statements must be interpreted allegorically. This view, however, did not mean that Maimonides discarded the teaching of theology whenever Aristotle held something different to that which the Scripture taught. For example, theology teaches the creation of the world in time out of nothing, and this means both that God must be the author of matter as well as of form and that the world cannot be eternal. If the eternity of the world could be demonstrated by reason in such a way that the opposite was clearly seen to be an impossibility, then we should have to interpret the Scriptural teaching accordingly; but, as a matter of fact, the Scriptural teaching is clear and the philosophical arguments adduced to prove the eternity of the world are inconclusive: we must, then, reject Aristotle's teaching on this point. Plato came nearer to the truth than Aristotle, but even he accepted an uncreated matter. The creation out of nothing of both matter and form is also necessary, according to Maimonides, if the fact of miracles, plainly taught in the Old Testament, is to be allowed, since, if God is able to suspend the operation of natural laws, He must be the absolute Sovereign of nature and He would not be that unless He were Creator in the full sense of the word. To the fanatics Maimonides's allegorical interpretation of some of the Scriptural pictures of God seemed to be a selling of the Holy Scripture to the Greeks, and some Jews in France even went so far as to try to enlist the aid of the Inquisition against this

'heresy'; but in point of fact he was merely saying that there can
be a fountain of certain truth besides theology. In other words, he
gave a charter to philosophy, and he thus influenced the growth of
philosophical interest among the Jews in Spain, even if his chief
influence lay in the province of theology. That he was no blind
worshipper of Aristotle has been shown already. Aristotle, thought
Maimonides, went wrong in teaching the eternity of the world, and
even if philosophy cannot demonstrate creation in time, it can at
least show that the arguments brought up in favour of the
Aristotelian position are inconclusive and unsound.

Relying partly on the natural theology of Alfarabi and Avicenna,
Maimonides proved the existence of God in various ways, arguing
from creatures to God as first Mover, as necessary Being and as
first Cause. These arguments he supported from statements of
Aristotle in the *Physics* and *Metaphysics*. But if Maimonides
anticipated most of the types of proof given later by St. Thomas,
he was more insistent than the latter on the inapplicability of
positive predicates to God. God is pure Act, without matter and
without potency, infinitely removed from creatures, and, in regard
to 'qualities', we can say what God is *not*, rather than what He is.
He is one and transcendent (between God and the world there is a
hierarchy of Intelligences or pure spirits), but we cannot form any
adequate positive idea of God. St. Thomas, of course, would admit
this, but Maimonides was rather more insistent on the *via negativa*.
We can, however, ascribe to God activities, the activities of creation and providence, for example, provided that we realise that
the difference of names does not correspond to any difference in
God Himself and that God Himself is unchangeable. Unlike
Avicebron, Maimonides admitted a special providence on God's
part in regard to particular creatures, though this is true only of
men, so far as the material world is concerned. The active intellect
is the tenth Intelligence (the Intelligences are without 'matter'),
but the passive intellects of the just are immortal. Immortality,
then, he admitted only in a limited extension, for the just; but he
maintained the freedom of the will, whereby men become just,
and he denied the determining influence of the celestial bodies and
spheres in regard to human conduct. In fine, Moses Maimonides
made a better business of reconciling Greek philosophy with
Jewish orthodoxy than Avicebron had made of it, and it is noteworthy that the influence of the Aristotelian system is more in
evidence in the former's philosophy than in the latter's.

CHAPTER XXI

THE TRANSLATIONS

*The translated works—Translations from Greek and from Arabic
—Effects of translations and opposition to Aristotelianism.*

1. BEFORE the twelfth century part of the *Organon* of Aristotle
(the *Categories* and the *De Interpretatione*) had been available to
mediaeval philosophers in the Latin version by Boethius (*Logica
vetus*), but the entire *Organon* became available fairly early in the
twelfth century. Thus about 1128 James of Venice translated the
Analytics, the *Topics* and the *Sophistical Arguments* from Greek into
Latin, the newly translated books of the *Organon* being known as
the *Logica nova*. It appears that portions at least of other books
of the *Organon* besides the *Categories* and the *De Interpretatione*
had survived into the twelfth century in the translation of
Boethius; but in any case a complete translation of the *Organon*
into Latin had been effected by the middle of the century. It is
to be noted that the translation by James of Spain was made from
the Greek, as was also the translation of the fourth book of the
Meteorologica made by Henricus Aristippus before 1162. Henricus
Aristippus was Archdeacon of Catania in Sicily, an island which
was an important centre in the work of translation. Thus it was
in twelfth-century Sicily that Ptolemy's μεγάλη σύνταξις and the
Optics, some of the works of Euclid and Proclus's *Elementatio
physica* were translated from Greek into Latin.

Sicily was one centre of the work of translation; Spain was
another, the most famous school of translators being that of
Toledo. Thus under Archbishop Raymond (1126–51) Joannes
Hispanus (Avendeath) translated from the Arabic into Latin (*via*
Spanish) the Logic of Avicenna, while Dominicus Gundissalinus
translated (with help from other scholars) the *Metaphysics* of
Avicenna, parts of his *Physics*, his *De Sufficientia, De Caelo et
Mundo* and *De Mundo*, the *Metaphysics* of Algazel and the *De
Scientiis* of Alfarabi. Dominicus Gundissalinus and John of Spain
also translated from Arabic into Latin the *Fons Vitae* of Avicebron.

A distinguished member of this group of scholars was Gerard of
Cremona, who took up work at Toledo in 1134 and died in 1187.
He translated from Arabic into Latin Aristotle's *Posterior Analytics*

(together with the commentary of Themistius), *Physics, De Caelo
et Mundo, De Generatione et Corruptione, Meteorologica* (first three
books); Alkindi's *De Intellectu, De Somno et Visione, De quinque
Essentiis*; the *Liber de Causis* and some other works.

The Toledo school of translators was still of importance in the
thirteenth century. Thus Michael Scot (Michael Scottus, died
c. 1235) translated at Toledo the *De Caelo et Mundo*, the *De Anima*,
the zoological writings and also (probably) the *Physics of Aristotle*,
as well as Averroes's commentaries on the *De Caelo et Mundo* and
the *De Anima*, Avicenna's compendium of the *De Animalibus*,
while Herman the German, who died in 1272, as Bishop of Astorga,
translated Averroes's 'middle commentary' on the *Nicomachean
Ethics* and also his compendium of the same work and his commentaries on the *Rhetoric* and the *Poetics*.

2. It will be seen from what has already been said that it is a
mistake to imagine that the Latin Scholastics were entirely dependent on translations from Arabic or even that translation from the
Arabic always preceded translation from the Greek. Thus Henricus
Aristippus's translation of the fourth book of the *Meteorologica*
from the Greek preceded Gerard of Cremona's translation of the
first three books of the same work from the Arabic. Moreover,
some of the *Metaphysics* had been translated from the Greek before
the Arabic translation was made. The translation from the Greek,[1]
which did not comprise simply the first three books and a small
part of book four, as was formerly supposed, was in use at Paris
by 1210 and was known as the *Metaphysica vetus*, in distinction
from the translation from the Arabic, which was made by Gerard
of Cremona or Michael Scot and was known (in the first half of the
thirteenth century) as the *Metaphysica nova*. Books K, M, N, as
well as smaller passages, were missing in this translation. In the
second half of the century the title *Metaphysica nova* or *Translatio
nova* was given to the translation from the Greek by William of
Moerbeke (after 1260), upon which translation St. Thomas based
his commentary. It has also been shown that there was a *translatio
media* from the Greek, on which St. Albert the Great based his
commentary and which was known to St. Thomas.

As regards the ethical writings of Aristotle, a translation of
Books 2 and 3 of the *Nicomachean Ethics* was available by the end
of the twelfth century. This translation had been made from the
Greek (possibly it was the work of Boethius himself) and was

---

[1] St. Thomas's *Translatio Boethii*.

known as the *Ethica vetus*, while a later translation (of Book 1) was known as the *Ethica nova*. A full translation, generally ascribed to Robert Grosseteste (d. 1253), was then made from the Greek, the first three books being a recension of the *Ethica vetus* and the *Ethica nova*. The *Magna Moralia* were translated by Bartholomew of Messina in the reign of King Manfred (1258–66); but only the seventh book of the *Eudemian Ethics* was known in the thirteenth century.

The *De Anima* was translated from the Greek before 1215, the translation from the Arabic by Michael Scot being somewhat later. William of Moerbeke produced a further version from the Greek or a corrected edition of the first translation from the Greek. Similarly there was a translation of the *Physics* from the Greek before the two translations from the Arabic by Gerard of Cremona and Michael Scot, while a translation of the *De Generatione et Corruptione* from the Greek preceded the translation from the Arabic by Gerard of Cremona. The *Politics* were translated from the Greek about 1260 by William of Moerbeke (there was no translation from the Arabic), who probably also translated the *Economics* about 1267. This eminent man, who was born about 1215 and died in 1286, as Archbishop of Corinth, not only translated Aristotle's works from the Greek and re-edited earlier translations (thus enabling his friend, St. Thomas Aquinas, to write his commentaries), but also translated from the Greek some commentaries by Alexander of Aphrodisias, Simplicius, Joannes Philoponus and Themistius, as also some works of Proclus and the latter's exposition of the *Timaeus* of Plato.[1] His translation of Proclus's *Elementatio theologica* brought to St. Thomas the realisation that the *Liber de Causis* was not the work of Aristotle, as it was previously supposed to be, but was based on the work of Proclus. It was also William of Moerbeke who translated the *Rhetoric* of Aristotle. As to the *Poetics*, the mediaevals possessed only Herman the German's translation of Averroes's commentary.[2]

As modern investigation has shown that translations from the Greek generally preceded translations from the Arabic, and that, even when the original translation from the Greek was incomplete, the Arabic-Latin version soon had to give place to a new and

[1] The *Timaeus* of Plato was known to the West, thanks to Cicero and Chalcidius, but it was not until the twelfth century that the *Meno* and *Phaedo* were translated (by Henricus Aristippus).
[2] How far St. Thomas actually used William's translation has been much discussed.

better translation from the Greek, it can no longer be said that the mediaevals had no real knowledge of Aristotle, but only a caricature of his doctrine, a picture distorted by the hand of Arabian philosophers. What can, however, be said is that they were not always able to distinguish what was to be ascribed to Aristotle from what was not to be ascribed to Aristotle. A great step forward was taken when St. Thomas came to realise that the *Liber de Causis* was not the work of Aristotle. He was already quite conscious of the fact that Averroes's commentaries were not to be taken as the unquestionable interpretation of Aristotle's philosophy, but even he seems to have thought, at least for a time, that the Pseudo-Dionysius was not far from being a follower of Aristotle. The fact of the matter is, not that the mediaevals had no reliable texts of Aristotle, but that they were deficient in historical knowledge: they did not, for example, adequately realise the relation of Aristotle to Plato or of neo-Platonism to Plato and Aristotle. That St. Thomas was an able commentator on Aristotle can be denied only by those unacquainted with his commentaries; but it would be foolish to claim even for St. Thomas a knowledge of the history and development of Greek philosophy such as is open to the modern scholar. He made good use of the information available to him; but that information was rather limited.

3. The translation of works of Aristotle and his commentators, as well as of the Arabian thinkers, provided the Latin Scholastics with a great wealth of intellectual material. In particular they were provided with the knowledge of philosophical systems which were methodologically independent of theology and which were presented as the human mind's reflection on the universe. The systems of Aristotle, of Avicenna, of Averroes, opened up a wide vista of the scope of the human reason and it was clear to the mediaevals that the truth attained in them must have been independent of Christian revelation, since it had been attained by a Greek philosopher and his Greek and Islamic commentators. In this way the new translations helped to clarify in the minds of the mediaevals the relation between philosophy and theology and contributed very largely to the delimitation of the provinces of the two sciences. It is, of course, true that Aristotle's system not unnaturally took the limelight in preference to those of his commentators, and his philosophy tended to appear in the eyes of those Latins who were favourably impressed as the *ne plus ultra* of human intellectual endeavour, since it constituted the

most sustained and extensive effort of the human mind with which they were acquainted; but they were quite well aware that it was the work of reason, not a set of revealed dogmas. To us, looking back from a long way off, it may seem that some of the mediaevals exaggerated the genius of Aristotle (we also know that they did not realise the existence of different strata or periods in Aristotle's thought), but we should put ourselves for a moment in their place and try to imagine the impression which would be made on a mediaeval philosopher by the sight of what in any case is one of the supreme achievements of the human mind, a system which, in regard to both completeness and close reasoning, was unparalleled in the thought of the early Middle Ages.

However, the system of Aristotle did not meet with universal welcome and approbation, though it could not be ignored. Largely because the *Liber de Causis* (until St. Thomas discovered the truth), the so-called *Theologia Aristotelis* (extracts from the *Enneads* of Plotinus) and the *De secretis secretorum* (composed by an Arab philosopher in the eleventh or beginning of the twelfth century) were wrongly attributed to Aristotle, the latter's philosophy tended to appear in a false light. Moreover, the attribution of these books to Aristotle naturally made it appear that the Arab commentators were justified in their neo-Platonic interpretation. Hence it came about that in 1210 the Provincial Council of Paris, meeting under the presidency of Peter of Corbeil, Archbishop of Sens, forbad the public or private teaching of Aristotle's 'natural philosophy' or of the commentaries on them. This prohibition was imposed under pain of excommunication and applied to the University of Paris. In all probability 'natural philosophy' included the metaphysics of Aristotle, since when the statutes of the university were sanctioned by Robert de Courçon, Papal Legate, in 1215 Aristotle's works on metaphysics and natural philosophy, as well as compendia of these works and the doctrines of David of Dinant, Amalric of Bene and Maurice of Spain (probably Averroes, the Moor or *Maurus*) were prohibited, though the study of Aristotle's logic was ordered. The study of the *Ethics* was not forbidden.

The reason for the prohibition was, as already indicated, largely due to the ascription to Aristotle of works which were not by him. Amalric of Bene, whose writings were included in the prohibition of 1215, maintained doctrines which were at variance with Christian teaching and which would naturally appear to find some support in the philosophy of Aristotle, if the latter were interpreted in the light of all the books attributed to him, while David of Dinant, the other heretical philosopher whose writings were prohibited, had actually appealed to the *Metaphysics*, which had been translated into Latin from the Greek version brought from Byzantium before 1210. To these considerations must be added the undoubted fact that Aristotle maintained the eternity of the world. It was, therefore, not unnatural that the Aristotelian system, especially when coupled with the philosophies of David of Dinant, Amalric of Bene and Averroes, should appear as a danger to orthodoxy in the eyes of the traditionalists. The logic of Aristotle had long been in use, even if the full *Organon* had come into circulation only comparatively recently, but the complete metaphysical and cosmological teaching of Aristotle was a novelty, a novelty rendered all the more dangerous through association with heretical philosophies.

However, in 1231 Pope Gregory IX, while maintaining the prohibition, appointed a commission of theologians, William of Auxerre, Stephen of Provins and Simon of Authie, to correct the prohibited books of Aristotle, and as this measure obviously implied that the books were not fundamentally unsound, the prohibition tended to be neglected. It was extended to Toulouse in 1245 by Innocent IV, but by that date it was no longer possible to check the spread of Aristotelianism and from 1255 all the known works of Aristotle were officially lectured on in the University of Paris. The Holy See made no move against the university, though in 1263 Urban IV renewed the prohibition of 1210, probably out of a fear of Averroism, the renewed prohibition remaining a dead letter. The Pope must have known perfectly well that William of Moerbeke was translating the prohibited works of Aristotle at his own court, and the prohibition of 1263 must have been designed as a check to Averroism, not as a seriously meant attempt to put an end to all study of the Aristotelian philosophy. In any case the prohibition was of no effect, and finally in 1366 the Legates of Urban V required from all candidates for the Licentiate of Arts at Paris a knowledge of all the known works of Aristotle. It had by then long been clear to the mediaevals that a work like the *Liber de Causis* was not Aristotelian and that the philosophy of Aristotle was not, except, of course, in the eyes of the Latin Averroists, bound up with the interpretation given it by Averroes but could be harmonised with the Christian faith. Indeed the dogmas of faith themselves had by then been expressed by theologians in terms taken from the Aristotelian system.

This brief summary of the official attitude to Aristotle on the part of ecclesiastical and academic authority shows that Aristotelianism triumphed in the end. This does not mean, however, that all mediaeval philosophers of the thirteenth and fourteenth centuries extended an equal welcome to Aristotle or that they all understood him in the same way: the vigour and variety of mediaeval thought will be made clear in succeeding chapters. There is truth in the statement that the shadow of Aristotle hung over and dominated the philosophic thought of the Middle Ages, but it is not the whole truth, and we would have a very inadequate idea of mediaeval philosophy in the thirteenth and fourteenth centuries if we imagined that it was inspired and characterised by a slavish acceptance of every word of the great Greek philosopher.

PART V

THE THIRTEENTH CENTURY

CHAPTER XXII

INTRODUCTION

The University of Paris—Universities closed and privileged corporations—Curriculum—Religious Orders at Paris—Currents of thought in the thirteenth century.

1. THE leading philosophers and theologians of the thirteenth century were all associated, at some period, with the University of Paris, which arose out of the body of professors and students attached to the Cathedral School of Notre Dame and the other schools of Paris, the statutes of the university being sanctioned by Robert de Courçon, Papal Legate, in 1215. Alexander of Hales, St. Bonaventure, St. Albert the Great, St. Thomas Aquinas, Matthew of Aquasparta, Roger Marston, Richard of Middleton, Roger Bacon, Giles of Rome, Siger of Brabant, Henry of Ghent, Raymond Lull, Duns Scotus (d. 1308), all either studied or taught (or both) at Paris. Other centres of higher education were, however, growing in importance and acquiring a tradition of their own. Thus with the University of Oxford were associated the names of men like Robert Grosseteste, Roger Bacon and Duns Scotus, and whereas Paris was the scene of the triumph of Aristotelianism, the name of Oxford recalls a characteristic mingling of the Augustinian tradition with 'empiricism', as in the philosophy of Roger Bacon. Yet in spite of the importance of Oxford, Bologna and, at times, the Papal Court, the University of Paris was easily the most important centre of higher studies in the Christendom of the thirteenth century. Scholars might come to Paris for their studies and then return to Oxford or Bologna to teach, thus carrying with them the spirit and ideals of the great university, and even those scholars who never themselves set foot in Paris were subject to Parisian influence. Robert of Grosseteste, for instance, who possibly never studied at Paris, was certainly influenced by professors of Paris.

The international character of the University of Paris, with its consequent importance in the intellectual expression and defence of Christianity, naturally made the maintenance of religious orthodoxy within its precincts one of the interests of the Holy See. Thus the Averroistic controversy must be seen in the light of the university's international standing: it represented in itself the intellectual culture of the Middle Ages, as far as philosophy and theology were concerned, and the spread within its walls of a system of thought which was irreconcilable with Christianity could not be a matter of indifference to Rome. On the other hand it would be a mistake to suppose that there was any rigid imposition of one particular tradition. St. Thomas Aquinas met with difficulties, it is true, in his acceptance and propagation of Aristotelianism; but such difficulties did not last, and even if the philosophy of Aristotle came in the end to dominate the intellectual life of the university, in the thirteenth and fourteenth centuries there was still plenty of room for different philosophical outlooks.

2. The universities, to be constituted as such, had to receive a formal charter, either from pope or emperor (the University of Naples received its charter from Frederick II) or, later, from kings. These charters conferred considerable privileges on professors and students, privileges which were jealously guarded. The two most important privileges were those of internal jurisdiction (which still survives at Oxford, for example) and of power to give the degree, which carried with it licence to teach. The students were exempt from military service, except in special circumstances, and the university was generally exempt from a great deal of taxation, particularly local taxation. In northern Europe the professors controlled the university, the rector being elected, whereas the universities of southern Europe were often distinctly democratic in their governmental arrangements, but in either case the university was a largely independent and closed corporation, which maintained its privileges against Church and State. In this respect the universities of Oxford and Cambridge represent more faithfully the mediaeval tradition and practice than do those continental universities where rectors and professors are appointed by the State.

3. In mediaeval times, and the same is true of a much later period as well, students entered the university at a much earlier age than they do at present. Thus boys of thirteen or fourteen might begin attending the university, and if one remembers this fact, the number of years required in order to obtain the doctorate

will not appear so surprising. The course in arts lasted some four and a half to six years, according to the university (though at Oxford some seven years were required), and for a time at least the student had to qualify in the faculty of arts before he could proceed to theology. In the theological course he had to spend four years in attending lectures on the Bible and then two more years in attending lectures on the *Sentences*, after which, if by then twenty-six years of age, he became a Baccalaureate and lectured for the two following years on two books of the Bible. He could then lecture on the *Sentences* and finally, after several years spent in study and disputations, he could take the doctorate and teach theology, the minimum age for this being thirty-four. For teaching the arts the minimum age required was twenty. At Paris the tendency was to increase the number of years required for obtaining the doctorate, though at Oxford the arts course was longer and the theological course shorter than at Paris.

Those students who took the doctorate and left the university were known as *magistri non regentes*, whereas those who remained to teach were known as *magistri regentes*; but, however many students there may have been who fell into the first class, it is clear that the long university course was designed to produce professors and teachers by career.

As for the curriculum, the general practice in the university of the thirteenth century was to lecture or listen to lectures on certain texts. Thus, apart from the writings of the grammarians like Priscian and Donatus and certain other classical texts, the writings of Aristotle came to dominate the arts school altogether in the course of time, and it is significant that 'Latin Averroism' was represented principally by professors in that faculty. In theology the Bible and the *Sentences* of Peter Lombard dominated the scene, and the professor gave his own views by way of commentary. Besides the lectures there was another essential feature of the curriculum, namely the disputation, which took the form either of an 'ordinary' disputation (*disputatio ordinaria*) or the 'general' disputation (*de quolibet*). The *disputationes de quolibet*, in which a choice was made from a great variety of topics, were held at solemn feasts, and after the disputation in the strict sense, that is, between a defendant or *respondens* and the objectors, *opponentes*, the professor summed up the whole matter, arguments, objections and replies, and finished by giving his considered solution (*determinatio*) of the point at issue, in which he began with the words,

Respondeo dicendum. The final result, arranged by the professor, was then published as a *Quodlibet*. (St. Thomas left some eleven or twelve *Quodlibets*.) The *disputatio ordinaria* was also followed by a *determinatio* and was published as a *quaestio disputata*. There were other forms of disputation as well; but these two, the *disputatio ordinaria* and the *disputatio de quolibet*, were the most important. They were designed to increase the student's understanding of a particular theme, and his power of argument and of refuting objections. In fact, generally speaking, mediaeval university education aimed rather at imparting a certain body of knowledge and dexterity in dealing with it than at increasing factual knowledge as in a modern research institute. Of course, scholars certainly aimed at increasing knowledge speculatively; but the increase of scientific knowledge, for example, had little place in mediaeval education, though in the fourteenth century science made some progress at Paris and at Vienna.

4. Of considerable importance in the life of Paris and Oxford were the religious Orders, particularly the two mendicant Orders founded in the thirteenth century, the Dominicans and the Franciscans. The former Order established itself in Paris in 1217, the latter a few years later, and both Orders then proceeded to claim chairs of theology in the university, i.e. they claimed that their chairs of theology should be incorporated in the university and that their professors and students should enjoy the university privileges. There was considerable opposition to this claim from the teaching body of the university; but in 1229 the Dominicans received one chair and in 1231 a second, in the same year that the Franciscans obtained their first chair (they did not receive a second). Roland of Cremona and John of St. Giles were the first Dominican professors, Alexander of Hales the first Franciscan professor. In 1248 the General Chapter of the Dominican Order decreed the erection of *studia generalia* (houses of study for the whole Order, distinct from the houses of study of particular provinces) at Cologne, Bologna, Montpellier and Oxford, while the Franciscans meanwhile erected *studia generalia* at Oxford and Toulouse. In 1260 the Augustinians opened a house at Paris, the first official doctor being Giles of Rome, while the Carmelites opened houses at Oxford in 1253 and at Paris in 1259. Other Orders also followed suit.

The religious Orders, particularly the Dominicans and Franciscans, accomplished a great work in the intellectual field and produced men of outstanding eminence (we have only to think of St. Albert the Great and St. Thomas Aquinas in the Dominican, of Alexander of Hales and St. Bonaventure in the Franciscan Order); but they had to put up with a good deal of opposition, doubtless inspired in part by jealousy. Not only did their opponents demand that no religious Order should occupy more than one chair at one time, but they even set about attacking the religious state itself. Thus in 1255 William of St. Amour published a pamphlet, *De periculis novissimorum temporum*, which drew from St. Thomas's pen the *Contra impugnantes Dei cultum*. William of St. Amour's pamphlet was condemned and in 1257 the seculars were forbidden to publish writings against the regulars; but in spite of this prohibition Gerard of Abbeville restarted the opposition with his *Contra adversarium perfectionis christianae*. St. Bonaventure and St. Thomas, however much they might disagree on matters philosophical, were united in a determination to defend the religious Orders, and both published replies to Gerard's work, and these in their turn evoked a counterblast from Nicholas of Lisieux, writing on behalf of the seculars. The quarrel between regulars and seculars broke out again on various later occasions, but, as far as the main point was concerned, the incorporation into the university of the regular chairs, judgement had been given in favour of the regulars and it was not revoked. One result followed, however, which is worthy of mention, and that is the founding of the College of the Sorbonne in 1253 by Robert de Sorbon, chaplain to Louis IX, for the education of students in theology, secular students being admitted. If I call the founding of the College of the Sorbonne and similar colleges a 'result' of the controversy between seculars and regulars, all I mean is that such colleges were founded partly perhaps to counterbalance the influence and position of the regulars and certainly in order to extend to a wider field the benefits of the type of education and training provided by the religious.

5. In the thirteenth century one can distinguish various currents of thought which tended eventually, in the religious Orders, to become more or less fixed in traditional schools. First of all there is the Augustinian current of thought, conservative in character and generally reserved in its attitude towards Aristotelianism, its attitude varying from marked hostility to partial acceptance. This current is characteristic of the Franciscan thinkers (and indeed of the first Dominicans), represented by Grosseteste, Alexander of

Hales and St. Bonaventure. Secondly there is the Aristotelian current of thought, which became characteristic of the Dominicans, represented by St. Albert the Great (in part) and (fully) by St. Thomas Aquinas. Thirdly there are the Averroists, represented by Siger of Brabant. Fourthly one has to take into consideration the independent and eclectic thinkers like Giles of Rome and Henry of Ghent. Fifthly, at the turn of the century, there is the great figure of Duns Scotus who revised the Franciscan tradition in the light of Aristotelianism and who, rather than St. Bonaventure, became the accepted Doctor of his order. I cannot enter in detail into the thought of all the philosophers of the thirteenth century; but I shall endeavour to put in clear relief their salient characteristics, show the variety of thought within a more or less common framework and indicate the formation and development of the different traditions.

CHAPTER XXIII

WILLIAM OF AUVERGNE

Reasons for treating of William of Auvergne—God and creatures;
essence and existence—Creation by God directly and in time—
Proofs of God's existence—Hylomorphism—The soul—Know-
ledge—William of Auvergne a transition-thinker.

1. WILLIAM OF AUVERGNE (or William of Paris), author of a *De
Trinitate* or *De primo principio* (c. 1225), a *De Anima* (1230), a
De universo creaturarum (c. 1231) and other smaller treatises, was
Bishop of Paris from 1228 to 1249, the year in which he died. He
is not, it is true, one of the best-known thinkers of the Middle
Ages; but he claims our attention as a philosopher and theologian
who was Bishop of Paris at the time when Grégory IX appointed
the commission of theologians to amend the works of Aristotle and
thus tacitly modified the Church's attitude towards the pagan
philosopher. Indeed William of Auvergne represents the attitude
adopted by Gregory IX when he (William) says in his *De Anima*
that although Aristotle often contradicts the truth and so must be
rejected, his teaching should be accepted when it conforms to the
truth, that is, when it is compatible with Christian doctrine. In his
fundamental line of thought William continues the tradition of
Augustine, Boethius and Anselm, but he knew not only the works
of Aristotle, but also the writings of the Arabian and Jewish
philosophers and he did not hesitate to utilise their ideas exten-
sively. In general, therefore, one may say that in William of
Auvergne we see an intelligent and open-minded adherent of the
old tradition who was willing to utilise the new currents of thought
but who was perfectly conscious of the points in which the Arabians
and Aristotle himself were at variance with Christian doctrine. He
is, then, an embodiment of the meeting of the twelfth and thirteenth centuries and has a title to be considered when one is
treating of the earlier thinkers of the latter century. Moreover,
he was a secular priest who occupied the episcopal see of Paris at
the time when the mendicant Orders obtained their first chairs,
and on this count too there is justification for discussing his
philosophical ideas before proceeding to deal with the thinkers of
the Franciscan and Dominican Orders. Nor is he himself a

negligible figure: on the contrary, his thought is vigorous, original and systematic.

2. From Avicenna, William of Auvergne adopted the distinction between essence and existence and made it the explanation of the creature's finitude and dependence. *Esse*, existence, does not belong to the *ratio* or essence of any object save that one object (God) in which it is identical with the essence; of all other objects existence is predicated only 'accidentally', i.e. it belongs to them by participation (*per participationem*). If we consider any finite object, we realise that there is a distinction between its *ratio* or essential nature and its existence, it is not necessary that it should exist; but if we consider the necessary Being, we realise that its essence cannot be conceived without existence. In fine, 'in everything (other than God) *ens* is one thing, *esse* or *entitas* another'.[1] This means that God alone is pure existence, existence being His essence, whereas objects do not exist essentially, because they must, but because their existence is acquired, received. The relation, then, of objects other than God to God must be one of creature to Creator, from which it follows that the theory of emanation is false:[2] God is absolutely simple. Things did not pre-exist in God as parts of God, as they would have had to do if they flowed from God as the waters from a fountain, but only in the *formae exemplares*, which are identical with God. God sees Himself as the exemplary cause of all creatures.[3]

3. If William of Auvergne rejects the neo-Platonist-Arabian theory of emanation, he rejects also the notion of creation by way of intermediaries. The hierarchy of Intelligences posited by Aristotle and his followers has no foundation in reality:[4] God created the world directly. From this it follows that He exercises providence in regard to individual things and William appeals at length to the instinctive activities of the brutes as an illustration of the operation of divine providence.[5] Again, the Aristotelian doctrine of the eternity of the world is rejected. Whatsoever people may say and however much they may try to excuse Aristotle, it is a certain fact that he held that the world is eternal and that it did not begin to be, and Avicenna followed him in this opinion.[6] Accordingly William not only gives the reasons why Aristotle and Avicenna held this opinion, but he even tries to put them in the best light by improving on their arguments, after

[1] Cf. *De Universo*, 1, 3, 26; 2, 2, 8; *De Trinitate*, 1 and 2.
[2] *De Universo*, 1, 1, 17.   [3] *Ibid.*, 1, 1, 17.   [4] *Ibid.*, 1, 1, 24 ff.
[5] *Ibid.*, 1, 3, 2-3.   [6] *Ibid.*, 1, 2, 8.

which he refutes the arguments. For example, the idea that if God preceded the creation of the world, an infinite duration would have to be passed through before creation, and the idea that there would be empty time before creation both rest on a confusion of time with eternity. The idea of infinite duration elapsing before creation would have significance only if eternity were the same as time, i.e. if it were not eternity, if God were in time; and the idea of empty time before creation is also meaningless, since before creation there can be no time. We have to speak of God preceding creation, of existing before the world, it is true, but at the same time we must remember that such phrases are borrowed from temporal duration and that when applied to what is eternal, they are used in an analogical, not in a univocal sense.

However, as William of Auvergne remarks,[1] it is not sufficient to contradict one's opponents and to show the insufficiency of their arguments unless one goes on to prove one's own position positively. He, therefore, gives various arguments for the creation of the world in time, some of which appear again in St. Bonaventure and are declared inconclusive by St. Thomas. For example, William argues, taking the words out of his adversary's mouth, as it were, that if the world had been eternally in existence, an infinite time would have been passed through before the present moment. But it is impossible to pass through an infinite time. Therefore the world cannot have existed from eternity. Therefore it was created in time, that is, a first moment of time is assignable. Again, supposing that the revolutions of Saturn stand to the revolutions of the sun in a proportion of one to thirty, the sun will have made thirty times as many revolutions since creation as Saturn. But if the world exists from eternity, both Saturn and the sun will have made an infinite number of revolutions. Now, how can an infinity be thirty times greater than another infinity?

From what has been already said it is clear that William of Auvergne did not simply deny the neo-Platonic conception of emanation and the Aristotelian idea of an eternal world, while maintaining the Augustinian doctrine of direct and free creation by God in time. On the contrary, he vigorously and exactly detailed and refuted the arguments of his opponents and elaborated systematic proofs of his own thesis. That he was able to do this was largely due to the fact that he was acquainted at first hand with the writings of Aristotle and the Arabians and did not

[1] *De Universo*, I, 2, 11.

hesitate to utilise not only the Aristotelian logic and the Aristotelian categories but also the ideas of Aristotle, Avicenna and others, when they were acceptable. His utilisation of Avicenna's distinction between essence and existence, for instance, has been already mentioned, and indeed he was the first mediaeval Scholastic to make this distinction an explicit and fundamental point in his philosophy. To this distinction, which enabled him to develop clearly the relation of creature to Creator, William added the doctrine of analogy. Apropos of the statement that finite things possess *esse* 'by participation', he observes that the reader is not to be upset or troubled by the fact that the same word or concept is applied to both God and creatures, since it is not applied in the same sense (*univoce*) or equally: it is applied primarily to God, who *is esse*, and only secondarily to creatures who *have esse*, who participate, that is, in existence in virtue of receiving it through God's creative act. Health, he comments, is predicated of man, of urine, of medicine and of food, but it is not predicated in the same sense or in the same way.[1] The illustration of health is somewhat hackneyed, but it shows that William of Auvergne had apprehended the doctrine of analogy, which is essential to a theistic philosophy.

4. In regard to proofs of God's existence it is a curious fact that William of Auvergne made little use of the proofs used by Aristotle or even by Maimonides. The Aristotelian proof of God as first unmoved mover is not given, and although William certainly looks on God as the first efficient cause, his characteristic proof is one that recalls at least the line of argument adopted by St. Anselm, even though Anselm's argument is not reproduced. The argument in question is from the being which exists by participation to the being which exists essentially, *per essentiam*. This immediately suggests the proof from contingency, which appears in the Arabian and Jewish philosophy, but William prefers to argue from the one concept to the other. For example, the concept *esse adunatum* has as its correlative concept *esse non causatum*, *esse causatum* involves *esse non causatum*, *esse secundarium*, *esse primum*, and so on.[2] William speaks of the *analogia oppositorum* and points out how the one concept or word necessarily involves its correlative concept or word, so that Grunwald[3] can say that William prefers a purely logical or even grammatical mode of proof, in that from one word

[1] *De Trinit.*, 7.   [2] *Ibid.*, 6.
[3] *Gesch. der Gottesbeweise im Mittelalter; Beiträge*, 6, 3, p. 92.

he concludes to another word which is contained in or presupposed by the first word. That the argument does tend to give this impression is true, and, if it were a purely verbal argument, it would be open to the retort that the words, or concepts, *esse participatum* or *esse causatum* certainly involve the words, or concepts, *esse per essentiam* or *esse non causatum*, but this is no proof that *esse per essentiam* or *esse non causatum* actually exists, unless it has first been shown that there is an *esse participatum* or an *esse causatum*. Otherwise the proof would be no more a demonstration of God's existence than is St. Anselm's *a priori* argument. However, although William does not sufficiently develop the experiential character of the proof in regard to its starting-point, his argument is by no means purely verbal, since he shows that the object which comes into being cannot be self-dependent or self-caused. *Esse indigentiae* demands *esse sufficientiae* as the reason for its existence, just as *esse potentiale* requires being in act to bring it into a state of actuality. The whole universe requires necessary Being as its cause and reason. In other words, though one may often get the impression that William is simply analysing concepts and hypostasising them, he gives a proof which is not merely logical or verbal but also metaphysical.

5. William of Auvergne accepted the Aristotelian doctrine of hylomorphic composition, but he refused to admit Avicebron's notion that the Intelligences or angels are hylomorphically composed.[1] It is clear that Aristotle did not think that the rational soul contains *materia prima*, since he clearly asserts that it is an immaterial form, and the account of prime matter given by Averroes, according to which prime matter is the potentiality of sensible substance and sensible substance the final act of prime matter, clearly implies the same, that is, that prime matter is the matter of sensible substance only. Moreover, what could be the use of prime matter in the angels, what function could it serve? Matter in itself is something dead; it cannot contribute in any way to intellectual and spiritual operations or even receive them. As he had already utilised the distinction between essence and existence to explain the finitude of creatures and their radical difference from God, William did not require universal hylomorphic composition for this purpose, and as he considered that to postulate the presence of prime matter in the angels would hinder rather than facilitate the explanation of their purely spiritual

[1] *De Universo*, 2, 2, 8.

operations, he restricted prime matter to the sensible world, as St. Thomas did after him.

6. In his psychology, as set forth in the *De Anima*, William of Auvergne combines Aristotelian and Augustinian themes. Thus he expressly adopts the Aristotelian definition of the soul as *perfectio corporis physici organici potentia vitam habentis*,[1] though he warns the reader that he is not quoting Aristotle as an unquestionable authority, but proposes to show the truth of the definition. That he has a soul should be clear to every man, since he is conscious that he understands and judges;[2] but the soul is not the whole of man's nature. If it were, then a human soul joined to an aerial body, for example, would still be a man, whereas in point of fact it would not be. Aristotle, then, was correct in saying that the soul is to the body, as form is to matter.[3] However, that does not prevent him from saying that the soul is a substance on the ground that it must be either substance or accident and cannot be an accident, and he uses the Augustinian comparison of the soul with a harpist, the body being the harp. It might appear that in man there are three souls, one being the principle of life (vegetative soul), the second being the principle of sensation (animal or sensitive soul) and the third being the principle of intellection (rational soul); but a little reflection will show that this cannot be so. If there was an animal soul in man, distinct from the rational or human soul, then humanity, human nature, would not involve animality, whereas in point of fact a man is an animal because he is man, animality belonging to human nature.[4] There is, then, one soul in man, which exercises various functions. It is created and infused by God alone, neither generated by the parents nor educed from the potentiality of matter,[5] and it is, moreover, immortal, as William proceeds to show by arguments, some of which are of Platonic origin. For example, if the malice of an evil soul does not injure or destroy its *esse*, how can bodily death destroy it?[6] Again, since the body receives life from the soul and the soul's power is such that it vivifies a body which, considered in itself, is dead, that is, lacking life, the fact that the body ceases to live cannot destroy the vital power inherent in the soul.[7] Further, the soul can communicate with *substantiae separatae* and is thus like to them, immortal; but as the human soul is indivisible and one, it

[1] *De Anima*, 1, 1.   [2] *Ibid.*, 1, 3.   [3] *Ibid.*, 1, 2.
[4] *Ibid.*, 4, 1–3.   [5] *Ibid.*, 5, 1 ff.   [6] *Ibid.*, 6, 1.
[7] *Ibid.*, 6, 7.

follows that the whole human soul is immortal, not simply a rational part.[1]

But though he accepts the Peripatetic doctrine of the soul as form of the body (one must make the reservation that he sometimes uses Platonic-Augustinian expressions in regard to the soul's union with the body), William of Auvergne follows St. Augustine in refusing to recognise a real distinction between the soul and its faculties.[2] Only a substance can understand or will, an accident could not do so. Therefore it is the soul itself which understands or wills, though it exercises itself in regard to different objects, or to the same objects, in different ways, now by apprehending them, now by desiring them. From this it would naturally follow that the Aristotelian distinction between the active and the passive intellects must be rejected, and indeed William of Auvergne rejects the doctrines of the active intellect and of the *species intelligibilis* altogether. The followers of Aristotle and of his commentators swallow the theory of the active intellect without any real reflection, whereas not only are the arguments adduced to prove the theory insufficient, but also very good arguments can be adduced to prove the contrary, the argument from the simplicity of the soul, for example. The active intellect is, then, to be rejected as a useless fiction.[3] *A fortiori*, of course, William rejects the Arabian idea of a *separate* active intellect, an idea which, following Averroes, he ascribed (and probably rightly) to Aristotle himself.

7. In regard to the active intellect, then, William of Auvergne parts company with Aristotle and the Arabians in favour of Augustine, and the Augustinian influence is observable also in his theory of knowledge. Like Augustine he emphasises the soul's knowledge of itself, its direct self-consciousness, and, again like Augustine, he minimises the importance of the senses. It is true that man is inclined to concentrate on bodily things, the objects of the senses; that is why a man may neglect the data of self-consciousness and even be so foolish as to deny the very existence of the immaterial soul. It is also true that for sense-perception the senses are necessary, obviously enough, and that corporeal objects produce a physical impression on the organs of sense. But the intelligible forms, abstract and universal, by which we know the objects of the corporeal world, cannot arise either from the objects themselves or from the phantasms of such objects, since both the

objects and the images are particular. How, then, are our abstract and universal ideas of sensible objects produced? They are produced by the understanding itself, which is not purely passive, but active, *effectrix earum (scientiarum quae a parte sensibilium ei advenire videntur) apud semetipsam et in semetipsa.*[1] This activity is an activity of the soul itself, though it is exercised on the occasion of sense-impressions.

What guarantee is there, then, of the objective character of abstract and universal ideas? The guarantee is the fact that the intellect is not merely active but also passive, though it is in regard to God that it is passive, not in regard to the things of sense. God impresses on the intellect not only the first principles, but also our abstract ideas of the sensible world. In the *De Anima*[2] William teaches explicitly that it is not only the first principles (*regulae primae et per se notae*) and the laws of morality (*regulae honestatis*) which are known in this way, but also the intelligible forms of sensible objects. The human soul occupies a position on the bounds of two worlds (*velut in horizonte duorum mundorum naturaliter esse constitutam et ordinatam*), the one being the world of sensible objects, to which it is joined by the body, the other being, not Plato's universal Ideas or Aristotle's separate Intelligence, but God Himself, *creator ipse*, who is the *exemplar*, the *speculum*, the *liber vivus*, so present to the human intellect that the latter reads off, as it were, in God (*absque ullo alio medio*) the principles and rules and intelligible forms. In this way William of Auvergne makes the active intellect of Aristotle and the Arabians to be God Himself, combining this theory with the Augustinian theory of illumination, interpreted ideogenetically.

8. It may cause surprise that a special chapter has been dedicated to a man whose name is not among the most famous of mediaeval thinkers; but William of Auvergne is of interest not only as a vigorous and systematic philosopher, but also as an illustration of the way in which the metaphysical, cosmological and psychological ideas of Aristotle and the Arabians could affect an open-minded man who stood, generally speaking, in the line of the older tradition. William of Auvergne was quite ready to accept ideas from the Aristotelians; he adopted Aristotle's definition of the soul, for instance, and utilised Avicenna's distinction between essence and existence; but he was first and foremost a Christian philosopher and, apart from any personal predilection

[1] *De Anima*, 5, 6.   [2] 7, 6.

for Augustine, he was not the type of man to adopt Aristotelian or supposedly Aristotelian doctrines when these seemed to him to be incompatible with the Christian faith. Thus the Aristotelian doctrine of the eternity of the world, the neo-Platonic-Arabian notions of emanation and of 'creation' by intermediaries, the theory of a separate, unitary and infra-divine active intellect, he unhesitatingly rejected. It would, however, be a mistake to suppose that he rejected these ideas as incompatible with Christianity and left it at that, for he was clearly satisfied in his own mind that the arguments for the offending positions were inconclusive and insufficient, while the arguments for his own tenets were conclusive. In other words, he was a philosopher and wrote as a philosopher, even though in his works we find theological and philosophical themes treated together in the same book, a feature common to most other mediaeval thinkers.

One may say, then, that William of Auvergne was a transition-thinker. He helped, through his intimate acquaintance with the writings of Aristotle and of the Arabian and Jewish philosophers, and through his limited acceptance of their theories, to pave the way for the completer Aristotelianism of St. Albert and St. Thomas, while, on the other hand, his clear rejection of some leading notions of Aristotle and his followers paved the way for the explicitly anti-Aristotelian attitude of an Augustinian like St. Bonaventure. He is, as I have said earlier, the embodiment of the meeting of the twelfth and thirteenth centuries: he is, one might say, the twelfth century meeting the thirteenth century sympathetically, yet by no means with uncritical admiration or acceptance.

But though we are entitled to regard William of Auvergne as a transition-thinker in respect of the rising influence and growing acceptance of Aristotelianism, i.e. as a stage in the development of thought from the older Augustinianism to the Christian Aristotelianism of St. Thomas, we are also entitled to look upon his philosophy as a stage in the development of Augustinianism itself. St. Anselm had made comparatively little use of Aristotelianism, of which he had but a very restricted knowledge; but later Augustinians were forced to take account of Aristotle, and we find Duns Scotus in the thirteenth century attempting the construction of a synthesis in which Augustinianism would be expounded and defended with the help of Aristotle. Of course, whether one should regard these thinkers as Augustinians who modified and enriched Augustinianism under the influence of Aristotle or as incomplete

Aristotelians, is disputable, and one's estimate of William's philos phy will differ, according as one adopts the one or the other point of view, but unless one is determined to view mediaeval philosophy simply in function of Thomism, one should be prepared to admit that William of Auvergne could be regarded as preparing the way for Duns Scotus just as well as preparing the way for St. Thomas. Probably both judgements are true, though from different viewpoints. In a sense any pre-Thomistic mediaeval philosopher who made some use of Aristotle was preparing the way for a more complete adoption of Aristotelianism, and there can be no difficulty in admitting it; yet it is also legitimate to ask whether Aristotelian elements were employed in the service of the Augustinian tradition, so that the resulting philosophy was one in which characteristic Augustinian themes predominated, or whether they were employed in the construction of a philosophy which was definitely orientated towards Aristotelianism as a system. If one asks this question, there can be little doubt about the answer so far as William of Auvergne is concerned; so that M. Gilson can affirm that 'the complex Augustinian of the thirteenth century is almost completely represented by the doctrine of William of Auvergne' and that while nothing could stop the invasion of the Schools by Aristotle, 'the influence of William certainly did much to retard and limit its progress'.[1]

[1] *La Philosophie au Moyen Age*, third edition, 1944, pp. 423-4.

CHAPTER XXIV

ROBERT GROSSETESTE AND ALEXANDER OF HALES

(a) Robert Grosseteste's life and writings—Doctrine of light—God and creatures—Doctrine of truth and of illumination.
(b) Alexander of Hales's attitude to philosophy—Proofs of God's existence—The divine attributes—Composition in creatures— Soul, intellect, will—Spirit of Alexander's philosophy.

WHEN one is treating of mediaeval philosophy, it is not easy to decide in what way one will group the various thinkers. Thus one might very well treat Oxford and Paris separately. At Oxford the general tendency in metaphysics and psychology was conservative, Augustinian, while at the same time an interest was developed in empirical studies, and the combination of these two factors would afford some reason for tracing the course of philosophy at Oxford from Robert Grosseteste to Roger Bacon in a continuous line; while as regards Paris the Augustinianism of Alexander of Hales and St. Bonaventure on the one hand and the Aristotelianism of St. Albert and St. Thomas on the other hand, together with the relation between the two Schools, might make it desirable to treat them in close proximity. However, such a method has its disadvantages. For example, Roger Bacon died (*c.* 1292) long after Alexander of Hales (1245), in regard to whose writings he made some slighting remarks, and also after St. Albert the Great (1280), towards whom he seems to have felt a special hostility, so that it would seem desirable to consider Roger Bacon after considering these two thinkers. One might, even then, leave over Robert Grosseteste for consideration with Roger Bacon, but the fact remains that Grosseteste died (1253) well before the Oxford condemnation of series of theses, among which figured some of those maintained by St. Thomas (1277 and 1284), whereas Roger Bacon was alive at the time of the condemnations and criticised that of 1277, in so far as he felt that it concerned him personally. While admitting, then, that there would be a great deal to say in favour of another mode of grouping, in which more attention would be paid to spiritual affinities than to chronology, I decided to treat first of Robert Grosseteste at Oxford and Alexander of Hales at Paris, then of Alexander's disciple St. Bonaventure, the greatest representative of the Augustinian tradition in the thirteenth

century, then of the Aristotelianism of St. Albert and St. Thomas
and of the ensuing controversies, and only afterwards to consider
Roger Bacon, in spite of his spiritual affinity with Grosseteste.

(a) ROBERT GROSSETESTE

1. Robert Grosseteste was born in Suffolk about 1170 and
became Chancellor of Oxford University about 1221. From 1229
to 1232 he was Archdeacon of Leicester and in 1235 he became
Bishop of Lincoln, a post which he occupied until his death in
1253. Besides translations (it has already been mentioned that he
probably translated the *Ethics* directly from the Greek), Robert
Grosseteste composed commentaries on the *Posterior Analytics*,
the *Sophistical Arguments*, the *Physics*, though the 'commentary'
on the *Physics* was rather a compendium than a commentary, and
on the writings of the Pseudo-Dionysius. The statement by Roger
Bacon to the effect that Grosseteste *neglexit omnino libros Aristotelis et vias eorum*[1] cannot, therefore, be taken as meaning that
he was ignorant of the writings of Aristotle, but must be understood in the sense that, though acquainted with the thought of
Aristotle, Grosseteste approached philosophical problems in a
different manner. Bacon's further words make this clear, as he
says that Grosseteste was dependent on other authors than
Aristotle and that he also relied on his own experience.

Of original works Robert Grosseteste published books: *De unica
forma omnium, De Intelligentiis, De statu causarum, De potentia et
actu, De veritate, De veritate propositionis, De scientia Dei, De ordine
emanandi causatorum a Deo* and *De libero arbitrio*, the authenticity of the *De Anima* not being certain. In works such as those
just named it is quite clear that Grosseteste stood in the Augustinian tradition, although he knew the philosophy of Aristotle and
utilised some of his themes. But with his Augustinianism he
combined an interest in empirical science which influenced Roger
Bacon and excited his admiration, so that Bacon was led to say of
his master that he knew the sciences better than other men[2] and
was able to explain causes by the aid of mathematics.[3] Thus
Grosseteste wrote *De utilitate artium, De generatione sonorum, De
sphaera, De computo, De generatione stellarum, De cometis, De
impressione aeris, De luce, De lineis, angulis et figuris, De natura
locorum, De iride, De colore, De calore solis, De differentiis localibus,*

---

[1] *Compendium studii*, ed. Brewer, p. 469. [2] *Ibid.*, p. 472.
[3] *Opus Maius*, ed. Bridges, 1, 108.

De impressionibus elementorum, De motu corporali, De motu super-caelestium, De finitate motus et temporis and *Quod homo sit minor mundus.*

2. The philosophy of Robert Grosseteste centres round the idea of light, so dear to the mind of the Augustinian. In the *De luce*[1] Grosseteste remarks that the first corporeal form, which some call corporeity, is in his judgement light. Light unites with matter, that is, with Aristotelian prime matter, to form a simple substance without dimensions. Why does Grosseteste make light the first corporeal form? Because it is the nature of light to diffuse itself and he uses this property of light to explain how a substance composed of non-dimensional form and non-dimensional matter acquires tridimensionality. If we suppose that the function of light is to multiply itself and to diffuse itself and so to be responsible for actual extension, we must conclude that light *is* the first corporeal form, since it would not be possible for the first corporeal form to produce extension through a secondary or consequent form. Moreover, light is the noblest of all forms and bears the greatest resemblance to the separate intelligences, so that on this title also it is the first corporeal form.

Light (*lux*) diffuses itself in all directions, 'spherically', forming the outermost sphere, the firmament, at the farthest point of its diffusion, and this sphere consists simply of light and prime matter. From every part of the firmament light (*lumen*) is diffused towards the centre of the sphere, this light (the light of experience) being *corpus spirituale, sive mavis dicere spiritus corporalis*.[2] This diffusion takes place by means of a self-multiplication and generation of light, so that at intervals, so to speak, there arises a new sphere, until the nine celestial and concentric spheres are complete, the innermost being the sphere of the moon. This sphere in turn produces light, but the rarefaction or diffusion is less as the light approaches the centre, and the four infra-lunar spheres, of fire, air, water and earth are produced. There are, then, thirteen spheres in all in the sensible world, the nine celestial spheres, which are incorruptible and changeless, and the four infra-celestial spheres, which are corruptible and capable of change.

The degree of light possessed by each kind of body determines its place in the corporeal hierarchy, light being the *species et perfectio corporum omnium*.[3] Grosseteste also explains colour in terms of light, declaring that it is *lux incorporata perspicuo*.[4] An

[1] Ed. Baur, p. 51.   [2] P. 55.   [3] P. 56.   [4] *De colore*, p. 78.

abundance of light *in perspicuo puro* is whiteness, while *lux pauca in perspicuo impuro nigredo est*, and he explains in this sense the statement of Aristotle[1] and Averroes that blackness is a privation. Light again is the principle of motion, motion being nothing else but the *vis multiplicativa lucis*.[2]

3. So far light has been considered as something corporeal, as a component of the corporeal; but Grosseteste extends the conception of light to embrace the spiritual world as well. Thus God is pure Light, the eternal Light (not in the corporeal sense, of course), and the angels are also incorporeal lights, participating in the eternal Light. God is also the 'Form of all things', but Grosseteste is careful to explain that God is not the form of all things as entering into their substance, uniting with their matter, but as their exemplary form.[3] God precedes all creatures, but 'precedes' must be understood as meaning that God is eternal, the creature temporal: if it is understood as meaning that there is a common duration in which both God and creatures exist, the statement will be incorrect, since the Creator and the creature do not share any common measure.[4] We naturally *imagine* a time in which God existed before creation, just as we naturally imagine space outside the universe; but reliance on the imagination in such matters is a source of error.

4. In the *De veritate propositionis*[5] Grosseteste says that *veritas sermonis vel opinionis est adaequatio sermonis vel opinionis et rei*, but he concentrates more on 'ontological truth', on the Augustinian view of truth. He is willing to accept the Aristotelian view of the truth of enunciation as *adaequatio sermonis et rei* or *adaequatio rei ad intellectum*, but truth really means the conformity of things to the eternal Word *quo dicuntur* and consists in their conformity to the divine Word.[6] A thing is true, in so far as it is what it ought to be, and it is what it ought to be when it is conformed to the Word, that is, to its exemplar. This conformity can be perceived only by the mind, so that truth may also be defined with St. Anselm as *rectitudo sola mente perceptibilis*.[7]

From this it follows that no created truth can be perceived except in the light of the supreme Truth, God. Augustine bore witness to the fact that a created truth is visible only in so far as the light of its *ratio eterna* is present to the mind.[8] How is it, then,

---

[1] *Physics*, 201 a 6; *Metaph.*, 1065 b 11. [2] *De motu corporali et luce*, p. 92.
[3] *De unica forma omnium*, p. 109.
[4] *De ordine emanandi causatorum a Deo*, p. 149. [5] P. 144.
[6] *De veritate*, pp. 134-5. [7] *Ibid.*, p. 135. [8] *Ibid.*, p. 137.

that the wicked and impure can attain truth? They cannot be supposed to see God, who is seen only by the pure of heart. The answer is that the mind does not perceive the Word or the *ratio eterna* directly, but perceives truth in the light of the Word. Just as the bodily eye sees corporeal objects in the light of the sun without looking directly at the sun or even perhaps adverting to it at all, so the mind perceives truth in the light of the divine illumination without thereby perceiving God, the *Veritas summa*, directly or even without necessarily realising at all that it is only in the divine light that it sees truth.[1] Thus Grosseteste follows the Augustinian doctrine of divine illumination, but explicitly rejects any interpretation of the doctrine which would involve a vision of God.

Into Grosseteste's views on mathematics, perspective, etc., I cannot enter: enough has been said to show how Grosseteste's philosophy was built upon Augustinian lines by a man who yet knew and was willing to utilise Aristotelian ideas.

(b) ALEXANDER OF HALES

5. There was within the Franciscan Order a party of zealots who adopted a hostile attitude towards learning and other accommodations to the needs of life, which they regarded as treason to the simple idealism of the Seraphic Father; but these 'Spirituals' were frowned upon by the Holy See, and in point of fact the Franciscan Order produced a long line of distinguished theologians and philosophers, the first eminent figure being that of the Englishman, Alexander of Hales, who was born in Gloucestershire between 1170 and 1180, entered the Franciscan Order about 1231 and died in 1245. He was the first Franciscan professor of theology at Paris and occupied the chair until within a few years of his death, having as his successor John of la Rochelle.

It is difficult to ascertain exactly what contributions to philosophy are to be ascribed to Alexander of Hales in person, since the *Summa theologica* which passes under his name, and which drew caustic comments from Roger Bacon, comprises elements, particularly in the latter portion, taken from the writings of other thinkers and seems to have attained its final form some ten years or more after Alexander's death.[2] In any case, however, the work represents a stage in the development of western philosophy and

[1] *De veritate*, p. 138.
[2] References below are to the *Summa theologica* in the Quaracchi edition, according to volume and section.

a tendency in that development. It represents a stage, since the Aristotelian philosophy as a whole is clearly known and utilised: it represents a tendency, since the attitude adopted towards Aristotle is critical, in the sense that Alexander not only attacks certain doctrines of Aristotle and the Aristotelians but also considers that the pagan philosophers were unable to formulate a satisfactory 'philosophy', in the wide sense, owing to the fact that they did not possess the Christian revelation: a man on a hill can see more even of the valley than the man at the foot of the hill can see. He followed, therefore, his Christian predecessors (the Fathers, especially St. Augustine, Boethius, the Pseudo-Dionysius, St. Anselm, the Victorines) rather than Aristotle.

6. The doctrine of the Blessed Trinity cannot be attained by man's unaided reason, owing to the weakness of the human intellect,[1] but God's existence can be known by all men, whether they are good or bad.[2] Distinguishing God's existence (*quia est*) from His nature (*quid est*) Alexander teaches that all can know God's existence by means of creatures, recognising God as efficient and final cause.[3] Moreover, though the natural light of reason is insufficient to attain to a knowledge of the divine nature as it is in itself, that does not mean that all knowledge of God's nature is barred to the natural intellect, since it can come to know something of God, for example, His power and wisdom, by considering His operation in creatures, a degree of knowledge open to those who are not in a state of grace.[4] This type of knowledge is not univocal but analogical.[5] For example, goodness is predicated of God and of creatures, but while it is predicated of God *per naturam*, as being identical with His nature and as the self-existent source of all goodness, it is predicated of creatures *per participationem*, inasmuch as creatures depend on God, are God's effects, and receive a limited degree of goodness from Him.

In proving God's existence Alexander makes use of a variety of arguments. Thus he uses Richard of St. Victor's proof from contingency, St. John Damascene's argument from causality and Hugh of St. Victor's argument from the soul's knowledge that it had a beginning; but he also employs St. Augustine's and St. Anselm's proof from the eternity of truth and accepts the latter's proof from the idea of the Perfect, as given in the *Proslogium*.[6] In addition he maintains that it is impossible to be ignorant of God's

---

[1] I, no. 10. [2] I, no. 15. [3] I, no. 21. [4] I, no. 15.
[5] I, no. 21. [6] I, no. 25.

existence.[1] This is a startling proposition, but it is necessary to bear in mind certain distinctions. For instance, we must distinguish habitual knowledge and actual knowledge (*cognitio habitu, cognitio actu*). The former, says Alexander, is a habit naturally impressed on the intellect, enabling the intellect to know God, and would seem to be little more than implicit knowledge, if 'implicit knowledge' can be called knowledge at all. St. Albert the Great comments, rather sarcastically, that this distinction is a *solutio mirabilis*.[2] Actual knowledge itself must also be distinguished, since it may comprise the soul's recognition that it is not *a se* or it may mean a concentration on creatures. In so far as actual knowledge of the first sort is concerned, the soul cannot fail to know God's existence, though it would appear that the actual recognition of God may even here be 'implicit', but in so far as the soul is turned away from God by sin and error and rivets its attention on creatures, it may fail to realise God's existence. In this latter case, however, a further distinction must be introduced between knowledge of God *in ratione communi* and knowledge of God *in ratione propria*. For example, the man who places his happiness in riches or sensual pleasures knows God in a sense, since God is Beatitude, but he does not have a true notion of God, *in ratione propria*. Similarly the idolater recognises God *in communi*, for example, as 'Something', but not as He really is, *in ratione propria*. Such distinctions may indeed appear somewhat far-fetched, but Alexander is taking into account such facts as St. Paul's[3] saying that the heathen know God but have not glorified Him as God or St. John Damascene's declaration that the knowledge of God is naturally impressed on the mind.[4] The view that the human mind cannot be without any knowledge of God is characteristic of the Augustinian School; but, in view of the fact that idolaters and, at least, professed atheists exist, any writer who wishes to maintain such a view is bound to introduce the distinction between implicit and explicit knowledge or between knowledge of God *in ratione communi* and knowledge of God *in ratione propria*.

7. Alexander treats of the divine attributes of immutability, simplicity, infinity, incomprehensibility, immensity, eternity, unity, truth, goodness, power and wisdom, giving objections, his own reply to the general question and answers to the objections.

---

[1] 1, no. 26.   [3] *S.T.*, p.l., tr. 4, q. 19.
Romans 1.   [4] *De fide orthod.*, 1, cc. 1 and 3; *P.G.*, 94, 790 and 794.

Appeals to former writers and quotations from authorities like Augustine and Anselm are frequent, nor is the doctrine developed in a particularly original fashion, but the arrangement is systematic and careful, and a considerable amount of general philosophical reflection is included. For instance, when treating of the unity of the divine nature, Alexander begins by considering unity in general, defining *unitas* as *indivisio entis* and *unum* as *ens indivisum in se, divisum autem ab aliis*,[1] and goes on to consider the relation of unity to being, truth and goodness.[2] As regards the divine knowledge, Alexander maintains, following Augustine and Anselm, that God knows all things in and through Himself. The exemplar or eternal 'ideas' of creatures are in God, though, considered in themselves, they do not form a plurality but are identical with the one divine essence, so that it is by knowing Himself that God knows all things. How, then, does He know evil and sin? Only as defect, i.e. a defect from goodness. If light, says Alexander, following the Pseudo-Dionysius, were gifted with the power of knowing, it would know that this or that object was unreceptive of its action: it would not know darkness in itself without any relation to light. This involves, of course, the view that evil is nothing positive but rather a privation,[3] for, if evil were something positive, it would be necessary either to maintain dualism or to say that evil has an exemplar in God.

In treating of the divine will Alexander raises the question whether or not God can order actions which are against the natural law. The immediate origin of the question is a problem of Scriptural exegesis; how, for example, to explain God's order to the Israelites to despoil the Egyptians, but the question has, of course, a much wider significance. God, he answers, cannot order an action which would be formally contrary to the natural law, since this would be to contradict Himself; He cannot, for instance, will that man should have any other end but God, since God is essentially the final end. Nor could God order the Israelites to steal in the proper sense of the word, as implying an act directed against God Himself, a sin. God can, however, deprive the Egyptians of their property and so order the Israelites to take it. He can also order the Israelites to take something that belongs to another, since this affects only the *ordo ad creaturam*, but cannot order them to take it *ex cupiditate*, since this affects the *ordo ad Deum* and would involve self-contradiction on God's part.[4]

[1] I, no. 72.   [2] I, no. 73.   [3] Cf. I, nos. 123 ff.   [4] I, no. 276.

Similarly, God could order the prophet Osee to have intercourse with a woman who was not his wife, in so far as this act involved the *ordo ad creaturam*, but He could not order Osee to do this *ex libidine*, since this would involve the *ordo ad Deum*. Alexander's distinctions on this matter are somewhat obscure and not always satisfactory, but it is in any case clear that he did not believe that the moral law depends on God's arbitrary *fiat*, as Ockham was later to maintain.

8. God is the immediate Creator of the world, in regard both to matter and form, and the non-eternity of the world can be proved.[1] Thus Alexander rejects the Aristotelian notion of the eternity of the world, but he accepts the doctrine of hylomorphic composition. This composition is found in every creature, since 'matter' equals potentiality, but a more fundamental composition, also found in every creature, is that between the *quo est* and the *quod est*.[2] It may appear that this is the distinction between essence and existence, but it seems rather that the *quod est* refers to the concrete being, a man, for instance, and the *quo est* to the abstract essence, humanity, for example. In any case the distinction is a 'rational' distinction, since we can predicate the *quo est* of the *quod est*, in a certain sense at least, as when we say that this being is a man. There is no real distinction between a man and his humanity; yet the humanity is received. In God there is no dependence, no reception, and so no composition between the *quod est* (*Deus*) and the *quo est* (*Deitas*).

9. In accordance with his general spirit of reliance on tradition, Alexander of Hales gives and defends seven definitions or descriptions of the human soul.[3] For example, the soul may be defined as *Deiforme spiraculum vitae*,[4] or as *substantia quaedam rationis particeps, regendo corpori accommodata*[5] or as *substantia spiritualis a Deo creata, propria sui corporis vivificatrix*.[6] Other definitions are taken from St. Augustine, St. John Damascene and Seneca. The soul, insists Alexander, is not a substance simply in the sense that it is a substantial form, but it is an *ens in se*, a substance *simpliciter*, composed of 'intellectual' matter and form. If in this respect he follows the Platonic-Augustinian tradition, even suggesting that the soul must be a substance since it stands to the body as the sailor to the ship, he also insists that the soul vivifies the body.

[1] 2, no. 67. [2] 2, nos. 59-61. [3] 2, no. 321.
[4] Cf. *De sp. et an.*, c. 42, (placed among works of Augustine; P. L. 40, 811) and St. Aug., *De Gen. ad litt.*, 7 cc. 1-3.
[5] St. Aug., *De quant. an.*, c. 13, n. 22. [6] Cassiodorus, *De Anima*, c. 2.

An angel is also *spiraculum vitae*, but an angel is not *spiraculum vitae corporis*, whereas the soul is the principle of the body's life.

Each human soul is created by God out of nothing.[1] The human soul is not an emanation of God, part of the divine substance,[2] nor is it propagated in the manner postulated by the traducianists. Original sin can be explained without recourse to a traducianist theory.[3] The soul is united with the body after the manner of the union of form with matter (*ad modum formae cum materia*),[4] but this must be interpreted in an Augustinian sense, since the rational soul is joined to its body *ut motor mobili et ut perfectio formalis suo perfectibili*.[5] The soul has the three powers of the *vis vegetativa*, the *vis sensitiva* and the *vis intellectiva*, and though these powers are not to be called parts of the soul, in the strict sense of the word 'part',[6] they are yet distinct from one another and from the essence of the soul. Alexander, therefore, explains Augustine's assertion of the identity of the soul and its powers by saying that this identity is to be referred to the substance, not to the essence of the soul.[7] The soul cannot subsist without its powers nor are the powers intelligible apart from the soul, but just as *esse* and *operari* are not identical, so are *essentia* and *potentia* not identical.

The active and passive intellects are *duae differentiae* of the rational soul, the former referring to the spiritual form of the soul, the latter to its spiritual matter, and the active intellect is not separate from the soul but belongs to it.[8] But together with the Aristotelian classification of the rational powers of the soul Alexander gives also the classifications of St. Augustine and St. John Damascene and attempts to reconcile them. For example, 'intellect' in the Aristotelian philosophy refers to our power of acquiring knowledge of intelligible forms by means of abstraction,[9] and it corresponds, therefore, to the Augustinian *ratio*, not to the Augustinian *intellectus* or *intelligentia*, which has to do with spiritual objects. Intellect in the Aristotelian sense has to do with embodied forms and abstracts them from the *phantasmata*, but intellect in the Augustinian sense has to do with non-embodied, spiritual forms, and when there is question of knowing those forms which are superior to the human soul, the intellect is powerless unless it is illuminated by God.[10] Alexander provides no clear

[1] 2, nos. 329 and 322. [2] 2, no. 322. [3] 2, no. 327. [4] 2, no. 347.
[5] 2, no. 345. [6] 2, no. 351. [7] 2, no. 349. [8] 2, no. 372.
[9] 2, no. 368. [10] 2, no. 372.

explanation of what this illumination precisely is, but he at least makes it clear that he accepts the Aristotelian doctrine of abstraction in regard to the corporeal world, though in regard to the spiritual world the doctrine of Aristotle has to be supplemented by that of Augustine. One may also remark that Alexander was quite right in seeing in the Peripatetic classification a psychological analysis and in the Augustinian classification a division according to the objects of knowledge.

Alexander gives three definitions of free will, that of St. Anselm (*potestas servandi rectitudinem propter se*), that of St. Augustine (*facultas rationis et voluntatis, qua bonum eligitur gratia assistente et malum eadem desistente*) and that of St. Bernard (*consensus ob voluntatis inamissibilem libertatem et rationis indeclinabile iudicium*) and attempts to reconcile them.[1] *Liberum arbitrium* is common to God and the soul, but it is predicated neither universally nor equivocally, but analogically, primarily of God, secondarily of the creature.[2] In man it is one faculty or function of reason and will in union, and it is in this sense only that it may be termed distinct from reason and will: it is not in reality a separate power of the soul. Moreover, inasmuch as it is bound up with the possession of reason and will, it is inseparable from the soul, that is, as far as natural liberty is concerned. Following St. Bernard, Alexander distinguishes *libertas arbitrii* and *libertas consilii et complaciti* and declares that, while the latter may be lost, the former cannot.

10. Alexander of Hales is of interest, since his main work is a sustained effort of systematic thought, being a Scholastic presentation of the Christian theology and philosophy. In regard to form it belongs to the mediaeval period of the *Summas*, sharing in the merits and defects of that type of compilation, in their succinctness and orderly arrangement as in their aridity and absence of developments which, from our point of view, might be desirable. As regards content, on the one hand Alexander's *Summa* stands in close connection with the past, as the author is determined to be faithful to tradition and very frequently quotes Augustine or Anselm, Bernard or John Damascene, instead of developing his own arguments. This does not mean that he appeals simply to authority, in the sense of merely citing famous names, since he often quotes the arguments of his predecessors; but it does mean that the developed arguments which would have been desirable even at the time he wrote, are absent. However, his work is, of

---

[1] Cf. 2, nos. 393–6.   [2] 2, no. 402.

course, a *Summa*, and a *Summa* is admittedly a summary. On the other hand the work shows a knowledge of Aristotle, though he is not often explicitly mentioned, and it makes some use of the Peripatetic doctrine. There is always present, however, the desire to harmonise the elements taken from Aristotle with the teaching of Augustine and Anselm, and the general tendency is towards a contrast between the God-enlightened Christian thinkers on the one hand and the Philosophers on the other hand. It is not that Alexander gives the impression of being a polemical writer nor that he confuses philosophy and theology,[1] but he is chiefly concerned with the knowledge of God and of Christ. To say that, is simply to say that he was faithful to the tradition of the Augustinian School.

[1] Cf. 1, no. 2.

CHAPTER XXV

ST. BONAVENTURE—I

Life and works—Spirit—Theology and philosophy—Attitude to Aristotelianism.

1. St. Bonaventure, Giovanni Fidanza, was born at Bagnorea in Tuscany in the year 1221. Healed of a sickness while a child, through his mother's invocation of St. Francis of Assisi, he entered the Franciscan Order at a date which cannot be exactly determined. It may have been shortly before or after 1240, but in any case Bonaventure must have become a Franciscan in time to study under Alexander of Hales at Paris before the latter's death in 1245. The teaching of Alexander evidently made a great impression on his pupil, for in his *Praelocutio prooemio in secundum librum Sententiarum praemissa* Bonaventure declares that just as in the first book of the *Sentences* he has adhered to the common opinions of the masters, and especially to those of 'our master and father of happy memory Brother Alexander', so in the following books he will not stray from their footsteps.[1] In other words Bonaventure imbibed the Franciscan, i.e. the Augustinian, tradition, and he was determined to keep to it. It might perhaps be thought that this determination indicated simply a pious conservatism and that Bonaventure was ignorant of or at least ignored and adopted no definite and positive attitude towards the new philosophical tendencies at Paris; but the Commentary on the *Sentences* dates from 1250–1 (he started lecturing in 1248, on St. Luke's Gospel) and at that date Bonaventure cannot have made his studies at Paris and yet have been ignorant of the Aristotelian philosophy. Moreover, we shall see later that he adopted a very definite attitude towards that philosophy, an attitude which was not simply the fruit of ignorance but proceeded from reflection and reasoned conviction.

St. Bonaventure was involved in the same difficulties between regulars and seculars in which St. Thomas Aquinas was involved, and in 1255 he was excluded from the university, that is, he was refused recognition as a doctor and professor of the university

---

[1] Alexander appears again as 'our father and master' in 2 *Sent.*, 23, 2, 3; II, p. 547.

staff. He may have been readmitted in 1256, but in any case he was accepted, along with Aquinas, in October 1257, as a result of Papal intervention. He was then a professor of theology at the university, as far as acceptance was concerned, and would doubtless have proceeded to exercise that office had he not been elected Minister General of his Order on February 2nd, 1257. The fulfilment of the normal functions of his office would by itself have prevented his living the settled life of a university professor, but in addition there were differences of opinion at the time within the Order itself in regard to its spirit, practice and function, and Bonaventure was faced with the difficult task of maintaining or restoring peace. However, in 1259 he wrote the *Itinerarium mentis in Deum*, in 1261 his two lives of St. Francis, in 1267 or 1268 the *Collationes de decem praeceptis* (Lenten sermons), the *De decem donis Spiritus sancti* (about 1270), the *Collationes in Hexaëmeron* in 1273. The *Breviloquium* was written before 1257. The Commentaries on the Scriptures, short mystical treatises, sermons, and letters on points connected with the Franciscan Order make up his other writings at various periods of his life.

Although in 1265 Bonaventure had succeeded in inducing the Pope to rescind his appointment to the Archbishopric of York, he was appointed Bishop of Albano and Cardinal in 1273. In 1274 he was present at the Council of Lyons, where he preached on the reunion of the Eastern Church with Rome, but on the conclusion of the Council he died (July 15th, 1274) and was buried at Lyons in the presence of Pope Gregory X.

2. St. Bonaventure was not only himself a man of learning, but he also encouraged the development of studies within the Franciscan Order, and this may appear strange in the case of a Franciscan saint, when it can hardly be said that the founder had envisaged his friars devoting themselves to erudition. But it is, of course, perfectly clear to us, as it was to Bonaventure, that an order consisting largely of priests, with a vocation which involved preaching, could not possibly fulfil its vocation unless its members, at least those who were destined for the priesthood, studied the Scriptures and theology. But it was impossible to study Scholastic theology without acquiring a knowledge of philosophy, so that philosophical and theological studies were both necessary. And once this general principle was admitted, as admitted it must be, it was hardly practicable to set a limit to the degree of study. If the students were to be trained in philosophy and theology, they

had to have professors and the professors had not only to be competent themselves but to educate their successors. Moreover, if apostolic work might involve contact with learned men, perhaps also with heretics, one could not set on *a priori* grounds a limit to the study which might be advisable.

One might indeed multiply such practical considerations, which justified the development of studies within the Franciscan Order; but, as far as Bonaventure is concerned, there is an equally important consideration to be mentioned. St. Bonaventure was perfectly faithful to the spirit of St. Francis in regarding union with God as the most important aim in life; but he saw very well that this would scarcely be attained without knowledge of God and the things of God, or at least that such knowledge, so far from being a hindrance to union with God, should predispose the soul to closer union. After all, it was the study of the Scriptures and of theology which he recommended and himself pursued, not the study of questions which had no connection with God, and this was one of the reasons why he disliked and mistrusted the metaphysical philosophy of Aristotle, which had no place for personal communion with the Godhead and no place for Christ. There is, as M. Gilson has pointed out, a certain parallel between the life of St. Francis and the teaching of St. Bonaventure. For just as the former's personal life culminated in mystical communion with God, so the latter's teaching culminated in his mystical doctrine, and just as Francis had approached God through Christ and had seen, *concretely*, all things in the light of the divine Word, so Bonaventure insisted that the Christian philosopher must see the world in its relation to the creative Word. Christ, as he expressly says, is the *medium* or Centre of all sciences, and so he could not accept the Aristotelian metaphysic, which, so far from knowing anything of Christ, had rejected even the exemplarism of Plato.

In the end the Franciscan Order accepted Duns Scotus as its doctor *par excellence*; but though it was doubtless right in so doing and though Scotus was undoubtedly a man of genius, a thinker of great speculative and analytic ability, one may perhaps say that it was St. Bonaventure who stood nearer in thought, as in time, to the spirit of the Seraphic Father. Indeed, it is not without reason that he was accorded the title of the Seraphic Doctor.

3. St. Bonaventure's view of the purpose and value of study, determined as much by his own inclinations and spiritual tendencies as by his intellectual training under Alexander of Hales and

his membership of the Franciscan Order, naturally placed him in the Augustinian tradition. St. Augustine's thought centred round God and the soul's relation to God, and, since the man who is related to God is the concrete and actual man of history, who has fallen from grace and who has been redeemed by grace, Augustine dealt with man in the concrete and not with the 'natural man', not, that is, with man considered apart from his supernatural vocation and in abstraction from the operation of supernatural grace. This meant that St. Augustine could make no very rigid distinction between philosophy and theology, even though he distinguished between the natural light of reason and supernatural faith. There is, of course, adequate justification for treating in philosophy of man in 'the state of nature', since the order of grace is super-natural and one can distinguish between the order of grace and the order of nature; but the point I want to make is simply this, that if one is principally interested in the soul's advance to God, as Augustine and Bonaventure were, then one's thought will centre round man in the concrete, and man in the concrete is man with a supernatural vocation. Man considered in the 'state of nature', is a legitimate abstraction; but this legitimate abstraction will not appeal to one whose thought centres round the actual historical order. It is largely a question of approach and method. Neither Augustine nor Bonaventure would deny the distinction between the natural and the supernatural, but since they were both primarily interested in the actual historical man, who, be it repeated, is man with a supernatural vocation, they naturally tended to mingle theological and philosophical themes in one Christian wisdom rather than to make a rigid, methodological distinction between philosophy and theology.

It may be objected that in this case St. Bonaventure is simply a theologian and not a philosopher at all; but one can give a similar answer in the case of Bonaventure as in that of Augustine. If one were to define a philosopher as one who pursues the study of Being or the ultimate causes, or whatever other object one is pleased to assign to the philosopher, without any reference to revelation and prescinding *completely* from dogmatic theology, the Christian dispensation and the supernatural order, then of course neither Augustine nor Bonaventure could be termed a philosopher; but if one is willing to admit into the ranks of the philosophers all those who pursue what are generally recognised as philosophical themes, then both men must be reckoned philosophers. Bonaventure may sometimes treat, for instance, of the stages of the soul's ascent from knowledge of God through creatures to immediate and interior experience of God and he may speak of the stages without any clear demarcation of what is proper to theology and what is proper to philosophy; but that does not alter the fact that in treating of knowledge of God through creatures, he develops proofs of God's existence and that these proofs are reasoned arguments and so can be termed philosophical arguments. Again, Bonaventure's interest in the material world may be principally an interest in that world as the manifestation of God and he may delight to see therein *vestigia* of the Triune God, but that does not alter the fact that he holds certain opinions about the nature of the world and its constitution which are cosmological, philosophical, in character. It is true that to isolate Bonaventure's philosophical doctrines is in a sense to impair the integrity of his system; but there are philosophical doctrines in his system and this fact entitles him to a place in the history of philosophy. Moreover, as I shall mention shortly, he adopted a very definite attitude towards philosophy in general and the Aristotelian system in particular, and on this count alone he merits a place in the history of philosophy. One could hardly exclude Kierkegaard from the history of philosophy, although his attitude towards philosophy, in his understanding of the term, was hostile, for he philosophised about philosophy: still less can one exclude Bonaventure whose attitude was less hostile than that of Kierkegaard and who represents a particular standpoint in regard to philosophy, the standpoint of those who maintain not only that there is such a thing as Christian philosophy, but also that every independent philosophy is bound to be deficient and even partly erroneous as philosophy. Whether this standpoint is right or wrong, justified or unjustified, it deserves consideration in a history of philosophy.

Bonaventure was, then, of the Augustinian tradition; but it must be remembered that a great deal of water had flowed under the bridge since the time of Augustine. Since that time Scholasticism had developed, thought had been systematised, the Aristotelian metaphysic had been fully made known to the western Christian world. Bonaventure commented on the *Sentences* of Peter Lombard and he was acquainted with the thought of Aristotle: we would only expect, then, to find in his writings not only far more elements of Scholasticism and of the Scholastic method than in Augustine but also an adoption of not a few

Aristotelian ideas, for Bonaventure by no means rejected Aristotle lock, stock and barrel: on the contrary he respected him as a natural philosopher, even if he had no high opinion of his metaphysics, of his theology at least. Thus from the point of view of the thirteenth century the Bonaventurian system was a modern Augustinianism, an Augustinianism developed through the centuries and re-thought in relation to Aristotelianism.

4. What then was Bonaventure's view of the general relation of philosophy to theology and what was his view of Aristotelianism? The two questions can be taken together, since the answer to the first determines the answer to the second.

As has already been remarked, Augustine distinguished faith and reason, and Bonaventure naturally followed him, quoting Augustine's words to the effect that what we believe we owe to authority, what we understand to reason.[1] It follows from this, one might think, that philosophy and theology are two separate sciences and that an independent philosophy of a satisfactory character is, at least theoretically, possible. Indeed Bonaventure actually makes an explicit and clear distinction between dogmatic theology and philosophy. For example, in the *Breviloquium*[2] he says that theology begins with God, the supreme Cause, with whom philosophy ends. In other words, theology takes its data from revelation and proceeds from God Himself to His effects, whereas philosophy starts with the visible effects and argues to God as cause. Again, in the *De Reductione Artium ad Theologiam*[3] he divides 'natural philosophy' into physics, mathematics and metaphysics, while in the *In Hexaëmeron*[4] he divides philosophy into physics, logic and ethics.

In view of the above, how can it be maintained that St. Bonaventure did not admit of any rigid distinction between philosophy and theology? The answer is that he admitted a methodological distinction between the sciences and also a distinction of subject-matter, but insisted that no satisfactory metaphysic or philosophical system can be worked out unless the philosopher is guided by the light of faith and philosophises in the light of faith. For instance, he was well aware that a philosopher can arrive at the existence of God without the aid of revelation. Even if he had not been convinced of this by his own reason and by the testimony of the Scriptures, the philosophy of Aristotle would have been

---

[1] Aug., *De utilitate credendi*, 11, 25; Bonav., *Breviloq.*, 1, 1, 4.
[2] 1, 1.   [3] 4.   [4] 4, 2.

sufficient to persuade him of the fact. But he was not content to say that the knowledge of God so attained is incomplete and stands in need of the completion provided by revelation: he went further and stated that such purely rational knowledge is, and must be, in important points erroneous. This point he proved empirically. For example, 'the most noble Plotinus of the sect of Plato and Tully of the academic sect', in spite of the fact that their views on God and the soul were preferable to those of Aristotle, fell into error since they were unaware of the supernatural end of man, of the true resurrection of the body and of eternal felicity.[1] They could not know these things without the light of faith, and they fell into error precisely because they had not got the light of faith. Similarly, a mere metaphysician may come to the knowledge of the supreme Cause, but if he is a mere metaphysician he will stop there, and if he stops there he is in error, since he thinks of God otherwise than He is, not knowing that God is both one and three. 'Philosophical science is the way to other sciences; but he who wishes to stop there, falls into darkness.'[2] In other words, Bonaventure is not denying the power of the philosopher to attain truth, but he maintains that the man who is satisfied with philo- sophy, who is a mere philosopher, necessarily falls into error. It is one thing if a man comes by reason to know that there exists one God and then goes on to recognise, in the light of faith, that this unity is a unity of Nature in Trinity of Persons, and quite another thing if a man stops short at the unity of God. In the latter case the man affirms the unity of Nature to the exclusion of the Trinity of Persons, and to do this is to fall into error. If it is objected that it is not necessary to exclude the Trinity, since a philosopher may prescind from revelation altogether, so that his philosophical know- ledge, though incomplete, remains valid and true, Bonaventure would doubtless answer that if the man is simply a philosopher and rests in philosophy, he will be convinced that God is one in Nature and not three in Persons. In order to make due allowance for the completion, he must already possess the light of faith. The light of faith does not supply the rational arguments for God's existence (there is such a thing as philosophy), but it ensures that the philosophy remains 'open' and that it does not close in on itself in such a way that error results.

Bonaventure's view of Aristotelianism follows easily enough from these premises. That Aristotle was eminent as a natural

---

[1] *In Hexaëm.*, 7, 3 ff.   [2] *De Donis*, 3, 12.

philosopher, that is, in regard to sensible objects, Bonaventure admits: what he will not admit is that Aristotle was a true meta-physician, that is, that the metaphysics of Aristotle are satis-factory. Some people, seeing that Aristotle was so eminent in other sciences, have imagined that he must also have attained truth in metaphysics; but this does not follow, since the light of faith is necessary in order to form a satisfactory metaphysical system. Moreover, Aristotle was so competent in other sciences precisely because his mind and interests were of such a kind that he was not inclined to form a philosophy which should point beyond itself. Thus he refused to find the principle of the world outside the world: he rejected the ideas of Plato[1] and made the world eternal.[2] From his denial of the Platonic theory of ideas there followed not only the denial of creationism, but also the denial of God's knowledge of particulars, and of divine foreknow-ledge and providence.[3] Again, the doctrine of the unicity of the intellect is at least attributed to Aristotle by Averroes, and from this there follows the denial of individual beatitude or punishment after death.[4] In short, though all pagan philosophers have fallen into error, Aristotle was more involved in error than Plato or Plotinus.

Possibly one may obtain a clearer view of Bonaventure's notion of the relation of philosophy to theology if one bears in mind the attitude of the Catholic philosopher in practice. The latter works out arguments for the existence of God, for example, but he does not make himself an atheist for the time being nor does he deny his faith in the dogma of the Trinity: he philosophises in the light of what he already believes and he will not conclude to a unity in God of such a kind that it will exclude the Trinity of Persons. On the other hand his arguments for God's existence are rational arguments: in them he makes no reference to dogma, and the value of the proofs as such rests on their philosophical merits or demerits. The philosopher pursues his arguments, psychologically speaking, in the light of the faith which he already possesses and which he does not discard during his philosophical studies, and his faith helps him to ask the right questions and to avoid untrue conclu-sions, though he does not make any formal use of the faith in his philosophic arguments. The Thomist would, of course, say that the faith is to the philosopher an extrinsic norm, that the philo-sopher prescinds from his faith, even though he does not deny it,

[1] *In Hexaëm.*, 6, 2.   [2] *Ibid.*, 4.   [3] *Ibid.*, 2–3.   [4] *Ibid.*, 4.

and that a pagan could, theoretically at least, reach the same conclusions in philosophy. St. Bonaventure, however, would reply that, even though the philosopher may make no formal use of dogma in this or that metaphysical argument, he certainly philosophises in the light of faith and that this is something positive: the action of faith is a positive influence on the mind of the philosopher and without it he will inevitably fall into error. One cannot exactly say that St. Bonaventure believed only in a total Christian wisdom comprising indifferently philosophical and theological truths, since he admitted a classification of the sciences in which philosophy figures; but, this latter point once admitted, one can say that his ideal was the ideal of a Christian wisdom in which the light of the Word is shed not only on theological but also on philosophical truths, and without which those truths would not be attained.

I have argued that since St. Bonaventure certainly treated of philosophical questions, he has a claim to be included in a history of philosophy, and I do not see how this contention can be seriously disputed; but it remains true that he was a theologian, that he wrote as a theologian and that he did not really consider philosophical questions and problems for their own sake. St. Thomas Aquinas was also primarily a theologian, and he wrote primarily as a theologian; but he did consider philosophical problems at length and even composed some philosophical works, which St. Bonaventure did not do. The Commentary on the *Sentences* was not what we would to-day call a philosophical work. It seems, therefore, to constitute something of an exaggeration when M. Gilson maintains, in his magnificent study of St. Bonaventure's philosophical thought, that there is a Bonaventurian philosophical system, the spirit and content of which can be sharply defined. We have seen that St. Bonaventure recognised philosophy as a definite science, separate from theology; but as far as he himself is concerned, he might be called a philosopher *per accidens*. In a sense the same is true, of course, of any mediaeval thinker who was primarily a theologian, even of St. Thomas; but it is most relevant in the case of a thinker who was chiefly concerned with the soul's approach to God. Moreover, M. Gilson probably tends to exaggerate St. Bonaventure's hostility to pagan philosophy and to Aristotle in particular. I have indeed admitted that St. Bonaventure attacked the Aristotelian metaphysic (this is a fact which cannot be denied) and that he considered that any philosopher who is merely a philosopher will inevitably fall into error; but it is desirable in this connection to call to mind the fact that St. Thomas himself insisted on the moral necessity of revelation. On that point St. Bonaventure and St. Thomas were in agreement. They both rejected pagan philosophy where it was incompatible with Christianity, though they differed as to what precise points were to be rejected and how far one could go in following Aristotle.

However, though I think that M. Gilson's genius for capturing the peculiar spirit of the individual thinker and for setting it in clear relief leads him to exaggerate the systematic aspect of St. Bonaventure's philosophy and to find a greater opposition between the views of Bonaventure and Thomas in regard to the pagan philosophers than probably exists in actual fact, I cannot subscribe to the judgement of M. Fernand Van Steenberghen[1] that 'the philosophy of St. Bonaventure is an eclectic and neo-platonising Aristotelianism, put at the service of an Augustinian theology'. That Bonaventure made considerable use of Aristotelianism is perfectly true; but the inspiration of his philosophy is, in my opinion, what for want of a better word we call 'Augustinian'. As I remarked in regard to William of Auvergne, it depends to a large extent on one's point of view whether one calls those Augustinian theologians who adopted selected Aristotelian doctrines in philosophy incomplete Aristotelians or modified Augustinians; but in the case of a man whose whole interest centred round the soul's ascent to God, who laid such stress on the illuminative action of God and who, as M. Van Steenberghen himself states when criticising M. Gilson, never worked out a philosophy for its own sake, it seems to me that 'Augustinian' is the only fit word for describing his thought, if for no better reason than the principle that *maior pars trahit minorem* and that the spirit must take precedence of the letter.

---

[1] *Aristote en Occident*, p. 147.

CHAPTER XXVI

ST. BONAVENTURE—II: GOD'S EXISTENCE

Spirit of Bonaventure's proofs of God's existence—Proofs from sensible world—A priori knowledge of God—The Anselmian argument—Argument from truth.

1. WE have seen that St. Bonaventure, like St. Augustine, was principally interested in the soul's relation to God. This interest had an effect on his treatment of the proofs for God's existence; he was chiefly concerned to exhibit the proofs as stages in the soul's ascent to God or rather to treat them in function of the soul's ascent to God. It must be realised that the God to whom the proofs conclude is not, then, simply an abstract principle of intelligibility, but is rather the God of the Christian consciousness, the God to whom men pray. I do not, of course, mean to suggest that there is, ontologically, any discrepancy or any irreconcilable tension between the God of the 'philosophers' and the God of experience; but since Bonaventure is primarily interested in God as Object of worship and prayer and as goal of the human soul, he tends to make the proofs so many acts of drawing attention to the self-manifestation of God, whether in the material world or within the soul itself. Indeed, as one would expect, he lays more emphasis on proofs from within than on proofs from the material world, from without. He certainly does prove God's existence from the external sensible world (St. Augustine had done this) and he shows how from the knowledge of finite, imperfect, composite, moving and contingent beings man can rise to the apprehension of the infinite, perfect, simple, unchanging and necessary Being; but the proofs are not systematically elaborated, the reason for this being, not any inability on Bonaventure's part to develop the proofs dialectically, but rather his conviction that the existence of God is so evident to the soul through reflection on itself that extra-mental creation serves mainly to remind us of it. His attitude is that of the Psalmist, when he says: *Coeli enarrant gloriam Dei, et opera manuum eius annuntiat firmamentum.* Thus it is quite true that the imperfection of finite and contingent things demands and proves the existence of absolute perfection, God; but, asks St. Bonaventure in a truly Platonic manner, 'how could the intellect

know that this being is defective and incomplete, if it had no
knowledge of Being without any defect?'[1] In other words, the
idea of imperfection presupposes the idea of perfection, so that
the idea of perfection or the perfect cannot be obtained simply by
way of negation and abstraction, and consideration of creatures in
their finiteness and imperfection and dependence serves simply to
remind the soul or to bring the soul to a clearer awareness of what
is in some sense already evident to it, already known to it.

2. St. Bonaventure does not deny for a moment that God's
existence can be proved from creatures: on the contrary he affirms
it. In the Commentary on the *Sentences*[2] he declares that God can
be known through creatures as Cause through effect, and he goes
on to say that this mode of cognition is natural to man inasmuch
as for us sensible things are the means by which we arrive at the
knowledge of '*intelligibilia*', that is, objects transcending sense.
The Blessed Trinity cannot be proved in the same way, however,
by the natural light of reason, since we cannot conclude to the
Trinity of Persons either by denying certain properties or limitations of creatures or by the positive way of attributing to God
certain qualities of creatures.[3] St. Bonaventure thus teaches
clearly enough the possibility of a natural and 'philosophic'
knowledge of God, and his remark on the psychological naturalness
of this approach to God through sensible objects is Aristotelian in
character. Again, in the *In Hexaëmeron*[4] he argues that if there
exists being which is produced, there must be a first Being, since
there must be a cause: if there is being *ab alio*, there must be
Being *a se*: if there is a composite being, there must be simple
Being: if there is changeable being, there must be unchanged
Being, *quia mobile reducitur ad immobile*. The last statement is
obviously a reference to the Aristotelian proof of the existence of
the unmoved mover, though Bonaventure mentions Aristotle only
to say that he argued on these lines to the eternity of the world
and that on this point the Philosopher was wrong.

Similarly in the *De Mysterio Trinitatis*[5] Bonaventure gives a
series of brief arguments to show how clearly creatures proclaim
the existence of God. For instance, if there is *ens ab alio*, there
must exist *ens non ab alio*, because nothing can bring itself out of
a state of non-being into a state of being, and finally there must
be a first Being which is self-existent. Again, if there is *ens*

[1] *Itin.*, 3, 3.   [2] I, 3, 2: *Utrum, Deus sit cognoscibilis per creaturas.*
[3] I *Sent.*, 3, 4.   [4] 5, 29.   [5] I, I, 10-20.

possibile, Being which can exist and can not exist, there must be *ens necessarium*, being which has no possibility of non-existence, since this is necessary in order to explain the eduction of possible being into a state of existence; and if there is *ens in potentia*, there must be *ens in actu*, since no potency is reducible to act save through the agency of what is itself in act; and ultimately there must be *actus purus*, a Being which is pure Act, without any potentiality, God. Again, if there is *ens mutabile*, there must be *ens immutabile* because, as the Philosopher proves, motion has as its principle an unmoved being and exists for the sake of unmoved being, which is its final cause.

It might indeed appear from such passages, where Bonaventure employs Aristotelian arguments, that the statements to the effect that Bonaventure regarded the witness of creatures to God's existence in function of the soul's ascent to God and that he regarded the existence of God as a self-evident truth, cannot stand. But he makes it quite clear in various places[1] that he regards the sensible world as the mirror of God and sense-knowledge or knowledge obtained through sense and reflection on sensible objects as, formally, the first step in the stages of the soul's spiritual ascent, the highest stage of which in this life is the experimental knowledge of God by means of the *apex mentis* or *synderesis scintilla* (on this point he shows himself faithful to the tradition of Augustine and the Victorines), while in the very article of the *De Mysterio Trinitatis* where he gives the proofs cited he affirms emphatically that God's existence is indubitably a truth naturally implanted in the human mind (*quod Deum esse sit menti humanae indubitabile, tanquam sibi naturaliter insertum*). He goes on to declare that, in addition to what he has already said on this matter, there is a second way of showing that the existence of God is an indubitable truth. This second way consists in showing that what every creature proclaims is an indubitable truth, and it is at this point that he gives his succession of proofs or rather of indications that every creature really does proclaim God's existence. Subsequently he adds that there is a third way of showing that God's existence cannot be doubted and proceeds to give his version of St. Anselm's proof in the *Proslogium*. There can, then, be no doubt at all that Bonaventure affirmed that God's existence is self-evident and cannot be doubted: the question is rather what exactly he meant by this, and we will consider this in the next section.

[1] For example, in the *Itinerarium mentis in Deum*, c. 1.

3. In the first place St. Bonaventure did not suppose that everyone has an explicit and clear knowledge of God, still less that he has such a knowledge from birth or from the first use of reason. He was well aware of the existence of idolaters and of the *insipiens*, the fool who said in his heart that there is no God. The existence of idolaters does not, of course, cause much difficulty since idolaters and pagans do not so much deny the existence of God as possess a wrong idea of God; but what of the *insipiens*? The latter sees, for example, that the impious are not always punished in this world or at least that they sometimes appear to be better off in this world than many good people, and he concludes from this that there is no divine Providence, no divine Ruler of the world.[1] Moreover, he explicitly affirms,[2] in answer to the objection that it is useless to prove the existence of that which is self-evident, of that concerning which no one doubts, that though the existence of God is indubitable so far as objective evidence is concerned, it can be doubted *propter defectum considerationis ex parte nostra* because of want of due consideration and reflection on our part. Does not this look as if Bonaventure is saying no more than that objectively speaking, the existence of God is indubitable (i.e. the evidence, when considered, is indubitable and conclusive), but that subjectively speaking it may be doubted (i.e. because this or that human being does not give sufficient attention to the objective evidence); and if this is what he means when he says that God's existence is indubitable and self-evident, how does his position differ from that of St. Thomas?

The answer seems to be this. Although St. Bonaventure did not postulate an explicit and clear idea of God in every human being, still less any immediate vision or experience of God, he certainly postulated a dim awareness of God in every human being, an implicit knowledge which cannot be fully denied and which can become an explicit and clear awareness through interior reflection alone, even if it may sometimes need to be supported by reflection on the sensible world. The universal knowledge of God is, therefore, implicit, not explicit; but it is implicit in the sense that it can at least be rendered explicit through interior reflection alone. St. Thomas admitted an implicit knowledge of God, but by this he meant that the mind has the power of attaining to the knowledge of God's existence through reflection on the things of sense and by arguing from effect to cause, whereas St. Bonaventure meant

<hr/>

[1] *De Mysterio Trinitatis*, I, I, *conclusio*.   [2] *Ibid.*, 12.

something more by implicit knowledge, that is, virtual knowledge of God, a dim awareness which can be rendered explicit without recourse to the sensible world.

Application of this view to Bonaventure's concrete instances may make the understanding of it easier. For instance, every human being has a natural desire for happiness (*appetitus beatitudinis*). But happiness consists in the possession of the supreme Good, which is God. Therefore every human being desires God. But there can be no desire without some knowledge of the object (*sine aliquali notitia*). Therefore the knowledge that God or the supreme Good exists is naturally implanted in the soul.[1] Similarly, the rational soul has a natural knowledge of itself, because it is present to itself and is knowable by itself. But God is most present to the soul and is knowable. Therefore a knowledge of its God is implanted in the soul. If it be objected that while the soul is an object proportionate to its own power of knowing, God is not, the reply can be made that, if that were true, the soul could never come to the knowledge of God, which is obviously false.[2]

According to the above line of argument, then, the human will is naturally orientated towards the supreme Good, which is God, and not only is this orientation of the will inexplicable unless the supreme Good, God, really exists, but it also postulates an *a priori* knowledge of God.[3] This knowledge is not necessarily explicit or clear, since if it were there could be no atheists, but it is implicit and vague. If it is objected that an implicit and vague knowledge of this kind is not knowledge at all, it may be answered that an unprejudiced man who reflects on the orientation of his will towards happiness can come to realise that the direction of his will implies the existence of an adequate object and that this object, the complete Good, must exist and is what we call God. He will realise not only that in seeking happiness he is seeking God, but that this search implies an inkling, as it were, of God, since there can be no search for what is *entirely* unknown. Therefore, by reflecting on itself, on its own dependence and on its own desires for wisdom, peace or felicity, the soul can recognise God's existence and even God's presence, God's activity within it: it is not necessary for it to seek without, it has only to follow Augustine's

---

[1] *De Mysterio Trinitatis*, 1, 1, 7.   [2] *Ibid.*, 10.

[3] When speaking here of a 'natural' orientation of the will, I do not mean to use the term in a strictly theological sense, but rather in the sense that the will of man in the concrete is directed to the attainment of God, prescinding altogether from the question whether or not there is a *desiderium naturale videndi Deum*.

advice and enter within itself, when it will see that it was never without some inkling, some dim awareness, a 'virtual' knowledge of God. To seek for happiness (and every human being must seek for happiness) and to deny God's existence is really to be guilty of a contradiction, to deny with the lips what one affirms with the will and, in the case of wisdom at least, with the intellect. Whether this line of argument is valid or not, I do not propose to discuss here. It is obviously open to the objection, cogent or otherwise, that if there were no God, then the desire for happiness might be *frustra* or might have some other cause than the existence of God. But it is at least clear that St. Bonaventure did not postulate an innate idea of God in the crude form under which Locke later attacked innate ideas. Again, when St. Bonaventure declares that the soul knows God as most present to it, he is not affirming ontologism or saying that the soul sees God immediately: he means that the soul, recognising its dependence, recognises, if it reflects, that it is the image of God: it sees God in His image. As it necessarily knows itself, is conscious of itself, it necessarily knows God in at least an implicit manner. By contemplating itself it can make this implicit awareness explicit, without reference to the external world. Whether the absence of reference to the external world is more than formal, in the sense that the external world is not explicitly mentioned, is perhaps disputable.

4. We have seen that for St. Bonaventure the very arguments from the external world presuppose some awareness of God, for he asks how the mind can know that sensible things are defective and imperfect if it has no previous awareness of perfection, in comparison with which it recognises the imperfections of creatures. This point of view must be borne in mind when considering his statement of St. Anselm's proof, which he adopted from the *Proslogium*.

In the Commentary on the *Sentences*[1] St. Bonaventure resumes the Anselmian argument. God is that than which no greater can be thought. But that which cannot be thought not to exist is greater than that which can be thought not to exist. Therefore, since God is that than which no greater can be thought, God cannot be thought not to exist. In the *De Mysterio Trinitatis*[2] he quotes and states the argument at somewhat greater length and points out[3] that doubt may arise if someone has an erroneous notion of God and does not realise that He is that than which no

[1] I, 8, I, 2.   [2] I, I, 21–4.   [3] *Ibid., conclusio.*

greater can be thought. Once the mind realises what the idea of
God is, then it must also realise not only that the existence of God
cannot be doubted, but also that His non-existence cannot even
be thought. As regards Gaunilo's objection about the best of all
possible islands St. Bonaventure answers[1] that there is no parity,
for while there is no contradiction involved in the concept of a
Being than which no greater can be thought the idea of an island
than which no better can be thought is a contradiction in terms
(*oppositio in adiecto*), since 'island' denotes an imperfect being
whereas 'than which no better can be thought' denotes a perfect
being.

This method of argument may appear to be purely dialectical,
but, as already mentioned, Bonaventure did not regard the idea
of the perfect as obtained simply through a negation of the
imperfection of creatures, but as something presupposed by our
recognition of the imperfection of creatures, at least in the sense
that man's desire of the perfect implies a previous awareness. In
accordance with the Platonic-Augustinian tradition Bonaventure
presupposed, then, a virtual innate idea of the perfect, which can
be nothing else but God's imprint on the soul, not in the sense that
the soul is perfect but in the sense that the soul receives the idea
of the perfect or forms the idea of the perfect in the light of God,
through the divine illumination. The idea is not something
negative, the realisation of which in concrete existence can be
denied, for the presence of the idea itself necessarily implies God's
existence. On this point we may note the resemblance at least
between St. Bonaventure's doctrine and that of Descartes.[2]

5. St. Augustine's favourite argument for the existence of God
had been that from truth and the existence of eternal truths: St.
Bonaventure utilised this argument as well. For example, every
affirmative proposition affirms something as true; but the affirmation of any truth affirms also the cause of all truth.[3] Even if
someone says that a man is an ass, this statement, whether correct
or not, affirms the existence of the primal truth, and even if a man
declares that there is no truth, he affirms this negation as true and
so implies the existence of the foundation and cause of truth.[4] No
truth can be seen save through the first truth, and the truth

[1] *De Mysterio Trinitatis*, 1, 1, 6.
[2] Cf. E. Gilson's Commentary on the *Discours de la Méthode*, concerning the idea
of the perfect.
[3] 1 *Sent.*, 8, 1, 2, *conclusio*.
[4] *Ibid.*, 5 and 7. Cf. *De Mysterio Trinitatis*, 1, 1, 26.

through which every other truth is seen, is an indubitable truth: therefore, since the first Truth is God, God's existence is indubitable.[1]

But here again St. Bonaventure is not pursuing a merely verbal and dialectical argument. In a passage of the *In Hexaëmeron*,[2] where he points out that the man who says there is no truth contradicts himself, since he affirms it as true that there is no truth, he remarks that the light of the soul is truth, which so enlightens the soul that it cannot deny truth's existence without contradicting itself, and in the *Itinerarium mentis in Deum*[3] he maintains that the mind can apprehend eternal truths and draw certain and necessary conclusions only in the divine light. The intellect can apprehend no truth with certainty save under the guidance of Truth itself. To deny God's existence, then, is not simply to be guilty of a dialectical contradiction; it is also to deny the existence of the Source of that light which is necessary for the mind's attainment of certitude, the light *quae illuminat omnem hominem venientem in hunc mundum*: it is to deny the Source in the name of that which proceeds from the Source.

[1] *De Mysterio Trinitatis*, 1, 1, 25.   [2] 4, 1.   [3] 3, 2 ff.

CHAPTER XXVII

ST. BONAVENTURE—III
RELATION OF CREATURES TO GOD

Exemplarism—The divine knowledge—Impossibility of creation from eternity—Errors which follow from denial of exemplarism and creation—Likeness of creatures to God, analogy—Is this world the best possible world?

1. WE have seen that the lines of proof adopted by St. Bonaventure lead, not to the transcendent and self-enclosed unmoved Mover of Aristotle (though he does not hesitate to utilise the Philosopher's thought and to cite him when he considers it apposite), but to the God, at once transcendent and immanent, who is the Good which draws the will, the Truth which is not only foundation of all particular truths but also the Light which through its radiation within the soul makes the apprehension of certain truth possible, the Original which is mirrored in the human soul and in nature, and the Perfect which is responsible for the idea of the perfect within the human soul. In this way the arguments for God's existence stand in close relation to the spiritual life of the soul, revealing to it the God whom it has always sought, if only in a semi-conscious fashion, and the God who has always operated within it. The further knowledge of God which is given by revelation crowns the philosophic knowledge and opens up to the soul higher levels of spiritual life and the possibility of a closer union with God. Philosophy and theology are thus integrated together, the former leading on to the latter, the latter shedding light on the deeper meaning of the former.

A similar integration of philosophy and theology is seen in Bonaventure's doctrine of exemplarism, which in his eyes was a matter of the greatest importance. In the *In Hexaëmeron*[1] he makes exemplarism the central point of metaphysics. The metaphysician, he says, proceeds from the consideration of created, particular substance to the uncreated and universal substance (not in the pantheistic sense, of course), and so, in so far as he deals in general with the originating Principle of all things, he is akin to the natural philosopher who also considers the origins of

[1] 1, 13.

things, while in so far as he considers God as final end he shares his subject-matter to some degree with the moral philosopher, who also considers the supreme Good as the last end, giving his attention to happiness in the practical or speculative order. But in so far as the metaphysician considers God, the supreme Being, as exemplary cause of all things, he shares his subject-matter with no one else (*cum nullo communicat et verus est metaphysicus*). The metaphysician, however, if he will attain the truth concerning exemplarism, cannot stop at the mere fact that God is the exemplary Cause of all things, for the *medium* of creation, the express image of the Father and the exemplar of all creatures, is the divine Word. Precisely as a philosopher he cannot come to a certain knowledge of the Word, it is true;[1] but then if he is content to be a mere philosopher, he will fall into error: he must, enlightened by faith, proceed beyond mere philosophy and realise that the divine Word is the exemplary Cause of all things. The purely philosophic doctrine of exemplarism thus prepares the way for the theology of the Word and, conversely, the theology of the Word sheds light on the truth attained by philosophy, and in this sense Christ is the *medium* not only of theology, but also of philosophy.

An obvious conclusion in regard to Aristotle follows from this position. Plato had maintained a doctrine of archetypal ideas or essences and, whatever Plato himself may or may not have thought, the neo-Platonists at least 'located' these ideas in the divine mind, so that St. Augustine was enabled to praise Plato and Plotinus on this account; but Aristotle rejected the ideas of Plato and attacked his theory with bitterness (*in principio Metaphysicae et in fine et in multis aliis locis exsecratur ideas Platonis*).[2] In the *Ethics* too he attacks the doctrine, though the reasons he gives are worthless (*nihil valent rationes suae*).[3] Why did he attack Plato? Because he was simply a natural philosopher, interested in the things of the world for their own sake, and gifted with the *sermo scientiae* but not with the *sermo sapientiae*. In refusing to despise the sensible world and in refusing to restrict certainty to knowledge of the transcendent Aristotle was right as against Plato, who, in his enthusiasm for the *via sapientiae*, destroyed the *via scientiae*, and he rightly censured Plato on this point, but he himself went to the opposite extreme and destroyed the *sermo sapientiae*.[4] Indeed, by denying the doctrine of exemplarism,

---

[1] *In Hexaëm.*, 1, 13.   [2] *Ibid.*, 6, 2.   [3] *Ibid.*   [4] *Serm.*, 18.

Aristotle necessarily involved himself also in a denial of divine creation and divine providence, so that his error was worse than that of Plato. Now, exemplarism, on which Plato insisted, is, as we have seen, the key to and centre of metaphysics, so that Aristotle, by rejecting exemplarism, excluded himself from the rank of metaphysicians, in Bonaventure's understanding of the term.

But we have to go beyond Plato and learn from Augustine, to whom was given both the *sermo sapientiae* and the *sermo scientiae*,[1] for Augustine knew that the ideas are contained in the divine Word, that the Word is the archetype of creation. The Father knows Himself perfectly and this act of knowledge is the image and expression of Himself: it is His Word, His *similitudo expressiva*.[2] As proceeding from the Father the Word is divine, the divine Son (*filius* denotes the *similitudo hypostatica*, the *similitudo connaturalis*),[3] and as representing the Father, as *Imago*, as *similitudo expressa*, the Word expresses also, represents, all that the Father can effect (*quidquid Pater potest*).[4] If anyone could know the Word, he would know all knowable objects (*si igitur intelligis Verbum, intelligis omnia scibilia*).[5] In the Son or Word the Father expressed all that He could make (i.e. all possible beings are ideally or archetypally represented in the Word) and all that He would make.[6] The 'ideas' of all creatures, therefore, possible and actual, are contained in the Word, and these ideas extend not only to universals (*genera* and *species*), but also to singular or individual things.[7] They are infinite in number, as representing all possibles, as representing the infinite power of God.[8] But when it is said that there is an infinity of ideas in the Word, it is not meant that the ideas are really distinct in God, for there is no distinction in God save the distinctions of Persons: considered as existent in God, they are not distinct from the divine Essence or from one another (*ideae sunt unum secundum rem*).[9] It follows that, not being distinct from one another, they cannot form a real hierarchy.[10] However, although the ideas are ontologically one and there is no real distinction between them, there is a distinction of reason, so that they are *plures secundum rationem intelligendi*.[11] The foundation of the distinction cannot be any real distinction in the divine Essence, since not only are the ideas ontologically identical with the simple divine Essence, but also there is no real relation on the part of God to creatures, for He is in no way

---

[1] *Serm.*, 4, 19. [2] *Breviloq.*, 1, 3. [3] *Ibid.* [4] *In Hexaëm.*, 3, 4.
[5] *Ibid.* [6] *Ibid.*, 1, 13. [7] *1 Sent.*, 35, *art. unicus*, 4. [8] *Ibid.*, 5.
[9] *Ibid.*, 2. [10] *Ibid.*, 6. [11] *Ibid.*, 3.

dependent on creatures, though there is a real relation on the part of creatures to God and God and creatures are not the same, so that from the point of view of the things signified or connoted the ideas are distinct *secundum rationem intelligendi*. In God the ideas are one, but from our point of view they stand midway, as it were, between God the knower and the thing known, the distinction between them being, not a distinction in what they are (i.e. not a real distinction) but a distinction in what they connote, and the foundation of the distinction being the real multiplicity of the things connoted (i.e. creatures), not any real distinction in the divine Essence or in the divine knowledge.

Plato was working towards this theory of ideas, but as he lacked the light of faith, he could not ascend to the true doctrine but necessarily stopped short: in order to possess the true doctrine of ideas, it is necessary to have knowledge of the Word. Moreover, just as creatures were produced through the medium of the Word and could not have been produced save through the Word, so they cannot be truly known save in the light of their relation to the Word. Aristotle may have been, indeed was, an eminent natural philosopher, but he could not know truly even the selected objects of his studies, since he did not see them in their relation to the Word, as reflections of the divine Image.

2. God, then, in knowing Himself knows also all ways in which His divine essence can be mirrored externally. He knows all the finite good things which will be realised in time, and this knowledge Bonaventure calls the *cognitio approbationis*, the knowledge of those things to which His *beneplacitum voluntatis* extends. He knows too, not only all the good things which have been, are and will be in the course of time, but also all the evil things, and this knowledge Bonaventure calls the *cognitio visionis*. Needless to say St. Bonaventure does not mean to imply that evil has its exemplary idea in God: evil is rather the privation in the creature of that which it ought to have according to its idea in God. God knows too all possible things, and this knowledge Bonaventure terms *cognitio intelligentiae*. Its objects, the possibles, are infinite in number, whereas the objects of the two former types of knowledge are finite.[1] The three types of knowledge are, however, not accidents in God, distinct from one another: considered ontologically, as in God, they are one act of knowledge, identical with the divine essence.

[1] Cf. 1 *Sent.*, 39, 1, 2 and 3; *De Scientia Christi*, 1.

God's act of knowledge is infinite and eternal, so that all things are present to Him, even future events: there is no succession in the divine knowledge, and if we speak of God's 'foreknowledge' we must understand the futurity as concerning the objects themselves (in the sense that they succeed one another in time and are known by God to succeed one another in time), not as concerning the divine knowledge itself. God knows all things by one eternal act and there is no temporal succession in that act, no before and after; but God knows eternally, through that one act, things as succeeding one another in time. Bonaventure therefore makes a distinction in regard to the statement that God knows all things *praesenter*, pointing out that this *praesentialitas* must be understood in reference to God (*a parte cognoscentis*), not in reference to the objects known (*a parte cognitorum*). If it were understood in the latter sense, the implication would be that all things are present to one another, which is false, for they are not all present to one another, though they are all present to God.[1] Imagine, he says,[2] an eye fixed and motionless on a wall and observing the successive movements of all persons and things down below with a single act of vision. The eye is not changed, nor its act of vision, but the things under the wall are changed. This illustration, remarks Bonaventure, is really in no way like what it illustrates, for the divine knowledge cannot be pictured in this way; but it may help towards an understanding of what is meant.

3. If there were no divine ideas, if God had no knowledge of Himself and of what He can effect and will effect, there could be no creation, since creation demands knowledge on the Creator's part, knowledge and will. It is not a matter for surprise, then, that Aristotle, who rejected the ideas, rejected also creation and taught the eternity of the world, a world uncreated by God. At least he is judged to have held this by all the Greek Doctors, like Gregory of Nyssa, Gregory Nazianzen, Damascene and Basil, and by all the Arabian commentators, while you will never find Aristotle himself saying that the world had a beginning: indeed he censures Plato, the only Greek philosopher who seems to have declared that time had a beginning.[3] St. Bonaventure need not have spoken so cautiously, since Aristotle certainly did not believe in a divine creation of the world out of nothing.

St. Thomas saw no incompatibility, from the philosophical standpoint, between the idea of creation on the one hand and of

[1] Cf. 1 *Sent.*, 39, 2, 3, *conclusio*.   [2] *Ibid.*, 2, *conclusio*.   [3] *In Hexaëm.*, 6, 4.

the world's eternity on the other, so that for him the world might have had no beginning in time and yet have been created, that is, God might have created the world from eternity; but St. Bonaventure considered that the eternity of the world is impossible and that God could not have created it from eternity: if it is created, then time necessarily had a beginning. It follows that to deny that time had a beginning is to deny that the world was created, and to prove that eternal motion or time without a beginning is impossible is to prove that the world was created. St. Bonaventure, therefore, regarded the Aristotelian idea of the world's eternity as *necessarily* bound up with a denial of creation, and this opinion, which Aquinas did not share, sharpened his opposition to Aristotle. Both Bonaventure and Aquinas naturally accepted the *fact* of the world having had a beginning in time, since this is taught by theology; but they differed on the question of the abstract possibility of creation from eternity, and Bonaventure's conviction of its impossibility naturally made him resolutely hostile to Aristotle, since the latter's assertion of it as a fact, and not merely as a possibility, necessarily seemed to him an assertion of the independence of the world in relation to God, an assertion which he thought was primarily due to the Philosopher's rejection of exemplarism.

For what reasons did Bonaventure hold eternal motion or time without a beginning to be impossible? His arguments are more or less those which St. Thomas treats as objections to his own position. I give some examples.

(i) If the world had existed from eternity, it would follow that it is possible to add to the infinite. For instance, there would have been already an infinite number of solar revolutions, yet every day another revolution is added. But it is impossible to add to the infinite. Therefore the world cannot have always existed.[1]

St. Thomas answers[2] that if time is supposed eternal, it is infinite *ex parte ante*, but not *ex parte post*, and there is no cogent objection to an addition being made to the infinity at the end at which it is finite, that is, terminates in the present. To this St. Bonaventure retorts that, if one considers simply the past, then one would have to admit an infinite number of lunar revolutions. But there are twelve lunar revolutions to one solar revolution. Therefore we are faced with two infinite numbers, of which the one is twelve times greater than the other, and this is an impossibility.

---

[1] *2 Sent.*, 1, 1, 1, 2, 1.   [2] *Contra Gent.*, 2, 38.

(i:) It is impossible to pass through an infinite series, so that if time were eternal, that is, had no beginning, the world would never have arrived at the present day. But it is clear that it has.[1] To this St. Thomas answers[2] that every passing through or *transitus* requires a beginning term and a final term. But if time is of infinite duration, there was no first term and consequently no *transitus*, so that the objection cannot arise. St. Bonaventure retorts, however, that there is either a revolution of the sun which is infinitely distant, in the past, from to-day's revolution or there is not. If there is not, then the distance is finite and the series must have had a beginning. If there is, then what of the revolution immediately following that which is infinitely distant from to-day's? Is this revolution also infinitely distant from to-day's or not? If not, then the hypothetically infinitely distant revolution cannot be infinitely distant either, since the interval between the 'first' and second revolution is finite. If it is, then what of the third and fourth revolutions, and so on? Are they also infinitely distant from to-day's revolution? If they are, then to-day's revolution is no less distant from them than from the first. In this case there is no succession and they are all synchronous, which is absurd.

(iii) It is impossible for there to be in existence at the same time an infinity of concrete objects. But, if the world existed from eternity, there would be in existence now an infinity of rational souls. Therefore the world cannot have existed from eternity.[3]

To this Aquinas answers[4] that some say that human souls do not exist after the death of the body, while others maintain that only a (common) intellect remains: others again hold a doctrine of reincarnation, while certain writers maintain that an infinite number in act is possible in the case of things which are not ordered (*in his quae ordinem non habent*). St. Thomas naturally held none of the first three positions himself; as to the fourth position his own final attitude seems to be doubtful, so that Bonaventure was able to remark rather caustically that the theory of reincarnation is an error in philosophy and is contrary to the psychology of Aristotle, while the doctrine that a common intellect alone survives is an even worse error. As to the possibility of an infinite number in act he believed that it was an erroneous notion, on the ground that an infinite multitude could not be ordered and

---

[1] 2 *Sent.*, 1, 1, 1, 2, 3.   [3] *Contra Gent.*, 2, 38: *S.T.*, Ia, 46, 2, ad 6.
[2] 2 *Sent.*, 1, 1, 1, 2, 5.   [4] *Contra Gent.*, 2, 38.

so could not be subject to divine providence, whereas in fact all that God has created is subject to His providence.

Bonaventure was thus convinced that it can be philosophically proved, as against Aristotle, that the world had a beginning and that the idea of creation from eternity involves a 'manifest contradiction', since, if the world was created from nothing, it has being after not-being (*esse post non-esse*)[1] and so cannot possibly have existed from eternity. St. Thomas answers that those who assert creation from eternity do not say that the world was made *post nihilum*, but that it was made out of nothing, the opposite of which is 'out of something'. The idea of time, that is to say, is in no way implicated. In Bonaventure's eyes it is bad enough to say that the world is eternal and is uncreated (that is an error which can be philosophically disproved), but to say that it was created eternally out of nothing is to be guilty of a glaring contradiction, 'so contrary to reason that I should not have believed that any philosopher, of however little understanding, could have asserted it'.[2]

4. If the doctrine of exemplarism is denied, and if God did not create the world, it is only natural to conclude that God knows only Himself, that He moves only as final Cause, as object of desire and love (*ut desideratum et amatum*) and that He knows no particular thing outside Himself.[3] In this case God can exercise no providence, not having in Himself the *rationes rerum*, the ideas of things, by which He may know them.[4] The doctrine of St. Bonaventure is, of course, that God knows things other than Himself, but that He knows them in and through Himself, through the exemplary ideas. If he did not hold this, he would have to say that the divine knowledge receives a complement or perfection from things outside of God, depends in some way on creatures. In reality it is God who is completely independent: creatures are dependent on Him and cannot confer on His Being any perfection.[5] But if God is wrapped up in Himself, in the sense of having no knowledge of creatures and exercising no providence, it follows that the changes or movements of the world proceed either from chance, which is impossible, or from necessity, as the Arabian philosophers held, the heavenly bodies determining the movements of things in this world But if this be so, then all doctrine of reward or punishment in this life disappears, and in point of

---

[1] 2 *Sent.*, 1, 1, 1, 2, 6.   [2] *Ibid., conclusio.*   [3] *In Hexaëm.*, 6, 2.
[4] *Ibid.*, 3.   [5] Cf. 1 *Sent.*, 39, 1, 1, *conclusio.*

fact you will never find Aristotle speaking of a beatitude after the present life.[1] All these erroneous conclusions follow, then, from a denial of exemplarism, and it is more than ever clear that exemplarism is the key to a true metaphysic and that without it a philosopher will inevitably fall into errors if he discusses metaphysical themes.

5. From the doctrine of exemplarism it follows that there is some resemblance between creatures and God; but we have to distinguish various kinds of resemblance (*similitudo*) in order to attain to a correct idea of the relation of creatures to God, in order to avoid pantheism on the one hand and an independent world on the other hand. In the Commentary on the *Sentences*[2] Bonaventure says that *similitudo* may mean the agreement of two things in a third (and this he calls *similitudo secundum univocationem*), or it may mean the likeness of one thing to another without any agreement in a third thing being implied, and it is in this sense that the creature is said to be a likeness of God. In the same *conclusio* (*ad* 2) he distinguishes *similitudo univocationis sive participationis* and *similitudo imitationis, et expressionis*, going on to remark that the former does not hold good of the relation between creatures and God, because there is no common term (*quia nihil est commune*, because there is nothing common to God and the creature, that is). What he means is that God and the creature do not participate in Being, for example, *univocally* (precisely in the same sense), for if they did, the creature would be God and pantheism would result. The creature is, however, an imitation of God, of the idea of it in God, and God expresses the idea externally in the finite creature. Therefore, when Bonaventure rejects *similitudo participationis*, we must understand participation as referring here to participation in something common to both God and creatures in a univocal sense, in a *tertium commune* as he puts it.

It may be objected that if there is nothing common between God and creatures, there can be no likeness; but the community which St. Bonaventure wishes to exclude is *univocal* community, to which he opposes *analogy*. The likeness of the creature to God or of God to the creature (*exemplaris ad exemplatum*) is one kind of analogy, the other being that of *proportionalitas* (*habitudo duorum ad duo*), which exists between sets of things belonging to different genera, though in the case of the relation between creatures and

---

[1] *In Hexaëm.*, 6, 3.   [2] I, 35, *art. un.*, 1, *conclusio*.

God it is only the creature which is a member of a generic class. Thus a teacher is to his school what a pilot is to his ship, since both direct.[1] In the latter place Bonaventure distinguishes proportion in a wide sense, which includes proportionality, from proportion in a strict sense, which exists between members of the same class, arithmetical numbers, for example. Proportion in this strict sense cannot, of course, exist between God and creatures.

But though Bonaventure speaks of analogy of proportionality, the analogies to which he gives most attention are those of likeness, for he loved ever to find expressions, manifestations, images and *vestigia* of God in the world of creatures. Thus in the Commentary on the *Sentences*,[2] after excluding *similitudo per convenientiam omnimodam in natura*, which holds good between the three divine Persons, each of whom is identical with the divine Nature, and *similitudo per participationem alicuius naturae universalis*, which holds good between man and ass, in virtue of their common sharing in the *genus* animal, he admits proportionality, *similitudo secundum proportionalitatem* (giving here the example of the pilot and the charioteer in relation to the objects they direct) and *similitudo per convenientiam ordinis* (*sicut exemplatum assimilatur exemplari*), and proceeds to discuss these latter types of analogy, both of which, as already mentioned, hold good between the creature and God.

Every creature, says Bonaventure, is a *vestigium* of God, and the two types of analogy (that of the *exemplatum* to the *exemplar* and that of proportionality) apply to every creature, the first inasmuch as every creature is the effect of God and is conformed to God through the divine idea, the second inasmuch as the creature also produces an effect, although not in the same way as God produces His effect (*sicut enim Deus producit suum effectum, sic et agens creatum, licet non omnino*—for the creature is not the total cause of its effect). But though every creature is a *vestigium Dei*, this general conformity of the creature to God is comparatively remote (*magis de longinquo*): there is another type of likeness which is closer (*de proximo*) and more express and which applies only to certain creatures. All creatures are ordered to God, but only rational creatures are directed immediately (*immediate*) to God, the irrational creatures being directed to God mediately (*mediante creatura rationali*). The rational creature alone can know God, can

---

[1] Cf. 1 *Sent.*, 3, 1, *art. un.*, 2, 3 and 1 *ibid.*, 48, 1, 1, *conclusio.*
[2] 2 *Sent.*, 16, 1, 1, *conclusio.*

praise God and serve God consciously, and so has a greater conformity to God, a greater *convenientia ordinis* than the irrational creature. Now, the greater the *convenientia ordinis*, the greater and closer and more express is the resemblance or *similitudo*. This closer resemblance is called by Bonaventure *imago*. Every creature is, then, a *vestigium Dei*, but only the rational creature is an *imago Dei*, for it resembles God in the possession of spiritual powers through which it can become ever more and more conformed to God.

A similar difference between the rational creature and the irrational creature can be observed if we consider the analogy of proportionality. We can say, if we make the due allowances and reservations, that as God is to the creature, as Cause, that is, to His effect, so is the creature to its effect, and this holds good of all creatures in so far as they are active agents: but the effect considered is *extrinsic* to the agent, whereas in the case of rational creatures, and of them alone, there is an *intrinsic* proportion. In God there is a unity of Nature in a Trinity of Persons, and in man there is a unity of essence with a trinity of powers which are ordered to one another, the relation between them resembling in some way the relations in God (*quasi consimili modo se habentium, sicut se habent personae in divinis*). Bonaventure does not mean that we can prove the doctrine of the Trinity by the natural light of reason from a consideration of human nature, for he denies the possibility of any strict philosophical proof of the mystery, but rather that, guided by the light of faith, we can find an analogy to the Trinity in human rational nature. As the divine Nature is to the three divine Persons, so (*quasi consimili modo*) is the human nature or essence to its three powers. This is an 'express' resemblance of proportion and on this count, too, man is to be called the image of God. The word 'express' means that the Blessed Trinity has expressed itself, manifested itself to some degree in the constitution of human nature, and it is clear that for Bonaventure the analogy of resemblance (i.e. *exemplati ad exemplar*) is more fundamental than the analogy of proportionality, the latter being really treated in function of the former and having no concrete value or meaning apart from it.

In this way Bonaventure is enabled to order the hierarchy of being according to the closeness or remoteness of the likeness of the creature to God. The world of purely sensible things is the *vestigium* or *umbra Dei*, though here too he finds analogies of the

Trinity; it is the *liber scriptus forinsecus*. When considered by the
natural philosopher who is nothing else but a natural philosopher
it is simply *natura*: such a man cannot read the book of nature,
which is to him no *vestigium Dei* but something considered for its
own sake and without reference to God.[1] The rational creation
stands above the purely sensible creation and is *imago Dei*, God's
image in a special sense. But the phrase 'image of God' is itself
of wide application, for it covers not only the natural substance of
men and angels, but also that supernatural likeness which is the
result of the possession of grace. The soul in grace is the image of
God in a higher sense than is the purely natural essence of man,
and the soul in heaven, enjoying the beatific vision, is God's image
in a yet deeper sense. Thus there are many grades of analogy, of
likeness to God, and every grade must be seen in the light of the
Word, who is the consubstantial image of the Father and the
Exemplar of all creation, reflected in creatures according to various
degrees of 'expression'. We may note not only the constant
integration of theology and philosophy, but also the fact that the
various degrees of likeness stand in close relation to the intellectual
and spiritual life of man. The ascent to God on the part of the
individual involves a turning from the *umbra* or pure *vestigium*,
contemplated by the senses, from the *liber scriptus forinsecus*, to
the interior reflection of God, the *imago Dei*, the *liber scriptus
intrinsecus*, in obedience to the command of Augustine to go
within oneself, and so ultimately to the contemplation of God in
Himself, the *exemplatum*. The fact that St. Bonaventure does not
treat theology and philosophy in watertight compartments of their
own enables him to link up his vision of the universe with the
ascetical and mystical life and so to deserve the name of a
specifically Christian thinker.

6. Is this world, which reflects so admirably the Divine Creator,
the best of all possible worlds? We must first of all distinguish
two questions. Could God make a better world than this world?
Could God have made this world better than it is? Bonaventure
answers to the first question that God could have made a better
world than this one, by creating nobler essences, and that this
cannot be denied without thereby limiting the divine power. As
to the second question, it all depends on what you mean by
'world' and by 'better'. If you refer to the substances which go
to make up the world, are you asking if God could make these

[1] *In Hexaëm.*, 12, 15.

substances better in the sense of making them nobler essences or substances, that is, of a higher kind, or are you asking if God could make these substances accidentally better, that is, while remaining within their own class? If the former, then the answer is that God could indeed change the substances into nobler ones, but it would not be the same world and God would not be making *this* world better. If the latter, then God could make this world better. To take an example. If God changed a man into an angel, the man would no longer be a man and God would not be making the man better; but God could make a man better by increasing his intellectual power or his moral qualities.[1] Again, while God could make *this* man or *this* horse a better man or horse, we must make another distinction if it is asked whether or not God could make man as such better, in the sense of placing him in better conditions. Absolutely speaking He could; but if one takes into consideration the purpose for which He has placed man in these conditions or allowed him to be in these conditions it may very well be that He could not make man better. For instance, if God brought it about that all men served Him well, He would be making man better, from the abstract viewpoint; but if you consider the purpose for which God has permitted man to serve Him well or ill, He would not be making man better by practically overriding his free will. Finally, if anyone asks why, if God could have made or could make the world better, He has not done so or does not do so, no answer can be given save this, that He so willed and that He Himself knows the reason (*solutio non potest dari nisi haec, quia voluit, et rationem ipse novit*).[2]

---

[1] *1 Sent.*, 44, 1, 1, *conclusio*.   [2] *Ibid., ad* 4.

CHAPTER XXVIII

ST. BONAVENTURE—IV: THE MATERIAL CREATION

*Hylomorphic composition in all creatures—Individuation—Light—Plurality of forms—*Rationes seminales.

1. ST. BONAVENTURE accepted from his master, Alexander of Hales, the doctrine of the hylomorphic composition of all creatures, the doctrine, that is, that all creatures are composed of matter and form. By 'matter' he naturally meant in this connection the principle of potentiality in the widest sense, not 'matter' in the sense in which matter is opposed to spirit. 'Matter *considered in itself* is neither spiritual nor corporeal', and so in itself it is indifferent to the reception either of a spiritual or of a corporeal form; but as matter never exists on its own, apart from a definite form, and as, once united with a corporeal or a spiritual form, it always remains corporeal or spiritual as the case may be, it follows that the matter actually present in a corporeal substance is different in kind from that in a spiritual substance.[1] 'Matter' may be regarded in more than one way. If one considers it from the point of view of 'privation' (*per privationem*), abstracting from all forms, whether substantial or accidental, one must admit that it is essentially the same in all creatures, 'for if either kind of matter is separated from all forms and all accidents, no difference at all will be seen.' But if matter is looked at 'analogically' (*secundum analogiam*), that is, as potentiality, as a foundation for form, one must make a distinction. In so far as matter is looked on as providing a foundation for form in regard simply to being (*in ratione entis*), it is essentially the same in both spiritual and material creatures, since both spiritual and material creatures exist and subsist, and one can consider their existence by itself, without going on to consider the precise way in which they exist or the kind of things they are. This is the way in which the metaphysician considers matter, and so in the eyes of the metaphysician matter is similar in the spiritual and in the material creation. If, however, matter is simply looked on in its relation to motion in the wide sense, understood, that is, as change, then it is not the same in creatures which cannot undergo substantial

[1] 2 *Sent.*, 3, 1, 1, 2, *conclusio ad* 3.

change or receive corporeal forms and in creatures which can undergo substantial change and receive corporeal forms, though it can be considered as *analogically* similar, inasmuch as angels are susceptible of, for example, divine influence. It is the natural philosopher or *physicus* who considers matter in this light.

Without going into the further distinctions made by Bonaventure and without attempting a judgement on his doctrine, one can say, then, that his teaching on the hylomorphic composition of all creatures is this, that matter is the principle of potentiality as such. Both spiritual creatures and material creatures are dependent beings, not self-existent beings, so that if one considers potentiality in abstraction from all form, looking on it as a co-principle of being, one can say with the metaphysician that it is essentially the same in both. If, however, one considers it as actually existent, as standing in relation to a concrete form, spiritual or material, it is not the same in both. The natural philosopher considers bodies and is concerned with matter, not its abstract essence but as existent in a particular type of being, as standing in a concrete relation to a certain kind of form, material form; and matter considered in this light is not to be found in spiritual beings. One might, of course, object that if matter as concretely existing, as united with form, is of different kinds and remains different, there must be something in the matter itself which makes it of different kinds so that its similarity in the spiritual and material created orders cannot be more than analogical; but Bonaventure admits that matter never actually exists apart from form and only states that if it is considered, as it can be considered, in abstraction from all form, as mere potentiality, then it can justly be said to be essentially the same. If the angels have an element of possibility, of potency in them, as they have, they must possess matter, for matter, considered in itself, is simply possibility or potency. It is only in the Being who is pure Act, without any potency or possibility, that there is no matter.

2. Is matter the principle of individuation? Some thinkers, says St. Bonaventure,[1] have held this, relying on the words of Aristotle, but it is very difficult to see how that which is common to all can be the principal cause of distinction, of individuality. On the other hand, to say that form is the principle of individuation and to postulate an individual form, following on that of the species, is to go to the opposite extreme and forget that every created form

---

[1] 2 *Sent.*, 3, 1, 2, 3, *conclusio.*

is capable of having another like it. It is better to hold that individuation arises from the actual union of matter and form, which appropriate one another, as it were, through their union. Seals are made by different impressions in wax, and without the wax there would be no plurality of seals, but without the different impressions the wax would not become many. Similarly, matter is necessary if there is to be distinction and multiplicity, number, but form is also necessary, for distinction and multiplication presuppose the constitution of a substance through the elements composing it. That an individual substance is something definite, of a definite kind, it owes to the form; that it is *this* something, it owes principally to matter, by which the form acquires position in place and time. Individuation denotes principally something substantial, a substance composed of matter and form, but it also denotes something which can be considered an accident, namely number. Individuality (*discretio individualis*) denotes two things: individuation, which arises from the union of the two principles, matter and form, and secondly distinction from other things, which is the origin of number; but the former, individuation, is the more fundamental.

Personality (*discretio personalis*) arises when the form united with matter is a rational form, and it thus adds to individuality the dignity of rational nature, which holds the highest place among created natures and is not in potency to a higher substantial form. But there is something more needed to constitute personality, namely that within the *suppositum* there should be no other nature of a greater eminence and dignity, that within the *suppositum* rational nature should possess *actualem eminentiam*. (In Christ the human nature, though perfect and complete, does not possess *actualem eminentiam* and so is not a person.) 'We must say, then, that just as individuality arises from the existence of a natural form in matter, so personality arises from the existence of a noble and supereminent nature in the substance.'[1]

As St. Bonaventure attributes matter, that is, a spiritual matter, to the angels, he is able to admit a plurality of individual angels within the same species without being compelled like St. Thomas to postulate as many angelic species as there are angels. The Scriptures show us some angels as exercising similar functions and this argues similarity of being, while the 'love of charity' also demands the multiplicity of angels within the same species.[2]

[1] 2 *Sent.*, 3, 1, 2, 2, *conclusio.*   [2] *Ibid.*, 3, 1, 2, 1.

3. In the corporeal creation there is one substantial form which all bodies possess, and that is the form of light.[1] Light was created on the first day, three days before the production of the sun, and it is corporeal in Bonaventure's opinion, although St. Augustine interpreted it as meaning the angelic creation. It is not, properly speaking, a body but the form of a body, the first substantial form, common to all bodies and the principle of their activity, and the different kinds of body form a graded hierarchy according as they participate more or less in the form of light. Thus the 'empyrean' stands at one end of the scale, while the earth stands at the other, the lower end. In this way the light-theme, so dear to the Augustinian School and going back to Plotinus and to Plato's comparison of the Idea of the Good with the sun, finds a prominent place in the philosophy of St. Bonaventure.

4. Obviously if Bonaventure holds that light is a substantial form, possessed by all bodies, he must also hold that there can be a plurality of substantial forms in one substance. For him there was no difficulty in holding this, since he looked on form as that which prepares the body for the reception of other and higher perfections. While for St. Thomas substantial form was limitative and definitive, so that there could not be more than one substantial form in a body, for St. Bonaventure form looked forward and upward, so to speak, not so much rounding off the body and confining it as preparing it for fresh possibilities and perfections. In the *In Hexaëmeron*[2] he went so far as to say that it is mad (*insanum*) to say that the final form is added to prime matter without there being something which is a disposition for it or in potency to it, without there being any intermediate form, and he loved to trace a parallel between the order of grace and that of nature. Just as the gift of knowledge disposes for the gift of wisdom and is not itself annulled by the gift of wisdom, and as the gifts do not annul the theological virtues, so one form predisposes for a higher form and the latter, when received, does not expel the former but crowns it.

5. It is only to be expected that St. Bonaventure, who avowedly walked in the path of the Augustinian tradition, would accept the doctrine of *rationes seminales*, especially as this doctrine lays emphasis on the work of the Creator and diminishes the independence of the natural agent, though it was no more a 'scientific' doctrine in the modern sense of the word with St. Bonaventure

[1] Cf. *2 Sent.*, 13.   [2] 4, 10.

than it was with St. Augustine: for both men it was required by true Scriptural exegesis or rather by a philosophy which took account of the data of revelation, with the added reason in the case of Bonaventure that it was held by his great predecessor, the Christian philosopher *par excellence*, who was endowed with both the *sermo sapientiae* and the *sermo scientiae*. 'I believe that this position should be held, not only because reason inclines us to it, but also because the authority of Augustine, in his literal commentary on Genesis, confirms it.'[1]

Bonaventure thus maintained a certain *latitatio formarum* of things in matter; but he refused to accept the view that the forms of things which appear in time were originally in matter in an *actual* state, like a picture covered with a cloth, so that the particular agent only uncovers them, like the man who takes away the cloth from the picture and lets the painting appear. On this view contrary forms, which exclude one another, would have been together at the same time in the same subject, which is impossible. Nor will he accept the view that God is the only efficient cause in the eduction of forms, for this would mean that God creates all forms in the way in which He creates the rational human soul and that the secondary agent really does nothing at all, whereas it is clear that its activity really does contribute something to the effect. The second of these two views would reduce or do away altogether with the activity of the created agent, while the first would reduce it to a minimum, and Bonaventure is unwilling to accept either of them. He prefers the view 'which seems to have been that of Aristotle, and which is now commonly held by the doctors of philosophy and theology' that 'almost all the natural forms, corporeal forms at least, such as the forms of the elements and the forms of mixtures, are contained in the potency of matter and are reduced to act (*educuntur in actum*) through the action of a particular agent.' But this may be understood in two ways. It may mean that matter has both the potency to receive the form and the inclination to co-operate in the production of the form and that the form to be produced is in the particular agent as in its effective and original principle, so that the eduction of the form takes place by the multiplication of the form of the agent, as one burning candle may light a multitude of candles, or it may mean that matter contains the form to be educed not only as that in which and, to a certain extent, by which the form is produced, but

[1] *2 Sent.*, 7, 2, 2, 1, *resp.*

also as that from which it is produced, though in the sense that it is concreated with matter and in matter, not as an actual, but as a virtual form. On the first hypothesis the forms are not indeed said to be created by the agent, since they do not come out of nothing, though all the same a new essence would seem to be produced in some way, whereas on the second hypothesis no new essence or quiddity is produced, but the form which existed in potency, virtually, is reduced to act, is given a new *dispositio*. The second hypothesis, therefore, attributes less to the created agent than does the first, since the created agent simply brings it about that what formerly existed in one way now exists in another way, whereas on the first hypothesis the created agent would produce something positively new, even if not by way of creation out of nothing. If a gardener tends the rose-tree so that the rose-buds can blossom into roses he does something, it is true, but less than he would do, were he to produce a rose-tree from some other form of tree. Bonaventure, then, anxious to avoid attributing even the semblance of creative powers to a created agent, chooses the hypothesis which attributes less to the work of the created agent and more to the work of the Creator.

The forms which are educed were, therefore, originally in matter in a virtual state. These virtual forms are the *rationes seminales*. A *ratio seminalis* is an active power, existing in matter, the active power being the essence of the form to be educed, standing to the latter in the relation of *esse incompletum* to *esse completum* or of *esse in potentia* to *esse in actu*.[1] Matter is thus a *seminarium* or seed-bed in which God created in a virtual state corporeal forms which would be successively educed therefrom. This applies not only to the forms of inorganic things, but also to the souls of brutes and vegetables. Needless to say, Bonaventure is aware that the activity of particular agents is necessary for the birth of an animal, but he will not admit the traducianist theory, according to which the soul of a new animal is produced by 'multiplication' of the soul of the parent, yet without any diminution on the latter's part, as this theory implies that a created form can produce a similar form out of nothing.[2] What happens is that the parent animals act upon what they have themselves received, the seminal principle, the seminal principle being an active power or potency containing the new soul in germ, though the activity of the parents is necessary in order that the virtual should become actual. Bonaventure thus

[1] 2 *Sent.*, 18, 1, 3, *resp.*   [2] *Ibid.*, 2, 15, 1, 1, *resp.*

steers a middle course between attributing too little or nothing to the created agent and attributing what seemed to him too much, his general principle being that while God produces things out of nothing, a created agent can only produce something which already existed in potency, by which he means in a virtual state.[1] It is, however, useless to look for an exact description and explanation of the concrete working of his theory of *rationes seminales*, since it is founded partly on authority and partly on *a priori* philosophic reasoning, not on empirical observation or scientific experiment.

[1] Cf. 2 *Sent.*, 7, 2, 2, 2, *resp*.

CHAPTER XXIX

ST. BONAVENTURE—V: THE HUMAN SOUL

Unity of human soul—Relation of soul to body—Immortality of the human soul—Falsity of Averroistic monopsychism—Knowledge of sensible objects and of first logical principles—Knowledge of spiritual realities—Illumination—The soul's ascent to God—Bonaventure as philosopher of the Christian life.

1. WE have seen that, according to St. Bonaventure, the souls of animals are produced *seminaliter*; but this does not, of course, apply to the human soul, which is produced immediately by God, created by Him out of nothing. The human soul is the image of God, called to union with God, and on this count (*propter dignitatem*) its production was fittingly reserved by God to Himself. This reasoning involves theology, but Bonaventure also argues that since the human soul is immortal, incorruptible, its production can be effected only by that Principle which has life and perpetuity of itself. The immortality of the human soul implies a 'matter' in the soul which is incapable of being an element in substantial change; but the activity of created agents is confined to working on transmutable matter and the production of a substance with unchangeable matter transcends the power of such agents. It follows that the traducianist view must be rejected, even if Augustine inclined to it on occasion because he thought that thereby he could explain the transmission of original sin.[1]

What is it that God creates? It is the entire human soul, not the rational faculty alone. There is one soul in man, endowed with rational and sensitive faculties, and it is this soul which God creates. The body was contained *seminaliter* in the body of Adam, the first man, and it is transmitted by means of the seed, but this does not mean that the body has a sensitive soul, educed from the potency of matter and distinct from the created and infused rational soul. The seed contains, it is true, not only the superfluity of the father's nourishment, but also something of his *humiditas radicalis*, so that there is in the embryo, before the infusion of the soul, an active disposition towards the act of sensation, a kind of inchoate sensibility; but this disposition is a

[1] 2 *Sent.*, 18, 2, 3, *resp.*

disposition to accomplishing the act of sensation through the power of the soul, once it has been infused: at the complete animation of the embryo by the infusion of the soul this inchoate sensibility ceases or rather it is subsumed under the activity of the soul, which is the principle of sensation as well as of intellection. In other words, St. Bonaventure is careful to maintain the continuity of life and the reality of parentage while avoiding any splitting of the human soul into two.[1]

2. The human soul is the form of the body: St. Bonaventure uses the Aristotelian doctrine against those who hold that the souls of all men are one substance. 'The rational soul is the act and entelechy of the human body: therefore since human bodies are distinct, the rational souls which perfect those bodies will also be distinct':[2] the soul is an existent, living, intelligent form, endowed with liberty.[3] It is present wholly in every part of the body, according to the judgement of St. Augustine, which Bonaventure approves as preferable to the theory that the soul is primarily present in a determinate part of the body, the heart for instance. 'Because it is the form of the whole body, it is present in the whole body; because it is simple, it is not present partly here and partly there; because it is the sufficient moving principle (*motor sufficiens*) of the body, it has no particular situation, is not present at one point or in a determinate part.'[4]

But though Bonaventure accepts the Aristotelian definition of the soul as the form of the body, his general tendency is Platonic and Augustinian in character, inasmuch as he insists that the human soul is a spiritual substance, composed of spiritual form and spiritual matter. It is not enough to say that there is in the soul composition of *ex quo est* and *quod est*, since the soul can act and be acted upon, move and be moved, and this argues the presence of 'matter', the principle of passivity and mutability, though this matter transcends extension and corruptibility, being spiritual and not corporeal matter.[5] This doctrine may seem to contradict the admitted simplicity of the human soul, but Bonaventure points out[6] that 'simplicity' has various meanings and degrees. Thus 'simplicity' may refer to absence of quantitative parts, and this the soul enjoys, being simple in comparison with corporeal things; or it may refer to absence of constitutive parts, and this the soul does not enjoy. The main point, however,

---

[1] Cf. 2 *Sent.*, 30, 3, 1 and 31, 1, 1.   [2] *Ibid.*, 18, 2, 1, *contra* 1.
[3] *Breviloq.*, 2, 9.   [4] 1 *Sent.*, 8, 2, *art. un.*, 3, *resp.*   [5] 2 *Sent.*, 17, 1, 2, *resp.*
[6] *Ibid.*, *ad* 5.

is that the soul, though form of the body and moving principle of the body, is also much more than this, and can subsist by itself, being *hoc aliquid*, though as a *hoc aliquid* which is partly passive and mutable it must have in it spiritual matter. The doctrine of the hylomorphic composition of the human soul is thus calculated to ensure its dignity and its power of subsistence apart from the body.

If the soul is composed of form and spiritual matter, it follows that it is individuated by its own principles.[1] If this is so, however, why is it united with the body, for it is an individual spiritual substance in its own right? The answer is that the soul, even though a spiritual substance, is so constituted that it not only can inform a body but also has a natural inclination to do so. Conversely, the body, though also composed of matter and form, has an *appetitus* for being informed by the soul. The union of the two is thus for the perfection of each and is not to the detriment of either soul or body.[2] The soul does not exist simply, or even primarily, to move the body[3] but to enjoy God; yet it exercises its powers and potentialities fully only in informing the body and it will one day, at the resurrection, be reunited with the body. Aristotle was ignorant of this, and it is not to be wondered at that he was ignorant of it, for 'a philosopher necessarily falls into some error, unless he is aided by the light of faith'.[4]

3. The doctrine of the hylomorphic composition of the human soul naturally facilitates the proof of its immortality, since Bonaventure does not link the soul so closely to the body as does the Aristotelian doctrine; but his favourite proof is the one drawn from the consideration of the ultimate purpose of the soul (*ex consideratione finis*). The soul seeks for perfect happiness (a fact which no one doubts, 'unless his reason is entirely perverted'). But no one can be perfectly happy if he is afraid of losing what he possesses: on the contrary, it is this very fear which makes him miserable. Therefore, as the soul has a natural desire for perfect happiness, it must be naturally immortal. This proof presupposes the existence of God, of course, and the possibility of attaining perfect happiness, as also the existence of a natural desire for human happiness; but it was Bonaventure's favourite proof because of its spiritual character, because of its connection with

---

[1] 2 *Sent.*, 18, 2, 1, *ad* 1.
[2] *Ibid.*, 18, 2, 1, *ad* 6.
[3] Cf., *ibid.* 17, 1, 2, *ad* 6.
[4] *Ibid.*

the movement of the soul towards God: it is for him the *ratio principalis*, the principle argument.[1]

In a rather similar way he argues[2] from consideration of the formal cause, from the nature of the soul as the image of God. Because the soul has been made for the attainment of happiness, which consists in the possession of the supreme Good, God, it must be capable of possessing God (*capax Dei*) and so must be made in His image and likeness. But it would not be made in the likeness of God if it were mortal. Therefore it must be immortal. Again (arguing *ex parte materiae*), Bonaventure declares that the form of the rational soul is of such dignity that it makes the soul like to God, with the result that the matter which is united to this form (i.e. the spiritual matter) finds its satisfaction and completion in union with this form alone, so that it must be likewise immortal.

Bonaventure gives other arguments, such as that from the necessity of sanctions in an after life[3] and from the impossibility of God's bringing the good to frustration. In the latter proof he argues that it would be against divine justice for that which has been well done to tend towards evil and frustration. Now, according to all moral teaching a man ought to die rather than commit injustice. But if the soul were mortal, then its adhesion to justice, lauded by all moral philosophers, would come to nothing, and this is contrary to divine justice. More Aristotelian in character are the arguments drawn from the soul's power of reflection on itself and from its intellectual activity, which has no intrinsic dependence on the body, to prove its superiority to corporeal matter and its incorruptibility.[4] But though these Aristotelian proofs are probably more acceptable to us, as presupposing less and as involving no theology, in Bonaventure's eyes it was the proofs borrowed from Augustine or dependent on his line of thought which were more telling, especially that from the desire of beatitude. The Augustinian proof from the soul's apprehension of and assimilation to abiding truth is given by Bonaventure,[5] but it does not appear as a *potissimus modus* of proving the soul's immortality. This qualification is reserved for the proofs drawn from the desire for beatitude.

If it were objected against Bonaventure that this form of proof presupposes the desire for union with God, for beatitude in the full sense, and that this desire is elicited only under the action of grace

---

[1] 2 *Sent.*, 19, 1, 1, *resp.*   [2] *Ibid.*   [3] *Ibid., sed contra* 3, 4.
[4] *Ibid.*, 7 ff.; cf. *De Anima*, Bk. 3.   [5] 2 *Sent.*, 11.

and so belongs to the supernatural order and not to the order of nature, which is the object of the philosopher's study, the Saint would doubtless answer that he had not the slightest intention of denying the work of grace or its supernatural character, but that, on the other hand, the true philosopher considers the world and human life as they are and that one of the data is precisely the desire for complete happiness. Even though the desire may imply the operation of grace, it is a datum of experience and so can be taken into account by the philosopher. If the philosopher cannot explain it without recourse to theology, that is only another proof of Bonaventure's principle that no philosophy can be satisfactory unless it is illumined by the light of faith. In other words, whereas the 'Thomist' systematically eliminates from the data of experience all he knows to be supernatural and then, as philosopher, considers the resulting 'nature', the Bonaventurian philosopher starts from nature in the sense of the given. It is perfectly true that grace is not something 'given' in the sense of visible or apprehensible with certainty by unaided reason, but some of its effects are given in experience and these the philosopher will take into account, though he cannot explain them without reference to theology. The Thomist approach and the Bonaventurian approach are therefore different and one cannot force them into the same mould without thereby distorting one or the other.

4. All that has been said on the human soul implies the individuality of the soul, but Bonaventure was quite aware of the Averroistic interpretation of Aristotle and argued explicitly against it. Averroes maintained that both the active and passive intellects survive death, and, whatever Aristotle himself may have taught, his commentator, Averroes, certainly held that these intellects are not individual to each man, are not parts or faculties of individual men, but rather unitary substances, cosmic intelligences. Such a position, however, is not only heretical and contrary to the Christian religion, but also against reason and experience.[1] It is against reason since it is clear that the intellectual soul is a perfection of man as man, and men differ from one another, are individual persons, as men and not merely as animals, which would be the case if the rational soul were numerically one in all men. It is against experience, since it is a matter of experience that different men have different thoughts. And it is no good saying that this difference of thoughts comes simply from the diversity of *species*

<hr>

[1] 2 *Sent.*, 18, 2, 1, *resp.*

in the imaginations of different men, that is, that it is only the perishable imagination, fed by the senses, which is different in different individuals, since men differ in ideas, for example, of the virtues, which are not founded on sense-perception and which are not abstracted from imaginative *species*. Nor, from the point of view of Bonaventure, is it a good argument to say that the intellectual soul is independent of the body and cannot therefore be individuated by it, for the soul is not individuated by the body but by the union of its two constitutive principles, spiritual matter and spiritual form.

5. In regard to the content of the soul's knowledge of sensible objects, this is dependent on sense-perception, and St. Bonaventure agrees with Aristotle that the soul does not of itself have either knowledge or species of sensible objects: the human intellect is created in a state of 'nudity' and is dependent on the senses and imagination.[1] The sensible object acts upon the sense organ and produces therein a sensible species, which in turn acts upon the faculty of sensation, and then perception takes place. It will be noted that St. Bonaventure, in admitting a passive element in sensation, departs from the teaching of St. Augustine; but at the same time he holds that the faculty of sensation or sensitive power of the soul judges the content of sensation, for example, that this is white, the passive reception of the species being attributed primarily to the organ, the activity of the judgement to the faculty.[2] This judgement is not, of course, a reflective judgement, it is rather a spontaneous awareness; but it is possible because the faculty of sensation is the sensitive faculty of a rational soul, for it is the soul which communicates to the body the act of sensation.[3] The separate sensations, for example, of colour and touch, are unified by the 'common sense' and preserved in the imagination, which is not the same as 'memory' if the latter is taken as meaning *recordatio* or recalling at will.[4] Finally the active and passive intellects, working in co-operation, abstract the species from the imagination. The active and passive intellects are not two powers, one of which can work without the other, but are two 'differences' of the same intellectual faculty of the soul. We can indeed say that the active intellect abstracts and the passive intellect receives, but Bonaventure qualifies this statement by affirming that the

---

[1] 2 *Sent.*, 3, 2, 2, 1, *resp.* and *ad* 4.   [2] *Ibid.*, 8, 1, 3, 2, *ad* 7.
[3] *Ibid.*, 25, 2, *art. un.*, 6, *resp*.
[4] *Ibid.*, 7, 2, 1, 2, *resp.*, where Bonaventure distinguishes memory as habit, *retentio speciei*, from the act of remembering or *recordatio*.

passive intellect has the power of abstracting the species and judging it, though *only* with the help of the active intellect, while the active intellect is dependent for its activity of knowing on the information of the passive intellect by the species. There is, in fact, only one complete act of intellection and the active and passive intellects co-operate inseparably in that act.[1]

Clearly, then, apart from various 'Augustinianisms', such as the refusal to make a real distinction between the faculties of the soul, Bonaventure's view of the way in which we acquire our knowledge of sensible objects approximates more or less closely to the Aristotelian theory. He admits that the soul, in regard to knowledge of such objects, is originally a *tabula rasa*,[2] and he has no place for innate ideas. Moreover, this rejection of innate ideas applies also to our knowledge of first principles. Some people have said that these principles are innate in the active intellect, though acquired as far as the possible intellect is concerned; but such a theory agrees neither with the words of Aristotle nor with the truth. For if these principles were innate in the active intellect, why could it not communicate them to the possible intellect without the help of the senses, and why does it not know these principles from the very beginning? A modified version of innatism is that the principles are innate in their most general form while the conclusions or particular applications are acquired, but it would be difficult on such a view to show why a child does not know the first principles in their general form. Moreover, even this modified innatism contradicts both Aristotle and Augustine. Bonaventure doubtless considered that a theory which united against it both Aristotle and Augustine could not possibly be true. It remains then to say that the principles are innate only in the sense that the intellect is endowed with a natural light which enables it to apprehend the principles in their universality when it has acquired knowledge of the relevant species or ideas. For example, no one knows what a whole is or a part until he has acquired the species or idea in dependence on sense-perception; but once he has acquired the idea, the light of the intellect enables him to apprehend the principle that the whole is greater than the part.[3] On this matter, therefore, St. Bonaventure is at one with St. Thomas.

6. But though we have no innate knowledge of sensible objects or of their essences or of the first principles, logical or mathematical,

[1] 2 *Sent.*, 24, 1, 2, 4.   [2] *Ibid., resp.*   [3] *Ibid.*, 39,˙1, 2, *resp.*

it does not follow that our knowledge of purely spiritual realities is acquired through sense-perception. 'God is not known by means of a likeness drawn from sense',[1] but rather by the soul's reflection on itself. It has no intuitive vision of God, of the divine Essence, in this life, but it is made in the image of God and is orientated towards God in desire and will, so that reflection on its own nature and on the direction of the will enables the soul to form the idea of God without recourse to the external sensible world. In this sense the idea of God is 'innate', though not in the sense that every man has from the beginning a clear, explicit and accurate knowledge of God. The direction of the will, its desire for complete happiness, is the effect of the divine action itself, and reflection on this desire manifests to the soul the existence of the Object of the desire, which indeed it already knows in a kind of vague awareness, though not necessarily in an explicit idea. 'The knowledge of this truth (God's existence) is innate in the rational mind, inasmuch as the mind is an image of God, by reason of which it has a natural appetite and knowledge and memory of Him in whose image it has been made and towards whom it naturally tends, that it may find its beatitude in Him.'[2] The knowledge of God is of various kinds: God has a comprehensive knowledge of Himself, the Blessed know Him clearly (*clare et perspicue*), we know Him partly and in a hidden way (*ex parte et in aenigmate*), this last knowledge being contained implicitly in or implied by the knowledge which each soul has that it did not always exist and must have had a beginning.[3]

The knowledge of the virtues too must be 'innate' in the sense that it is not derived from sense-perception. An unjust man can know what justice is; but obviously he cannot know justice through its presence in his soul, since he does not possess it, nor can he know it through abstraction from sensible species, since it is not an object of sense and has no likeness in the world of sense. He cannot know it by its effects, since he would not recognise the effects of justice unless he previously knew what justice is, just as one cannot recognise the effects of a man's activity as the effects of a man's activity unless one previously knows what a man is.[4] There must, therefore, be some *a priori* or innate knowledge of the virtues. In what sense is it innate? There is no innate idea (*species innata*) in the sense of a clear idea or intellectual likeness of the

[1] 2 *Sent.*, 39, 1, 2, *resp.*   [2] *De Myst. Trinit.*, 1, 1, *resp.*
[3] *Ibid.*, 1, 2, *ad* 14.   [4] *De Scientia Christi*, 4, 23.

virtue in the mind from its beginning; but there is present in the
soul a natural light by which it can recognise truth and rectitude,
and there is present also an affection or inclination of the will.
The soul knows, therefore, what rectitude is and what an affection
or inclination of the will is, and in this way it recognises what
rectitudo affectionis is. As this is charity, it knows what charity is,
even though it does not actually possess the virtue of charity.[1]

Thus the knowledge of the virtues is innate in much the same
sense as knowledge of God is innate, not as an innate explicit
species or idea, but in the sense that the soul has in itself all the
material needed to form the explicit idea, without its being
necessary for it to have recourse to the sensible world. The innate
idea of Bonaventure is a virtually innate idea. Of course, there is
one big difference between our knowledge of the virtues and our
knowledge of God, for while we can never apprehend the essence
of God in this life, it is possible to apprehend the essence of the
virtues. However, the ways in which we arrive at the knowledge
of the virtues and of God are similar, and we can say that the soul
possesses an innate knowledge of the principles necessary to its
conduct. It knows by self-reflection what God is, what fear is and
what love is, and so it knows what it is to fear and to love God.[2]
If anyone quotes in opposition the Philosopher's dictum *nihil est
in intellectu, quod prius non fuerit in sensu*, the answer is that the
dictum must be understood as having reference only to our knowledge of sensible objects or to the acquisition of ideas which are
capable of being formed by abstraction from sensible species.[3]

7. But though Bonaventure will not admit that the first principles relating to the world about us or indeed even the first
principles of conduct are explicit in the mind from the beginning
or infused into it from outside apart from any activity on
the part of the mind itself, it does not follow that he is prepared
to dispense with the Augustinian doctrine of illumination; on the
contrary, he regards it as one of the cardinal truths of metaphysics.

Truth is the *adaequatio rei et intellectus*,[4] involving the object
known and the knowing intellect. In order that truth in this
sense, truth apprehended, may exist, conditions are required on
the part of both subject and object, immutability on the part of
the latter and infallibility on the part of the former.[5] But if
Bonaventure is prepared to echo in this way the words of the

[1] *1 Sent.*, 17, 1, *art. un.*, 4, *resp.*   [2] *2 Sent.*, 39, 1, 2, *resp.*   [3] *Ibid.*
[4] *1 Sent.*, *resp.*, *ad* 1, 2, 3; cf. *Breviloq.*, 6, 8.   [5] *De Scientia Christi*, 4, *resp.*

Theaetetus, demanding these two conditions in order that *cognitio certitudinalis*, certain knowledge, may exist, he is necessarily faced by problems similar to those with which Plato and Augustine were faced, since no created object is strictly immutable and all sensible objects are perishable, while the human mind is not *of itself* infallible in regard to any class of object. It must, therefore, receive help from outside, and naturally Bonaventure had recourse to the Augustinian theory of illumination, which commended itself to him, not only because St. Augustine had held it but also because it emphasised both the dependence of the human intellect on God and the interior activity of God in the human soul. For him it was both an epistemological truth and a religious truth, something that could be established as a necessary conclusion from a study of the nature and requirements of certainty and also something upon which one could profitably meditate in the religious sense. Indeed for him the intellectual life and the spiritual life cannot properly be separated.

The human mind, then, is subject to change, doubt, error, while the phenomena which we experience and know are also changeable. On the other hand it is an indubitable fact that the human mind does possess certainties and knows that it does so and that we apprehend unchanging essences and principles. It is only God, however, who is unchanging, and this means that the human mind is aided by God and that the object of its certain knowledge is seen in some way as rooted in God, as existing in the *rationibus aeternis* or divine ideas. But we do not apprehend these divine ideas directly, in themselves, and Bonaventure points out with Augustine that to follow the Platonic doctrine is to open the door to scepticism, since if the only certain knowledge attainable is direct knowledge of the eternal archetypes or exemplars and if we have no direct knowledge of these archetypes, the necessary conclusion is that true certainty is unattainable by the human mind.[1] On the other hand it is not sufficient to say that the *ratio aeterna* influences the mind in this sense only, that the knowing mind attains not the eternal principle itself but only its influence, as a *habitus mentis*, for the latter would be itself created and subject to the same conditions as the mind of which it is a disposition.[2] The *rationes aeternae*, then, must have a direct regulative action on the human mind, though remaining themselves unseen. It is they which move the mind and rule the mind in its certain judgements,

---

[1] *De Scientia Christi*, 4, resp.   [2] *Ibid.*

enabling it to apprehend the certain and eternal truths in the speculative and moral orders and to make certain and true judgements even concerning sensible objects: it is their action (which is the divine illumination) which enables the mind to apprehend the unchanging and stable essences in the fleeting and changing objects of experience. This does not mean that Bonaventure contradicts the approval he has given to Aristotle's doctrine about our knowledge of the sensible world, but it does mean that he considers it insufficient. Without sense-perception we would never indeed know sensible objects and it is quite true that the intellect abstracts, but the divine illumination, the direct action of the *ratio aeterna*, is necessary in order that the mind should see in the object the reflection of the unchanging *ratio* and be able to make an infallible judgement concerning it. Sense-perception is required in order that our ideas of sensible objects should arise, but the stability and necessity of our judgements concerning them are due to the action of the *rationes aeternae*, since neither are the sensible objects of our experience unchanging nor are the minds which know them infallible of themselves. The dim (*obtenebratae*) species of our minds, affected by the obscurity of *phantasmata*, are thus illumined in order that the mind should know. 'For if to have real knowledge means to know that a thing cannot possibly be otherwise, it is necessary that He alone should cause us to know, who knows the truth and has the truth in Himself.'[1] Thus it is through the *ratio aeterna* that the mind judges all those things which we know by the senses.[2]

In the *Itinerarium Mentis in Deum*[3] St. Bonaventure describes how the exterior sensible objects produce a likeness of themselves (*similitudo*) first in the medium and then through the medium on the organ of sense, and so on the interior sense. The particular sense, or the faculty of sensation acting through the particular sense, judges that this object is white or black or whatever it is, and the interior sense that it is pleasing, beautiful, or the reverse. The intellectual faculty, turning itself towards the species, asks why the object represented is beautiful and judges that it is beautiful because it possesses certain characteristics. But this judgement implies a reference to an idea of beauty which is stable and unchanging, not bound to place or time. This is where the divine illumination comes in, namely to explain the judgement in its unchanging and supertemporal aspect by reference to the

---

[1] *In Hexaëm.*, 12, 5.   [2] *Itin. Mentis in Deum*, 2, 9.   [3] 2, 4-6.

directing and regulating *ratio aeterna*, not to supersede or annul the work of the senses or the activity of abstraction. All sensible objects which are known enter the mind through the three psychical operations of *apprehensio, oblectatio* and *diiudiçatio*, but the latter operation, to be true and certain, must be a judgement made in the light of the *rationes aeternae*.

Now, as we have seen earlier, the *rationes aeternae* are ontologically identified and are in fact identical with the Word of God. It follows then that it is the Word which illuminates the human mind, that Word which enlightens every man who comes into the world. 'Christ is the interior teacher and no truth is known except through Him, not by His speaking as we speak, but by His enlightening us interiorly. . . . He is intimately present to every soul and by His most clear ideas He shines upon the dark ideas of our minds.'[1] We have no vision of the Word of God and though the light is so intimately within us, it is invisible, *inaccessibilis*: we can only reason to its presence from observation of its effects.[2] Thus Bonaventure's doctrine of illumination and his interpretation of Augustine do not involve ontologism. His doctrine completes his seemingly Aristotelian affirmation of abstraction and his denial of the properly innate character of even the first principles, giving to his teaching a peculiar and non-Aristotelian, an Augustinian flavour and colour. We abstract, yes, but we could not seize the intelligible and stable merely through abstraction, we need also the divine illumination: we can attain knowledge of moral principles by interior reflection, yes, but we could not apprehend their unchanging and necessary character without the regulative and guiding action of the divine light. Aristotle failed to see this, he failed to see that as we cannot know creatures fully unless we see them as *exemplata* of the divine *exemplar*, so we cannot form certain judgements about them without the light of the divine Word, of the *Ratio Aeterna*. Exemplarism and illumination are closely connected, the true metaphysician recognises them both: Aristotle recognised neither.

8. There are only four faculties of the soul, the vegetative and sensitive powers, the intellect and the will; but Bonaventure distinguishes various 'aspects' of the soul and, in particular, of the intellect or mind according to the objects to which its attention is directed and according to the way in which it is directed. It would, then, be a mistake to suppose that he meant that *ratio*,

---

[1] *In Hexaëm.*, 12, 5.   [2] *Ibid.*, 12, 11.

intellectus, intelligentia and *apex mentis* or *synderesis scintilla*[1] are all different faculties of the soul:. they denote rather different functions of the rational soul in its upward ascent from sensible creatures to God Himself. In the Commentary on the *Sentences*[2] he says expressly that the division of the reason into lower and higher (*ratio inferior* and *ratio superior*) is not a division into different faculties: it is a division into *officia* and *dispositiones*, which is something more than a division into aspects (*aspectus*). The lower reason is reason turned towards sense-objects, the higher reason is reason turned towards intelligible objects, and the term 'lower' and 'higher' thus refer to different functions or *officia* of the same faculty; but there is this further point to be added, that the reason as directed to intelligibles is strengthened and invigorated, whereas, directed to sensibles, it is in a manner weakened and drawn down, so that although there is only one *ratio*, the distinction between higher and lower reason corresponds not only to different functions, but also to different dispositions of the one reason.

The stages of the upward ascent of the mind scarcely need much elaboration, as they are more connected with ascetical and mystical theology than with philosophy in our sense; but since they are connected with philosophy in Bonaventure's understanding of the term, it is as well to touch very briefly on them, as they illustrate his tendency to integrate philosophy and theology as closely as possible. Walking in the footsteps of Augustine and the Victorines Bonaventure traces the ascending stages of the soul's life, stages which correspond to different potentialities in the soul and lead him from the sphere of nature into that of grace. Starting from the soul's sensitive powers (*sensualitas*) he shows how the soul may see in sensible objects the *vestigia Dei*, as it contemplates sensible things first as God's effects, then as things wherein God is present, and he accompanies it, with Augustine, as it retires within itself and contemplates its natural constitution and powers as the image of God. The intelligence is then shown contemplating God in the soul's faculties renewed and elevated by grace, being enabled to do so by the Word of God. In this stage, however, the soul still contemplates God in His image, which is the soul itself, even if elevated by grace, and it can proceed yet further, to the contemplation of God *supra nos*, first as Being, then as the Good. Being is good, and the contemplation of God as Being, the perfection of being, leads to the realisation of Being as the Good, as

[1] *Itin. Mentis in Deum*, 1, 6.   [2] *2 Sent.*, 24, 1, 2, 2, *resp.*

diffusivum sui, and so to the contemplation of the Blessed Trinity. Further than this the intellect cannot go: beyond lies the luminous darkness of mystical contemplation and ecstasy, the *apex affectus* outstripping the mind. The will, however, is a faculty of the one human soul and, though issuing from the substance of the soul, it is not a distinct accident, so that to say that the affection of the will outruns the intellect is simply to say that the soul is united to God by love so closely that the light infused into it blinds it. There can be but one higher stage, reserved for the next life, and that is the vision of God in heaven.

9. It will be remembered that the three cardinal points of metaphysics for Bonaventure are creation, exemplarism and illumination. His metaphysical system is thus a unity in that the doctrine of creation reveals the world as proceeding from God, created out of nothing and wholly dependent on Him, while the doctrine of exemplarism reveals the world of creatures as standing to God in the relation of imitation to model, of *exemplatum* to *exemplar*, while the doctrine of illumination traces the stages of the soul's return to God by way of contemplation of sensible creatures, of itself and finally of Perfect Being. The divine action is always emphasised. Creation out of nothing can be proved, as also God's presence and activity in creatures and especially in the soul itself: God's action enters into the apprehension of every certain truth, and even though for the establishment of the higher stages of the soul's ascent the data of theology are required, there is in a sense a continuity of divine action in increasing intensity. God acts in every man's mind when he attains truth, but at this stage the activity of God is not all-sufficient, man is also active through the use of his natural powers: in the higher stages God's action progressively increases until in ecstasy God takes possession of the soul and man's intellectual activity is superseded.

Bonaventure may thus be termed the philosopher of the Christian life, who makes use of both reason and faith in order to produce his synthesis. This integration of reason and faith, philosophy and theology, is emphasised by the place he accords to Christ, the Word of God. Just as creation and exemplarism cannot be properly understood apart from the realisation that it is through the Word of God that all things are created and that it is the Word of God, the consubstantial image of the Father, whom all creatures mirror, so illumination in its various stages cannot be properly understood apart from the realisation that it is the Word of God who illumines every man, the Word of God who is the door through which the soul enters into God above itself, the Word of God who, through the Holy Spirit whom He has sent, inflames the soul and leads it beyond the limitations or its clear ideas into the ecstatic union. Finally it is the Word of God who shows us the Father and opens to us the beatific vision of heaven. Christ in fact is the *medium omnium scientiarum*,[1] of metaphysics as of theology, for though the metaphysician as such cannot attain to knowledge of the Word through the use of the natural reason, he can form no true and certain judgements without the illumination of the Word, even if he is quite unaware of this, and in addition his science is incomplete and vitiated by its incompleteness unless it is crowned by theology.

[1] *In Hexaëm.*, I, II.

CHAPTER XXX

ST. ALBERT THE GREAT

Life and intellectual activity—Philosophy and theology—God—
Creation—The soul—Reputation and importance of St. Albert.

1. ALBERT THE GREAT was born in 1206 at Lauingen in Swabia, but left Germany in order to study the arts at Padua, where he entered the Dominican Order in 1223. After having lectured in theology at Cologne and other places he received the doctorate at Paris in 1245, having Thomas Aquinas among his pupils from 1245 to 1248. In the latter year he returned to Cologne accompanied by Thomas, in order to establish the Dominican house of studies there. His purely intellectual work was interrupted, however, by administrative tasks which were laid upon him. Thus from 1254 until 1257 he was Provincial of the German Province and from 1260 until 1262 Bishop of Ratisbon. Visits to Rome and the preaching of a Crusade in Bohemia also occupied his time, but he seems to have adopted Cologne as his general place of residence. It was from Cologne that he set out for Paris in 1277, to defend the opinions of Thomas Aquinas (died 1274), and it was at Cologne that he died on November 15th, 1280.

It is clear enough from his writings and activities that Albert the Great was a man of wide intellectual interests and sympathies, and it is hardly to be expected that a man of his type would ignore the rise of Aristotelianism in the Parisian Faculty of Arts, especially as he was well aware of the stir and trouble caused by the new tendencies. As a man of open mind and ready intellectual sympathy he was not one to adopt an uncompromisingly hostile attitude to the new movement, though, on the other hand, he was not without strong sympathy for the neo-Platonist and Augustinian tradition. Therefore, while he adopted Aristotelian elements and incorporated them into his philosophy, he retained much of the Augustinian and non-Aristotelian tradition, and his philosophy bears the character of a transitional stage on the way to that fuller incorporation of Aristotelianism which was achieved by his great pupil, St. Thomas Aquinas. Moreover, being primarily a theologian, Albert could not but be sensible of the important points on which Aristotle's thought clashes with Christian doctrine, and that uncritical acceptance of Aristotle which became fashionable in a section of the Faculty of Arts was impossible for him. It is indeed no matter for surprise that though he composed paraphrases on many of the logical, physical (for example, on the *Physics* and *De Caelo et Mundo*), metaphysical and ethical works (*Nicomachean Ethics* and *Politics*) of Aristotle, he did not hesitate to point out errors committed by the Philosopher and published a *De unitate intellectus* against Averroes. His declared intention in composing the paraphrases was to make Aristotle intelligible to the Latins, and he professed to give simply an objective account of Aristotle's opinions; but in any case he could not criticise Aristotle without showing something of his own ideas, even if his commentaries are for the most part impersonal paraphrases and explanations of the Philosopher's works.

It has not been found possible to determine with any degree of accuracy the dates of Albert's writings or even the order in which he published them, but it seems that the publication of his Commentary on the *Sentences* of Peter Lombard and the *Summa de Creaturis* antedate the publication of his paraphrases of Aristotle's works. He also published Commentaries on the books of the Pseudo-Dionysius. The *De unitate intellectus* appears to have been composed after 1270, and the *Summa theologiae*, which may be a compilation due to other hands, remained unfinished.

One cannot pass over in silence a remarkable side of Albert's interest and activity, his interest in the physical sciences. In an enlightened manner he insisted on the necessity of observation and experiment in these matters, and in his *De vegetalibus* and *De animalibus* he gives the results of his own observations as well as ideas of earlier writers. Apropos of his description of trees and plants he remarks that what he has set down is the result of his own experience or has been borrowed from authors whom he knows to have confirmed their ideas by observation, for in such matters experience alone can give certainty.[1] His speculations are often very sensible, as when, in opposition to the idea that the earth south of the equator is uninhabitable, he affirms that the reverse is probably true, though the cold at the poles may be so excessive as to prevent habitation. If, however, there are animals living there, we must suppose that they have coats thick enough to protect them against the climate and these coats are probably white in colour. In any case it is unreasonable to suppose that

[1] *Liber* 6, *de Veget. et Plantis*, Tract. I, c. I.

people living on the lower part of the earth would fall off, since the term 'lower' is only relative to us.[1] Naturally Albert relies very much on the opinions, observations and guesses of his predecessors; but he frequently appeals to his own observation, to what he has personally noticed of the habits of migrating birds, or of the nature of plants, for example, and he shows a robust common sense, as when he makes it plain that *a priori* arguments for the uninhabitable character of the 'torrid zone' cannot outweigh the evident fact that parts of lands which we know to be inhabited lie in that zone. Again, when speaking of the lunar halo or 'rainbow',[2] he remarks that according to Aristotle this phenomenon occurs only twice in fifty years, whereas he and others have observed it twice in one year, so that Aristotle must have been speaking from hearsay and not from experience. In any case, whatever value the particular conclusions drawn by St. Albert have, it is the spirit of curiosity and the reliance on observation and experiment which is remarkable and helps to distinguish him from so many Scholastics of a later period. Incidentally this spirit of inquiry and wide interests brings him near, in this respect, to Aristotle, since the Philosopher himself was well aware of the value of empirical research in scientific matters, however much later disciples may have received all his dicta as unquestionable and lacked his inquiring spirit and many-sided interests.

2. St. Albert the Great is quite clear as to the distinction between theology and philosophy, and so between the theology which takes as its foundation the data of revelation and the theology which is the work of the unaided natural reason and belongs to metaphysical philosophy. Thus metaphysics or first theology treats of God as the first Being (*secundum quod substat proprietatibus entis primi*), while theology treats of God as known by faith (*secundum quod substat attributis quae per fidem attribuuntur*). Again, the philosopher works under the influence of the general light of reason given to all men, by which light he sees the first principles, while the theologian works by the supernatural light of faith, through which he receives the revealed dogmas.[3] St. Albert has, therefore, little sympathy for those who deny or belittle philosophy, since not only does he make use of dialectic in theological reasoning, but he also recognises philosophy itself as an independent science. Against those who assert that it is wrong

---

[1] Cf. *De Natura Locorum*, Tract. 1, cc. 6, 7, 8, 12.
[2] *Liber* 3, *Meteorum*, Tract. 4, c. 11.   [3] 1 *Summa Theol.*, 1, 4, *ad* 2 *et* 3.

to introduce philosophic reasoning into theology, he admits that such reasoning cannot be primary, since a dogma is proved *tamquam ex priori*, that is, a dogma is shown by the theologian to have been revealed and is not a conclusion from philosophic argument; but he goes on to say that philosophic arguments can be of real utility in a secondary capacity, when dealing with objections brought by hostile philosophers, and speaks of the ignorant people who want to attack in every way the employment of philosophy and who are like 'brute animals blaspheming against that of which they are ignorant'.[1] Even in the Order of Preachers there was opposition to philosophy and the study of such 'profane' science, and one of the greatest services rendered by St. Albert was to promote the study and use of philosophy in his own Order.

3. The doctrine of St. Albert is not a homogeneous system, but rather a mixture of Aristotelian and neo-Platonic elements. For instance, he appeals to Aristotle when giving a proof for God's existence from motion,[2] and he argues that an infinite chain of *principia* is impossible and contradictory, since there would in reality be no *principium*. The *primum principium* or first principle must, by the very fact that it is the first principle, have its existence from itself and not from another: its existence (*esse*) must be its substance and essence.[3] It is the necessary Being, without any admixture of contingence or of potency, and Albert shows also that it is intelligent, living, omnipotent, free, and so on, in such a way that it is its own intelligence; that in God's knowledge of Himself there is no distinction between subject and object; that His will is not something distinct from His essence. Finally he carefully distinguishes God, the first Principle, from the world by observing that none of the names which we ascribe to God can be predicated of Him in their primary sense. If, for example, He is called substance, this is not because He falls within the category of substance, but because He is above all substances and the whole category of substance. Similarly, the term 'being' primarily refers to the general abstract idea of being, which cannot be predicated of God.[4] In fine, it is truer to say of God that we know what He is not rather than what He is.[5] One may say, then, that in the philosophy of St. Albert God is depicted, in dependence on Aristotle, as first unmoved Mover, as pure Act and as the self-

[1] *Comm. in Epist. 9 B. Dion. Areop.*, 7, 2.
[2] *Lib. 1, de causis et proc. universitatis*, 1, 7.   [3] *Ibid.*, 1, 8.   [4] *Ibid.*, 3, 6.
[5] *Comm. in Epist. 9 B. Dion. Areop.*, 1.

knowing Intellect, but emphasis is laid, in dependence on the writings of the Pseudo-Dionysius, on the fact that God transcends all our concepts and all the names we predicate of Him.

4. This combination of Aristotle and the Pseudo-Dionysius safeguards the divine transcendence and is the foundation for a doctrine of analogy; but when it comes to describing the creation of the world Albert interprets Aristotle according to the doctrine of the *Peripatetici*, that is to say, according to what are in reality neo-Platonic interpretations. Thus he uses the words *fluxus* and *emanatio* (*fluxus est emanatio formae a primo fonte, qui omnium formarum est fons et origo*)[1] and maintains that the first principle, *intellectus universaliter agens*, is the source whence flows the second intelligence, the latter the source whence flows the third intelligence, and so on. From each subordinate intelligence is derived its own proper sphere, until eventually the earth comes into being. This general scheme (Albert gives several particular schemes, culled from the 'ancients') might seem to impair the divine transcendence and immutability, as also the creative activity of God; but St. Albert does not, of course, think of God as becoming less through the process of emanation or as undergoing any change, while he also insists that a subordinate cause works only in dependence on, with the help of, the higher cause, so that the whole process must ultimately be referred to God. This process is variously represented as a graded diffusion of goodness or as a graded diffusion of light. However, it is clear that in this picture of creation St. Albert is inspired far more by the *Liber de causis*, the neo-Platonists and the neo-Platonising Aristotelians than by the historic Aristotle, while on the other hand he does not appear to have realised that the neo-Platonic notion of emanation, though not strictly pantheistic, since God remains distinct from all other beings, is yet not fully in tune with the Christian doctrine of free creation out of nothing. I do not mean to suggest for a moment that St. Albert intended to substitute the neo-Platonic emanation process for the Christian doctrine: rather did he try to express the latter in terms of the former, without apparently realising the difficulties involved in such an attempt.

St. Albert departs from the Augustinian-Franciscan tradition by holding that reason cannot demonstrate with certainty the world's creation in time, that is, that the world was not created from eternity,[2] and also by denying that angels and the human soul are

[1] *Lib. I, de causis et proc. universitatis,* 4, 1.　　[2] *In Phys.,* 8, 1, 13.

composed of matter and form, in this evidently thinking of matter as related to quantity; but on the other hand he accepts the doctrine of the *rationes seminales* and that of light as the *forma corporeitatis*. Moreover, besides adopting doctrines sometimes from Aristotelianism and sometimes from Augustinianism or neo-Platonism, St. Albert adopts phrases from the one tradition while interpreting them in the sense of the other, as when he speaks of seeing essences in the divine light, while meaning that the human reason and its operation is a reflection of the divine light, an effect thereof, but not that a special illuminating activity of God is required over and above the creation and conservation of the intellect. In general he follows the Aristotelian theory of abstraction. Again, Albert by no means always makes his meaning clear, so that it remains doubtful whether or not he considered that the distinction between essence and existence is real or conceptual. As he denied the presence of matter in the angels, while affirming that they are composed of 'essential parts', it would indeed seem reasonable to suppose that he maintained the theory of the real distinction, and he speaks in this sense on occasion; but at other times he speaks as if he held the Averroist theory of a conceptual distinction. We are left in difficulty as to the interpretation of his thought on this and other points owing to his habit of giving various different theories without any definite indication of which solution to the problem he himself adopted. It is not always clear how far he is simply reporting the opinions of others and how far he is committing himself to the affirmation of the opinions in question. It is impossible, then, to speak of a completed 'system' of Albert the Great: his thought is really a stage in the adoption of the Aristotelian philosophy as an intellectual instrument for the expression of the Christian outlook. The process of adopting and adapting the Aristotelian philosophy was carried much further by St. Albert's great pupil, Thomas Aquinas; but it would be a mistake to exaggerate the Aristotelianism even of the latter. Both men remained to a great extent in the tradition of Augustine, though both men, St. Albert in an incomplete, St. Thomas in a more complete fashion, interpreted Augustine according to the categories of Aristotle.

5. St. Albert was convinced that the immortality of the soul can be demonstrated by reason. Thus in his book on the nature and origin of the soul[1] he gives a number of proofs, arguing, for

---

[1] *Liber de natura et origine animae*, 2, 6; cf. also *De Anima*, 3.

example, that the soul transcends matter in its intellectual operations, having the principle of such operations in itself, and so cannot depend on the body *secundum esse et essentiam*. But he will not allow that the arguments for the unicity of the active intellect in all men are valid, arguments which, if probative, would deny personal immortality. He treats of this matter not only in the *De Anima*, but also in his special work on the subject, the *Libellus de unitate intellectus contra Averroem*. After remarking that the question is very difficult and that only trained philosophers, accustomed to metaphysical thinking, should take part in the dispute,[1] he goes on to expose thirty arguments which the Averroists bring forward or can bring forward to support their contention and observes that they are very difficult to answer. However, he proceeds to give thirty-six arguments against the Averroists, outlines his opinion on the rational soul and then answers in turn[2] the thirty arguments of the Averroists. The rational soul is the form of man, so that it must be multiplied in individual men: but what is multiplied numerically must also be multiplied substantially. If it can be proved, then, as it can be proved, that the rational soul is immortal, it follows that the multiplicity of rational souls survive death. Again, *esse* is the act of the final form of each thing (*formae ultimae*), and the final or ultimate form of man is the rational soul. Now, either individual men have their own separate *esse* or they have not. If you say that they do not possess their own individual *esse*, you must be prepared to admit that they are not individual men, which is patently false, while if you admit that each man has his own individual *esse*, then he must also have his own individual rational soul.

6. St. Albert the Great enjoyed a high reputation, even during his own lifetime, and Roger Bacon, who was far from being an enthusiastic admirer of his work, tells us that 'just as Aristotle, Avicenna and Averroes are quoted (*allegantur*) in the Schools, so is he'. Roger Bacon means that St. Albert was cited by name, which was contrary to the custom then in vogue of not mentioning living writers by name and which gives witness to the esteem he had won for himself. This reputation was doubtless due in large part to the Saint's erudition and to his many-sided interests, as theologian, philosopher, man of science and commentator. He had a wide knowledge of Jewish and Arabian philosophy and frequently

quotes the opinions of other writers, so that, in spite of his frequent
indefiniteness of thought and expression and his mistakes in
historical matters, his writings give the impression of a man of
extensive knowledge who had read very widely and was interested
in many lines of thought. His disciple, Ulric of Strasbourg, a
Dominican, who developed the neo-Platonic side of St. Albert's
thought, called him 'the wonder and miracle of our time';[1] but,
apart from his devotion to experimental science, St. Albert's
thought is of interest to us primarily because of its influence on
St. Thomas Aquinas, who, unlike Ulric of Strasbourg and John of
Fribourg, developed the Aristotelian aspect of that thought. The
master, who outlived his pupil, was devoted to the latter's
memory, and we are told that when St. Albert, as an old man,
used to think of Thomas at the commemoration of the dead in the
Canon of the Mass, he would shed tears as he thought of the death
of him who had been the flower and glory of the world.

St. Albert's reputation as a man of learning and wide-ranging
interests was justly merited; but his chief merit, as several
historians have noticed, was that he saw what a treasure for the
Christian West was contained in the system of Aristotle and in
the writings of the Arabian philosophers. Looking back on the
thirteenth century from a much later date, one is inclined to
contemplate the invasion and growing dominance of Aristotelianism in the light of the arid Scholastic Aristotelianism of a later
period, which sacrificed the spirit to the letter and entirely mis-
understood the inquiring mind of the great Greek philosopher, his
interest in science and the tentative nature of many of his conclusions; but to regard the thirteenth century in this light is to be
guilty of an anachronism, for the attitude of the decadent
Aristotelians of a later period was not the attitude of St. Albert.
The Christian West possessed nothing of its own in the way of
pure philosophy or of natural science which could compare with
the philosophy of Aristotle and the Arabians. St. Albert realised
this fact clearly; he saw that a definite attitude must be adopted
towards Aristotelianism, that it could not simply be disregarded,
and he was rightly convinced that it would be wasteful and even
disastrous to attempt to disregard it. He saw too, of course, that
on some points Aristotle and the Arabians held doctrines which
were incompatible with dogma; but at the same time he realised
that this was no reason for rejecting in its entirety what one had

[1] *Summa de bono*, 4, 3, 9.

to reject in part. He endeavoured to make Aristotelianism intelligible to the Latins and to show them its value, while pointing out its errors. That he accepted this or that point, rejected this or that theory, is not so important as the fact that he realised the general significance and value of Aristotelianism, and it is surely not necessary to be a rigid Aristotelian oneself in order to be able to appreciate his merits in this respect. It is a mistake so to stress St. Albert's independence, in regard to some of Aristotle's scientific observations, for example, that one loses sight of the great service he did in drawing attention to Aristotle and displaying something of the wealth of Aristotelianism. The passage of years certainly brought a certain unfortunate ossification in the Aristotelian tradition; but the blame for that cannot be laid at the door of St. Albert the Great. If one tries to imagine what mediaeval philosophy would have been without Aristotle, if one thinks away the Thomistic synthesis and the philosophy of Scotus, if one strips the philosophy of St. Bonaventure of all Aristotelian elements, one will hardly look on the invasion of Aristotelianism as an historical misfortune.

CHAPTER XXXI

ST. THOMAS AQUINAS—I

Life—Works—Mode of exposing St. Thomas's philosophy—The spirit of St. Thomas's philosophy.

1. THOMAS AQUINAS was born in the castle of Roccasecca, not far from Naples, at the end of 1224 or beginning of 1225, his father being the Count of Aquino. At the age of five years he was placed by his parents in the Benedictine Abbey of Monte Cassino as an oblate, and it was there that the future Saint and Doctor made his first studies, remaining in the monastery from 1230 to 1239, when the Emperor Frederick II expelled the monks. The boy returned to his family for a few months and then went to the University of Naples in the autumn of the same year, being then fourteen years old. In the city there was a convent of Dominican friars, and Thomas, attracted by their life, entered the Order in the course of the year 1244. This step was by no means acceptable to his family, who no doubt wished the boy to enter the abbey of Monte Cassino, as a step to ecclesiastical preferment, and it may have partly been due to this family opposition that the Dominican General resolved to take Thomas with him to Bologna, where he was himself going for a General Chapter, and then to send him on to the University of Paris. However, Thomas was kidnapped by his brothers on the way and was kept a prisoner at Aquino for about a year. His determination to remain true to his Order was proof against this trial, and he was able to make his way to Paris in the autumn of 1245.

Thomas was probably at Paris from 1245 until the summer of 1248, when he accompanied St. Albert the Great to Cologne, where the latter was to found a house of studies (*studium generale*) for the Dominican Order, remaining there until 1252. During this period, first at Paris, then at Cologne, Thomas was in close contact with Albert the Great, who realised the potentialities of his pupil, and while it is obvious that his taste for learning and study must in any case have been greatly stimulated by intimate contact with a professor of such erudition and such intellectual curiosity, we can hardly suppose that St. Albert's attempt to utilise what was valuable in Aristotelianism was without direct influence on his pupil's mind. Even if St. Thomas did not at this early date in his career conceive the idea of completing what his master had begun, he must at least have been profoundly influenced by the latter's open-mindedness. Thomas did not possess the all-embracing curiosity of his master (or one might say perhaps that he had a better sense of mental economy), but he certainly possessed greater powers of systematisation, and it was only to be expected that the meeting of the erudition and open-mindedness of the older man with the speculative power and synthesising ability of the younger would result in splendid fruit. It was St. Thomas who was to achieve the expression of the Christian ideology in Aristotelian terms, and who was to utilise Aristotelianism as an instrument of theological and philosophical analysis and synthesis; but his sojourn at Paris and Cologne in company with St. Albert was undoubtedly a factor of prime importance in his intellectual development. Whether or not we choose to regard St. Albert's system as incomplete Thomism is really irrelevant: the main fact is that St. Albert (*mutatis mutandis*) was Thomas's Socrates.

In 1252 St. Thomas returned from Cologne to Paris and continued his course of studies, lecturing on the Scriptures as *Baccalaureus Biblicus* (1252–4) and on the *Sentences* of Peter Lombard as *Baccalaureus Sententiarius* (1254–6), at the conclusion of which period he received his Licentiate, the licence or permission to teach in the faculty of theology. In the course of the same year he became *Magister* and lectured as Dominican professor until 1259. Of the controversy which arose concerning the Dominican and Franciscan chairs in the university mention has already been made. In 1259 he left Paris for Italy and taught theology at the *studium curiae* attached to the Papal court until 1268. Thus he was at Anagni with Alexander IV (1259–61), at Orvieto with Urban IV (1261–4), at Santa Sabina in Rome (1265–7), and at Viterbo with Clement IV (1267–8). It was at the court of Urban IV that he met the famous translator, William of Moerbeke, and it was Urban who commissioned Thomas to compose the Office for the feast of Corpus Christi.

In 1268 Thomas returned to Paris and taught there until 1272, engaging in controversy with the Averroists, as also with those who renewed the attack on the religious Orders. In 1272 he was sent to Naples in order to erect a Dominican *studium generale*, and he continued his professorial activity there until 1274, when Pope Gregory X summoned him to Lyons to take part in the

Council. The journey was begun but never completed, as St. Thomas died on the way on March 7th, 1274, at the Cistercian monastery of Fossanuova, between Naples and Rome. He was forty-nine years of age at the time of his death, having behind him a life devoted to study and teaching. It had not been a life of much external activity or excitement, if we except the early incident of his imprisonment, the more or less frequent journeys and the controversies in which the Saint was involved; but it was a life devoted to the pursuit and defence of truth, a life also permeated and motivated by a deep spirituality. In some ways Thomas Aquinas was rather like the professor of legend (there are several stories concerning his fits of abstraction, or rather concentration, which made him oblivious to his surroundings), but he was a great deal more than a professor or theologian, for he was a Saint, and even if his devotion and love are not allowed to manifest themselves in the pages of his academic works, the ecstasies and mystical union with God of his later years bear witness to the fact that the truths of which he wrote were the realities by which he lived.

2. St. Thomas's Commentary on the *Sentences* of Peter Lombard dates probably from 1254 to 1256, the *De principiis naturae* from 1255, the *De ente et essentia* from 1256 and the *De Veritate* from between 1256 and 1259. It may be that the *Quaestiones quodlibetales* 7, 8, 9, 10 and 11 were also composed before 1259, i.e. before Thomas left Paris for Italy. The *In Boethium de Hebdomadibus* and the *In Boethium de Trinitate* are also to be assigned to this period. While in Italy St. Thomas wrote the *Summa contra Gentiles*, the *De Potentia*, the *Contra errores Graecorum*, the *De emptione et venditione* and the *De regimine principum*. To this period belong also a number of the Commentaries on Aristotle: for example, those on the *Physics* (probably), the *Metaphysics*, the *Nicomachean Ethics*, the *De Anima*, the *Politics* (probably). On his return to Paris, where he became engaged in controversy with the Averroists, St. Thomas wrote the *De aeternitate mundi contra murmurantes* and the *De unitate intellectus contra Averroistas*, the *De Malo* (probably), the *De spiritualibus creaturis*, the *De anima* (i.e. the *Quaestio disputata*), the *De unione Verbi incarnati*, as well as the *Quaestiones quodlibetales* 1 to 6 and the commentaries on the *De causis*, the *Meteorologica*[1] and the *Perihermeneias*, also

---

[1] The supplement to the Commentary on the *Meteorologica* seems to have been completed by an anonymous writer, drawing on Peter of Auvergne.

belong to this period, while during his stay at Naples St. Thomas wrote the *De mixtione elementorum*, the *De motu cordis*, the *De virtutibus*, and the commentaries on Aristotle's *De Caelo* and *De generatione et corruptione*. As to the *Summa Theologica*, this was composed between 1265 (at the earliest) and 1273, the *Pars prima* being written in Paris, the *Prima secundae* and *Secunda secundae* in Italy, and the *Tertia pars* in Paris between 1272 and 1273. The *Supplementum*, made up from previous writings of St. Thomas, was added by Reginald of Piperno, St. Thomas's secretary from the year 1261. One must add that Peter of Auvergne completed the commentary on the *De Caelo* and that on the *Politics* (from Book 3, *lectio* 7), while Ptolemy of Lucca was responsible for part of the *De regimine principum*, St. Thomas having written only the first book and the first four chapters of the second book. The *Compendium theologiae*, an unfinished work, was a product of the later years of St. Thomas's life, but it is not certain if it was written before or after his return to Paris in 1268.

A number of works have been attributed to St. Thomas which were definitely not written by him, while the authenticity of certain other small works is doubtful, for example, the *De natura verbi intellectus*. The chronology which has been given above is not universally agreed upon, Mgr. Martin Grabmann and Père Mandonnet, for instance, ascribing certain works to different years. On this subject the relevant works mentioned in the Bibliography can be consulted.

3. To attempt to give a satisfactory outline of the 'philosophical system' of the greatest of the Schoolmen is to attempt a task of considerable magnitude. It does not indeed appear to me an acute question whether one should attempt a systematic or a genetic exposition, since the literary period of St. Thomas's life comprises but twenty years and though there were modifications and some development of opinion in that period, there was no such considerable development as in the case of Plato and still less was there any such succession of phases or periods as in the case of Schelling.[1] To treat the thought of Plato genetically might well be considered desirable (though actually, for purposes of convenience and clarity, I adopted a predominantly systematic form of exposition in my first volume) and to treat the thought of Schelling genetically is essential; but there is no real reason against

---

[1] Recent research, however, tends to show that there was more development in St. Thomas's thought than is sometimes supposed.

presenting the system of St. Thomas systematically: on the contrary, there is every reason why one should present it systematically.

The difficulty lies rather in answering the question, what precise form the systematic exposition should take and what emphasis and interpretation one should give to the component parts of its content. St. Thomas was a theologian and although he distinguished the sciences of revealed theology and philosophy, he did not himself elaborate a systematic exposition of philosophy by itself (there is theology even in the *Summa contra Gentiles*), so that the method of exposition is not already decided upon by the Saint himself.

Against this it may be objected that St. Thomas certainly did fix the starting-point for an exposition of his philosophy, and M. Gilson, in his outstanding work on St. Thomas,[1] argues that the right way of exposing the Thomistic philosophy is to expose it according to the order of the Thomistic theology. St. Thomas was a theologian and his philosophy must be regarded in the light of its relation to his theology. Not only is it true to say that the loss of a theological work like the *Summa Theologica* would be a major disaster in regard to our knowledge of St. Thomas's philosophy, whereas the loss of the Commentaries on Aristotle, though deplorable, would be of less importance; but also St. Thomas's conception of the content of philosophy or of the object which the philosopher (i.e. theologian-philosopher) considers, was that of *le révélable*, that which could have been revealed but has not been revealed and that which has been revealed but need not have been revealed, in the sense that it can be ascertained by the human reason, for example, the fact that God is wise. As M. Gilson rightly remarks, the problem for St. Thomas was not how to introduce philosophy into theology without corrupting the essence and nature of *philosophy*, but how to introduce philosophy without corrupting the essence and nature of *theology*. Theology treats of the revealed, and revelation must remain intact; but some truths are taught in theology which can be ascertained without revelation (God's existence, for example), while there are other truths which have not been revealed but which might have been revealed and which are of importance for a total view of God's creation. St. Thomas's philosophy should thus be regarded in the light of its relation to theology, and it is a mistake to collect

---

[1] *Le Thomisme*, 5th edition, Paris, 1944.

the philosophical items from St. Thomas's works, including his theological works, and construct a system out of them according to one's own idea of what a philosophical system should be, even though St. Thomas would very likely have refused to recognise such a system as corresponding with his actual intentions. To reconstruct the Thomistic system in such a way is legitimate enough for a philosopher, but it is the part of the historian to stick to St. Thomas's own method.

M. Gilson argues his point with his customary lucidity and cogency, and it seems to me that his point must, in general, be admitted. To begin an historical exposition of St. Thomas's philosophy by a theory of knowledge, for example, especially if the theory of knowledge were separated from psychology or the doctrine of the soul, would scarcely represent St. Thomas's own procedure, though it would be legitimate in an exposition of 'Thomism' which did not pretend to be primarily historical. On the other hand, St. Thomas certainly wrote some philosophical works before he composed the *Summa Theologica*, and the proofs of the existence of God in the latter work obviously presuppose a good many philosophical ideas. Moreover, as those philosophical ideas are not mere ideas, but are, on the principles of St. Thomas's own philosophy, abstracted from experience of the concrete, there seems to me ample justification for starting with the concrete sensible world of experience and considering some of St. Thomas's theories about it before going on to consider his natural theology. And this is the procedure which I have actually adopted.

Another point. St. Thomas was an extremely clear writer; but none the less there have been and are divergences of interpretation in regard to certain of his doctrines. To discuss fully the *pros* and *cons* of different interpretations is, however, not possible in a general history of philosophy: one can do little more than give the interpretation which commends itself in one's own eyes. At the same time, as far as the present writer is concerned, he is not prepared to state that on points where a difference of interpretation has arisen, he can give what is the indubitably correct interpretation. After all, concerning which great philosopher's system is there complete and universal agreement of interpretation? Plato, Aristotle, Descartes, Leibniz, Kant, Hegel? In the case of some philosophers, especially in the case of those who have expressed their thought clearly and carefully, like St. Thomas, there is a pretty generally accepted interpretation as to the main body of the system; but it is doubtful if the consent ever is or ever will be absolute and universal. A philosopher may write clearly and yet not express his final thought on all problems which arise in connection with his system, especially as some of those problems may not have occurred to him: it would be absurd to expect of any philosopher that he should have answered all questions, settled all problems, even that he should have rounded off and sealed his system in such a way that there could be no possible ground for divergence of interpretation. The present writer has the greatest respect and reverence for the genius of St. Thomas Aquinas, but he does not see that anything is to be gained by confusing the finite mind of the Saint with Absolute Mind or by claiming for his system what its author himself would certainly never have dreamed of claiming.

4. The philosophy of St. Thomas is essentially realist and concrete. St. Thomas certainly adopts the Aristotelian statement that first philosophy or metaphysic studies being as being; but it is perfectly clear that the task he sets himself is the explanation of existent being, so far as this is attainable by the human mind. In other words, he does not presuppose a notion from which reality is to be deduced; but he starts from the existent world and inquires what its being is, how it exists, what is the condition of its existence. Moreover, his thought concentrates on the supreme Existence, on the Being which does not merely possess existence, but is Its own existence, which is the very plenitude of existence, *ipsum esse subsistens*: his thought remains ever in contact with the concrete, the existent, both with that which has existence as something derived, something received, and with that which does not receive existence but is existence. In this sense it is true to say that Thomism is an 'existential philosophy', though it is very misleading, in my opinion, to call St. Thomas an 'existentialist', since the *Existenz* of the existentialists is not the same thing as St. Thomas's *esse*; nor is St. Thomas's method of approach to the problem of existence the same as that of the philosophers who are now called existentialists.

It has been maintained that St. Thomas, by bringing *esse* to the forefront of the philosophic stage, advanced beyond the philosophies of essence, particularly beyond Plato and the philosophies of Platonic inspiration. There is certainly truth in this contention: although Plato did not disregard the question of existence, the salient characteristic of his philosophy is the explanation of the world in terms of essence rather than of existence, while even for Aristotle, God, although pure Act, is primarily Thought, or Idea, the Platonic Good rendered 'personal'. Moreover, although Aristotle endeavoured to explain form and order in the world and the intelligible process of development, he did not explain the existence of the world; apparently he thought that no explanation was needed. In neo-Platonism again, though the derivation of the world is accounted for, the general scheme of emanation is primarily that of an emanation of essences, though existence is certainly not left out of account: God is primarily the One or the Good, not *ipsum esse subsistens*, not the *I am who am*. But one should remember that creation out of nothing was not an idea at which any Greek philosopher arrived without dependence on Judaism or Christianity and that without this idea the derivation of the world tends to be explained as a necessary derivation of essences. Those Christian philosophers who depended on and utilised neo-Platonic terminology spoke of the world as flowing from or emanating from God, and even St. Thomas used such phrases on occasion; but an orthodox Christian philosopher, whatever his terminology, regards the world as created freely by God, as receiving *esse* from *ipsum esse subsistens*. When St. Thomas insisted on the fact that God is subsistent existence, that His essence is not primarily goodness or thought but existence, he was but rendering explicit the implications of the Jewish and Christian view of the world's relation to God. I do not mean to imply that the idea of creation cannot be attained by reason; but the fact remains that it was not attained by the Greek philosophers and could hardly be attained by them, given their idea of God.

Of St. Thomas's general relation to Aristotle I shall speak later; but it may be as well to point out now one great effect which Aristotelianism had on St. Thomas's philosophical outlook and procedure. One might expect that St. Thomas, being a Christian, a theologian, a friar, would emphasise the soul's relation to God and would begin with what some modern philosophers call 'subjectivity', that he would place the interior life in the foreground even of his philosophy, as St. Bonaventure did. In point of fact, however, one of the chief characteristics of St. Thomas's philosophy is its 'objectivity' rather than its 'subjectivity'. The immediate object of the human intellect is the essence of the material thing, and St. Thomas builds up his philosophy by reflection on sense-experience. In the proofs which he gives of God's existence the process of argument is always from the sensible world to God. No doubt certain of the proofs could be applied to the soul itself as a starting-point and be developed in a different way; but in actual fact this was not the way of St. Thomas, and the proof which he calls the *via manifestior* is the one which is most dependent on Aristotle's own arguments. This Aristotelian 'objectivity' of St. Thomas may appear disconcerting to those for whom 'truth is subjectivity'; but at the same time it is a great source of strength, since it means that his arguments can be considered in themselves, apart from St. Thomas's own life, on their own merits or demerits, and that observations about 'wishful thinking' are largely irrelevant, the relevant question being the objective cogency of the arguments themselves. Another result is that St. Thomas's philosophy appears 'modern' in a sense in which the philosophy of St. Bonaventure can hardly do. The latter tends to appear as essentially bound up with the general mediaeval outlook and with the Christian spiritual life and tradition, so that it seems to be on a different plane from the 'profane' philosophies of modern times, whereas the Thomistic philosophy can be divorced from Christian spirituality and, to a large extent, from the mediaeval outlook and background, and can enter into direct competition with more recent systems. A Thomistic revival has taken place, as everybody knows; but it is a little difficult to imagine a Bonaventurian revival, unless one were at the same time to change the conception of philosophy, and in this case the modern philosopher and the Bonaventurian would scarcely speak the same language.

Nevertheless, St. Thomas was a Christian philosopher. As already mentioned, St. Thomas follows Aristotle in speaking of metaphysics as the science of being as being; but the fact that his thought centres round the concrete and the fact that he was a Christian theologian led him to emphasise also the view that 'first philosophy is wholly directed to the knowledge of God as the last end' and that 'the knowledge of God is the ultimate end of every human cognition and operation'.[1] But actually man was created for a profounder and more intimate knowledge of God than he can attain by the exercise of his natural reason in this life, and so revelation was morally necessary in order that his mind might be raised to something higher than his reason can attain to in this life and that he should desire and zealously strive towards

[1] *Contra Gent.*, 3, 25.

something 'which exceeds the whole state of this life.'[1] Metaphysics has its own object, therefore, and a certain autonomy of its own, but it points upwards and needs to be crowned by theology: otherwise man will not realise the end for which he was created and will not desire and strive towards that end. Moreover, as the primary object of metaphysics, God, exceeds the apprehension of the metaphysician and of the natural reason in general, and as the full knowledge or vision of God is not attainable in this life, the conceptual knowledge of God is crowned in this life by mysticism. Mystical theology does not enter the province of philosophy, and St. Thomas's philosophy can be considered without reference to it; but one should not forget that for St. Thomas philosophical knowledge is neither sufficient nor final.

[1] *Contra Gent.*, 1, 5.

CHAPTER XXXII

ST. THOMAS AQUINAS—II
PHILOSOPHY AND THEOLOGY

Distinction between philosophy and theology—Moral necessity of revelation—Incompatibility of faith and science in the same mind concerning the same object—Natural end and supernatural end—St. Thomas and St. Bonaventure—St. Thomas as 'innovator'.

1. THAT St. Thomas made a formal and explicit distinction between dogmatic theology and philosophy is an undoubted and an indubitable fact. Philosophy and the other human sciences rely simply and solely on the natural light of reason: the philosopher uses principles which are known by the human reason (with God's natural concurrence, of course, but without the supernatural light of faith), and he argues to conclusions which are the fruit of human reasoning. The theologian, on the other hand, although he certainly uses his reason, accepts his principles on authority, on faith; he receives them as revealed. The introduction of dialectic into theology, the practice of starting from a revealed premiss or from revealed premisses and arguing rationally to a conclusion, leads to the development of Scholastic theology, but it does not turn theology into philosophy, since the principles, the data, are accepted as revealed. For instance, the theologian may attempt with the aid of categories and forms of reasoning borrowed from philosophy to understand a little better the mystery of the Trinity; but he does not thereby cease to act as a theologian, since all the time he accepts the dogma of the Trinity of Persons in one Nature on the authority of God revealing: it is for him a datum or principle, a revealed premiss accepted on faith, not the conclusion of a philosophical argument. Again, while the philosopher starts from the world of experience and argues by reason to God in so far as He can be known by means of creatures, the theologian starts with God as He has revealed Himself, and the natural method in theology is to pass from God in Himself to creatures rather than to ascend from creatures to God, as the philosopher does and must do.

It follows that the principal difference between theology and

312

philosophy lies in the fact that the theologian receives his principles as revealed and considers the objects with which he deals as revealed or as deducible from what is revealed, whereas the philosopher apprehends his principles by reason alone and considers the objects with which he deals, not as revealed but as apprehensible and apprehended by the natural light of reason. In other words, the fundamental difference between theology and philosophy does not lie in a difference of objects concretely considered. Some truths are proper to theology, since they cannot be known by reason and are known only by revelation, the mystery of the Trinity, for example, while other truths are proper to philosophy alone in the sense that they have not been revealed; but there are some truths which are common to both theology and philosophy, since they have been revealed, though at the same time they can be established by reason. It is the existence of these common truths which makes it impossible to say that theology and philosophy differ primarily because each science considers different truths: in some instances they consider the same truths, though they consider them in a different manner, the theologian considering them as revealed, the philosopher as conclusions of a process of human reasoning. For example, the philosopher argues to God as Creator, while the theologian also treats of God as Creator; but for the philosopher the knowledge of God as Creator comes as the conclusion of a purely rational argument, while the theologian accepts the fact that God is Creator from revelation, so that it is for him a premiss rather than a conclusion, a premiss which is not hypothetically assumed but revealed. In technical language it is not *primarily* a difference of truths considered 'materially', or according to their content, which constitutes the difference between a truth of theology and a truth of philosophy, but rather a difference of truths considered 'formally'. That is to say, the same truth may be enunciated by both the theologian and the philosopher; but it is arrived at and considered by the theologian in a different way from that in which it is arrived at and considered by the philosopher. *Diversa ratio cognoscibilis diversitatem scientiarum inducit.* . . . 'There is, therefore, no reason why another science should not treat of the very same objects, as known by the light of divine revelation, which the philosophical sciences treat of according as they are knowable by the light of natural reason. Hence the theology which belongs to sacred doctrine differs generically from that theology which is a part of philosophy.'[1] Between dogmatic theology and natural theology there is a certain overlapping; but the sciences differ generically from one another.

2. According to St. Thomas, almost the whole of philosophy is directed to the knowledge of God, at least in the sense that a good deal of philosophical study is presupposed and required by natural theology, that part of metaphysics which treats of God. Natural theology, he says, is the last part of philosophy to be learnt.[2] Incidentally, this statement does not support the view that one should start the exposition of the Thomist philosophy with natural theology; but in any case the point I now want to make is that St. Thomas, seeing that natural theology, if it is to be properly grasped, requires much previous study and reflection, insists that revelation is morally necessary, given the fact that God is man's end. Moreover, not only does natural theology require more reflection and study and ability than most men are in a position to devote to it, but also, even when the truth is discovered, history shows that it is often contaminated by error. Pagan philosophers have certainly discovered God's existence; but error was often involved in their speculations, the philosopher either not realising properly the unity of God or denying divine providence or failing to see that God is Creator. If it were a question simply of astronomy or natural science, errors would not matter so much, since man can perfectly well attain his end even if he holds erroneous opinions concerning astronomical or scientific matters; but God is Himself man's end, and knowledge of God is essential in order that man should direct himself rightly towards that end, so that truth concerning God is of great importance and error concerning God is disastrous. Granted, then, that God is man's end, we can see that it is morally necessary that the discovery of truths so important for life should not be left simply to the unaided powers of those men who have the ability, the zeal and the leisure to discover them, but that these truths should also be revealed.[3]

3. At once the question arises whether the same man can at the same time believe (accept on authority by faith) and know (as a result of rational demonstration) the same truth. If God's existence, for instance, has been demonstrated by a philosopher, can he at the same time believe it by faith? In the *De Veritate*[4]

---

[1] *S.T.*, Ia, 1, 1, ad 2.
[2] *Contra Gent.*, 1, 4.
[3] Cf. *S.T.*, Ia, 1, 1; *Contra Gent.*, 1, 4.
[4] 14, 9.

St. Thomas answers roundly that it is impossible for there to be faith and knowledge concerning the same object, that the same truths should be both known scientifically (philosophically) and at the same time believed (by faith) by the same man. On this supposition it would seem that a man who has proved the unity of God cannot believe that same truth by faith. In order, then, that it should not appear that this man is failing to give assent to articles of faith, St. Thomas finds himself compelled to say that such truths as the unity of God are not properly speaking articles of faith, but rather *praeambula ad articulos*.[1] He adds, however, that nothing prevents such truths being the object of belief to a man who cannot understand or has no time to consider the philosophical demonstration,[2] and he maintains his opinion that it was proper and fitting for such truths to be proposed for belief.[3] The question whether a man who understands the demonstration but who is not attending to it or considering it at the moment, can exercise faith in regard to the unity of God he does not explicitly answer. As to the opening phrase of the Creed (*Credo in unum Deum*, I believe in one God), which might seem to imply that faith in the unity of God is demanded of all, he would, on his premisses, have to say that the unity of God is here not to be understood by itself but together with what follows, that is, as a unity of Nature in a Trinity of Persons.

To go into this question further and to discuss with what sort of faith the uneducated believe the truths which are known (demonstratively) by the philosopher, would be inappropriate here, not only because it is a theological question, but also because it is a question which St. Thomas does not explicitly discuss: the main point in mentioning the matter at all is to illustrate the fact that St. Thomas makes a real distinction between philosophy on the one hand and theology on the other. Incidentally, if we speak of a 'philosopher', it must not be understood as excluding the theologian: most of the Scholastics were both theologians and philosophers, and St. Thomas distinguishes the sciences rather than the men. That St. Thomas took this distinction seriously can also be seen from the position he adopted towards the question of the eternity of the world (to which I shall return later). He considered that it can be demonstrated that the world was created, but he did not think that reason can demonstrate that the world

[1] *S.T.*, Ia, 2, 2, ad 1; *De Verit.*, 14, 9, ad 9.
[2] *S.T.*, Ia, 2, 2, ad 1.   [3] *Contra Gent.*, 1, 4.

was not created from eternity, although it can refute the proofs adduced to show that it *was* created from eternity. On the other hand we know by revelation that the world was not created from eternity but had a beginning in time. In other words, the theologian knows through revelation that the world was not created from eternity, but the philosopher cannot prove this—or rather no argument which has been brought forward to prove it is conclusive. This distinction obviously presupposes or implies a real distinction between the two sciences of philosophy and theology.

4. It is sometimes said that St. Thomas differs from St. Augustine in that while the latter considers man simply in the concrete, as man called to a supernatural end, St. Thomas distinguishes two ends, a supernatural end, the consideration of which he assigns to the theologian, and a natural end, the consideration of which he assigns to the philosopher. Now, that St. Thomas distinguishes the two ends is quite true. In the *De Veritate*[1] he says that the final good as considered by the philosopher is different from the final good as considered by the theologian, since the philosopher considers the final good (*bonum ultimum*) which is proportionate to human powers, whereas the theologian considers as the final good that which transcends the power of nature, namely life eternal, by which he means, of course, not simply survival but the vision of God. This distinction is of great importance and it has its repercussion both in morals, where it is the foundation of the distinction between the natural and the supernatural virtues, and in politics, where it is the foundation of the distinction between the ends of the Church and the State and determines the relations which should exist between the two societies; but it is not a distinction between two ends which correspond to two mutually exclusive orders, the one supernatural, the other that of 'pure nature': it is a distinction between two orders of knowledge and activity in the same concrete human being. The concrete human being was created by God for a supernatural end, for perfect happiness, which is attainable only in the next life through the vision of God and which is, moreover, unattainable by man by his own unaided natural power; but man can attain an imperfect happiness in this life by the exercise of his natural powers, through coming to a philosophic knowledge of God through creatures and through the attainment and exercise of the natural

virtues.[1] Obviously these ends are not exclusive, since man can attain the imperfect felicity in which his natural end consists without thereby putting himself outside the way to his supernatural end; the natural end, imperfect beatitude, is proportionate to human nature and human powers, but inasmuch as man has been created for a supernatural final end, the natural end cannot satisfy him, as St. Thomas argues in the *Contra Gentiles*[2]; it is imperfect and points beyond itself.

How does this affect the question of the relation between theology and philosophy? In this way. Man has one final end, supernatural beatitude, but the existence of this end, which transcends the powers of mere human nature, even though man was created to attain it and given the power to do so by grace, cannot be known by natural reason and so cannot be divined by the philosopher: its consideration is restricted to the theologian. On the other hand, man can attain through the exercise of his natural powers to an imperfect and limited natural happiness in this life, and the existence of this end and the means to attain it are discoverable by the philosopher, who can prove the existence of God from creatures, attain some analogical knowledge of God, define the natural virtues and the means of attaining them. Thus the philosopher may be said to consider the end of man in so far as this end is discoverable by human reason, i.e. only imperfectly and incompletely. But both theologian and philosopher are considering man in the concrete: the difference is that the philosopher, while able to view and consider human nature as such, cannot discover all there is in man, cannot discover his supernatural vocation; he can only go part of the way in discovering man's destiny, precisely because man was created for an end which transcends the powers of his nature. It is, therefore, not true to say that for St. Thomas the philosopher considers man in a hypothetical state of pure nature, that is, man as he would have been, had he never been called to a supernatural end: he considers man in the concrete, but he cannot know all there is to be known about that man in the concrete. When St. Thomas raises the question whether God could have created man *in puris naturalibus*[3] he is asking simply if God could have created man (who even in this hypothesis was created for a supernatural end) without

---

[1] Cf. *In Boethium de Trinitate*, 6, 4, 5; *In 1 Sent., prol.*, 1, 1; *De Veritate*, 14, 2; S.T., Ia, IIae, 5, 5.   [2] 3, 27 ff.
[3] *In 2 Sent.*, 29, 1, 2; *ibid.*, 29, 2, 3; S.T., Ia, 95, 1, 4; *Quodlibet*, 1, 8.

sanctifying grace, that is to say, if God could have first created man without the means of attaining his end and then afterwards have given it; he is not asking if God could have given man a purely natural ultimate end, as later writers interpreted him as saying. Whatever, then, the merit of the idea of the state of pure nature considered in itself may be (this is a point I do not propose to discuss), it does not play a part in St. Thomas's conception of philosophy. Consequently he does not differ from St. Augustine so much as has been sometimes asserted, though he defined the spheres of the two sciences of philosophy and theology more clearly than Augustine had defined them: what he did was to express Augustinianism in terms of the Aristotelian philosophy, a fact which compelled him to utilise the notion of natural end, though he interpreted it in such a way that he cannot be said to have adopted a starting-point in philosophy totally different from that of Augustine.

Actually the idea of the state of pure nature seems to have been introduced into Thomism by Cajetan. Suarez, who himself adopted the idea, remarks that 'Cajetan and the more modern theologians have considered a third state, which they have called purely natural, a state which can be thought of as possible, although it has not in fact existed'.[1] Dominicus Soto[2] says that it is a perversion of the mind of St. Thomas, while Toletus[3] observes that there exist in us a natural desire and a natural appetite for the vision of God, though this opinion, which is that of Scotus and seems to be that of St. Thomas, is contrary to that of Cajetan.

5. St. Thomas certainly believed that it is *theoretically* possible for the philosopher to work out a true metaphysical system without recourse to revelation. Such a system would be necessarily imperfect, inadequate and incomplete, because the metaphysician is primarily concerned with the Truth itself, with God who is the principle of all truth, and he is unable by purely human rational investigation to discover all that knowledge of Truth itself, of God, which is necessary for man if he is to attain his final end. The mere philosopher can say nothing about the supernatural end of man or the supernatural means of attaining that end, and as the knowledge of these things is required for man's salvation, the insufficiency of philosophical knowledge is apparent. On the other

---

[1] *De Gratia, Prolegom.*, 4, c. 1, n. 2. [2] *In* 4 *Sent.*, 49, 2, 1; p. 903, 1613 edit.
[3] *In Summam Sancti Thomae*, Ia, 1, 1, t. 1, pp. 17-19, 1869 edit.

hand, incompleteness and inadequacy do not necessarily mean falsity. The truth that God is one is not vitiated by the very fact that nothing is said or known of the Trinity of Persons; the further truth completes the first, but the first truth is not false, even taken by itself. If the philosopher states that God is one and simply says nothing about the Trinity, because the idea of the Trinity has never entered his head; or if he knows of the doctrine of the Trinity and does not himself believe it, but simply contents himself with saying that God is one; or even if he expresses the view that the Trinity, which he understands wrongly, is incompatible with the divine unity; it still remains true that the statement that God is one in Nature is a correct statement. Of course, if the philosopher states positively that God is one Person, he is stating what is false; but if he simply says that God is one and that God is personal, without going on to state that God is one Person, he is stating the truth. It may be unlikely that a philosopher would stop short at saying that God is personal, but it is at least theoretically possible. Unless one is prepared to condemn the human intellect as such or at any rate to debar it from the discovery of a true metaphysic, one must admit that the establishment of a satisfactory metaphysic is abstractly possible, even for the pagan philosopher. St. Thomas was very far from following St. Bonaventure in excluding Aristotle from the ranks of the metaphysicians: on the contrary, the latter was in Thomas's eyes the philosopher *par excellence*, the very embodiment of the intellectual power of the human mind acting without divine faith, and he attempted, wherever possible, to interpret Aristotle in the most 'charitable' sense, that is, in the sense which was most compatible with Christian revelation.

If one emphasises simply this aspect of St. Thomas's attitude towards philosophy, it would seem that a Thomist could not legitimately adopt a consistently hostile and polemical attitude towards modern philosophy. If one adopts the Bonaventurian position and maintains that a metaphysician cannot attain truth unless he philosophises in the light of faith (though without, of course, basing his philosophical proofs on theological premisses), one would only expect that a philosopher who rejected the supernatural or who confined religion within the bounds of reason alone, should go sadly astray; but if one is prepared to admit the possibility of even a pagan philosopher elaborating a more or less satisfactory metaphysic, it is unreasonable to suppose that in

several centuries of intensive human thought, no truth has come
to light. It would seem that a Thomist should expect to find fresh
intellectual illumination in the pages of the modern philosophers
and that he should approach them with an initial sympathy and
expectancy rather than with an *a priori* suspicion, reserve and
even hostility.

On the other hand, though St. Thomas's attitude towards the
pagan philosophers, and towards Aristotle in particular, differed
from that of St. Bonaventure, it is not right to exaggerate their
difference of outlook. As has already been mentioned, St. Thomas
gives reasons why it is fitting that even those truths about God
which can be discovered by reason should be proposed for men's
belief. Some of the reasons he gives are not indeed relevant to the
particular point I am discussing. For example, it is perfectly true
that many people are so occupied with earning their daily bread
that they have not the time to give to metaphysical reflection,
even when they have the capacity for such reflection, so that it is
desirable that those metaphysical truths which are of importance
for them in their lives should be proposed for their belief: otherwise they will never know them at all,[1] just as most of us would
have neither the time nor the energy to discover America for
ourselves, did we not already accept the fact that it exists on the
testimony of others; but it does not necessarily follow that those
who have the time and ability for metaphysical reflection will
probably draw wrong conclusions, except in so far as metaphysical
thinking is difficult and requires prolonged attention and concentration, whereas 'certain people', as St. Thomas remarks, are lazy.
However, there is this further point to be borne in mind,[2] that on
account of the weakness of our intellect in judging and on account
of the intrusion of the imagination falsity is generally (*plerumque*)
mixed with truth in the human mind's conclusions. Among the
conclusions which are truly demonstrated there is sometimes
(*aliquando*) included a false conclusion which has not been demonstrated but is asserted on the strength of a probable or sophistical
reasoning passing under the name of demonstration. The practical
result will be that even certain and sure conclusions will not be
whole-heartedly accepted by many people, particularly when they
see philosophers teaching different doctrines while they themselves
are unable to distinguish a doctrine which has been truly demonstrated from one which rests on a merely probable or sophistical

[1] *Contra Gent.*, 1, 4.   [2] *Ibid.*

argument. Similarly, in the *Summa Theologica*, St. Thomas observes that the truth about God is arrived at by the human reason only by a few men and after a long time and 'with the admixture of many errors'.[1] When the Saint says that it is desirable that even those truths about God which are rationally demonstrable should be proposed as objects of belief, to be accepted on authority, he emphasises indeed the practical requirements of the many rather than the speculative insufficiency of metaphysics as such, but he does admit that error is frequently mixed with the truth, either because of over-hastiness in jumping to conclusions or because of the influence of passion and emotion or of imagination. Possibly he did not himself apply this idea with perfect consistency in regard to Aristotle and was too ready to interpret Aristotle in the sense which was most compatible with Christian doctrine, but the fact remains that he acknowledges theoretically the weakness of the human intellect in its present condition, though not its radical perversion. Accordingly, though he differs from St. Bonaventure in that he admits the abstract possibility, and indeed, in Aristotle's case, the concrete fact, of a 'satisfactory' metaphysic being elaborated by a pagan philosopher and also refuses to allow that its incompleteness vitiates a metaphysical system, he also admits it is likely that any independent metaphysical system will contain error.

Perhaps it is not fanciful to suggest that the two men's abstract opinions were largely settled by their attitude towards Aristotle. It might, of course, be retorted that this is to put the cart before the horse, but it will appear more reasonable if one considers the actual circumstances in which they lived and wrote. For the first time Latin Christendom was becoming acquainted with a great philosophical system which owed nothing to Christianity and which was represented by its fervent adherents, such as Averroes, as being the last word in human wisdom. The greatness of Aristotle, the depth and comprehensiveness of his system, was a factor which could not be ignored by any Christian philosopher of the thirteenth century; but it could be met and treated in more than one way. On the one hand, as expounded by Averroes, Aristotelianism conflicted on several very important points with Christian doctrine, and it was possible to adopt a hostile and unreceptive attitude towards the Aristotelian metaphysic on this count. If, however, one adopted this course, as St. Bonaventure

[1] *S.T.*, Ia, 1, 1, *in corpore.*

did, one had to say either that Aristotle's system affirmed philoso-phical truth but that what was true in philosophy might not be true in theology, since God could override the demands of natural logic, or else that Aristotle went wrong in his metaphysics. St. Bonaventure adopted the second course. But why, in Bona-venture's view, did Aristotle go wrong, the greatest systematiser of the ancient world? Obviously because any independent philo-sophy is bound to go wrong on important points simply because it is independent: it is only in the light of the Christian faith that one can elaborate anything like a complete and satisfactory philosophical system, since it is only in the light of the Christian faith that the philosopher will be enabled to leave his philosophy open to revelation: if he has not that light, he will round it off and complete it, and if he rounds it off and completes it, it will be thereby vitiated in part at least, especially in regard to those parts, the most important parts, which deal with God and the end of man. On the other hand, if one saw in the Aristotelian system a magnificent instrument for the expression of truth and for the welding together of the divine truths of theology and philosophy, one would have to admit the power of the pagan philosopher to attain metaphysical truth, though in view of the interpretation of Aristotle given by Averroes and others one would have also to allow for and explain the possibility of error even on the part of the Philosopher. This was the course adopted by St. Thomas.

6. When one looks back on the thirteenth century from a much later date, one does not always recognise the fact that St. Thomas was an innovator, that his adoption of Aristotelianism was bold and 'modern'. St. Thomas was faced with a system of growing influence and importance, which seemed in many respects to be incompatible with Christian tradition, but which naturally capti-vated the minds of many students and masters, particularly in the faculty of arts at Paris, precisely because of its majesty, apparent coherence and comprehensiveness. That Aquinas boldly grasped the bull by the horns and utilised Aristotelianism in the building up of his own system was very far from being an obscurantist action: it was, on the contrary, extremely 'modern' and was of the greatest importance for the future of Scholastic philosophy and indeed for the history of philosophy in general. That some Scholastics in the later Middle Ages and at the time of the Renaissance brought Aristotelianism into discredit by their obscu-rantist adherence to all the Philosopher's *dicta*, even on scientific

matters, does not concern St. Thomas: the plain fact is that they were not faithful to the spirit of St. Thomas. The Saint rendered, on any count, an incomparable service to Christian thought by utilising the instrument which presented itself, and he naturally interpreted Aristotle in the most favourable sense from the Christian standpoint, since it was essential to show, if he was to succeed in his undertaking, that Aristotle and Averroes did not stand or fall together. Moreover, it is not true to say that St. Thomas had no sense of accurate interpretation: one may not agree with all his interpretations of Aristotle, but there can be no doubt that, given the circumstances of the time and the paucity of relevant historical information at his disposal, he was one of the most conscientious and the finest commentators of Aristotle who have ever existed.

In conclusion, however, it must be emphasised that though St. Thomas adopted Aristotelianism as an instrument for the expression of his system, he was no blind worshipper of the Philosopher, who discarded Augustine in favour of the pagan thinker. In theology he naturally treads in the footsteps of Augustine, though his adoption of the Aristotelian philosophy as an instrument enabled him to systematise, define and argue logically from theological doctrines in a manner which was foreign to the attitude of Augustine: in philosophy, while there is a great deal which comes straight from Aristotle, he often interprets Aristotle in a manner consonant with Augustine or expresses Augustine in Aristotelian categories, though it might be truer to say that he does both at once. For instance, when treating of divine knowledge and providence, he interprets the Aristotelian doctrine of God in a sense which at least does not exclude God's knowledge of the world, and in treating of the divine ideas he observes that Aristotle censured Plato for making the ideas independent both of concrete things and of an intellect, with the tacit implication that Aristotle would not have censured Plato, had the latter placed the ideas in the mind of God. This is, of course, to interpret Aristotle *in meliorem partem* from the theological standpoint, and although the interpretation tends to bring Aristotle and Augustine closer together, it most probably does not represent Aristotle's actual theory of the divine knowledge. However, of St. Thomas's relation to Aristotle I shall speak later.

CHAPTER XXXIII

ST. THOMAS AQUINAS—III
PRINCIPLES OF CREATED BEING

Reasons for starting with corporeal being—Hylomorphism—Rejection of rationes seminales*—Rejection of plurality of substantial forms—Restriction of hylomorphic composition to corporeal substances—Potentiality and act—Essence and existence.*

1. IN the *Summa Theologica*, which, as its name indicates, is a theological synopsis, the first philosophical problem of which St. Thomas treats is that of the existence of God, after which he proceeds to consider the Nature of God and then the divine Persons, passing subsequently to creation. Similarly, in the *Summa contra Gentiles*, which more nearly resembles a philosophical treatise (though it cannot be called simply a philosophical treatise, since it also treats of such purely dogmatic themes as the Trinity and the Incarnation), St. Thomas also starts with the existence of God. It might seem, then, that it would be natural to begin the exposition of St. Thomas's philosophy with his proofs of God's existence; but apart from the fact (mentioned in an earlier chapter) that St. Thomas himself says that the part of philosophy which treats of God comes after the other branches of philosophy, the proofs themselves presuppose some fundamental concepts and principles, and St. Thomas had composed the *De ente et essentia*, for example, before he wrote either of the *Summae*. It would not in any case be natural, then, to start immediately with the proofs of God's existence, and M. Gilson himself, who insists that the natural way of expounding St. Thomas's philosophy is to expound it according to the order adopted by the Saint in the *Summae*, actually begins by considering certain basic ideas and principles. On the other hand, one can scarcely discuss the whole general metaphysic of St. Thomas and all those ideas which are explicitly or implicitly presupposed by his natural theology: it is necessary to restrict the basis of one's discussion.

To a modern reader, familiar with the course and problems of modern philosophy, it might seem natural to begin with a discussion of St. Thomas's theory of knowledge and to raise the question whether or not the Saint provides an epistemological justification of the possibility of metaphysical knowledge. But although St. Thomas certainly had a 'theory of knowledge' he did not live after Kant, and the problem of knowledge did not occupy that position in his philosophy which it has come to occupy in later times. It seems to me that the natural starting-point for an exposition of the Thomist philosophy is the consideration of corporeal substances. After all, St. Thomas expressly teaches that the immediate and proper object of the human intellect in this life is the essence of material things. The fundamental notions and principles which are presupposed by St. Thomas's natural theology are not, according to him, innate, but are apprehended through reflection on and abstraction from our experience of concrete objects, and it seems, therefore, only reasonable to develop those fundamental notions and principles first of all through a consideration of material substances. St. Thomas's proofs of God's existence are *a posteriori*; they proceed from creatures to God, and it is the creature's nature, the lack of self-sufficiency on the part of the immediate objects of experience, which reveals the existence of God. Moreover, we can, by the natural light of reason, attain only that knowledge of God which can be attained by reflection on creatures and their relation to Him. On this count too it would seem only 'natural' to begin the exposition of the Thomist philosophy with a consideration of those concrete objects of experience by reflection on which we arrive at those fundamental principles which lead us on to develop the proofs of God's existence.

2. In regard to corporeal substances St. Thomas adopts from the very outset the common-sense standpoint, according to which there are a multiplicity of substances. The human mind comes to know in dependence on sense-experience, and the first concrete objects the mind knows are material objects into relation with which it enters through the senses. Reflection on these objects, however, at once leads the mind to form a distinction, or rather to discover a distinction, in the objects themselves. If I look out of my window in the spring I see the beech-tree with its young and tender green leaves, while in the autumn I see that the leaves have changed colour, though the same beech-tree stands out there in the park. The beech is substantially the same, a beech-tree, in spring and autumn, but the colour of its leaves is not the same: the colour changes without the beech-tree changing substantially. Similarly, if I go to the plantation, one year I see the larches as small trees, newly planted; later on I see them as bigger trees: their

size has changed but they are still larches. The cows in the field I see now in this place, now in that, now in one posture, now in another, standing up or lying down, now doing one thing, now another, eating the grass or chewing the cud or sleeping, now undergoing one thing, now another, being milked or being rained on or being driven along, but all the time they are the same cows. Reflection thus leads the mind to distinguish between substance and accident, and between the different kinds of accident, and St. Thomas accepts from Aristotle the doctrine of the ten categories, substance and the nine categories of accident.

So far reflection has led us only to the idea of accidental change and the notion of the categories: but further reflection will introduce the mind to a profounder level of the constitution of material being. When the cow eats grass, the grass no longer remains what it was in the field, but becomes something else through assimilation, while on the other hand it does not simply cease to be, but something remains in the process of change. The change is substantial, since the grass itself is changed, not merely its colour or size, and the analysis of substantial change leads the mind to discern two elements, one element which is common to the grass and to the flesh which the grass becomes, another element which confers on that something its determination, its substantial character, making it to be first grass, then cow-flesh. Moreover, ultimately we can conceive any material substance changing into any other, not necessarily directly or immediately, of course, but at least indirectly and mediately, after a series of changes. We come thus to the conception on the one hand of an underlying substrate of change which, *when considered in itself*, cannot be called by the name of any definite substance, and on the other hand of a determining or characterising element. The first element is 'prime matter', the indeterminate substrate of substantial change, the second element is the substantial form, which makes the substance what it is, places it in its specific class and so determines it as grass, cow, oxygen, hydrogen, or whatever it may be. Every material substance is composed in this way of matter and form.

St. Thomas thus accepts the Aristotelian doctrine of the hylomorphic composition of material substances, defining prime matter as pure potentiality and substantial form as the first act of a physical body, 'first act' meaning the principle which places the body in its specific class and determines its essence. Prime matter is in potentiality to all forms which can be the forms of bodies, but considered in itself it is without any form, pure potentiality: it is, as Aristotle said, *nec quid nec quantum nec quale nec aliud quidquam eorum quibus determinatur ens*.[1] For this reason, however, it cannot exist by itself, for to speak of a being actually existing without act or form would be contradictory: it did not, then, precede form temporally, but was created together with form.[2] St. Thomas is thus quite clear on the fact that only concrete substances, individual compositions of matter and form, actually exist in the material world. But though he is at one with Aristotle in denying the separate existence of universals (though we shall see presently that a reservation must be made in regard to this statement), he also follows Aristotle in asserting that the form needs to be individuated. The form is the universal element, being that which places an object in its class, in its species, making it to be horse or elm or iron: it needs, then, to be individuated, in order that it should become the form of this particular substance. What is the principle of individuation? It can only be matter. But matter is of itself pure potentiality: it has not those determinations which are necessary in order that it should individuate form. The accidental characteristics of quantity and so on are logically posterior to the hylomorphic composition of the substance. St. Thomas was, therefore, compelled to say that the principle of individuation is *materia signata quantitate*, in the sense of matter having an exigency for the quantitative determination which it receives from union with form. This is a difficult notion to understand, since although matter, and not form, is the foundation of quantitative multiplication, matter considered in itself is without quantitative determination: the notion is in fact a relic of the Platonic element in Aristotle's thought. Aristotle rejected and attacked the Platonic theory of forms, but his Platonic training influenced him to the extent of his being led to say that form, being of itself universal, requires individuation, and St. Thomas followed him in this. Of course, St. Thomas did not think of forms first existing separately and then being individuated, for the forms of sensible objects do not exist in a state of temporal priority to the composite substances; but the idea of individuation is certainly due originally to the Platonic way of thinking and speaking of forms: Aristotle substituted the notion of the immanent substantial form for that of the 'transcendent' exemplar form, but it would

---

[1] *In 7 Metaph., lectio 2.*   [2] *S.T.*, Ia, 66, 1, *in corpore.*

not become an historian to turn a blind eye to the Platonic legacy in Aristotle's thought and consequently in that of St. Thomas.

3. As a logical consequence of the doctrine that prime matter as such is pure potentiality, St. Thomas rejected the Augustinian theory of *rationes seminales*:[1] to admit this theory would be to attribute act in some way to what is in itself without act.[2] Non-spiritual forms are educed out of the potentiality of matter under the action of the efficient agent, but they are not previously in prime matter as inchoate forms. The agent does not, of course, work on prime matter as such, since this latter cannot exist by itself; but he or it so modifies or changes the dispositions of a given corporeal substance that it develops an exigency for a new form, which is educed out of the potentiality of matter. Change thus presupposes, for Aquinas as for Aristotle, a 'privation' or an exigency for a new form which the substance has not yet got but 'demands' to have in virtue of the modifications produced in it by the agent. Water, for example, is in a state of potentiality to becoming steam, but it will not become steam until it has been heated to a certain point by an external agent, at which point it develops an exigency for the form of steam, which does not come from outside, but is educed out of the potentiality of matter.

4. Just as St. Thomas rejected the older theory of *rationes seminales*, so he rejected the theory of the plurality of substantial forms in the composite substance, affirming the unicity of the substantial form in each substance. In his Commentary on the *Sentences* St. Thomas seems indeed to accept the *forma corporeitatis* as the first substantial form in the corporeal substance;[3] but even if he accepted it at first, he certainly rejected it afterwards. In the *Contra Gentiles*[4] he argues that if the first form constituted the substance as substance, the subsequent forms would arise in something which was already *hoc aliquid in actu*, something actually subsisting, and so could be no more than accidental forms. Similarly he argues against the theory of Avicebron[5] by pointing out that only the first form can be the substantial form, since it would confer the character of substance, with the result that other

---

[1] *In 2 Sent.*, 18, 1, 2.

[2] St. Thomas certainly employed the name, *rationes seminales*, but he meant thereby primarily the active forces of concrete objects, e.g. the active power which controls the generation of living things and restricts it to the same species, not the doctrine that there are inchoate forms in prime matter. This last theory he either rejected or said that it did not fit in with the teaching of St. Augustine (cf. *loc. cit.*, S.T., Ia, 115, 2; *De Veritate*, 5, 9, *ad* 8 and *ad* 9).

[3] Cf. *In* I *Sent.*, 8, 5, 2; 2 *Sent.*, 3, 1, 1.

[4] 4, 81.　　　　　[5] *Quodlibet*, 11, 5, 5, *in corpore*.

subsequent forms, arising in an already constituted substance, would be accidental. (The necessary implication is, of course, that the substantial form directly informs prime matter.) This view aroused much opposition, being stigmatised as a dangerous innovation, as we shall see later when dealing with the controversies in which St. Thomas's Aristotelianism involved him.

5. The hylomorphic composition which obtains in material substances was restricted by St. Thomas to the corporeal world: he would not extend it, as St. Bonaventure did, to the incorporeal creation, to angels. That angels exist, St. Thomas considered to be rationally provable, quite apart from revelation, for their existence is demanded by the hierarchic character of the scale of being. We can discern the ascending orders or ranks of forms from the forms of inorganic substances, through vegetative forms, the irrational sensitive forms of animals, the rational soul of man, to the infinite and pure Act, God; but there is a gap in the hierarchy. The rational soul of man is created, finite and embodied, while God is uncreated, infinite and pure spirit: it is only reasonable, then, to suppose that between the human soul and God there are finite and created spiritual forms which are without body. At the summit of the scale is the absolute simplicity of God: at the summit of the corporeal world is the human being, partly spiritual and partly corporeal: there must, therefore, exist between God and man beings which are wholly spiritual and yet which do not possess the absolute simplicity of the Godhead.[1]

This line of argument was not new: it had been employed in Greek philosophy, by Poseidonius, for example. St. Thomas was also influenced by the Aristotelian doctrine of separate Intelligences connected with the motion of the spheres, this astronomical view reappearing in the philosophy of Avicenna, with which St. Thomas was familiar; but the argument which weighed most with him was that drawn from the exigencies of the hierarchy of being. As he distinguished the different grades of forms in general, so he distinguished the different 'choirs' of angels, according to the object of their knowledge. Those who apprehend most clearly the goodness of God in itself and are inflamed with love thereat are the Seraphim, the highest 'choir', while those who are concerned with the providence of God in regard to particular creatures, for example, in regard to particular men, are the angels in the narrower sense of the word, the lowest choir. The choir which is

[1] Cf. *De spirit. creat.*, 1, 5.

concerned with, *inter alia*, the movement of the heavenly bodies (which are universal causes affecting this world) is that of the Virtues. Thus St. Thomas did not postulate the existence of angels primarily in order to account for the movement of the spheres.

Angels exist therefore; but it remains to be asked if they are hylomorphically composed. St. Thomas affirmed that they are not so composed. He argued that the angels must be purely immaterial, since they are intelligences which have as their correlative object immaterial objects, and also that their very place in the hierarchy of being demands their complete immateriality.[1] Moreover, as St. Thomas places in matter an exigency for quantity (which possibly does not altogether square with its character of pure potentiality), he could not in any case attribute hylomorphic composition to the angels. St. Bonaventure, for example, had argued that angels must be hylomorphically composed, since otherwise they would be pure act and God alone is pure act; but St. Thomas countered this argument by affirming that the distinction between essence and existence in the angels is sufficient to safeguard their contingency and their radical distinction from God.[2] To this distinction I shall return shortly.

A consequence of the denial of the hylomorphic composition of the angels is the denial of the multiplicity of angels within one species, since matter is the principle of individuation and there is no matter in the angels. Each angel is pure form: each angel, then, must exhaust the capacity of its species and be its own species. The choirs of angels are not, then, so many species of angels; they consist of angelic hierarchies distinguished not specifically but according to function. There are as many species as there are angels. It is of interest to remember that Aristotle, when asserting in the *Metaphysics* a plurality of movers, of separated intelligences, raised the question how this could be possible if matter is the principle of individuation, though he did not answer the question. While St. Bonaventure, admitting the hylomorphic composition of angels, could and did admit their multiplicity within the species, St. Thomas, holding on the one hand that matter is the principle of individuation and denying its presence in the angels on the other hand, was forced to deny their multiplicity within the species. For St. Thomas, then, the intelligences really became separate universals, though not, of course, in the

---

[1] *S.T.*, Ia, 50, 2; *De spirit. creat.*, I, I.
[2] *De spirit. creat.*, I, I; *S.T.*, Ia, 50, 2, ad 3; *Contra Gent.*, 2, 30; *Quodlibet*, 9, 4, I.

sense of hypostatised concepts. It was one of the discoveries of Aristotle that a separate form must be intelligent, though he failed to see the historic connection between his theory of separate intelligences and the Platonic theory of separate forms.

6. The establishment of the hylomorphic composition of material substances reveals at once the essential mutability of those substances. Change is not, of course, a haphazard affair, but proceeds according to a certain rhythm (one cannot assume that a given substance can become immediately any other substance one likes, while change is also guided and influenced by the general causes, such as the heavenly bodies); yet substantial change cannot take place except in bodies, and it is only matter, the substrate of change, which makes it possible. On the principle which St. Thomas adopted from Aristotle that what is changed or moved is changed or moved 'by another', *ab alio*, one might argue at once from the changes in the corporeal world to the existence of an unmoved mover, with the aid of the principle that an infinite regress in the order of dependence is impossible; but before going on to prove the existence of God from nature, one must first penetrate more deeply into the constitution of finite being.

Hylomorphic composition is confined by St. Thomas to the corporeal world; but there is a more fundamental distinction, of which the distinction between form and matter is but one example. Prime matter, as we have seen, is pure potentiality, while form is act, so that the distinction between matter and form is a distinction between potency and act, but this latter distinction is of wider application than the former. In the angels there is no matter, but there is none the less potentiality. (St. Bonaventure argued that because matter is potentiality, therefore it can be in angels. He was thus forced to admit the *forma corporeitatis*, in order to distinguish corporeal matter from matter in the general sense. St. Thomas, on the other hand, as he made matter pure potentiality and yet denied its presence in the angels, was forced to attribute to matter an exigency for quantity, which comes to it through form. Obviously there are difficulties in both views.) The angels can change by performing acts of intellect and will, even though they cannot change substantially: there is, therefore, some potentiality in the angels. The distinction between potentiality and act runs, therefore, through the whole of creation, whereas the distinction between form and matter is found only in the corporeal creation. Thus, on the principle that the reduction of potentiality to act requires a principle which is itself act, we should be in a position to argue from the fundamental distinction which obtains in all creation to the existence of pure Act, God; but first of all we must consider the basis of potentiality in the angels. In passing, one can notice that the distinction of potency and act is discussed by Aristotle in the *Metaphysics*.

7. We have seen that hylomorphic composition was restricted by St. Thomas to corporeal substance; but there is a profounder composition which affects every finite being. Finite being is being because it exists, because it has existence: the substance is that which is or has being, and 'existence is that in virtue of which a substance is called a being'.[1] The essence of a corporeal being is the substance composed of matter and form, while the essence of an immaterial finite being is form alone; but that by which a material substance or an immaterial substance is a real being (*ens*) is existence (*esse*), existence standing to the essence as act to potentiality. Composition of act and potentiality is found, therefore, in every finite being and not simply in corporeal being. No finite being exists necessarily; it has or possesses existence which is distinct from essence as act is distinct from potentiality. The form determines or completes in the sphere of essence, but that which actualises the essence is existence. 'In intellectual substances which are not composed of matter and form (in them the form is a subsistent substance), the form is that which is; but existence is the act by which the form is; and on that account there is in them only one composition of act and potentiality, namely composition of substance and existence. . . . In substances composed of matter and form, however, there is a double composition of act and potentiality, the first a composition in the substance itself, which is composed of matter and form, the second a composition of the substance itself, which is already composite, with existence. This second composition can also be called a composition of the *quod est* and *esse*, or of the *quod est* and the *quo est*.'[2] Existence, then, is neither matter nor form; it is neither an essence nor part of an essence; it is the act by which the essence is or has being. '*Esse* denotes a certain act; for a thing is not said to be (*esse*) by the fact that it is in potentiality, but by the fact that it is in act.'[3] As neither matter nor form, it can be neither a substantial nor an accidental form; it does not belong to the sphere of essence, but is that by which forms are.

[1] *Contra Gent.*, 2, 54.   [2] *Ibid.*   [3] *Ibid.*, 1, 22.

Controversy has raged in the Schools round the question whether St. Thomas considered the distinction between essence and existence to be a real distinction or a conceptual distinction. Obviously the answer to this question depends largely on the meaning attached to the phrase 'real distinction'. If by real distinction were meant a distinction between two things which could be separated from one another, then certainly St. Thomas did not hold that there is a real distinction between essence and existence, which are not two separable physical objects. Giles of Rome practically held this view, making the distinction a physical distinction; but for St. Thomas the distinction was metaphysical, essence and existence being the two constitutive metaphysical principles of every finite being. If, however, by real distinction is meant a distinction which is independent of the mind, which is objective, it seems to me not only that St. Thomas maintained such a distinction as obtaining between essence and existence, but that it is essential to his system and that he attached great importance to it. St. Thomas speaks of *esse* as *adveniens extra*, in the sense that it comes from God, the cause of existence; it is act, distinct from the potentiality which it actualises. In God alone, insists St. Thomas, are essence and existence identical: God exists necessarily because His essence is existence: all other things receive or 'participate in' existence, and that which receives must be distinct from that which is received.[1] The fact that St. Thomas argues that that whose existence is other than its essence must have received its existence from another, and that it is true of God alone that His existence is not different from or other than His essence, seems to me to make it perfectly clear that he regarded the distinction between essence and existence as objective and independent of the mind. The 'third way' of proving the existence of God appears to presuppose the real distinction between essence and existence in finite things.

Existence determines essence in the sense that it is act and through it the essence has being; but on the other hand existence, as act, is determined by essence, as potentiality, to be the existence of this or that kind of essence.[2] Yet we must not imagine that essence existed before receiving existence (which would be a contradiction in terms) or that there is a kind of neutral existence which is not the existence of any thing in particular until it is united with essence: the two principles are not two physical things

---

[1] Cf. *S.T.*, Ia, 3, 4; *Contra Gent.*, I, 22.   [2] *De Potentia*, 7, 2, ad 9.

united together, but they are two constitutive principles which are concreated as principles of a particular being. There is no essence without existence and no existence without essence; the two are created together, and if its existence ceases, the concrete essence ceases to be. Existence, then, is not something accidental to the finite being: it is that by which the finite being is a being. If we rely on the imagination, we shall think of essence and existence as two things, two beings; but a great deal of the difficulty in understanding St. Thomas's doctrine on the subject comes from employing the imagination and supposing that if he maintained the real distinction, he must have understood it in the exaggerated and misleading fashion of Giles of Rome.

The Moslem philosophers had already discussed the relation of existence to essence. Alfarabi, for example, had observed that analysis of the essence of a finite object will not reveal its existence. If it did, then it would be sufficient to know what human nature is, in order to know that man exists, which is not the case. Essence and existence are, therefore, distinct, and Alfarabi drew the somewhat unfortunate conclusion that existence is an accident of the essence. Avicenna followed Alfarabi in this matter. Although St. Thomas certainly did not regard existence as an 'accident', in the *De ente et essentia*[1] he follows Alfarabi and Avicenna in their way of approaching the distinction. Every thing which does not belong to the concept of the essence comes to it from without (*adveniens extra*) and forms a composition with it. No essence can be conceived without that which forms part of the essence; but every finite essence can be conceived without existence being included in the essence. I can conceive 'man' or 'phoenix' and yet not know if they exist in nature. It would, however, be a mistake to interpret St. Thomas as though he maintained that the essence, prior to the reception of existence, was something on its own, so to speak, with a diminutive existence proper to itself: it exists only through existence, and created existence is always the existence of this or that kind of essence. Created existence and essence arise together, and although the two constitutive principles are objectively distinct, existence is the more fundamental. Since created existence is the act of a potentiality, the latter has no actuality apart from existence, which is 'among all things the most perfect' and 'the perfection of all perfections'.[2]

St. Thomas thus discovers in the heart of all finite being a certain instability, a contingency or non-necessity, which immediately points to the existence of a Being which is the source of finite existence, the author of the composition between essence and existence, and which cannot be itself composed of essence and existence but must have existence as its very essence, existing necessarily. It would indeed be absurd and most unjust to accuse Francis Suarez (1548–1617) and other Scholastics who denied the 'real distinction' of denying the contingent character of finite being (Suarez denied a real distinction between essence and existence and maintained that the finite object is limited because *ab alio*); but I do not personally feel any doubt that St. Thomas himself maintained the doctrine of the real distinction, provided that the real distinction is not interpreted as Giles of Rome interpreted it. For St. Thomas, existence is not a state of the essence, but rather that which places the essence in a state of actuality.

It may be objected that I have evaded the real point at issue, namely the precise way in which the distinction between essence and existence is objective and independent of the mind. But St. Thomas did not state his doctrine in such a manner that no controversy about its meaning is possible. Nevertheless it seems clear to me that St. Thomas held that the distinction between essence and existence is an objective distinction between two metaphysical principles which constitute the whole being of the created finite thing, one of these principles, namely existence, standing to the other, namely essence, as act to potency. And I do not see how St. Thomas could have attributed that importance to the distinction which he did attribute to it, unless he thought that it was a 'real' distinction.

CHAPTER XXXIV

ST. THOMAS AQUINAS—IV: PROOFS OF GOD'S EXISTENCE

Need of proof—St. Anselm's argument—Possibility of proof—
The first three proofs—The fourth proof—The proof from finality
—The 'third way' fundamental.

1. BEFORE actually developing his proofs of God's existence St.
Thomas tried to show that the provision of such proofs is not a
useless superfluity, since the idea of God's existence is not,
properly speaking, an innate idea nor is 'God exists' a proposition
the opposite of which is inconceivable and cannot be thought. To
us indeed, living in a world where atheism is common, where
powerful and influential philosophies eliminate or explain away
the notion of God, where multitudes of men and women are
educated without any belief in God, it seems only natural to think
that God's existence requires proof. Kierkegaard and those philosophers and theologians who follow him may have rejected natural
theology in the ordinary sense; but normally speaking we should
not dream of asserting that God's existence is what St. Thomas
calls a *per se notum*. St. Thomas, however, did not live in a world
where theoretic atheism was common, and he felt himself compelled to deal not only with statements of certain early Christian
writers which seemed to imply that knowledge of God is innate in
man, but also with the famous argument of St. Anselm which
purports to show that the non-existence of God is inconceivable.
Thus in the *Summa Theologica*[1] he devotes an article to answering
the question *utrum Deum esse sit per se notum*, and two chapters
in the *Summa contra Gentiles*[2] to the consideration *de opinione
dicentium quod Deum esse demonstrari non potest, quum sit per se
notum.*

St. John Damascene[3] asserts that the knowledge of God's
existence is naturally innate in man; but St. Thomas explains
that this natural knowledge of God is confused and vague and
needs elucidation to be made explicit. Man has a natural desire
of happiness (*beatitudo*), and a natural desire supposes a natural
knowledge; but although true happiness is to be found only in
God, it does not follow that every man has a natural knowledge

---

[1] Ia, 2, 1.   [2] I, 10–11.   [3] *De fide orthodoxa*, I, 3.

of God as such: he has a vague idea of happiness since he desires it, but he may think that happiness consists in sensual pleasure or in the possession of wealth, and further reflection is required before he can realise that happiness is to be found only in God. In other words, even if the natural desire for happiness may form the basis for a proof of God's existence, a proof is none the less required. Again, in a sense it is *per se notum* that there is truth, since a man who asserts that there is no truth inevitably asserts that it is true that there is no truth, but it does not follow that the man knows that there is a primal or first Truth, a Source of truth, God: further reflection is necessary if he is to realise this. Once again, although it is true that without God we can know nothing, it does not follow that in knowing anything we have an actual knowledge of God, since God's influence, which enables us to know anything, is not the object of direct intuition but is known only by reflection.[1]

In general, says St. Thomas, we must make a distinction between what is *per se notum secundum se* and what is *per se notum quoad nos*. A proposition is said to be *per se nota secundum se* when the predicate is included in the subject, as in the proposition that man is an animal, since man is precisely a rational animal. The proposition that God exists is thus a proposition *per se nota secundum se*, since God's essence is His existence and one cannot know God's nature, what God is, without knowing God's existence, that He is; but a man has no *a priori* knowledge of God's nature and only arrives at knowledge of the fact that God's essence is His existence after he has come to know God's existence, so that even though the proposition that God exists is *per se nota secundum se*, it is not *per se nota quoad nos*.

2. In regard to the 'ontological' or *a priori* proof of God's existence given by St. Anselm, St. Thomas answers first of all that not everyone understands by God 'that than which no greater can be thought'. Possibly this observation, though doubtless true, is not altogether relevant, except in so far as St. Anselm considered that everyone understands by 'God' that Being whose existence

[1] It may appear that St. Thomas's attitude in regard to 'innate' knowledge of God does not differ substantially from that of St. Bonaventure. In a sense this is true, since neither of them admitted an explicit innate idea of God; but St. Bonaventure thought that there is a kind of initial implicit awareness of God, or at least that the idea of God can be rendered explicit by interior reflection alone, whereas the proofs actually given by St. Thomas all proceed by way of the external world. Even if we press the 'Aristotelian' aspect of Bonaventure's epistemology, it remains true that there is a difference of emphasis and approach in the natural theology of the two philosophers.

he intended to prove, namely the supremely perfect Being. It must not be forgotten that Anselm reckoned his argument to be an argument or proof, not the statement of an immediate intuition of God. He then argues, both in the *Summa contra Gentiles* and in the *Summa Theologica*, that the argument of St. Anselm involves an illicit process or transition from the ideal to the real order. Granted that God is conceived as the Being than which no greater can be thought, it does not follow necessarily that such a Being exists, apart from its being conceived, that is, outside the mind. This, however, is not an adequate argument, when taken by itself at least, to disprove the Anselmian reasoning, since it neglects the peculiar character of God, of the Being than which no greater can be thought. Such a Being is its own existence and if it is possible for such a Being to exist, it must exist. The Being than which no greater can be thought is the Being which exists necessarily, it is the necessary Being, and it would be absurd to speak of a merely possible necessary Being. But St. Thomas adds, as we have seen, that the intellect has no *a priori* knowledge of God's nature. In other words, owing to the weakness of the human intellect we cannot discern *a priori* the positive possibility of the supremely perfect Being, the Being the essence of which is existence, and we come to a knowledge of the fact that such a Being exists not through an analysis or consideration of the idea of such a Being, but through arguments from its effects, *a posteriori*.

3. If God's existence cannot be proved *a priori*, through the idea of God, through His essence, it remains that it must be proved *a posteriori*, through an examination of God's effects. It may be objected that this is impossible since the effects of God are finite while God is infinite, so that there is no proportion between the effects and the Cause and the conclusion of the reasoning process will contain infinitely more than the premises. The reasoning starts with sensible objects and should, therefore, end with a sensible object, whereas in the proofs of God's existence it proceeds to an Object infinitely transcending all sensible objects.

St. Thomas does not deal with this objection at any length, and it would be an absurd anachronism to expect him to discuss and answer the Kantian Critique of metaphysics in advance; but he points out that though from a consideration of effects which are disproportionate to the cause we cannot obtain a perfect knowledge of the cause, we can come to know that the cause exists. We can argue from an effect to the existence of a cause, and if the effect is of such a kind that it can proceed only from a certain kind of cause, we can legitimately argue to the existence of a cause of that kind. (The use of the word 'effect' must not be taken as begging the question, as a *petitio principii*: St. Thomas argues from certain facts concerning the world and argues that these facts require a sufficient ontological explanation. It is true, of course, that he presupposes that the principle of causality is not purely subjective or applicable only within the sphere of 'phenomena' in the Kantian sense; but he is perfectly well aware that it has to be shown that sensible objects are effects, in the sense that they do not contain in themselves their own sufficient ontological explanation.)

A modern Thomist, wishing to expound and defend the natural theology of the Saint in the light of post-mediaeval philosophic thought, would rightly be expected to say something in justification of the speculative reason, of metaphysics. Even if he considered that the onus of proof falls primarily on the opponent of metaphysics, he could not neglect the fact that the legitimacy and even the significance of metaphysical arguments and conclusions have been challenged, and he would be bound to meet this challenge. I cannot see, however, how an historian of mediaeval philosophy in general can justly be expected to treat St. Thomas as though he were a contemporary and fully aware not only of the Kantian criticism of the speculative reason, but also of the attitude towards metaphysics adopted by the logical positivists. Nevertheless, it is true that the Thomist theory of knowledge itself provides, apparently at least, a strong objection against natural theology. According to St. Thomas the proper object of the human intellect is the *quidditas* or essence of the material object: the intellect starts from the sensible objects, knows in dependence on the phantasm and is proportioned, in virtue of its embodied state, to sensible objects. St. Thomas did not admit innate ideas nor did he have recourse to any intuitive knowledge of God, and if one applies strictly the Aristotelian principle that there is nothing in the intellect which was not before in the senses (*Nihil in intellectu quod non prius fuerit in sensu*), it might well appear that the human intellect is confined to knowledge of corporeal objects and cannot, owing to its nature or at least its present state, transcend them. As this objection arises out of the doctrine of Thomas himself, it is relevant to inquire if the Saint attempted to meet it and, if so, how he met it. With the Thomist theory of human knowledge I shall deal later;[1] but I shall give immediately a brief statement of what appears to be St. Thomas's position on this point without development or references.

Objects, whether spiritual or corporeal, are knowable only in so far as they partake of being, are in act, and the intellect as such is the faculty of apprehending being. Considered simply in itself, therefore, the intellect has as its object all being; the primary object of intellect is being. The fact, however, that a particular kind of intellect, the human intellect, is embodied and is dependent on sense for its operation, means that it must start from the things of sense and that, naturally speaking, it can come to know an object which transcends the things of sense (consideration of self-knowledge is here omitted) only in so far as sensible objects bear a relation to that object and manifest it. Owing to the fact that the human intellect is embodied its natural and proper object, proportionate to its present state, is the corporeal object; but this does not destroy the primary orientation of the intellect to being in general, and if corporeal objects bear a discernible relation to an object which transcends them, the intellect can know that such an object exists. Moreover, in so far as material objects reveal the character of the Transcendent, the intellect can attain some knowledge of its nature; but such a knowledge cannot be adequate or perfect, since sense-objects cannot reveal adequately or perfectly the nature of the Transcendent. Of our natural knowledge of God's nature I shall speak later:[2] let it suffice to point out here that when St. Thomas says that the corporeal object is the natural object of the human intellect, he means that the human intellect in its present state is orientated towards the essence of the corporeal object, but that just as the embodied condition of the human intellect does not destroy its primary character as intellect, so its orientation, in virtue of its embodied state, towards the corporeal object does not destroy its primary orientation towards being in general. It can therefore attain to some natural knowledge of God, in so far as corporeal objects are related to Him and reveal Him; but this knowledge is necessarily imperfect and inadequate and cannot be intuitive in character.

4. The first of the five proofs of God's existence given by St. Thomas is that from motion, which is found in Aristotle[3] and was utilised by Maimonides and St. Albert. We know through sense-perception that some things in the world are moved, that motion

is a fact. Motion is here understood in the wide Aristotelian sense of reduction of potency to act, and St. Thomas, following Aristotle, argues that a thing cannot be reduced from potency to act except by something which is already in act. In this sense 'every thing which is moved is moved by another'. If that other is itself moved, it must be moved by yet another agent. As an infinite series is impossible, we come in the end to an unmoved mover, a first mover, 'and all understand that this is God'.[1] This argument St. Thomas calls the *manifestior via*.[2] In the *Summa contra Gentiles*[3] he develops it at considerable length.

The second proof, which is suggested by the second book of Aristotle's *Metaphysics*[4] and which was used by Avicenna, Alan of Lille and St. Albert, also starts from the sensible world, but this time from the order or series of efficient causes. Nothing can be the cause of itself, for in order to be this, it would have to exist before itself. On the other hand, it is impossible to proceed to infinity in the series of efficient causes: therefore there must be a first efficient cause, 'which all men call God'.

The third proof, which Maimonides took over from Avicenna and developed, starts from the fact that some beings come into existence and perish, which shows that they can not be and can be, that they are contingent and not necessary, since if they were necessary they would always have existed and would neither come into being nor pass away. St. Thomas then argues that there must exist a necessary being, which is the reason why contingent beings come into existence. If there were no necessary being, nothing at all would exist.

There are several remarks which must be made, though very briefly, concerning these three proofs. First of all, when St. Thomas says that an infinite series is impossible (and this principle is utilised in all three proofs), he is not thinking of a series stretching back in time, of a 'horizontal' series, so to speak. He is not saying, for example, that because the child owes its life to its parents and its parents owe their lives to their parents and so on, there must have been an original pair, who had no parents but were directly created by God. St. Thomas did not believe that it can be proved philosophically that the world was not created from eternity: he admits the abstract possibility of the world's creation from eternity and this cannot be admitted without the possibility of a beginningless series being admitted at the same time. What he

---

[1] *S.T.*, Ia, 2, 3, *in corpore*.   [2] *Ibid*.   [3] I, 13.   [4] C. 2.

denies is the possibility of an infinite series in the order of actually
depending causes, of an infinite 'vertical' series. Suppose that the
world had actually been created from eternity. There would be
an infinite horizontal or historic series, but the whole series would
consist of contingent beings, for the fact of its being without
beginning does not make it necessary. The whole series, therefore,
must depend on something outside the series. But if you ascend
upwards, without ever coming to a stop, you have no explanation
of the existence of the series: one must conclude with the existence
of a being which is not itself dependent.

Secondly, consideration of the foregoing remarks will show that
the so-called mathematical infinite series has nothing to do with
the Thomist proofs. It is not the possibility of an infinite series
as such which St. Thomas denies, but the possibility of an infinite
series in the ontological order of dependence. In other words, he
denies that the movement and contingency of the experienced
world can be without any ultimate and adequate ontological
explanation.

Thirdly, it might seem to be rather cavalier behaviour on St.
Thomas's part to assume that the unmoved mover or the first
cause or the necessary being is what we call God. Obviously if
anything exists at all, there must be a necessary Being: thought
must arrive at this conclusion, unless metaphysics is rejected
altogether; but it is not so obvious that the necessary being must
be the personal Being whom we call God. That a purely philosophical argument does not bring us to the full revealed notion of
God needs no elaboration; but, even apart from the full notion
of God as revealed by Christ and preached by the Church, does a
purely philosophical argument give us a personal Being at all?
Did St. Thomas's belief in God lead him perhaps to find more in
the conclusion of the argument than was actually there? Because
he was looking for arguments to prove the existence of the God
in whom he believed, was he not perhaps over-hasty in identifying
the first mover, the first cause and the necessary being with the
God of Christianity and religious experience, the personal Being
to whom man can pray? I think that we must admit that the
actual phrases which St. Thomas appends to the proofs given in
the *Summa Theologica* (*et hoc omnes intelligunt Deum, causam
efficientem primam quam omnes Deum nominant, quod omnes dicunt
Deum*) constitute, if considered in isolation, an over-hasty conclusion; but, apart from the fact that the *Summa Theologica* is a

summary (and mainly) theological text-book, these phrases should not be taken in isolation. For example, the actual summary proof of the existence of a necessary being contains no explicit argument to show whether that being is material or immaterial, so that the observation at the end of the proof that this being is called by everyone God might seem to be without sufficient warrant; but in the first article of the next question St. Thomas asks if God is material, a body, and argues that He is not. The phrases in the question should, therefore, be understood as expressions of the fact that God is recognised by all who believe in Him to be the first Cause and necessary Being, not as an unjustifiable suppression of further argument. In any case the proofs are given by St. Thomas simply in outline: it is not as though he had in mind the composition of a treatise against professed atheists. If he had to deal with Marxists, he would doubtless treat the proofs in a different, or at least in a more elaborate and developed manner: as it is, his main interest is to give a proof of the *praeambula fidei*. Even in the *Summa contra Gentiles* the Saint was not dealing primarily with atheists, but rather with the Mohammedans, who had a firm belief in God.

5. The fourth proof is suggested by some observations in Aristotle's *Metaphysics*[1] and is found substantially in St. Augustine and St. Anselm. It starts from the degrees of perfection, of goodness, truth, etc., in the things of this world, which permit of one making such comparative judgements as 'this is more beautiful than that', 'this is better than that'. Assuming that such judgements have an objective foundation, St. Thomas argues that the degrees of perfection necessarily imply the existence of a best, a most true, etc., which will be also the supreme being (*maxime ens*).

So far the argument leads only to a relatively best. If one can establish that there actually are degrees of truth, goodness and being, a hierarchy of being, then there must be one being or several beings which are comparatively or relatively supreme. But this is not enough to prove the existence of God, and St. Thomas proceeds to argue that what is supreme in goodness, for example, must be the cause of goodness in all things. Further, inasmuch as goodness, truth and being are convertible, there must be a supreme Being which is the cause of being, goodness, truth, and so of all perfection in every other being; *et hoc dicimus Deum*.

[1] 2, 1; 4, 4.

As the term of the argument is a Being which transcends all sensible objects, the perfections in question can obviously be only those perfections which are capable of subsisting by themselves, pure perfections, which do not involve any necessary relation to extension or quantity. The argument is Platonic in origin and presupposes the idea of participation. Contingent beings do not possess their being of themselves, nor their goodness or onto-logical truth; they receive their perfections, share them. The ultimate cause of perfection must itself be perfect: it cannot receive its perfection from another, but must be its own perfection: it is self-existing being and perfection. The argument consists, then, in the application of principles already used in the foregoing proofs to pure perfections: it is not really a departure from the general spirit of the other proofs, in spite of its Platonic descent. One of the main difficulties about it, however, is, as already indicated, to show that there actually are objective degrees of being and perfection before one has shown that there actually exists a Being which is absolute and self-existing Perfection.

6. The fifth way is the teleological proof, for which Kant had a considerable respect on account of its antiquity, clarity and persuasiveness, though, in accordance with the principles of the *Kritik der reinen Vernunft*, he refused to recognise its demonstra-tive character.

St. Thomas argues that we behold inorganic objects operating for an end, and as this happens always or very frequently, it cannot proceed from chance, but must be the result of intention. But inorganic objects are without knowledge: they cannot, then, tend towards an end unless they are directed by someone who is intelligent and possessed of knowledge, as 'the arrow is directed by the archer'. Therefore there exists an intelligent Being, by whom all natural things are directed to an end; *et hoc dicimus Deum.* In the *Summa contra Gentiles* the Saint states the argu-ment in a slightly different manner, arguing that when many things with different and even contrary qualities co-operate towards the realisation of one order, this must proceed from an intelligent Cause or Providence; *et hoc dicimus Deum.* If the proof as given in the *Summa Theologica* emphasises the internal finality of the inorganic object, that given in the *Summa contra Gentiles* emphasises rather the co-operation of many objects in the realisa-tion of the one world order or harmony. By itself the proof leads to a Designer or Governor or Architect of the universe, as Kant observed; further reasoning is required in order to show that this Architect is not only a 'Demiurge', but also Creator.

7. The proofs have been stated in more or less the same bold and succinct way in which St. Thomas states them. With the exception of the first proof, which is elaborated at some length in the *Summa contra Gentiles*, the proofs are given only in very bare outline, both in the *Summa Theologica* and in the *Summa contra Gentiles*. No mention has been made, however, of Aquinas's (to our view) somewhat unfortunate physical illustrations, as when he says that fire is the cause of all hot things, since these illustrations are really irrelevant to the validity or invalidity of the proofs as such. The modern disciple of St. Thomas naturally has not only to develop the proofs in far greater detail and to consider difficulties and objections which could hardly have occurred to St. Thomas, but also to justify the very principles on which the general line of proof rests. Thus, in regard to the fifth proof given by St. Thomas, the modern Thomist must take some account of recent theories which profess to render intelligible the genesis of the order and finality in the universe without recourse to the hypothesis of any spiritual agent distinct from the universe, while in regard to all the proofs he has not only, in face of the Kantian Critique, to justify the line of argument on which they rest, but he has to show, as against the logical positivists, that the word 'God' has some significance. It is not, however, the task of the historian to develop the proofs as they would have to be developed to-day, nor is it his task to justify those proofs. The way in which St. Thomas states the proofs may perhaps cause some dissatisfaction in the reader; but it must be remembered that the Saint was primarily a theologian and that, as already mentioned, he was concerned not so much to give an exhaustive treatment of the proofs as to prove in a summary fashion the *praeambula fidei*. He, therefore, makes use of traditional proofs, which either had or seemed to have some support in Aristotle and which had been employed by some of his predecessors.

St. Thomas gives five proofs, and among these five proofs he gives a certain preference to the first, to the extent at least of calling it the *via manifestior*. However, whatever we may think of this assertion, the fundamental proof is really the third proof or 'way', that from contingency. In the first proof the argument from contingency is applied to the special fact of motion or change, in the second proof to the order of causality or causal production, in the fourth proof to degrees of perfection and in the fifth proof to finality, to the co-operation of inorganic objects in the attainment of cosmic order. The argument from contingency itself is based on the fact that everything must have its sufficient reason, the reason why it exists. Change or motion must have its sufficient reason in an unmoved mover, the series of secondary causes and effects in an uncaused cause, limited perfection in absolute perfection, and finality and order in nature in an Intelligence or Designer. The 'interiority' of the proofs of God's existence as given by St. Augustine or St. Bonaventure is absent from the five ways of St. Thomas; but one could, of course, apply the general principles to the self, if one so wished. As they stand, the five proofs of St. Thomas may be said to be an explicitation of the words of the *Book of Wisdom*[1] and of St. Paul in *Romans*[2] that God can be known from His works, as transcending His works.

[1] Ch. 13. [2] Ch. 1.

CHAPTER XXXV

ST. THOMAS AQUINAS—V: GOD'S NATURE

The negative way—The affirmative way—Analogy—Types of analogy—A difficulty—The divine ideas—No real distinction between the divine attributes—God as existence itself.

1. ONCE it has been established that the necessary Being exists, it would seem only natural to proceed to the investigation of God's nature. It is very unsatisfactory simply to know that a necessary Being exists, unless at the same time we can know what sort of a Being the necessary Being is. But a difficulty at once arises. We have in this life no intuition of the divine essence; we are dependent for our knowledge on sense-perception, and the ideas which we form are derived from our experience of creatures. Language too is formed to express these ideas and so refers primarily to our experience and would seem to have objective reference only within the sphere of our experience. How, then, can we come to know a Being which transcends sense-experience? How can we form ideas which express in any way the nature of a Being which transcends the range of our experience, the world of creatures? How can the words of any human language be at all applicable to the Divine Being?

St. Thomas was well aware of this difficulty, and indeed the whole tradition of Christian philosophy, which had undergone the influence of the writings of the Pseudo-Dionysius, himself dependent on neo-Platonism, would have helped, if help had been needed, to prevent him indulging in any over-confidence in the power of the human reason to penetrate the divine essence. Rationalism of the Hegelian type was quite foreign to his mind, and we find him saying that we cannot come to know of God *quid sit*, what He is (His essence), but only *an sit* or *quod sit*, that He is (His existence). This statement, if taken alone, would seem to involve complete agnosticism as regards the divine nature, but this is not St. Thomas's meaning, and the statement must be interpreted according to his general doctrine and his explanation of it. Thus in the *Summa contra Gentiles*[1] he says that 'the divine substance exceeds by its immensity every form which our intellect

[1] I, 14.

attains; and so we cannot apprehend it by knowing what it is, but we have some notion of it by coming to know what it is not.' For example, we come to know something of God by recognising that He is not, and cannot be, a corporeal substance: by denying of Him corporeality we form some notion of His nature, since we know that He is not body, though this does not give us of itself a positive idea of what the divine substance is in itself, and the more predicates we can deny of God in this way, the more we approximate to a knowledge of Him.

This is the famous *via remotionis* or *via negativa*, so dear to the Pseudo-Dionysius and other Christian writers who had been strongly influenced by neo-Platonism; but St. Thomas adds a very useful observation concerning the negative way.[1] In the case of a created substance, he says, which we can define, we first of all assign it to its genus by which we know in general what it is, and then we add the difference by which it is distinguished from other things; but in the case of God we cannot assign Him to a genus, since He transcends all genera, and so we cannot distinguish Him from other beings by positive differences (*per affirmativas differentias*). Nevertheless, though we cannot approach to a clear idea of God's nature in the same way in which we can attain a clear idea of human nature, that is, by a succession of positive or affirmative differentiations, such as living, sensitive or animal, rational, we can attain some notion of His nature by the negative way, by a succession of negative differentiations. For example, if we say that God is not an accident, we distinguish Him from all accidents; if we say that He is not corporeal, we distinguish Him from some substances; and thus we can proceed until we obtain an idea of God which belongs to Him alone (*propria consideratio*) and which suffices to distinguish Him from all other beings.

It must, however, be borne in mind that when predicates are denied of God, they are not denied of Him because He lacks any perfection expressed in that predicate, but because He infinitely exceeds that limited perfection in richness. Our natural knowledge has its beginning in sense and extends as far as it can be led by the help of sensible objects.[2] As sensible objects are creatures of God, we can come to know that God exists, but we cannot attain by means of them any adequate knowledge of God, since they are effects which are not fully proportionate to the divine power. But we can come to know about Him what is necessarily true of Him

---

[1] *Contra Gent.*, 1, 14.　　[2] *S.T.*, Ia, 12, 12, *in corpore.*

precisely as cause of all sensible objects. As their cause, He transcends them and is not and cannot be a sensible object Himself: we can, then, deny of Him any predicates which are bound up with corporeality or which are inconsistent with His being the first Cause and necessary Being. But *haec non removentur ab eo propter ejus defectum, sed quia superexcedit.*[1] If we say, therefore, that God is not corporeal, we do not mean that God is less than body, that He *lacks* the perfection involved in being body, but rather that He is *more than* body, that He possesses none of the imperfections necessarily involved in being a corporeal substance.

Arguing by means of the negative way St. Thomas shows that God cannot be corporeal, for example, since the unmoved Mover and the necessary Being must be pure Act, whereas every corporeal substance is in potentiality. Again, there cannot be any composition in God, either of matter and form or of substance and accident or of essence and existence. If there were composition of essence and existence, for instance, God would owe His existence to another being, which is impossible, since God is the first Cause. There cannot in fine be any composition in God, as this would be incompatible with His being as first Cause, necessary Being, pure Act. We express this absence of composition by the positive word 'simplicity', but the idea of the divine simplicity is attained by removing from God all the forms of composition which are found in creatures, so that 'simplicity' here means absence of composition. We cannot form an adequate idea of the divine simplicity as it is in itself, since it transcends our experience: we know, however, that it is at the opposite pole, so to speak, from simplicity or comparative simplicity in creatures. In creatures we experience the more complex substance is the higher, as a man is higher than an oyster; but God's simplicity means that He possesses the fullness of His being and perfection in one undivided and eternal act.

Similarly, God is infinite and perfect, since His *esse* is not something received and limited, but is self-existent; He is immutable, since the necessary Being is necessarily all that it is and cannot be changed; He is eternal, since time requires motion and in the immutable Being there can be no motion. He is one, since He is simple and infinite. Strictly speaking, however, says St. Thomas, God is not eternal, but is eternity, since He is His own subsistent *esse* in one undivided act. To go through all the various attributes of God which can be known by the negative way is unnecessary:

[1] *S.T.*, Ia, 12, 12, *in corpore*.

it is sufficient to have given some examples to show how, after
proving that God exists as unmoved Mover, first Cause, and
necessary Being, St. Thomas then proceeds to remove from God,
to deny of God, all those predicates of creatures which are incompatible with God's character as unmoved Mover, first Cause and
necessary Being. There cannot be in God corporeality, composition, limitation, imperfection, temporality, etc.

2. Predicates or names such as 'immutable' and 'infinite' suggest
by their very form their association with the negative way, immutable being equivalent to not-mutable and infinite to not-finite;
but there are other predicates applied to God which suggest no
such association, such as good, wise, etc. Moreover, while a
negative predicate, says St. Thomas,[1] refers directly not to the
divine substance, but to the 'removal' of something from the
divine substance, that is, the denial of some predicate's applica-
bility to God, there are positive predicates or names which are
predicated of the divine substance affirmatively. For example, the
predicate 'non-corporeal' denies corporeality of God, removes it
from Him, whereas the predicate good or wise is predicated
affirmatively and directly of the divine substance. There is, then,
an affirmative or positive way, in addition to the negative way.
But what is its justification if these perfections, goodness, wisdom,
etc., are experienced by us as they are in creatures, and if the
words we use to express these perfections express the ideas we
derive from creatures? Are we not applying to God ideas and
words which have no application save within the realm of experience? Are we not faced with the following dilemma? Either we
are predicating of God predicates which apply only to creatures,
in which case our statements about God are false, or we have
emptied the predicates of their reference to creatures, in which
case they are without content, since they are derived from our
experience of creatures and express that experience?

First of all, St. Thomas insists that when affirmative predicates
are predicated of God, they are predicated positively of the divine
nature or substance. He will not allow the opinion of those who,
like Maimonides, make all predicates of God equivalent to negative
predicates, nor the opinion of those who say that 'God is good' or
'God is living' means simply 'God is the cause of all goodness' or
'God is the cause of life'. When we say that God is living or God
is life, we do not mean merely that God is not non-living: the

[1] S.T., Ia, 13, 2, *in corpore.*

statement that God is living has a degree of affirmation about it that is wanting to the statement that God is not a body. Nor does the man who states that God is living mean only that God is the cause of life, of all living things: he means to say something positive about God Himself. Again, if the statement that God is living meant no more than that God is the cause of all living things, we might just as well say that God is body, since He is the cause of all bodies. Yet we do not say that God is body, whereas we do say that God is living, and this shows that the statement that God is living means more than that God is the cause of life, and that a positive affirmation is being made concerning the divine substance.

On the other hand, none of the positive ideas by means of which we conceive the nature of God represent God perfectly. Our ideas of God represent God only in so far as our intellects can know Him; but we know Him by means of sensible objects in so far as these objects represent or mirror God, so that inasmuch as creatures represent God or mirror Him only imperfectly, our ideas, derived from our experience of the natural world, can themselves represent God only imperfectly. When we say that God is good or living, we mean that He contains, or rather is the perfection of, goodness or life, but in a manner which exceeds and excludes all the imperfections and limitations of creatures. As regards *what is predicated* (goodness, for example), the affirmative predicate which we predicate of God signifies a perfection without any defect; but as regards the *manner of predicating it* every such predicate involves a defect, for by the word (*nomen*) we express something in the way it is conceived by the intellect. It follows, then, that predicates of this kind may, as the Pseudo-Dionysius observed, be both affirmed and denied of God; affirmed *propter nominis rationem*, denied *propter significandi modum*. For example, if we make the statement that God is wisdom, this affirmative statement is true in regard to the perfection as such; but if we meant that God is wisdom in precisely that sense in which we experience wisdom, it would be false. God is wise, but He is wisdom in a sense transcending our experience; He does not possess wisdom as an inhering quality or form. In other words, we affirm of God the essence of wisdom or goodness or life in a 'supereminent' way, and we deny of God the imperfections attendant on human wisdom, wisdom as we experience it.[1] When, therefore, we say that God is good, the

---

[1] *Contra Gent.*, 1, 30.

meaning is not that God is the cause of goodness or that God is not evil, but that what we call goodness in creatures pre-exists in God *secundum modum altiorem*. From this it does not follow that goodness belongs to God inasmuch as He causes goodness, but rather that because He is good, He diffuses goodness into things, according to the saying of Augustine, 'because He is good, we exist'.[1]

3. The upshot of the foregoing considerations is, therefore, that we cannot in this life know the divine essence as it is in itself, but only as it is represented in creatures, so that the names we apply to God signify the perfections manifested in creatures. From this fact several important conclusions must be drawn, the first being this, that the names we apply to God and to creatures are not to be understood in an univocal sense. For example, when we say that a man is wise and that God is wise, the predicate 'wise' is not to be understood in an univocal sense, that is, in precisely the same sense. Our concept of wisdom is drawn from creatures, and if we applied precisely this concept to God, we should be saying something false about God, since God is not, and cannot be, wise in precisely the same sense in which a man is wise. On the other hand, the names we apply to God are not purely equivocal, that is to say, they are not entirely and completely different in meaning from the meaning they bear when applied to creatures. If they were purely equivocal, we should have to conclude that we can gain no knowledge of God from creatures. If wisdom as predicated of man and wisdom as predicated of God signified something completely different, the term 'wise' as applied to God would have no content, no significance, since our knowledge of wisdom is drawn from creatures and is not based on direct experience of the divine wisdom. Of course, it might be objected that, though it is true that if the terms predicated of God were used in an equivocal sense, we should know nothing of God from creatures, it does not follow that we can know anything about God from creatures; but St. Thomas's insistence that we can know something of God from creatures is based on the fact that creatures, as effects of God, must manifest God, though they can do this only imperfectly.

Yet if the concepts derived from our experience of creatures and then applied to God are used neither in an univocal nor in an equivocal sense, in what sense are they used? Is there any half-way house? St. Thomas replies that they are used in an analogical

[1] *S.T.*, Ia, 13, 2.

sense. When an attribute is predicated analogically of two different beings, this means that it is predicated according to the relation they have to some third thing or according to the relation the one has to the other. As an example of the first type of analogical predication St. Thomas gives his favourite example, health.[1] An animal is said to be healthy because it is the subject of health, possesses health, while medicine is said to be healthy as being the cause of health, and a complexion is said to be healthy as being the sign of health. The word 'healthy' is predicated in different senses of the animal in general, the medicine and the complexion, according to the different relations they bear to health; but it is not predicated in a purely equivocal sense, for all three bear some real relation to health. Medicine is not healthy in the same sense that animal is healthy, for the term 'healthy' is not employed univocally, but the senses in which it is used are not equivocal or purely metaphorical, as when we speak of a smiling meadow. But this, says St. Thomas, is not the way in which we predicate attributes of God and creatures, for God and creatures have no relation to any third object: we predicate attributes of God and creatures, in so far as the creature has a real relation to God. When, for example, we predicate being of God and creatures, we attribute being first and foremost to God, as self-existing being, secondarily to creatures, as dependent on God. We cannot predicate being univocally of God and creatures, since they do not possess being in the same way, nor do we predicate being in a purely equivocal sense, since creatures have being, though their being is not like the divine being but is dependent, participated being.

As regards what is meant by the words we apply to God and creatures, it is attributed primarily to God and only secondarily to creatures. Being, as we have seen, belongs essentially to God, whereas it does not belong essentially to creatures but only in dependence on God: it is being, but it is a different kind of being from the divine being, since it is received, derived, dependent, finite. Nevertheless, though the thing signified is attributed primarily to God, the name is predicated primarily of creatures. The reason is tnat we know creatures before we know God, so that since our knowledge of wisdom, for example, is derived from creatures and the word primarily denotes the concept derived from our experience of creatures, the idea of wisdom and the word

[1] *Contra Gent.*, 1, 34; *S.T.*, Ia, 13, 5.

are predicated primarily of creatures and analogically of God, even though in actual fact wisdom itself, the thing signified, belongs primarily to God.

4. Analogical predication is founded on resemblance. In the *De Veritate*[1] St. Thomas distinguishes resemblance of proportion (*convenientia proportionis*) and resemblance of proportionality (*convenientia proportionalitatis*). Between the number 8 and the number 4 there is a resemblance of proportion, while between the proportions of 6 to 3 and of 4 to 2 there is a resemblance of proportionality, that is, a resemblance or similarity of two proportions to one another. Now, analogical predication in a general sense may be made according to both types of resemblance. The predication of being in regard to created substance and accident, each of which has a relation to the other, is an example of analogical predication according to proportion, while the predication of vision in regard to both ocular and intellectual vision is an example of analogical predication according to proportionality. What corporeal vision is to the eye, that intellectual apprehension or vision is to the mind. There is a certain similarity between the relation of the eye to its vision and the relation of mind to its intellectual apprehension, a similarity which enables us to speak of 'vision' in both cases. We apply the word 'vision' in the two cases neither univocally nor purely equivocally, but analogically.

Now, it is impossible to predicate anything analogically of God and creatures in the same way that it is possible to predicate being of substance and accident, for God and creatures have no mutual real relationship: creatures have a real relation to God, but God has no real relation to creatures. Nor is God included in the definition of any creature in the way that substance is included in the definition of accident. It does not follow, however, that there can be no analogy of proportion between God and creatures. Though God is not related to creatures by a real relation, creatures have a real relation to God, and we are able to apply the same term to God and creatures in virtue of that relation. There are perfections which are not bound up with matter and which do not necessarily imply any defect or imperfection in the being of which they are predicated. Being, wisdom and goodness are examples of such perfections. Obviously we gain knowledge of being or goodness or wisdom from creatures; but it does not follow

---

[1] 2, 11, *in corpore.*

that these perfections exist primarily in creatures and only secondarily in God, or that they are predicated primarily of creatures and only secondarily of God. On the contrary, goodness, for instance, exists primarily in God, who is the infinite goodness and the cause of all creaturely goodness, and it is predicated primarily of God and only secondarily of creatures, even though creaturely goodness is what we first come to know. Analogy of proportion is possible, then, in virtue of the creature's relation and likeness to God. To this point I shall return shortly.

It has been argued that St. Thomas came to abandon analogy of proportionality in favour of the analogy of proportion (in the acceptable sense); but this does not seem to me likely. In the Commentary on the *Sentences*[1] he gives both types of analogy, and even if in later works, like the *De Potentia*, the *Summa contra Gentiles* and the *Summa Theologica*, he seems to emphasise analogy of proportion, that does not seem to me to indicate that he ever abandoned analogy of proportionality. This type of analogical predication may be used in two ways, symbolically or properly. We can speak of God as 'the Sun', meaning that what the sun is to the bodily eye, that God is to the soul; but we are then speaking symbolically, since the word 'sun' refers to a material thing and can be predicated of a spiritual being only in a symbolic sense. We can say, however, that there is a certain similarity between God's relation to His intellectual activity and man's relation to his intellectual activity, and in this case we are not speaking merely symbolically, since intellectual activity as such is a pure perfection.

The foundation of all analogy, then, that which makes analogical predication possible, is the likeness of creatures to God. We do not predicate wisdom of God merely because God is the cause of all wise things, for in that case we might just as well call God a stone, as being the cause of all stones; but we call Him wise because creatures, God's effects, manifest God, are like to Him, and because a pure perfection like wisdom can be formally predicated of Him. But what is this likeness? In the first place it is only a one-way likeness, that is, the creature is like to God, but we cannot properly say that God is like the creature. God is the absolute standard, as it were. In the second place creatures are only imperfectly like God; they cannot bear a perfect resemblance to Him. This means that the creature is *at the same time* both like and unlike God. It is like God in so far as it is an imitation of Him; it is unlike God in

[1] *In* 4 *Sent.*, 49, 2, 1, *ad* 6.

so far as its resemblance to Him is imperfect and deficient. Analogical predication, therefore, lies between univocal and equivocal predication. In analogical predication the predicate is applied to God and creatures neither in precisely the same sense nor in totally different senses; it is applied at the same time in similar and dissimilar senses.[1] This notion of simultaneous similarity and difference is fundamental in analogy. The notion may, it is true, occasion considerable difficulties from the logical standpoint; but it would be inappropriate to discuss here the objections of modern positivists to analogy.

St. Thomas distinguishes, then, *analogy of proportion* (*analogia secundum convenientiam proportionis*) and *analogy of proportionality* (*analogia secundum convenientiam proportionalitatis*). As we have seen, he does not admit in regard to God and creatures that analogy of proportion which is applicable to substance and accident in respect of being; by analogy of proportion in natural theology he means that analogy in which a predicate is applied primarily to one analogue, namely God, and secondarily and imperfectly to the other analogue, namely the creature, in virtue of the creature's real relation and likeness to God. The perfection attributed to the analogues is really present in both of them, but it is not present in the same way, and the one predicate is used at the same time in senses which are neither completely different nor completely similar. Terminology has changed since the time of St. Thomas, and this kind of analogy is now called analogy of attribution. Analogy of proportionality, the resemblance of proportions, is sometimes called analogy of proportion, in distinction from the analogy of attribution; but not all Scholastics and commentators on St. Thomas employ the terms in precisely the same way.

Some Scholastics have maintained that being, for example, is predicable of God and creatures only by analogy of proportionality and not by analogy of attribution. Without, however, wishing to enter on a discussion of the value of analogy of proportionality as such, I do not see how we could know that God has any perfection save by way of the analogy of attribution. All analogical predication rests on the real relation and likeness of creatures to God, and it seems to me that the analogy of proportionality presupposes analogy of proportion or attribution and that the latter is the more fundamental of the two kinds of analogy.

5. If one reads what St. Thomas has to say of analogy, it may

[1] Cf. *S.T.*, Ia, 13, 5, *in corpore.*

appear that he is simply examining the way in which we speak about God, the verbal and conceptual implications of our statements, and that he is not actually establishing anything about our real knowledge of God. But it is a fundamental principle with St. Thomas that the perfections of creatures must be found in the Creator in a super-eminent manner, in a manner compatible with the infinity and spirituality of God. For example, if God has created intellectual beings, God must be possessed of intellect; we cannot suppose that He is less than intellectual. Moreover, a spiritual being must be an intellectual form, as Aristotle says, and the infinite spiritual being must be possessed of infinite intelligence. On the other hand, God's intelligence cannot be a faculty distinct from His essence or nature, since God is pure Act and not a composite being, nor can God know things successively, since He is changeless and incapable of accidental determination. He knows future events in virtue of His eternity, by which all things are present to Him.[1] God must possess the perfection of intellectuality, but we cannot form any adequate concept of what the divine intelligence is, since we have no experience of it: our knowledge of the divine intelligence is imperfect and inadequate, but it is not false; it is analogical knowledge. It would be false only if we were unaware of its imperfection and actually meant to ascribe to God finite intelligence as such: we cannot help thinking and speaking of the divine intelligence in terms of human concepts and language, since there are no others available to us, but at the same time we are aware that our concepts and language are imperfect. We cannot, for instance, help speaking as though God 'foresaw' future events, but we are aware that for God there is not past or future. Similarly we must ascribe to God the perfection of free will in respect of other objects than Himself, but God's free will cannot involve changeableness: He willed freely to create the world in time, but He willed it freely from all eternity, in virtue of the one act of will which is identical with His essence. Of the divine free will we can, therefore, form no adequate conception; but the relation of creatures to God shows us that God must possess free will and we can realise some of the things which the divine free will cannot mean; yet the positive reality of the divine free will exceeds our comprehension, precisely because we are creatures and not God. Only God can comprehend Himself.

It can scarcely be denied, however, that a grave difficulty arises

[1] Cf. *S.T.*, Ia, 14, 13.

in connection with the doctrine of analogy. If our idea of intelligence, for example, is derived from human intelligence, it obviously cannot, as such, be applied to God, and St. Thomas insists that no predicate which is applied to God and creatures is applied univocally. On the other hand, unless we were willing to acquiesce in agnosticism, we could not allow that such predicates are used in a purely equivocal sense. What, then, is the positive content of our concept of the divine intelligence? If St. Thomas adhered simply to the *via negativa* the difficulty would not arise: he would be saying simply that God is not not-intelligent or that He is superintelligent, admitting that we have no positive idea of what the divine intelligence is. But St. Thomas does not stick simply to the *via negativa*: he admits the *via affirmativa*. Our idea of divine intelligence has, therefore, a positive content; but what can that positive content be? Is the reply that a positive content is obtained by denying the limitations of human intelligence, its finiteness, discursive character, potentiality and so on? In this case, however, we either attain a positive concept of the divine intelligence as such or we attain a concept of the 'essence' of intelligence, apart from finitude or infinity, which would seem to be univocal in respect of God and creatures. It might even appear that the negations either cancel out the content altogether or make it into an idea of the essence of intelligence which would be univocal in respect of divine and human intelligence. It was for this reason that Duns Scotus later insisted that we can form univocal concepts applicable to both God and creatures, though there is no univocity in the real order in respect of God and creatures. It is sometimes said that analogical concepts are partly the same as and partly different from univocal concepts; but the same difficulty recurs. The element of 'sameness' will be an univocal element, while the element of 'difference' will either be negative or it will have no content, since we have no immediate experience of God from which the idea can be derived. But further consideration of this point is best reserved for our treatment of St. Thomas's doctrine of knowledge.[1]

6. Mention of the divine intelligence naturally leads one on to raise the question what St. Thomas thought of the doctrine of the divine ideas. In the first place he establishes that there must be ideas in the divine mind, *necesse est ponere in mente divina ideas*,[2] since God has created things not by chance, but intelligently,

---

[1] Cf. Ch. XXXVIII, sect. 4.   [2] *S.T.*, Ia, 15, 1.

according to the exemplary idea He conceived in His mind. He remarks that Plato erred in asserting the existence of ideas which were not in any intellect, and he observes that Aristotle blamed Plato on this account. As a matter of fact, Aristotle, who did not believe in any free creation by God, did not blame Plato for making the ideas independent of the divine mind, but for maintaining their subsistence apart from the human mind, if one is considering their subjective reality, and apart from things, if one is considering their objective reality as forms. In asserting the existence of ideas in the divine mind St. Thomas is therefore following in the wake of the tradition which began with Plato, was developed in Middle Platonism and neo-Platonism and lived on, in a Christian setting, in the philosophy of Augustine and those who followed him.

One of the reasons why the neo-Platonists placed the ideas in the *Nous*, the second hypostasis or first emanating divine being, and not in the One or supreme Godhead was that the presence of a multiplicity of ideas in God would, they thought, impair the divine unity. How did St. Thomas meet this difficulty, when the only real distinction he could admit in God was the distinction between the three divine Persons in the Trinity (and with this distinction he was not, of course, concerned as philosopher)? His answer is that from one point of view we must say that there is a plurality of ideas in God, as Augustine said, since God knows each individual thing to be created, but that from another point of view there cannot be a plurality of ideas in God, since this would contradict the divine simplicity. What he means is this. If by idea one refers to the content of the idea, then one must admit a plurality of ideas in God, since God knows many objects; but if by idea one means the subjective mental determination, the species, then one cannot admit a plurality of ideas in God, since God's intellect is identical with His undivided essence and cannot receive determinations or any sort of composition. God knows His divine essence not only as it is in itself, but also as imitable outside itself in a plurality of creatures. This act of knowledge, as it exists in God, is one and undivided and is identical with His essence; but since God not only knows His essence as imitable in a multiplicity of creatures, but also knows that in knowing His essence He knows a multiplicity of creatures, we can and must speak of a plurality of ideas in God, for 'idea' signifies, not the divine essence as it is in itself, but the divine essence as the exemplar of this or that object. And it is the exemplar of many objects. In other words, the truth or falsity of our statements in regard to God must be estimated in terms of human language. To deny a plurality of ideas in God without qualification would be to deny that God knows a plurality of objects; but the truth that God knows His essence as imitable by a plurality of creatures must not be stated in such a way as to imply that there is a multiplicity of real species or really distinct modifications in the divine intellect.[1]

This discussion of the divine ideas is of some interest because it shows that St. Thomas is by no means simply an Aristotelian, but that in this respect at least he adheres to the Platonic-Augustinian tradition. Indeed, although he sees clearly that he has to provide against any impairing of the divine simplicity, he is not content with saying that God by one act of His intellect, one 'idea', knows His essence as imitable in a plurality of creatures, but he asserts that there is a plurality of ideas in God. He certainly gives his reasons for doing so, but one has the impression that one unstated reason was his reverence for Augustine and Augustine's mode of speaking. However, it is true that a distinction must be made. When we to-day use the term 'idea' we naturally refer to the subjective idea or mental modification, and in this sense St. Thomas does not admit in God a plurality of ideas really distinct from one another; but St. Thomas was primarily thinking of 'idea' in the sense of exemplary form, and since the divine essence as known by the divine intellect is known as imitable in a plurality of creatures, as the exemplar of many objects, he felt himself entitled to speak of a plurality of *rationes* in God, though he had to insist that this plurality consists simply in God's knowledge of His essence in respect of the multiplicity of creatures and not in a real distinction in God.

7. We have spoken of the divine intelligence and the divine will, the divine goodness, unity, simplicity and so on. Are these attributes of God really distinct from one another? And if they are not distinct from one another, what is our justification for speaking of them as though they were distinct? The attributes of God are not really distinct from one another, since God is simple: they are identical with the divine essence. The divine intelligence is not really distinct from the divine essence, nor is the divine will: the divine justice and the divine mercy are identical as they exist in God. Nevertheless, apart from the fact that the structure of

---

[1] Cf. *S.T.*, Ia, 15, 1–3; *Contra Gent.*, 1, 53–4.

our language compels us to speak in terms of subject and predicate, we apprehend the divine perfection piecemeal, as it were. We attain our natural knowledge of God only by considerations of creatures, God's effects, and since the perfections of creatures, the manifestations or reflections of God in creatures are different, we use different names to signify those different perfections. But if we could comprehend the divine essence as it is in itself and if we could give it its proper name, we should use one alone.[1] We cannot, however, comprehend the divine essence, and we know it only by means of diverse concepts: we have, therefore, to employ diverse words to express the divine essence, though we know at the same time that the actual reality corresponding to all those names is one simple reality. If it is objected that to conceive an object otherwise than it is is to conceive it falsely, the answer is that we do not conceive the object to exist otherwise than it actually exists, for we know that God is actually a simple Being, but we conceive in a composite manner the object which we know to be non-composite. This means simply that our intelligences are finite and discursive and that they cannot apprehend God save by means of His different reflections in creatures. Our knowledge of God is thus inadequate and imperfect, but it is not false.[2] There is indeed a certain foundation in God for our composite and distinct concepts, this foundation, however, not being any real distinction in God between the divine attributes but simply His infinite perfection which, precisely because of its infinite richness, cannot be apprehended by the human mind in one concept.

8. According to St. Thomas[3] the most appropriate name of God is the name He gave to Moses at the burning bush,[4] *Qui est*, He who is. In God there is no distinction between essence and existence; He does not receive His existence, but is His existence; His essence is to exist. In no creature, however, is the distinction between essence and existence absent. Every creature is good and every creature is true; but no creature is its own existence: it is not the essence of any creature to exist. Existence itself *ipsum esse*, is the essence of God, and the name which is derived from that essence is most appropriate to God. God is goodness, for example, and His goodness is identical with His essence, but goodness, in our human experience, follows on and accompanies *esse*; though not really distinct, it is conceived as secondary; but

---

[1] *Contra Gent.*, 1, 31.   [2] Cf. *S.T.*, Ia, 13, 12, *in corpore* and *ad* 3.
[3] *S.T.*, Ia, 13, 11; *Contra Gent.*, 1, 22.   [4] Exodus 3. 14.

to say that God is *ipsum esse* is to give, as it were, His inner nature. Every other name is in some way inadequate. If we say, for example, that God is infinite Justice, we say what is true, but as our intelligences necessarily distinguish Justice and Mercy, even though we know that they are identical in God, the statement that God is infinite Justice is an inadequate expression of the divine essence. The names we employ in speaking of God are derived from our experience of determinate forms and express primarily those forms; but the name *He who is* signifies not a determinate form, but 'the infinite ocean of substance'.

CHAPTER XXXVI

ST. THOMAS AQUINAS—VI: CREATION

Creation out of nothing—God alone can create—God created freely—The motive of creation—Impossibility of creation from eternity has not been demonstrated—Could God create an actually infinite multitude?—Divine omnipotence—The problem of evil.

1. SINCE God is the first Cause of the world, since finite beings are contingent beings owing their existence to the necessary Being, finite beings must proceed from God through creation. Moreover, this creation must be creation out of nothing. If creatures were made out of a pre-existent material, this material would be either God Himself or something other than God. But God cannot be the material of creation, since He is simple, spiritual, unchangeable; nor can there be any thing independent of the first Cause: there can be but one necessary Being. God, therefore, is absolutely prior, and if He cannot change, cannot exteriorise Himself in creation, He must have created the world out of nothing, *ex nihilo*. This phrase must not be taken to imply that nothing, *nihil*, is a material out of which God made the world: when it is said that God created the world out of nothing, it is meant either that first there was nothing and then there was something or the phrase *ex nihilo* must be understood as equivalent to *non ex aliquo*, not out of something. The objection that out of nothing comes nothing is, therefore, irrelevant, since nothing is looked on neither as efficient cause nor as material cause; in creation God is the efficient Cause and there is no material cause whatsoever.[1] Creation is thus not a movement or change in the proper sense, and since it is not a movement, there is no succession in the act of creation.

Creation, considered in the term of the act of creation, that is, in the creature, is a real relation to God as the principle of the creature's being. Every creature, by the very fact that it is created, has a real relation to God as Creator. But one cannot argue the other way round, that God has a real relation to the creature. Such a relation in God would either be identical with the divine substance or it would be an accident in God; but the divine substance cannot be necessarily related to creatures, since

---

[1] On the sense of *creatio ex nihilo*, cf. *De Potentia*, 3, 1, *ad* 7; *S.T.*, Ia, 45, 1, *ad* 3.

in that case God would depend in some way on creatures for His very existence, while on the other hand God, as absolutely simple, cannot receive or possess accidents.[1] The statement that God as Creator has no real relation to creatures certainly sounds rather strange at first hearing, as it might seem to follow that God has no care for His creatures; but it is a strictly logical conclusion from St. Thomas's metaphysic and doctrine of the divine Nature. That God is related to creatures by His very substance St. Thomas could not possibly admit, since in that case not only would creation necessarily be eternal, and we know from revelation that it is not eternal, but God could not exist apart from creatures: God and creatures would form a Totality and it would be impossible to explain the generation and perishing of individual creatures. On the other hand, if one is speaking of relation as falling within one of the nine categories of accidents, such a relation also is inadmissible in God. The acquisition of such an accident would allow of creation in time, it is true; but such an acquisition on the part of God is impossible if God is pure act, without potentiality. It was, therefore, impossible for St. Thomas to admit that God as Creator has a real relation to creatures; he had to say that the relation is a mental relation of reason alone (*relatio rationis*), attributed to God by the human intellect. The attribution is, however, legitimate, since God is Creator and we cannot express this fact in human language without speaking as though God were related to creatures: the important point is that, when we speak of creatures as related to God and of God as related to creatures, we should remember that it is creatures which depend on God and not God on creatures, and that consequently the real relation between them, which is a relation of dependence, is found in creatures alone.

2. The power of creation is a prerogative of God alone and cannot be communicated to any creature.[2] The reason why some philosophers, Avicenna, for example, introduced intermediary beings was because they thought of God as creating by a necessity of nature, so that there must be intermediary stages between the absolute simplicity of the supreme Godhead and the multiplicity of creatures; but God does not create by a necessity of nature and there is no reason why He should not create directly a multiplicity of creatures. Peter Lombard thought that the power of creation is communicable by God to a creature in such a way

[1] *Contra Gent.*, 2, 11–13; *S.T.*, Ia, 45, 3; *De Potentia*, 3, 3.
[2] Cf. *De Potentia*, 3, 4.

that the latter could act as an instrument, not by its own power; but this is impossible, since if the creature is to contribute in any way to creation, its own power and activity will be involved, and this power, being finite like the creature itself, cannot accomplish an act which demands infinite power, the act of bridging the infinite gulf between not-being and being.

3. But if God does not create by a necessity of nature, how does He create? An intellectual being, in whom there is, so to speak, no element of unconsciousness, but who is perfectly self-luminous and 'self-possessed', cannot act in any other way than according to wisdom, with full knowledge. To put the matter crudely, God must act for a motive, in view of a purpose, a good. But God's nature is not only infinite intelligence, but also infinite will, and that will is free. God loves Himself necessarily, since He is Himself the infinite good, but objects distinct from Himself are not necessary to Him, since, as infinite perfection, He is self-sufficient: His will is free in their regard. Therefore, although we know that God's intellect and will are not really distinct from His essence, we are bound to say that God chose freely an object or end conceived by Him as good. The language employed is certainly anthropomorphic, but we have only human language at our disposal, and we cannot express the truth that God created the world freely without making it clear that the act-of will by which God created was neither a blind act nor a necessary act, but an act which followed, to speak in human fashion, the apprehension of a good, apprehended as a good though not as a good necessary to God.

4. What was the motive for which God acted in creation? As infinite perfection God cannot have created in order to acquire anything for Himself: He created, not in order to obtain, but to give, to diffuse His goodness (*intendit solum communicare suam perfectionem quae est ejus bonitas*).[1] When it is said, then, that God created the world for His own glory the statement must not be taken to mean that God needed something which He had not already got; still less that He wanted to obtain, if one may so speak without irreverence, a chorus of admirers; but rather that God's will cannot depend on anything apart from God, that He Himself as the infinite good must be the end of His infinite act of will, and that in the case of the act of creation the end is His own goodness as communicable to beings outside Himself. The divine goodness is represented in all creatures, though rational creatures

[1] *S.T.*, Ia, 44, 4.

have God as their end in a manner peculiar to themselves, since
they are able to know and to love God: all creatures glorify God
by representing and participating in His goodness, while rational
creatures are capable of consciously appreciating and loving the
divine goodness. God's glory, the manifestation of His goodness,
is thus not something separate from the good of creatures, for
creatures attain their end, do the best for themselves, by mani-
festing the divine goodness.[1]

5. That God created the world freely, does not of itself show
that He created it in time, that time had a beginning. As God is
eternal, He might have created the world from eternity. That this
had been shown to be an impossible supposition St. Thomas
refused to allow. He believed that it can be philosophically proved
that the world was created out of nothing, but he maintained that
none of the philosophical proofs adduced to prove that this
creation took place in time, that there is, ideally, a first assignable
moment of time, were conclusive, differing on this point from
St. Albert. On the other hand, St. Thomas maintained, against
the Averroists, that it cannot be shown philosophically that the
world cannot have begun in time, that creation in time is an
impossibility. In other words, though well aware that the world
was actually created in time and not from eternity, St. Thomas
was convinced that this fact is known only through revelation,
and that the philosopher cannot settle the question whether the
world was created in time or from eternity. Thus he maintained,
against the *murmurantes*, the possibility (as far as we can see) of
creation from eternity. In practice this meant that he showed, or
at least was satisfied that he could show, that the type of argument
brought forward by St. Bonaventure to prove the impossibility of
creation from eternity was inconclusive. It is, however, unnecessary to mention St. Thomas's replies again, since these, or some
of them at least, have already been given when we were considering
the philosophy of St. Bonaventure.[2] Let it suffice to recall the fact
that St. Thomas saw no contradiction in the notion of a series
without a beginning. In his eyes the question whether it would be
possible for the world to have passed through infinite time does not
arise, since there is strictly no passing through an infinite series if
there is no first term in the series. Moreover, for St. Thomas a
series can be infinite *ex parte ante* and finite *ex parte post*, and it
can be added to at the end at which it is finite. In general, there

is no contradiction between being brought into existence and existing from eternity: if God is eternal, God could have created from eternity.

On the other hand, St. Thomas rejects the arguments adduced to show that the world must have been created from eternity. 'We must hold firmly, as the Catholic faith teaches, that the world has not always existed. And this position cannot be overcome by any physical demonstration.'[1] It may be argued, for example, that as God is the Cause of the world and as God is eternal, the world, God's effect, must also be eternal. As God cannot change, as He contains no element of potentiality and cannot receive new determinations or modifications, the creative act, God's free act of creation, must be eternal. The effect of this act must, therefore, also be eternal. St. Thomas has to agree, of course, that the creative act as such, that is, God's act of will, is eternal, since it is identical with God's essence; but he argues that what follows from this is simply that God willed freely from eternity to create the world, not that the world came into existence from eternity. If we consider the matter merely as philosophers, if, that is, we prescind from our knowledge, gained from revelation, that God actually created the world in time, all we can say is that God may have willed freely from eternity that the world should come into existence in time or that God may have willed freely from eternity that the world should come into existence from eternity: we are not entitled to conclude that God *must* have willed from eternity that the world should exist from eternity. In other words, God's creative act is certainly eternal, but the external effect of that act will follow in the way willed by God, and if God willed that the external effect should have *esse post non-esse* it will not have *esse ab aeterno*, even though the creative act, considered precisely as an act in God, is eternal.[2]

6. One of the reasons adduced by St. Bonaventure to show that the world must have been created in time and could not have been created from eternity was that, if it had been created from eternity, there would be in existence now an infinite number of immortal human souls and that an infinite actual multitude is an impossibility. What did St. Thomas maintain concerning God's power to create an infinite multitude? The question arises in connection with a multitude *extra genus quantitatis*, since St. Thomas followed

[1] *De Potentia*, 3, 17.
[2] On this subject see *Contra Gent.*, 2, 31-7; *S.T.*, Ia, 46, 1; *De Potentia*, 3, 17; *De aeternitate mundi contra murmurantes*.

Aristotle in rejecting the possibility of an infinite quantity. In the *De Veritate*[1] the Saint remarks that the only valid reason for saying that God could not create an actual infinite multitude would be an essential repugnance or contradiction in the notion of such an infinity, but he defers any decision on the matter. In the *Summa Theologica*[2] he affirms categorically that there cannot be an actual infinite multitude, since every created multitude must be of a certain number, whereas an infinite multitude would not be of a certain number. But in the *De aeternitate mundi contra Murmurantes*, when dealing with the objection against the possibility of the world's creation from eternity that there would then be in existence an infinite number of immortal human souls, he replies that God might have made the world without men, or that He could have made the world from eternity but have made man only when He did make him, while on the other hand 'it has not yet been demonstrated that God cannot make an infinity in act'. It may be that the last remark indicates a change of mind on St. Thomas's part or a hesitancy concerning the validity of his own previous demonstration; but he does not explicitly recall what he said in the *Summa Theologica*, and the remark might be no more than an *argumentum ad hominem*, '*you* have not yet demonstrated that an existing infinite multitude is impossible'. In any case, in view of the statement in the *Summa Theologica* and in view of the proximity in time of the *De aeternitate mundi* to the first part of the *Summa Theologica*, it would seem rash to conclude to more than a possible hesitancy on St. Thomas's part as to the impossibility of an infinite multitude in act.

7. The mention of God being able or unable to create an actually infinite multitude naturally raises the wider question of the sense in which the divine omnipotence is to be understood. If omnipotence means the ability to do all things, how can God be omnipotent if He cannot make it come about that a man should be a horse or that what has happened should not have happened? In answer St. Thomas observes first of all that the divine attribute of omnipotence means that God can do all that is possible. But 'all that is possible' must not be understood, he goes on to say, as equivalent to 'all that is possible to God', for in this case when we say that God is omnipotent we should mean that God is able to do all that He is able to do a statement which would tell us nothing. How, then, are we to understand the phrase 'all that is possible'? Tha

---

is possible which has no intrinsic repugnance to being, in other words, that the existence of which would not involve a contradiction. That which involves a contradiction in its very notion is neither actual nor possible, but not-being. For example, that a man, while remaining a man, should also be a horse, involves a contradiction: man is rational, a horse irrational, and rational and irrational are contradictories. We can certainly speak of a human horse or an equine man, but the phrases do not indicate a thing, whether actual or possible; they are mere verbiage, signifying nothing conceivable. To say, therefore, that God's omnipotence means that God can do all that is possible does not indicate a limit to God's power, for power has meaning only in regard to the possible. Whatever has or can have being is the object of divine omnipotence, but that which is intrinsically contradictory is not an object at all. 'So it is better to say that what involves contradiction cannot be done rather than that God cannot do it.'[1]

It must not, however, be imagined that there is a principle of contradiction which stands behind God and to which God is subject as the Greek gods were subject to *Moira* or Destiny. God is supreme Being, *ipsum esse subsistens*, and His will to create is a will to create His own similitude, something, that is, which can participate in being. That which involves a contradiction is at the utmost remove from Being; it neither has nor ever can have any likeness to God, any being. If God could will what is self-contradictory He could depart from His own nature, could love that which bears no resemblance whatsoever to Himself, that which is nothing at all, that which is utterly unthinkable. But if God could act in this way, He would not be God. It is not that God is subject to the principle of contradiction, but rather that the principle of contradiction is founded on the nature of God. To suppose, then, with St. Peter Damian (or with Leo Chestov) that God is superior to the principle of contradiction, in the sense that God can do what is self-contradictory, is to suppose that God can act in a manner inconsistent with and contrary to His own nature, and this is an absurd supposition.[2]

But this does not mean that God can do only what He actually does. It is certainly true that since God actually wills the order of things which He has created and which actually exists, He cannot will another order, since the divine will cannot change, as

---

[1] Cf. *S.T.*, Ia, 25, 3–4; *De Potentia*, 1, 7.   [2] Cf. *Contra Gent.*, 1, 84.

our finite wills can change; but the question is not concerning the divine power *ex suppositione*, on the supposition that God has already chosen, but concerning the absolute divine power, i.e. whether God was restricted to willing the actual order He has willed or whether He could have willed another order. The answer is that God did not will this present order of things necessarily, and the reason is that the end of creation is the divine goodness which so exceeds any created order that there is not and cannot be any link of necessity between a given order and the end of creation. The divine goodness and the created order are incommensurable, and there cannot be any one created order, any one universe, which is necessary to a divine goodness that is infinite and incapable of any addition. If any created order were proportionate to the divine goodness, to the end, then the divine wisdom would be determined to choose that particular order; but since the divine goodness is infinite and creation necessarily finite, no created order can be proportionate in the full sense to the divine goodness.[1]

From the above is made apparent the answer to the questions whether God could make better things than He has made or could make the things which He has made better than they are.[2] In one sense God must always act in the best possible manner, since God's act is identical with His essence and with infinite goodness; but we cannot conclude from this that the extrinsic object of God's act, creatures, must be the best possible and that God is bound, on account of His goodness, to produce the best possible universe if He produces one at all. As God's power is infinite, there can always be a better universe than the one God actually produces, and why He has chosen to produce a particular order of creation is His secret. St. Thomas says, therefore, that absolutely speaking God could make something better than any given thing. But if the question is raised in regard to the existent universe, a distinction must be drawn. God could not make a given thing better than it actually is in regard to its substance or essence, since that would be to make another thing. For example, rational life is in itself a higher perfection than merely sensitive life; but if God were to make a horse rational it would no longer be a horse and in that case God could not be said to make the horse better. Similarly, if God changed the order of the universe, it would not

---

[1] Cf. *S.T.*, Ia, 19, 3; 1, 25, 5; *Contra Gent.*, 2, 26–7; *De Potentia*, 1, 5.
[2] *S.T.*, Ia, 25, 6.

be the same universe. On the other hand, God could make a thing accidentally better; He could, for example, increase a man's bodily health or, in the supernatural order, his grace.

It is plain, then, that St. Thomas would not agree with the Leibnizian 'optimism' or maintain that this is the best of all possible worlds. In view of the divine omnipotence the phrase 'the best of all possible worlds' does not seem to have much meaning: it has meaning only if one supposes from the start that God creates from a necessity of His nature, from which it would follow, since God is goodness itself, that the world which proceeds from Him necessarily must be the best possible. But if God creates not from a necessity of nature, but according to His nature, according to intelligence and will, that is, freely, and if God is omnipotent, it must always be possible for God to create a better world. Why, then, did He create this particular world? That is a question to which we cannot give any adequate answer, though we can certainly attempt to answer the question why God created a world in which suffering and evil are present: that is to say, we can attempt to answer the problem of evil, provided that we remember that we cannot expect to attain any comprehensive solution of the problem in this life, owing to the finitude and imperfection of our intelligences and the fact that we cannot fathom the divine counsel and plans.

8. In willing this universe God did not will the evils contained in it. God necessarily loves His own essence, which is infinite goodness, and He freely wills creation as a communication of His goodness; He cannot love what is opposed to goodness, namely evil. But did not God, to speak in human language, foresee the evils in the world; and if He foresaw the evils in the world and yet willed the world, did He not will the evils in the world? If evil were a positive entity, something created, then it would have to be ascribed to God as Creator, since there is no ultimate principle of evil, as the Manichaeans thought; but evil is not a positive entity; it is, as St. Augustine taught, following Plotinus, a *privation*. It is not *aliquid*, a positive thing, and God cannot have created it, since it is not creatable, but it only exists as a privation in what itself, as being, is good. Moreover, evil as such cannot be willed even by a human will, for the object of the will is necessarily the good or what appears as such. The adulterer, says St. Thomas, does not will the evil, the sin, precisely as such; he wills the sensible pleasure of an act which involves evil. It might be objected that

some people have indulged in diabolic wickedness, have committed acts precisely because they were an offence against God; but even in this case it is some apparent good, complete independence, for example, which is the object of the will: the evil defiance of God appears as a good and is willed *sub specie boni*. No will, therefore, can desire evil precisely as such, and God, in creating a world the evils of which He 'foresaw', must be said, not to have willed the evils but to have willed the world which, as such, is good and to have willed to permit the evils which He foresaw.

It must not, however, be imagined that by maintaining the doctrine that evil as such is a privation St. Thomas means to imply that evil is unreal, in the sense of being an illusion. This would be to misunderstand his position completely. Evil is not a being, *entitas*, in the sense that it falls under any of the ten categories of being, but in reply to the question whether evil exists or not, the answer must be in the affirmative. This certainly sounds paradoxical, but St. Thomas means that evil exists as a privation in the good, not in its own right as a positive entity. For example, lack of ability to see is not a privation in a stone, for it does not pertain to a stone to see, and 'blindness' in a stone is the mere absence of a power which would be incompatible with the nature of the stone; but blindness in a man is a privation, the absence of something which belongs to the fullness of man's nature. This blindness is not, however, a positive entity, it is a privation of sight; yet the privation exists, is real, it is by no means an unreal illusion. It has no meaning or existence apart from the being in which it exists, but as existing in that being the privation is real enough. Similarly, evil cannot of and by itself cause anything, but it exists and can be a cause through the good being in which it exists. For example, the difformity in the will of a fallen angel cannot by itself be a cause, but it is a real privation and can be a cause by means of the positive being in which it exists. Indeed, the more powerful the being in which it exists, the greater are its effects.[1]

God did not, then, create evil as a positive entity, but must He not be said to have willed evil in some sense, since He created a world in which He foresaw that evil would exist? It is necessary to consider separately physical evil and moral evil (*malum culpae*). Physical evil was certainly permitted by God and it can in a sense be even said to have been willed by God. God did not will it for its own sake, of course, *per se*, but He willed a universe, a natural order, which involved at least the possibility of physical defect and suffering. By willing the creation of sensitive nature God willed that capacity for feeling pain as well as pleasure which is, naturally speaking, inseparable from human nature. He did not will suffering as such, but He willed that nature (a good) which is accompanied by the capacity for suffering. Moreover, the perfection of the universe requires, says St. Thomas, that there should be, besides incorruptible beings, corruptible beings, and if there are corruptible beings, corruption, death, will take place according to the natural order. God, then, did not will corruption (needless to say, the word is not being used in the moral sense) for its own sake, but He can be said to have caused it *per accidens*, in that He willed to create and created a universe the order of which demanded the capacity for defect and corruption on the part of some beings. Again, the preservation of the order of justice demands that moral evil should meet with punishment (*malum poenae*), and God may be said to will and cause that punishment not for its own sake, but so that the order of justice may be preserved.

In treating of physical evil, therefore, St. Thomas tends to treat God as an artist and the universe as a work of art. The perfection of that work of art requires a variety of beings, among which will be found beings which are mortal and capable of suffering, so that God may be said to have willed physical evil not *per se* but *per accidens*, for the sake of a good, the good of the whole universe. But when it is a question of the moral order, the order of freedom, and of considering human beings precisely as free agents, his attitude is different. Freedom is a good and without it human beings could not give God that love of which He is worthy, could not merit and so on: freedom makes man more like to God than he would be, were he not free. On the other hand, man's liberty, when he has not got the vision of God, involves the power of choosing against God and the moral law, of sinning. God did not will moral disorder or sin in any sense, but He permitted it. Why? For the sake of a greater good, that man might be free and that he might love and serve God of his own free choice. The physical perfection of the universe required the presence of some beings who could and would die, so that God, as we have seen, can be said to have willed death *per accidens*; but though the perfection of the universe required that man should be free, it did not require that he should misuse his freedom, should sin, and God cannot be said to have willed moral evil either *per se* or *per accidens*. Nevertheless, it was impossible for there to be a human being in the natural order who should be free and at the same time incapable of sinning, so that it is true to say that God permitted a moral evil, though He permitted it only for the sake of a greater good.

There would, of course, be a great deal more to say on this subject, were one to introduce considerations drawn from theology, and any purely philosophical consideration of the problem is necessarily far less satisfactory than a treatment in which both theological and philosophical truths are utilised. The doctrines of the Fall and the Redemption, for instance, throw a light on the problem of evil which cannot be shed by purely philosophical reasoning. However, arguments based on revelation and dogmatic theology must be omitted here. St. Thomas's philosophical answer to the problem of evil in its relation to God can be summed up in the two statements, first that God did not will moral evil in any sense whatever but only permitted it for a greater good than could be attained by preventing it, that is, by not making man free, and secondly that though God did not will physical evil for its own sake, He may be said to have willed certain physical evils *per accidens*, for the perfection of the universe. I say 'certain *physical evils*', since St. Thomas does not mean to imply that God can be said to have willed all physical evils, even *per accidens*. Corruptibility or death pertains to a certain kind of being, but many physical evils and sufferings are not bound up with the perfection or good of the universe at all, but are the result of moral evil on man's part: they are not 'inevitable'. Such physical evils God only permitted.[1]

---

[1] On the subject of evil and its relation to God see, for example, *S.T.*, Ia, 19, 9; Ia, 48–9; *Contra Gent.*, 3, 4–5; *De Malo*, questions 1–3; *De Potentia*, 1, 6.

CHAPTER XXXVII

ST. THOMAS AQUINAS—VII: PSYCHOLOGY

One substantial form in man—The powers of the soul—The interior senses—Free will—The noblest faculty—Immortality—The active and passive intellects are not numerically the same in all men.

1. WE have already seen[1] that St. Thomas maintained the Aristotelian doctrine of hylomorphism and that, departing from the views of his predecessors, he defended the unicity of the substantial form in the substance. It may be that at first St. Thomas accepted the existence of a *forma corporeitatis* as the first substantial form in a material substance;[2] but in any case he soon opposed this opinion and held that the specific substantial form informs prime matter immediately and not by the medium of any other substantial form. This doctrine he applied to man, maintaining that there is but one substantial form in the human *compositum*. This one substantial form is the rational soul, which informs matter directly: there is no *forma corporeitatis*, still less are there vegetative and sensitive substantial forms. The human being is a unity, and this unity would be impaired, were we to suppose a plurality of substantial forms. The name 'man' applies neither to the soul alone nor to the body alone, but to soul and body together, to the composite substance.

St. Thomas, then, follows Aristotle in stressing the unity of the human substance. It is the one soul in man which confers on him all his determinations as man, his corporeity (by informing prime matter), his vegetative, sensitive and intellectual operations. In a plant there is present only the vegetative principle or soul, conferring life and the powers of growth and reproduction; in the brute there is present only the sensitive soul which acts as the principle not only of vegetative life, but also of sensitive life; in man there is present only the rational principle or soul, which is not only the principle of the operations peculiar to itself, but also of the vegetative and sensitive functions. When death comes and the soul is separated from the body, the body disintegrates: it is not merely that rational functions cease, for the sensitive and

---

[1] Ch. XXXIII.   [2] Cf. *In* 1 *Sent.*, 8, 5, 2; *In* 2 *Sent.*, 3, 1, 1.

vegetative functions also cease: the one principle of all these operations no longer informs the matter which it previously informed
and instead of the unified human substance there results a multiplicity of substances, the new substantial forms being educed from
the potentiality of matter.

Clearly, therefore, the Platonic idea of the relation of soul to
body was unacceptable to St. Thomas. It is the one individual
man who perceives not only that he reasons and understands, but
also that he feels, and exercises sensation. But one cannot have
sensation without a body, so that the body, and not the soul only,
must belong to man.[1] A man is generated when the rational soul
is infused and a man dies when the rational soul departs from the
body: there is no other substantial form in man than the rational
soul and this soul exercises the functions of inferior forms, itself
performing in the case of man what the vegetative soul does in
the case of plants and the sensitive soul in the case of irrational
animals.[2] It follows from this that the union of soul with body
cannot be something unnatural: it cannot be a punishment to the
soul for sin in a preceding state, as Origen thought. The human
soul has the power of sensation, for example, but it cannot exercise
this function without a body; it has the power of intellection, but
it has no innate ideas and has to form its ideas in dependence on
sense-experience, for which it needs a body; the soul, then, is
united to a body because it needs it, because it is naturally the
form of a body. The union of soul and body is not to the detriment,
but to the good of the soul, *propter animam*. Matter exists for the
form and not the other way about, and the soul is united to the
body in order that it (the soul) may act according to its
nature.[3]

2. But though St. Thomas emphasised the unity of man, the
close union between soul and body, he held that there is a real
distinction between the soul and its faculties, and between the
faculties themselves. In God alone are the power of acting and
the act itself identical with the substance, since in God alone is
there no potentiality: in the human soul there are faculties or
powers of acting which are in potentiality to their acts and which
are to be distinguished according to their respective acts and
objects.[4] Some of these powers or faculties belong to the soul as
such and are not intrinsically dependent on a bodily organ, while

[1] *S.T.*, Ia, 76, 1.   [2] *Ibid.*, Ia, 76, 4.   [3] Cf. *ibid.*, Ia, 76, 5; Ia, 89, 1.
[4] *Ibid.*, Ia, 77, 1–3; *De Anima*, 1, *lectio* 2.

others belong to the *compositum* and cannot be exercised without the body: the former, therefore, remain in the soul even when it is separated from the body, whereas the latter remain in the separated soul only potentially or virtually (*virtute*), in the sense that the soul still has the remote power to exercise the faculties, but only if it were reunited with the body: in its separated state it cannot use them. For instance, the rational or intellectual faculty is not intrinsically dependent on the body, though in the state of union with the body there is a certain dependence in regard to the material of knowledge (in a sense to be explained later); but the power of sensation can obviously not be exercised without the body. On the other hand it cannot be exercised by the body without the soul. Its 'subject', therefore, is neither soul alone nor body alone but the human *compositum*. Sensation cannot be attributed simply to the soul using a body (as St. Augustine thought); body and soul play their respective parts in producing the act of sensation, and the power of sensation belongs to both in union rather to either of them separately.

In the powers or faculties there is a certain hierarchy. The vegetative faculty, comprising the powers of nutrition, growth and reproduction, has as its object simply the body united to the soul or living by means of the soul. The sensitive faculty (comprising the exterior senses, of sight, hearing, smell, taste, touch, and the interior senses of *sensus communis*, *phantasia* or imagination, *vis aestimativa* and *vis memorativa* or memory) has as its object, not simply the body of the sentient subject but rather every sensible body. The rational faculty (comprising the active and passive intellects) has as its object, not only sensible bodies but being in general. The higher the power, therefore, the wider and more comprehensive its object. The first general faculty is concerned with the subject's own body; but the other two faculties, the sensitive and intellectual, are also concerned with objects extrinsic to the subject itself, and a consideration of this fact shows us that there are other powers in addition to those already mentioned. If we consider the aptitude of the external object to be received in the subject through cognition, we find there are two kinds of faculty, sensitive and intellective, the former of which is more restricted in scope than the latter; but if we consider the inclination and tendency of the soul towards the external object, we find that there are two other powers, that of locomotion, by which the subject attains the object through its own motion, and that of appetition, by which the object is desired as an end or *finis*. The power of locomotion belongs to the level of sensitive life; but the power of appetition is twofold, comprising desire on the sensitive level, the sensitive appetite, and desire on the intellectual level, volition. On the vegetative level of life, therefore, we find the three powers of nutrition, growth and reproduction, on the sensitive level the five exterior senses, the four interior senses, the power of locomotion and the sensitive appetite, on the rational level of life the active intellect, the passive intellect and the will. In man they are all present.

These powers and faculties proceed from the essence of the soul as from their principle, but they are really distinguished from one another. They have different formal objects (sight, for example, has colour as its object), their activities are different, and so they are really distinct powers (*operatio sequitur esse*). But real distinctions must not be multiplied without a sufficient reason. For instance, one of the interior senses is the *vis memorativa* or sensitive memory, by means of which the animal remembers friend or foe, what has given it pleasure and what has injured it, and according to St. Thomas the memory of the past as past belongs to the sensitive memory, since the past as past refers to particulars and it is the sensitive memory which is concerned with particulars. If, however, we mean by memory the conservation of ideas or concepts, it is necessary to refer this to the intellect, and we can speak of the intellectual memory; but the intellectual memory is not a power really distinct from the intellect itself, more precisely the passive intellect: it is the intellect itself regarded under one of its aspects or functions. Again, the act of apprehending a truth, of resting in the apprehension of the truth, does not proceed from a power or faculty different from the faculty by which we reason discursively: *intellectus* and *ratio* are not distinct faculties, for it is the same mind which apprehends truth and reasons from that truth to another truth. Nor is the 'higher reason' (*ratio superior*) concerned with eternal things, a faculty different from the *ratio inferior*, by which we attain rational knowledge of temporal things. The two are one and the same faculty, though the faculty receives different names according to the objects of its different acts, as Augustine said. The same applies to the speculative and practical intellects, which are but one faculty.

3. It may be as well to say a few more words on the subject of the 'interior senses', which are common to animal as well as

human beings. St. Thomas observes[1] that Avicenna in his book *On the Soul* postulated five interior senses, but that in reality there are only four. What does St. Thomas mean by 'senses' in this connection? Obviously not senses in our use of the term, since when we use the word senses, we refer to the five exterior senses. Why, then, does he call them senses? To indicate that they are operations belonging to the level of sensitive life and that they do not involve reason. There must, for example, be an instinctive operation by which the bird 'judges' that the twigs it sees will be useful for building a nest: it cannot see the utility simply by vision, which is directed to colour, while on the other hand it does not reason or judge in the proper sense: it has, therefore, an 'interior sense' by which it apprehends the utility of the twigs.

First of all, there must be an interior sense by which the data of the special exterior senses are distinguished and collated. The eye sees colour, the ear hears sounds, but though the sense of sight distinguishes one colour from another, it cannot distinguish colour from sound, since it cannot hear; and for the same reason it cannot refer the sound to the coloured object seen, for example, when a man is talking to his dog. This function of distinction and collation is performed by the general sense or *sensus communis*. Secondly, the animal is able to conserve the forms apprehended by sense, and this function is performed by the imagination (*phantasia* or *imaginatio*), which is 'a certain treasury of the forms received through the senses'. Thirdly, the animal is able to apprehend things which it cannot perceive through the senses, for example, that something is useful to it, that someone or something is friendly or unfriendly, and this task is performed by the *vis aestimativa*, while, lastly, the *vis memorativa* conserves such apprehensions. As regards sensible forms, there is, says St. Thomas, no difference between men and animals, since they are affected by exterior sensible objects in the same way; but in regard to apprehensions of things which are not directly perceived by the exterior senses, there is a difference between men and animals. The latter perceive such things as utility and inutility, friendliness and hostility by a natural instinct, whereas man compares particular things. What in animals, therefore, he calls the *vis aestimativa naturalis*, St. Thomas calls *vis cogitativa* in the case of human beings. Something more than mere instinct is involved.

4. Besides the five exterior senses, the four interior senses, the

[1] *S.T.*, Ia, 78, 4.

power of locomotion, the sensitive appetite and the rational cognitive faculties (to which I shall return in the next chapter, when treating of St. Thomas's theory of knowledge), man has also will (*voluntas*). The will differs from the sensitive appetite, since it desires the good as such or the good in general (*bonum sub communi ratione boni*), whereas the sensitive appetite does not desire good in general, but the particular objects of desire presented by the senses. Moreover, the will is of its very nature orientated towards good in general, and it necessarily desires the good in general. This necessity is not, however, a necessity of coercion, a necessity which bears upon the will with violence; it proceeds from the will itself, which of its very nature desires the last end or happiness (*beatitudo*). The will, since it is an appetitive faculty, cannot be understood apart from its natural object of desire, its natural *finis*, and this object, says St. Thomas, following Aristotle, is beatitude, happiness, the good in general. We necessarily desire to be happy, we cannot help desiring it; but the necessity in question is not a necessity imposed from without by violence (*necessitas coactionis*) but a necessity of nature (*necessitas naturalis*) proceeding from the nature of the will.

Yet although man necessarily desires happiness, this does not mean that he is not free in regard to his particular choices. There are some particular goods which are not necessary to happiness, and a man is free to will them or not. Moreover, even though true happiness is to be found only in the possession of God, only in the attainment of the infinite Good, that does not mean that every man must have a conscious desire of God or that he must necessarily will those means which will bring him to God. In this life the intellect has not got that clear vision of God as the infinite good and only source of happiness which would be needed to determine the will: man necessarily desires happiness, but the connection between happiness and God is not so steadfastly clear to him that he is unable to will something other than God. In a sense, of course, he is always willing God, because he necessarily wills happiness and, *de facto*, happiness is to be found only in the attainment of God, the infinite Good; but owing to his lack of clear vision of God as the infinite Good, objects may appear to him as necessarily related to his happiness which are not so related, and he can place his happiness in something other than God. Whatever he wills, he wills as a good, real or apparent (he necessarily wills *sub ratione boni*), but he does not necessarily will the actual infinite Good. In an interpretative sense he may be said to be always willing God; but as far as conscious choice is concerned, he may will something other than God, even to the exclusion of God. If he shuts his eyes to the truth and turns his attention to sensual pleasures, for example, placing his happiness in them, he is morally guilty; but that does not alter the fact that the incompatibility between indulgence in inordinate sensual pleasure and the attainment of true happiness is not so compellingly self-evident to him that he cannot take indulgence in inordinate pleasure of sense as his end. One can take a parallel example from the activity of the intellect. If a man knows what the terms mean, it is impossible for him not to assent to the first principles in the intellectual order, for example, the principle of identity, but when a chain of reasoning is involved, as in a metaphysical proof of God's existence, he may refuse his assent, not because the argument is insufficient, but because he does not wish to assent and turns away his intellect from perceiving or dwelling on the necessary connection of the conclusion with the premises. Similarly, a man necessarily wills *sub ratione boni*, he necessarily desires happiness; but he can turn his attention away from the necessary connection between happiness and God and allow something other than God to appear to him as the source of true happiness.

Free will (*liberum arbitrium*) is not a power or faculty different from the will; but there is a mental distinction between them, since the term 'will signifies the faculty as principle of all our volition, whether necessary (in regard to the end, happiness) or free (in regard to the choice of means to the end), whereas 'free will' signifies the same faculty as principle of our free choice of means to the end. As already mentioned, St. Thomas maintained that though man necessarily wills the end, happiness, he has no compelling vision of the connection between particular means and this end, and therefore he is free in regard to the choice of these means, being necessitated neither from without nor from within. That man is free follows from the fact that he is rational. A sheep 'judges' by a natural instinct that the wolf is to be avoided, but man judges that some good is to be attained or some evil to be avoided by a free act of his intelligence.[1] The reason, unlike instinct, is not determined in its judgement concerning particular choices. Choice concerns the means to the final end (happiness), and it is possible for a man to consider any particular object from

---

[1] *S.T.*, Ia, 83, 1.

more than one point of view: he may consider it under its aspect as a good and judge that it should be chosen or he may consider it under its aspect as evil, that is, as lacking some good, and judge that it should be avoided.[1] *Liberum arbitrium* is thus the power by which a man is able to judge freely.[2] It might seem, then, that freedom belongs to the intellect and not to will; but St. Thomas observes[3] that when it is said that *liberum arbitrium* is the power by which a man is able to judge freely, the reference is not to any kind of judgement but to the decisive judgement of choice which puts an end to the deliberation which arises from the fact that a man can consider a possible object of choice from different points of view. For example, if there is a question of my going for a walk or not going for a walk, I can regard the walk as a good, as healthy exercise, or as evil, as taking up time which should be given to writing a letter for the afternoon post. The decisive judgement which says that I will go for a walk (or not, as the case may be) is made under the influence of the will. *Liberum arbitrium*, therefore, is the will, but it designates the will not absolutely, but in its relation to the reason. Judgement as such belongs to the reason, but freedom of judgement belongs immediately to the will. Still, it is true that St. Thomas's account of freedom is intellectualist in character.

5. This intellectualism is apparent in his answer to the question whether the intellect or the will is the nobler faculty. St. Thomas answers that, absolutely speaking, the intellect is the nobler faculty, since the intellect through cognition possesses the object, contains it in itself through mental assimilation, whereas the will tends towards the object as external, and it is more perfect to possess the perfection of the object in oneself than to tend towards it as existing outside oneself. In regard to corporeal objects, therefore, knowledge of them is more perfect and nobler than volition in respect to them, since by knowledge we possess the forms of these objects in ourselves, and these forms exist in a nobler way in the rational soul than they do in the corporeal objects. Similarly, the essence of the beatific vision consists in the act of knowledge by which we possess God. On the other hand, although possession of the object by the intellect is in itself more perfect than tending towards the object by volition, the will may be nobler than the intellect in certain respects, *secundum quid*, because of accidental reasons. For example, in this life our knowledge

of God is imperfect and analogical, we know God only indirectly, whereas the will tends to God directly: love of God is, therefore, more perfect than knowledge of God. In the case of objects which are less noble than the soul, corporeal objects, we can have immediate knowledge, and such knowledge is more perfect than volition; but in the case of God, an object which transcends the human soul, we have only mediate knowledge in this life, and our love of God is more perfect than our knowledge of God. In the beatific vision in heaven, however, when the soul sees the essence of God immediately, the intrinsic superiority of intellect to will reasserts itself, as it were. In this way St. Thomas, while adopting the intellectualist attitude of Aristotle, interprets it in a Christian setting.[1]

6. We have seen that St. Thomas rejected the Platonic-Augustinian view of the relation of soul to body and adopted the Aristotelian view of the soul as form of the body, emphasising the closeness of the union between the two. There is no *forma corporeitatis*, there is but one substantial form in man, the rational soul, which directly informs prime matter and is the cause of all human activities on the vegetative, sensitive and intellectual levels: sensation is an act not of the soul using a body, but of the *compositum*; we have no innate ideas, but the mind is dependent on sense-experience for its knowledge. The question arises, therefore, whether the closeness of the union between soul and body has not been so emphasised that the possible subsistence of the human soul apart from the body must be ruled out. In other words, is not the Aristotelian doctrine of the relation of soul to body incompatible with personal immortality? If one starts with the Platonic theory of the soul, immortality is assured, but the union of soul and body is rendered difficult to understand; whereas if one starts with the Aristotelian theory of the soul, it might seem that one has to sacrifice immortality, that the soul is so closely bound to the body that it cannot subsist apart from the body.

The soul is indeed the form of the body and, according to St. Thomas, it always retains its aptitude to inform a body, precisely because it is naturally the form of the body; but it is none the less a rational soul and its powers are not exhausted in informing the body. When actually dealing with the immortality of the soul St. Thomas argues that the soul is incorruptible because it is a subsistent form. A thing which corrupts is corrupted either by

---

[1] *De Veritate*, 22, 11; cf. *S.T.*, Ia, 82, 3.

itself (*per se*) or accidentally (*per accidens*), that is, through the corruption of something else on which it depends for existence. The soul of the brute is dependent on the body for all its operations and corrupts when the body corrupts (*corruptio per accidens*): the rational soul, however, being a subsistent form, cannot be affected by the corruption of the body on which it does not intrinsically depend.[1] If this were all St. Thomas had to say by way of proving immortality, he would obviously be guilty of a gross *petitio principii*, since it is presupposed that the human soul is a *forma subsistens*, and this is precisely the point which has to be proved. St. Thomas argues, however, that the rational soul must be spiritual and a subsistent form, because it is capable of knowing the natures of all bodies. If it were material, it would be determined to a specified object, as the organ of vision is determined to the perception of colour. Again, if it depended intrinsically on a bodily organ, it would be confined to the knowledge of some particular kind of bodily object, which is not the case,[2] while if it were itself a body, material, it could not reflect on itself.[3] For these and other reasons the human soul, which is a rational soul, must be immaterial, i.e. spiritual, from which it follows that it is incorruptible or naturally immortal. Physically speaking, it could, of course, be annihilated by the God who created it; but its immortality follows from its nature and is not simply gratuitous, save in the sense that its very existence, like the existence of any other creature, is gratuitous.

St. Thomas argues also from the desire of persistence in being. There is a natural desire for immortality and a natural desire, as implanted by God, cannot be in vain.[4] 'It is impossible for a natural appetite to be in vain. But man has a natural appetite for perpetual persistence in being. This is clear from the fact that existence (*esse*) is desired by all things, but a man has an intellectual apprehension of *esse* as such, and not only of *esse* here and now as the brutes have. Man therefore attains immortality as regards his soul, by which he apprehends *esse* as such and without temporal limit.'[5] Man, as distinct from the irrational animal, can conceive perpetual existence, divorced from the present moment, and to this apprehension there corresponds a natural desire for immortality. As this desire must have been implanted by the Author of Nature, it cannot be in vain (*frustra* or *inane*). Against

[1] *S.T.*, Ia, 75, 6; *Contra Gent.*, 2, 79. [2] *S.T.*, Ia, 75, 2. [3] *Contra Gent.*, 2, 49.
[4] *S.T.*, Ia, 75, 6. [5] *Contra Gent.*, 2, 79.

this Duns Scotus later argued that, as far as a natural desire (*desiderium naturale*) is concerned, man and brute are on a level in that both naturally shun death, while in regard to an elicited or conscious desire we have first to show that its fulfilment is possible before we can argue that it must be fulfilled.[1] One might reply that the possibility of the fulfilment of the desire is shown by proving that the soul is not intrinsically dependent on the body but is spiritual. This would be to admit that the argument from the spirituality of the soul is fundamental.

In view of St. Thomas's epistemology, of his insistence on the origin of human ideas in sense-experience and on the rôle of the phantasm in the formation of such ideas, it might appear that he contradicts himself when he says that the human mind is not intrinsically dependent on the body, and it might also appear that the soul in a state of separation would be incapable of intellectual activity. In regard to the first point, however, he maintains that the mind needs the body for its activity not as an organ of mental activity, for this is an activity of the mind alone, but because of the natural object of the human mind in this life, when conjoined to a body. In other words, the mind is not intrinsically dependent on the body for its subsistence. Can it, then, exercise its activity in a state of separation from the body? Yes, for its mode of cognition follows the state in which it is. When united to the body, the rational soul does not come to know things save *convertendo se ad phantasmata*; but when it is in a state of separation it is no longer unable to know itself and other souls perfectly and directly, the angels imperfectly. It might seem indeed that in this case it is better for the soul to be in a state of separation from the body than united to it, since spirits are nobler objects of knowledge than corporeal things; but St. Thomas cannot admit this, since he has insisted that it is natural for the soul to be united to the body and that their union is for the good of the soul. He does not hesitate, then, to draw the conclusion that the state of separation is *praeter naturam* and that the soul's mode of cognition in the state of separation is also *praeter naturam*.[2]

7. When St. Thomas proves the immortality of the soul, he is naturally referring to personal immortality. Against the Averroists he argues that the intellect is not a substance distinct from the human soul and common to all men, but that it is multiplied 'according to the multiplication of bodies'.[3] It is impossible to

---

[1] *Opus Oxon.*, 4, 43, 2, nos. 29 ff.   [2] *S.T.*, Ia, 89, 1 ff.   [3] *Ibid.*, Ia, 76, 2.

explain the diversity of ideas and intellectual operations in different men on the supposition that all men have but one intellect. It is not only sensations and phantasms which differ from man to man but their intellectual lives and activities as well. It is as absurd to suppose that they have one intellect as it would be to suppose that they have one vision.

It is important to realise that it is not the opinion of Avicenna concerning the unicity and separate character of the *active* intellect which necessarily does away with personal immortality (some mediaeval philosophers who certainly maintained personal immortality identified the active intellect with God or God's activity in the soul), but rather the opinion of Averroes concerning the unicity and separate character of the *passive* as well as of the active intellect. That Averroes was the chief enemy on this point St. Thomas makes quite clear at the beginning of his *De unitate intellectus contra Averroistas*. If the Averroistic theory is accepted 'it follows that after death nothing remains of men's souls but one intellect; and in this way the bestowal of rewards and punishments is done away with.' This is not to say, of course, that St. Thomas accepted the theory of the unicity of the active intellect: he argues against it in the *Summa contra Gentiles*, for example,[1] as also in the *Summa Theologica*.[2] One of his arguments is to the effect that if the active intellect were one in all men, then its functioning would be independent of the individual's control and would be constant, whereas in point of fact we can pursue intellectual activity at will and abandon it at will. Incidentally, St. Thomas interprets the notoriously obscure passage in Aristotle's *De Anima*[3] as teaching the individual character of the active intellect in individual men. It is impossible to say with certainty that the Thomist interpretation of Aristotle is wrong, though I incline to this opinion; but the rightness or wrongness of his interpretation of Aristotle obviously does not affect the question of the truth or falsity of his own idea of the active intellect.[4]

Against the unicity of the passive intellect St. Thomas argues in the *De unitate intellectus contra Averroistas* and in the *Summa contra Gentiles*.[5] His arguments presuppose for the most part the Aristotelian psychology and epistemology; but the presupposition is only to be expected, not only because St. Thomas accepted the Aristotelian doctrine as he understood and interpreted it, but also

[1] 2, 76.   [2] Ia, 79, 4-5.   [3] 3, 5; 430 a. 17 ff.
[4] On Aristotle, see *Summa contra Gentiles*, 2, 78, and the Commentary on the *De Anima*, 3, *lectio* 10.   [5] 2, 73-5.

because the Averroists were Aristotelians. To say, then, that St. Thomas presupposed the Aristotelian psychology and epistemology is simply to say that he tried to show the Averroists that their notion of the unitary and separate character of the passive intellect was inconsistent with their own principles. If the soul is the form of the body, how could the passive intellect be one in all men? One principle could not be the form of a plurality of substances. Again, if the passive intellect were a separate principle, it would be eternal; it should, then, contain all the *species intelligibiles* which have ever been received, and every man should be able to understand all those things which have ever been understood by men, which is manifestly not the case. Furthermore, if the active intellect were separate and eternal, it would be functioning from eternity and the passive intellect, also supposed to be separate and eternal, would be receiving from eternity; but this would render the senses and imagination unnecessary for intellectual operations, whereas experience shows that they are indispensable. And how could one explain the different intellectual capacities of different men? Men's differences in this respect certainly depend to some extent on their different infra-intellectual capacities.

It may be somewhat difficult for us to-day to understand the excitement produced by the Averroistic theory and the interest it aroused; but it was obviously incompatible with the Christian doctrines of immortality and of sanctions in the next life, and even if St. Thomas shows a desire to dissociate Aristotle from Averroes, the moral and religious consequences of the Averroistic doctrine were more important to him than Averroes's attempt to father his doctrine on the Greek philosopher. Against the Averroists Augustinians and Aristotelians made common cause. One might compare the reaction provoked by modern metaphysical and psychological systems which appear to endanger the human personality. On this point absolute idealism, for instance, aroused opposition on the part of philosophers who were otherwise sharply divided among themselves.

CHAPTER XXXVIII

ST. THOMAS AQUINAS—VIII: KNOWLEDGE

'Theory of knowledge' in St. Thomas—The process of knowledge; knowledge of the universal and of the particular—The soul's knowledge of itself—The possibility of metaphysics.

1. To look for an epistemology in St. Thomas, in the sense of a justification of knowledge, a proof or attempted proof of the objectivity of knowledge in face of subjective idealism of one kind or another, would be to look in vain. That everyone, even the self-styled sceptic, is convinced that knowledge of some sort is attainable was as clear to St. Thomas as it was to St. Augustine, and so far as there is a problem of knowledge for St. Thomas it is rather how to safeguard and justify metaphysics in face of the Aristotelian psychology than to justify the objectivity of our knowledge of the extramental world in face of a subjective idealism which had not yet arisen or to show the legitimacy of metaphysics in face of a Kantian criticism which still lay far in the future. This is not to say, of course, that the Thomist principles cannot be developed in such a way as to afford answers to subjective idealism and Kantianism; but one should not be guilty of the anachronism of making the historic Thomas answer questions with which he was not actually faced. Indeed, to treat St. Thomas's theory of knowledge separately from his psychological doctrine is itself something of an anachronism, yet I think it is capable of being justified, since it is out of the psychology that a problem of knowledge arises, and one can, for the sake of convenience at least, treat this problem separately. For the purpose of making this problem clear it is necessary first of all to give a brief sketch of the way in which we attain our natural ideas and knowledge, according to Aquinas.

2. Corporeal objects act upon the organs of sense, and sensation is an act of the *compositum*, of soul and body, not of the soul alone using a body, as Augustine thought. The senses are naturally determined to the apprehension of particulars, they cannot apprehend universals. Brutes have sensation, but they have no grasp of general ideas. The phantasm or image, which arises in the imagination and which represents the particular material object

perceived by the senses, is itself particular, the phantasm of a particular object or objects. Human intellectual cognition, however, is of the universal: the human being in his intellectual operations apprehends the form of the material object in abstraction; he apprehends a universal. Through sensation we can apprehend only particular men or trees, for example, and the interior images or phantasms of men or trees are always particular. Even if we have a composite image of man, not representing any one actual man distinctly but representing many confusedly, it is still particular, since the images or parts of the images of particular actual men coalesce to form an image which may be 'generic' in respect of actual particular men but which is itself none the less particular, the image of a particular imagined man. The mind, however, can and does conceive the general idea of man as such, which includes all men in its extension. An image of man certainly will not apply to all men, but the intellectual idea of man, even though conceived in dependence on the sensitive apprehension of particular men, applies to all men. The image of a man must be either of a man who has or of a man who has not some hair on his head. If the former, it does not in that respect represent bald men; if the latter, it does not in that respect represent men who are not bald; but if we form the concept of man as a rational animal, this idea covers all men, whether they are bald or not, white or black, tall or short, because it is the idea of the essence of man.

How, then, is the transition from sensitive and particular knowledge to intellectual cognition effected? Although sensation is an activity of soul and body together, the rational and spiritual soul cannot be affected directly by a material thing or by the phantasm: there is need, therefore, of an activity on the part of the soul, since the concept cannot be formed simply passively. This activity is the activity of the active intellect which 'illumines' the phantasm and abstracts from it the universal or 'intelligible species'. St. Thomas thus speaks of illumination, but he does not use the word in the full Augustinian sense (not at least according to what is probably the true interpretation of Augustine's meaning); he means that the active intellect by its natural power and without any special illumination from God renders visible the intelligible aspect of the phantasm, reveals the formal and potentially universal element contained implicitly in the phantasm. The active intellect then abstracts the universal element by itself, producing in the passive intellect the *species impressa*. The reaction of the passive intellect to this determination by the active intellect is the *verbum mentis* (*species expressa*), the universal concept in the full sense. The function of the active intellect is purely active, to abstract the universal element from the particular elements of the phantasm, to cause in the passive intellect the *species impressa*. The intellect of man contains no innate ideas but is in potentiality to the reception of concepts: it has, therefore, to be reduced to act, and this reduction to act must be effected by a principle itself in act. As this active principle has no ready-made ideas of itself to supply, it must draw its materials from what is provided by the senses, and this means that it must abstract the intelligible element from the phantasm. To abstract means to isolate intellectually the universal apart from the particularising notes. Thus the active intellect abstracts the universal essence of man from a particular phantasm by leaving out all particular notes which confine it to a particular man or particular men. As the active intellect is purely active, it cannot impress the universal on itself; it impresses it on the potential element of the human intellect, on the passive intellect, and the reaction to this impression is the concept in the full sense, the *verbum mentis*.

It is important to realise, however, that the abstract concept is not the object of cognition, but the means of cognition. If the concept, the modification of the intellect, were itself the object of knowledge, then our knowledge would be a knowledge of ideas, not of things existing extramentally, and the judgements of science would concern not things outside the mind but concepts within the mind. In actual fact, however, the concept is the likeness of the object produced in the mind and is thus the means by which the mind knows the object: in St. Thomas's language it is *id quo intelligitur*, not *id quod intelligitur*.[1] Of course, the mind has the power of reflecting on its own modifications and so can turn the concept into an object; but it is only secondarily an object of knowledge, primarily it is the instrument of knowledge. By saying this St. Thomas avoids putting himself in a position which would be that of subjective idealism and which would land him in the difficulties attending that form of idealism. The theory he actually contrasts with his own is the theory of Plato; but that does not alter the fact that by adopting the attitude he did he escaped a snare from which it is practically impossible to extricate oneself.

[1] *S.T.*, Ia, 5, 2.

As he held that the intellect knows directly the essence, the universal, St. Thomas drew the logical conclusion that the human mind does not know directly singular material things. The emphasis is, of course, on 'mind' and 'know', since it cannot be denied that the human being apprehends particular material objects sensitively: the object of sense is precisely the sensible particular. The intellect, however, comes to know by abstracting the intelligible species from the individualising matter, and in this case it can have direct knowledge of universals only. Nevertheless, even after abstracting the intelligible species, the intellect exercises its activity of knowing only through a 'conversion', a turning of attention to the phantasms in which it apprehends the universals, and in this way it has a reflexive or indirect knowledge of the particular things represented by the phantasms. Thus the sensitive apprehension of Socrates enables the mind to abstract the universal 'man'; but the abstract idea is a means of knowledge, an instrument of knowledge to the intellect only in so far as the latter adverts to the phantasm, and so it is able to form the judgement that Socrates is a man. It is thus not true to say that the intellect, according to St. Thomas, has no knowledge of corporeal particulars: what he held was that the mind has only an indirect knowledge of such particulars, the direct object of knowledge being the universal.[1] But this should not be taken to imply that the primary object of intellectual cognition is the abstract idea as such: the mind apprehends the formal element, the potentially universal element in Socrates, for example, and abstracts this from the individualising matter. In technical language its primary object of knowledge is the direct universal, the universal apprehended in the particular: it is only secondarily that it apprehends the universal precisely as universal, the reflexive universal.

Two explanatory remarks should be added. St. Thomas explains that when he says that the mind abstracts the universal from the corporeal particular by abstracting it from the individualising matter, he means that when the mind abstracts the idea of man, for example, it abstracts it from *this* flesh and *these* bones, that is, from the particular individualising matter, not from matter in general, 'intelligible matter' (i.e. substance as subject to quantity). Corporeality enters into the idea of man as such, though particular matter does not enter into the universal idea of man.[2] Secondly, St. Thomas does not mean to imply that it is the particular thing

---

[1] *S.T.*, Ia, 86, 1.   [2] *Ibid.*, Ia, 85, 1.

as such which cannot be the direct object of intellectual cognition, but rather the particular sensible or corporeal object. In other words, the particular corporeal object is debarred from being the direct object of intellectual cognition not precisely because it is particular but because it is material and the mind knows only by abstracting from matter as principle of individuation, that is, from this or that matter.[1]

3. According to St. Thomas, then, the human mind is originally in potentiality to knowledge; but it has no innate ideas. The only sense in which ideas are innate is that the mind has a natural capacity for abstracting and forming ideas: as far as actual ideas go, the mind is originally a *tabula rasa*. Moreover, the source of the mind's knowledge is sense-perception, since the soul, the form of the body, has as its natural object of knowledge the essences of material objects. The rational soul knows itself only by means of its acts, apprehending itself, not directly in its essence but in the act by which it abstracts intelligible species from sensible objects.[2] The soul's knowledge of itself is not, therefore, an exception to the general rule that all our knowledge begins with sense-perception and is dependent on sense-perception. This fact St. Thomas expresses by saying that the intellect, when united to a body in the present life, cannot come to know anything *nisi convertendo se ad phantasmata*.[3] The human mind does not think without the presence of a phantasm, as is clear from introspection, and it is dependent on the phantasm, as is shown by the fact that a disordered power of imagination (as in mad people) hinders knowledge; and the reason for this is that the cognitive power is proportioned to its natural object.[4] In brief, the human soul, as Aristotle said, understands nothing without a phantasm, and we can say, *nihil in intellectu quod prius non fuerit in sensu*.

4. From this it obviously follows that the human mind cannot in this life attain a direct knowledge of immaterial substances, which are not and cannot be the object of the senses.[5] But the problem also arises whether there can be metaphysical knowledge at all on these premises, whether the human mind can rise above the things of sense and attain any knowledge of God, for example, since God cannot be an object of sense. If our intellects are dependent on the phantasm, how can they know those objects of which there are no phantasms, which do not act on the senses?[6]

---

[1] *S.T.*, Ia, 86, 1, *ad* 3. [2] *Ibid.*, Ia, 87, 1. [3] *Ibid.*, Ia, 84, 7.
[4] *Ibid.*, Ia, 84, 7. [5] *Ibid.*, Ia, 88, 1. [6] *Ibid.*, Ia, 84, 7, *ad* 3.

On the principle, *nihil in intellectu quod prius non fuerit in sensu*, how can we attain knowledge of God when we cannot say *quod Deus prius fuerit in sensu*? In other words, once given the Thomist psychology and epistemology, it would appear that the Thomist natural theology is inevitably invalidated: we cannot transcend the objects of sense and are debarred from any knowledge of spiritual objects.

In order to understand St. Thomas's reply to this serious objection, it is necessary to recall his doctrine of intellect as such. The senses are necessarily determined to one particular kind of object, but the intellect, being immaterial, is the faculty of apprehending being. Intellect as such is directed towards all being. The object of the intellect is the intelligible: nothing is intelligible except in so far as it is in act, partakes of being, and all that is in act is intelligible in so far as it is in act, i.e. partakes of being. If we consider the human intellect precisely as intellect, we must admit, then, that its primary object is being. *Intellectus respicit suum obiectum secundum communem rationem entis; eo quod intellectus possibilis est quo est omnia fieri.*[1] *Primo autem in conceptione intellectus cadit ens; quia secundum hoc unumquodque cognoscibile est, inquantum est actu . . . Unde ens est proprium obiectum intellectus.*[2] The first movement of the intellect is thus towards being, not towards sensible being in particular, and the intellect can know the essence of a material thing only in so far as it is being: it is only in the second place that a particular kind of intellect, the human intellect, is directed towards a particular kind of being. Owing to its embodied state and the necessity of the *conversio ad phantasma* the human intellect has, in its embodied state, the sensible object as the natural and 'proper' object of its apprehension, but it does not lose its orientation towards being in general. As *human* intellect it must start from sense, from material beings, but as human *intellect* it can proceed beyond sense, not being confined to material essences, though it can do this only in so far as the immaterial objects are manifested in and through the sensible world, in so far as the material things have a relation to immaterial objects. As embodied intellect, as a *tabula rasa*, the natural object of which is the material essence, the intellect does not and cannot by its own power apprehend God directly; but sensible objects, as finite and contingent, reveal their relation to God, so that the intellect can know that God exists. Moreover,

[1] *S.T.*, Ia, 79, 7. [2] *Ibid.*, Ia, 5, 2.

sensible objects, as the effects of God, manifest God to some extent, so that the intellect can come to know something of God's nature, though this knowledge cannot (naturally) be more than analogical. The necessity of the *conversio ad phantasma* means that we cannot know God directly, but we can know Him in so far as sensible objects manifest His existence and enable us to attain an analogical, indirect and imperfect knowledge of His nature: we can know God *ut causam, et per excessum, et per remotionem.*[1]

A presupposition of this position is the activity of the human intellect. If the human intellect were merely passive, if the *conversio ad phantasma* meant that ideas were caused simply passively, there could obviously be no natural knowledge of God, since sensible objects are not God and of God and other immaterial beings *non sunt phantasmata.* It is the active power of the intellect which enables it to read off, as it were, the relation to immaterial being in sensible being. Sensible cognition is not the total and perfect cause of our intellectual cognition, but is rather the *materia causae* of intellectual cognition: the phantasm is made actually intelligible by the active intellect through its abstractive operation. Inasmuch, then, as sensitive cognition is not the total cause of intellectual cognition, 'it is nothing to be astonished at if intellectual cognition extends farther than sensitive cognition'.[2] The human intellect, as united to a body, has as its natural object the essences of material things, but by means of these essences it can ascend to 'some sort of knowledge of invisible things'. These immaterial objects we can know only *per remotionem*, by denying of them the characteristics peculiar to sensible objects, or analogically; but we could not know them at all, were it not for the active power of the intellect.[3]

A further difficulty, already mentioned, remains. How can there be any positive content to our idea of God, or indeed of any spiritual object? If we say, for example, that God is personal, we obviously do not mean to ascribe to God human personality. If, however, we simply mean that God is not less than what we know as personal, is there any positive content to our idea of divine personality? Is 'not-less-than-personal' a positive idea? If we state it in affirmative terms, 'more-than-personal', has it a positive content? If it has not, then we are confined to the *via negativa* and can know God only *per remotionem*. But St. Thomas does not

---

[1] *S.T.*, Ia, 84, 7 *ad* 3.   [2] *Ibid.*, Ia, 84, 6, *in corpore* and *ad* 3.
[3] Cf. *ibid.*, Ia, 84, 7, *in corpore* and *ad* 3.

adhere simply to the *via negativa*: he utilises also the *via affirmativa*, maintaining that we can know God *per excessum*. Now, if when we ascribe wisdom, for instance, to God, we say that we are ascribing wisdom *modo eminentiori*, it is difficult to see what the content of our idea of divine wisdom actually is. It must be based on human wisdom, which is the only wisdom we experience naturally and directly; and yet it cannot be precisely human wisdom. But if it is human wisdom without the limitations and forms of human wisdom, what positive content does the idea possess, when we have no experience of wisdom without limitations? It would seem that if one is determined to maintain that the idea has a positive content, one must say either that the idea of human wisdom plus a negation of its limitations is a positive idea or, with Scotus, that we can attain an idea of the essence of wisdom, so to speak, which can be predicated univocally of God and man. The latter theory, though helpful in some ways, is not altogether satisfactory, since neither St. Thomas nor Scotus would hold that wisdom or any other perfection is realised univocally in God and creatures. As to the first answer, it may seem at first hearing to constitute an evasion of the difficulty; but reflection will show that to say that God is wise, meaning that God is more than wise (in the human sense), is not at all the same thing as saying that God is not wise (in the human sense). A stone is not wise (in the human sense), neither is it more than wise: it is less than wise. It is true that if we use the word 'wise' as signifying precisely the wisdom we experience, namely human wisdom, we can say with truth not only that the stone is not wise, but also that God is not wise; but the meaning of the two statements is not the same, and if the meaning is not the same, there must be a positive content in the statement that God is not wise (i.e. that God is more than wise in the specifically human sense). The statement, therefore, that God is wise ('wise' meaning infinitely more than wise in the human sense) has a positive content. To demand that the content of analogical ideas should be perfectly clear and expressible, so that they could be understood perfectly in terms of human experience, would be to misunderstand altogether the nature of analogy. St. Thomas was no rationalist, though he allowed that we can attain to *aliqualis cognitio Dei*. The infinity of the object, God, means that the finite human mind can attain no adequate and perfect idea of God's nature; but it does not mean that it cannot attain an imperfect and inadequate notion of God's nature. To know that

God understands is to know something positive about God, since it tells us at the very least that God is not irrational like a stone or a plant, even though to know what the divine understanding is in itself exceeds our power of comprehension.

To return to the example of personality. The assertion that God is personal depends on the argument that the necessary Being and first Cause cannot be less perfect than what proceeds from it and depends on it. On the other hand, the Aristotelian-Thomist psychology and epistemology prevent one from saying that an argument of this kind will afford any adequate idea of what the divine personality is in itself. If one claimed that one had such an idea, it would be derived from experience and it would inevitably represent the data of experience. In practice this would mean that one would affirm that God is *a* Person, and the consequence would be a contradiction between revelation and philosophy. If, however, one realises that one can by philosophical argument alone attain no adequate idea of the divine personality, one will realise that all one is entitled to say from the philosophical viewpoint is that God is personal, not that God is *a* Person. When revelation informs us that God is three Persons in one Nature, our knowledge of God is extended, but no contradiction between theology and philosophy is involved. Moreover, when we say that God is personal, we really mean that He is not less than what we experience as personality, in the sense that the perfection of personality must be in Him in the only manner in which it can be in an infinite Being. If it is objected that this is to beg the question, since the question is precisely whether personality and infinity are compatible, one can reply that the proofs of God's personality and of His infinity are independent, so that we know that personality and infinity must be compatible, even though we have no direct experience of the divine personality or of the divine infinity. That there is a positive content of some sort to our idea of divine personality is shown by the fact that the meaning in the statement 'God is super-personal' (i.e. more than that which we directly experience as personality) is different from the meaning in the statement 'God is not personal' (i.e. in any sense, just as a stone is not personal). If we had reason to believe that God were not personal in the sense in which a stone is not personal, we should see the uselessness of worship and prayer; but the statement that God is personal suggests immediately that worship and prayer are in place, even though we have no adequate idea of what the divine personality is in itself. Of an infinite Being we can have but a finite and analogical natural knowledge, precisely because we ourselves are finite; but a finite and imperfect knowledge is not the same thing as no knowledge at all.

CHAPTER XXXIX

ST. THOMAS AQUINAS—IX: MORAL THEORY

*Eudaemonism—The vision of God—Good and bad—The virtues
—The natural law—The eternal law and the foundation of
morality in God—Natural virtues recognised by St. Thomas
which were not recognised by Aristotle; the virtue of religion.*

To treat the moral theory of St. Thomas in detail would be impracticable here, but a discussion of some important points may help to show its relation to the Aristotelian ethic.

1. In the *Nicomachean Ethics* Aristotle argues that every agent acts for an end and that the human agent acts for happiness, with a view to the acquisition of happiness. Happiness, he says, must consist in an activity, primarily in the activity which perfects the highest faculty in man directed to the highest and noblest objects. He comes to the conclusion, therefore, that human happiness consists primarily in *theoria*, in contemplation of the highest objects, chiefly in the contemplation of the unmoved Mover, God, though he held that the enjoyment of other goods, such as friendship and, in moderation, external goods, is necessary to perfect happiness.[1] Aristotle's ethic was thus eudaemonistic in character, teleological, and markedly intellectualist, since it is clear that for him contemplation meant philosophical contemplation: he was not referring to a religious phenomenon, such as the ecstasy of Plotinus. Moreover, the end (*telos*) of moral activity is an end to be acquired in this life: as far as the ethics of Aristotle are concerned there is no hint of any vision of God in the next life, and it is indeed questionable whether he believed in personal immortality at all. Aristotle's truly happy man is the philosopher, not the saint.

Now, St. Thomas adopted a similar eudaemonological and teleological standpoint, and his theory of the end of human conduct is in some respects intellectualist; but a change of emphasis soon becomes visible which marks a very considerable difference between his ethical theory and that of Aristotle. The only acts of man which fall properly within the moral sphere are free acts, acts which proceed from man precisely as man, as a rational and free

[1] For a fuller treatment of the Aristotelian ethic, see the first volume of this history, pp. 332–50.

being. These human acts (*actiones humanae*, as distinguished from *actiones hominis*) proceed from man's will, and the object of the will is the good (*bonum*). It is the prerogative of man to act for an end which he has apprehended, and every human act is performed for an apprehended end; but the particular end or good, for the attainment of which a particular human act is performed, does not and cannot fully perfect and satisfy the human will, which is set towards the universal good and can find its satisfaction only in the attainment of the universal good. What is the universal good in the concrete? It cannot consist in riches, for example, for riches are simply a means to an end, whereas the universal good is necessarily the final end and cannot be itself a means to a further end. It cannot consist in sensible pleasure, since this perfects only the body, not the whole man; nor can it consist in power, which does not perfect the whole man or satisfy the will completely and which, moreover, can be abused, whereas it is inconceivable that the ultimate and universal good can be abused or employed for an unworthy or evil purpose. It cannot consist even in consideration of the speculative sciences, since philosophic speculation certainly does not satisfy completely the human intellect and will. Our natural knowledge is drawn from sense-experience; yet man aspires to a knowledge of the ultimate cause as it is in itself, and this cannot be acquired by metaphysics. Aristotle may have said that the good of man consists in the consideration of the speculative sciences, but he was speaking of imperfect happiness, such as is attainable in this life. Perfect happiness, the ultimate end, is not to be found in any created thing, but only in God, who is Himself the supreme and infinite Good. God is the universal good in the concrete, and though He is the end of all things, of both rational and irrational creatures, it is only rational creatures who can attain this final good by way of knowledge and love: it is only rational creatures who can attain the vision of God in which alone perfect happiness lies. In this life man can know that God exists and he can attain an imperfect and analogical notion of God's nature, but it is only in the next life that he can know God as He is in Himself and no other end can fully satisfy man.[1]

Aristotle, says St. Thomas, was speaking of imperfect happiness such as is attainable in this life; but Aristotle, as I have already mentioned, says nothing in the *Ethics* of any other happiness. His

[1] On the foregoing, see particularly *S.T.*, Ia, IIae, questions 1-3.

ethic was an ethic of human conduct in this life, whereas St. Thomas has not proceeded far before he has brought in consideration of the perfect happiness attainable only in the next life, this happiness consisting principally in the vision of God, though it also includes, of course, satisfaction of the will, while other goods, such as the society of friends, contribute to the *bene esse* of beatitude, though no good save God is *necessary* for happiness.[1] At once, therefore, St. Thomas's moral theory is seen to move on a different plane from that of Aristotle, since however much St. Thomas may use Aristotle's language, the introduction of the next life and of the vision of God into moral theory is foreign to the thought of Aristotle.[2] What Aristotle calls happiness, St. Thomas calls imperfect happiness or temporal happiness or happiness as attainable in this life, and this imperfect happiness he regards as ordered to perfect happiness, which is attainable only in the next life and consists principally in the vision of God.

2. St. Thomas's statement that the perfect happiness of man consists in the vision of God raises a very difficult problem for any interpreter of the Saint's moral theory, a problem which is of much greater importance than might at first appear. The ordinary way of presenting the Thomist ethic has been to assimilate it to the ethic of Aristotle so far as is consistent with St. Thomas's position as a Christian, and to say that St. Thomas as moral philosopher considers man 'in the natural order' without reference to his supernatural end. When he speaks of beatitude as a moral philosopher he would, therefore, be speaking of natural beatitude, that attainment of the supreme Good, God, which is open to man in the natural order, without supernatural grace being necessary. His difference from Aristotle would lie in the fact that he, unlike the latter, introduces consideration of the next life, concerning which Aristotle is silent. Beatitude would consist principally in the natural knowledge and love of God attainable in this life (imperfect natural beatitude) and in the next life (perfect natural beatitude). Those actions would be good which lead to or are compatible with the attainment of such beatitude, while those actions would be bad which are incompatible with the attainment of such beatitude. The fact that St. Thomas speaks of the attainment of the vision of the divine essence (which is man's supernatural end and is unattainable without supernatural grace) when

---

[1] See *S.T.*, Ia, IIae, 4.

[2] This is true of St. Thomas's moral teaching in the *Summae*. I do not mean to imply that St. Thomas rejected the possibility of a purely philosophical ethic.

we would expect him to continue speaking as a moral philosopher would, then, be due to the fact that he makes in practice no very methodical separation between the rôles of philosopher and theologian and speaks sometimes as the one, sometimes as the other, without any clear indication of the change. Alternatively one would have to explain away references to the vision of God as meaning not the supernatural vision of the divine essence, but merely the knowledge of God which would be attainable by man in the next life, had man no supernatural end. In some such way one would make of St. Thomas a moral philosopher who completed the Aristotelian ethic by introducing consideration of the next life.

Unfortunately for upholders of this interpretation not only does St. Thomas seem to refer to the vision of God in the proper sense, but he even speaks of a 'natural desire' for the vision of God. 'Ultimate and perfect beatitude can consist only in the vision of the divine essence.' This, say some commentators, does not refer to the vision of God as supreme good, as He is in Himself, but only to the vision of God as first cause. But how could St. Thomas speak of knowledge of God as first cause as though such knowledge were or could be a vision of the divine essence? By the natural light of reason we can know that God is first cause, but St. Thomas states that 'for perfect beatitude it is required that the intellect should arrive at the very essence of the first cause'.[1] Again, 'Ultimate beatitude consists in the vision of the divine essence, which is the very essence of goodness.'[2] For the attainment of that vision there is in man a natural desire, as man naturally desires to know the essence, the nature of the first cause.[3] Whether or not St. Thomas was right in saying this, it is to me inconceivable that he meant to refer only to what Cajetan calls a *potentia obedientialis*: what can a 'natural desire' be, if it is not something positive? On the other hand, it is out of the question to suppose that St. Thomas meant to deny the supernatural and gratuitous character of the beatific vision of God. Some commentators (Suarez, for example) have got rid of the difficulty by saying that St. Thomas meant to affirm the presence in man of a *conditional* natural desire, that is, conditional on God's elevating man to the supernatural order and giving him the means to attain the supernatural end. This is a reasonable position, no doubt; but is it necessary to suppose that by a natural desire St. Thomas meant more than a desire to know the nature of the first cause, a desire

[1] *S.T.*, Ia, IIae, 3, 8.   [2] *Ibid.*, 4, 4.   [3] *Ibid.*, 3, 8.

which *in the concrete*, that is, given man's elevation to the supernatural order and his being destined for a supernatural end, means
a desire for the vision of God? In other words, I suggest that
St. Thomas is considering man in the concrete and that when he
says that there is in man a 'natural desire' to know God's essence,
and so to attain the vision of God, he means that man's natural
desire to know as much as possible of the ultimate cause is, in the
concrete and actual order, a desire to see God. Just as the will is
naturally set towards the universal good and this movement of the
will can reach satisfaction and quiescence only in the possession of
God, so the intellect is made for truth and can be satisfied only by
the vision of the absolute Truth.

It may be objected that this implies either that man has a
natural desire for the beatific vision (using the word natural as
opposed to supernatural), and in this case it is difficult to safeguard the gratuity of the supernatural order, or that by 'natural'
St. Thomas means simply natural in the sense in which we
frequently use the word, as opposed to 'unnatural' rather than
supernatural, which is to interpret him in an arbitrary and unjustifiable fashion. But what I am suggesting is that St. Thomas is
speaking pretty well as St. Augustine might speak, that he is
considering man in the concrete, as called to a supernatural end,
and that when he says that man has a natural desire to know the
essence of God, he does not mean to imply that man in a hypothetical state of nature would have had such a natural desire,
whether absolute or conditional, of seeing God, but simply that
the term of the natural movement of the human intellect towards
truth is *de facto* the vision of God, not because the human intellect
can of itself see God, whether in this life or the next, but because
de facto the only end of man is a supernatural end. I do not think
that St. Thomas is considering the hypothetical state of nature at
all, when he speaks of the *desiderium naturale*, and if this is so, it
obviously means that his moral theory is not and cannot be a
purely philosophical theory. His moral theory is partly theological
and partly philosophical: he utilises the Aristotelian ethic but fits
it into a Christian setting. After all, Aristotle was himself considering man in the concrete, as far as he knew what man in the
concrete actually is, and St. Thomas, who knew much better than
Aristotle what man in the concrete actually is, was fully justified
in utilising the thought of Aristotle when he believed it to be
correct and found it compatible with his Christian standpoint.

It is perfectly true that St. Thomas speaks of imperfect beatitude, of man's temporal good, and so on; but that does not mean that he is considering man in a hypothetical state of pure nature. If St. Thomas says that the Church is instituted to help man to attain his supernatural good, and the State to help man to attain his temporal good, it would be absurd to conclude that in considering man in relation to the State he is considering man in a purely hypothetical condition: he is considering actual man in certain aspects and functions. It is not that St. Thomas ignores the fact that the attainment of man's true end exceeds man's unaided powers, but that in his moral theory he considers man as set towards, as called to that end. When answering the question if beatitude, once attained, can be lost, he answers that the imperfect beatitude of this life can be lost, but that the perfect beatitude of the next life cannot be lost, since it is impossible for anyone who has once seen the divine essence to desire not to see it.[1] This shows clearly enough that he is speaking of supernatural beatitude. In the reply to the second objection he says that the will is ordered to the last end by a natural necessity;[2] but this does not mean either that the last end in question is purely natural or, if it is supernatural, that God *could not* have created man without directing him to this end. The will necessarily desires happiness, beatitude, and *de facto* this beatitude can be found only in the vision of God: we can say, therefore, that the concrete human being necessarily desires the vision of God.

It seems to me that this interpretation is confirmed by the doctrine of the *Summa contra Gentiles*. First of all[3] St. Thomas argues that the end of every intellectual substance is to know God. All creatures are ordered to God as to their last end,[4] and rational creatures are ordered to God principally and peculiarly by way of their highest faculty, the intellect. But though the end and happiness of man must consist principally in the knowledge of God, the knowledge in question is not that knowledge which is obtained philosophically, by demonstration. By demonstration we come to know rather what God is not than what He is, and man cannot be happy unless he knows God as He is.[5] Nor can human happiness consist in the knowledge of God which is obtained through faith, even though by faith we are able to know more about God than we can learn through philosophical demonstration. The 'natural desire' is satisfied by the attainment of the

---

[1] *S.T.*, Ia, IIae, 5, 4.   [2] *Ibid.*   [3] 3, 25.   [4] 3, 18.   [5] 3, 39.

final end, complete happiness, but 'knowledge by faith does not satisfy the desire, but rather inflames it, since everyone desires to see what he believes'.[1] Man's final end and happiness must consist, therefore, in the vision of God as He is in Himself, in the vision of the divine essence, a vision which is promised us in the Scriptures and by which man will see God 'face to face'.[2] It is only necessary to read St. Thomas in order to see that he is talking of the vision of the divine essence properly speaking. On the other hand, it is only necessary to read St. Thomas in order to see that he is perfectly aware that 'no created substance can by its natural power come to see God in His essence'[3] and that to attain this vision supernatural elevation and aid are required.[4]

What, then, of the 'natural desire'? Does not St. Thomas explicitly say that 'since it is impossible for a natural desire to be in vain (inane), and since this would be the case if it were not possible to arrive at the knowledge of the divine substance, which all minds naturally desire, it is necessary to say that it is possible for the substance of God to be seen by the intellect',[5] even though this vision cannot be attained in this life?[6] If there is really a 'natural desire' for the vision of God, is not the gratuitous character of supernatural beatitude endangered? In the first place it may be pointed out once again that St. Thomas explicitly states that man cannot attain to the vision of God by his own efforts: its attainment is made possible only through the grace of God, as he clearly affirms.[7] But there certainly is a difficulty in seeing how the grace of God, which alone makes possible the attainment of the final end, is not in some sense due to man, if there is a 'natural desire' for the vision of God and if it is impossible for a natural desire to be in vain. To come to a definitive conclusion as to what St. Thomas precisely understood by desiderium naturale in this connection may not be possible; but it seems legitimate to suppose that he was regarding the natural desire of the intellect to know absolute Truth in the light of the actual and concrete order. Man's intellect has a natural orientation towards happiness, which must consist primarily in the knowledge of the absolute Truth; but man in the concrete actual order has been destined for a supernatural end and cannot be satisfied with anything less. Regarding the natural desire in the light of the facts known by revelation, one can say, then, that man has a 'natural desire' for the vision of God.

[1] 3, 40.   [2] 3, 51.   [3] 3, 52.   [4] 3, 52-4.   [5] 3, 51.
[6] 3, 47-8.   [7] 3, 52.

In the *De Veritate*[1] St. Thomas says that man, according to his nature, has a natural appetite for *aliqua contemplatio divinorum*, such as it is possible for a man to obtain by the power of nature, and that the inclination of his desire towards the supernatural and gratuitous end (the vision of God) is the work of grace. In this place, then, St. Thomas does not admit a 'natural desire' in the strict sense for the vision of God, and it seems to me only reasonable to suppose that when in the *Summa Theologica* and the *Summa contra Gentiles* he speaks of a natural desire for the vision of God, he is not speaking strictly as a *philosopher*,[2] but as a theologian and philosopher combined, that is, presupposing the supernatural order and interpreting the data of experience in the light of that presupposition. In any case what has been said should be sufficient to show the difference between Aristotle's and St. Thomas's views of the end of man.[3]

3. The will, therefore, desires happiness, beatitude, as its end, and human acts are good or bad in so far as they are or are not means to the attainment of that end. Happiness must, of course, be understood in relation to man as such, to man as a rational being: the end is that good which perfects man as a rational being, not indeed as a disembodied intellect, for man is not a disembodied intellect, but in the sense that the perfecting of his sensitive and vegetative tendencies must be accomplished in subordination to his primary tendency, which is rational: the end is that which perfects man as such, and man as such is a rational being, not a mere animal. Every individual human act, that is to say, every deliberate act, is either in accordance with the order of reason (its immediate end being in harmony with the final end) or out of accordance with the order of reason (its immediate end being incompatible with the final end), so that every human act is either good or bad. An indeliberate act, such as the reflex act of brushing away a fly, may be 'indifferent'; but no human, deliberate act, can be indifferent, neither good nor bad.[4]

4. St. Thomas follows Aristotle in treating the moral and intellectual virtues as habits, as good qualities or habits of the mind, by which a man lives rightly.[5] The virtuous habit is formed by good acts and facilitates the performance of subsequent acts for

[1] 27, 2.   [2] Cf. *De Veritate, loc. cit.*, and cf. also *De Malo*, 5, 1, 15.
[3] On the question of the 'natural desire' for the vision of God, cf. the summary and discussion of the opinions by A. Motte in the *Bulletin Thomiste*, 1931 (nos. 651–76) and 1934 (nos. 573–90).
[4] *S.T.*, Ia, IIae, 18, 9.   [5] *Ibid.*, Ia, IIae, 55 ff.

the same end. It is possible to have the intellectual virtues with the exception of prudence without the moral virtues, and it is possible to have the moral virtues without the intellectual virtues, with the exception of prudence and of understanding.[1] Moral virtue consists in a mean (*in medio consistit*). The object of moral virtue is to secure or facilitate conformity to the rule of reason in the appetitive part of the soul; but conformity implies the avoidance of the extremes of excess and defect, it means that the appetite or passion is reduced to the rule of reason. Of course, if one is considering simply conformity to reason, virtue is an extreme and all difformity with the rule of reason, whether by excess or defect, constitutes the other extreme (to say that virtue consists in a mean is not to say that it consists in mediocrity); but if one considers moral virtue in regard to the matter with which it is concerned, the passion or appetite in question, it is then seen to consist in a mean. The adoption of this theory of Aristotle might seem to make it difficult to defend virginity or voluntary poverty, for example, but St. Thomas points out that complete chastity, for instance, is virtuous only when it is in conformity with reason enlightened by God. If it is observed in accordance with God's will or invitation and for man's supernatural end, it is in accord with the rule of reason and so is, in St. Thomas's use of the word, a mean: if, however, it were observed out of superstition or vainglory, it would be an excess. In general, a virtue may be looked at as an extreme in relation to one circumstance, as a mean in regard to another.[2] In other words, the fundamental factor in virtuous action is conformity to the rule of reason, directing man's acts to his final end.

5. The rule and measure of human acts is the reason, for it belongs to the reason to direct a man's activity towards his end.[3] It is reason, therefore, which gives orders, which imposes obligation. But this does not mean that the reason is the arbitrary source of obligation or that it can impose whatever obligations it likes. The primary object of the practical reason is the good, which has the nature of an end, and the practical reason, recognising the good as the end of human conduct, enunciates its first principle, *Bonum est faciendum et prosequendum, et malum vitandum*, good is to be done and pursued, and evil avoided.[4] But the good for man is that which befits his nature, that to which he has a natural

---

[1] *S.T.*, Ia, IIae, 58, 4–5.
[2] *Ibid.*, Ia, IIae, 64, 1.
[3] *Ibid.*, Ia, IIae, 90, 1.
[4] *Ibid.*, Ia, IIae, 94, 2.

inclination as a rational being. Thus man, in common with all other substances, has a natural inclination to the preservation of his being, and reason, reflecting on this inclination, orders that the means necessary to the preservation of life are to be taken. Conversely, suicide is to be avoided. Again, man, in common with other animals, has a natural inclination to the propagation of the species and the bringing up of children, while as a rational being he has a natural inclination to seek out the truth, especially concerning God. Reason, therefore, orders that the species is to be propagated and children educated, and that truth is to be sought, especially that truth which is necessary to the attainment of man's end. Obligation, therefore, is imposed by reason, but it is founded immediately on human nature itself; the moral law is rational and natural, in the sense of not being arbitrary or capricious: it is a natural law, *lex naturalis*, which has its basis in human nature itself, though it is enunciated and dictated by reason.

As the natural law is founded in human nature as such, in that nature which is the same in all men, it has regard primarily to those things which are necessary to human nature. There is an obligation, for example, to preserve one's life, but that does not mean that every man has to preserve his life in exactly the same way: a man must eat, but it does not follow that he is under an obligation to eat this or that, this much or that much. In other words, acts may be good and according to nature without being obligatory. Moreover, though reason sees that no man can preserve his life without eating and that no man can order his life rightly without knowledge of God, it also sees that the precept of propagating the species falls not on the individual, but on the multitude, and that it is fulfilled, even though not all individuals actually fulfil it. (This would be St. Thomas's answer to the objection that virginity is contrary to the natural law.)[1]

From the fact that the natural law is founded on human nature itself it follows that it cannot be changed, since human nature remains fundamentally the same, and that it is the same for all. It can be 'added to', in the sense that precepts useful for human life can be promulgated by divine law and by human law, even though these precepts do not fall directly under the natural law; but it cannot be changed, if by change is meant subtraction from the law.[2]

[1] Cf. *S.T.*, IIa, IIae, 152, 2.   [2] *Ibid.*, Ia, IIae, 94, 5.

The primary precepts of the natural law (e.g. life is to be preserved) are entirely unchangeable, since their fulfilment is absolutely necessary for the good of man, while the proximate conclusions from the primary precepts are also unchangeable, though St. Thomas admits that they may be changed in a few particular cases on account of special reasons. But St. Thomas is not thinking here of what we call 'hard cases': he is thinking rather of cases like that of the Israelites who made off with the goods of the Egyptians. His meaning is that in this case God, acting as supreme lord and owner of all things rather than as legislator, transferred the ownership of the goods in question from the Egyptians to the Israelites, so that the Israelites did not really commit theft. Thus St. Thomas's admission of the changeability of the secondary precepts of the natural law in particular cases refers rather to what the Scholastics call a *mutatio materiae* than to a change in the precept itself: it is rather that the circumstances of the act are so changed that it no longer falls under the prohibition than that the prohibition itself is changed.

Moreover, precisely because the natural law is founded on human nature itself, men cannot be ignorant of it in regard to the most general principles, though it is true that they may fail on account of the influence of some passion to apply a principle to a particular case. As regards the secondary precepts men may be ignorant of these through prejudice or passion, and that is all the more reason why the natural law should be confirmed by positive divine law.[1]

6. Obligation, as we have seen, is the binding of the free will to perform that act which is necessary for the attainment of the last end, an end which is not hypothetical (an end which may or may not be desired) but absolute, in the sense that the will cannot help desiring it, the good which must be interpreted in terms of human nature. So far the ethic of St. Thomas follows closely that of Aristotle. Is there nothing further? Is the natural law, promulgated by reason, without any transcendental foundation? Aristotle's eudaemonological ethic fitted in, of course, with his general finalistic outlook; but it was not grounded in God and could not be, since the Aristotelian God was not Creator nor did He exercise providence: He was final cause, but not first efficient cause or supreme exemplary cause. In St. Thomas's case, however, it would be extremely strange were ethics to be left without demonstrable

---

[1] *S.T.*, Ia, IIae, 95, 6; 99, 2, *ad* 2.

connection with metaphysics, and in fact we find that connection insisted on.

On the supposition that God created and rules the world (the proof of this does not pertain to ethics), it follows that the divine wisdom must be conceived as ordering man's actions towards his end. God, to speak somewhat anthropomorphically, has an exemplar idea of man and of the acts which fulfil man's nature and which are required for the attainment of man's end, and the divine wisdom as directing man's acts to the attainment of that end constitutes the eternal law. As God is eternal and His idea of man eternal, the promulgation of the law is eternal *ex parte Dei*, though it is not eternal *ex parte creaturae*.[1] This eternal law, existing in God, is the origin and fount of the natural law, which is a participation of the eternal law. The natural law is expressed passively in man's natural inclinations, while it is promulgated by the light of reason reflecting on those inclinations, so that inasmuch as every man naturally possesses the inclinations to the end of man and possesses also the light of reason, the eternal law is sufficiently promulgated for every man. The natural law is the totality of the universal dictates of right reason concerning that good of nature which is to be pursued and that evil of man's nature which is to be shunned, and man's reason could, at least in theory, arrive by its own light at a knowledge of these dictates or precepts. Nevertheless, since, as we have seen, the influence of passion and of inclinations which are not in accordance with right reason may lead men astray and since not all men have the time or ability or patience to discover the whole natural law for themselves, it was morally necessary that the natural law should be positively expressed by God, as was done by the revelation of the Decalogue to Moses. It must also be added that man has *de facto* a supernatural end, and in order that he should be able to attain this supernatural end, it was necessary that God should reveal the supernatural law, over and above the natural law. 'Since man is destined to the end of eternal beatitude, which exceeds the capacity of the human natural faculty, it was necessary that besides the natural law and human law he should also be directed to his end by a divinely given law.'[2]

It is very important to realise clearly that the foundation of the natural law in the eternal law, the metaphysical foundation of the natural law, does not mean that the natural law is capricious

---

[1] *S.T.*, Ia, IIae, 9, 1; 93, 1 ff.   [2] *Ibid.*, Ia, IIae, 91, 4.

or arbitrary; that it could be otherwise than it is: the eternal law does not depend primarily on the divine will but on the divine reason, considering the exemplar idea of human nature. Given human nature, the natural law could not be otherwise than it is. On the other hand, we must not imagine that God is subject to the moral law, as something apart from Himself. God knows His divine essence as imitable in a multiplicity of finite ways, one of those ways being human nature, and in that human nature He discerns the law of its being and wills it: He wills it because He loves Himself, the supreme Good, and because He cannot be inconsistent with Himself. The moral law is thus ultimately founded on the divine essence itself and so cannot change: God wills it certainly, but it does not depend on any arbitrary act of the divine will. Hence to say that the moral law does not depend primarily on the divine will is not at all equivalent to saying that there is a moral law which in some mysterious way stands behind God and rules God: God is Himself the supreme Value and the source and measure of all value: values depend on Him, but in the sense that they are participations or finite reflections of God, not in the sense that God arbitrarily confers on them their character as values. St. Thomas's doctrine of the metaphysical foundation, the theistic foundation, of the moral law in no way threatens its rational or necessary character: ultimately the moral law is what it is because God is what He is, since human nature, the law of whose being is expressed in the natural law, itself depends on God.

7. Finally one can point out that St. Thomas's realisation of God as Creator and supreme Lord led him, in company, of course, with other Scholastics, to recognise natural values which Aristotle did not envisage and could not envisage once given his view of God. To take one example, that of the virtue of religion (*religio*). Religion is the virtue by which men pay to God the worship and reverence which they owe Him as 'first Principle of the creation and government of things'. It is superior to the other moral virtues, inasmuch as it is more closely concerned with God, the last end.[1] It is subordinate to the virtue of justice (as a *virtus annexa*), inasmuch as through the virtue of religion a man pays to God his debt of worship and honour, a debt which is owing in justice.[2] Religion is thus grounded in man's relationship to God, as creature to Creator, as subject to Lord. As Aristotle did not

---

[1] On the virtue of religion, cf. *S.T.*, IIa, IIae, 81, 1–8.
[2] *S.T.*, Ia, IIae, 80, *articulus unicus*.

look upon God as Creator nor as exercising conscious government and providence, but regarded Him as the final Cause alone, wrapped up in Himself and drawing the world unconsciously, he could not envisage a personal relationship between man and the unmoved Mover, though he expected, of course, that man would recognise and in a sense honour the unmoved Mover, as the noblest object of philosophic contemplation. St. Thomas, however, with his clear idea of God as Creator and as provident Governor of the universe, could and did envisage as man's primary duty the expression in act of the relationship which is bound up with his very being. The virtuous man of Aristotle is, in a sense, the most independent man, whereas the virtuous man of St. Thomas is, in a sense, the most dependent man, that is, the man who realises truly and fully expresses his relation of dependence on God.

CHAPTER XL

ST. THOMAS AQUINAS—X: POLITICAL THEORY

St. Thomas and Aristotle—The natural origin of human society and government—Human society and political authority willed by God—Church and State—Individual and State—Law—Sovereignty—Constitutions—St. Thomas's political theory an integral part of his total system.

1. ST. THOMAS's ethical theory or theory of the moral life was based philosophically on the moral theory of Aristotle, though St. Thomas supplied it with a theological basis which was lacking in Aristotle's theory. In addition, the Thomist theory is complicated by the fact that St. Thomas believed, as a Christian, that man has *de facto* only one end, a supernatural end, so that a purely philosophical ethic was bound to be in his eyes an insufficient guide to practice: he could not simply adopt Aristotelianism lock, stock and barrel. The same is true of his political theory, in which he adopted the general framework of Aristotle's treatment, but had at the same time to leave the political theory 'open'. Aristotle certainly supposed that the State satisfied or ideally could satisfy all the needs of man;[1] but St. Thomas could not hold this, since he believed that man's end is a supernatural end and that it is the Church and not the State which caters for the attainment of that end. This meant that a problem which was not, and could not be, treated by Aristotle had to be considered by St. Thomas, as by other mediaeval writers on political theory, the problem of the relations of Church and State. In other words, though St. Thomas borrowed largely from Aristotle in regard to the subject-matter and method of treatment of political theory, he considered the matter in the light of the Christian mediaeval outlook and modified or supplemented his Aristotelianism in accordance with the exigencies of his Christian faith. The Marxist may like to point to the influence of mediaeval economic, social and political conditions on St. Thomas's theory, but the important difference between Aristotle and St. Thomas is not that the former lived in a Greek City-state and the latter in the feudal epoch; it is rather that for the former the natural end of man is self-sufficient and is attained

---

[1] This at least was the view which Aristotle took over and which he can hardly be said to have repudiated expressly, though it is true that the individualistic ideal of theoretic contemplation tended to break through the ideal of the City-state's self-sufficiency.

through life in the State, whereas for the latter the end of man is supernatural and is fully attainable only in the next life. Whether the amalgamation of Aristotelianism with the Christian view of man and his end constitutes a fully consistent and coherent synthesis or a somewhat fragile partnership, is a further question; what is insisted on at the moment is that it is a mistake to place a greater emphasis on the influence of mediaeval conditions on St. Thomas than on the influence of the Christian religion as such, which did not grow up in the Middle Ages and is not confined to the Middle Ages. The precise form taken by the problem of the relations of Church and State must of course be seen in the light of mediaeval conditions; but ultimately the problem arises from the confrontation of two different conceptions of man and his destiny; its precise formulation at any given time or by one thinker is incidental.

2. The State is for St. Thomas, as for Aristotle, a natural institution, founded on the nature of man. At the beginning of the *De regimine principum*[1] he argues that every creature has its own end, and that whereas some creatures attain their end necessarily or instinctively, man has to be guided to its attainment by his reason. But man is not an isolated individual who can attain his end simply as an individual by using his own individual reason; he is by nature a social or political being, born to live in community with his fellows. Indeed, man needs society more than other animals do. For whereas nature has provided the animals with clothing, means of defence, etc., she has left man unprovided, in a condition where he has to provide for himself by the use of his reason, and this he can do only through co-operation with other men. Division of labour is necessary, by which one man should devote himself to medicine, another to agriculture, and so on. But the most evident sign of the social nature of man is his faculty of expressing his ideas to other men through the medium of language. Other animals can express their feelings only through very general signs, but man can express his concepts completely (*totaliter*). This shows that man is naturally fitted for society more than any other gregarious animal, more even than the ants and the bees.

Society, therefore, is natural to man; but if society is natural, so also is government. Just as the bodies of men and animals disintegrate when the controlling and unifying principle (the soul) has left them, so would human society tend to disintegrate owing

---
[1] I, I.

to the number of human beings and their natural preoccupation with self, unless there was someone to take thought for the common good and direct the activities of individuals with a view to the common good. Wherever there is a multitude of creatures with a common good to be attained there must be some common ruling power. In the body there is a principal member, the head or the heart; the body is ruled by the soul, and in the soul the irascible and concupiscible parts are directed by the reason; in the universe at large inferior bodies are ruled by the superior, according to the disposition of divine providence. What is true, then, of the universe at large, and of man as an individual, must be true also of human society.

3. If human society and government are natural, are prefigured in human nature, it follows that they have a divine justification and authority, since human nature has been created by God. In creating man God willed human society and political government, and one is not entitled to say that the State is simply the result of sin. If no one did wrong, then obviously some activities and institutions of the State would be unnecessary; but even in the state of innocence, if it had persisted, there would have to have been an authority to care for the common good. 'Man is by nature a social animal. Hence in the state of innocence men would have lived in society. But a common social life of many individuals could not exist, unless there were someone in control, to attend to the common good.'[1] Moreover, there would have been some inequality of gifts even in the state of innocence, and if one man had been supereminent in knowledge and righteousness, it would not have been proper that he should have no opportunity to exercise his outstanding talents for the common good by direction of common activities.

4. By declaring the State a natural institution St. Thomas gave it, in a sense, a utilitarian foundation, but his utilitarianism is Aristotelian; he certainly did not consider the State simply the creation of enlightened egoism. He recognised the force of egoism, of course, and its centrifugal tendency in regard to society; but he also recognised the social tendency and impulse in man, and it is this social tendency which enables society to endure in spite of the tendency to egoism. As Hobbes regarded egoism as the only fundamental impulse, he had to find the practical principle of cohesion in force, once society had been rounded by the prudential

[1] *S.T.*, Ia, 96, 4.

dictates of enlightened egoism; but in point of fact neither force nor enlightened egoism would be sufficient to make society endure, if man had no social tendency implanted by nature. In other words, the Christianised Aristotelianism of St. Thomas enabled him to avoid both the notion that the State is the result of original sin, a notion to which St. Augustine seems to have tended, and the notion that the State is simply the creation of egoism: it is prefigured in human nature, and since human nature is God's creation, it is willed by God. From this there follows the important consequence that the State is an institution in its own right, with an end of its own and a sphere of its own. St. Thomas could not, then, adopt an extremist position in regard to the problem of the relations between Church and State: he could not, if he was to be logical, turn the Church into a super-State and the State into a kind of dependency of the Church. The State is a 'perfect society' (*communitas perfecta*), that is, it has at its disposal all the means necessary for the attainment of its end, the *bonum commune* or common good of the citizens.[1] The attainment of the common good postulates first of all peace within the State, among the citizens, secondly the unified direction of the activities of the citizens *ad bene agendum*, thirdly the adequate provision for the needs of life; and the government of the State is instituted to secure these necessary conditions of the common good. It is also necessary for the common good that hindrances to the good life, such as danger from foreign enemies and the disintegrating effects of crime within the State, should be averted, and the monarch has at his disposal the means necessary to avert these hindrances, namely armed force and the judiciary system.[2] The end of the Church, a supernatural end, is higher than that of the State, so that the Church is a society superior to the State, which must subordinate itself to the Church in matters bearing upon the supernatural life; but that does not alter the fact that the State is a 'perfect society', autonomous within its own sphere. In terms of later theology, then, St. Thomas must be reckoned as an upholder of the *indirect power* of the Church over the State. When Dante in his *De Monarchia* recognises the two spheres of Church and State, he is at one with St. Thomas, as far at least as the Aristotelian aspect of the latter's political theory is concerned.[3]

[1] Cf. *S.T.*, Ia, IIae, 90, 2.   [2] Cf. *De regimine principum*, 1, 15.

[3] Dante was actually more concerned to uphold the authority of the Emperor against that of the Pope and was somewhat behind the times in his imperial dreams; but he carefully adhered to the two spheres theory.

However, the attempted synthesis between the Aristotelian idea of the State and the Christian idea of the Church was somewhat precarious. In the *De regimine principum*[1] St. Thomas declares that the end of society is the good life and that the good life is a life according to virtue, so that a virtuous life is the end of human society. He then goes on to observe that the *final* end of man is not to live virtuously, but by living virtuously to attain to the enjoyment of God, and that the attainment of this end exceeds the powers of human nature. 'Because man does not attain the end of enjoyment of God by human power, but by divine power, according to the words of the Apostle "the grace of God, life eternal",[2] to lead man to this end will pertain not to human but to divine rule': the leading of man to his final end is entrusted to Christ and His Church, so that under the new Covenant of Christ kings must be subject to priests. St. Thomas certainly recognises that the king has in his hands the direction of human and earthly matters, and he cannot be rightly interpreted as meaning to deny that the State has its own sphere; but he insists that it pertains to the king to procure the good life of his subjects with a view to the attainment of eternal beatitude: 'he should order those things which lead to heavenly beatitude and prohibit, as far as possible, their contraries.'[3] The point is that St. Thomas does not say that man has, as it were, two final ends, a temporal end which is catered for by the State and a supernatural, eternal end which is catered for by the Church: he says that man has one final end, a supernatural end, and that the business of the monarch, in his direction of earthly affairs, is to facilitate the attainment of that end.[4] The power of the Church over the State is not a *potestas directa*, since it is the business of the State, not the Church, to care for economic concerns and the preservation of peace; but the State must care for these concerns with an eye on the supernatural end of man. In other words, the State may be a 'perfect society', but the elevation of man to the supernatural order means that the State is very much a handmaid of the Church. This point of view is based not so much on mediaeval practice as on the Christian faith, and it is, needless to say, not the view of Aristotle who knew nothing of man's eternal and supernatural end. That there is a certain synthesis between the Aristotelian political theory and the demands of the Christian faith in the thought of St. Thomas,

[1] I, 14.   [2] Romans 6. 23.   [3] *De regimine principum*, I, 15.
[4] St. Thomas is, of course, addressing a Christian prince.

I should not attempt to deny; but I do think that the synthesis is, as I have already suggested, somewhat precarious. If the Aristotelian elements were pressed, the result would be a theoretical separation of Church and State of a kind which would be quite foreign to the thought of St. Thomas. In fact, his view of the relation of Church and State is not unlike his view of the relation between Faith and Reason. The latter has its own sphere, but philosophy is none the less inferior to theology: similarly, the State has its own sphere, but it is none the less, to all intents and purposes, the handmaid of the Church. Conversely, if one adheres to the historic Aristotle so closely as to make philosophy absolutely autonomous in its own sphere, one will naturally, in political theory, tend to make the State absolutely autonomous within its own sphere: this is what the Averroists did, but St. Thomas was most emphatically not an Averroist. One may say, then, that St. Thomas's political theory does represent to some extent the actual situation, in which the nation-State was becoming self-conscious but in which the authority of the Church had not yet been expressly repudiated. St. Thomas's Aristotelianism allowed him to make the State a perfect society, but his Christianity, his conviction that man has but one ultimate end, effectually prevented him from making the State an absolutely autonomous society.

5. A similar ambiguity shows itself in St. Thomas's doctrine of the relation of the individual to the State. In the *Summa Theologica*[1] he remarks that since the part is ordered to the whole as what is imperfect to what is perfect, and since the individual is a part of the perfect society, it is necessary that law should properly be concerned with the common happiness. It is true that he is trying to show simply that law is concerned primarily with the common good rather than with the good of the individual, but he does speak as though the individual citizen were subordinated to the whole of which he forms a part. The same principle, that the part exists for the whole, is applied by St. Thomas in more than one place to the individual's relation to the community. For example,[2] he argues that it is right for the public authority to deprive an individual citizen of life for the graver crimes on the ground that the individual is ordered to the community, of which he forms a part, as to an end. And it is really an application of this principle when he insists in the Commentary on the *Ethics*[3] that

[1] Ia, IIae, 90, 2.   [2] *S.T.*, IIa, IIae, 65, 1.   [3] 3 *Ethic., lect.* 4.

courage is shown by giving one's life for the best things, as is the case when a man dies in defence of his country.

If this principle, that the part is ordered to the whole, which represents St. Thomas's Aristotelianism, were pressed, it would seem that he subordinates the individual to the State to a remarkable degree; but St. Thomas also insists that he who seeks the common good of the multitude seeks his own good as well, since one's own good cannot be attained unless the common good is attained, though it is true that in the *corpus* of the article in question he remarks that right reason judges that the common good is better than the good of the individual.[1] But the principle should not be over-emphasised, since St. Thomas was a Christian theologian and philosopher as well as an admirer of Aristotle, and he was well aware, as we have already seen, that man's final end is outside the sphere of the State: man is not simply a member of the State, indeed the most important thing about him is his supernatural vocation. There can, then, be no question of 'totalitarianism' in St. Thomas, though it is obvious that his Aristotelianism would make it impossible for him to accept such a theory of the State as that of Herbert Spencer: the State has a positive function and a moral function. The human being is a person, with a value of his own; he is not simply an 'individual'.

6. That totalitarianism is foreign to St. Thomas's thought is shown clearly by his theory of law and of the origin and nature of sovereignty. There are four kinds of law: the eternal law, the natural law, the divine positive law and human positive law. The divine positive law is the law of God as positively revealed, imperfectly to the Jews, perfectly through Christ,[2] while the law of the State is human positive law. Now, the function of the human legislator is primarily to apply the natural law[3] and to support the law by sanctions.[4] For example, murder is forbidden by the natural law, but reason shows the desirability of positive enactments whereby murder is clearly defined and whereby sanctions are added, since the natural law does not of itself clearly define murder in detail or provide immediate sanctions. The legislator's primary function is, therefore, that of defining or making explicit the natural law, of applying it to particular cases and of making it effective. It follows that human positive law is derived from the natural law, and that every human law is a true law only in

[1] *S.T.*, IIa, IIae, 47, 10, *in corpore* and *ad* 2.   [2] *Ibid.*, Ia, IIae, 91, 5.
[3] *Ibid.*, 3.   [4] *Ibid.*, 95, 1.

so far as it is derived from the natural law. 'But if it disagrees with the natural law in something, it will not be a law, but the perversion of law.'[1] The ruler is not entitled to promulgate laws which go counter to or are incompatible with the natural law (or, of course, the divine law): he has his legislative power ultimately from God, since all authority comes from God, and he is responsible for his use of that power: he is himself subject to the natural law and is not entitled to transgress it himself or to order his subjects to do anything incompatible with it. Just human laws bind in conscience in virtue of the eternal law from which they are ultimately derived; but unjust laws do not bind in conscience. Now, a law may be unjust because it is contrary to the common good or because it is enacted simply for the selfish and private ends of the legislator, thus imposing an unjustifiable burden on the subjects, or because it imposes burdens on the subjects in an unjustifiably unequal manner, and such laws, being more acts of violence than laws, do not bind in conscience, unless perhaps on occasion their non-observance would produce a greater evil. As for laws which are contrary to the divine law, it is never licit to obey them, since we ought to obey God rather than men.[2]

7. It will be seen, then, that the legislator's power is very far from being absolute in the thought of St. Thomas; and the same is clear from a consideration of his theory of sovereignty and government. That St. Thomas held that political sovereignty comes from God is admitted by all, and it seems probable that he maintained the view that sovereignty is given by God to the people as a whole, by whom it is delegated to the actual ruler or rulers; but this latter point does not seem to me to be quite so certain as some writers have made out, since texts can be alleged to show that he held otherwise. Yet it is undeniable that he speaks of the ruler as representing the people[3] and that he states roundly[4] that the ruler possesses legislative power only in so far as he stands in place (*gerit .personam*) of the people,[5] and such statements may reasonably be taken to imply that he did hold that sovereignty comes to the ruler from God *via* the people, though at the same time it must be admitted that St. Thomas scarcely discusses the question in a formal and explicit manner. In any case, however, the ruler possesses his sovereignty only for the good of the whole

[1] *S.T.*, Ia, IIae, 95, 2. [2] Cf. *ibid.*, Ia, IIae, 96, 4. [3] Cf. *ibid.*, Ia, IIae, 90, 3.
[4] Though apparently referring to elected government.
[5] *S.T.*, Ia, IIae, 97, 3, *ad* 3.

people, not for his private good, and if he abuses his power, he becomes a tyrant. Assassination of a tyrant was condemned by St. Thomas and he speaks at some length of the evils which may attend rebellions against a tyrant. For example, the tyrant may become more tyrannical, if the rebellion fails, while if it is successful, it may simply result in the substitution of one tyranny for another. But deposition of a tyrant is legitimate, especially if the people have the right of providing themselves with a king. (Presumably St. Thomas is referring to an elective monarchy.) In such a case the people do no wrong in deposing the tyrant, even if they had subjected themselves to him without any time limit, for he has deserved deposition by not keeping faith with his subjects.[1] Nevertheless, in view of the evils which may attend rebellion, it is far preferable to make provision beforehand to prevent a monarchy turning into a tyranny than to have to put up with or to rebel against tyranny once established. If feasible, no one should be made ruler if he is likely to turn himself into a tyrant; but in any case the power of the monarch should be so tempered that his rule cannot easily be turned into a tyranny. The best constitution will in fact be a 'mixed' constitution, in which some place is given to aristocracy and also to democracy, in the sense that the election of certain magistrates should be in the hands of the people.[2]

8. In regard to classification of forms of government St. Thomas follows Aristotle. There are three good types of government (law-abiding democracy, aristocracy and monarchy) and three bad forms of government (demagogic and irresponsible democracy, oligarchy and tyranny), tyranny being the worst of the bad forms and monarchy the best of the good forms. Monarchy gives stricter unity and is more conducive to peace than other forms: moreover, it is more 'natural', bearing an analogy to the rule of reason over the other functions of the soul and of the heart over the other members of the body. Moreover, the bees have their monarch, and God rules over all creation.[3] But the ideal of the best man as monarch is not easily attainable, and in practice the best constitution, as we have seen, is a mixed constitution, in which the power of the monarch is tempered by that of magistrates elected by the people. In other words and in modern terms St. Thomas favours limited or constitutional monarchy, though

[1] *De regimine principum*, I, 6.   [2] *S.T.*, Ia, IIae, 105, 1.
[3] *De regimine principum*, I, 2.

he does not regard any particular form of decent government as divinely ordained: it is not the precise form of government which is of importance, but the promotion of the public good, and if in practice the form of government is an important consideration, it is its relation to the public good which makes it of importance. St. Thomas's political theory, therefore, is flexible in character, not rigid and doctrinaire, and while he rejects absolutism, he also implicitly rejects the *laissez-faire* theory. The ruler's task is to promote the public good, and this he will not do unless he promotes the economic well-being of the citizens. In fine, St. Thomas's political theory is characterised by moderation, balance and common sense.

9. In conclusion one may point out that St. Thomas's political theory is an integral part of his total philosophical system, not just something added on. God is supreme Lord and Governor of the universe, but He is not the only cause, even though He is the first Cause and the final Cause; He directs rational creatures to their end in a rational manner through acts the fitness and rightness of which are shown by reason. The right of any creature to direct another, whether it be the right of the father of the family over the members of the family or of the sovereign over his subjects, is founded on reason and must be exercised according to reason: as all power and authority is derived from God and is given for a special purpose, no rational creature is entitled to exercise unlimited, capricious or arbitrary authority over another rational creature. Law is defined, then, as 'an ordinance of reason for the common good, made by him who has care of the community, and promulgated'.[1] The sovereign occupies a natural place in the total hierarchy of the universe, and his authority must be exercised as part of the general scheme by which the universe is directed. Any idea of the sovereign being completely independent and irresponsible would thus be essentially alien to St. Thomas's philosophy. The sovereign has his duties and the subjects have their duties: 'legal justice', which should exist both in the sovereign and in his subjects, directs the acts of all the virtues to the common good;[2] but these duties are to be seen in the light of the relationship of means to end which obtains in all creation. As man is a social being, there is need for political society, in order that his nature may be fulfilled; but man's vocation to live in political society must itself be seen in the light of the final end

[1] *S.T.*, Ia, IIae, 90, 4.   [2] *Ibid.*, IIa, IIae, 58, 6.

for which man was created. Between the supernatural end of man and the natural end of man there must be due harmony and the due subordination of the latter to the former; so that man must prefer the attainment of the final end to anything else, and if the sovereign orders him to act in a manner incompatible with the attainment of the final end, he must disobey the sovereign. Any idea of the complete and total subordination of the individual to the State would be necessarily abhorrent to St. Thomas, not because he was an extreme 'Papalist' in political affairs (he was not), but because of his total theological-philosophical system, in which order, proportion and subordination of the lower to the higher reign, though without the enslavement or moral annihilation of the lower. In the whole scheme of creation and providence man has his place: abuses and practical exaggerations cannot alter the ideal order and hierarchy which are ultimately based on God Himself. Forms of government may alter; but man himself has a fixed and abiding essence or nature, and on that nature the necessity and moral justification of the State are grounded. The State is neither God nor Antichrist: it is one of the means by which God directs the rational embodied creation to its end.

Note on St. Thomas's aesthetic theory.

One cannot say that there is a formal discussion of aesthetic theory in the philosophy of St. Thomas, and what he does have to say on the matter is mostly borrowed from other writers, so that though his remarks may be taken as the starting-point of an aesthetic theory, it would be a mistake to develop an aesthetic theory on the basis of his remarks and then attribute that theory to him, as if he had himself developed it. Nevertheless, it may be as well to point out that when he remarks that *pulchra dicuntur quae visa placent*[1], he does not mean to deny the objectivity of beauty. The beautiful consists, he says, in proper proportion and belongs to the formal cause: it is the object of the cognitive power, whereas the good is the object of desire.[2] For beauty three elements are required, integrity or perfection, proper proportion and clarity:[3] the form shines out, as it were, through colour, etc., and is the object of disinterested (non-appetitive) apprehension. St. Thomas recognises, therefore, the objectivity of beauty and the fact that aesthetic appreciation or experience is something *sui generis*, that it cannot be identified simply with intellectual cognition and that it cannot be reduced to apprehension of the good.

[1] *S.T.*, Ia, 5, 4, *ad* 1.　　　[2] *Ibid*.　　　[3] *Ibid*., Ia, 39, 8.

CHAPTER XLI

ST. THOMAS AND ARISTOTLE: CONTROVERSIES

St. Thomas's utilisation of Aristotle—Non-Aristotelian elements in Thomism—Latent tensions in the Thomist synthesis—Opposition to Thomist 'novelties'.

1. ALTHOUGH St. Albert had gone some way in the utilisation of the Aristotelian philosophy, it was left to St. Thomas to attempt the full reconciliation of the Aristotelian system with Christian theology. The desirability of attempting this reconciliation was clear, since to reject the Aristotelian system would mean rejecting the most powerful and comprehensive intellectual synthesis known to the mediaeval world. Moreover, St. Thomas, with his genius for systematisation, saw clearly the use that could be made of the principles of the Aristotelian philosophy in achieving a systematic theological and philosophical synthesis. But when I say that St. Thomas saw the 'usefulness' of Aristotelianism, I do not mean to imply that his approach was pragmatic. He regarded the Aristotelian principles as true and, because true, as useful; he did not regard them as 'true' because they were useful. It would be absurd, of course, to suggest that the Thomist philosophy is simply Aristotelianism, since he makes use of other writers like St. Augustine and the Pseudo-Dionysius, as also of his mediaeval predecessors and of Jewish (Maimonides in particular) and Arabian philosophers; but none the less the Thomist synthesis is unified by the application of fundamental Aristotelian principles. A great deal of St. Thomas's philosophy is indeed the doctrine of Aristotle, but it is the doctrine of Aristotle re-thought by a powerful mind, not slavishly adopted. If St. Thomas adopted Aristotelianism, he adopted it primarily because he thought it true, not simply because Aristotle was a great name or because an 'unbaptised' Aristotle might constitute a grave danger to orthodoxy: a man of St. Thomas's serious mind, devoted to truth, would certainly not have adopted the system of a pagan philosopher, had he not considered it to be in the main a true system, especially when some of the ideas he put forward ran contrary to tradition and created some scandal and lively opposition. Yet his conviction as to the truth of the philosophy which he adopted did not lead

St. Thomas to adopt mechanically an ill-digested system: he gave a great deal of thought and attention to Aristotelianism, as can be seen from his commentaries on Aristotle's works, and his own works bear evidence of the care with which he must have considered the implications of the principles he adopted and their relation to Christian truth. If I suggest presently that the synthesis of Christianity and Aristotelianism in St. Thomas's thought was in some respects rather precarious, I do not mean to take back what I have just said and to imply that the Saint adopted Aristotelianism purely mechanically, though I think it is true that he did not fully realise the latent tension, in regard to certain points, between his Christian faith and his Aristotelianism. If this is really the case, however, it need cause no surprise; St. Thomas was a great theologian and philosopher, but he was not infinite mind, and a much smaller intellect can look back and discern possibly weak points in the system of a great mind, without the latter's greatness being thereby impugned.

Of St. Thomas's utilisation of Aristotelian themes for the purpose of systematisation one can afford space for only one or two examples. One of the fundamental ideas in the Aristotelian philosophy is that of act and potency or potentiality. St. Thomas, like Aristotle before him, saw the interplay, the correlation of act and potency in the accidental and substantial changes of the material world and in the movements (in the broad Aristotelian sense) of all creatures. Adopting the Aristotelian principle that nothing is reduced from potentiality to act, save by the agency of that which is itself in act, he followed Aristotle in arguing from the observed fact of movement, of change, to the existence of the unmoved Mover. But St. Thomas saw deeper than Aristotle: he saw that in every finite thing there is a duality of principles, of essence and existence, that the essence is in potency its existence, that it does not exist necessarily, and so he was enabled to argue not merely to the Aristotelian unmoved Mover, but to the necessary Being, God the Creator. He was able, moreover, to discern the essence of God as existence, not simply as self-thinking thought but as *ipsum esse subsistens*, and thus while following in the footsteps of Aristotle he was able to go beyond Aristotle. Not distinguishing clearly essence and existence in finite being, Aristotle could not arrive at the idea of Existence itself as the essence of God, from whom all limited existence comes.

Again, a fundamental idea in the Aristotelian philosophy is that of finality; indeed, this idea is in one sense more fundamental than that of act and potency, since all reduction from potentiality to act takes place in view of the attainment of an end, and potency exists only for the realisation of an end. That St. Thomas uses the idea of finality in his cosmological, psychological, ethical and political doctrines is a point which needs no labouring; but one may point out the help it was to him in explaining creation. God, who acts according to wisdom, created the world for an end, but that end can be none other than God Himself: He created the world, therefore, in order to manifest His own perfection, by communicating it to creatures by participation, by diffusing His own goodness. Creatures exist *propter Deum*, for God, who is their ultimate end, though He is not the ultimate end of all creatures in the same way; it is only rational creatures who can possess God by knowledge and love. Creatures have, of course, their proximate ends, the perfecting of their natures, but this perfecting of creatures' natures is subordinate to the final end of all creation, the glory of God, the manifestation of His divine perfection, which is manifested precisely by the perfecting of creatures, so that the glory of God and the good of creatures are by no means antithetical ideas. In this way St. Thomas was able to utilise the Aristotelian doctrine of finality in a Christian setting or rather in a way which would harmonise with the Christian religion.

Among the individual ideas borrowed by St. Thomas from Aristotle or thought out in dependence on the philosophy of Aristotle one may mention the following. The soul is the form of the body, individualised by the matter it informs; it is not a complete substance in its own right, but soul and body together make up a complete substance, a man. This stressing of the close union of soul and body, with the rejection of the Platonic theory on this point, makes it much easier to explain why the soul should be united to the body (the soul is by nature the form of the body), but it suggests that, granted the immortality of the soul, the resurrection of the body is demanded by the soul.[1] As for the doctrine of matter as the principle of individuation, which has as its consequence the doctrine that angelic beings, because devoid of matter, cannot be multiplied within the same species, this

---

[1] The answer can only be that it is *conveniens*, but not a strict debt, since it cannot be realised by natural means. We would then seem to be faced by the dilemma, that either the soul after death would, apart from God's intervention, remain in an 'unnatural' condition or that the doctrine of the soul's union with the body must be revised.

doctrine excited the hostility of critics of Thomism, as we shall see presently. The same can be said of the doctrine that there is only one substantial form in any substance, a doctrine which, when applied to the human substance, means the rejection of any *forma corporeitatis*.

The adoption of Aristotelian psychology naturally went hand in hand with the adoption of Aristotelian epistemology and with insistence on the fact that human knowledge is derived from sense-experience and reflection thereon. This meant the rejection of innate ideas, even in a virtual form, and the rejection of the theory of divine illumination or rather the interpretation of divine illumination as equivalent to the natural light of the intellect with the ordinary and natural concurrence of God. This doctrine raises difficulties, as we have seen earlier on, in regard to man's analogical knowledge of God.

But though St. Thomas did not hesitate to adopt an Aristotelian position even when this led him into conflict with traditional theories, he did so only when he considered that the Aristotelian positions were true in themselves and were thus compatible with Christian revelation. When it was a question of positions which were clearly incompatible with the Christian doctrine, he rejected them, or maintained that the Averroistic interpretation of Aristotle on such points was not the true interpretation or at least was not rendered necessary by Aristotle's actual words. For example, commenting on Aristotle's description of God as self-thinking Thought, St. Thomas observes that it does not follow that things other than God are unknown to Him, for by knowing Himself He knows all other things.[1] Probably, however, the historic Aristotle did not think of the unmoved Mover as knowing the world or as exercising any providence: He is the cause of movement as final, not as efficient, cause. Similarly, as already mentioned, when commenting on the very obscure words of Aristotle in the *De Anima* concerning the active intellect and its persistence after death, St. Thomas interprets the passage *in meliorem partem* and not in the Averroistic sense: it is not necessary to conclude that for Aristotle the intellect is one in all men and that there is no personal immortality. St. Thomas was anxious to rescue Aristotle from the toils of Averroes and to show that his philosophy did not necessarily involve the denial of divine providence or of personal immortality, and in this he succeeded, even if his interpretation of

[1] *In 12 Metaph., lect.* 11.

what Aristotle actually thought on these matters is probably not the correct one.

2. St. Thomas's Aristotelianism is so obvious that one sometimes tends to forget the non-Aristotelian elements in his thought, though such elements certainly exist. For example, the God of Aristotle's *Metaphysics*, though final cause, is not efficient cause; the world is eternal and was not created by God. Moreover, Aristotle envisaged the possibility at least of a multiplicity of unmoved movers corresponding to the different spheres, the relation of which to one another and to the highest unmoved mover he left in obscurity.[1] The God of St. Thomas's natural theology on the other hand is first efficient cause and Creator, as well as final cause: He is not simply wrapped in splendid isolation, the object of *eros*, but He acts *ad extra*, creating, preserving, concurring, exercising providence. St. Thomas made a certain concession to Aristotle perhaps in allowing that the possibility of creation from eternity had not been disproved; but even if the world could have had no beginning in time, its creation, its utter dependence on God, can none the less be proved. All that St. Thomas admits is that the idea of *creatio ab aeterno* has not been shown to be self-contradictory, not that creation cannot be demonstrated. It may be said that St. Thomas's position in natural theology constituted a supplement to or a completion of Aristotle's position and that it cannot be said to be non-Aristotelian; but it must be remembered that for St. Thomas God creates according to intelligence and will and that He is efficient cause, Creator, as exemplary cause: that is to say, He creates the world as a finite imitation of His divine essence, which He knows as imitable *ad extra* in a multiplicity of ways. In other words, St. Thomas utilises the position of St. Augustine in regard to the divine ideas, a position which, philosophically speaking, was derived from neo-Platonism, which in turn was a development of the Platonic philosophy and tradition. Aristotle rejected the exemplary ideas of Plato, as he rejected the Platonic Demiurge; both of these notions, however, are present in the thought of St. Augustine, transmuted and rendered philosophically consistent, coupled also with the doctrine of *creatio ex nihilo*, at which the Greeks did not arrive; and St. Thomas's acceptance of these notions links him on this point with Augustine, and so with Plato through Plotinus, rather than with Aristotle.

[1] Cf. the first volume of this history, pp. 315-16.

Again, St. Thomas's Christian faith frequently impinges on or has some effect on his philosophy. For instance, convinced that man has a supernatural final end, and a supernatural final end alone, he was bound to envisage the term of man's intellectual ascent as the knowledge of God as He is in Himself, not as the knowledge of the metaphysician and astronomer; he was bound to place the final goal of man in the next life, not in this, thus transmuting the Aristotelian conception of beatitude; he was bound to recognise the insufficiency of the State for fulfilling the needs of the whole man; he was bound to acknowledge the subordination of State to Church in point of value and dignity; he was bound, not only to allow for divine sanctions in the moral life of man, but also to link up ethics with natural theology, and indeed to admit the insufficiency of the natural moral life in regard to the attainment of beatitude, since the latter is supernatural in character and cannot be attained by purely human means. Instances of this impinging of theology on philosophy could no doubt be multiplied; but what I want to draw attention to now is the latent tension on some points between St. Thomas's Christianity and his Aristotelianism.

3. If one looks on the philosophy of Aristotle as a complete system, a certain tension is bound to be present when one attempts to combine it with a supernatural religion. For the Aristotelian philosopher it is the universal and the totality which really matters, not the individual as such: the viewpoint is what one might call that of the physicist, and partly that of the artist. Individuals exist for the good of the species: it is the species which persists through the succession of individuals; the individual human being attains his beatitude in this life or he does not attain it at all: the universe is not a setting for man, subordinate to man, but man is an item in, a part of, the universe; to contemplate the heavenly bodies is really more worth while than to contemplate man. For the Christian on the other hand the individual human being has a supernatural vocation and his vocation is not an earthly vocation, nor is his final beatitude attainable in this life or by his own natural efforts; the individual stands in a personal relation to God, and however much one may stress the corporate aspect of Christianity, it remains true that each human person is ultimately of more value than the whole material universe, which exists for the sake of man, though both man and the material universe exist ultimately for God. One can, it is true, legitimately adopt a point

of view from which man is regarded as a member of the universe, since he is a member of the universe, rooted in the material universe through his body, and if one adopts, as St. Thomas adopted, the Aristotelian psychology, the doctrine of the soul as by nature the form of the body, individualised by the body and dependent on the body for its knowledge, one emphasises the more man's place as a member of the cosmos. It is from this point of view, for instance, that one is led to regard physical defects and physical suffering, the death and corruption of the individual, as contributing to the good and harmony of the universe, as the shadows that throw into relief the lights of the total picture. It is from this point of view too that St. Thomas speaks of the part as existing for the whole, the member for the whole body, using an analogy taken from the organism. There is, as has been admitted, truth in this point of view, and it has been strenuously defended as a corrective to false individualism and to anthropo-centricism: the created universe exists for the glory of God, and man is a part of the universe. No doubt; but there is another point of view as well. Man exists for the glory of God and the material universe exists for man; it is not quantity, but quality which is truly significant; man is small from the point of view of quantity, but qualitatively all the heavenly bodies together pale into insigni-ficance beside one human person; moreover, 'man', existing for the glory of God, is not simply the species man, but a society of immortal persons, each of whom has a supernatural vocation. To contemplate man is more worth while than to contemplate the stars; human history is more important than astronomy; the sufferings of human beings cannot be explained simply 'artisti-cally'. I am not suggesting that the two viewpoints cannot be combined, as St. Thomas attempted to combine them; but I do suggest that their combination involves a certain tension and that this tension is present in the Thomist synthesis.

Since, historically speaking, Aristotelianism was a 'closed' system, in the sense that Aristotle did not and could not envisage the supernatural order, and since it was a production of reason unaided by revelation, it naturally brought home to the mediaevals the potentialities of the natural reason: it was the greatest intel-lectual achievement they knew. This meant that any theologian who accepted and utilised the Aristotelian philosophy as St. Thomas did was compelled to recognise the theoretical autonomy of philosophy, even though he also recognised theology as an extrinsic norm and criterion. As long as it was a question of theologians, the balance between theology and philosophy was, of course, preserved; but when it was a question of thinkers who were not primarily theologians, the charter granted to philosophy tended to become a declaration of independence. Looking back from the present day and bearing in mind human inclinations, characters, temperaments and intellectual bents, we can see that the acceptance of a great system of philosophy known to have been thought out without the aid of revelation was almost certain sooner or later to lead to philosophy going her own way independently of theology. In this sense (and the judgement is an historical, not a valuational judgement) the synthesis achieved by St. Thomas was intrinsically precarious. The arrival of the full Aristotle on the scene almost certainly meant in the long run the emergence of an independent philosophy, which would first of all stand on its own feet while trying to keep the peace with theology, sometimes sincerely, sometimes perhaps insincerely, and then in the end would try to supplant theology, to absorb the content of theology into itself. At the beginning of the Christian era we find the theologians utilising this or that element of Greek philosophy to help them in their statement of the data of revelation and this process continued during the stages of mediaeval Scholastic development; but the appearance of a fully-fledged system of philosophy, though an inestimable boon in the creation of the Thomist synthesis, could hardly be anything else but a challenge in the long run. It is not the purpose of the present writer to dispute the utility of the Aristotelian philosophy in the creation of a Christian theological and philosophical synthesis or in any way to belittle the achievement of St. Thomas Aquinas, but rather to point out that when philosophic thought had become more or less full-grown and had won a certain autonomy, it was not to be expected that it should for ever be content to sit at home like the elder son in the parable of the prodigal. St. Thomas's baptism of philosophy in the person of Aristotle could not, historically speaking, arrest the development of philosophy, and in that sense his synthesis contained a latent tension.

4. To turn finally, but of necessity briefly, to the opposition caused by the Thomist adoption of Aristotle. This opposition must be looked at against the background of the alarm caused by Averroism, i.e. the Averroistic interpretation of Aristotle, which we shall consider in the next chapter. The Averroists were

accused, and certainly not without justice, of preferring the authority of a pagan philosopher to that of St. Augustine and the *Sancti* in general, and of impairing the integrity of revelation; and St. Thomas was regarded by some zealous traditionalists as selling the pass to the enemy. They accordingly did their best to involve Thomism in the condemnations levelled against Averroism. The whole episode reminds us that St. Thomas in his own day was an innovator, that he struck out on new paths: it is useful to remember this at a time when Thomism stands for tradition, for theological soundness and security. Some of the points on which St. Thomas was most bitterly attacked by the hot-heads may not appear particularly startling to us to-day; but the reasons why they were attacked were largely theological in character, so that it is clear that Thomist Aristotelianism was once regarded as 'dangerous' and that the man who now stands before us as the pillar of orthodoxy was once regarded, by hot-heads at least, as a sower of novelties. Nor was the attack confined to people outside his own religious Order; he had to bear the hostility even of Dominicans, and it was only by degrees that Thomism became the official philosophy of the Dominican Order.

One of the principal points attacked was St. Thomas's theory of the unicity of the substantial form. It was combated at a debate in Paris, before the bishop, about 1270, Dominicans and Franciscans, especially the Franciscan Peckham, accusing St. Thomas of maintaining an opinion which was contrary to the teaching of the saints, particularly Augustine and Anselm. Peckham and the Dominican Robert Kilwardby maintained this point of view vigorously in their letters, the chief ground of complaint being that the Thomist doctrine was unable to explain how the dead body of Christ was the same as the living body, since according to St. Thomas there is only one substantial form in the human substance and this form, the soul, is withdrawn at death, other forms being educed out of the potentiality of matter. St. Thomas certainly held that the dead body of a man is not precisely the same as the living body, but is the same only *secundum quid*,[1] and Peckham and his friends regarded this theory as fatal to the veneration of the bodies and relics of the saints. St. Thomas, however, maintained that the dead body of Christ remained united to the Divinity, so that it was, even in the tomb, united to the Word of God and worthy of adoration. The doctrine of the

---

[1] *S.T.*, IIIa, 50, 5.

passivity of matter and that of the simplicity of the angels were also among the novel opinions to which exception was taken.

On March 7th, 1277, Stephen Tempier, Bishop of Paris, condemned two hundred and nineteen propositions, threatening with excommunication anyone who should uphold them. This condemnation was levelled chiefly against the Averroists, particularly Siger of Brabant and Boethius of Dacia, but a number of propositions were common to Siger of Brabant and St. Thomas so that Thomism was affected by the bishop's act. Thus the theories of the necessary unicity of the world, of matter as the principle of individuation, of the individualisation of angels and their relation to the universe were condemned, though that of the unicity of substantial form does not appear in the condemnation and seems never to have been formally condemned at Paris, apart from being censured in Scholastic debates and disputations.

The Parisian condemnation was followed, on March 18th, 1277, by a condemnation at Oxford, inspired by Robert Kilwardby, O.P., Archbishop of Canterbury, in which figured, among other propositions, those of the unicity of the substantial form and the passivity of matter. Kilwardby remarked in a letter that he forbad the propositions as dangerous, without condemning them as heretical, and indeed he does not seem to have been oversanguine as to the probable results of his prohibition since he offered an indulgence of forty days to anyone who would abstain from propounding the offending ideas. Kilwardby's condemnation was repeated by his successor in the Archbishopric of Canterbury, the Franciscan Peckham, on October 29th, 1284, though by that time Thomism had been officially approved in the Dominican Order. However, Peckham again prohibited the novel propositions on April 30th, 1286, declaring them to be heretical.

Meanwhile Thomism had been growing in popularity among the Dominicans as was indeed only to be expected in the case of such a splendid achievement by one of their number. In the year 1278 the Dominican Chapter at Milan and in 1279 the Chapter of Paris took steps to counteract the hostile attitude which was evident among the Oxford Dominicans, the Paris Chapter forbidding the condemnation of Thomism, though not enjoining its acceptance. In 1286 another Chapter of Paris declared that professors who showed hostility to Thomism should be relieved of their office, though it was not until the fourteenth century that its acceptance was made obligatory on members of the Order. The growing popularity of Thomism in the last two decades of the thirteenth century, however, naturally led to the publication by Dominican authors of replies to the attacks levelled against it. Thus the *Correctorium Fratris Thomas*, published by William de la Mare, a Franciscan, called forth a series of Corrections of the Correction, such as the *Apologeticum veritatis super corruptorium* (as they called the *Correctorium*), published by Rambert of Bologna near the end of the century, to which the Franciscans replied in their turn. In 1279 the latter, in their General Chapter at Assisi, prohibited the acceptance of the propositions condemned at Paris in 1277, while in 1282 the General Chapter of Strasbourg ordered that those who utilised Thomas's *Summa Theologica* should not do so without consulting William de la Mare's *Correctorium*. However, the attacks of Franciscans and others naturally diminished after the canonisation of St. Thomas on July 18th, 1323, and in 1325 the then Bishop of Paris withdrew the Parisian censures. At Oxford there does not seem to have been any formal withdrawal of this kind, but Peckham's successors did not confirm or repeat his censures and the battle gradually came to an end. Early in the fourteenth century Thomas of Sutton speaks of Aquinas as being, according to the testimony of all, the Common Doctor (*in ore omnium communis doctor dicitur*).

Thomism naturally established itself in the estimation of Christian thinkers owing to its completeness, its lucidity and its depth: it was a closely reasoned synthesis of theology and philosophy which drew on the past and incorporated it into itself, while at the same time it utilised the greatest purely philosophical system of the ancient world. But though the suspicion and hostility which Thomism, or certain aspects of it, at first aroused were destined to die a natural death in face of the undeniable merits of the system, it must not be supposed that Thomism ever acquired in the Middle Ages that official position in the intellectual life of the Church which it has occupied since the Encyclical *Aeterni Patris* of Pope Leo XIII. The *Sentences* of Peter Lombard, for example, continued to be commented upon for very many years, while at the time of the Reformation there existed Chairs in the universities for the exposition of the doctrines not only of St. Thomas and Duns Scotus and Giles of Rome, but also of Nominalists like William of Ockham and Gabriel Biel. Variety was in fact the rule, and though Thomism became at an early date the official system of the Dominican Order, many centuries elapsed before it became in any real sense the official system of the Church. (I do not mean to imply that even after *Aeterni Patris* Thomism, in the sense in which it is distinguished from Scotism, for example, is imposed on all religious Orders and ecclesiastical institutes of higher studies; but Thomism is certainly proposed as a norm from which the Catholic philosopher should dissent only when inspired by reasons which seem to him compelling, and then without disrespect. The singular position now accorded to Thomism must be looked at in the light of the historical circumstances of recent times, in order to be understood; these circumstances were not those obtaining in the Middle Ages.)

CHAPTER XLII

LATIN AVERROISM: SIGER OF BRABANT

*Tenets of the 'Latin Averroists'—Siger of Brabant—Dante and
Siger of Brabant—Opposition to Averroism; condemnations.*

1. THE term 'Latin Averroism' has become so common that it is
difficult not to make use of it, but it must be recognised that the
movement characterised by this name was one of integral or
radical Aristotelianism: Aristotle was the real patron of the movement, not Averroes, though the latter was certainly looked on as
the commentator *par excellence* and was followed in his mono-
psychistic interpretation of Aristotle. The doctrine that the
passive intellect, no less than the active intellect, is one and the
same in all men and that this unitary intellect alone survives at
death, so that individual personal immortality is excluded, was
understood in the thirteenth century as being the characteristic
tenet of the radical Aristotelians, and as this doctrine was
supported by the Averroistic interpretation of Aristotle its upholders came to be known as the Averroists. I do not see how
exception can really be taken to the use of this term, provided
that it is clearly realised that the 'Averroists' regarded themselves
as Aristotelians rather than as Averroists. They seem to have
belonged to the faculty of arts of Paris and to have pushed their
adherence to Aristotle as interpreted by Averroes so far that they
taught doctrines in philosophy which were incompatible with
Christian dogma. The salient point in their doctrine, and the one
which attracted most attention, was the theory that there is only
one rational soul in all men. Adopting Averroes's interpretation
of Aristotle's obscure and ambiguous teaching on this matter, they
maintained that not only the active intellect, but also the passive
intellect is one and the same in all men. The logical consequence
of this position is the denial of personal immortality and of
sanctions in the next life. Another of their heterodox doctrines,
and one which incidentally was an undoubtedly Aristotelian
doctrine, was that of the eternity of the world. On this point it
is important to note the difference between the Averroists and
St. Thomas. Whereas for St. Thomas the eternity of the (created)
world has not been proved impossible, though it certainly has not

been proved true (and we know from revelation that as a matter of fact the world was not created from eternity), the Averroists held that the eternity of the world, the eternity of change and movement, can be philosophically demonstrated. Again, it appears that some of them, following Aristotle, denied divine providence and followed Averroes in maintaining determinism. It can, therefore, be understood without difficulty why the theologians attacked the Averroists, either, like St. Bonaventure, attacking Aristotle himself or, like St. Thomas, arguing not only that the peculiar Averroistic positions were intrinsically false, but also that they did not represent the real thought, or at least the clear teaching, of Aristotle.

The Averroists or radical Aristotelians were thus forced to reconcile their philosophical doctrines with theological dogmas, unless they were prepared (and they were not prepared) simply to deny the latter. In other words, they had to provide some theory of the relation of reason to faith which would permit them to assert with Aristotle that there is only one rational soul in all men and at the same time to assert with the Church that every man has his own individual rational soul. It is sometimes said that in order to effect this conciliation they had recourse to the theory of the double truth, maintaining that a thing can be true in philosophy or according to reason and yet that its opposite can be true in theology or according to faith; and indeed Siger of Brabant speaks in this way, implying that certain propositions of Aristotle and Averroes are irrefutable, though the opposite propositions are true according to faith. Thus it can be rationally proved that there is but one intellectual soul in all men, though faith makes us certain that there is one intellectual soul to each human body. Looked at from the logical standpoint this position would lead to the rejection of either theology or philosophy, faith or reason; but the Averroists seem to have meant that in the natural order, with which the philosopher deals, the intellectual soul would have been one in all men, but that God has miraculously multiplied the intellectual soul. The philosopher uses his natural reason, and his natural reason tells him that the intellectual soul is one in all men, while the theologian, who treats of the supernatural order and expounds the divine revelation, assures us that God has miraculously multiplied what by nature could not be multiplied. It is in this sense that what is true in philosophy is false in theology and *vice versa*. This mode of self-defence naturally did not appeal to the theologians, who were quite unprepared to admit that God intervened to perform miraculously what was rationally impossible. Nor had they much sympathy with the alternative method of self-defence adopted by the Averroists, namely the contention that they were simply reporting the teaching of Aristotle. According to a contemporary sermon, perhaps by St. Bonaventure, 'there are some students of philosophy who say certain things which are not true according to faith; and when they are told that something is contrary to faith, they reply that Aristotle says it, but that they themselves do not assert it and are only reporting Aristotle's words'. This defence was treated as a mere subterfuge by the theologians, and justifiably, in view of the Averroists' attitude towards Aristotle.

2. The foremost of the Averroists or radical Aristotelians was *Siger of Brabant*, who was born about the year 1235 and became a teacher in the faculty of arts at Paris. In 1270 he was condemned for his Averroistic doctrines, and it appears that he not only defended himself by saying that he was simply reporting Aristotle and did not intend to assert what was incompatible with the Faith, but also somewhat modified his position. It has been suggested that he was converted from Averroism by the writings of St. Thomas, but there is no certain evidence that he definitely abandoned his Averroism. If he did so, it would be difficult to explain why he was involved in the condemnation of 1277 and why in that year the Inquisitor of France, Simon du Val, ordered him to appear before his court. In any case the question of the changes in Siger's opinions cannot be settled with certainty until the chronology of his works has been settled. The works which have been discovered include the *De anima intellectiva*, *De aeternitate mundi*, *De necessitate et contingentia causarum*, *Compendium de generatione et corruptione*, some *Quaestiones naturales*, some *Quaestiones morales*, some *Quaestiones logicales*, *Quaestiones in Metaphysicam*, *Quaestiones in Physicam*, *Quaestiones in libros tres de Anima*, six *Impossibilia*, and fragments of the *De intellectu* and the *Liber de felicitate*. It appears that the *De intellectu* was a reply to St. Thomas's *De unitate intellectus contra Averroistas* and that in his reply Siger maintained that the active intellect is God, and that man's beatitude on earth consists in union with the active intellect. Whether Siger was still a monopsychist at this time or not, depends, however, on what he thought about the unicity or multiplication of the passive intellect: it cannot be concluded

without more ado from the identification of the active intellect with God that he was still a monopsychist in the Averroistic sense. If Siger appealed from the Inquisition to Rome, it may be that he felt he had been unjustly accused of heterodoxy. He died at Orvieto about 1282, being assassinated by his mad secretary.

To mention Siger of Brabant simply in connection with the Averroistic controversy is to give a partial view of his thought, since it was a system that he expounded, and not simply isolated points in regard to which he followed Averroes. His system, however, though professedly a system of true Aristotelianism, differed very much in important respects from the philosophy of the historic Aristotle, and this was bound to be so if he followed Averroes. For example, while Aristotle looked on God as the first mover in the sense of ultimate final cause, not in the sense of first efficient cause, Siger followed Averroes in making God the first creative cause. God operates mediately, however, through intermediate causes, the successively emanating intelligences, and in this respect Siger followed Avicenna rather than Averroes, so that, as M. Van Steenberghen has noted, Siger's philosophy cannot, with strict accuracy, be called radical Averroism. Nor for the matter of that can it accurately be termed radical Aristotelianism, if one is thinking of the historic Aristotle, though it is a convenient enough term if one is thinking of Siger's intentions. On the question of the eternity of creation Siger follows 'Aristotle', but rather because the Arabian philosophers followed 'Aristotle' on this point than because of what Aristotle himself said on the matter, since the latter did not envisage creation at all. Similarly, Siger's notion that all terrestrial events are determined by the movements of the heavenly bodies smacks of the Islamic philosophy. Again, while the idea that no species can have had a beginning, so that there can have been no first man, is Aristotelian in origin, the idea of the eternal recurrence or cyclic process of determined events is not found in Aristotle.

As regards the salient Averroistic theses of monopsychism and the eternity of the world, Siger seems to have retracted his heterodox opinions. Commenting on the *De Anima*, for example, he not only admits that the monopsychism of Averroes is not true, but proceeds to admit the weight of the objections brought against it by St. Thomas and others. Thus he allows that it is impossible for two different individual acts in two different human beings to proceed simultaneously from an intellectual faculty or principle which is numerically one. Similarly, in his Questions on the *Physics*, he concedes that motion is not eternal and that it had a beginning, although this beginning cannot be rationally demonstrated. However, as has already been noted, it is difficult to ascertain with certainty whether this apparent change of front involved a real change of opinion or whether it was a prudential course adopted in view of the condemnation of 1270.

3. The fact that Dante not only places Siger of Brabant in Paradise, but even puts his praises on the lips of St. Thomas, his adversary, is difficult to explain. Mandonnet, believing on the one hand that Siger of Brabant was a real Averroist and on the other hand that Dante was an anti-Averroist, was forced to suggest that Dante was probably unacquainted with Siger's doctrines. But, as M. Gilson has pointed out, Dante also places in Paradise and attaches to St. Bonaventure the Abbot Joachim of Flores, whose doctrines were rejected by both St. Bonaventure and St. Thomas, and it is extremely unlikely that Dante was unaware of what he was doing in the case of either Joachim or Siger. M. Gilson himself has suggested that Siger of Brabant, as he appears in the *Divine Comedy*, is not so much the actual historical Siger of Brabant as a symbol. St. Thomas symbolises speculative theology, St. Bernard mystical theology, and while Aristotle represents philosophy in limbo Siger, being a Christian, represents it in Paradise. When, therefore, Dante makes St. Thomas praise Siger of Brabant, he is not intending to make the historic Thomas praise the historic Siger, but rather to make speculative theology pay her compliments to philosophy. (M. Gilson explains in an analogous manner St. Bonaventure's praise of Joachim in the *Divine Comedy*.)

M. Gilson's explanation of the problem seems to me to be reasonable. There are, however, other possibilities. Bruno Nardi argued (and he was followed by Miguel Asín) that the explanation of the problem lies in the fact that Dante was not a pure Thomist, but that he incorporated doctrines not only from other Scholastic sources, but also from the Moslem philosophers, notably Averroes, whom he particularly admired. As Dante could not place Avicenna and Averroes in Paradise, he consigned them to limbo, whereas Mohammed he placed in hell proper; but as Siger was a Christian he placed him in Paradise. Dante would thus have acted with deliberation, showing his appreciation of Siger's devotion to Islamic philosophy.

Even if what Bruno Nardi says of Dante's philosophical sources is true, it seems to me that his explanation could well be combined with that of M. Gilson. If Dante admired the Moslem philosophers and was influenced by them, it would explain why he placed Siger in Paradise; but would it explain why he placed Siger's praises on the lips of St. Thomas? If Dante knew that Siger was an Averroist, he certainly knew also that St. Thomas was an anti-Averroist. May it not have been that Dante made St. Thomas the symbol of speculative theology, as Gilson suggests, and Siger, the Averroist, he made the symbol of philosophy, precisely because Siger was a member of the faculty of arts and not a theologian? In that case, as M. Gilson says, St. Thomas's praise of Siger would simply represent theology's tribute to philosophy.

The question has been complicated by M. Van Steenberghen's contention that Siger of Brabant abandoned Averroism inasmuch as it conflicted with theology and approximated to St. Thomas's position. If this is true, and if Dante were aware of the fact that Siger changed his opinions, the difficulty of explaining how St. Thomas could be made to praise Siger would obviously be greatly lessened. In other words, in order to obtain an adequate explanation of the fact why the poet not only placed Siger in heaven, but also made his adversary, St. Thomas, speak his praises, one would have to obtain first an adequate and accurate idea not only of Dante's philosophical sympathies, but also of the evolution of Siger's opinions.[1]

4. We have seen that the philosophy of St. Thomas aroused considerable opposition on the part of other Scholastic philosophers; but even if an attempt was made to implicate St. Thomas in the condemnation of Averroistic Aristotelianism, it remains true that the controversy over such Thomist doctrines as the unicity of the substantial form was a domestic controversy which can be distinguished from the Averroistic controversy proper in which the theologians in general, including St. Thomas, were united in a common front against the heterodox philosophers. Thus the Franciscans, from Alexander of Hales and St. Bonaventure to Duns Scotus, were at one with Dominicans like St. Albert and St. Thomas, Augustinians like Giles of Rome and secular clergy like Henry of Ghent, in opposing what they regarded as a dangerous movement. From the philosophic standpoint the most important

[1] Cf. P. Mandonnet: *Siger de Brabant*, second edit., 1911; B. Nardi: *Sigieri di Brabante nella Divina Commedia* and *le fonti della filosofia di Dante*, 1912; F. Van Steenberghen: *Les œuvres et la doctrine de Siger de Brabant*, 1938; E. Gilson: *Dante et la philosophie*, 1939 (English translation, 1948).

feature of their opposition was, of course, their critical refutation of the offending theories, and in this respect one may mention St. Albert's *De unitate intellectus contra Averroem* (1256), St. Thomas's *De unitate intellectus contra Averroistas* (1270), Giles of Rome's *De purificatione intellectus possibilis contra Averroem* and his *Errores Philosophorum* (which lists the errors of Aristotle and the Moslem philosophers, but does not treat of Siger of Brabant), and Raymund Lull's *Liber contra errores Boetii et Segerii* (1298), *Liber reprobationis aliquorum errorum Averrois, Disputatio Raymundi et Averroistae* and *Sermones contra Averroistas.*

The theologians were not, however, content with writing and speaking against the Averroists; they also endeavoured to secure their official condemnation by ecclesiastical authority. This was only natural, as can be seen from considering the clash on important points between Averroistic philosophy and the Faith, and also from considering the theoretical and possible practical consequences of such theories as those of monopsychism and determinism. Accordingly, in 1270 the Bishop of Paris, Stephen Tempier, condemned the doctrines of monopsychism, denial of personal immortality, determinism, eternity of the world and denial of divine providence. In spite of this condemnation, however, the Averroists continued to teach in secret ('in corners and before boys', as St. Thomas puts it), although in 1272 the professors of the faculty of arts were forbidden to treat of theological matters, and in 1276 secret teaching in the university was prohibited. This led to a further condemnation on March 7th, 1277, when the Bishop of Paris condemned 219 propositions and excommunicated anyone who should persist in maintaining them. The condemnation was aimed principally at the teaching of Siger of Brabant and Boethius of Dacia, and it involved the 'double truth' subterfuge. Boethius of Dacia, who was a contemporary of Siger of Brabant, upheld the intellectualist idea of beatitude expounded by Aristotle, maintaining that only philosophers can attain true happiness, while non-philosophers sin against the natural order. The condemned propositions, that 'there is no more excellent state than to devote oneself to philosophy' and that 'the wise men of the world are the philosophers alone', seem to have been taken from or to have summarised the teaching of Boethius, who, as professor of the faculty of arts, omitted all mention of the supernatural order and treated the Aristotelian conception of beatitude as adequate, at least from the standpoint of reason.

CHAPTER XLIII

FRANCISCAN THINKERS

Roger Bacon, life and works—Philosophy of Roger Bacon—
Matthew of Aquasparta—Peter John Olivi—Roger Marston
—Richard of Middleton—Raymond Lull.

1. ONE of the most interesting of mediaeval thinkers is *Roger Bacon*
(*c.* 1212 to after 1292), called the *Doctor Mirabilis.* He would be of
interest, were it only for his interest in and respect for experimental
science and the application of mathematics in science; but what
makes him considerably more interesting is that his scientific
interests are combined with a lively interest in philosophy proper,
and that both these interests were combined with a typically
Franciscan emphasis on mysticism. Traditional elements were
thus fused with a scientific outlook which was really foreign to the
mentality of the majority of contemporary theologians and philosophers.[1] Moreover, Roger Bacon, impulsive, somewhat intolerant
and hot-headed, convinced of the truth and value of his own
opinions and of the obscurantism of many of the leading thinkers
of his time, particularly those of Paris, is interesting not only as
philosopher, but also as a man. He was something of a stormy
petrel in his Order, but he is at the same time one of the glories of
that Order and one of the leading figures of British philosophy. If
a comparison were instituted between Roger Bacon and Francis
Bacon (1561–1626), the comparison would by no means be to the
unqualified advantage of the latter. As Professor Adamson
remarked, 'it is more than probable that in all fairness, when we
speak of the Baconian reform of science, we should refer to the
forgotten monk of the thirteenth century rather than to the
brilliant and famous Chancellor of the seventeenth',[2] while Bridges
observes that though Francis Bacon was 'immeasurably superior
as a writer, Roger Bacon had the sounder estimate and the firmer
grasp of that combination of deductive with inductive matters
which marks the scientific discoverer'.[3]

Born at Ilchester, Roger Bacon studied at Oxford under Adam
Marsh and Robert Grosseteste. For the latter Bacon had the

[1] I refer, of course, to experimental science.
[2] *Roger Bacon: The Philosophy of Science in the Middle Ages,* p. 7.
[3] J. H. Bridges: Introduction to *Opus Maius,* pp. xci–xcii.

442

liveliest admiration, remarking that he knew mathematics and perspective, and that he could have known everything; Grosseteste also knew enough of languages to understand the wise men of antiquity.[1] From Oxford, Bacon went to Paris, where he apparently taught for a few years. For the Parisian professors he had little respect. Thus of Alexander of Hales's *Summa* he remarks that it weighed more than a horse, though he contests its authenticity,[2] while he blames the theologians for their incursions into philosophy, for their ignorance of the sciences, and for the unmerited deference they paid to Alexander of Hales and Albert the Great.[3] Ignorance of the sciences and of languages were his chief charges against contemporary thinkers, though he also found fault with the veneration given to the *Sentences* of Peter Lombard, which, he says, was preferred to the Bible itself, and with faulty Scriptural exegesis. In other words, his criticism (which was often unfair, as in regard to St. Albert) shows the twofold character of his thought, a devotion to science coupled with a traditional or conservative attitude in respect to theology and metaphysics. As regards Aristotle, Bacon was an admirer of the Philosopher, but he detested what he regarded as bad and misleading Latin translations of his works and declared that he would have them all burnt, if it lay in his power to do so.[4]

But though Bacon had little use for the great figures of the University of Paris and contrasted the Parisian thinkers unfavourably with his fellow countrymen, he met at Paris one man at least who had a lasting influence on his thought, Peter of Maricourt, a Picard and author of an *Epistola de magnete* and a *Nova compositio Astrolabii particularis*.[5] According to Roger Bacon[6] he was the one man who could safely be praised for his achievements in scientific research. 'For the last three years he has been working at the production of a mirror which shall produce combustion at a distance; a problem which the Latins have neither solved nor attempted, though books have been written upon the subject.' Peter evidently stimulated Roger Bacon's leaning to experimental science and won his respect by putting his questions to Nature herself instead of attempting to answer them *a priori* and without recourse to experiment.

About the year 1250 Bacon entered the Franciscan Order and

[1] *Opus Tertium*, c. 25.   [2] *Opus Minus*, edit. J. S. Brewer, p. 326.
[3] *Ibid.*, p. 322 ff.   [4] *Compendium philosophiae*, p. 469.
[5] Peter's name of *Peregrinus* seems to be due to the fact that he went on a crusade.   [6] *Opus Tertium*, c. 13.

taught at Oxford until 1257, when he had to abandon public teaching, having incurred the suspicion or hostility of his superiors. He was still permitted to write, however, though not to publish his works. In June 1266 Pope Clement IV, a friend of Bacon, told the latter to send him his works; but the Pope died shortly afterwards and it is not known with certainty if the manuscripts ever reached Rome and, if they did, what reception was accorded them. In any case Bacon got into trouble in 1277 by writing the *Speculum astronomiae* in order to defend his ideas on astrology and to criticise Stephen Tempier's condemnation of astrology. The Franciscan General of the time, Jerome of Ascoli, had Bacon brought before a Chapter in Paris under suspicion of teaching novelties, and this resulted in Bacon's imprisonment in 1278. He seems to have remained in prison until 1292, and it was in this year or not long afterwards that he died, being buried at Oxford in the Franciscan Church.

Bacon's chief work was the *Opus Maius*, which may have been completed and sent to the Pope. The *Opus Minus* and the *Opus Tertium* are more or less summaries of material incorporated in the *Opus Maius*, though they contain additional matter as well. It is in the *Opus Minus* that Bacon treats of the seven sins of theology, for example. A number of other works, such as the *Quaestiones supra libros octo Physicorum Aristotelis* and the *Quaestiones supra libros Primae Philosophiae*, have been published in the fourteen volumes of the *Opera hactenus inedita Rogeri Baconi* of which sixteen fascicules have so far appeared. Some of these works seem to have been written as parts of a projected *Scriptum Principale*. Bacon also wrote a *Compendium Philosophiae*, a *Compendium studii Philosophiae* and a *Compendium studii Theologiae*.

2. In the first part of the *Opus Maius* Bacon enumerates four principal causes of human ignorance and failure to attain truth: subjection to unworthy authority, the influence of habit, popular prejudice, and making a show of apparent wisdom to cover one's own ignorance. The first three causes of error were recognised by men like Aristotle, Seneca, Averroes; but the fourth is the most dangerous, as it makes a man conceal his own ignorance by holding up as true wisdom the result of worshipping untrustworthy authority, of habit and of popular prejudice. For example, because Aristotle said something, it is considered true; but Avicenna may have corrected Aristotle on the point, and Averroes may have corrected Avicenna. Again, because the Fathers did not pursue scientific studies, it is taken for granted that such studies are

valueless; but the circumstances of that time were quite different, and what was an excuse for them is not necessarily an excuse for us. Men do not realise the value of studying mathematics and languages, and so they belittle these studies out of prejudice.

In the second part Bacon emphasises the dominating character of theology among the sciences: all truth is contained in the Scriptures. But for the elucidation of the Scriptures we need the help of canon law and of philosophy. Philosophy and the use of reason in general cannot be condemned, since reason is of God. God is the active intellect (so Bacon interpreted St. Augustine, appealing also to Aristotle and Avicenna), and He enlightens the individual human mind, concurring with it in its activity. Philosophy has as its purpose to lead man to the knowledge and service of God; it culminates in moral philosophy. The speculative and moral sciences of the pagans were certainly inadequate and find their completion only in Christian theology and the Christian ethic; but it is not right to condemn or to neglect any particle of truth. As a matter of fact, says Bacon, philosophy was not a pagan invention, but was revealed to the Patriarchs. Subsequently the revelation was obscured through human depravity, but the pagan philosophers helped to rediscover it, or part of it. The greatest of these philosophers was Aristotle, and Avicenna is his principal expounder. As for Averroes, he was a man of real wisdom who improved in many points on what his predecessors had said, though his own theories also stand in need of correction. In fine, we should use pagan philosophy in an intelligent manner, without ignorant rejection and condemnation on the one hand or slavish adherence to any particular thinker on the other. It is our business to carry on and perfect the work of our predecessors, remembering that though it is the function of truth to lead man to God, we should not regard as valueless studies which have at first sight no immediate relation to theology: all truth of whatever kind leads ultimately to God.

The third part Bacon devotes to the subject of language, emphasising the practical importance of the scientific study of languages. Without a real knowledge of Hebrew and Greek the Scriptures cannot be properly interpreted and translated, nor can manuscripts be corrected when faulty; and good translations of Greek and Arabian philosophers are also needed. But for purposes of translation something more than a smattering of a language is necessary, if slavish translations are to be avoided.

In the fourth part Bacon discusses mathematics, the 'door and key' of other sciences. Mathematics were studied by the Patriarchs and came to the knowledge of the Greeks by way of the Chaldeans and Egyptians; but among the Latins they have fallen into neglect. Yet mathematical science is *quasi innata*, or at least it is learnt more easily and immediately and with less dependence on experience than other sciences, so that it may be said to be presupposed by other sciences. Logic and grammar are dependent to a certain extent on mathematics, while it is obvious that without mathematics no advance can be made in astronomy, and they are useful even for theology: mathematical astronomy can, for instance, demonstrate the comparative insignificance of the earth as compared with the heavens, not to speak of the facts that mathematics are useful for solving the chronological problems in the Scriptures and that they show the inadequacy of the Julian Calendar, a matter to which the Pope would do well to attend. Bacon proceeds to speak about light, its propagation, reflection and refraction; about eclipses, tides, the spherical shape of the earth, the unicity of the universe, and so on; and then passes to geography and astrology. Astrology is regarded with suspicion as it is thought to involve determinism; but this suspicion is unjust. The influence and movements of the heavenly bodies affect terrestrial and human events and produce even natural dispositions in human beings, but they do not destroy free will: it is only prudent to gain all the knowledge we can and use it for a good end. Bacon approves Aristotle's advice to Alexander concerning the treatment to be meted out to certain tribes of perverse ways: change their climate, that is, change their place of abode and thus change their morals.

Optics form the subject of the fifth part, in which Bacon treats of the structure of the eye, the principles of vision and the conditions of vision, reflection, refraction, and finally the practical application of the science of optics. Mirrors, he suggests, might be erected in elevated spots in order that the layout and movements of an enemy's camp might be observed, while by the use of refraction we could make small things appear great and distant objects appear near. There is no evidence to show that Bacon actually invented the telescope; but he conceived the possibility of such a thing.

In the sixth part Bacon considers experimental science. Reasoning may guide the mind to a right conclusion, but it is only confirmation by experience which removes doubt. That is one reason why diagrams and figures are employed in geometry. Many beliefs are refuted by experience. Experience, however, is of two kinds. In one kind of experience we employ our bodily senses, aided by instruments and by the evidence of trustworthy witnesses, while the other kind is experience of spiritual things and needs grace. This latter type of experience advances through various stages to the mystical states of rapture. The former type of experience can be used to prolong life (by improving the science of medicine, and discovering antidotes to poisons), to invent explosive substances, to transmute baser metals into gold and to refine gold itself, and so to disabuse the heathen of their false magical beliefs.

Finally, in the seventh part of the *Opus Maius*, Bacon treats of moral philosophy, which stands on a higher level than philology, or mathematics and experimental science. These sciences are related to action of various kinds, whereas moral philosophy is related to the actions by which we become good or bad, and it instructs man about his relations with God, his fellow men and himself. It is thus closely related to theology and shares in the latter's dignity. Supposing the 'principles of metaphysics', which include Christian revelation, Bacon treats of civic morality and then, more at length, of personal morality, making use of the writings of Greek, Roman and Moslem philosophers, particularly of Seneca, the Roman Stoic. In conclusion he treats of the grounds for accepting the Christian religion. Revelation is necessary and the Christian accepts the Faith on authority; but in dealing with non-Christians we cannot appeal simply to authority, but must have recourse to reason. Thus philosophy can prove the existence of God, His unity and infinity, while the credibility of the sacred writers is established by their personal sanctity, their wisdom, the evidence of miracles, their firm steadfastness under persecution, the uniformity of their faith, and their victory in spite of their humble origin and temporal condition. Bacon ends with the doctrine of man's incorporation with Christ and his participation through Christ in the divine life. *Et quid potest homo plus petere in hac vita?* And what more can a man seek in this life?

From what has been said, the twofold character of Bacon's philosophy is clear. His emphasis on the relation of philosophy to theology, on the former's function of leading man to God, and on the practical or moral aspect of philosophy, the place he attributes in his philosophy to inner knowledge of God and spiritual things, culminating in rapture, the close relation he establishes between theology and philosophy, his doctrine of God as the illuminating active intellect,[1] his adoption of the theories of 'seminal reasons' (for the development of which matter has a kind of active appetite), of the universal hylomorphic composition of creatures, and of the plurality of forms (from the form of corporeity up to the *forma individualis*), all mark him as an adherent, to a large extent, of the Augustinian tradition. In spite of his respect for Aristotle he not infrequently misinterprets him and even ascribes to him doctrines which he certainly never held. Thus he discerns elements of the Christian revelation in the philosophy of Aristotle which were actually not there; and though he refers to St. Thomas he does not seem to have been influenced by the Thomist positions or to have been particularly interested in them. On the other hand, the breadth of his interests and the vigour of his insistence on experimental science in general, on the development of astronomy by the aid of mathematics, and on the practical applications of science mark him out as a herald of the future. By temperament he was somewhat self-assured, inclined to impatience and to sometimes unjust criticism and condemnation; but he laid his finger on many weak points in contemporary science as also in contemporary moral and ecclesiastical life. For his scientific theories he depended very much on other thinkers, as was only natural; but he was quick to see the possibility of their development and application, and, as has already been remarked, he had a firmer grasp of scientific method, of the combination of deduction and induction, than was possessed by Francis Bacon, the Chancellor of England, whose insistence on experiment and observation and the practical applications of knowledge has sometimes been depicted as if without parallel or anticipation among philosophers of an earlier period.

3. An Augustinian of a different type was *Matthew of Aquasparta* (c. 1240–1302), who studied at Paris, taught at Bologna and Rome, and became General of the Franciscan Order in 1287, being created a cardinal in 1288. The author of, among other works, a Commentary on the *Sentences, Quaestiones disputatae* and *Quaestiones quodlibetales*, Matthew adhered in general to the position of St. Bonaventure, regarding St. Augustine as the great fount of wisdom. Thus, while he admitted that man's ideas of corporeal objects are formed only in dependence on sense-experience, he

---

[1] Obviously this doctrine is not Averroistic. The latter's monopsychism Bacon condemned as error and heresy.

refused to admit that corporeal objects can affect more than the body: it is the soul itself which is responsible for sensation as such, as St. Augustine had held, though, of course, sensation requires that a sense-organ should be affected by a sensible object. Again, it is the active intellect which transforms the *species sensibilis* and produces the idea in the passive intellect. Matthew appeals explicitly to St. Augustine on this matter.[1] Yet the soul's activity alone is not sufficient to explain knowledge: the divine illumination is required. What is this divine illumination? It is really God's immediate concurrence with the operation of the human intellect, a concurrence by the aid of which the intellect is moved to know the object. God moves us to know the object of which we receive the *species sensibilis*, this movement being the divine illumination. The object is related to its eternal exemplar foundation, the *ratio aeterna* or divine idea, and it is the divine light which enables us to discern this relation, the *rationes aeternae* exercising a regulative effect on the intellect. But we do not discern the divine light or concurrence, nor are the eternal ideas objects directly perceived; we know them rather as principles which move the intellect to know the created essence, *ut obiectum movens et in aliud ducens*, not as *obiectum in se ducens*.[2] There is, then, no difficulty in seeing how the divine light operates in all men, good or bad, since there is no question of a vision of the divine ideas and of the divine essence as such, in themselves. God co-operates in all the activities of creatures; but the human mind is made in the image of God in a special manner and God's concurrence with the mind's activity is rightly termed illumination.

In the same *De cognitione* to which reference has already been made, Matthew mentions the Thomist doctrine that the intellect knows the singular thing *per quandam reflexionem*, by a certain act of reflection[3] and rejects it. It is difficult to understand this position, he says, for the knowledge of the singular thing *per reflexionem ad phantasma* means that the intellect knows the singular thing either in the phantasm or directly in itself. The latter supposition is ruled out by the Thomist view, while on the other hand the phantasm is not actually intelligible (*intelligibile actu*), but the *species intelligibilis* has to be abstracted. In opposition to the Thomist view Matthew asserts that the intellect knows singular things in themselves and directly, by means of *species singulares*. It is sense intuition which apprehends the object as existing and intellectual intuition which apprehends the individual quiddity or essence; but unless the mind had first of all an intuition of the singular thing, it could not abstract the universal notion. The *species universalis* thus presupposes the *species singularis*. Of course, the singular thing is not intelligible if by intelligible you mean deductively demonstrable, since it is contingent and passing; but if by intelligible you mean what can be apprehended by the intellect, then in this case it must be allowed that the singular thing is intelligible.[1] Otherwise it is not possible to explain satisfactorily the abstraction and real foundation of the universal idea.

Another theory of St. Thomas which Matthew rejects is the theory that the soul while united to the body has no direct intuition of itself and its dispositions and powers, but knows indirectly that it itself and its dispositions exist, through its perception of the act by which it knows objects through *species* abstracted from phantasms. This theory of the soul's purely indirect knowledge of itself Matthew rejects, as being contrary to the teaching of St. Augustine and also to what reason demands. It is unreasonable to suppose that the soul is so immersed in the body that it can apprehend nothing without an image or phantasm and that it can apprehend itself and its dispositions only indirectly. 'It seems altogether absurd to suppose the intellect so blind that it does not see itself, when it is by the intellect that the soul knows all things.'[2] His own theory Matthew states with considerable care. As regards the *beginning* of knowledge 'I say without any doubt that the soul can intuit neither itself nor the habits which are in it, nor can the first act of knowledge be directed to itself or the things which are in it.'[3] The soul needs a stimulus from the bodily senses for the beginning of knowledge, and then by reflecting on its own perceived act of knowing it comes to know its powers and itself as existent. But afterwards the soul turns in on itself, as it were (*quadam spirituali conversione in semetipsam revocata est*),[4] and then it can have a direct intuition of itself and its habits, these being no longer simply the non-intuited conclusions of a process of reasoning, but the direct object of a mental vision. In order that this intellectual vision should take place, four conditions are required, just as for sensitive vision, namely a visible object which is present as visible, a properly disposed power of vision, mutual proportion, and illumination. All these conditions are or can be fulfilled. The soul is an intellectually visible object and it is present

---

[1] *De cognitione*, p. 311.   [2] *Ibid.*, p. 328.   [3] *Ibid.*, p. 329.   [4] *Ibid.*, p. 329.

to the intellect; the intellect is an immaterial power and is not intrinsically dependent on a sense-organ; both the intellect and the soul itself are intellectual finite objects, and nothing is so proportioned to the soul as the soul itself; lastly the divine illumination is always present.[1]

Matthew of Aquasparta thus adhered closely, though reasonably and with moderation, to the Augustinian tradition, and it is only to be expected that he would maintain the theories of the *rationes seminales* and the *forma corporeitatis*. In addition he upheld the Bonaventurian doctrine of the universal hylomorphic composition of creatures, rejecting the real distinction of essence and existence as an adequate explanation of their finitude and contingence.

4. A much less faithful Augustinian was *Peter John Olivi* (c. 1248–98), a prominent figure among the Franciscan 'spirituals'. Thus while he clung to the theory of the hylomorphic composition of all creatures and the multiplicability of angels in the same species, as also to the doctrine of plurality of forms, he not only denied the existence of *rationes seminales*, but even maintained that this denial was in accordance with the doctrine of St. Augustine. An anticipation of Scotus's *distinctio formalis a parte rei*, intermediate between a real distinction and a conceptual distinction, is to be found in his philosophy; and it exists between the divine attributes, for instance, as Scotus also thought. Olivi is also remarkable for having adopted the *impetus* theory of Joannes Philoponus, i.e. the theory that when a projectile is set in motion, the mover or thrower confers an impetus or *impulsus* on the projectile which carries the projectile on even when it is no longer in contact with the mover, though it may be overcome by the resistance of the air and other opposing forces. But consideration of this theory, which meant the abandonment of the Aristotelian theory of 'unnatural' motion, is best reserved for the next volume, in connection with those thinkers who drew some novel conclusions from the doctrine and paved the way for a new conception of the corporeal world. Further consideration of the *distinctio formalis a parte rei* will be reserved for the treatment of the Scotist system. My real reason for mentioning Olivi here is to allude briefly to his theory of the soul and its relation to the body. This theory, or part of it, was condemned at the Council of Vienne in 1311, and the matter is worth mentioning since certain

[1] The doctrines of the soul's intuition of itself and of the intellectual knowledge of the singular thing appear also in the teaching of the Franciscan *Vital du Four* (d. 1327).

writers in the past have claimed that the Council meant to condemn what they certainly did not mean to condemn.

According to Olivi, there are three constitutive 'parts' in the human soul, the vegetative principle or form, the sensitive principle or form, and the intellectual principle or form. These three forms together constitute the one human soul, the rational soul, as constitutive parts of the whole soul. There was no particular novelty in maintaining a doctrine of plurality of forms; but Olivi drew from his theory the peculiar conclusion that the three formal parts are united by the spiritual matter of the soul in such a way that the higher form influences and moves the lower forms only through the mediation of the spiritual matter. He concluded further that while the vegetative and sensitive parts inform the body, the intellectual part does not of itself inform the body, though it moves the others parts as its instruments and subjects. He maintained that the rooting of all three parts in the spiritual matter of the soul safeguarded the unity of man and the substantial union of soul and body; but at the same time he refused to allow that the intellectual part of the soul informs the body directly. This last point aroused opposition among the Franciscans themselves. One of the reasons of their opposition was that if it were true that the intellectual form did not inform the body directly but only mediately, through the sensitive form, it would follow that Christ was not, as Man, composed of a rational soul and a body, as the Faith teaches.[1] The end of the matter was that in 1311 the Council of Vienne condemned as heretical the proposition that the rational or intellectual soul does not inform the body directly (*per se*) and essentially (*essentialiter*). The Council did not, however, condemn the doctrine of the plurality of forms and affirm the Thomist view, as some later writers have tried to maintain. The Fathers of the Council, or the majority of them at least, themselves held the doctrine of the plurality of forms. The Council simply wished to preserve the unity of man by affirming that the intellectual soul informs the body directly. This is shown clearly by the reference to Christology. The human nature of Christ consists of a passible human body and a rational human soul which informs the body, the two together forming human nature. The Council did not concern itself with the question of the *forma corporeitatis* or with the question whether there

[1] In support of Olivi's thesis the reason was given that if the intellectual form informed the body directly, it would either give its own immortality to the body or lose its own immortality through informing the body.

are or are not various 'parts' in the human soul: what it says is simply that the rational soul informs the body directly and so is a principle integral to man: it was the separation between the intellectual soul and the human body which it condemned, not the doctrine of the plurality of forms. It is, therefore, quite erroneous to state that the Council of Vienne declared that the human soul informs prime matter directly and that the Thomist theory is imposed by the Church.

5. If Peter John Olivi was an independent thinker who departed on some points from the Augustinian tradition and prepared the way for later stages in Franciscan thought, *Roger Marston* (d. 1303), who was for a time Minister of the English Franciscan province, was a whole-hearted Augustinian. He embraced all the characteristic 'Augustinian' theories, such as the intellectual apprehension of the singular thing, the pre-eminence of will over intellect, universal hylomorphic composition in creatures, plurality of forms, and he criticised St. Thomas for admitting the apparent possibility of creation from eternity and for throwing overboard the *rationes seminales*. Indeed, this resolute English conservative found even Matthew of Aquasparta too accommodating and firmly rejected any attempt to water down what he regarded as the genuine doctrine of St. Augustine and St. Anselm. We should prefer the 'saints' to those 'infernal men', the pagan philosophers.

In his *De Anima* Roger Marston gives an uncompromising interpretation of St. Augustine's teaching on the divine illumination. The active intellect may indeed be called a part of the soul if by active intellect is meant a natural disposition in the soul for the knowledge of truth (*sicut perspicuitas naturalis in oculo*); but if by active intellect is meant the act of illumination, we must say that it is a separate substance, God Himself.[1] The active intellect is the uncreated or eternal light which impresses on the mind, as a seal on the wax, a certain active impression which leaves a passive impression that is the formal principle in the knowledge of unchanging truths.[2] It is not the concepts or terms of the judgement which are provided by the eternal light, God; but the eternal truth.[3] For example, the eternal light does not infuse into the mind the concept of the whole and the concept of the part, but it is the radiation of the eternal light which enables the mind to apprehend infallibly the relation between the terms, the eternal truth that the whole is greater than the part. The eternal ideas

---

[1] *De Anima*, p. 259. [2] *Ibid.*, p. 263. [3] *Ibid.*, p. 262.

are thus the ultimate foundation of the certain and infallible judgement (*rationes aeternae aliqualiter attinguntur*). The explanation of the fact that the human race agrees about the fundamental truths is to be found in the common illumination of all minds by the one divine light, and Roger Marston refuses to allow that this divine light consists simply in the creation of the human intellect as a finite imitation of the divine intellect. Those who deny that the active intellect is the primal and uncreated light are people who are 'drunk with the nectar of philosophy' and who pervert the meaning of St. Augustine and the *Sancti*.[1] If St. Augustine had not intended to say any more than these people make him say, then his arguments would be without point and would beg the question, since if the human intellect was assumed to be the source of its own light, one could not argue to the existence of an uncreated light, as St. Augustine certainly does.[2]

6. Another English Franciscan of note was *Richard of Middleton*, who studied at Oxford and Paris. He went to Paris in 1278, and after taking his degree he occupied one of the Franciscan chairs of theology until 1286, when he became tutor to St. Louis of Toulouse, the son of Charles II of Sicily. The date of his death is uncertain, but it must have occurred about the turn of the century. He composed the customary Commentary on the *Sentences* of Peter Lombard and was responsible for *Quaestiones Disputatae* and *Quodlibets*.

In some points Richard of Middleton followed the general Franciscan tradition, maintaining, for example, the impossibility of creation from eternity, since this would involve a created infinite, universal hylomorphic composition in creatures, the plurality of forms and the primacy of the will. On other points, however, he approximated to the Thomist position, and in this matter he represents the new movement among Franciscan thinkers towards a modified Augustinianism, the greatest exponent of which was Duns Scotus. Thus Richard insists not only that all valid demonstrations of God's existence are *a posteriori*, but also that our intellectual knowledge of spiritual as well as of corporeal beings is abstracted from sense-experience and that it is unnecessary to postulate any special illumination or to identify the active intellect with God. On the other hand, the mind apprehends the singular, though it does so by means of the same concept by which it apprehends the universal.

---

[1] *De Anima*, p. 273.   [2] *Ibid.*, p. 256.

In addition, Richard maintained some more or less original ideas. One of the less happy of these ideas was the notion that what the mind directly attains is not the individual existent thing itself, but its *esse repraesentatum*. He also invented a *principium pure possibile*, in order to explain how new forms can appear under the action of a created agent. It might appear at first that this is nothing else but prime matter; but matter, which differs in kind in spiritual and corporeal beings and so is not homogeneous, has some actuality of its own in Richard's eyes, whereas the *principium pure possibile* has no actuality of its own, is concreated with matter and cannot exist separately. If matter is understood as the primary foundation of natural change, as that which is common to corrupted and generated bodies and receives form, then it is really distinct from the purely potential principle, which is transmuted into the form itself. The purely potential principle may then be called the potentiality of matter (*potentia materiae*), if the potentiality of matter is understood as meaning the principle out of which the created agent educes the form and which is transmuted into the form educed; but in this case the *potentia materiae* is really distinct from matter itself. Conversely, if by *potentia materiae* is meant matter's power to receive form, it is the same as matter itself; but in this case it is really distinct from the *principium pure possibile*.[1] In other words, the power to receive form is not the same as the power to become form. Besides prime matter as the subject of change, which has some actuality of its own and which receives form, Richard postulates, then, a kind of receptacle of forms, a purely potential principle which is transmuted into those forms which are received in matter. He considered that this theory constituted an improvement on the theory of *rationes seminales*, and he tried to interpret St. Augustine as teaching the existence, not of active forces (which would amount to a *latitatio formarum*), but of a purely potential principle which becomes forms. In virtue of this positive potentiality forms may be said to be created from the beginning in potency, but this must not be taken to imply the presence of 'seeds'. The principle in question is in matter, and Richard calls it the more intimate part of matter and the passive potentiality of matter; but, as we have seen, it is not identical with matter as subject of change and recipient of form.[2] It is not, therefore, something altogether separate from matter, but it is distinct from matter in the ordinary

[1] *In 2 Sent.*, 12, 1, 10.   [2] *Ibid.*, 12, 1, 1.

sense. This may appear to involve an approximation to the Thomist view of prime matter, and to a certain extent this seems to be true; but Richard refused to abandon the traditional view of matter as having some actuality of its own, and so he had to distinguish matter as element in the composite thing from the potential principle which becomes forms under the action of the created agent.

In addition to being composed of matter and form every creature is also composed of essence and existence. But existence is not something really distinct from the essence, to which it comes as an accident. On the other hand, existence is not merely conceptually distinct from essence, since it does add something to essence. What does it add? A twofold relation: a *relatio rationis* to itself, inasmuch as existence confers on essence the dignity of being an hypostasis or substance, and a real relation to the Creator.[1] On this matter Richard of Middleton accepted the position of Henry of Ghent.

At the end of his work *Richard de Middleton*[2] Père E. Hocedez, S.J., remarks: *Richard finit une époque.* The last representative of the Seraphic School, he attempted a synthesis (*prudemment nouvelle*) in which the main positions of Bonaventure, deepened and perfected, should be integrated with what he considered best in Aristotelianism and in the theology of St. Thomas. That Richard of Middleton incorporated ideas from outside the Augustinian tradition is clear enough; but I cannot agree with Père Hocedez that this movement of thought 'had no morrow' and that Scotus directed Franciscan philosophy 'in new ways which were soon to end in nominalism'. Rather did Richard's philosophy form a stage on the way to Scotism, which opened the door wider to Aristotelianism, but was certainly not nominalistic or favourable to nominalism.

7. One of the most interesting of the Franciscan philosophers is *Raymond Lull* (1232/35-1315). Born in Majorca, Raymond Lull was for a time at the court of King James II; but about 1265 he underwent a religious conversion and abandoned his family in order to devote himself to what he considered his great task in life, to fight against Islam and to help in the rooting out of Averroism. With this end in view he devoted nine years to the study of Arabic and philosophy, the first fruit of the period of study being his *Ars Magna*, followed by the *Liber principiorum*

---

[1] *In 2 Sent.*, 3, 1, 1; *Quodlibet*, 1, 8.   [2] Paris, 1925.

philosophiae. He joined the Third Order of St. Francis and travelled to Africa to convert the Moors; he taught at Paris and combated Averroism; he wrote logic, philosophy, theology and poetry, writing in his native Catalan and in Arabic, as well as in Latin. Finally he was martyred in Tunisia in 1315. Besides the two above-mentioned works one may mention the *Ars demonstrativa*, the *Ars brevis*, the *Ars generalis ultima*, and the anti-Averroistic works such as the *Liber contra errores Boetii et Segerii* (i.e. against Boethius of Dacia and Siger of Brabant), the *De naturali modo intelligendi*, the *Liber reprobationis aliquorum errorum Averrois*, the *Disputatio Raymundi et Averroistae* and the *Sermones contra Averroistas*. But this forms but a selection of the astonishing literary output of a man who was apostle and traveller, poet and mystic.

The apostolic interests of Raymond Lull were by no means irrelevant to his philosophy; they were partly responsible for the general attitude he adopted towards philosophy, whose ancillary relation to theology he stressed. He was quite aware of the distinction between faith and reason, and he compared faith to oil which continues to rest unmixed on the water, even if the water is increased; but his interest in the conversion of the Moslems naturally led to an insistence, not only on philosophy's subordinate relation to theology, but also on reason's ability to make acceptable the dogmas of the Faith. It is in the light of this general attitude that we must understand his proposal to 'prove' the articles of faith by 'necessary reasons'. He no more proposed to rationalise (in the modern sense) the Christian mysteries than did St. Anselm or Richard of St. Victor, when they spoke of 'necessary reasons' for the Trinity, and he expressly declares that faith treats of objects which the human reason cannot understand; but he wished to show the Moslems that Christian beliefs are not contrary to reason and that reason can meet the objections adduced against them. Moreover, believing that the accusation brought against the Averroists that they held a 'double truth' theory was justified and that the theory in question was contradictory and absurd, he was concerned to show that there is no need to have recourse to any such radical separation of theology and philosophy, but that theological dogmas harmonise with reason and cannot be impugned by reason. In regard to the peculiar theories of the Averroists themselves, he argued that these are contrary both to faith and reason. Monopsychism, for instance, contradicts the testimony of consciousness: we are conscious that our acts of thought and will are our own.

If one looked merely at the familiar 'Augustinian' theories maintained by Lull, such as the impossibility of creation from eternity, universal hylomorphic composition of creatures, plurality of forms, the primacy of will over intellect, and so on, there would not appear to be any particularly interesting feature in his philosophy; but we find such a feature in his *Ars combinatoria*. Raymond Lull supposes first of all that there are certain general principles or categories, which are self-evident and which are common to all sciences, in the sense that without them there can be neither philosophy nor any other science. The most important of these are the nine absolute predicates, goodness, greatness, eternity, power, wisdom, will, virtue, truth, glory. (These predicates express attributes of God.) There are nine other concepts which express relations (between creatures): difference, agreement, contrariety, beginning, middle, end, majority, equality, minority. In addition, there are sets of fundamental questions, such as how, when, where, etc., of virtues and of vices. Lull cannot have attached any particular importance to the number nine, which appears in the *Ars generalis*, as elsewhere he gives other numbers of divine attributes or absolute predicates; for example, in the *Liber de voluntate infinita et ordinata* he gives twelve, while in the *De possibili et impossibili* he gives twenty: the main point is that there are certain fundamental ideas which are essential to philosophy and science.

These fundamental ideas being presupposed, Raymond Lull speaks as though through their combination one could discover the principles of the particular sciences and even discover new truths, and in order that the work of combination might be facilitated, he had recourse to symbolism, the fundamental concepts being symbolised by letters, and to mechanical means of tabulating and grouping. For example, God was represented by the letter A, and, in the later writings, nine *principia*, also symbolised by letters representing the divine attributes, surround Him. These principles could be combined in a hundred and twenty ways through the use of figures and concentric circles. It is not to be wondered at, therefore, that some writers have seen in Lull's scheme an anticipation of Leibniz's dream of the *caracteristica universalis* and *Ars combinatoria*, of an algebraic symbolism, the use of which would permit the deduction from fundamental concepts not only of already ascertained truths, but even

of new truths. As already mentioned, Lull does seem to imply
such an aim on occasion, and if this had been his real object, he
would obviously have to be considered as separating himself from
the Scholastic tradition; but in point of fact he expressly asserts[1]
that his aim was to facilitate the use of the memory. Moreover,
we must remember his apostolic interests, which suggest that his
scheme was designed for purposes of exposition and explanation
rather than of deduction in the strict sense. The fact that Leibniz
was influenced by Lull proves nothing as to the latter's intentions,
of course. According to Dr. Otto Keicher, O.F.M.,[2] it is the
principia which form the essence not only of the *Ars generalis*, but
of the whole system of Raymond Lull; but though it is obvious
enough that what Lull regarded as fundamental concepts formed
in a sense the basis of his system, it does not seem that one can
reduce his 'art' to the establishment of certain principles or
categories: the philosopher himself regarded it as something more
than that. Of course, if one stresses the expository, didactic aspect
of the art, it is scarcely necessary to debate what are the essential
and unessential elements in it; but if one chooses to regard it as
an anticipation of Leibniz, then it would be relevant to make a
distinction between Lull's schematism and mechanical technique
on the one hand and on the other hand the general notion of
deducing the principles of the sciences from a combination of
fundamental concepts, since Lull might have anticipated Leibniz
in regard to the latter's general principle, even though his 'logical
algebra' was radically deficient. This is more or less the view of
Dr. Bernhard Geyer,[3] and I believe it to be correct. That Lull
pursues his deduction in reliance on three main principles;[4] to
hold as true everything which affirms the greatest harmony
between God and created being, to attribute to God that which
is the most perfect, and to assume that God has made whatever
truly appears.to be the better, is no argument against this interpretation: it doubtless shows the spiritual kinship between Lull
and the Augustinian tradition, but it also reminds one of important
points in the system of Leibniz some centuries later.

---

[1] *Compendium artis demonstrativae*, prol.   [2] *Beiträge*, 7, 4–5, p. 19.
[3] Ueberweg-Geyer, *Die patristische und scholastische Philosophie*, p. 460.
[4] Cf. Article, 'Lulle' by Père E. Longpré in *Dictionnaire de théologie catholique*,
vol. 9.

CHAPTER XLIV

GILES OF ROME AND HENRY OF GHENT

(a) Giles of Rome. *Life and works—The independence of Giles as a thinker—Essence and existence—Form and matter; soul and body—Political theory.*

(b) Henry of Ghent. *Life and works—Eclecticism, illustrated by doctrines of illumination and innatism—Idea of metaphysics—Essence and existence—Proofs of God's existence—General spirit and significance of Henry's philosophy.*

(a) Giles of Rome

1. Giles (Aegidius) of Rome was born in 1247 or a little earlier and entered the Order of the Hermits of St. Augustine about 1260. He made his studies at Paris and seems to have attended the lectures of St. Thomas Aquinas from 1269 to 1272. It appears that he composed the *Errores Philosophorum* about 1270, in which he enumerates the errors of Aristotle, Averroes, Avicenna, Algazel, Alkindi and Maimonides. The Commentaries on the *De generatione et corruptione*, the *De Anima*, the *Physics*, the *Metaphysics* and the logical treatises of Aristotle, the Commentary on the first book of the *Sentences* and the works entitled *Theoremata de Corpore Christi* and *De plurificatione intellectus possibilis* were apparently also written before 1277. In that year occurred the famous condemnation by Stephen Tempier, Bishop of Paris (March 7th); but between Christmas 1277 and Easter 1278 Giles wrote the *De gradibus formarum*, in which he came out strongly against the doctrine of plurality of forms. For this and similar offences Giles was called upon to make a retractation; but he refused and was excluded from the University of Paris before he had completed his theological studies. In his period of absence from Paris he wrote the *Theoremata de esse et essentia* and his Commentary on the second and third books of the *Sentences*.

In 1285 Giles returned to Paris and was permitted to receive the licentiate in theology, though he had to make a public retractation first. He then taught theology at Paris, until he was elected General of the Order in 1292. In 1295 he was appointed Archbishop of Bourges. The works he wrote after his return to Paris in 1285 include *Quaestiones disputatae de esse et essentia*, *Quaestiones Quodlibetales*, a Commentary on the *Liber de Causis*, exegetical works such as the *In Hexaëmeron* and political treatises like the *De regimine principum* and the *De potestate ecclesiastica*. Giles died at Avignon in 1316.

2. Giles of Rome has sometimes been represented as a 'Thomist'; but though he found himself in agreement with St. Thomas on some points, as against the Franciscans, he can scarcely be called a disciple of St. Thomas: he was an independent thinker, and his independence shows itself even in matters where he might at first sight appear to be following St. Thomas. For instance, though he certainly maintained a real distinction between essence and existence, he equally certainly went beyond what St. Thomas taught on this question. Moreover, though he rejected the plurality of forms in 1277, going so far as to declare that this doctrine was contrary to the Catholic faith,[1] it has been shown that this had not always been his view. In the Commentary on the *De Anima*[2] he spoke hesitantly and doubtfully on the unicity of the substantial form in man, and the same is true in regard to the *Theoremata de Corpore Christi*,[3] while in the *Errores Philosophorum* he had stated that the doctrine of the unicity of the substantial form in man is false.[4] It is clear, then, that he began with the 'Augustinian' or Franciscan view, and that he advanced to the opposite theory only gradually.[5] No doubt he was influenced by St. Thomas in the matter, but it does not look as though he simply accepted Thomas's doctrine without question. He did not hesitate to criticise Thomist positions or to deviate from them when he wished to; and when he agreed with them, it is evident that he agreed as a result of personal thought and reflection, not because he was or had been a disciple of St. Thomas. The legend of Giles of Rome as a 'Thomist' was really a conclusion from the fact that he listened to lectures by St. Thomas for a period; but attendance at a professor's lectures is not a sure guarantee of discipleship.

3. Giles of Rome was considerably influenced by the neo-Platonist theory of participation. Existence (*esse*) flows from God and is a participation of the divine existence. It is received by essence and is really distinct from essence. That it is received by essence can be empirically established as regards corporeal things, since they have a beginning of existence and are not always joined to existence, a fact which shows that they are in potentiality to existence, and that existence is really distinct from the essence

[1] *De gradibus formarum*, f. 211 v.   [2] I, 12, 16.   [3] Prop. 47, f. 36 v.   [4] I, 11.
[5] On the question of the dating and authenticity of the *Errores Philosophorum* see the edition by J. Koch, listed in the bibliography.

of the sensible thing. Indeed, if existence were not really distinct from essence in all created things, creatures would not be creatures: they would exist in virtue of their own essence and would thus be independent of God's creative activity. The real distinction is, therefore, an essential safeguard of the doctrine of creation. Needless to say, the statement that created existence is a participation of the divine existence was not meant to imply pantheism. It was precisely the created character of finite things, of the participations, which Giles wanted to uphold. By essence Giles meant, in the case of material things, the composite of form and matter. The composite or corporeal essence possesses a mode of being (*modus essendi*) which is derived from the union of form and matter (in the case of immaterial creatures the mode of being comes from the form alone); but it does not of itself possess existence in the proper sense (*esse simpliciter*), which is received. The attribution of a *modus essendi* to the essence would seem to make of the latter a thing, and this aspect of the theory is accentuated by Giles's explicit teaching that essence and existence are not only really distinct, but also separable. In fact, he does not hesitate to speak of them as separable things.

This exaggerated version of the theory of the real distinction led to a lively controversy between Giles of Rome and Henry of Ghent, who attacked Giles's doctrine in his first *Quodlibet* (1276). The *Quaestiones disputatae de esse et essentia* contained Giles's answer to Henry; but the latter returned to the attack in his tenth *Quodlibet* (1286), to which Giles retorted in his twelfth *Quaestio disputata*, maintaining therein that unless existence and essence were really distinct, in the sense in which he taught the real distinction, annihilation of a creature would be impossible. He continued to hold, therefore, that his real distinction is absolutely necessary, in order to safeguard the creature's total dependence on God. The fact that he taught a real distinction between essence and existence links him with St. Thomas; but St. Thomas certainly did not teach that essence and existence are two separable things: this was an original, if somewhat strange contribution of Giles himself.

4. Giles of Rome was inclined, as his theory of essence and existence shows, to suppose that wherever the mind detects a real distinction there is separability. Thus the mind abstracts the universal from the individual (abstraction being the work of the passive intellect, when the active intellect has illumined the passive

intellect and the phantasm) by apprehending the form of the object without the matter. Therefore, form and matter are really distinct and separable. Now, matter, which is found only in corporeal things, is the principle of individuation, and it follows that if matter and all the individual conditions which follow from it could be removed, the individuals of any given species would be one. Perhaps this is a legitimate conclusion from the doctrine of matter as the principle of individuation; but in any case the tendency to ultra-realism is obvious, and Giles's inclination to equate 'really distinct from' with 'separable from' is partly responsible.

Again, form (soul) and body are really distinct and separable. There is nothing novel in this idea, of course; but Giles suggested that the body may remain a body, that is, numerically the same body, after separation from the form, since before actual separation it was separable, and actual separation does not change its numerical identity.[1] Body in this sense would mean extended and organised matter. Incidentally, this theory afforded him a simple explanation of the way in which Christ's body was numerically identical before and after Christ's death on the Cross. He neither had to have recourse to the doctrine of a *forma corporeitatis* (in which he did not believe) nor was he compelled to refer the numerical identity of Christ's body in the sepulchre with His body before death simply to its union with the Divinity. Moreover, one of the reasons why Giles of Rome attacked the doctrine of plurality of forms as incompatible with theological orthodoxy was that, in his opinion, it endangered the doctrine of Christ's death. If there are several forms in man and only one of them, which is peculiar to man and is not found in other animals, is separated at death, then Christ could not be said to have undergone bodily death. The theological reason was not his only reason by any means for attacking the plurality of forms; he believed, for instance, that different forms are contrary and cannot be found together in the same substance.

5. The *De ecclesiastica potestate* is of interest not merely intrinsically, as treating of the relation between Church and State, but also because it was one of the works which were utilised by Pope Boniface VIII in the composition of his famous Bull, *Unam*

[1] It might appear that on Giles's theory the soul (i.e. the form) in a state of separation from the body would not be individual; but it must be remembered that for him, as for St. Thomas, it was individuated by union with matter and retained its individuality.

Sanctam (November 18th, 1302). In his *De regimine principum*, written for the prince who was to become Philip the Fair of France, Giles wrote in dependence on Aristotle and St. Thomas; but in the *De potestate ecclesiastica* he propounded a doctrine of papal absolutism and sovereignty and of the Pope's jurisdiction even in temporal matters which was aimed especially against the pretensions of monarchs and which was most acceptable to Boniface VIII. In this work he relied much more on the attitude shown by St. Augustine towards the State than on the political thought of St. Thomas, and what St. Augustine had said with the pagan empires principally in mind was applied by Giles to contemporary kingdoms, the doctrine of Papal supremacy being added.[1] There are indeed two powers, two swords, that of the Pope and that of the king; but temporal power is subject to the spiritual. 'If the earthly power goes wrong, it will be judged by the spiritual power as by its superior; but if the spiritual power, and especially the power of the supreme pontiff, acts wrongly, it can be judged by God alone.'[2] When Philip IV of France accused Boniface VIII of asserting, in the *Unam Sanctam*, that the Holy See has direct power over kings even in temporal matters, the Pope replied that that had not been his intention: he did not mean to usurp the power of kings, but to make it clear that kings, like any other members of the Church, were subject to the Church *ratione peccati*. It would appear, however, that Giles of Rome, who spoke, of course, simply as a private theologian, went much further in this matter than Boniface VIII. He admits that there are two swords and two powers and that the one power is vested in the monarch, the other in the Church, and especially in the Papacy; but he goes on to say that although priests and especially the supreme pontiff ought not under the new law, that is, in the Christian dispensation, to wield the material sword as well as the spiritual sword; this is not because the Church does not possess the material sword, but rather because it possesses the material sword, *non ad usum, sed ad nutum*. In other words, just as Christ possessed all power, spiritual and temporal, but did not actually use His temporal power, so the Church possesses power in temporal matters, though it is not expedient for her to exercise this power immediately and continually. Just as the body is ordered to the soul and should be subject to the soul, so the temporal power is ordered to the

[1] I do not mean to imply that Augustine rejected the pre-eminence of the Roman See; but it would be absurd to say that he maintained the doctrine of Papal jurisdiction in temporal affairs.   [2] I, 5.

spiritual power and should be subject to it, even in temporal matters. The Church has, then, supreme jurisdiction even in temporal matters; and the logical consequence is that kings are little more than lieutenants of the Church.[1] 'All temporal things are placed under the dominion and power of the Church and especially of the supreme pontiff.'[2] This theory was followed by James of Viterbo in his *De regimine Christiano* before September 1302.

In 1287 the signal honour was paid to Giles of Rome of being made the Doctor of his Order during his own lifetime, not only in regard to what he had already written, but also in regard to what he should write in the future.

(b) Henry of Ghent

6. Henry of Ghent was born at Tournai or at Ghent at a date which cannot be determined. (His family came originally from Ghent in any case; but it was not a noble family, as legend had it.) By 1267 he was a Canon of Tournai, and in 1276 he became Archdeacon of Bruges. In 1279 he was made principal Archdeacon of Tournai. His archidiaconal duties do not seem to have been very exacting, as he taught at Paris, first in the faculty of arts and later (from 1276) in that of theology. In 1277 he was a member of the commission of theologians which assisted Stephen Tempier, Bishop of Paris. His works include a *Summa Theologica*, fifteen *Quodlibets, Quaestiones super Metaphysicam Aristotelis* (1–6), *Syncathegorematum Liber* and a *Commentum in Librum de Causis*; but it does not appear that the last three works can be attributed to him with certainty, and the same can be said of the Commentary on the *Physics* of Aristotle. It is, therefore, the *Summa Theologica* and the *Quodlibets* which constitute the sure source for our knowledge of Henry's teaching. He died on June 29th, 1293. He was never a member of the Servite Order, as was once maintained.

7. Henry of Ghent was an eclectic thinker and can be called neither an Augustinian nor an Aristotelian. This eclecticism may be illustrated by his theory of knowledge. If one read a proposition such as *omnis cognitio nostra a sensu ortum habet,*[3] one might suppose that Henry was a decided Aristotelian, with little sympathy for Augustinianism, and especially if one read the proposition in conjunction with his statement that man can know that which is true in the creature without any special divine illumination, but simply through his natural powers aided by God's ordinary

concurrence.[1] But this is only one aspect of his thought. The knowledge of creatures which we can attain through sense-experience is but a superficial knowledge, and though we can without illumination know what is true in the creature, we cannot without illumination know its truth. The reason why knowledge based simply on sense-experience is superficial, is this. The *species intelligibilis* contains no more than was contained in the *species sensibilis*: by the latter we apprehend the object in its singularity and by the former we apprehend the object in its universal aspect; but neither the one nor the other gives us the intelligible essence of the object in its relation to the divine ideas, and without the apprehension of the intelligible essence we cannot form a certain judgement concerning the object. The 'truth' (*Veritas*) of the object consists in its relation to the unchanging truth, and in order to apprehend this relation we need the divine illumination.[2] Thus when Henry of Ghent says that our knowledge comes from sense, he restricts the extension of 'knowledge': 'it is one thing to know concerning a creature that which is true in it, and it is another thing to know its truth.' The 'truth' of a thing is conceived by him in an Augustinian manner, and to apprehend it illumination is necessary. He may have made comparatively little use of the illumination theory and watered down Augustinianism to a certain extent, but the Augustinian element was certainly present in his thought: the natural operations of sense and intellect explain what one might call man's normal knowledge, which is a comparatively superficial knowledge of objects, but they do not and cannot explain the whole range of possible human knowledge.

A similar eclectic tendency can be seen in his doctrine of innatism. He rejected the Platonic doctrine of innatism and reminiscence and he rejected the theory of Avicenna that in this life ideas are impressed by the *Dator formarum*; but he did not accept the doctrine of Aristotle (as commonly interpreted) that all our ideas are formed by reflection on the data of sense-experience. Henry made his own the statement of Avicenna that the ideas of being, thing, and necessity are of such a kind that they are imprinted immediately on the soul by an impression which owes nothing to anterior and better-known ideas.[3] On the other hand, the primary ideas, of which the most important and the ultimate is that of being, are not innate in the strict sense, but are conceived

---

[1] *Summa*, 1, 2, 11 and 13. [2] *Ibid.*, 1, 2, 26.
[3] Avicenna, *Metaphysics*, 1, 2, 1; Henry, *Summa*, 1, 12, 9; 3, 1, 7.

together with experience of sense-objects, even if they are not derived from that experience.[1] The mind seems to draw these ideas out of itself or rather to form them from within on the occasion of sense-experience.[2] As the idea of being embraces both uncreated and created being,[3] the idea of God may be called innate in a certain sense; but this does not mean that man has from birth an actual idea of God, the origin of which is quite independent of experience: the idea is only virtually innate, in the sense that a man forms it from the idea of being, which is itself presupposed by experience of concrete objects but does not arise in clear consciousness, is not actually formed, until experience is enjoyed. As metaphysics really consist in an investigation of the idea of being and in the realisation of the relation between the intelligible essences of created being and uncreated being, one would expect that the necessity of illumination would be emphasised; but Henry frequently describes the genesis of ideas and of knowledge without any reference to a special illumination, possibly under the influence of Aristotle and of Avicenna. His tendency to eclecticism seems to have led to a certain carelessness in regard to consistency.

8. While the natural philosopher or *physicus* starts with the singular object and then forms by abstraction the universal notion of the sensible object, the metaphysician starts with the idea of being (or *res* or *aliquid*) and proceeds to discover the intelligible essences virtually contained in that idea.[4] There is a certain overlapping, of course, between the provinces of physics and metaphysics, since, for example, when the metaphysician says that man is a rational animal, he apprehends the same object as the physicist, who says that man is a body and a soul; but the starting-point and the mode of approach of the metaphysician is different from that of the physicist. The metaphysician, proceeding from the more universal to the less universal, from genus to species, defines the intelligible essence of man, whereas the physicist starts from the individual man and by abstraction apprehends and states the physical components of all men.

Being or *res* in the widest sense comprises *res secundum opinionem* (such as a golden mountain) which have only mental being, and *res secundum veritatem*, which have an actual or possible extramental existence,[5] and it is being in the second sense which

---

[1] Cf. *Summa*, 1, 11, 6; 1, 5, 5.   [2] Cf. *ibid.*, 1, 11, 18.
[3] For the qualification which makes this statement not strictly true, see section 10.   [4] *Quodlibet*, 4, 4, 143.   [5] *Ibid.*, 7, 1, 389.

is *ens metaphysicum*, the object of metaphysics. Just as *ens* in the widest sense is divided analogically, so is *ens metaphysicum* divided analogically into that which is *ipsum esse*, God, and that *cui convenit esse*, creatures. Being is thus not a genus or predicament. Again, being in the last sense, *aliquid cui convenit vel natum est convenire esse*, comprises and is divided analogically into substances, to which it pertains to exist in themselves (*esse in se*) and accidents, to which it pertains to exist in another (*esse in alio*), that is, in a substance. It is quite true that for Aristotle too metaphysics was the science of being as being; but for Aristotle the idea of being was not the starting-point, the analysis of which leads to the discovery of the analogical divisions of being: Henry of Ghent was inspired in this matter by the thought of Avicenna, whose philosophy was also influential in the building of the Scotist system. According to both Henry of Ghent and Scotus the metaphysician studies the idea of being, and metaphysics move primarily on the conceptual level.

It might appear that on this view not only is it difficult to effect a passage from the essential level to the existential level, but also that there would be confusion between the *res secundum opinionem* and the *res secundum veritatem*. However, Henry maintained that essences which are actualised or which are objectively possible have and can be discerned as having a certain reality of their own, an *esse essentiae*, the possession of which distinguishes them from pure *entia rationis*. The theory of *esse essentiae*, which Henry took from Avicenna, must not be understood, however, to imply a kind of inchoate existence, as though the essence had an extramental existence of a rudimentary sort; Henry accused Giles of Rome of maintaining a theory of this kind: it means that the essence exists actually in thought, that it is definable, that it is an intelligible essence.[1] Its intelligibility, its intrinsic possibility, distinguishes it from the *res secundum opinionem*, from the notion, for example, of a being half man and half goat, which is a contradictory notion. As to the relation between the essential level and the existential level, it is evident enough that we can know the existence of the singular only through experience of the singular (there is no question in Henry's philosophy of any deduction of singulars), while the intelligible essence, which is universal in character, is not deduced from the notion of being so much as 'arranged' under the notion of being. As we have seen, the natural philosopher detects

---

[1] Cf. *Quodlibet*, 3, 2, 80.

in man his physical components, body and soul; but man is defined by the metaphysician as a rational animal, in terms of genus and species, in terms of his intelligible essence. This intelligible essence is thus arranged under the notion of being and its (analogical) 'contractions', as a particular kind of substance; but that man actually exists is known only by experience. On the other hand, the intelligible essence is a reflection (an *exemplatum* or *ideatum*) of the Idea in God, the exemplar or absolute essence, and God knows singular things through essence considered as multipliable in numerically different substances or *supposita*: there are no ideas of singular things as such in God, but the latter are known by Him in and through the specific essence.[1] From this it would seem to follow either that singular things are contained in the universal idea in some way and are, theoretically at least, deducible from it or that one must relinquish any prospect of rendering singular things intelligible.[2] Henry would not allow that individuality adds any real element to the specific essence:[3] individual things differ from one another simply in virtue of the fact that they exist actually and extramentally. If, then, the individuation cannot be explained in terms of a real added element, it must be explained in terms of a negation, a double negation, that of internal or intrinsic division and that of identity with any other being. Scotus attacked this view on the ground that the principle of individuation cannot be a negation and that the negation must presuppose something positive; but, of course, Henry did presuppose something positive, namely existence.[4]

The above may seem a confusing and perhaps somewhat irrelevant account of varied items of Henry's doctrine, but it is meant to bring out a fundamental difficulty in his system. In so far as metaphysics are a study of the idea of being and of intelligible essences and in so far as individuals are considered as intelligible only as contained in the essence, Henry's metaphysic is of a Platonic type, whereas his theory of individuation looks forward to the Ockhamist view that there is no need to seek for any principle of individuation, since a thing is individual by the very fact that it exists. If the first point of view demands an explanation of objects in terms of essence, the second demands an explanation in terms of existence, of creation and making; and

---

[1] Scotus attacked this theory of Henry of Ghent.
[2] Cf. *Quodlibet*, 2, 1, 46.   [3] *Ibid.*, 8, 57 f.
[4] For Henry's doctrine of the double negation, cf. *Quodlibet*, 5, 8, 245 ff.

Henry juxtaposes the two points of view without achieving any adequate reconciliation.

9. We have seen that Henry of Ghent endowed the intelligible essence with an *esse essentiae*, as distinguished from the *esse existentiae*. What is the nature of the distinction in question? In the first place Henry rejected the theory of Giles of Rome, who transported the distinction on to the physical plane and made it a distinction between two separable things, essence and existence. Against this view Henry argued in his first (9), tenth (7) and eleventh (3) *Quodlibets*. If existence were distinct from essence in the sense postulated by Giles of Rome, existence would itself be an essence and would require another existence in order to exist; so that an infinite process would be involved. Moreover, what would existence, really distinct from essence, be? Substance or accident? One could maintain neither answer. Furthermore, Henry rejected the real distinction understood as a metaphysical distinction: the essence of an existent object is in no way indifferent to existence or non-existence; in the concrete order a thing either is or it is not. Existence is not a constitutive element or principle of a thing, of such a kind that the thing would be a synthesis of essence and existence; any synthesis there may be, that is, by way of addition of existence to essence, is the work of the mind.[1] On the other hand, the content of the concept of essence is not identical with the content of the concept of existence: the idea of an existent essence contains more, to our view, than the mere idea of essence as such. The distinction, therefore, though not a real distinction, is not a purely logical distinction, but an 'intentional' distinction, expressing different *intentiones* concerning the same simple thing.[2]

But if the actualised essence contains more than the essence conceived as possible and if the real distinction between essence and existence is not to be reintroduced, what can this 'more' be? According to Henry of Ghent, it consists in a relation, the relation of effect to Cause, of creature to Creator. It is one and the same thing for a creature to exist and to depend on God:[3] to be an effect of God and to have *esse existentiae ab ipso* are the same, namely a *respectus* or relation to God. The essence considered merely as possible is an *exemplatum* and depends on the divine knowledge, whereas the actualised or existent essence depends on

[1] Cf. *Quodlibet*, 3, 9, 100; *Summa*, 21, 4, 10.
[2] Cf. *Summa*, 21, 4, 7 ff.; 27, 1, 25; 28, 4, 7.   [3] *Quodlibet*, 10, 7, 153.

the divine creative power,[1] so that the notion of the latter contains more than the notion of the former; but though the relation of the actualised essence to God is a real relation of dependence, it is not distinct from the essence in the concrete order with a real distinction. From the metaphysical point of view, then, God alone can be thought without relation to any other being; the creature, apart from the twofold relationship to God (as *exemplatum* to Exemplar and as effect to Cause), is nothing. Through the first relationship *by itself* the essence does not exist 'outside' God; by the second relationship it exists as an actualised essence; but apart from that relationship it has no *esse existentiae*, since the *esse existentiae* and the *respectus ad Deum* are the same.

10. Henry of Ghent admitted the *a posteriori* proofs of God's existence; but he regarded them as physical in character (his ideas of physics or natural philosophy and of metaphysics could lead to no other conclusion) and as inferior to the *a priori* proof. The physical proofs can lead us to the recognition of a pre-eminent Being, but they cannot reveal to us the essence of that Being: as far as these proofs are concerned, the existence of God is an existence of fact, which is not revealed as also an existence of right. The metaphysical proof, however, makes us see God's existence as necessarily contained in, or rather identical with His essence.[2] Similarly, it is only the metaphysical proof which can firmly establish the unicity of God, by showing that the divine essence has an intrinsic repugnance to any multiplication.[3]

The *a priori* idea of God, that of the supreme conceivable simple Perfection, which cannot not exist, was assumed by Henry of Ghent as one of the primary notions, namely Being, thing or essence, and Necessity. One might expect that he would attempt to deduce the notions of necessary Being and contingent being from an original univocal concept of being; but in point of fact he refused to admit the univocal character of the concept of being. Our realisation of what necessary Being is and our realisation of what contingent being is grow *pari passu*: we cannot have an imperfect knowledge of the latter without an imperfect knowledge of the former, nor a perfect knowledge of the latter without a perfect knowledge of the former.[4] There is no one univocal concept of being common to God and creatures: there are two concepts, that of necessary Being and that of contingent being, and our

---

[1] *Summa*, 21, 4, 10.
[2] Cf. *ibid.*, 24, 6, 7; 22, 4; 22, 5.
[3] *Ibid.*, 22, 3; 25, 2-3.
[4] *Ibid.*, 24, 8, 6; 7, 7.

concept of being must be one or the other. We can, however, confuse the two. There are two sorts of indetermination, negative indetermination and privative indetermination. A being is negatively indeterminate when it excludes all possibility of determination in the sense of finitude, and God alone is indeterminate in this sense, while a being is privatively indeterminate when it can or must be determined but is not yet determined or is considered in abstraction from its determinations.[1] Thus if one considers being in abstraction from its determinations, one is considering *created* being, which must in the concrete be either substance or accident but which can be considered in abstraction from these determinations, and this concept of the *privative indeterminatum* does not comprise God, the *negative indeterminatum*. But the mind can easily confuse the two concepts and conceive them as one, although they are in reality two. In saying this and in excluding any univocal concept of being common to God and creatures Henry of Ghent wished to avoid the Avicennian idea of necessary creation, which would seem to follow if one could deduce from an original univocal concept of being both necessary and created being; but he came perilously near to teaching, and he was accused by Scotus of so teaching, that the two concepts of being are equivocal. It is perfectly true that Henry expounded a doctrine of analogy and asserted that 'being' is not used purely equivocally of God and creatures;[2] but he insisted so much that the concept of being is either the concept of God or the concept of creatures and that there is no positive community between them, but only negative, (without there being any positive foundation whatsoever for the negation, i.e. the 'indetermination') that there would seem to be considerable justification for Scotus's accusation.[3] Scotus objected that on Henry's view every argument from creatures to God must be fallacious, and it would indeed appear that if that aspect of Henry's thought to which Scotus objected is emphasised, the only way of safeguarding man's philosophical knowledge of God would be to recognise the existence of an *a priori* idea of God, not derived from experience of creatures.

11. Henry of Ghent was, it has been said, an eclectic, and of this eclecticism some examples have been given. While he combated the theory of the real distinction put forward by Giles of Rome (and even that of St. Thomas, though Giles was the

---

[1] Cf. *Summa*, 21, 2, 14.   [2] Cf. *ibid.*, 21, 2, 6 and 8.
[3] Cf. *ibid.*, 21, 2, 17; 21, 2, *ad* 3.

particular object of attack), while he refused to allow the possibility of creation from eternity, and while he rejected the Thomist theory of individuation, he also rejected the doctrine of universal hylomorphism in creatures and opposed the doctrine of plurality of forms so far as material beings other than man were concerned. In the first *Quodlibet* Henry adopted the Thomist theory of the unicity of the substantial form in man, but in the second *Quodlibet* he changed his opinion and admitted the *forma corporeitatis* in man. On the other hand, while he postulated special illumination of a restricted type and while he maintained the superiority of the free will to the intellect, he borrowed a good deal from Aristotle, was strongly influenced by the philosophy of Avicenna and, in his doctrine of individuation, bears more resemblance to the thinkers of the Ockhamist movement than to his predecessors. Yet to call a philosopher an 'eclectic' without qualification implies that he achieved no synthesis and that his philosophy is a collection of juxtaposed opinions borrowed from various sources. In the case of Henry of Ghent, to picture him in this light would be to commit an injustice. He was certainly not always consistent, nor do his opinions and tendencies of thought always harmonise well with one another; but he belonged definitely to the Platonic tradition in Christian thought and his borrowings from Aristotle and Aristotelian thinkers do not really affect this fact; St. Bonaventure himself had utilised Aristotle, but he was none the less an Augustinian. The main tendency of Henry as metaphysician was to construct a metaphysic of the intelligible, a metaphysic of essences rather than of the concrete, and this marks him off as a philosopher of the Platonic tradition.

But if Henry belonged to the Platonic tradition, he was also a Christian philosopher. Thus he maintained clearly the doctrine of free creation out of nothing. He did not attempt to deduce created existence from the idea of being, and in his desire to avoid making creation necessary he rejected the univocity of the concept of being as a starting-point for metaphysical deduction. Plato himself, of course, never attempted an 'idealist' deduction of this type; but Henry, unlike Plato or any other pagan Greek philosopher, had a clear idea of creation and he stressed the dependence of all created things on God, maintaining that they were nothing apart from their relationship to Him. This prominent Christian element in his thought sets him in the Augustinian tradition, from which he drew his doctrines of illumination and of virtually innate

Ideas, of ideas which can be formed from within. On the other hand, while he tried to avoid what he considered to be the faults of the philosophy of Avicenna, his metaphysic was strongly influenced by the Moslem philosopher's thought, so that M. Gilson has been able to speak in this connection of an *augustinisme avicennisant*. Apart from the fact that Henry brings together God in His function as illuminator (St. Augustine) with the separate active intellect of Avicenna (a *rapprochement* which was not peculiar to Henry), his doctrine of mitigated innatism naturally inclined him to a metaphysic of intelligible essences rather than to a metaphysic of the concrete, and, like Avicenna, he attributed a certain reality or objectivity, though not independent of God, to essences considered as possible, essences which follow necessarily from the divine intellect and so are, in themselves at least, deducible. But when it was a question of existence, of the concrete existent world of creation, he had to part company with Avicenna. The latter, regarding the divine will as subject to the same necessity as the divine intellect, made the emergence of existences parallel to the emergence of essences, the subordinate Intelligences being responsible for prolonging the activity of the first Cause and bringing about the transition from the universal to the particular; but Henry of Ghent, as a Christian thinker, could not hold this: he had to admit free creation and also creation in time. He saw quite well that the sensible and concrete cannot be rendered fully intelligible, if to render fully intelligible means to explain in terms of essence, and therefore he made a sharp distinction between metaphysics and physics, each of the sciences having its own starting-point and mode of procedure.

In spite, however, of the Platonic and Avicennian tendencies in his thought, Henry of Ghent helped in a certain sense to prepare the way for nominalism. Insistence on illumination easily leads to a certain scepticism concerning the mind's power of achieving a metaphysical system based on experience, while Henry's tendency to simplification when dealing with the created world (for example, by the denial of any real distinction between essence and existence and by his theory of individuation, which involves the rejection of realism) may, if considered by itself, be regarded as heralding the simplifying tendencies and the conceptualism of the fourteenth century. Of course, this is but one aspect of his philosophy and it is not the most important and characteristic, but it is a real aspect none the less. Ockham criticised Henry of

Ghent's thought under its other aspects; but that does not mean that Henry's thought was without influence on the movement of which Ockham was the chief figure. Henry has been called an 'intermediary' figure, intermediary between the thirteenth and fourteenth centuries, and this can hardly be denied; but before Ockhamism arose, Duns Scotus, who so frequently criticised Henry, as Henry had criticised Giles of Rome, was to attempt to develop and justify a synthesis of Augustinianism and Aristotelianism, thus endeavouring, in spite of his polemics against Henry of Ghent, to accomplish satisfactorily what Henry had not accomplished satisfactorily.

CHAPTER XLV

SCOTUS—I

Life—Works—Spirit of Scotus's philosophy.

1. JOHN DUNS SCOTUS, *Doctor Subtilis*, was born in Scotland, at Maxton in the county of Roxburgh, his family name, Duns, being originally taken from a place in the county of Berwick. That he was a Scotsman can be now taken as certain, not simply from the fact that by his time Scotsmen and Irishmen were no longer called indiscriminately *Scoti*, but also as having been proved by the discovery of a series of documents, the authority of which can scarcely be called in question. But if the country of his birth is certain, the date is not so certain, though it is probable that he was born in 1265 or 1266, and that he entered the Order of Friars Minor in 1278, taking the habit in 1280 and being ordained priest in 1291. The traditional date of his death is November 8th, 1308. He died at Cologne and was buried in the Franciscan Church in that city.

The dates of Scotus's academic career are by no means certain; but it appears that he studied at Paris under Gonsalvus of Spain from 1293 to 1296, after a brief sojourn at Oxford. According to the traditional view Scotus then went to Oxford, where he commented on the *Sentences* and produced the *Opus Oxoniense* or Oxford Commentary on the *Sentences*. The fact that in the fourth book of the *Opus Oxoniense* Scotus quotes a bull of Benedict XI, of January 31st, 1304, is no certain argument against the traditional view, as Scotus certainly retouched and made later additions to the work.[1] In 1302 Scotus returned to Paris and commented there on the *Sentences*; but in 1303 he was banished from Paris, as he had supported the Papal party against King Philip the Fair. Where he spent the time of banishment is not quite clear: Oxford, Cologne and Bologna have all been suggested. In any case he taught at Oxford in the academic year 1303–4, returning to Paris in 1304 and receiving the doctorate in theology in 1305. It is possible that he returned to Oxford again for a short while, but he was certainly at Paris, engaged in commenting on the *Sentences*,

---

[1] Scotus is said to have taught at Cambridge also, either before or after his teaching at Oxford.

when he was sent to Cologne in the summer of 1307. At Cologne
he resumed his work of teaching; but in 1308, as already mentioned,
he died, when about forty-two or forty-three years of age.

2. The uncertainty concerning the exact course of Scotus's life
is to be regretted; but far more to be regretted is the uncertainty
concerning the authentic character of some works attributed to
him in the edition of Luke Wadding. Happily, however, the
general authenticity of the two great commentaries on the
Sentences is not in question, though neither the *Opus Oxoniense*
nor the *Reportata Parisiensia* in their traditional form can be
ascribed in their totality to Scotus. As to the *Opus Oxoniense*,
the original text as Scotus left it (the *Ordinatio*, of which no
manuscript has yet been discovered) was added to by disciples
who wished to complete the work of the master by presenting a
complete exposition of his thought, though in some subsequent
codices the scribes attempted to note the additions which had
been made. A similar situation presents itself in regard to the
Reportata Parisiensia, since in their case too the desire to give a
complete account of Scotus's teaching led the master's disciples
to assemble together partial accounts from various sources, without, however, making any serious attempt to discover the respective authority and value of the different parts of the mosaic. The
task of the Commission appointed to superintend the production
of the critical edition of Scotus's works is, then, no easy one; but
although the Oxford and Paris Commentaries represent basically
the thought of Scotus, no secure and final picture of that thought
can be given until the critical edition of the Commentaries appears,
more especially until the original *Ordinatio* or *Liber Scoti* is
published, free from accretions.

The authentic character of the *De primo principio* is not in
question, though the arguments adduced by Father Ciganotto to
show that it was Scotus's last work, written at Cologne, do not
appear to be decisive. The *Quaestiones Quodlibetales* are also
authentic,[1] as are also the forty-six *Collationes* (Wadding knew of
only forty, but C. Balic discovered another six) and the first nine
books of the *Quaestiones subtilissimae super libros Metaphysicorum
Aristotelis*. As to the *De Anima*, the question of its authenticity
has been a matter for dispute. Pelster maintained that it was
authentic, while Longpré tried to show that it was unauthentic,

---

[1] P. Glorieux: *La littérature quodlibétique*, t. 2 (Bibliothèque thomiste, 21),
Paris, 1935.

though his arguments were declared insufficient by Fleig. It is now generally accepted as authentic, even by Longpré. On the other hand, the *Grammatica speculativa* is to be attributed to Thomas of Erfurt, while the *De rerum principio* is also unauthentic, being probably, in part at least, a plagiarism from the *Quaestiones Quodlibetales* of Godfrey of Fontaines. Also unauthentic are the *Metaphysica textualis* (probably to be attributed to Antoine André), the *Conclusiones metaphysicae* and the commentaries on Aristotle's *Physics* and *Meteorology*.

To determine with certainty which are and which are not authentic works of Scotus is obviously a matter of importance. Some doctrines which appear in the *De rerum principio*, for example, do not appear in the certainly authentic works, so that if one were to accept the authenticity of the *De rerum principio* (as already mentioned, it is now rejected), one would have to assume that Scotus first taught a doctrine which he later abandoned, since it would clearly be out of the question to assume that his thought contained patent contradictions. To assert a change of opinion on some comparatively minor doctrine when no such change actually took place might not perhaps be a mistake of great importance, even if it resulted in an inaccurate account of Scotus's doctrinal development; but the question of authenticity or unauthenticity is of much greater importance where the *Theoremata* are concerned. In this work the author states that it cannot be proved that there is only one ultimate Principle or that God is infinite or that He is intelligent, and so on, such statements being, at first sight at least, in clear contradiction with the teaching of the certainly authentic works of Scotus. If, then, one were to accept the *Theoremata* as authentic, one would either have to assume an astonishing *volte-face* on Scotus's part or one would have to attempt a difficult task of interpretation and conciliation.

The first attack on the authenticity of the *Theoremata* was that of Father de Basly in the year 1918, and this attack was continued by Father Longpré. The latter argued that no manuscript had yet been discovered which explicitly attributed the work to Scotus, that the teaching contained in the work is contrary to that contained in Scotus's certainly authentic works, that Ockham and Thomas of Sutton, who attacked Scotus's natural theology, never quote the work as his, that the doctrine of the *Theoremata* is nominalistic in character and must be attributed to the Ockhamist School, and that John of Reading, who knew Scotus, quotes from the authentic works when he is dealing with the question whether God's existence can be proved or not by the natural light of reason, but does not mention the *Theoremata*. These arguments appeared to be convincing and were generally accepted as settling the question, until Father Balic brought forward other arguments to contest Longpré's view. Noting that Longpré's arguments were, for the most part, based on internal evidence, Balic tried to show not only that the arguments drawn from internal evidence were unconvincing, but also that there were good arguments drawn from external evidence to prove that the *Theoremata* were really the work of Scotus. Thus four codices explicitly attribute the work to Scotus, while in the fourth chapter of the *De primo principio* occur the words *In sequenti, scilicet in Theorematibus, ponentur credibilia*. The phrase *scilicet in Theorematibus* cannot have been added by Wadding, since it is found in some codices. In addition, the *Theoremata* are given as the work of Scotus by, among others, Joannes Canonicus, a fourteenth-century Scotist. Baudry then tried to show that even if some of the theories contained in the *Theoremata* betray a nominalistic spirit, the fundamental doctrines of the work are not of Ockhamist origin, and Gilson (in the *Archives d'histoire doctrinale et littéraire du moyen âge*, 1937–8) attempted to prove that the first sixteen *Theoremata* do not stand in contradiction with the certainly authentic works of Scotus. According to Gilson, Scotus speaks in the *Theoremata* (supposing that the work is really by him) as a philosopher showing what the unaided human reason can achieve, while in the *Opus Oxoniense*, which is a theological work, he shows what can be achieved by metaphysics aided by theology. Even if the conclusions arrived at in the *Theoremata* seem to approximate to those of Ockham, the spirit is different, since Scotus believed that the theologian can give metaphysical and demonstrative arguments for God's existence and attributes, whereas Ockham denied this and had recourse to faith alone. In the latest edition (1944) of his work, *La philosophie au moyen âge*, Gilson leaves the question of the authenticity or unauthenticity of the *Theoremata* an open question; but he maintains that if the *Theoremata* are the work of Scotus, there is no difficulty in reconciling the doctrine they contain with the doctrine of the *Opus Oxoniense*. The pure philosopher treats of being in a universal sense and can never get beyond a first mover who is first in the chain of causes but who is nevertheless in the chain; he cannot arrive at the conception of God which can be attained by the philosopher who is also a theologian.

I feel rather doubtful of the validity of M. Gilson's contention. In the Oxford Commentary Scotus states that many essential attributes of God can be known by the metaphysician,[1] and in both commentaries he asserts that man can attain a natural knowledge of God, although he cannot *ex puris naturalibus* come to know such truths as that of the Trinity.[2] I find it hard to suppose that when Scotus said that man can come to know truths about God *ex puris naturalibus*, he was thinking of a metaphysician who is also a theologian. Nor do I see that Scotus meant to confine the pure philosopher's knowledge of God to knowledge of Him as first Mover: he says clearly that the metaphysician can proceed further than the *physicus*.[3] Moreover, it seems to me extremely odd, supposing that the *Theoremata* are Scotus's work, that Scotus should prove in the *De primo principio* that God or the first Principle is, for example, intelligent, and that then in the *Theoremata* he should declare that this truth is a *credibile* and cannot be proved. He certainly restricted somewhat the scope of the natural reason in regard to God (he did not think that God's omnipotence is capable of strict proof by the natural reason); but it would seem from the *Commentaries*, from the *De primo principio* and from the *Collationes* that Scotus undoubtedly considered a natural theology to be possible, irrespective of the question whether the philosopher is also a theologian or not.[4] Of course, if it were ever proved conclusively by external evidence that the *Theoremata* are the authentic work of Scotus, one would have to have recourse to some such theory as that of M. Gilson in order to explain the apparently flat contradiction between the *Theoremata* and the other works of Scotus; but meanwhile it seems to me to be pressing conciliation too far to suggest that there is no contradiction, and I propose in my exposition of Scotus's natural theology to disregard the *Theoremata*. But, while disregarding the *Theoremata*, I admit, as just mentioned, that in the event of the work's authenticity being satisfactorily proved, one would be

---

[1] *Ox.*, Prol., 4, no. 32.
[2] *Ibid.*, 1, 3, 1; *Rep.*, 1, 3, 1; *Rep.*, Prol., 3, nos. 1 and 4.   [3] *Rep.*, Prol., 3, 1.
[4] Minges, accepting the *Theoremata*, tries to show that in that work Scotus understands demonstration in the strictest Aristotelian sense, as *demonstratio ex causis*. If that could be proved, there would, of course, be no contradiction between the *Theoremata* and the certainly authentic works of Scotus. Longpré, however, argues against this interpretation of the author's meaning. Cf. Minges, Vol. 2, pp. 29–30; Longpré, p. 109 (cf. Bibliography).

compelled to say with Gilson that in that work Scotus is considering simply the power of the natural philosopher (the *physicus*) in
regard to the attainment of natural knowledge of God. My point
is, however, that until the authenticity of the *Theoremata* is
proved, there does not seem to be any adequate or compelling
reason for affirming that the metaphysician of the certainly
authentic works is necessarily a metaphysician who possesses the
background of faith. I shall, therefore, treat the *Theoremata* for
practical purposes as unauthentic, without, however, pretending
to settle the question definitively or to add any further grounds
than those already alleged by other writers for rejecting the work
as spurious.

The problem of the *Theoremata* has been discussed at some
length in order to show the difficulty there is in interpreting
accurately the mind of Scotus. Even if one maintains that the
doctrines of the *Theoremata* and of the *Opus Oxoniense* are not at
variance, but can be reconciled, the very reconciliation results in
a picture of Scotus's philosophy which would hardly be that
suggested by a first acquaintance with the *Opus Oxoniense*. Still,
even if the authenticity of the *Theoremata* has not been demonstrated and even if it would appear preferable to reject it, convenience of exposition is no sure criterion of authenticity or
unauthenticity, and one cannot, in view of recent attempts to
rehabilitate the work, exclude the possibility that it may at some
future date be shown to be certainly authentic, even though
internal evidence may suggest the contrary.

3. Various general interpretations of Scotus's philosophy have
been given, ranging from the interpretation of Scotus as a revolutionary, as a direct precursor of Ockham and of Luther, to the
attempt to soften down the sharp differences between Scotism and
Thomism and to interpret Scotus as a continuator of the work of
St. Thomas. The first interpretation, that of Landry, can be
dismissed, in its extreme form at least, as extravagant and
insufficiently grounded, while on the other hand it is impossible
to deny that Scotism does differ from Thomism. But is Scotus
to be regarded as a continuator of the Franciscan tradition who
at the same time adopted a great deal from Aristotle and from
non-Franciscan mediaeval predecessors, or is he to be regarded
as a thinker who carried on the Aristotelian tradition of St.
Thomas but at the same time corrected St. Thomas in the light of
what he himself considered to be the truth, or is he simply to be

regarded as an independent thinker who at the same time depended, as all philosophers must, on preceding thinkers in regard to the problems raised and discussed? The question is not an easy one to answer, and any attempt to answer it definitively must be postponed until the production of the critical edition of Scotus's works; but it would seem that there is truth in each of the foregoing suggestions. Scotus was, indeed, a Franciscan Doctor, and even if he discarded a number of doctrines which were generally held in common by former Franciscan thinkers, he certainly regarded himself as faithful to the Franciscan tradition. Again, although Scotus certainly criticised St. Thomas's views on important points, he can also be regarded as continuing the work of synthesis to which St. Thomas had devoted himself. Finally, Scotus certainly was an independent thinker; but at the same time he built on already existing foundations. But although Scotism did not involve a complete break with the past, it is only reasonable to lay stress on its comparatively original and independent aspects and thus draw attention to the difference between Scotism and other systems.

In some aspects of his thought Scotus did indeed carry on the Augustinian-Franciscan tradition: in his doctrine of the superiority of will to intellect, for example, as also in his admission of plurality of forms and in his utilisation of the Anselmian argument for God's existence. Moreover, it has been shown that Scotus did not invent the *distinctio formalis a parte rei*, but that it had been employed by some preceding Franciscan thinkers. Nevertheless, Scotus often gave a peculiar stamp or emphasis to the elements he adopted from tradition. Thus in his treatment of the relation of will to intellect he emphasised freedom rather than love, though he held, it is true, to the superiority of love to knowledge, a superiority which is closely connected with his theory that the supreme practical principle is that God should be loved above all things. Again, though he utilised the Anselmian argument, the so-called 'ontological argument', he did not accept it as a conclusive proof of God's existence but maintained, not only that it must be 'coloured' before it can be usefully employed, but also that even then it is not a demonstrative proof of God's existence, since the only demonstrative arguments are *a posteriori*.

But if Scotus in some respects carried on the Augustinian-Franciscan tradition, in other respects he departed from that tradition. It is not quite clear whether he did or did not teach the hylomorphic composition of angels; but he expressly rejected as unnecessary the theories of *rationes seminales* and of a special illumination of the human intellect, while he saw no contradiction, as St. Bonaventure had seen, in the idea of creation from eternity, even though he speaks more hesitantly than St. Thomas on this matter. In Scotism, then, the influence of Aristotelianism had penetrated further than it had in the philosophy of St. Bonaventure, and one must mention in particular the influence of Avicenna. For example, Scotus insists that the object of the metaphysician is being as being, and in his insistence on this point, as in his treatment of the problem of God, he seems to have been influenced by the Islamic philosopher, whose name occurs not infrequently in the pages of Scotus's works. It is true that Aristotle himself had declared that metaphysics, or rather first philosophy, is the science of being as being; but the Aristotelian metaphysic centres in practice round the doctrine of the four causes, whereas Scotus treats at length of the idea and nature of being, and the impulse thereto seems to have been partly derived from Avicenna. Scotus's discussion of universals, for instance, was also not without a debt to Avicenna.

Yet even if Scotus owed much more to Aristotle and his commentators than did St. Bonaventure, and even if he appeals to the authority of Aristotle in support of this or that theory, he was far from being a mere follower of 'the Philosopher', whom he does not hesitate to criticise. But, apart from individual pieces of criticism, Scotus's philosophical inspiration, so to speak, was different from that of Aristotle. In his eyes the conception of God as first Mover was a very inadequate conception, as it does not pass beyond the physical world and attain the transcendent, infinite Being on which all finite beings essentially depend. Again, it follows from Scotus's ethical doctrine that the Aristotelian ethic must be insufficient, as the notion of obligation, depending on the divine will, does not appear therein. It may be said, of course, that any Christian philosopher would find Aristotle deficient on such matters, and that St. Thomas was compelled to supplement Aristotle with Augustine; but the point is that Scotus did not go out of his way to 'explain' Aristotle or to 'reconcile' his opinions with what he himself considered to be the truth. In so far, for example, as there is a moral philosophy in the strict sense in Scotism, its dependence on or borrowing from Aristotelianism is far from being conspicuous.

Scotus's attitude to St. Thomas has been depicted in recent years in a rather different light to that in which it was formerly sometimes depicted: there has been, and not unnaturally, a tendency to minimise his divergences from Thomism. It has been pointed out, for example, that in his polemics he often has other thinkers in mind, Henry of Ghent, for example. This is quite true, of course; but the fact remains that he frequently criticises Thomist positions, giving St. Thomas's arguments and refuting them. But whatever the justice or injustice of this or that individual criticism may be, Scotus certainly did not criticise for the sake of criticism. If he insisted, for example, on some intellectual intuition of the singular object and if he emphasised the reality of the 'common nature', without however, falling into the exaggerated realism of early mediaeval philosophers, he did so, not simply in order to differ from St. Thomas, but in order to safeguard, as he believed, the objectivity of knowledge. Similarly, if he insisted on the univocal character of the concept of being, he did so because he considered his own doctrine to be absolutely necessary if agnosticism were to be avoided, that is, in order to safeguard the objective character of natural theology. If he made extensive use of the *distinctio formalis a parte rei*, this was not simply in order to display his subtlety, though he certainly was a subtle and sometimes a tortuous thinker and dialectician, but because he considered that such use was necessitated by the facts and by the objective reference of our concepts. In so far, then, as Scotus can be looked on as a successor of St. Thomas or as a continuator of Thomism, one must recognise that he endeavoured to correct what he regarded, rightly or wrongly, as dangerous deficiencies and tendencies in the Thomist philosophy.

It is well to bear in mind Scotus's concern for the theoretical safeguarding of the objectivity of human knowledge and of natural theology in particular, since the realisation of this concern acts as a counterbalance to the tendency to look on him as predominantly a destructive critic. It is true that Scotus was somewhat rigorous in his idea of what constitutes a proof, and he would not allow that the proofs adduced for the soul's immortality, for example, were conclusive, demonstrative; but all the same his philosophy remains one of the great mediaeval syntheses, an effort of constructive and positive thought. Moreover, it had a religious inspiration, as one can see from the invocations of God which sometimes appear in his writings and which one cannot simply dismiss as literary convention.

Nevertheless, if one looks on Scotism in its position as a stage in the development of mediaeval thought, it would be idle to deny that *de facto* it helped to stimulate the critical movement of the fourteenth century. When Scotus asserted that certain of the divine attributes cannot be proved by natural reason and when he denied the demonstrative character of the arguments adduced for the immortality of the human soul, he did not intend to undermine positive philosophy; but, looking at the matter from the purely historical viewpoint, his criticism obviously helped to prepare the way for the much more radical criticism of Ockham. That the latter regarded Scotism with hostility is not really relevant to the point at issue. Similarly, though it is quite untrue that Scotus made the whole moral law to depend on the arbitrary choice of the divine will, it can hardly be denied that the elements of voluntarism in his philosophy helped to prepare the way for the authoritarianism of Ockham. For example, his doctrine of moral obligation and his assertion that the secondary precepts of the decalogue do not belong, in the strict sense, to the natural law and are subject to divine dispensation in particular cases. I am not suggesting that Ockhamism is the legitimate child of Scotism, but simply that after the attainment of the supreme mediaeval synthesis of Thomism the work of the critical intellect or of the critical function of philosophy was only to be expected, and that the restricted and moderate use of criticism by Scotus prepared the way, as a matter of fact, for the radical and destructive criticism which is characteristic of Ockhamism. An historical judgement of this type does not necessarily mean that Scotus's criticism was not justified and the radical criticism of later thinkers unjustified: that is a matter for the philosopher to decide, not the historian. Of course, if the *Theoremata* were ever proved to be authentic, that would but serve to emphasise the critical aspect of Scotism.

In fine, then, the philosophy of Scotus looks backward as well as forward. As a positive and constructive system it belongs to the thirteenth century, the century which witnessed the philosophies of St. Bonaventure and, above all, of St. Thomas; but in its critical aspects and in its voluntaristic elements, associated though the latter are with the Augustinian-Franciscan tradition, it looks forward to the fourteenth century. A triumph of dialectical skill and of careful and patient thought the philosophy of Scotus is the work of a man who was, though impregnated with tradition, a powerful, vigorous and original thinker, a man who really belonged to the closing epoch of 'dogmatic philosophy' but who at the same time heralded the new movement.

CHAPTER XLVI

SCOTUS—II: KNOWLEDGE

The primary object of the human intellect—Why the intellect depends on the phantasm—The soul's inability to intuit itself in this life—Intellectual apprehension of the individual thing—Is theology a science?—Our knowledge is based on sense-experience, and no special illumination is required for intellectual activity—Intuitive and abstractive knowledge—Induction.

1. THE primary natural object of our intellect is being as being, from which it follows that every being, every thing which is intelligible, falls within the scope of the intellect.[1] Scotus gives, among other proofs, one taken from Avicenna to the effect that if being were not the primary object of the intellect, being could be described or explained in terms of something more ultimate, which is impossible. But if being as being is the natural object of the intellect and if being is taken to include every intelligible object, does it not follow that infinite Being, God, is a natural object of the human intellect? In a sense the answer must be in the affirmative, since being includes infinite being and finite being, but it does not follow that man has an immediate natural knowledge of God, since man's intellect in its present state is directed immediately to sensible things. But, says Scotus, if we are speaking of the primary object of the intellect, it is only reasonable to assign as its primary object that which is the primary object of intellect as such, not that which is the primary object of the intellect in this or that particular case. We do not say, for example, that the primary object of vision is that which the eye can see in candlelight; but we assign as its primary object that which is its object simply as a power or faculty.[2] Therefore, even if man in his present state (*homo viator*) comes first of all to know creatures, this does not mean that the primary adequate object of his intellect is not being as being. It may be added that this doctrine does not mean that the human intellect has a natural power of knowing the divine essence in itself or the divine Persons in the Trinity, since the general (and univocal) concept of being does not include *this particular essence as particular*, while creatures are not such perfect imitations of God that they reveal the divine

---

[1] *Ox.*, Prol., q. 1.   [2] *Ibid.*, 1, 3, 3, no. 24.

essence as it is in itself.[1] The divine essence as such moves (*movet*) naturally, is the natural object of the divine intellect only; it can be known by the human intellect only through God's free choice and activity, not through the human intellect's natural power.

But if Scotus in assigning being as being as the primary adequate object of the human intellect certainly did not confuse supernatural and natural knowledge, he equally certainly meant to reject St. Thomas's view, or what he regarded as such, of the primary object of the human mind. St. Thomas[2] maintained that the natural object of the human intellect is the essence of the material thing, which essence becomes intelligible to the intellect when it is abstracted from the individualising matter. It is natural to the angelic intellect to know natures which do not exist in matter; but the human intellect cannot do this in its present state, when united to the body. And to be united to the body is the natural state of the human intellect; to be separated from the body is *praeter naturam*. So St. Thomas argues that, inasmuch as the natural object of the human intellect is the form of the material thing and inasmuch as we know this kind of form by abstracting it from the 'phantasm', the human intellect necessarily depends on the 'phantasm', and so on sense-experience, for its knowledge.[3] Scotus[4] interprets St. Thomas as teaching that the quiddity or essence, known by way of abstraction from the phantasm, is the primary object of the human intellect considered not simply as being in a certain state, that is, in the present life, but in its nature as a power or faculty of a certain kind, and he replies that this opinion is untenable by a theologian, i.e. by a man who accepts the next life and the doctrine of eternal happiness. In heaven the soul knows immaterial things directly. Now, the intellect remains the same power in heaven as it was on earth. Therefore, if it can know immaterial things in heaven, we cannot say that its primary object is the essence of the material thing: its primary object, if we consider the intellect as a power, must embrace both immaterial and material things, even if in this life it cannot know immaterial things directly. Its restriction in this life to a certain type of object must be secondary, not primary. If it is answered that in heaven the intellect is elevated, so that it can know immaterial objects directly, Scotus replies that this knowledge either exceeds the power of the intellect or it does not.

[1] *Ox.*, 3, 2, 16, cf. *Quodlibet* 14: *Utrum anima suae naturali perfectioni relicta possit cognoscere Trinitatem personarum in Divinis.*
[2] *S.T.*, Ia, 12. 4.   [3] Cf. *ibid.*, Ia, 85, 1.   [4] *Ox.*, 1, 3, 3, nos. 1 ff.

If the latter is the case, then the primary object of the intellect considered *ex natura potentiae* cannot be the quiddity of the material thing, whereas, if the former is the case, then the intellect in heaven becomes another power, which St. Thomas certainly does not intend to teach.

Scotus also argues that if St. Thomas's view were correct, metaphysical science would be impossible for our intellects, since metaphysics are the science of being as being. If the primary object of the human intellect were the essence of the material thing, it could no more know being as being than the power of vision could extend further than its natural object, colour and light.[1] If the Thomist view were true, metaphysics would either be impossible, if understood in its proper sense, or it would not transcend physics. In fine, 'it does not seem fitting to confine the intellect, considered as a power, to the sensible thing, so that it transcends the senses only through its mode of cognition', that is, not through its object as well.

Since Scotus also maintains[2] that there is in the human intellect a natural desire to know 'the cause' distinctly and that a natural desire cannot be in vain, and since he concludes that the primary object of the intellect cannot, therefore, be material things, which are the effect of the immaterial cause, it might appear that he is contradicting his assertion that we cannot have a natural knowledge of the divine essence; but it must be remembered that he does not deny that the human intellect in its present state is limited in range, though he insists that the object of a power in a certain condition must not be confused with the object of the power considered in itself. Moreover, he did not consider that an analysis of being as being can yield knowledge of the divine essence as it is in itself, for even if being is the primary and adequate object of the human intellect, it does not follow that we form our idea of being by any other way than abstraction. In general, we may say that Scotus accepted the Aristotelian account of abstraction, though he considered that the active and passive intellects are not two distinct powers, but are two aspects or functions of one power.[3]

2. As to the reason why the human intellect in its present state, in this life, depends on the phantasm, Scotus declares that it is due to the order established by divine wisdom, either as a penalty for original sin or with a view to the harmonious operation of our

[1] *Ox.*, 1, 3, 3, nos. 1 ff. [2] *Ibid.*, 1, 3, 3, no. 3. [3] *De Anima*, 13.

various powers (*propter naturalem concordiam potentiarum animae in operando*), sense and imagination apprehending the individual thing, the intellect apprehending the universal essence of that thing, or else on account of our infirmity (*ex infirmitate*). The intellect in its present condition, he repeats, is moved immediately only by what is imaginable or sensible, and the reason for this may be punitive justice (*forte propter peccatum, sicut videtur Augustinus dicere*) or it may be a natural cause, inasmuch as the order or harmony of powers may require it so far as this present state is concerned. 'Nature' in this connection means, therefore, nature in a particular state or condition, not nature absolutely considered: on this point Scotus insists.[1] This is not a very satisfactory or a very clear or decided explanation; but what Scotus is quite clear about is that the intellect, absolutely considered, is the faculty of being as being, and he decisively rejects what he regards as the Thomist doctrine. Whether Scotus is fair in his interpretation of St. Thomas is another matter. Sometimes St. Thomas states explicitly that the proper object of the intellect is being.[2]

However, it is true that St. Thomas insists on the natural character of the necessity of the *conversio ad phantasma*,[3] arguing that if this necessity were simply the result of union with a body and not natural to the soul itself, it would follow that the union of soul and body takes place for the good of the body, not of the soul, since the soul would be hampered in its natural operations through its union with the body. Emphasising this aspect of the Thomist doctrine, Scotus concluded that Thomism is unable, logically speaking, to justify the possibility of metaphysical science.

3. Scotus's view on the primary object of the human intellect naturally had its effect on his treatment of the disputed question concerning the soul's knowledge of itself. According to St. Thomas Aquinas, the soul in its present state, which is its natural state, comes to know by means of ideas abstracted from sensible objects, and from this he concludes that the soul has no immediate knowledge of its own essence, but that it comes to know itself only indirectly, by reflecting on the acts by which it abstracts ideas and knows objects in those ideas.[4] Scotus, however, maintained that though the soul actually lacks an immediate intuition of itself in this life, it is a natural object of intellection to itself and

[1] Cf. *Ox.*, 1, 3, 3, no. 24; 2, 3, 8, no. 13.　　[2] As in *S.T.*, Ia, 5, 2, for instance.
[3] *S.T.*, Ia, 89, 1.　　[4] Cf. *ibid.*, Ia, 87, 1.

would actually intuit itself, 'were it not hindered'.[1] He then proceeds to suggest the causes of this hindrance which have already been mentioned. The difference between Scotus and St. Thomas concerns, then, the explanation of a fact rather than the fact itself. Both agree that the soul is actually without an immediate intuition of itself in this life; but, whereas St. Thomas explains this fact in terms of the nature of the human soul, attacking the Platonist view of the relation of soul to body, Scotus explains it, not in terms of the soul's nature, absolutely considered, but in terms of a hindrance, even suggesting that this hindrance may be due to sin and quoting St. Augustine in support of this suggestion. St. Thomas's attitude follows from his adoption of the Aristotelian psychology, whereas Scotus's position can be associated with the Augustinian tradition. On this matter one should regard Scotus not as an innovator or revolutionary or a destructive critic of Thomism, but rather as an upholder of the Augustinian-Franciscan tradition.

4. We have seen that Scotus considered his doctrine concerning the primary object of the intellect to be essential for the maintenance and justification of metaphysics: he also considered his doctrine of the intellectual apprehension of the individual thing as essential to the maintenance of the objectivity of human knowledge. According to St. Thomas[2] the intellect cannot know individual material things directly, since the intellect comes to know only by abstracting the universal from matter, the principle of individuation. He admits, however, that the mind has an indirect knowledge of individual things, since it cannot actually know the abstracted universal except through the 'conversion to the phantasm'. The imagination always plays its part, and the image is an image of the individual thing; but the primary and direct object of intellectual knowledge is the universal.

Scotus refused to accept this Thomist doctrine. The vehement repudiation of the doctrine wherein it is declared false and even heretical (on the ground that the Apostles believed that a certain visible, palpable, individual human being was God) comes from an unauthentic work, the *De rerum principio*; but the authentic works of Scotus make the latter's position perfectly clear. He accepted in general the Aristotelian account of abstraction, but he insists that the intellect has a confused primary intuition of the singular thing. His principle is that the higher power knows

[1] *Ox.*, 2, 3, 8, no. 13.   [2] *S.T.*, Ia, 86, 1.

what the lower power apprehends, though the higher power knows
the object in a more perfect manner than the lower power does,
so that the intellect, which co-operates in perception, knows
intuitively the singular thing apprehended by the senses. The
intellect knows true contingent propositions and reasons from
them; and such propositions concern individual things known
intuitively as existing. Therefore, although abstract and scientific
knowledge concerns universals, as Aristotle rightly taught, we
must also recognise an intellectual knowledge of the singular thing
as existent.[1] As already mentioned, the very vehement repudiation of the Thomist position, which is ascribed to Scotus by Father
Parthenius Minges, for example,[2] comes from the unauthentic *De
rerum principio*, and certain remarks which are found in the
authentic works might lead one to suppose that Scotus's position
on the question of the intellectual knowledge of the singular thing
is exactly parallel to his position in regard to the soul's intuition
of itself. He insists that the singular thing is intelligible in itself
and that the human intellect has at least the remote capability
of understanding it; but he seems to imply, or even to state
explicitly, that in its present condition it is unable to do so. 'The
singular thing is intelligible in itself, as far as the thing itself is
concerned; but if it is not intelligible to some intellect, to ours,
for example, this is not due to unintelligibility on the part of the
singular thing itself.'[3] Again, 'it is not an imperfection to know
the singular thing', but 'if you say that our intellect does not
understand the singular thing, I reply that this is an imperfection
(which obtains) in its present state'.[4] However, Scotus seems to
mean that while we have no clear knowledge of the singular thing
as singular, a deficiency which is due, not to the singular thing's
lack of intelligibility, but to the imperfection of our intellectual
operations in this life, we none the less have a primary, though
confused, intellectual intuition of the singular thing as existent.
This seems to be the view expressed in the *Quodlibet*[5] where
Scotus argues that if it is said that we have an intellectual knowledge of the universal and sense-experience of the singular, this is
not to be understood in the sense that the two powers are equal
and disparate, so that the intellect would not know the singular
at all, but in the sense that the lower power is subordinate to the
higher and that though the higher power can operate in a way that

---

[1] *Ox.*, 4, 45, 3, no. 17.
[2] *J. Duns Scoti Doctrina Philosophica et Theologica*, p. 247.
[3] *Ox.*, 2, 3, 6, no. 16.   [4] *Ibid.*, 2, 3, 9, no. 9.   [5] 13, 8-10.

the lower cannot, the opposite cannot be assumed as true. From the fact that sense cannot know the universal it does not follow that the intellect cannot know the singular. The intellect can have an intuitive knowledge of the singular as existent, even if its knowledge of the essence is knowledge of the universal.

If we are willing to accept the *De Anima* as authentic, Scotus's opinion is placed beyond doubt. In that work[1] Scotus rejects the Thomist doctrine on our knowledge of the singular, and also the Thomist doctrine of the principle of individuation, on which the first doctrine rests, and argues that the singular thing is (i) intelligible in itself; (ii) intelligible by us even in our present state; (iii) not intelligible by us in our present state so far as clear knowledge is concerned. The singular thing is intelligible in itself, since what is not intelligible in itself could not be known by any intellect, whereas the singular thing is certainly known by the divine and angelic intellects. It is intelligible by us even in our present state, as is shown by the process of induction and by the fact that we can love the individual thing, love presupposing knowledge. It is not, however, intelligible by us in our present state in a complete and clear manner (*sub propria ratione*). If two material things were deprived of all difference of accidents (of place, colour, shape, etc.), neither sense nor intellect could distinguish them from one another, even though their 'singularities' (Scotus's *haecceitas*) remained, and this shows that we have, in our present state, no clear and complete knowledge of the singularity of a thing. We can say, therefore, that the object of sense is the individual thing and the object of intellect the universal, if we mean that the intellect is not moved by singularity as such and does not know it clearly and completely in its present state; but we are not entitled to say that the intellect has no intuition of the individual thing as existent. If we say this, we destroy the objectivity of knowledge. 'It is impossible to abstract universals from the singular without previous knowledge of the singular; for in this case the intellect would abstract without knowing from what it was abstracting.'[2] It is clear that Scotus rejected the Thomist doctrine not merely because he rejected the Thomist idea of individuation, nor even merely because a process like induction seemed to him to prove the Thomist doctrine false; but also because he was convinced that the Thomist doctrine endangered the objectivity of that scientific and universal knowledge

[1] 22. [2] *De Anima*, 22, 3.

on which the Thomists laid such stress. Scotus did not mean to reject (he makes this quite clear) the Aristotelian doctrine that human science is of the universal; but he considered it essential to supplement that doctrine by accepting our intellectual intuition of the singular thing as existent, and he considered that this supplementation was necessitated by the facts. Concern for the safeguarding of the objectivity of human knowledge shows itself also in Scotus's handling of the problem of universals; but consideration of this problem is best left for the chapter on metaphysics, where it can be treated in connection with the problem of individuation.

5. From one point of view it would not be unreasonable to maintain, as has been maintained, that Scotus's ideal of science was mathematical science. If science is understood in the sense in which Aristotle uses the word in the first book of the *Posterior Analytics*, that is, as involving necessity of the object, as well as evidence and certainty, we cannot say that theology, as concerned with the Incarnation and with God's relations with man in general, is a science, since the Incarnation is not a necessary or a deducible event.[1] On the other hand, if we consider theology as concerned with its primary object, with God as He is in Himself, it treats of necessary truths like the Trinity of Persons, and is a science; but we must add that it is a science in itself and not for us, since the truths in question, though certain, are not self-evident to us. If someone were unable to understand the arguments of the geometers, but accepted their conclusions on their word, geometry would be for him an object of belief, not a science, even though it would still be a science in itself.[2] Theology considered as concerned with God in Himself, is thus a science in itself, though not for us, since, in spite of the necessity of the object, the data are accepted on faith. Theology as concerned with God's external operations, however, treats of 'contingent', that is, non-necessary events, and so is not a science in that sense. Scotus is clearly taking geometrical science as the model of science in the strict sense.

It should be added, however, that when Scotus denies that theology is a science in the senses above indicated, he does not intend to disparage theology or to cast doubts upon its certainty. He expressly says that if one understands 'science', not in the strictest sense, but as understood by Aristotle in the sixth book of the *Ethics*, namely as contrasted with opinion and conjecture,

[1] *Ox.*, Prol., 3, no. 28.   [2] *Ibid.*, Prol., 2 lat., no. 4.

it is a science, since it is certain and true, though it is more properly to be termed 'wisdom'.[1] Moreover, theology is not subordinate to metaphysics, since, although its object is in some degree comprised in the object of metaphysics, for God as knowable by the natural light of reason is comprised in the object of metaphysics, it does not receive its principles from metaphysics, nor are the truths of dogmatic theology demonstrable by means of the principles of being as such. The principles of dogmatic theology are accepted on faith, on authority; they are not demonstrated by natural reason nor are they demonstrable by the metaphysician. On the other hand, metaphysics are not, in the strict sense, a subordinate science to theology, since the metaphysician does not borrow his principles from the theologian.[2]

Theology, according to Scotus, is a practical science; but he explains very carefully and at length what he means by this.[3] 'Even necessary theology', that is, theological knowledge of necessary truths concerning God in Himself, is logically prior to the elicited act of will by which we choose God, and the first principles of salutary conduct are taken from it. Scotus discusses the views of Henry of Ghent and others, rejecting them in favour of his own view. He thus parts company with St. Thomas, who says[4] that theology is a speculative science, just as he parts company with St. Thomas when the latter declares that theology is a science.[5] Scotus, as one would expect in view of his doctrine of the priority of will over intellect, emphasises the aspect of theology under which it is a norm of salutary conduct for man.

The foregoing considerations may seem to be irrelevant, referring, as they do, to dogmatic theology; but if one understands Scotus's position in regard to dogmatic theology, one can see how unjust and false are some of the accusations which have been brought against him. If one said simply that whereas St. Thomas considered theology to be a science, a speculative science, Scotus declared that theology is not a science and that, in so far as it can be called a science, it is a practical science, one might conclude that theological doctrines were, for Scotus, postulates having only practical or pragmatic value; and in point of fact, Scotus has actually been compared with Kant. But if one considers Scotus's meaning, such an interpretation is obviously unjust and false. For example, Scotus does not deny that theology is a science as

[1] Ox., Prol., 3, no. 28.   [3] Ibid., Prol., 3, no. 29.   [3] Ibid., Prol. 4.
[4] S.T., Ia, 1, 4.   [5] Ibid., Ia, 1, 2.

far as certainty is concerned; he simply says that if you define science in the sense in which geometry is a science, then theology cannot be called a science. With this position St. Thomas would agree. Theology, he says, is a science, because its principles are derived from those of a higher science, proper to God and the blessed, so that they are absolutely certain; it is not a science in the same sense in which geometry and arithmetic are sciences, since its principles are not self-evident to the natural light of reason.[1] Again, Scotus says that theology is for us a practical science, mainly because revelation is given as a norm for salutary conduct, that we may attain our last end, whereas for St. Thomas[2] theology is primarily a speculative science, though not exclusively, because it deals more with divine things than with human acts. In other words, the main difference between them on this matter is one of emphasis: it is a difference which one would expect in view of St. Thomas's general emphasis on intellect and theoretic contemplation and Scotus's general emphasis on will and love, and it has to be seen in the light of the Aristotelian and Franciscan traditions rather than in the light of Kantianism and Pragmatism. If anyone wishes to make out that Scotus was a Kantian before Kant, he will find no solid reasons to support his contention in Scotus's doctrine concerning dogmatic theology.

6. Although Scotus insists, as we have seen, that the primary object of the intellect is being in general and not simply material essences, his Aristotelianism leads him also to emphasise the fact that our actual knowledge originates with sensation. There are no innate ideas, therefore. In the *Quaestiones subtilissimae super libros Metaphysicorum*[3] he affirms that the intellect does not, in virtue of its own constitution, possess any natural knowledge, either in simple or in complex notions, 'because all our knowledge arises from sensation'. This applies even to the knowledge of the first principles. 'For first the sense is moved by some simple, and not complex object, and through the movement of the sense the intellect is moved and apprehends simple objects: this is the intellect's first act. Secondly, after the apprehension of simple objects there follows another act, that of bringing together simple objects, and after this composition the intellect is able to assent to the truth of the complex, if it is a first principle.' Natural knowledge of the first principles means no more than that when the simple terms have been understood and combined, the intellect

---

[1] S.T., Ia, I, 2.   [2] Ibid., Ia, I, 4.   [3] 2, I, no. 2.

immediately assents, in virtue of its own natural light, to the truth of the principle; 'but the knowledge of the terms is acquired from sensible objects'. What Scotus means is this. We obtain the notions of 'whole' and 'part', for example, through sense-experience; but when the intellect brings together the terms, it sees immediately the truth of the proposition that the whole is greater than the part. The knowledge of what a whole is and what a part is comes from sense-experience; but the natural light of the intellect enables it to see immediately the truth of the complex object, the first principle. In answer to Averroes's objection that in this case all men would assent to the first principles, whereas in point of fact the Christians do not assent to the principle that 'out of nothing nothing is made', Scotus replies that he is speaking of first principles in the strict sense, such as the principle of contradiction and the principle that the whole is greater than its part, not of principles which some people think to be or which may be conclusions from the first principles. In the Paris Commentary, however,[1] he insists that the intellect cannot err in regard to those principles and conclusions which it sees to follow clearly from the first principles. In the same place he speaks of the intellect as a *tabula nuda*, which has no innate principles or ideas.

Scotus also rejects the doctrine that a special illumination of the intellect is necessary in order that it should apprehend certain truth. Thus he gives the arguments of Henry of Ghent on behalf of the illumination theory[2] and proceeds to criticise them, objecting that Henry's arguments seem to result in the conclusion that all certain and natural knowledge is impossible.[3] For example, if it were true that no certainty can be obtained concerning a continually changing object (and sensible objects are constantly changing, according to Henry), illumination would not help in any way, for we do not attain certainty when we know an object otherwise than it actually is. In any case, Scotus adds, the doctrine that sensible objects are continually changing is the doctrine of Heraclitus and is false. Similarly, if the changing character of the soul and its ideas are an obstacle to certainty, illumination will not remedy the defect. In fine, Henry's opinion would lead to scepticism.

Scotus thus defends the activity and natural power of the human intellect, and a similar preoccupation shows itself in his rejection of St. Thomas's doctrine that the soul, when separated from the

body, cannot acquire new ideas from things themselves.[1] He gives
the opinion of St. Thomas in more or less the same words that the
latter uses in his Commentary on the *Sentences*[2] and argues that it
belongs to the nature of the soul to know, to abstract, to will, so
that, since the soul is also of such a nature that it can exist in
separation from the body, we may legitimately conclude that it
can acquire fresh knowledge by natural means in this state of
separation. The opinion of St. Thomas, Scotus says, degrades the
human soul. Scotus's own opinion is, of course, connected with
his view that the soul's dependence on the senses in this life is
pro statu isto, forte ex peccato. It is also connected with his rejection
of the doctrine that the soul is purely passive and that the
phantasm causes the idea. The soul in the state of separation
from the body is, therefore, not cut off from the acquisition of
new knowledge, nor is it even confined to intuition: it can exercise
the power of abstraction too.

7. Scotus distinguishes intuitive and abstractive knowledge.
Intuitive knowledge is knowledge of an object as present in its
actual existence and it is against the nature of intuitive knowledge
that it should be knowledge of an object which is not actually
existent and present.[3] However, Scotus makes a distinction
between perfect intuitive knowledge, which is immediate knowledge of an object as present, and imperfect intuitive knowledge,
which is knowledge of an existent object as existing in the future,
as anticipated, or as existing in the past, as remembered.[4] Abstractive knowledge on the other hand is knowledge of the essence of
an object considered in abstraction from its existence or non-
existence.[5] The difference between intuitive and abstractive
knowledge is not, then, that the former is knowledge of an existent
object, the latter of a non-existent object, but rather that the
former is knowledge of an object as existent and actually present,
that is, in intuition properly speaking, whereas the latter is
knowledge of the essence of an object considered in abstraction
from existence, whether the object actually exists or not. 'There
can be abstractive knowledge of a non-existent object as well as
of an existent object, but there can be intuitive knowledge only
of an existent object as existent.'[6] We should have to add the
words 'and present', for 'it is against the nature of intuitive
knowledge that it should be of something which is not actually

[1] *Ox.*, 4, 45, 2.   [3] 4, 50, 1, 1; and cf. *S.T.*, Ia, 89, 1-4.
[2] *Ox.*, 1, 2, 7, no. 42; 2, 9, 2, no. 29.   [4] *Ibid.*, 3, 14, 3, no. 6.
[5] *Ibid.*, 2, 3, 9, no. 6.   [6] *Quodlibet*, 7, no. 8.

existent and present'.[1] Accordingly Scotus says that though the blessed could see him in God, that is, in the beatific vision, as existing and writing, this knowledge would not be intuitive knowledge, since 'I am not actually present in God, whom the blessed behold in heaven'.[2] Scotus's doctrine of abstractive knowledge, the knowledge of essences in abstraction from existence and non-existence, has led to the comparison of this aspect of his thought with the method of the modern Phenomenological School.

8. Scotus was sufficiently permeated by the spirit of the Aristotelian logic to lay stress on deduction and to have a rigorous idea of demonstrative proof; but he made some interesting remarks on induction. We cannot have experience of all instances of a particular type of natural event; but experience of a number of instances may be sufficient to show the scientist that the event in question proceeds from a natural cause and will always follow that cause. 'Whatever happens in most cases (that is, in the cases we have been able to observe) does not proceed from a free cause, but is the natural effect of the cause.' This proposition is recognised as true by the intellect, which sees that a free cause will not produce the same effect: if the cause could produce another effect, we should observe it doing so. If an effect is frequently produced by the same cause (Scotus means if the same effect is produced by the same cause, so far as our experience goes), the cause cannot be a free cause in that respect, nor can it be a 'casual' cause, but it must be the natural cause of that effect. Sometimes we have experience of the effect and are able to reduce the effect to a self-evident causal relation, in which case we can proceed to deduce the effect and so obtain a still more certain knowledge than we had through experience, while on other occasions we may have experience of the cause in such a way that we cannot demonstrate the necessary connection between cause and effect, but only that the effect proceeds from the cause as a natural cause.[3]

---

[1] *Ox.*, 2, 9, 2, no. 29.   [2] *Ibid.*, 4, 14, 3, no. 6.   [3] *Ibid.*, 1, 3, 4, no. 9.

CHAPTER XLVII

SCOTUS—III: METAPHYSICS

*Being and its transcendental attributes—The univocal concept of being—The formal objective distinction—Essence and existence —Universals—Hylomorphism—*Rationes seminales *rejected, plurality of forms retained—Individuation.*

1. METAPHYSICS is the science of being as being. The concept of being is the simplest of all concepts, and it is irreducible to other more ultimate concepts: being, therefore, cannot be defined.[1] We can conceive being distinctly by itself, for in its widest signification it simply means that which includes no contradiction, that which is not intrinsically impossible; but every other concept, every concept of a distinct kind of being, includes the concept of being.[2] Being in its widest sense thus includes that which has extramental being and that which has intramental being,[3] and it transcends all genera.[4]

There are various *passiones entis* (categories of being one might call them, provided that the word 'category' is not understood in the Aristotelian sense), the *passiones convertibiles* and the *passiones disiunctae.* The former are those categories of being which are designated by one name, which do not go in distinct pairs, and are convertible with being. For example, *one, true, good,* are *passiones convertibiles.* Every being is one, true, and good by the very fact that it is being, and there is no real distinction between these *passiones convertibiles* or between them and being, but there is a formal distinction, since they denote different aspects of being.[5] The *passiones disiunctae,* on the other hand, are not simply convertible with being if one takes them singly, though they are convertible if one takes them in pairs. For example, not every being is necessary and not every being is contingent; but every being is either necessary or contingent. Similarly, not every being is simply act and not every being is potency; but every being must be either act or potency or act in one respect and potency in another. Scotus speaks of the *passiones disiunctae* as transcendent,[6] since although no *passio disiuncta* comprises all being or is simply

---

[1] *Quodlibet,* 7, no. 14; 1, 39, no. 13.   [2] *Ox.,* 1, 3, 2, no. 24.
[3] *Quodlibet,* 3, no. 2.   [4] *Ox.,* 2, 1, 4, no. 26.
[5] *Ibid.,* 1, 3, 3, no. 7; 2, 16, no. 17.   [6] *Ibid.,* 1, 8, 3, no. 19.

convertible with the notion of being, it does not place an object in any definite genus or category, in the Aristotelian sense. The fact that a being is contingent, for example, does not tell one whether it is substance or accident.

As Scotus held that the concept of being is univocal, in the sense shortly to be discussed, it might appear that he tried to deduce the actuality of the *passiones disiunctae*; but this was not his intention. We can never deduce from the notion of being that contingent being exists, nor can we show that contingent being exists if necessary being exists, though we can show that if contingent being exists, necessary being exists and that if finite being exists, infinite being exists. In other words, we cannot deduce the existence of the less perfect *passio disiuncta* from the more perfect, though we can proceed the other way round. That contingent being actually exists is known only by experience.[1]

2. We have seen that in Scotus's opinion it is necessary to maintain that the primary object of the intellect is being in general, if one wishes to safeguard the possibility of metaphysics. By saying this I do not mean to suggest that Scotus's doctrine of the primary object of the intellect was motivated simply by pragmatic considerations. Rather did he hold that the intellect as such is the faculty of apprehending being in general, and, holding this, he then pointed out what appeared to him to be the unfortunate conclusion which followed from the Thomist position. Similarly, Scotus maintained that unless there is a concept of being which is univocal in respect of God and creatures, no metaphysical knowledge of God is possible; but he did not assert this doctrine of the univocal character of the concept of being for a purely utilitarian reason; he was convinced that there is actually a univocal concept of this kind, and then pointed out that unless its existence is admitted, one cannot safeguard the possibility of any metaphysical knowledge of God. Our concepts are formed in dependence on sense-perception and represent immediately material quiddities or essences. But no concept of a material quiddity as such is applicable to God, for God is not included among material things. Therefore, unless we can form a concept which is not restricted to the material quiddity as such, but is common to infinite being and to finite being, to immaterial and to material being, we can never attain a true knowledge of God by means of concepts which are proper to Him. If Henry of Ghent's doctrine of the equivocal

[1] *Ox.*, 1, 39, no. 13.

character of the concept of being as applied to God and to creatures were true, it would follow that the human mind was restricted (in this life at least) to the knowledge of creatures alone; agnosticism would thus be the consequence of Henry's theory.[1] If I have mentioned this aspect of the question first, I have done so not in order to imply that Scotus was motivated simply by utilitarian or pragmatic considerations, but rather in order to show that the question was not a purely academic one in Scotus's eyes.

What did Scotus mean by the univocal concept of being? In the Oxford Commentary[2] he says: *et ne fiat contentio de nomine univocationis, conceptum univocum dico, qui ita est unus, quod ejus unitas sufficit ad contradictionem, affirmando et negando ipsum de eodem. Sufficit etiam pro medio syllogistico, ut extrema unita in medio sic uno, sine fallacia aequivocationis, concludantur inter se unum.* Scotus's first point is, therefore, that a univocal concept means for him a concept the unity of which is sufficient to involve a contradiction if one affirms and denies the idea of the same subject at the same time. If one were to say 'the dog (i.e. the animal) is running' and at the same time 'the dog (meaning the star or the dog-fish) is not running', there would be no real contradiction, since 'running' and 'not running' are not affirmed of the same subject: the contradiction is purely verbal. Similarly, if one were to say 'the unicorn is' (meaning that the unicorn has an intramental existence) and 'the unicorn is not' (meaning that the unicorn has no extramental existence in nature), there would be no real contradiction. Scotus, however, is referring to a word the meaning of which is sufficiently the same to bring about a real contradiction if one were to affirm and deny it of the same subject at the same time. For instance, if one said that the unicorn is and that the unicorn is not, understanding 'is' in both judgements as referring to extramental existence, there would be a real contradiction. Similarly, if one said that God is and that God is not, referring in both cases to real existence, there would be a contradiction. What does Scotus mean by *sufficit*? In the judgements 'God is' and 'God is not' it is sufficient for the production of a contradiction that 'is' should mean opposed to nothingness or not-being. A contradiction is involved in saying both that God is opposed to nothingness and that God is not opposed to nothingness. It must be remembered that Scotus is maintaining the

---

[1] *Ox.*, 1, 8, 3, nos. 4 ff. This represents Scotus' interpretation of Henry's doctrine.
[2] 1, 3, 2, no. 5.

existence of a univocal concept of being which is applicable to
God and creatures, so that one can say that God is and the
creature is, using the word 'is' in the same sense. He is perfectly
well aware, of course, that God and the creature are actually
opposed to nothingness in different ways, and he does not mean
to deny this; but his point is that if you mean by 'is' simply the
opposite of nothingness or not-being, then you can use the word
'being' of God and creatures in the same sense, prescinding from
the concrete ways in which they are opposed to nothingness.
Accordingly he says *sufficit ad contradictionem* so as not to imply
that God and the creatures are opposed to nothingness in the
same way. But though they are opposed to nothingness in different ways, they are none the less both opposed to nothingness,
and if one forms a concept of being denoting sheer opposition to
nothingness, a concept which involves contradiction if affirmed
and denied of the same subject at the same time, this concept can
be predicated univocally of God and creatures.

As to the remark about the syllogism, Scotus says that a
univocal concept, as he understands it, is a concept which, when
employed as middle term in a syllogism, has a meaning 'sufficiently' the same in both premisses to prevent the fallacy of
equivocation being committed. To take a crude example, if one
argued 'every ram is an animal, this object (meaning an instrument for pumping water) is a ram, therefore this object is an
animal', the syllogism would involve the fallacy of equivocation
and would not be valid. Now take the following argument. If
there is wisdom in some creatures, there must be wisdom in God;
but there is wisdom in some creatures; therefore there is wisdom
in God. If the term 'wisdom' is used equivocally, in completely
different senses, in regard to God and in regard to creatures, the
argument would be fallacious: if the argument is to be valid, the
idea of wisdom as applied to God and to creatures must be
sufficiently the same for equivocation to be avoided. Scotus is
attacking Henry of Ghent, according to whose opinion the predicates we apply to God and creatures are equivocal, though the
two meanings so resemble one another that one word can be used
for both. Scotus objects that to admit the truth of Henry's
opinion would be to admit that every argument from creatures to
God employs the fallacy of equivocation and is fallacious. The
univocity which Scotus asserts is not restricted, then, to the
concept of being. 'Whatsoever things are common to God and

the creature are such as belong to being as indifferent to finite and finite.'[1] If one considers being in abstraction from the distinction between infinite and finite being, that is, as signifying mere opposition to nothing, one has a univocal concept of being, and the transcendental attributes of being, the *passiones convertibiles*, can also give rise to univocal concepts. If one can form a univocal concept of being, one can also form univocal concepts of *one, true, good*.[2] What, then, of wisdom? Goodness is a *passio convertibilis*, inasmuch as every being is good by the mere fact that it is a being; but not every being is wise. Scotus answers[3] that the *passiones disiunctae*, such as *necessary* or *possible, act* or *potency*, are transcendent in the sense that neither member determines its subject as belonging to any special genus, and that wisdom and suchlike attributes can also be called transcendent, that is, as transcending the division of being into genera.

Scotus lays a strong emphasis on this doctrine of univocity. Every metaphysical investigation concerning God involves the consideration of some attribute and the removal from our idea of it of the imperfection which attaches to that attribute as found in creatures. In this way we attain an idea of the essence of *ratio formalis* of the attribute, and then we can predicate it of God in a supremely perfect sense. Scotus takes the example of wisdom, intellect and will.[4] First we remove from the idea of wisdom, for example, the imperfections of finite wisdom and attain to a concept of the *ratio formalis* of wisdom, what wisdom is in itself. Then we attribute wisdom to God in the most perfect manner (*perfectissime*). 'Therefore every investigation concerning God supposes that the intellect has the same univocal concept, which it receives from creatures.'[5] If it is denied that we can thus form an idea of the *ratio formalis* of wisdom, and so on, the conclusion would follow that we could arrive at no knowledge of God. On the one hand our knowledge is founded on our experience of creatures, while on the other hand we cannot predicate of God any attribute precisely as it is found in creatures. Therefore, unless we can attain a common middle term with a univocal meaning, no argument from creatures to God is possible or valid. That we can form a univocal concept of being, without reference to infinite or finite, uncreated or created, Scotus regarded as a fact of experience.[6]

[1] *Ox.*, 1, 8, 3, no. 18.   [2] *Ibid.*, 1, 8, 3, no. 19.   [3] *Ibid.*
[4] *Ibid.*, 1, 3, 2, no. 10.   [5] *Ibid.*   [6] Cf. *ibid.*, 1, 3, 2, no. 6.

Scotus agrees with Henry of Ghent that God is not in a genus, but he will not agree with his denial of the univocal character of the concept of being. 'I hold my middle opinion, that it is compatible with the simplicity of God that there should be some concept common to Him and to the creature, but this common concept is not a generically common concept.'[1] Now, Henry of Ghent, in Scotus's view, maintained that the concept of being as applied to God and to creatures is equivocal, and it is easily understandable that Scotus rejects this opinion. But what was his attitude towards St. Thomas's doctrine of analogy? In the first place Scotus asserts firmly that God and the creature are completely different in the real order, *sunt primo diversa in realitate, quia in nulla realitate conveniunt*.[2] Hence to accuse Scotus of Spinozism is clearly absurd. In the second place Scotus does not reject the analogy of attribution, since he admits that being belongs primarily and principally to God and teaches that creatures are to God as *mensurata ad mensuram, vel excessa ad excedens*,[3] while in the *De Anima*[4] he says that *omnia entia habent attributionem ad ens primum, quod est Deus*. In the third place, however, he insists that analogy itself presupposes a univocal concept, since we could not compare creatures with God as *mensurata ad mensuram, vel excessa ad excedens*, unless there was a concept common to both.[5] God is knowable by man in this life only by means of concepts drawn from creatures, and unless these concepts were common to God and creatures, we should never be able to compare creatures with God as the imperfect with the perfect: there would be no bridge between creatures and God. Even those masters who deny univocity with their lips, really presuppose it.[6] If there were no univocal concepts, we should have only a negative knowledge of God, which is not the case. We may say that God is not a stone, but we can also say that a chimaera is not a stone, so that in saying that God is not a stone we know no more of God than we do of a chimaera.[7] Further, knowledge that something is an effect of God is not sufficient by itself to give us our knowledge of God. A stone is an effect of God; but we do not say that God is a stone, because He is the cause of the stone, whereas we do say that He is wise, and this presupposes a univocal concept of wisdom which is transcendent (in Scotus's sense). In fine, Scotus's teaching is that although all creatures have an essential relation of dependence

---

[1] *Ox.*, 1, 8, 3, no. 16.   [2] *Ibid.*, 1, 8, 3, no. 11.   [3] *Ibid.*, 1, 8, 3, no. 12.
[4] 21, no. 14.   [5] *Ox.*, 1, 8, 3, no. 12.   [6] *Rep.*, 1, 3, 1, no. 7.
[7] *Ox.*, 1, 3, 2; 1, 8, 3, no. 9.

to God, this fact would not be sufficient to afford us any positive knowledge of God, since we possess no natural intuition of God, unless we could form univocal concepts common to God and creatures. Therefore he says that 'all beings have an attribution to the first being, which is God . . .; yet in spite of this fact there can be abstracted from all of them one common concept which is expressed by this word *being*, and is one logically speaking, although it is not (one) naturally and metaphysically speaking', that is, speaking either as a natural philosopher or as a metaphysician.[1]

This last remark gives rise to the question whether or not Scotus considered the univocity of the concepts of being to be really restricted to the logical order. Some writers affirm that he did. The passage from the *De Anima* which has just been quoted seems to state it positively, and Scotus's observation, quoted above, that God and creatures *sunt primo diversa in realitate, quia in nulla realitate conveniunt*, would seem to teach the same. But if the univocal concept of being were restricted to the logical order in such a way that it was an *ens rationis*, how would it help to ensure objective knowledge of God? Moreover, in the Oxford Commentary[2] Scotus considers the objection to his theory that matter has an *esse* of its own. The objection is that in the case of analogues a thing or attribute is present really only in the primary analogue: in the other it is not present really, except by way of a relation to the primary analogue. Health is present really in the animal, whereas it is present in urine only *per attributionem ad illud*. *Esse* comes from the form: therefore it is not present really in matter, but only through its relation to the form. In answer to this objection Scotus says that the example given is valueless, since there are a hundred examples to the contrary, and then remarks, 'for there is no greater analogy than that of the creature to God *in ratione essendi*, and yet *esse*, existence, belongs primarily and principally to God in such a way that it yet belongs really and univocally to the creature; and similarly with goodness and wisdom and the like'.[3] Here he uses the words 'really and univocally' (*realiter et univoce*) together. If the doctrine of univocity is meant to ensure an objective knowledge of God from creatures, it would seem to be essential to that doctrine that the univocal concept should not be an *ens rationis* merely, but that it should have a real foundation or counterpart in extramental reality. On the other hand, Scotus is insistent that God is not in a genus and that God and creatures are in the real order *primo diversa*. How can the two sets of statements be reconciled?

The concept of being is abstracted from creatures, and it is the concept of being without any determination; it is logically prior to the division of being into infinite and finite being. But in actual fact every being must be either infinite or finite: it must be opposed to nothingness either as infinite being or as finite being: there is no actually existent being which is neither infinite nor finite. In this sense the univocal concept of being, as logically prior to the division of being into infinite and finite, possesses a unity which belongs to the logical order. The natural philosopher obviously does not consider being in this sense, nor does the metaphysician in so far as he is concerned with actually existent being and with possible being, since the concept of a being which would be neither infinite nor finite would not be the concept of a possible being. On the other hand, even though every actual being is either finite or infinite, every being is really opposed to nothingness, though in different ways, so that there is a real foundation for the univocal concept of being. As *intentio prima* the concept of being is founded on reality, for otherwise it could not be abstracted, and has objective reference, while as *intentio secunda* it is an *ens rationis*; but the concept of being as such, whether considered as *intentio prima* or *intentio secunda*, does not express something which has a formal existence outside the mind. It is, therefore, a logical concept. The logician 'considers second intentions as applied to first intentions', says Scotus when speaking of universals,[1] and what is univocal for the logician is equivocal[2] for the philosopher who is studying real things. One can say, then, that the univocal concept of being is an *ens rationis*. On the other hand, the univocal concept of being has a real foundation in actuality. The case is not without parallel to that of the universal. No doubt, Scotus did not consider adequately all the possible objections against his theory; but the truth of the matter seems to be that he was so intent on refuting the doctrine of Henry of Ghent, which he considered to endanger or render impossible any objective knowledge of God in this life, that he did not give his full attention to all the complexities of the problem and to the difficulties which

[1] *Ox.*, 2, 3, 1, no. 7.
[2] For Scotus 'equivocal' means, of distinct or different meanings. The scientist, for instance, considers actual bodies, which differ, but one can form a common concept of body in general.

might be raised against his own theory. It must be remembered, however, that Scotus postulated a formal distinction between the attributes of being and between the attributes and being. 'Being contains many attributes which are not different things from being itself, as Aristotle proves in the beginning of the fourth book of the *Metaphysics*, but which are distinguished formally and quidditatively, that is, by a formal, objectively grounded distinction, from one another, and also from being, by a real and quidditative formality, I say.'[1] In this case the univocal concept of being cannot be a mere *ens rationis*, in the sense of a purely subjective construction. There is no separate or separable thing, existing extramentally, which corresponds to the univocal concept of being; but there is an objective foundation for the concept none the less. One can say, then, that the univocal concept of being is not purely logical, provided that one does not mean to imply that there is any *thing* in extramental reality which corresponds to the concept.

3. I have treated the doctrine of univocity at some length, not only because the doctrine is one of the characteristics of Scotism, but also because Scotus attached very considerable importance to the doctrine, as a safeguard of natural theology. I turn now to a brief consideration of another characteristic doctrine of Scotus, that of the *distinctio formalis a parte rei*, the objective formal distinction, which plays an important rôle in the Scotist system and one use of which has just been mentioned.

The doctrine of the formal distinction was not an invention of Scotus: one finds it in the philosophy of Olivi, for example, and it has been ascribed to St. Bonaventure himself. In any case it became a common doctrine among the Franciscan thinkers, and what Scotus did was to take over the doctrine from his predecessors and make extensive use of it. In brief, the doctrine is that there is a distinction which is less than the real distinction and more objective than a virtual distinction. A real distinction obtains between two things which are physically separable, at least by divine power. It is obvious enough that there is a real distinction between a man's two hands, since these are distinct things; but there is also a real distinction between the form and matter of any material object. A purely mental distinction signifies a distinction made by the mind when there is no corresponding objective distinction in the thing itself. The distinction between a thing and its definition, for example, between 'man' and 'rational animal', is purely mental. A formal distinction obtains when the mind distinguishes in an object two or more *formalitates* which are objectively distinct, but which are inseparable from one another, even by divine power. For instance, Scotus asserted a formal distinction between the divine attributes. Mercy and justice are formally distinct, though the divine justice and the divine mercy are inseparable, since, in spite of the formal distinction between them, each is really identical with the divine essence.

An example from psychology may make Scotus's meaning clearer. There is only one soul in man, and there cannot be a real distinction between the sensitive soul and the intellectual or rational soul in man: it is in virtue of the one vital principle that a man thinks and exercises sensation. Not even God can separate a man's rational soul from his sensitive soul, for it would no longer be a human soul. On the other hand, sensation is not thought: rational activity can exist without sensitive activity, as in the angels, and sensitive activity can exist without rational activity, as in the case of the purely sensitive soul of the brute. In man, then, the sensitive and rational principles are formally distinct, with a distinction which is objective, that is, independent of the mind's distinguishing activity; but they are not really distinct *things*; they are distinct *formalitates* of one thing, the human soul.

Why did Scotus assert the existence of this formal distinction, and why was he not content to call it a *distinctio rationis cum fundamento in re*? The ultimate reason was, of course, that he thought the distinction to be not only warranted, but also demanded by the nature of knowledge and the nature of the object of knowledge. Knowledge is the apprehension of being, and if the mind is forced, so to speak, to recognise distinctions in the object, that is, if it does not simply construct actively a distinction in the object, but finds the recognition of a distinction imposed upon it, the distinction cannot be simply a mental distinction, and the foundation of the distinction in the mind must be an objective distinction in the object. On the other hand, there are cases when the foundation of the distinction cannot be the existence of distinct separable factors in the object. It is necessary, then, to find room for a distinction which is less than a real distinction, such as obtains between soul and body in man, but which at the same time is founded on an objective distinction in the object, a distinction which can be only between different, but not separable formalities of one and the same object. Such a distinction will maintain the objectivity of knowledge, without, however, impairing the unity of the object. It may be objected, of course, that the formal distinction as applied by Scotus does, in some cases at least, impair the requisite unity of the object and that it surrenders too much to 'realism'; but it would appear that Scotus considered the distinction to be necessary if the objectivity of knowledge is to be maintained.

4. One of the questions in which Scotus applies his formal distinction is the question of the distinction which obtains between essence and existence in the creature.[1] He refuses to admit a real distinction between essence and existence: 'it is simply false, that existence (*esse*) is something different from essence'.[2] Similarly, 'the proposition is false, that just as existence stands to essence, so operation (*operari*) stands to potency, for existence is really the same as the essence and does not proceed from the essence, whereas act or operation proceeds from potency and is not really the same as potency'.[3] The assertion, *simpliciter falsum est, quod esse sit aliud ab essentia*, would indeed appear to be directed against such statements of St. Thomas as *Ergo oportet quod omnis talis res, cuius esse est aliud a natura sua, habeat esse ab alio;*[4] but, given Scotus's conception of a real distinction, his denial of a real distinction between essence and existence in creatures is more relevant to the doctrine of Giles of Rome, for whom essence and existence were physically separable, than to that of St. Thomas Aquinas.

But when Scotus discusses the relation of essence and existence, his polemic is directed not so much against St. Thomas or even Giles of Rome as against Henry of Ghent. Henry did not maintain a real distinction between essence and existence in creatures, but he distinguished *esse essentiae* and *esse existentiae*, the former being the state of the essence as known by God, the latter being its state after creation, creation adding no positive element to the essence, but only a relation to God. Henry had asserted this doctrine of the *esse essentiae* in order to account for the fact of science, in the sense of knowledge of timeless truths about essences, irrespective of the actual existence of such objects, but Scotus argued that Henry's doctrine destroyed the Christian idea of creation. For example, creation is production out of

---

[1] It must be admitted that Scotus confines himself to denying the real distinction and does not explicitly apply the formal objective distinction to the relation of essence and existence in the creature; but the doctrine of Scotists on this point seems to me to be a reasonable interpretation of Scotus's meaning.

[2] *Ox.*, 4, 13, 1, no. 38.　　[3] *Ibid.*, 2, 16, no. 10.　　[4] *De ente et essentia*, 5.

nothing; but if a stone formerly, before its creation, had *esse verum reale*, then when it is produced by the efficient cause, it is not produced from nothing.[1] Moreover, as the essence is known eternally by God, it would follow from this notion that the essence before actual existence already possesses *esse reale* and that creation is eternal: one would thus have to admit other necessary beings besides God. Only that which actually exists has *esse reale*; possible existence (*esse possibile*) is only *esse secundum quid*.[2] The essence as known may be said to possess *esse diminutum*; but this existence (*esse*) of an essence in the divine mind before its actual production is simply *esse cognitum*. Scotus and St. Thomas are at one on this point, that creation means the production of the whole object out of nothing and that the essence before creation did not possess any *esse* of its own, though Scotus differed from St. Thomas in his view of the relationship which obtains between the essence and the existence in the created object, since he rejected a real distinction, though, as already remarked, this rejection was actually a rejection of the real distinction maintained by Giles of Rome rather than of that taught by St. Thomas.

5. The formal objective distinction was also employed by Scotus in his discussion of universals. In regard to universals Scotus was certainly not an exaggerated realist, and Suarez's assertion[3] that Scotus taught that the common nature is numerically the same in all individuals of the species, misrepresents Scotus's position, at least if taken out of its setting and out of relation to Suarez's own doctrine. Scotus states unambiguously that 'the universal in act does not exist except in the intellect' and that there is no actually existing universal which is predicable of another object than that in which it exists.[4] The common nature is not numerically the same in Socrates and in Plato; it cannot be compared to the divine essence, which is numerically the same in the three divine Persons.[5] Nevertheless, there is a unity which is less than numerical (*unitas minor quam numeralis*). Though the physical nature of an object is inseparable from the object's *haecceitas* (the object's 'thisness' or principle of individuation, which we shall consider shortly) and though it cannot exist in any other object, there is a formal objective distinction between the human nature and the 'Socratesness' or *haecceitas* in Socrates, but not a real distinction, so that the human nature can be considered simply as

---

[1] *Ox.*, 1, 36, no. 3.　　　　　　　[2] *Ibid.*, 1, 30, 2, no. 15.
[3] *Disputationes Metaphysicae*, 6, 1, no. 2.　　[4] *Rep.*, 2, 12, 5, no. 12.
[5] *Ibid.*, 2, 12, 5, no. 13.

such, without reference to individuality or to universality. Appealing to Avicenna,[1] Scotus observes that horseness is simply horseness (*equinitas est tantum equinitas*) and that of itself it has neither *esse singulare* nor *esse universale*.[2] In other words, there exists between the *haecceitas* and the nature in a concrete object a *distinctio formalis a parte rei*, and it is necessary to suppose such a distinction, since otherwise, that is, if the nature were *of itself* individual, if it were, for example, of itself the nature of Socrates, there would be no objective foundation, no valid ground for our universal statements. The abstraction of the logical universal presupposes a distinction in the object between the nature and the *haecceitas*.

It is, however, important to remember that this distinction is not a real distinction, not, that is, a distinction between two separable entities. Form and matter are separable; but the nature and the *haecceitas* are not separable. Not even the divine power can separate physically the 'Socratesness' of Socrates and the human nature of Socrates. Therefore, even though Scotus's assertion of the formal objective distinction is indeed a concession in one sense to realism, it does not imply that the human nature of Socrates is objectively and numerically identical with the human nature of Plato. Scotus is concerned, not to support exaggerated realism, but rather to account for the objective reference of our universal judgements. Whether or not one agrees with his theory is, of course, another matter; but in any case to accuse him of falling into the early mediaeval form of exaggerated realism is to misunderstand and misrepresent his position. Scotus is willing to say with Averroes,[3] *Intellectus est qui facit universalitatem in rebus*; but he insists that this proposition must not be understood as excluding the *unitas realis minor unitate numerali* which exists prior to the mind's operation, since this exclusion would make it impossible to explain why 'the intellect is moved to abstract one specific concept from Socrates and Plato rather than from Socrates and a stone'.[4] It is the objective reference of science which interests Scotus.

J. Kraus[5] has maintained that Duns Scotus distinguishes three universals. First, there is the physical universal, which is the specific nature existing really in individual objects; secondly, there is the metaphysical universal, which is the common nature, not

[1] In *Metaphysics*, 5, 1.   [2] *Ibid.*, 5, 11.   [3] *De Anima*, 1, 8.   [4] *Rep.*, 2, 12, 5, no. 13.
[5] *Die Lehre des J. Duns Skotus von der natura communis*, Fribourg, 1927.

as it actually exists in the concrete thing, but with the characteristics which it acquires through abstraction by the active intellect, namely positive indetermination or predicability of many individuals *in potentia proxima*; and thirdly, there is the logical universal, the universal in the strict sense, which is the metaphysical universal conceived reflexly in its predicability and analysed into its constitutive notes. But this threefold distinction must not be understood as implying that the physical universal is separable or really distinct from the individuality of the object in which it exists. The concrete object consists of the nature and the *haecceitas*, and between them there is, not a real distinction but a *distinctio formalis a parte rei*. Scotus's mention of the relation of matter to successive forms[1] should not mislead us, since for Scotus there is a real distinction between matter and form, and the same matter can exist under successive forms, though it cannot exist simultaneously under different ultimately determining forms. The physical universal, however, though indifferent, as considered *in itself*, to this or that *haecceitas*, cannot exist in itself extramentally and is physically inseparable from its *haecceitas*.

6. That Scotus taught the doctrine of hylomorphism is clear enough;[2] but it is not so clear whether or not he accepted the Bonaventurian attribution of hylomorphic composition to angels. If the *De rerum principio* were authentic, there could be no doubt as to Scotus's acceptance of the Bonaventurian view, but the *De rerum principio* is not the work of Scotus, and in his authentic writings the latter nowhere expressly states the Bonaventurian doctrine. Thus Father Parthenius Minges, O.F.M., who draws on the *De rerum principio* in his *Joannis Duns Scoti Doctrina philosophica et theologica*, has to admit that 'in the Commentaries on the *Sentences*, the *Quaestiones quodlibetales* and the *Questions on the Metaphysics of Aristotle* Scotus does not expressly state this doctrine, but only more or less touches on, insinuates or supposes it'.[3] It seems to me that Scotus's treatment of matter in the Commentaries can be said to 'suppose' the doctrine of the hylomorphic composition of rational soul and of angels only if one is determined on other grounds to assume that he held this doctrine, if, for example, one is determined to accept the *De rerum principio* as Scotus's work; but it is true that in the *De Anima*[4] he remarks that 'probably it can be said that in the soul there is matter'. However, Scotus is here engaged in showing that the presence of

---

[1] *Loc. cit.*   [2] Cf. *Ox.*, 2, 12, 1.   [3] p. 46.   [4] 15, no. 3 ff.

matter in the soul can be deduced with probability from the premisses of Aristotle and St. Thomas, even though St. Thomas did not hold the doctrine. For example, he argues that if matter is the principle of individuation, as St. Thomas (but not Scotus) held, then there must be matter in the rational soul. It is useless to say that the soul, when separated from the body, is distinguished from other souls by its relation to the body, first because the soul does not exist for the sake of the body, secondly because the relation or inclination to the body, which no longer exists, would be no more than a *relatio rationis*, and thirdly because the inclination or relation supposes a foundation, i.e. *this* soul, so that the thisness could not be due to the relation. Thus Scotus in the *De Anima* is trying to show that if one maintains with St. Thomas that matter is the principle of individuation, one ought to assert the presence of matter in the rational soul, in order to explain the individuality of the rational soul after death; he does not state that this conclusion represents his own opinion. It may be that it does represent Scotus's own opinion and that he wished to show that the Thomist ought, on his own premisses, to share that opinion; but one is hardly in a position to state positively that Scotus without a doubt maintained the Bonaventurian doctrine, and if one were prepared to reject the authenticity of the *De Anima*, there would seem to be no very cogent reason for stating that Scotus even probably maintained the doctrine.

But whatever Scotus's opinion on universal hylomorphism may have been, he certainly held that matter, really distinct from form, is an entity in its own right and that it is *potentia subjectiva* and not simply *potentia objectiva*, that is, that it is something existing, not something which is merely possible.[1] Moreover, matter is an *ens absolutum*, in the sense that it could exist by itself without form, at least through the divine power.[2] An entity which is distinct from and prior to another entity can exist apart from that other entity without any contradiction being involved. That matter is distinct from form is proved by the fact that together with form it makes a real composite being, while that it is prior to form, logically prior at least, is proved by the fact that it receives form and that what receives form must be logically prior to form.[3] Similarly, since God creates matter immediately, He could conserve it immediately, that is, without any secondary conserving agency. Again, form does not belong to the essence of

---

[1] *Ox.*, 2, 12, 1, no. 10.   [2] Cf. *ibid.*, 2, 12, 2; *Rep.* 2, 12, 2.   [3] *Ox., loc. cit.*, no. 3.

matter nor does the *esse* which form confers on matter belong to the matter itself, since it is removed in substantial change.[1] In other words, the reality of substantial change postulates the reality of matter. In answer to the Thomist objection that it is contradictory to speak of matter as a real entity, that is, as actually existing without form, since to say that matter actually exists on its own account and to say that it has a form is one and the same, Scotus answers that act and form are not necessarily convertible terms. Of course, if act is taken to mean act which is received and which actuates and distinguishes, then matter, which is receptive, is not act; but if act and potency are understood in a wider sense, every thing which is *extra causam suam* is in act, even privations, and in this sense matter is in act, though it is not form.[2]

7. Scotus rejects the theory of *rationes seminales*, on the ground that the theory is not needed in order to avoid the conclusion that the created efficient agent creates and annihilates in the changes it brings about, and that there is no other cogent reason for accepting it.[3] But though he rejects the theory of *rationes seminales*, he retains that of plurality of forms. Against the assertion of the Thomists that there is no need to postulate a form of corporeity, since *sine necessitate non est ponenda pluralitas*, Scotus replies that in this case there is a need, *hic enim est necessitas ponendi plura*, and he goes on to argue that although the body, when the soul has departed, is continually tending to dissolution, it remains a body, for a time at least, and must possess that form which makes a body a body.[4] Moreover, the Body of Christ in the tomb must have possessed a form of corporeity. From the fact that a human body naturally tends to dissolution when the soul has departed it does not follow that the body, in a state of separation from the soul, has no proper form of its own; it follows only that it has not got a *perfect* subsistence of its own, and the reason of this is that the form of corporeity is an imperfect form which disposes the body for a higher form, the soul.

But though Scotus affirms the existence of a form of corporeity in the human body, and, of course, in every organic body, which is transmitted by the parents at the same time that God infuses the rational soul and which is really distinct from the rational soul,

---

[1] *Rep.*, 2, 12, 2, no. 5.
[2] *Ox.*, 2, 12, 2, no. 7. The distinction of prime matter into *materia primo prima*, *materia secundo prima* and *materia tertio prima* is found only in the unauthentic *De rerum principio*.
[3] *Rep.*, 2, 18, 1.   [4] *Ox.*, 4, 11, 3, nos. 54 ff.

from which it can be separated, it should not be imagined that he breaks up the human soul into three really distinct forms or even parts, the vegetative, sensitive and intellective principles; and he rejects the theories which appear to him to impair the unity of the soul. The rational soul of man comprises these three powers *unitive*, 'although they are formally distinct'.[1] It would be false to suggest that Scotus taught the existence of three souls in man or that he maintained that the vegetative and sensitive powers are distinct from the rational power in the same way in which the form of corporeity is distinct. Whereas the distinction between the form of corporeity and the human soul is a real distinction, that between the powers within the soul itself is a formal distinction, which obtains between inseparable *formalitates* of one object, not between separable entities or forms.

8. It is necessary to say something about Scotus's somewhat obscure doctrine of individuation, the obscurity lying rather on the positive than on the negative side of the doctrine.

Scotus criticises and rejects St. Thomas's theory that prime matter is the principle of individuation. Prime matter cannot be the primary reason of distinction and diversity since it is of itself indistinct and indeterminate.[2] Moreover, if matter is the principle of individuation, it follows that in the case of substantial change the two substances, that corrupted and that generated, are precisely the same substance, since the matter is the same, even though the forms are different. St. Thomas's theory seems to imply that quantity is actually the principle of individuation; but quantity is an accident and a substance cannot be individuated by an accident. Incidentally, Scotus tries to show that Aristotle is wrongly cited as an authority for the Thomist view of individuation.

The principle of individuation is thus not prime matter, nor can it be the nature as such, since it is precisely with the individuation of the nature that we are concerned. What is it, then? It is an *entitas individualis*. 'This entity is neither matter nor form nor the composite thing, in so far as any of these is a nature; but it is the ultimate reality of the being which is matter or form or a composite thing.'[3] The *entitas singularis* and the *entitas naturae*, whether the latter is matter or form or a *compositum*, are formally distinct; but they are not, and cannot be, two things. They are not separable things; nor does the *entitas singularis* stand to the

---

[1] *Ox.*, 2, 16, no. 17.   [2] *Ibid.*, 2, 3, 5, no. 1.   [3] *Ibid.*, 2, 3, 6, no. 15.

entitas naturae as specific difference to genus.[1] The word *haecceitas* is not used for the principle of individuation in the Oxford Commentary, though it is so used in the *Reportata Parisiensia*[2] and in the *Quaestiones in libros Metaphysicorum*.[3]

It is not so easy to understand exactly what this *haecceitas* or *entitas singularis vel individualis* or *ultima realitas entis* actually is. It is, as we have seen, neither matter nor form nor the composite thing; but it is a positive entity, the final reality of matter, form and the composite thing. A human being, for instance, is *this* composite being, composed of *this* matter and *this* form. The *haecceitas* does not confer any further qualitative determination; but it seals the being as *this* being. Scotus's view certainly cannot be equated with the theory that every nature is of itself individual, since this he expressly denies, though in view of the fact that Scotus, while postulating a formal distinction between *haecceitas* and nature, denies their real distinction from one another, it seems to be implied that a thing has *haecceitas* or 'thisness' by the fact that it exists. His theory is not the same as that of the Nominalists, since he postulates contraction of the nature by the 'ultimate reality'; but the fact that he speaks of 'ultimate reality' would seem to imply that a nature acquires this ultimate reality through existence, though it is not, says Scotus, existence itself.[4]

[1] *Ox.*, 2, 3, 6, no. 15. [2] 2, 12, 5, nos. 1, 8, 13, 14.
[3] 7, 13, nos. 9 and 26. [4] *Quaestiones in libros Metaph.*, 7, 13, no. 7.

CHAPTER XLVIII

SCOTUS—IV: NATURAL THEOLOGY

Metaphysics and God—Knowledge of God from creatures—Proof of God's existence—Simplicity and intelligence of God—God's infinity—The Anselmian argument—Divine attributes which cannot be philosophically demonstrated—The distinction between the divine attributes—The divine ideas—The divine will—Creation.

1. GOD is not, properly speaking, an object of metaphysical science, says Scotus,[1] in spite of the fact that metaphysics are the science of being, and God is the first being. A truth belongs properly to that science in which it is known *a priori*, from the principles of that science, and the metaphysician knows truths about God only *a posteriori*. God is, therefore, the proper object of theology, in which science He is known as He is in His essence, in Himself; He is the object of metaphysics only *secundum quid*, inasmuch as the philosopher comes to know God only in and through His effects.

This statement certainly does not mean that for Scotus the philosopher or metaphysician is unable to attain any certain knowledge of God. 'By our natural power (*ex naturalibus*) we can know some truths concerning God', says Scotus,[2] and he goes on to explain that many things (*multa*) can be known about God by the philosophers through a consideration of God's effects. By the natural power of reason one can conclude that God is one, supreme, good, but not that God is three in Persons.[3] Theology deals more properly with the divine Persons than with the essential attributes of God, for most of the essential attributes (*essentialia plurima*) can be known by us in metaphysics.[4] Accordingly, the statement that God is, strictly speaking, the object of theology rather than of metaphysics does not mean that Scotus excludes the study of God from metaphysics, since although God is not the primary object of metaphysics, He is none the less considered in metaphysics in the noblest way in which He can be studied in any natural science.[5] In the *De primo principio*[6] Scotus recapitulates the perfections which the philosophers have proved to belong to

---

[1] *Rep.*, Prol., 3, no. 1. [2] *Ibid.*, Prol., 3, no. 6. [3] *Ox.*, 1, 1, 2, no. 2.
[4] *Ox.*, Prol., 4, no. 32. [5] *Ibid.*, Prol., 4, no. 20. [6] E.g. 4, nos. 36, 37.

God and distinguishes them from other perfections, such as omnipotence and universal and special providence, which belong more properly to the *credibilia*, truths which have not been proved by the philosophers but which are believed by *Catholici*. These latter truths, says Scotus, will be considered in *sequenti (tractatu)* and the words have been added, *scilicet in Theorematibus*. That an attempt was made to disprove this identification of the 'following' treatise with the *Theoremata* and that this attempt was largely due to the at least apparent contradiction between the *Theoremata* and the *De primo principio* has already been mentioned in Chapter XLV, and, as I there explained, I propose to expose the natural theology of Scotus on the supposition that the *Theoremata* is not the authentic work of Scotus, with the proviso that, were the authenticity of the *Theoremata* ever to be satisfactorily proved, one would have to explain the apparent contradiction on some such line as that adopted by M. Gilson. In any case, however, Scotus has made it perfectly clear in his certainly authentic works that the philosopher can prove many truths about God by the light of natural reason, without any actual employment of the data of revelation. Some of the points in regard to which Scotus restricted the scope of the unaided human intellect will be noted in the following pages; but it is important to note that Scotus was neither a sceptic nor an agnostic in regard to natural theology, and the *Theoremata*, even if authentic, would be quite insufficient to dispose of the clear and abundant evidence on this point which is afforded by the Commentaries on the *Sentences* and by the *De primo principio*.

2. Scotus certainly thought that the existence of God stands in need of rational proof and that this rational proof must be *a posteriori*. Of his use of the Anselmian argument I shall speak later.

First of all, man has no intuitive knowledge of God in this life, since the intuition of God is precisely that form of knowledge which places a man *extra statum viae*.[1] Our knowledge starts from the things of sense, and our natural conceptual knowledge of God is arrived at through reflection on the objects of experience.[2] By considering creatures as God's effects the human mind is able to form concepts which apply to God; but one must add that the concepts of God which are formed from creatures are imperfect,[3] in contrast, that is, with concepts based on the divine essence

---

[1] *Quodlibet*, 7, no. 8.   [2] *Ox.*, 1, 3, 2, nos. 1 and 30.   [3] *Ibid.*, Prol., 1, no. 17.

itself. It follows that our natural knowledge of God is indistinct and obscure, since it is not knowledge of God as immediately present to the intellect in His essence.[1]

Our natural knowledge of God rests on our capacity to form univocal concepts, as has been explained in the last chapter. Scotus affirms that 'creatures which impress their own ideas (*species*) on the intellect, can also impress the ideas of transcendent (attributes) which belong in common to them and to God';[2] but it would not be possible to proceed from a knowledge of creatures to the knowledge of God, were we not able to form from creatures univocal concepts. When the intellect has formed these concepts, it can combine them to form a composite quidditative idea of God. Just as the imagination can combine the images of mountain and gold to form the image of a golden mountain, so can the intellect combine the ideas of goodness, supreme and actuality to form the concept of a supremely good and actual being.[3] Needless to say, this comparison should not mislead us into thinking that for Scotus the combining activity of the mind in natural theology is exactly parallel to the combining work of imagination and fancy; the former activity is governed by the objective truth and apprehended logical necessity, whereas the imaginative construction of a golden mountain is 'imaginary', that is, arbitrary or the work of fancy.

3. How does Scotus prove the existence of God? In the Oxford Commentary[4] he states that the existence of the first cause is shown much more perfectly from the attributes (*passiones*) of creatures considered in metaphysics than from those which are considered by the natural philosopher. 'For it is a more perfect and immediate knowledge of the first being to know it as first or necessary being than to know it as first mover.' Scotus does not here deny that the natural philosopher can show that the fact of motion requires a first mover; but his point is that the argument from motion does not, of itself, transcend the physical order and arrive at the necessary being which is the ultimate total cause of its effects. The first mover, considered as such, is simply the cause of motion; it is not conceived as the cause of the being of all other things, but is a (necessary) hypothesis to explain the physical fact of motion. The argument from motion is thus very far from being Scotus's favourite proof. It may be noted in passing that if the

[1] *Rep.*, Prol., 3, 2, no. 4.   [3] *Ox.*, 1, 3, 2, no. 18.
[2] *Ibid.*   [4] Prol., 2 lateralis, no. 21.

Commentary on the *Physics*, which is now rejected as spurious, were authentic, the difficulty in accepting the *Theoremata* might perhaps be lessened. In the former work[1] the author makes clear his belief that the argument from motion does not, of itself, bring us to a recognisable concept of God, since it merely arrives at a first mover, without indicating the nature of the first mover. Thus if it could be maintained that the author of the *Theoremata* was speaking of natural philosophy when he said that it cannot be proved that God is living or intelligent, it would seem that the apparent contradiction between the *Theoremata* and Scotus's certainly authentic works could be resolved. However, as the *Questions on the Physics of Aristotle* is unauthentic and as the authenticity of the *Theoremata* has not been proved, it is hardly worth while pursuing the matter further. In any case it remains true that Scotus emphasised those proofs for the existence of God which are founded on *passiones metaphysicae*. Moreover, in the Oxford Commentary,[2] Scotus remarks that the proposition that mover and moved must be distinct 'is true only in corporeal things' and 'I also believe that (even) there it is not necessarily true', while 'I say at least that in regard to spiritual beings it is simply false . . .

In the *De primo principio*[3] Scotus argues from the fact of contingency to the existence of a first cause and a necessary being. That there are beings which can have being after not-being, which can come into existence, which are contingent, is clear; and such beings require a cause of their being, since they can neither cause themselves nor be caused by nothing (*nec a se nec a nihilo*). If *A* is the cause of the being of a contingent object, it must be itself either caused or uncaused. If it is itself caused, let *B* be the cause of *A*. But it is impossible to proceed to infinity; so there must ultimately be a cause which is itself uncaused. Scotus distinguishes clearly between the series of *essentialiter ordinata* and the series of *accidentaliter ordinata*, and he points out that what he is denying is not the possibility of an unending regress of successive causes, each of which, taken in itself, is contingent, but the possibility of an unending (vertical) series of simultaneous total causes. As he observes, even if we grant the possibility of an infinite series of successive causes, the whole chain requires an explanation, and this explanation must be outside the chain itself, since each member of the chain is caused, and so contingent. An infinite

---

[1] 3, 7.   [2] 2, 25, *quaestio unica*, no. 12.   [3] 3.

series of succeeding contingent beings cannot explain its own existence, since the whole series is contingent if each member is contingent: it is necessary to postulate a transcendent cause. 'The totality of ordered effects (*causatorum*) is itself caused; therefore (it has been caused) by some cause which does not belong to that totality.'[1] If, for example, one postulates that the human race goes back to infinity, there is an infinite succession of fathers and children. The father causes the child; but after the father's death the son continues to exist and continues to be contingent. An ultimate cause is required, not only of the son's being here and now, but also of the whole series of fathers and sons, since the infinite regress does not make the series necessary. The same principle must be extended to the universe of contingent beings in general: the universe of contingent beings requires an *actual* transcendent cause (itself uncaused). An infinite succession 'is impossible, except in virtue of some nature of infinite duration (*durante infinite*), on which the whole succession and every member of it depends'.[2]

Scotus then proceeds to show that the first cause in the essential order of dependence must exist actually and cannot be merely possible,[3] that it is necessary being, that is, that it cannot not exist[4] and that it is one.[5] There cannot be more than one necessary being. Scotus argues, for example, that if there were two beings with a common nature of necessary being, one would have to distinguish formally between the common nature and the individuality, which would be something other than necessary being. If it is answered that there is no such distinction in a necessary being, it follows that the two beings are indistinguishable and hence one. This argument, though based on Scotus's theory of the common nature and of individuation, reminds one of an analogous argument given by St. Anselm. Moreover, the one essential order of the universe postulates only one *primum effectivum*. Scotus then goes on to show that there is a first final cause, *primum finitivum*,[6] and a supreme being in the order of eminence,[7] and proceeds to show that the *primum effectivum*, the *primum finitivum* and the *primum eminens* (or *perfectissimum*) are identical.[8]

In the Oxford Commentary on the *Sentences*[9] Scotus argues in much the same way. We have to proceed from creatures to God

[1] *De primo principio*, 3, 3.   [3] *Ibid.*, 3, 4.   [5] *Ibid.*, 3, no. 5.
[4] *Ibid.*, 3, no. 6.   [6] *Ibid.*, 3, nos. 6–7.   [6] *Ibid.*, 3, no. 9.
[7] *Ibid.*, nos. 9–10.   [8] *Ibid.*, nos. 11–14.   [9] *Ox.*, 2, 2, nos. 10ff.

by considering the causal relation (in respect of either efficient or final causality) or the relation of *excessum* to *excedens* in the order of perfection. Contingent being, the *effectibile*, is caused by nothing or by itself or by another. As it is impossible for it to be caused by nothing or by itself, it must be caused by another. If that other is the first cause, we have found what we are seeking: if not, then we must proceed further. But we cannot proceed for ever in the vertical order of dependence. *Infinitas autem est impossibilis in ascendendo.*[1] Nor can we suppose that contingent beings cause one another, for then we shall proceed in a circle, without arriving at any ultimate explanation of contingency. It is useless to say that the world is eternal, since the eternal series of contingent beings itself requires a cause.[2] Similarly in the order of final causality there must be a final cause which is not directed to any more ultimate final cause,[3] while in the order of eminence there must be a most perfect being, a *suprema natura*.[4] These three are one and the same being. The first efficient cause acts with a view to the final end; but nothing other than the first being itself can be its final end. Similarly, the first efficient cause is not univocal with its effects, that is, it cannot be of the same nature, but must transcend them; and as first cause, it must be the 'most eminent' being.[5]

4. As the first being is uncaused, it cannot possess essential parts like matter and form nor can it possess accidents: it cannot, in short, be composed in any way but must be essentially simple.[6] It must be intelligent and possessed of will. The natural agents in the world which do not consciously act for an end do nevertheless act for an end; and this means that they do so by the power and knowledge of the agent which transcends them. If the natural agents of the world act teleologically, this supposes that the primary cause knows the end and wills it, since nothing can be directed to an end except in virtue of knowledge and will (as, we might say, the arrow is directed to an end by an archer who knows and wills the end). God loves Himself and wills Himself necessarily; but He does not will necessarily anything outside Himself, since nothing outside Himself is necessary to Him: He alone is necessary being. It follows that He causes His effects freely and not necessarily. God knows and understands from eternity all that He can produce; He has actual and distinct

[1] *Ox.*, 2, 2, no. 11. [2] *Ibid.*, nos. 14-15. [3] *Ibid.*, no. 17.
[4] *Ibid.*, no. 18. [5] *Ibid.* [6] *De primo principio*, 4, nos. 1-4.

understanding of every intelligible, and this understanding is identical with Himself (*idem sibi*).[1]

5. But Scotus gave his closest attention to the infinity of God. The simplest and most perfect concept of God which we can form is that of the absolutely infinite Being. It is simpler than the concept of goodness or the like, since infinity is not like an attribute or *passio* of the being of which it is predicated, but signifies the intrinsic mode of that being. It is the most perfect concept, since infinite being includes virtually infinite truth, infinite goodness and every perfection which is compatible with infinity.[2] It is true that every perfection in God is infinite, but 'it has its formal perfection from the infinity of the essence as its root and foundation'.[3] All the divine perfections are grounded in the divine essence, which is best described as the infinity of being: it is not correct, therefore, to state that for Scotus the divine essence consists in will. 'Although the will is formally infinite, it does not, however, include all intrinsic perfections formally in itself . . . but the essence alone includes all perfections in this way.'[4]

In the *Opus Oxoniense*[5] and in the *De primo principio*[6] Scotus gives a series of proofs of the divine infinity. Presupposing the compatibility of infinity with being Scotus takes as the text of his first argument Aristotle's words, *Primum movet motu infinito; ergo habet potentiam infinitam*, and argues that the conclusion is invalid if it is understood as following from motion which is infinite in duration, since length of duration does not make a thing more perfect, though it is valid if it is understood as following from the power to produce by motion infinite effects, that is, successively. God, as first efficient Cause, able to produce an infinity of effects, must be infinite in power. Moreover, as God possesses in Himself in a more eminent way the causality of all possible secondary causes, He must be infinite in Himself, *intensive*.[7] Secondly, God must be infinite since He knows an infinity of intelligible objects. This argument might seem to be a sheer *petitio principii*; but Scotus gives a somewhat singular reason for supposing that God knows an infinity of *intelligibilia*. 'Whatsoever things are infinite in potency, so that if they are taken one after the other they can have no end, are infinite in act, if they are together in act. But it is clear enough that intelligible objects are infinite in potency in

---

[1] *De primo principio*, 4, no. 14.   [2] *Ox.*, 1, 2, 3, no. 17.   [3] *Ibid.*, 4, 3, 1, no. 32.
[4] *Ibid.*, 4, 13, 1, no. 32.   [5] 2, 2, nos. 25 ff.   [6] 4, nos. 15 ff.
[7] Cf. *Ox.*, 1, 2, 2, nos. 25-9.

respect of the created intellect, and in the uncreated intellect all (the *intelligibilia*) which are successively intelligible by the created intellect are actually understood together. Therefore, there are there (in the uncreated intellect) an infinite number of actually apprehended objects.'[1] Thirdly, Scotus argues from the finality of the will. 'Our will can desire and love an object greater than any finite object . . . and what is more, there seems to be a natural inclination to love above all an infinite good. . . . It thus appears that in the act of loving we have experience of an infinite good; indeed, the will seems to find no perfect rest in any other object . . .' The infinite good must, therefore, exist.[2] The fourth argument of the Oxford Commentary[3] is to the effect that it is not incompatible with finite being that there should be a more perfect being, but that it is incompatible with the *ens eminentissimum* that there should be a more perfect being. But infinity is greater and more perfect than finitude, and infinity and being are compatible. The *ens eminentissimum* must, therefore, be infinite. The proof that infinity is compatible with being amounts to little more than saying that we can discern no incompatibility. In the *De primo principio*[4] Scotus also proves God's infinity from the fact that His intellect is identical with His substance, arguing that such identification is impossible in a finite being.

Having proved, to his satisfaction at least, God's infinity, Scotus is able to show that God must be one and one alone.[5]

6. In his discussion of the divine infinity Scotus introduces the so-called ontological argument of St. Anselm.[6] He has just remarked that the intellect, the object of which is being, finds no mutual repugnance between 'being' and 'infinite', and that it would be astonishing, supposing the two to be incompatible, if the intellect did not discern the incompatibility, 'when a discord in sound so easily offends the hearing'. If there is such an incompatibility, why does not the intellect 'shrink back' from the idea of the infinite, if it is incompatible with its own proper object, being? He then proceeds to state that the argument of St. Anselm in the first chapter of the *Proslogium* can be 'coloured' (*potest colorari*) and that it should be understood in this way: 'God is that than which, having been thought without contradiction, a greater cannot be thought without contradiction. That (the words) "without contradiction" must be added is clear, for that in the thought

[1] *Ox.*, 1, 2, 2, no. 30; cf. *De primo principio*, 15 ff. [2] *Ox.*, 1, 2, 2, no. 31.
[3] 1, 2, 2, nos. 31-2. [4] 4, no. 21.
[5] *Ox.*, 1, 2, 3; *De primo principio*, 4, nos. 38-40. [6] *Ox.*, 1, 2, 2, no. 32.

of which a contradiction is included (that is, involved), is unthink-able . . .' It has been asserted that since Scotus admits that the Anselmian argument must be 'coloured', he rejects it. But he obviously does not reject it without more ado. Why should he 'colour' it, except to use it? And in point of fact he does use it. First he tries to show that the idea of the *summum cogitabile* is without contradiction, i.e. that the essence or *esse quidditativum* is possible, and then he observes that if the *summum cogitabile* is possible, it must exist, that it must have *esse existentiae. Majus igitur cogitabile est, quod est in re quam quod est tantum in intellectu.* That which really exists is *majus cogitabile* than that which does not really exist but is merely conceived, inasmuch as that which really exists is 'visible' or capable of being intuited, and that which can be intuited is 'greater' than that which can be merely conceived or can be known by abstractive thought alone. It follows, then, that the *summum cogitabile* must really exist. Scotus is not saying that we have a natural intuition of God; he is giving a reason for the judgement that that which really exists is greater or more perfect than tnat which does not really exist extra-mentally.

There is no doubt, then, that Scotus makes use of the Anselmian argument. Two questions arise, therefore. First, in what does the *coloratio* of the argument consist? Secondly, how did Scotus think that his use of the argument was consistent with his clear assertion that we can demonstrate God's existence only *a posteriori?* First the *coloratio* consists in an attempt to show that the idea of the most perfect being is the idea of a possible being, and he does this primarily by observing that no contradiction is observable in the idea of the most perfect being. In other words, he anticipates Leibniz's attempt to show that the idea of God is the idea of a possible being, inasmuch as the idea does not involve any contra-diction, and the idea of a being which does not involve a contradic-tion constitutes the idea of a possible being. On the other hand, Scotus did not consider that the fact that we cannot observe any contradiction in the idea of the most perfect being is a demonstra-tive proof of the fact that no contradiction is involved. We cannot show apodeictically and *a priori* that the most perfect being is possible, and that is why he states elsewhere that the Anselmian argument belongs to the proofs which amount to no more than *persuasiones probabiles.*[1] This supplies the answer to our second

---

[1] *Rep.,* 1, 2, 3, no. 8.

question. Scotus considered his use of the Anselmian argument to be compatible with his assertion that we can demonstrate God's existence only *a posteriori* because he did not regard the Anselmian argument as a demonstration, but only as a 'probable persuasion', a probable proof. He did not simply reject the argument as St. Thomas did; but he was dissatisfied with the argument as it stood and thought that it needed 'colouring'. On the other hand, he did not think that the 'colouring', the proof that the idea of God is the idea of a possible being, is a demonstrative proof, and so he put forward the argument as probable. He used it as an auxiliary argument to show what is involved or implied in the idea of God rather than as a strict demonstration of God's existence. It is as though he had said: 'This is the best we can make of the argument, and it has its uses if you accept the premisses; but I do not regard the argument as a demonstration. If a strict demonstration of God's existence is wanted, it will have to proceed *a posteriori*.'

7. Scotus did not consider that we can demonstrate by the natural reason all God's essential attributes. Thus in the *De primo principio*[1] he says that consideration of the attributes of omnipotence, immensity, omnipresence, truth, justice, mercy and providence directed to all creatures, to intelligent creatures in particular, will be postponed until the next treatise, as they are *credibilia*, that is, revealed objects of faith. It might well appear strange to read that omnipotence, for instance, cannot be philosophically demonstrated as a divine attribute, when Scotus does not hesitate to conclude God's infinity from His infinite power; but he distinguishes between omnipotence in the proper theological sense (*proprie theologice*), which cannot be demonstrated with certainty by philosophers, and infinite power (*potentia infinita*), which can be demonstrated by philosophers.[2] The distinction consists in this. God's power to produce every possible effect, immediately *or* mediately, can be proved philosophically, but not His power to produce all possible effects immediately. Even though the first cause possesses in itself *eminentius* the causality of the secondary cause, it does not necessarily follow, says Scotus, that the first cause can produce the effect of the secondary cause immediately, without the co-operation of the secondary cause, not because the causality of the first cause needs adding to, so to speak, but because the imperfection of the effect may require, so far as the philosopher can see, the causal operation of the finite cause as its

[1] 4, no. 37. [2] *Ox.*, 1, 42, *quaestio unica*, no. 2.

explanation. Scotus is thus not attacking the demonstrability of God's creative power: what he is saying is that the proposition, 'whatever the first efficient cause can do with the co-operation of a secondary cause, that it can do immediately by itself', is neither self-evident nor philosophically demonstrable, but is known by faith (*non est nota ex terminis neque ratione naturali, sed est tantum credita*). The objection that God's universal immediate causality would destroy the proper causality of creatures cannot be solved by reason alone.[1]

As to the divine immensity and omnipresence, Scotus's denial of the demonstrability of this attribute of God depends on his denial of St. Thomas's rejection of *actio in distans*, action at a distance. According to St. Thomas[2] *actio in distans* is impossible, while for Scotus the greater the efficacy of the agent, the greater its power to act at a distance. 'Therefore, since God is the most perfect agent, it cannot be concluded concerning Him through the nature of action that He is together with (essentially present to) any effect caused by Him, but rather that He is distant.'[3] It is difficult to see what *actio in distans* could possibly mean in regard to God; but, as far as Scotus is concerned, he is not denying that God is omnipresent or that omnipresence is a necessary attribute of God, but only that God's omnipresence is philosophically demonstrable and, in particular, that the supposed impossibility of *actio in distans* is a valid reason for showing that God is omnipresent.

Probably 'truth' must be taken together with mercy and justice, as meaning in the context much the same as justice. At least, if this suggestion of commentators is not accepted, it is extremely difficult to see what Scotus did mean, since truth and veracity are listed among the divine attributes which are known by the natural reason.[4] As to justice, Scotus sometimes seems to say that the divine justice can be known by the natural light of reason;[5] but when he denies that the justice of God is philosophically demonstrable he appears to mean that it cannot be proved that God rewards and punishes in the next life, since it cannot be proved strictly by the philosopher that the soul is immortal,[6] or that we cannot justify by our reason all the ways of God in regard to man. That God is merciful, in the sense of forgiving sins and forgoing

---

[1] Cf. *Rep.* 1, 42, 2, no. 4; *Quodlibet*, 7, nos. 4 and 18.
[2] *S.T.*, Ia, 8, 1, *ad* 3.   [3] *Rep.*, 1, 37, 2, nos. 6ff.
[4] Cf. *De primo principio*, 4, nos. 36ff; *Ox.*, Prol., 2, no. 10; 3, 23, no. 5; 3, 24, no. 22.
[5] Cf. *ibid.*, 4, 17, no. 7; *Rep.*, 4, 17, no. 7.   [6] Cf. *Ox.*, 4, 43, 2, no. 27.

the exaction of punishment, cannot be philosophically demonstrated. Finally, as to divine providence, when Scotus says this cannot be philosophically proved, he appears to mean, not that no providence at all can be demonstrated, but that immediate or special providential action on the part of God, without the employment of secondary causes, cannot be philosophically demonstrated. Scotus certainly held that divine creation, conservation and government of the world can be demonstrated.

8. Scotus rejected the theories of St. Thomas and Henry of Ghent concerning the absence in God of any distinction other than the real distinction between the divine Persons and postulated a formal objective distinction between the divine attributes. The *ratio formalis* of wisdom, for example, is not identical with the *ratio formalis* of goodness. Now, 'infinity does not destroy the *ratio* of that to which it is added'.[1] If, therefore, the formal character of the univocal concept of wisdom is not the same as the formal character of the univocal concept of goodness, infinite wisdom will be formally distinct from infinite goodness. It follows, then, that the divine attributes of wisdom and goodness will be formally distinct, independently of the human mind's operation. On the other hand, there can be no composition in God, nor any real distinction in the technical sense between the divine attributes. The distinction between the divine attributes must be, therefore, not a real distinction, but a *distinctio formalis a parte rei*, and the formula will be that the attributes are really or substantially identical (*in re*), but formally distinct. 'So I allow that truth is identical with goodness *in re*, but not, however, that truth is formally goodness.'[2] Scotus contends that the distinction between the divine essence and the divine attributes and between the attributes themselves does not impair the divine simplicity, since the attributes are not accidents of God, nor do they inform God as finite accidents inform finite substances. As infinite they are really identical with the divine essence, and God can be called Truth or Wisdom or Goodness; but the fact remains that the *rationes formales* of truth, wisdom and goodness are formally and objectively distinct.[3]

9. It has been maintained in the past that the divine ideas depend, according to Scotus, on God's free will, so that the exemplar ideas are God's arbitrary creation. But as a matter of fact Scotus explicitly teaches that it is the divine intellect which

[1] *Ox.*, 1, 8, 4, no. 17.   [2] *Ibid.*, 1, 8, 4, no. 18.   [3] *Ibid.*, nos. 19 ff.

produces the ideas: 'the divine intellect, precisely as intellect, produces in God the *rationes ideales*, the ideal or intelligible natures'.[1] The divine essence, however, is the foundation of the ideas. 'God first knows His essence, and in the second instant He understands (*intelligit*) creatures by means of His essence, and then in that way the knowable object depends on the divine understanding in regard to its being known (*in esse cognito*), since it is constituted in its *esse cognito* by that understanding.'[2] The divine ideas do not, then, depend on the divine will. 'The divine intellect, as in some way, that is, logically prior to the act of the divine will, produces those objects in their intelligible being (*in esse intelligibili*), and so in respect of them it seems to be a merely natural cause, since God is not a free cause in respect of anything but that which presupposes in some way His will or an act of His will.'[3] Possibles are not produced by the divine omnipotence, but by the divine intellect, which produces them *in esse intelligibili*.[4]

The divine ideas are infinite in number, and they are substantially identical with the divine essence; but they are not formally identical with the divine essence:[5] they are necessary and eternal, but they are not formally necessary and eternal in precisely the same sense as the divine essence, since the divine essence has a certain logical priority. Again, 'although the divine essence was from eternity the exemplary cause of the stone in its intelligible being, yet by a certain order of priority the Persons were "produced" before the stone in its intelligible being ... even though it is eternal.'[6] Logically speaking, the divine essence is imitable before the divine intellect apprehends it as imitable.[7] The ideas are participations or possible imitations of the divine essence, apprehended by the divine intellect, and it is because the divine essence is infinite, because it is imitable in an infinite number of ways, that the ideas are infinite, though the presence of the ideas does not compel God to create corresponding objects.[8]

10. Scotus did not teach that the divine will acts in a simply capricious and arbitrary manner, though this doctrine has been ascribed to him. 'Will in God is His essence really, perfectly and identically',[9] and the divine volition is one act in itself.[10] The divine will and the act of the divine will, which are one *in re*, cannot change, therefore, though it does not follow that what God

---

[1] *Ox.*, 1, 36, no. 4, cf. no. 6.　[2] *Rep.*, 1, 36, 2, no. 33.　[3] *Ox.*, 1, 3, 4, no. 20.
[4] *Ibid.*, 2, 1, 2, no. 6.　[5] *Rep.*, 1, 36, 3, no. 27.　[6] *Collationes*, 31, no. 5.
[7] *Ox.*, 1, 35, no. 8.　[8] *Ibid.*, 1, 38, no. 5.　[9] *Rep.*, 1, 45, 2, no. 7.
[10] *Ox.*, 1, 17, 3, no. 18.

wills eternally must necessarily exist eternally. 'The operation (of the will) is in eternity, and the production of *esse existentiae* is in time.'[1] Logically speaking, even in God understanding precedes will, and God wills most rationally (*rationabilissime*). Although there is, ontologically, but one act of the divine will, we can distinguish the primary act by which God wills the end or *finis*, Himself, the secondary act by which He wills what is immediately ordered to the end, for example, by predestinating the elect, the third act by which He wills those things which are necessary to attain this end (e.g. grace), and the fourth act by which He wills more remote means, such as the sensible world.[2] But although the divine understanding logically precedes the divine volition, the divine will does not need direction as though it could err or choose something unsuitable, and *in this sense* the divine will is its own rule. Scotus sometimes states, indeed, that the divine will wills because it wills and that no reason can be given; but he makes his meaning clear enough. After citing Aristotle to the effect that it is the mark of an uneducated man to seek a demonstrative reason for everything, Scotus argues that it is not only ultimate principles which cannot be demonstrated, but also contingent things, because contingent things do not follow from necessary principles. The idea of human nature in God is necessary; but why God willed human nature to be represented in this or that individual, at this or that time, is a question to which no answer can be given save that 'because He willed it to be, therefore it was good that it should be'.[3] Scotus's point is that contingent things cannot be deduced by necessary demonstrations, since they would be necessary, and not contingent, if they could be so deduced. If you ask, he says, why heat heats, the only answer is that heat is heat: so the only answer to the question why God willed a contingent thing is that He willed it.[4] Scotus is not denying that God acts for an end, Himself, that He acts 'most rationally'; but he wants to show the absurdity of seeking a necessary reason for what is not necessary. 'From a necessary (principle) there does not follow something contingent.'[5] The free choice of God is the ultimate reason of contingent things, and we cannot legitimately go behind God's free choice and seek a necessary reason determining that choice. God's intellect does not determine His creative work by necessary reasons, since creation is free, nor is He

[1] *Ox.*, 1, 39, no. 21, cf. *ibid.*, 2, 1, 2, no. 7.   [2] *Ibid.*, 3, 32, no. 6.
[3] *Ibid.*, 2, 1, 2, no. 65.   [4] *Ibid.*, 1, 8, 5, nos. 23 f.; cf. *Quodlibet*, 16.
[5] *Rep.*, 1, 10, 3, no. 4.

determined by the goodness of objects, since the objects do not yet exist: rather are they good because He wills them to be. That God can create only what is an imitation of His essence and that He cannot, therefore, create anything evil, is understood.

Scotus thus insisted on God's freedom of will in regard to His operations *ad extra*; but he also maintained that though God loves Himself necessarily and cannot not will and love Himself, that love is none the less free. This theory certainly seems rather singular. That God's will is free in regard to finite objects other than Himself follows from the infinity of the divine will, which can have as its necessary object only an infinite object, God Himself; but that God should love Himself necessarily and freely at the same time would certainly appear, at first sight at least, to involve a contradiction. Scotus's position is as follows. Liberty belongs to the perfection of volition, and it must be present formally in God. As volition directed to the final end is the most perfect kind of volition, it must include what belongs to the perfection of volition. It must, therefore, be free. On the other hand, the divine will, identical with God, cannot but will and love the final end, God Himself. The principle of reconciliation of the two seemingly contradictory propositions is that necessity in the supreme act of the will does not take away, but rather postulates, what belongs to the perfection of will. 'The intrinsic condition of the power itself whether absolutely or in order to a perfect act is not incompatible with perfection in operation. But liberty is an intrinsic condition of the will absolutely or in order to the act of willing. Therefore liberty is compatible with a perfect possible condition in operation, and such a condition is necessity, especially when it is possible.'[1] Scotus gives an example to show what he means. 'If someone voluntarily hurls himself over a precipice (*voluntarie se praecipitat*) and, while falling, always continues to will it, he falls indeed necessarily by the necessity of natural gravity, and yet he freely wills that fall. So God, although He necessarily lives by His natural life, and that with a necessity which excludes all liberty, wills none the less freely that He should live by that life. Therefore, we do not place the life of God under necessity (i.e. we do not attribute necessity to God's life) if we understand by "life" life as loved by God by free will.'[2] Scotus appears to mean, then, that we can distinguish in God the natural necessity by which He loves Himself and His free ratification, as

[1] *Quodlibet*, 16, no. 8.   [2] *Ibid.*, 16, no. 9; cf. *Rep.*, 1, 10, 3, nos. 3 ff.

it were, of that necessity, so that necessary love of Himself and free love of Himself are not incompatible. One may think that this distinction is not particularly helpful; but in any case it is clear that Scotus's voluntaristic and libertarian doctrine does not imply that God could refrain from willing Himself or that His love for Himself is arbitrary. The truth of the matter is that Scotus attached so much value to liberty as a perfection of will that he was reluctant to exclude it even from those acts of will which he was compelled to regard as necessary. This will be apparent when we come to consider his doctrine concerning the human will.

11. Scotus maintained that God's power to create out of nothing is demonstrable by the natural light of reason. God as first efficient cause must be able to produce some effect immediately, since otherwise He would not be able to produce effects even mediately (taking as proved that He is *first* efficient cause). 'Therefore it is clear to the natural intellect that God can cause in such a way that something should be from Him (i.e. should have its being from God) without any element of itself being pre-supposed or any receptive element in which it is received. It is clear, then, to the natural reason that, although the Philosopher (Aristotle) did not say so, something can be proved to be capable of being caused by God in this way.' 'And I say that Aristotle did not affirm that God creates something in this way; but it does not thereby follow that the contrary (i.e. of Aristotle's opinion) cannot be known by the natural reason. . . .'[1] Moreover, it can be proved that God can create out of nothing.[2] But the relationship involved by creation is not mutual: the relation of the creature to God is a real relation, whereas the relation of God to the creature is a mental relation only (*relatio rationis*), since God is not essentially Creator and cannot be called Creator in the same sense in which He is called wise or good. He is really Creator; but His relationship to the creature is not a real relation, since He is not Creator by essence, in which case He would create necessarily, nor on the other hand can He receive an accidental relation.

As to the question whether creation in time can be proved, Scotus inclined to the opinion of St. Thomas, though he did not accept St. Thomas's reasons, that creation in time cannot be proved philosophically. The logical priority of *nihil* can be proved, 'since otherwise creation could not be admitted'; but it is not

---

[1] *Rep.*, 2, 1, 3, nos. 9–11; cf. *Ox.*, 2, 1, 2; *Collationes*, 13, no. 4.
[2] *Ox.*, 4, 1, 1, nos. 27 ff.

necessary that logical priority should involve temporal priority. Scotus speaks, however, with hesitation. 'It does not seem to be necessary that *nihil* should precede the world temporally; but it seems sufficient if it precedes the world logically.'[1] In other words, Scotus rejected the opinion of St. Bonaventure that the impossibility of creation from eternity can be philosophically demonstrated, and he inclined to the opinion of St. Thomas that creation in time is also incapable of philosophic demonstration; but he speaks more hesitantly on the point than does St. Thomas.

[1] *Ox.*, 2, 1, 3, no. 19.

CHAPTER XLIX

SCOTUS—V: THE SOUL

The specific form of man—Union of soul and body—Will and intellect—Soul's immortality not strictly demonstrated.

1. THAT the rational soul is the specific form of man can be philosophically proved,[1] and the opinion of Averroes that the intellect is a separate principle is unintelligible. 'All philosophers, generally speaking, have included "rational" in the definition of man as his special *differentia*, understanding by "rational" that the intellectual soul is an essential part of man.' No philosopher of note denies this, 'although that accursed Averroes in his fiction *On the Soul*, which, however, is intelligible neither to himself nor to anyone else, affirms that the intellect is a certain separate substance, which can be joined to us by means of the *phantasmata*; a union which neither he himself nor any disciple of his has hitherto been able to explain, nor has he been able by means of that union to preserve (the truth that) man understands. For according to him man would not be formally anything else but a kind of superior irrational animal, more excellent than other animals in virtue of his type of irrational, sensitive soul.'[2]

That the rational soul is the form of man Scotus proves by an enthymeme. 'Man understands (*intelligit*, apprehends intellectually) formally and properly; therefore the intellectual soul is the proper form of man.'[3] The antecedent, he says, seems to be clear enough through the authority of Aristotle; but in case anyone wantonly denies it, a rational proof must be given. To understand properly (*intelligere proprie*) means to understand by an act of knowledge which transcends every kind of sensitive knowledge, and that man understands in this sense can be proved as follows. To exercise intellectual activity in the proper sense is, as remarked, to exercise an activity transcending the power of sense. Now, sensitive apprehension is an organic function, since each of the senses has a determinate kind of object, the object of the special sense in question. Thus vision is determined to the perception of colour, hearing to that of sound. But the intellect is not determined in this way: its object is being, and it is not bound to a bodily organ in the sense in which sensation is bound. It can

[1] *Ox.*, 4, 43, 2, nos. 4-5.   [2] *Ibid.*, 4, 43, 2, no. 5.   [3] *Ibid.*, 4, 43, 2, no. 6.

apprehend objects which are not immediately given to sensation, such as generic and specific relations. Intellectual cognition, therefore, transcends the powers of sense, and it follows that man can *intelligere proprie*.[1]

That the conclusion of the original enthymeme ('therefore the intellectual soul is the proper form of man') follows from the antecedent can be shown in two ways. Intellectual cognition, as a function of man, must be 'received' in something in man himself which is not extended and which is neither a part nor the whole of the corporeal organism. If it was received in something extended, it would be itself extended and a purely organic function, which it has been proved not to be. When Scotus talks about intellectual cognition being 'received', he means that it is not identical with our substance, since we are not always exercising the power of intellectual cognition; so it must be the act of some principle in us. But it cannot be the act of the material part of man: therefore it must be the act of a spiritual formal principle, and what can this be but the intellectual soul, the principle which has the power of exercising intellectual activity? Secondly, man is master of his voluntary acts, he is free, and his will is not determined to any one kind of appetible object. Therefore it transcends organic appetite, and its acts cannot be the acts of any material form. It follows that our free, voluntary acts are the acts of an intellectual form, and if our free acts are *our* acts, as they are, then the form of which they are the acts must be *our* form. The intellectual soul is, then, the form of man: it is his specific form, which differentiates man from the brutes.[2]

2. In man there is only one soul, though there is, as already mentioned, a form of corporeity. There are, as we also saw earlier, various 'formalities' in the one human soul, which, though not really distinct (separable) from one another, are distinct with a *distinctio formalis a parte rei*, since the intellectual, sensitive and vegetative activities are formally and objectively distinct; but they are formalities of the one rational soul of man. This one rational soul is, therefore, not only the principle of man's rational cognition, but it is also the principle of his sensitive activity and of his life. It gives *esse vivum*, and it is the formal principle by which the organism is a living organism:[3] it is the substantial form of man.[4] The soul is, therefore, a part of man, and it is only

[1] *Ox.*, 4, 43, 2, nos. 6–11.   [2] *Ibid.*, 4, 43, 2, no. 12.
[3] *Ibid.*, 2, 16, no. 6.   [4] *Ibid.*, 2, 1, 4, no. 25.

improperly that it can be called subsistent, since it is part of a
substance rather than a substance by itself; it is the composite
being, soul and body, which is a *per se unum*.[1] The soul in the
state of separation from the body is not, properly speaking, a
person.[2] The soul perfects the body only when the latter is
properly disposed for it, and *this* soul has an aptitude for *this*
body. This means, says Scotus,[3] that the soul cannot be individuated by the matter it informs, since the soul, that is, a particular
soul, is infused into a body, and the creation of that soul is
logically prior to its union with the body.

Scotus differs also from St. Thomas in holding that the rational
soul does not confer *esse simpliciter*, but rather *esse vivum* and
esse sensitivum: there is, as already mentioned, a form of corporeity.
If the rational soul were to confer *esse simpliciter* on man, man
could not really be said to die. Death involves the corruption of
the 'entity' of man, and this implies that both soul and body have
a reality of their own, that the being of man as man is his being
as a *compositum*, not his being as a soul. If the soul conferred *esse
simpliciter* and there were no other form in the body, the separation
of soul from body would not mean a corruption of the being of
man as man. For death to take place, man must have a being as
compositum, a being distinct from that of his component parts,
taken separately or together, for it is this being of man as a
compositum which is corrupted at death. Moreover, St. Thomas,
according to Scotus, contradicts himself. 'Elsewhere he says that
the state of the soul in the body is more perfect than its state
outside the body, since it is a part of the *compositum*'; yet at the
same time he asserts that the soul confers, and therefore possesses,
esse simpliciter, and that it is not less perfect merely by the fact
that it does not communicate that *esse* to any thing other than
itself. 'According to you the soul possesses the same *esse* totally
in a state of separation which it possessed when united with the
body . . . therefore it is in no way more imperfect by the fact that
it does not communicate that *esse* to the body.'[4]

The soul is united to the body for the perfection of the whole
man, who consists of soul and body. According to St. Thomas,[5]
the soul is united to the body for the good of the soul. The soul
is naturally dependent on the senses for its cognition, the *conversio
ad phantasma* being natural to it,[6] and therefore the soul is united

---

[1] *Ox.*, 4, 12, 1, no. 19.   [2] *Quodlibet*, 9, no. 7, and 19, no. 19.   [3] *Ibid.*, 2, 3 ff.
[4] *Ox.*, 4, 43, 1, nos. 2–6.   [5] *S.T.*, Ia, 89, 1.   [6] Cf. *ibid.*, Ia, 84, 7.

to the body for the soul's good, in order that it may operate according to its nature. For Scotus, however, as we have already seen, the direction of the human intellect towards material things and its *de facto* dependence on the senses originate not so much in the nature of the human reason as such as in the present state of the soul, its condition in the body as wayfarer (with the alternative suggestion that sin may possibly be the responsible factor). St. Thomas would object that in this case its union with the body is for the good of the body, not of the soul, and that this is irrational, 'since matter is for the sake of form, and not conversely'. To such an objection Scotus's answer is that the soul is united to the body, not for the good of the body simply, but for the good of the composite being, man. It is man, the composite being, who is the term of the creative act, not soul taken by itself or body taken by itself, and the union of soul and body is effected in order that this composite being may be realised: the union exists, therefore, for the good of the whole man, *propter perfectionem totius*. The union of soul with body does not take place 'for the perfection of the body, nor for the perfection of the soul alone, but for the perfection of the whole which consists of these parts; and so although no perfection may accrue to this or that part which it would not have possessed without such a union, the union does not, however, take place in vain, since the perfection of the whole, which is principally intended by nature, could not be had except in that way.'[1]

3. Of Scotus's idea of human intellectual activity something has already been said in the chapter on knowledge; but a brief discussion must be given of his doctrine concerning the relation of will to intellect, as this has given rise to some misunderstanding concerning his general position.

The intellect is not, like the will, a free power. 'It is not in the power of the intellect to restrain its assent to the truths which it apprehends; for in so far as the truth of principles becomes clear to it from the terms or the truth of conclusions from principles, in so far must it give its assent on account of its lack of liberty.'[2] Thus if the truth of the proposition that the whole is greater than the part becomes clear to the intellect from the realisation of what a whole is and what a part is, or if the truth of the conclusion that Socrates is mortal becomes clear to the intellect from a considera- tion of the premisses that all men are mortal and that Socrates is a man, then the intellect is not free to withhold its consent to the proposition that the whole is greater than the part or the proposition that Socrates is mortal. The intellect is thus a *potentia naturalis*.

The will, however, is free, a *potentia libera*, and it is essentially free, its *ratio formalis* consisting more in its freedom than its character as appetite.[1] It is necessary to distinguish between will in the sense of a natural inclination and will as free, and it is only free will that is will in the proper sense; from which it follows that will is free of its very nature and that God could not, for example, create a rational will which would be *naturally* incapable of sinning.[2] By an elicited act of his free will, says Scotus, St. Paul willed 'to be dissolved and to be with Christ'; but this elicited act was contrary to his natural 'will', in the sense of natural inclination.[3] The two, therefore, are distinct, and this distinction is of importance when one considers man's desire of happiness or of his last end. The will as natural appetite or inclination to self-perfection necessarily desires happiness above all things, and since happiness or beatitude is, as a matter of concrete fact, to be found in God alone, there is in man a natural inclination to beatitude 'in particular', to God. But it does not follow that the will as free necessarily and perpetually desires the last end, nor that it necessarily elicits a conscious and deliberate act in regard to that object.[4] Scotus protests that he does not mean to imply that the will can choose misery *as such* or evil *as such*: 'I do not will beatitude' is not the same as 'I will the opposite of beatitude'; it means that I do not here and now elicit an act in its regard, not that I elicit a choice of its opposite, which cannot be an object of will. If I do elicit an act, however, that is, an act of willing beatitude, that act will be free, since every elicited act of the will is free.[5] Moreover, Scotus does not hesitate to draw the conclusion from his doctrine of the essential freedom of the will that the blessed in heaven will and love God freely.[6] He rejects, then, the doctrine of St. Thomas that when the *summum bonum* is clearly presented, the will chooses and loves it necessarily, and he even goes so far as to say that the blessed retain the power to sin. But when he says this, he does not mean to say any more than that the will as such remains free in heaven, since it is essentially free and heaven does not destroy its freedom: morally speaking, the blessed in heaven not only will not sin, but cannot sin, though this necessity is only *secundum*

[1] *Ox.*, 1, 17, 3, no. 5; 2, 25, no. 16.   [2] *Ibid.*, 2, 23, nos. 8 and 7.   [3] *Ibid.*, 3, 15, no. 37.
[4] Cf. *ibid.*, 4, 49, 10, no. 3; 2, 23, no. 8; 1, 1, 4, no. 16; *Collationes*, 16, no. 3.
[5] Cf. *Ox.*, 4, 49, 10, nos. 8f.   [6] *Ox.*, 1, 1, 4, nos. 13ff.

quid, proceeding from the 'habit of glory' (*habitus gloriae*) and the inclination produced in the will, not from a physical determination of the will.[1] The will of the blessed is thus morally impeccable, though not physically impeccable. Scotus does not differ from St. Thomas as to the actual fact that the blessed will not sin and he is willing to say that they cannot sin, provided that 'cannot' is not understood in a sense which would imply that the essence of the will is in any way impaired.[2]

The intellect, then, is a *potentia naturalis*, the will a *potentia libera*, and, given Scotus's insistence on liberty as a perfection, his position in the controversy regarding the primacy of intellect over will or of will over intellect cannot be in doubt. Knowledge certainly precedes every elicited act of the will, since the will cannot exercise choice in regard to an entirely unknown object (Scotus was no 'irrationalist'), and it is difficult, he says, though not impossible, for the will not to incline itself to what is finally dictated by the practical reason; but, on the other hand, the will can command the intellect. Scotus does not mean, of course, that the will can command the intellect to assent to propositions which are seen to be false: the will does not add anything to the act of understanding as such,[3] nor is it the cause of the intellect's act.[4] But the will can co-operate mediately, as an efficient cause, by moving the intellect to attend to this or that intelligible object, to consider this or that argument.[5] It follows that 'the will, by commanding the intellect, is a superior cause in respect of its act. But the intellect, if it is the cause of volition (that is, as a partial cause, by supplying the knowledge of the object) is a cause subservient to the will'.[6]

Scotus gives other reasons for affirming the primacy of the will. The will is more perfect than the intellect since the corruption of the will is worse than the corruption of the intellect; to hate God is worse than not to know God or not to think of God. Again, sin means willing something evil, whereas to think of something evil is not necessarily a sin: it is only a sin when the will gives some consent to or takes some pleasure in the evil thought of.[7] Again, love is a greater good than knowledge, and love resides in the will,[8] while it is the will which plays the principal part in final beatitude, uniting the soul with God, possessing and enjoying God. Though both powers, intellect and will, are involved in beatitude,

[1] *Ox.*, 4, 49, 6, no. 9.   [2] Cf. *Collatio*, 15.   [3] *Rep.*, 2, 42, 4, no. 7.
[4] *Collationes*, 2, no 7.   [5] *Rep.*, 1, 35, 1, no. 27.
[6] *Ox.*, 4, 49, *quaestio ex latere*, nos. 16 and 18.   [7] *Ibid.*, no. 17.   [8] *Ibid.*, no. 21.

the higher faculty, will, is the more immediate means of union with God.[1] Scotus thus rejected the Thomist doctrine of the primacy of the intellect and of the essence of beatitude and remained true to the tradition of the Augustinian-Franciscan School. It does not seem to be a matter of great moment, indeed, whether one adopts the Thomist or Scotist viewpoint, for both sides agree that beatitude, taken *extensive*, involves both powers; but it is necessary to explain Scotus's position, in order to show how foolish are accusations of irrationalism and of unmitigated voluntarism.

4. One might have expected, in view of Scotus's clear teaching, not only that the soul's intellectual activity transcends the powers of sense, but also that it can be proved philosophically to transcend the powers of sense and matter, that he would attempt to demonstrate the immortality of the human soul; but actually he did not believe that this truth can be strictly demonstrated in philosophy, and he criticised the proofs adduced by his predecessors. Of the three propositions, first that the rational soul is the specific form of man, secondly that the soul is immortal, and thirdly that the soul after death will not remain in a perpetual state of separation from the body (that is, that the body will rise again), the first is known by the natural light of reason, the error opposed to it, that of Averroes, being 'not only against the truth of theology, but also against the truth of philosophy' (that is, the Averroistic doctrine is not only against the truth as known by faith, but can also be philosophically refuted). 'But the other two (propositions) are not sufficiently known by the natural reason, although there are certain probable and persuasive arguments (*persuasiones probabiles*) for them. For the second, indeed, there are several more probable (arguments); hence the Philosopher seems to have held it *magis expresse*.' But for the third there are fewer reasons, and consequently the conclusion which follows from those reasons is not thereby sufficiently known through the natural reason.[2] Scotus's general position is, therefore, that we can prove philosophically that the rational soul is the specific form of man; but that we cannot prove demonstratively in philosophy either that the soul is immortal or that the body will rise again. The philosophical arguments for the soul's immortality have greater weight than those for the resurrection of the body, but they are none the less only probable arguments, the *a priori* arguments, namely those

[1] *Rep.*, 4, 49, 3, no. 7; *Ox.*, 4, 49, 3, nos. 5 ff.   [2] *Ox.*, 4, 43, 2, no. 26.

based on the soul's nature, being better than the *a posteriori* arguments, for example, those based on the need for sanctions in a future life. The soul's immortality may be said to be morally provable, *ex inductione*, and it is certainly more probable, philosophically speaking, than its opposite; but the arguments adduced for it are not demonstrative and necessary arguments, enjoying absolute certainty.[1]

As regards the authority of Aristotle, Scotus declares that his opinion is not really clear. 'For he speaks in various ways in different places, and he had different principles, from some of which one opposite (one opinion) seems to follow, from others another. It is probable, then, that he was always doubtful about that conclusion, and at one time he would approach the one side, at another time the other, according as he was treating a matter which harmonised more with one side than with the other.'[2] In any case not all the assertions of the philosophers were proved by them by necessary reasons; but 'frequently they had only some probable persuasions (some probable and persuasive arguments) or the general opinion of preceding philosophers.'[3] The authority of Aristotle is, therefore, no certain argument for the soul's immortality.

As to the arguments adduced by St. Thomas and other Christian philosophers, these are not absolutely conclusive. In the *Summa Theologica*[4] St. Thomas argues that the human soul cannot be corrupted *per accidens*, in virtue of the corruption of the body, since it is a subsistent form, nor can it be corrupted *per se*, since *esse* belongs to a subsistent form in such a way that the natural corruption of the form would mean the separation of the form from itself. To this Scotus answers that St. Thomas is begging the question, since he presupposes that the soul of man is a *forma per se subsistens*, which is the very point which has to be proved. The proposition that the human soul is a form of this kind is accepted as an object of belief, but it is not known by natural reason.[5] If it be objected that this criticism is unfair, in view of the fact that St. Thomas has previously devoted an article (2) to showing that the human soul is an incorporeal and subsistent principle, Scotus retorts that though it can be shown that the rational soul in its intellectual activity does not use a corporeal organ and that its intellectual activity transcends the power of

---

[1] Cf. *Rep.*, 4, 43, 2, nos. 15 ff.   [2] *Ox.*, 4, 43, 2, no. 16.   [3] *Ibid.*
[4] Ia, 75, 6.   [5] *Ox.*, 4, 43, 2, no. 23.

sense, it does not necessarily follow that the rational soul does not depend, as regards its being, on the whole *compositum*, which is certainly corruptible.[1] In other words, the fact that the human soul does not employ a corporeal organ in its purely intellectual activity does not necessarily prove that it is not naturally dependent for its existence on the continued existence of the *compositum*. It would have to be demonstrated that a form which transcends matter in a certain operation is necessarily independent in regard to existence, and this, according to Scotus, has not been conclusively proved.[2]

In regard to the argument drawn from the desire of beatitude, which involves immortality, Scotus observes that if by desire is meant a natural desire in the strict sense, one which is simply the inclination of nature to some thing, then it is clear that a natural desire for a thing cannot be proved, unless the latter's natural possibility has first been proved: to assert the existence of a natural inclination towards a state, the possibility of which is still unknown, is to be guilty of a *petitio principii*. If, however, by natural desire is meant a natural desire in a wider sense, that is, an elicited desire which is in accordance with a natural inclination, it cannot be shown that the elicited desire is natural in this sense until it has been proved that there is a natural desire in the strict sense. It may be said that an object which becomes the object of an elicited desire immediately it is apprehended must be the object of a natural desire or inclination; but in this case one might as well argue that because a vicious man is immediately inclined to desire the object of his vice when he apprehends it, he has a natural inclination or a natural desire for it, whereas in point of fact nature is not of itself vicious, and certainly not in everybody. It is no good saying that an object which, directly it is apprehended, is the object of an elicited desire according to right reason is the object of a natural desire, since the whole question is to discover whether the desire for immortality is or is not in accordance with right reason: this cannot legitimately be taken for granted. Furthermore, if it is said that man has a natural desire for immortality because he naturally flees from death, and that therefore immortality is at least a possibility, one might equally well argue that a brute has a natural desire for immortality and that it can and does survive.[3]

It may be as well to recall the fact that Scotus is not saying that the arguments for immortality are not probable or persuasive, still less that they are worthless: he is saying that they are not, in his opinion, demonstrative. The argument from desire does not conclude, because if one is speaking of the biological inclination to avoid death or what leads to death, brutes also possess this inclination, while if one is speaking of an elicited, conscious desire, one cannot legitimately argue from the desire of immortality to the fact of immortality unless one has first shown that immortality is a possibility, that the human soul can survive the disintegration of the *compositum*. It is all very well to say that the sufferings of this life demand a counterpoise in another life; but it remains true that man is exposed to suffering in this life, just as he is capable of pleasure and joy in this life, by the very fact of his nature, so that exposure to suffering is natural, and we cannot argue without more ado that suffering must be counterbalanced by other-worldly happiness. As to the argument that there must be sanctions in an after life, and that an after life therefore exists, the argument is not valid until you have shown that God does actually reward and punish people in this way, and Scotus did not think that this can be proved purely philosophically.[1] The best argument for the immortality of the human soul may be that drawn from the intellect's independence of a corporeal organ, from its spiritual activity; but although Scotus thought that this proof constituted a highly probable argument, he did not consider that it was an absolutely conclusive argument, since it might be that the soul, which is created as part of the *compositum*, cannot exist except as part of the *compositum*.

[1] *Ox.*, 4, 43, 2, no. 27.

CHAPTER L

SCOTUS—VI: ETHICS

Morality of human acts—Indifferent acts—The moral law and the will of God—Political authority.

MY aim in this chapter is not to propound all the ethical doctrines of Scotus, but rather to show that the accusation which has been brought against him of teaching the purely arbitrary character of the moral law, as though it depended simply and solely on the divine will, is, in the main, an unjust accusation.

1. An act is naturally good (*naturaliter bonus*) when it possesses all that is required for its *esse naturale*, just as a body is beautiful when it possesses all those characteristics of size, colour, shape, etc., which befit the body itself and harmonise with one another. An act is morally good when it possesses all that is required, not by the nature of the act taken merely in itself, but by right reason (*recta ratio*). To enter the moral order at all an act must be free, for 'an act is neither praiseworthy nor blameworthy unless it proceeds from the free will'; but obviously this is required for both morally good and morally bad acts; something more than freedom is required for a morally good act and that is conformity with right reason.[1] 'To attribute moral goodness is to attribute conformity to right reason.'[2] Every morally good act must be objectively good, in the sense of having an object conformable to right reason; but no act is good on this count alone, save the love of God, which can in no circumstances be morally evil, just as no act is morally evil on account of its object alone, save hatred of God, which cannot be morally good in any circumstances.[3] It is impossible, for instance, to love God with a bad intention, since there would then be no love, just as it is impossible to hate God with a good intention. In other cases, however, 'the goodness of the will does not depend on the object alone, but on all the other circumstances, and chiefly on the end' (*a fine*), which holds the primary place among the 'circumstances' of the act.[4] But though the end holds the primary place among the circumstances of the act, an act is not morally good merely because the end is good:

[1] *Ox.*, 2, 40, *quaestio unica*, nos. 2–3.   [2] *Ibid.*, 1, 17, 3, no. 14.
[3] *Rep.*, 4, 28, no. 6.   [4] *Ox.*, 1, *distinctio ultima*, nos. 1 and 2.

the end does not justify the means. 'It is necessary that all the (requisite) circumstances should occur together in any moral act, for it to be morally good; the defect of any one circumstance is sufficient in order that (the act) should be morally bad':[1] 'evil things must not be done in order that good (results) may eventuate.'[2] For an act to be morally good, then, it must be free, and it must be objectively good and be done with the right intention, in the right way, and so on. If it possesses these circumstances, it will be in accordance with right reason.

2. Every human act, that is, every free act, is good or evil in some way, not only in the sense that every act, considered purely ontologically, i.e. as a positive entity, is good, but also in the sense that every act has an object which is either in accordance with right reason or contrary to it. But inasmuch as goodness of all the circumstances is required for a completely good moral act, it is possible, if some circumstance is deficient in the goodness it should have, for an act to be 'indifferent'. For example, in order for almsgiving to be a completely good moral act, to have full moral value, it must be done with a moral intention. Now, to give alms with a bad intention would make the act bad; but it is possible to give alms simply from an immediate inclination, for example, and such an act, says Scotus, can be called morally indifferent: it is neither a bad act nor is it a fully moral act.[3] In the admission of indifferent elicited acts (and Scotus insisted that he was not speaking of reflex acts like brushing away a fly from one's face)[4] Scotus adopted an opinion opposed to that of St. Thomas Aquinas; but in order to understand his opinion, it is important to realise that for Scotus 'the first practical principle is: God ought to be loved'.[5] A man is not obliged always to refer his act to God either actually or virtually, because, says Scotus, God has not laid us under this obligation, but unless this is done, the act will not be completely good morally. On the other hand, since we are not obliged so to refer every act, it does not follow that an act which is not so referred is an evil act. If it is incompatible with the love of God, it will be evil; but it can be compatible with the love of God without being referred to God either actually or virtually. In this case it is an indifferent act. Apparently Scotus thought that 'habitual' reference is not sufficient to give an act full moral value.

3. We have seen that a morally good act must be in accordance

---

[1] *Ox.*, 1, *distinctio ultima*, nos. 1 and 2. [2] *Ibid.*, 4, 5, 2, no. 7.
[3] *Rep.*, 2, 41, no. 2. [4] Cf. *Ox.*, 2, 41, no. 4. [5] *Ibid.*, 4, 46, 1, no. 10.

with right reason. What, then, is the norm of right reason and of the morality of our actions? According to Scotus, 'the divine will is the cause of good, and so by the fact that He wills something it is good . . .'[1] This statement taken by itself naturally appears to imply that the moral law depends simply on the arbitrary will of God; but such was not Scotus's position, and he meant simply that what God wills is good because God of His very nature cannot will anything but what is good. Still, Scotus does make the moral law depend in one sense on the divine will, and his position must be made clear. Inasmuch as the divine intellect, considered as preceding an act of the divine will, perceives the acts which are in conformity with human nature, the eternal and immutable moral law is constituted in regard to its content; but it acquires obligatory force only through the free choice of the divine will. One can say, then, that it is not the content of the moral law which is due to the divine will, but the obligation of the moral law, its morally binding force. 'To command pertains only to the appetite or will.'[2] The intellect says that this is true or untrue, in the practical as in the speculative sphere, and though it inclines to action of a certain type, it does not dictate that one ought to act in that way. Scotus is not simply saying that obligation actually bears on human beings only because God has willed to create them, which would be obvious enough, since they could not be obliged if they did not exist; he is saying that the divine will is the fount of obligation. It seems to follow that if God had not chosen to impose obligation, morality would be a matter of self-perfection, in the sense that the intellect would perceive that a certain course of action is what befits human nature and would judge that it is reasonable and prudent to act in that way. One would have an ethic of the type represented by Aristotle's ethics. Actually, however, God has willed that course of action, and that will is reflected in moral obligation: to transgress the law is thus not simply irrational, it is sin in the theological sense of the word.

That the content of the moral law is not due simply to the arbitrary caprice or choice of God is made abundantly clear by Scotus. Speaking of the sin of Adam,[3] he observes: 'A sin which is a sin only because it is forbidden, is less of a sin formally than that which is evil in itself and not because it is forbidden. Now to eat of that tree was not more a sin, as far as the act was concerned,

---

[1] *Rep.*, 1, 48, *quaestio unica.*   [2] *Ox.*, 4, 14, 2, no. 5.
[3] *Rep.*, 2, 22, *quaestio unica*, no. 3.

than to eat of another tree, but only because it was forbidden. But all sins which concern the ten commandments are formally evil not merely because they are forbidden, but because they are evil; therefore they are forbidden, since by the law of nature the opposite of any commandment was evil, and by natural reason a man can see that any of those precepts is to be observed.' Here Scotus states clearly that the ten commandments are not simply arbitrary precepts and that a man can discern their validity through the natural use of reason, a statement which should involve the conclusion that God Himself could not change them, not because He is subject to them, as it were, but because they are ultimately founded on His nature.

The difficulty arises, however, that God seems to have dispensed in some of the secondary precepts of the decalogue (the precepts of the second table). For example, He told the Israelites to despoil the Egyptians, and He commissioned Abraham to sacrifice his son Isaac. Scotus, discussing this matter, asks first whether all the ten commandments belong to the law of nature, and he proceeds to make a distinction. Those moral laws which are self-evident or which follow necessarily from self-evident practical principles belong to the natural law in the strictest sense, and in the case of these principles and conclusions no dispensation is possible. God could not, for example, permit a man to have other gods than Himself or to take His name in vain, as such acts would be quite incompatible with man's end, the love of God as God, which necessarily involves exclusive worship and reverence. On the other hand, a moral law may belong to the law of nature, not as following necessarily from self-evident principles, but as being in accordance with the primary, necessary and self-evident practical principles; and of this type are the commandments of the second table. In the case of these moral commandments God can dispense.[1] Scotus proceeds to argue, or to suggest the argument,[2] that even if the love of the neighbour belongs to the natural law in the strict sense, so that I am necessarily bound to will that my neighbour should love God, it does not necessarily follow that I should will that he should have this or that particular good. This does not, however, prevent Scotus from going on to say[3] that the precepts of the decalogue are binding in every state and that before the giving of the written law all men were bound to observe

[1] Ox., 3, 37, quaestio unica, nos. 5–8.   [2] Ibid., 3, 37, quaestio unica, no. 11.
[3] Ibid., 3, 37, quaestio unica, nos. 13–15.

them, 'because they were written interiorly in the heart, or perhaps by some external teaching given by God which parents learnt and handed on to their sons.' Moreover, he explains that the children of Israel did not really need any dispensation when they despoiled the Egyptians, since God, as supreme lord, transferred to the Israelites the goods of the Egyptians, so that the former did not take what was not their own. Nevertheless, Scotus's general position is that the first two commandments of the first table of the decalogue belong to the natural law in the strictest sense (about the third commandment, that concerning sabbath observance, he expresses doubt), whereas the precepts of the second table do not belong to the natural law in the strictest sense, though they do so belong in the wider sense. God can, then, dispense in the case of the precepts of the second table, though He cannot dispense in the case of commandments which belong strictly to the natural law. On this matter of dispensation Scotus's opinion is at variance with that of the Thomists, who do not allow that God can, properly speaking, dispense in the case of any of the precepts of the decalogue, since they all derive immediately or mediately from primary practical principles. The Thomists explain the apparent dispensations which troubled Scotus as instances of *mutatio materiae*, that is, in much the same way as Scotus himself explained the spoliation of the Egyptians by the Israelites.

There is no call to discuss such Scriptural passages here, as they do not enter into philosophy; but it should be observed that even if Scotus admits the possibility of dispensation in the case of some commandments, the fact that he refused to allow that possibility in regard to moral precepts which belong strictly to the natural law shows clearly that he did not regard the whole moral law as due simply to the arbitrary decision of the divine will. He may have thought that the inviolability of private property, and the consequent wrongness of stealing, were not so bound up with the natural law that no exceptions would be legitimate, even in 'hard cases'; but he certainly stated that if a moral precept belonged to the natural law in the strict sense, it was unalterable. It cannot be denied that Scotus makes remarks such as that the divine will is the first rule of rectitude and that 'whatever does not include a contradiction is not repugnant to the divine will absolutely speaking, so that whatever God does or may do will be right and just';[1] but he certainly did not think that God can, without

[1] *Rep.*, 4, 46, 4, no. 8.

contradiction, order or permit acts which are contrary to self-evident practical principles or principles necessarily following therefrom. Probably one should view in close connection Scotus's doctrine concerning moral obligation and that concerning the secondary precepts of the decalogue. The primary precepts are self-evident or are so intimately connected with self-evident principles that their obligatory character is obvious. The secondary precepts, however, are not immediately deducible from primary practical principles, even if their harmony with those principles and their immediate derivatives is evident. Their obligatory character is thus not self-evident or necessary, but depends on the divine will. Their content is not purely arbitrary, since their harmony and consonance with necessary principles is clear; but the connection is not so strict that God cannot make exceptions. If it is His will which so reinforces the natural harmony of the secondary precepts with necessary principles that the former become obligatory in the full moral sense, His will can also dispense.

It would seem, then, that Scotus occupies a position midway, if one may so put it, between St. Thomas and Ockham. He agrees with the former that there are moral principles which are unalterable and he does not teach that the entire moral law depends on the arbitrary decision of God's will. On the other hand he attributed a much greater degree of prominence to the divine will in the determination of the moral order than St. Thomas had done, and he appears to have held that obligation, at least in regard to certain commandments, depends on that will as distinct from the divine intellect. While, then, if we look at Scotus's philosophy by itself, we must allow that his moral doctrine is not that of arbitrary divine authoritarianism, we must also allow, if we look at the historical development of thought, that his moral doctrine helped to prepare the way for that of Ockham, in whose eyes the moral law, including the whole decalogue, is the arbitrary creation of the divine will.

4. As regards political authority, Scotus distinguishes it carefully from paternal authority,[1] and appears to suggest that it rests on free consent. 'Political authority . . . can be right by common consent and the choice of the community itself.'[2] Scotus speaks of people who see that they cannot get on without some authority and who agree together to commit the care of the community to

---

[1] *Rep.*, 4, 15, 4, nos. 10-11.   [2] *Ox.*, 4, 15, 2, no. 7.

one person or to a community of persons, and either to one man for himself alone, so that his successor would have to be elected, or to one man for himself and his posterity.[1] Elsewhere[2] he speaks of many independent peoples who, 'in order to attain a continual state of peace, were able by the mutual consent of all to elect from among them one prince . . .'

Legitimate authority is one of the factors which are required in the legislators, the other factor being 'prudence', the ability to legislate in accordance with right reason.[3] The legislator must not pass laws for his private advantage, but for the common good, which is the end of legislation.[4] Moreover, the positive human law must not be in conflict either with the natural moral law or with the divine positive law. No more than St. Thomas Aquinas would Scotus have had any sympathy with the idea of despotic government or with that of the State as the fount of morality.

[1] *Ox.*, 4, 15, 2, no. 7. [2] *Rep.*, 4, 15, 4, no. 11.
[3] *Ox.*, 4, 15, 2, no. 6. [4] *Ibid.*, 4, 14, 2, no. 7.

CHAPTER LI

CONCLUDING REVIEW

Theology and philosophy—'Christian philosophy'—The Thomist synthesis—Various ways of regarding and interpreting mediaeval philosophy.

ANY general review of mediaeval philosophy must obviously be left to the conclusion of the next volume; but it may be worth while to indicate here some general aspects of the course of philosophy treated of in the present book, even though the omission of Ockhamism, which will be considered in the third volume, restricts the scope of one's reflections.

1. One can regard the development of philosophy in the Christian world from the days of the Roman Empire up to the thirteenth-century syntheses from the point of view of its relation to theology. In the first centuries of the Christian era there was scarcely any philosophy in the modern sense, in the sense, that is, of an autonomous science distinct from theology. The Fathers were aware, of course, of the distinction between reason and faith, between scientific conclusions and the data of revelation; but to distinguish reason and faith is not necessarily the same as to make a clear distinction between philosophy and theology. Christian apologists and writers who were anxious to show the reasonable character of the Christian religion, employed reason to show that there is, for example, but one God, and to that extent they may be said to have developed philosophical themes; but their aim was apologetic, and not primarily philosophic. Even those writers who adopted a hostile attitude towards Greek philosophy had to employ reason for apologetic purposes and they gave their attention to themes which were considered to belong to the province of philosophy; but though we can isolate those arguments and discussions which fall under the heading of philosophy, it would be idle to pretend that a Christian apologist of this kind was a professed philosopher; he may have borrowed from the philosophers to some extent, but he regarded 'philosophy' pretty well as a perverter of the truth and as a foe of Christianity. As to the Christian writers who adopted a predominantly favourable attitude to Greek philosophy, these tended to look on Greek philosophy as a preparation for Christian wisdom, the latter comprising not only the revealed

mysteries of faith but all truth about the world and human life looked at through the eyes of a Christian. Inasmuch as the Fathers not only applied reason to the understanding, correct statement and defence of the data of revelation, but also treated of themes which had been considered by Greek philosophers, they helped not only to develop theology, but also to provide material for the construction of a philosophy which would be compatible with Christian theology; but they were theologians and exegetes, not philosophers in the strict sense, save occasionally and incidentally; and even when they did pursue philosophic themes, they were rounding out, as it were, the total Christian wisdom rather than constructing a distinct philosophy or branch of philosophy. This is true even of St. Augustine, for although one can reconstruct a philosophy from his writings, he was above all a theologian and was not concerned to build up a philosophical system as such.

Fathers of the Church, like St. Gregory of Nyssa and St. Augustine, who in their writings utilised elements borrowed from neo-Platonism, found in neo-Platonism material which helped them in their development of a 'philosophy' of the spiritual life, to which, as Christians and saints, they paid much attention. It was only natural that they should speak of the soul, of its relation to the body, and of its ascent to God, in terms strongly reminiscent of Platonism and neo-Platonism; but since they could not (and in any case would not wish to) consider the soul's ascent to God in abstraction from theology and revelation, their philosophy, which concentrated so much on the soul and its ascent to God, was inevitably intertwined with and integrated into their theology. To treat St. Augustine's doctrine of illumination, for example, as a purely philosophic doctrine is not easy; it really ought to be looked at in the light of his general doctrine concerning the soul's relation to God and its ascent to God.

The general attitude of the Fathers set the tone, so to speak, for what we call 'Augustinianism'. St. Anselm, for instance, was a theologian, but he saw that the existence of the God who revealed the mysteries of the Christian religion needs in some way to be proved, and so he developed a natural theology, or helped towards the development of natural theology, though it would be a mistake to picture him as sitting down to elaborate a system of philosophy as such. *Fides quaerens intellectum* may, to speak rather crudely, work forwards or backwards. Working forwards from the data of revelation and applying reasoning to theological dogmas, in order to understand them as far as is possible, it produces Scholastic theology; working backwards, in the sense of considering the presuppositions of revelation, it develops the proofs of God's existence. But the mind at work in either case is really the mind of the theologian, even though in the second case it works within the province and with the methods of philosophy.

If the spirit of Augustinianism, born of the writings of the Fathers, was that of *fides quaerens intellectum*, it might also be called a spirit of *homo quaerens Deum*. This aspect of Augustinianism is especially marked in St. Bonaventure, whose thought was steeped so deeply in the affective spirituality of Franciscanism. A man may contemplate creatures, the world without and the world within, and discern their natures; but his knowledge is of little worth unless he discerns in nature the *vestigium Dei* and in himself the *imago Dei*, unless he can detect the operation of God in his soul, an operation which is itself hidden but is rendered visible in its effects, in its power. A number of 'Augustinians' no doubt maintained the doctrine of illumination, for example, out of conservatism and a respect for tradition; but in the case of a man like St. Bonaventure the retention of the doctrine was something much more than traditionalism. It has been said that of two doctrines, of which one attributes more to God and the other less, the Augustinian chooses the one which attributes more to God and less to the creature; but this is true only in so far as the doctrine is felt to harmonise with and express spiritual experience and in so far as it harmonises with and can be integrated into the general theological outlook.

If one understands the motto *fides quaerens intellectum* as expressing the spirit of Augustinianism and as indicating the place of philosophy in the mind of the Augustinian, it might be objected that such a description of Augustinianism is far too wide and that one might even have to class as Augustinians thinkers whom no one could reasonably call Augustinians. The passage from faith to 'understanding', to Scholastic theology on the one hand and to philosophy on the other hand, was ultimately the result of the fact that Christianity was given to the world as a revealed doctrine of salvation, not as a philosophy in the academic sense, nor even as a Scholastic philosophy. Christians believed first of all, and only afterwards, in the desire to defend, to explain and to understand what they believed, did they develop theology and, in subordination to theology, philosophy. In a sense this was the attitude not only of the early Christian writers and Fathers, but also of all those mediaeval thinkers who were primarily theologians. They believed first of all, and then they attempted to understand. This would be true of St. Thomas himself. But how could one call St. Thomas an Augustinian? Is it not better to confine the term 'Augustinian' to certain philosophical doctrines? Once one has done that, one has a means for distinguishing Augustinians from non-Augustinians: otherwise, one is involved in hopeless confusion.

There is a great deal of truth in this contention, and it must be admitted that in order to be able to discriminate between Augustinians and non-Augustinians in regard to the content of their philosophies, it is desirable to be clear first of all about what doctrines one is prepared to recognise as Augustinian and why; but I am speaking at present of the relation between theology and philosophy, and in regard to this point I maintain that, with an important qualification to be mentioned shortly, there is no essential difference in attitude between St. Augustine himself and the great theologian-philosophers of the thirteenth century. St. Thomas Aquinas certainly made a formal and methodological distinction between philosophy and theology, a distinction which was not clearly made by St. Gregory of Nyssa, St. Augustine, or St. Anselm; but the attitude of *fides quaerens intellectum* was none the less the attitude of St. Thomas. *On this point*, therefore, I should be willing to rank St. Thomas as an 'Augustinian'. In regard to doctrinal content one must adopt another criterion, it is true. St. Bonaventure too made a formal distinction between theology and philosophy, though he clung to and emphasised doctrines generally recognised as 'Augustinian', whereas St. Thomas rejected them, and in regard to these doctrines one can call the philosophy of Bonaventure 'Augustinian' and the philosophy of Thomas non-Augustinian. Again, St. Bonaventure, as we have seen, emphasised far more than St. Thomas the insufficiency of independent philosophy, so that it has even been said that the unity of Bonaventure's system must be sought on the theological and not on the philosophical level. All the same, St. Thomas himself did not believe that a purely independent philosophy would be, in actual fact and practice, completely satisfactory, and he, like St. Bonaventure, was primarily a theologian. There is a great deal to be said for M. Gilson's contention that for St. Thomas the sphere of philosophy is the sphere of *le révélable* (in the sense in which M. Gilson uses the term, and not, obviously enough, in every sense).

The 'important qualification' I mentioned above is this. Owing to the discovery of the complete Aristotle and his adoption by St. Thomas, so far as adoption was consistent with theological orthodoxy, St. Thomas provided the material for an independent philosophy. As I have suggested when treating of St. Thomas, the utilisation of the Aristotelian system helped philosophy to become self-conscious and to aspire after independence and autonomy. When philosophical material was comparatively scanty, as in the Patristic period and in the earlier centuries of the mediaeval era, there could be little question of an autonomous philosophy going its own way (it is not necessary to take the phenomenon of the *dialectici* very seriously); but once Aristotelianism, which appeared at least to be a complete philosophical system, elaborated independently of theology, had arrived on the scene and had won its right to be there, a parting of the ways was morally inevitable: philosophy had grown up, and would soon demand its birthright and wander out of the house. But this was by no means the intention of St. Thomas, who had meant to utilise Aristotelianism in the construction of a vast theologico-philosophical synthesis, in which theology should constitute the ultimate measuring-rod. Yet children, when they grow up, do not always behave exactly as their parents expected or wished. Bonaventure, Albert, Thomas utilised and incorporated an increasing amount of the new philosophical materials, and all the while they were rearing a child who would soon go his own way; but the three men, though differing from one another on many points of philosophical doctrine, were really at one in the ideal of a Christian synthesis. They belonged to the *Sancti*, not to the *philosophi*; and if one wishes to find a radical contrast between mediaeval thinkers in regard to their view of the relation between theology and philosophy, one should contrast not so much St. Anselm and St. Bonaventure on the one hand with St. Thomas on the other as St. Anselm, St. Bonaventure, St. Thomas and Scotus on the one hand with the Latin Averroists and, in the fourteenth century, the Ockhamist School on the other. The *philosophi* and radical Peripatetics stand over against the Fathers and theologians and *Sancti*.

2. What has already been said brings one to the question of 'Christian philosophy'. Can one speak of the 'Christian philosophy'

of the Middle Ages, and if so, in what sense? If philosophy is a legitimate and autonomous province of human study and knowledge ('autonomous' in the sense that the philosopher has his own method and subject-matter), it would appear that it is not and cannot be 'Christian'. It would sound absurd to speak of 'Christian biology' or 'Christian mathematics': a biologist or a mathematician can be a Christian, but not his biology or his mathematics. Similarly, it might be said, a philosopher can be a Christian, but not his philosophy. His philosophy may be true and compatible with Christianity; but one does not call a scientific statement Christian simply because it is true and compatible with Christianity. Just as mathematics can be neither pagan nor Moslem nor Christian, though mathematicians can be pagans or Moslems or Christians, so philosophy can be neither pagan nor Moslem nor Christian, though philosophers can be pagans or Moslems or Christians. The relevant question about a scientific hypothesis is whether it is true or false, confirmed by observation and experiment or refuted, not whether it is proposed by a Christian or a Hindoo or an atheist; and the relevant question about a philosophic doctrine is whether it is true or false, more or less adequate as an explanation of the facts it is supposed to explain, not whether it is expounded by a believer in Zeus, a follower of Mahomet or a Christian theologian. The most that the phrase 'Christian philosophy' can legitimately mean is a philosophy compatible with Christianity; if it means more than that, one is speaking of a philosophy which is not simply philosophy, but which is, partly at least, theology.

This is a reasonable and understandable point of view, and it certainly represents one aspect of St. Thomas's attitude towards philosophy, an aspect expressed in his formal distinction between theology and philosophy. The philosopher starts with creatures, the theologian with God; the philosopher's principles are those discerned by the natural light of reason, the theologian's are revealed; the philosopher treats of the natural order, the theologian primarily of the supernatural order. But if one adheres closely to this aspect of Thomism, one is placed in a somewhat difficult position. St. Bonaventure did not think that any satisfactory metaphysic can be achieved save in the light of the Faith. The philosophic doctrine of exemplary ideas, for example, is closely linked up with the theological doctrine of the Word. Is one to say, then, that St. Bonaventure had no philosophy properly speaking, or is one to sort out the theological elements from the philosophical elements? And if so, does not one run the risk of constructing a 'Bonaventurian philosophy' which St. Bonaventure himself would hardly have recognised as an adequate expression of his thought and intentions? Is it not perhaps simpler to allow that St. Bonaventure's idea of philosophy *was* that of a Christian philosophy, in the sense of a general Christian synthesis such as earlier Christian writers endeavoured to achieve? An historian is entitled to adopt this point of view. If one speaks simply as a philosopher who is convinced that philosophy either stands on its own feet or is not philosophy at all, one will not admit the existence of a 'Christian philosophy'; or, in other words, if one speaks simply as a 'Thomist', one will be forced to criticise any other and different conception of philosophy. But if one speaks as an historian, looking on from outside, as it were, one will recognise that there were two conceptions of philosophy, the one that of St. Bonaventure, the conception of a Christian philosophy, the other that of St. Thomas and Scotus, the conception of a philosophy which could not properly be called Christian, save in the sense that it was compatible with theology. From this point of view one can say that St. Bonaventure, even though he made a formal distinction between theology and philosophy, continued the tradition of the Fathers, whereas with St. Thomas philosophy received a charter. In this sense Thomism was 'modern' and looked forward to the future. As a system of self-sufficient philosophy Thomism can enter into competition and discussion with other philosophies, because it can prescind from dogmatic theology altogether, whereas a Christian philosophy of the Bonaventurian type can hardly do so. The true Bonaventurian could, of course, argue with modern philosophers on particular points, the proofs of God's existence, for example; but the total system could hardly enter the philosophical arena on equal terms, precisely because it is not simply a philosophical system but a Christian synthesis.

Yet is there not a sense in which the philosophies of St. Augustine and St. Bonaventure and St. Albert and St. Thomas can all be called Christian? The problems which they discussed were in large measure set by theology, or by the necessity of defending Christian truth. When Aristotle argued to the existence of an unmoved mover, he was answering a problem set by metaphysics (and by physics); but when St. Anselm and St. Bonaventure and St. Thomas proved God's existence, they were showing the rational foundation for the acceptance of a revelation in which they already believed. St. Bonaventure was concerned also to show God's immanent activity within the soul; and even though St. Thomas employed Aristotle's own argument, he was not answering simply an abstract problem nor was he interested simply in showing that there is an unmoved mover, an ultimate cause of motion; he was interested in proving the existence of God, a Being who meant a great deal more to St. Thomas than an unmoved mover. His arguments can naturally be considered in themselves and, from the philosophic standpoint, they must be so considered; but he approached the question from the viewpoint of a theologian, looking on the proof of God's existence as a *praeambulum fidei*. Moreover, although St. Thomas certainly spoke of philosophy or metaphysics as the science of being as being, and though his declaration that the rational knowledge of God is the highest part of philosophy, that to which other parts lead, can certainly be regarded as suggested by Aristotle's words, in his *Summae* (which are of the greatest importance from the philosophical, as well as from the theological standpoint) he follows the order suggested by theology, and his philosophy fits closely into his theology, making a synthesis. St. Thomas did not approach philosophical problems in the spirit of a professor of the Parisian faculty of arts; he approached them in the spirit of a Christian theologian. Moreover, in spite of his Aristotelianism and in spite of his repetition of Aristotelian statements, I think it can be maintained that for St. Thomas philosophy is not so much a study of being in general as a study of God, God's activity and God's effects, so far as the natural reason will take us; so that God is the centre of his philosophy as of his theology, the same God, though attained in different ways. I have suggested earlier on that St. Thomas's formal charter to philosophy meant that philosophy would in the end go her own way, and I think that this is true; but that is not to say that St. Thomas envisaged or desired the 'separation' of philosophy from theology. On the contrary, he attempted a great synthesis, and he attempted it as a Christian theologian who was also a philosopher; he would doubtless have considered that what would have appeared to him as the vagaries and errors of philosophers in later centuries were largely due to those very causes in view of which he declared revelation to be morally necessary.

3. More chapters have been devoted to the philosophy of St. Thomas Aquinas than to any other philosopher, and rightly so,

since Thomism is unquestionably the most imposing and comprehensive synthesis considered in this book. I may have emphasised
those aspects of Thomism which are of non-Aristotelian origin,
and one should, I think, bear these aspects in mind, lest one forget
that Thomism is a synthesis and not simply a literal adoption of
Aristotelianism; but none the less Thomism *can*, of course, be
regarded as the culminating process of a movement in the Christian
West towards the adoption and utilisation of Greek philosophy as
represented by Aristotle. Owing to the fact that philosophy in the
time of the Fathers meant, to all intents and purposes, neo-
Platonism, to utilise Greek philosophy meant, for the Fathers, to
utilise neo-Platonism: St. Augustine, for instance, did not know
much of the historic system of Aristotle, as distinct from neo-
Platonism. Moreover, the spiritual character of neo-Platonism
appealed to the mind of the Fathers. That the categories of
neo-Platonism should continue to dominate Christian thought in
the early Middle Ages was only natural, in view of the fact that
the Fathers had utilised them and that they were consecrated
through the prestige attaching to the writings of the Pseudo-
Dionysius, believed to be St. Paul's convert. Furthermore, even
when the *corpus* of Aristotle's writings had become available in
Latin translations from the Greek and the Arabic, the differences
between Aristotelianism proper and neo-Platonism proper were by
no means clearly recognised: they could not be clearly recognised
so long as the *Liber de causis* and the *Elementatio theologica* were
ascribed to Aristotle, especially when the great Moslem commentators had themselves drawn copiously on neo-Platonism. That
Aristotle had criticised Plato was, of course, perfectly clear from
the *Metaphysics*; but the precise nature and scope of the criticism
was not so clear. The adoption and utilisation of Aristotle did not
mean, therefore, the negation and rejection of all neo-Platonism,
and though St. Thomas recognised that the *Liber de causis* was not
the work of Aristotle, one can regard his interpretation of Aristotle
in a manner consonant with Christianity, not merely as an interpretation *in meliorem partem* (which it was, from the viewpoint of
anyone who is both a Christian and an historian), but also as
following from the general conception of Aristotle in his time. St.
Bonaventure certainly thought that Aristotle's criticism of Plato
involved a rejection of exemplarism (and in my opinion St.
Bonaventure was quite right); but St. Thomas did not think so,
and he interpreted Aristotle accordingly. One might be tempted to

think that St. Thomas was simply whitewashing Aristotle; but one should not forget that 'Aristotle' for St. Thomas meant rather more than Aristotle means to the modern historian of Greek philosophy; he was, to a certain extent at least, an Aristotle seen through the eyes of commentators and philosophers who were themselves not pure Aristotelians. Even the radical Aristotelians by intention, the Latin Averroists, were not pure Aristotelians in the strict sense. If one adopts this point of view, one will find it easier to understand how Aristotle could appear to St. Thomas as 'the Philosopher', and one will realise that when St. Thomas baptised Aristotelianism he was not simply substituting Aristotelianism for neo-Platonism, but that he was completing that process of absorbing Greek philosophy which had begun in the early days of the Christian era. In a sense we can say that neo-Platonism, Augustinianism, Aristotelianism and the Moslem and Jewish philosophies came together and were fused in Thomism, not in the sense that selected elements were juxtaposed mechanically, but in the sense that a true fusion and synthesis was achieved under the regulating guidance of certain basic ideas. Thomism, in the fullest sense, is thus a synthesis of Christian theology and Greek philosophy (Aristotelianism, united with other elements, or Aristotelianism, interpreted in the light of later philosophy) in which philosophy is regarded in the light of theology and theology itself is expressed, to a considerable extent, in categories borrowed from Greek philosophy, particularly from Aristotle.

I have asserted that Thomism is a synthesis of Christian theology and Greek philosophy, which might seem to imply that Thomism in the narrower sense, that is, as denoting simply the Thomist philosophy, is a synthesis of Greek philosophy and that it is nothing else but Greek philosophy. In the first place, it seems preferable to speak of Greek philosophy rather than of Aristotelianism, for the simple reason that St. Thomas's philosophy was a synthesis of Platonism (using the term in a wide sense, to include neo-Platonism) and of Aristotelianism, though one should not forget that the Moslem and Jewish philosophers were also important influences in the formation of his thought. In the first volume of my history I have argued that Plato and Aristotle should be regarded as complementary thinkers, in some respects at least, and that a synthesis is needed. St. Thomas Aquinas achieved this synthesis. We cannot speak of his philosophy, therefore, as simply Aristotelianism; it is rather a synthesis of

Greek philosophy, harmonised with Christian theology. In the second place, Thomism is a real synthesis and is not a mere juxtaposition of heterogeneous elements. For example, St. Thomas did not take over the Platonic-Plotinian-Augustinian tradition of exemplary ideas and merely juxtapose it with the Aristotelian doctrine of substantial form: he gave each element its ontological status, making the substantial form subordinate to the exemplary idea, and explaining in what sense one is entitled to speak of 'ideas' in God. Again, if he adopted the (originally) Platonic notion of participation, he did not employ it in a manner which would conflict with the Aristotelian elements of his metaphysic. St. Thomas went beyond the Aristotelian hylomorphism and discerned in the real distinction between essence and existence a profounder application of the principle of potentiality and act. This distinction enabled him to use the Platonic notion of participation to explain finite being, while at the same time his view of God as *ipsum esse subsistens* rather than as mere unmoved mover enabled him to use the idea of participation in such a way as to throw into relief the idea of creation, which was to be found neither in Plato nor in Aristotle. Needless to say, St. Thomas did not take participation, in the full sense, as a premiss; the complete idea of participation could not be obtained until God's existence had been proved, but the material for the elaboration of that idea was provided by the real distinction between essence and existence.

4. Some of the viewpoints adopted in this book may appear to be somewhat inconsistent; but one must remember that it is possible to adopt different viewpoints in regard to the history of mediaeval philosophy, or indeed in regard to the history of philosophy in any epoch. Apart from the fact that one will naturally adopt a different viewpoint and interpret the development of philosophy in a different light according as one is a Thomist, a Scotist, a Kantian, an Hegelian, a Marxist or a Logical Positivist, it is possible even for the same man to discern different principles or modes of interpretation, none of which he would be willing to reject as totally illegitimate and yet for none of which he would be prepared to claim complete truth and adequacy.

Thus it is possible, and from certain viewpoints perfectly legitimate, to adopt the linear or progressive mode of interpretation. It is possible to view the absorption and utilisation of Greek philosophy by Christian thinkers as starting practically from zero in the early years of the Christian era, as increasing through the thought of the Fathers up to the Scholasticism of the early Middle Ages, as being suddenly, comparatively speaking, enriched through the translations from the Arabic and the Greek, and as developing through the thought of William of Auvergne, Alexander of Hales, St. Bonaventure and St. Albert the Great, until it reached its culmination in the Thomist synthesis. According to this line of interpretation it would be necessary to regard the philosophy of St. Bonaventure as a stage in the development of Thomism, and not as a parallel and heterogeneous philosophy. One would regard the achievement of St. Thomas, not so much as an adoption of Aristotle in place of Augustine or of neo-Platonic Platonism, but rather as a confluence and synthesis of the various currents of Greek philosophy, and of Islamic and Jewish philosophy, as well as of the original ideas contributed by Christian thinkers. Mediaeval philosophy before St. Thomas one would regard, not as 'Augustinianism' as opposed to Aristotelianism, but as pre-Thomist Scholasticism or as the Scholasticism of the earlier Middle Ages. This line of interpretation seems to me to be perfectly legitimate, and it has the very great advantage of not leading to a distorted idea of Thomism as pure Aristotelianism. It would even be possible and legitimate to look on Thomism as an Aristotelianised Platonism rather than as a Platonised Aristotelianism. What has been said of the 'synthetic' character of Thomism and of its relation to Greek, and Islamic, philosophy in general rather than to Aristotelianism in particular supports this line of interpretation, which was also suggested by what was said in the first volume of this history concerning the complementary character of the Platonic and Aristotelian philosophies.

On the other hand, if one follows this line of interpretation exclusively, one runs the risk of missing altogether the rich variety of mediaeval philosophy and the individuality of the different philosophers. The spirit of St. Bonaventure was not the same as that of Roger Bacon nor the same as that of St. Thomas, and French historians like M. Gilson have done us a great service in drawing attention to and throwing into relief the peculiar genius of individual thinkers. This 'individualisation' of mediaeval philosophers is all the more to be welcomed in view of the fact that the Christian thinkers shared a common theological background, so that their philosophical differences were expressed within a comparatively restricted field, with the result that mediaeval philosophy might seem to consist of a series of repetitions on salient points and a series of differences on relatively insignificant points. If one said simply that St. Bonaventure postulated a special illumination and that St. Thomas rejected it, the difference between them would not present so much interest as it does if St. Bonaventure's theory of illumination is linked up with his total thought and if St. Thomas's denial of any special illumination is seen against the background of his system in general. But one cannot depict the total thought of Bonaventure or the general system of Thomas without setting in relief the peculiar spirit of each thinker. It may very well be true that M. Gilson, as I suggested earlier in this book, has exaggerated the differences between St. Bonaventure and St. Thomas, and that it is possible to look on St. Bonaventure's philosophy as a stage in the evolution of Thomism rather than as a parallel and different philosophy; but it is also possible for different men to have different conceptions of what philosophy is, and if a man does not accept the Thomist point of view, he will probably be no more inclined to look on Bonaventure as an incomplete Thomas than a Platonist would be inclined to look on Plato as an incomplete Aristotle. It is, I think, a mistake to insist so much on the linear type of interpretation that one rules out as illegitimate the type of interpretation represented by M. Gilson or, conversely, so to insist upon the individual characteristics and spirits of different thinkers as to lose sight of the general evolution of thought towards a complete synthesis. Narrowness of vision can hardly produce adequate understanding.

Again, while it is possible to view the development of mediaeval philosophy as a development towards the Thomist synthesis and to regard pre-Thomist philosophies as stages in that development, and while it is possible to concentrate more on the peculiarities of different philosophies and the individual geniuses of different thinkers, it is also possible to see and to throw into relief different general lines of development. Thus it is possible to distinguish different types of 'Augustinianism' instead of being content with one portmanteau word; to distinguish, for example, the typically Franciscan Augustinianism of St. Bonaventure from the Aristotelianised Augustinianism of Richard of Middleton or the Avicennian Augustinianism of Henry of Ghent and, in a certain measure, of Duns Scotus. It is possible to trace the respective influences on mediaeval thought of Avicenna, Averroes and Avicebron, and to attempt a corresponding classification. Hence phrases such as *augustinisme avicennisant*, *augustinisme avicebronisant*, *avicennisme latin*, of which French historians have made use. An investigation of such influences is certainly of value; but the classification produced by such an investigation cannot be regarded as a *complete* and entirely adequate classification of mediaeval philosophies, since insistence on the influence of the past tends to obscure original contributions, while it depends largely on what points of his philosophy one happens to have in mind whether one classes a philosopher as falling under the influence of Avicenna or Averroes or Avicebron.

Again, one can regard the development of mediaeval philosophy in regard to the relation of Christian thought to 'humanism', to Greek thought and culture and science in general. Thus if St. Peter Damian was a representative of the negative attitude towards humanism, St. Albert the Great and Roger Bacon represented a positive attitude, while from the political point of view Thomism represents a harmonisation of the natural and humanistic with the supernatural which is absent in the characteristic political theory of Giles of Rome. St. Thomas, again, through the greater part he attributes to human activity in knowledge and action compared with some of his predecessors and contemporaries, may be said to represent a humanistic tendency.

In fine, mediaeval philosophy can be considered under several aspects, each of which has its own justification, and it ought to be so considered if one is to attain anything like an adequate view of it; but any more extensive treatment of mediaeval philosophy in general must be reserved until the conclusion of the next volume, when the philosophy of the fourteenth century has been discussed. In the present volume the great synthesis of St. Thomas naturally and rightly occupies the central position, though, as we have seen, mediaeval philosophy and the philosophy of St. Thomas are not synonymous. The thirteenth century was the century of speculative thought, and the century was exceptionally rich in speculative thinkers. It was the century of original thinkers, whose thought had not yet become hardened into the dogmatic traditions of philosophical Schools. But though the great thinkers of the thirteenth century differed from one another in their philosophical doctrines and criticised one another, they did so against a background of commonly accepted metaphysical principles. One must distinguish criticism concerning the application of accepted metaphysical principles from criticism of the very foundations of metaphysical systems. The former was practised by all the great speculative thinkers of the Middle Ages; but the latter did not appear until the fourteenth century. I have concluded this volume with a consideration of Duns Scotus, who, from the chronological point of view, stands at the juncture of the thirteenth and fourteenth centuries; but even if one can discern in his philosophy the faint beginnings of the more radical spirit of criticism which was to characterise the Ockhamist movement of the fourteenth century, his criticism of his contemporaries and predecessors did not involve a denial of the metaphysical principles commonly accepted in the thirteenth century. Looking back on the Middle Ages, we may tend to see in the system of Scotus a bridge between the two centuries, between the age of St. Thomas and the age of Ockham; but Ockham himself certainly did not see in Scotus a kindred spirit, and I think that even if Scotus's philosophy did prepare the way for a more radical criticism his system must be regarded as the last of the great mediaeval speculative syntheses. It can hardly be denied, I think, that certain of Scotus's opinions in rational psychology, in natural theology and in ethics look forward, as it were, to the Ockhamist critique of metaphysics and the peculiar Ockhamist view of the nature of the moral law; but if one considers Scotus's philosophy in itself, without reference to a future which we know but he did not, we are forced to realise that it was just as much a metaphysical system as any of the great systems of the thirteenth century. It seemed to me, then, that Scotus's place was in this volume rather than in the next. In the next volume I hope to treat of fourteenth-century philosophy, of the philosophies of the Renaissance and of the revival of Scholasticism in the fifteenth and sixteenth centuries.

APPENDIX I

Honorific titles applied in the Middle Ages to philosophers treated of in this volume.

RHABANUS MAURUS:	Praeceptor Germaniae.
ABELARD:	Peripateticus Palatinus.
ALAN OF LILLE:	Doctor universalis.
AVERROES:	Commentator.
ALEXANDER OF HALES:	Doctor irrefragibilis.
ST. BONAVENTURE:	Doctor seraphicus.
ST. ALBERT THE GREAT:	Doctor universalis.
ST. THOMAS AQUINAS:	Doctor angelicus and Doctor communis.
ROGER BACON:	Doctor mirabilis.
RICHARD OF MIDDLETON:	Doctor solidus.
RAYMOND LULL:	Doctor illuminatus.
GILES OF ROME:	Doctor fundatissimus.
HENRY OF GHENT:	Doctor solemnis.
DUNS SCOTUS:	Doctor subtilis.

APPENDIX II
A SHORT BIBLIOGRAPHY

General Works on Mediaeval Philosophy

BRÉHIER, E. Histoire de la philosophie: tome 1, l'antiquité et le moyen âge. Paris, 1943.

CARLYLE, R. W. & A. J. A History of Mediaeval Political Theory in the West. 4 vols. London, 1903–22.

DEMPF, A. Die Ethik des Mittelalters. Munich, 1930.
Metaphysik des Mittelalters. Munich, 1930.

DE WULF, M. Histoire de la philosophie médiévale. 3 vols. Louvain, 1934–47 (6th edition). English translation of first two vols. by E. C. Messenger, London, 1935–8 (3rd edition).

GEYER, B. Die patristische und scholastische Philosophie. Berlin, 1928. (This is the second volume of the revised edition of Ueberweg.)

GILSON, E. La philosophie au moyen âge. Paris, 1944 (2nd edition, revised and augmented). English translation, 1936.
L'esprit de la philosophie médiévale. 2 vols. Paris, 1944 (2nd edition).
Études de philosophie médiévale. Strasbourg, 1921.
The Unity of Philosophical Experience. London, 1938.
Reason and Revelation in the Middle Ages. New York, 1939.

GRABMANN, M. Die Philosophie des Mittelalters. Berlin, 1921.
Mittelalterliches Geistesleben. 2 vols. Munich, 1926 and 1936.

GRUNWALD, G. Geschichte der Gottesbeweise im Mittelalter bis zum Ausgang der Hochscholastik. Münster, 1907.
(Beiträge zur Geschichte der Philosophie und Theologie des Mittelalters, 6, 3.)

HAURÉAU, B. Histoire de la philosophie scolastique. 3 vols. Paris, 1872–80.

HAWKINS, D. J. B. A Sketch of Mediaeval Philosophy. London, 1946.

LOTTIN, O. Psychologie et morale aux XIIe et XIIIe siècles. Tome 1: Problèmes de Psychologie. Louvain, 1942. Tome 2: Problèmes de Morale. 1948.
Le droit naturel chez S. Thomas d'Aquin et ses prédécesseurs. Bruges, 1931 (2nd edition).

PICAVET, F. Esquisse d'une histoire générale et comparée des philosophies médiévales. Paris, 1907 (2nd edition).
Essais sur l'histoire générale et comparée des théologies et des philosophies médiévales. Paris, 1913.

ROMEYER, B. La philosophie chrétienne jusqu'à Descartes. 3 vols. Paris, 1935–7.

RUGGIERO, G. DE. La filosofia del cristianesimo. 3 vols. Bari.

STÖCKL, A. Geschichte der Philosophie des Mittelalters. 3 vols. Mainz, 1864–6.

VIGNAUX, P. La pensée au moyen âge. Paris, 1938.

Chapter II: The Patristic Period

(a) Texts: General collections of

Migne (edit.), Patrologia Graeca. Paris.

Migne (edit.), Patrologia Latina. Paris.

Die griechischen christlichen Schriftsteller der ersten drei Jahrhunderte. Leipzig.

Corpus scriptorum ecclesiasticorum Latinorum. Vienna.

Ante-Nicene Christian Library, Translations of the writings of the Fathers down to A.D. 325. Edinburgh.

A Library of the Fathers (English translations). Oxford.

Ancient Christian Writers: the works of the Fathers in Translation. Westminster, Maryland, U.S.A., 1946 (edit. J. Quasten and J. C. Flumpe).

(b) Particular Texts

ARISTIDES. Apology. In *Zwei griechische Apologeten*, J. Geffcken. Leipzig, 1907.
       Apology. In *Texte und Untersuchungen*, IV. E. Hennecke (edit.). Leipzig, 1893.

ARNOBIUS. Libri 7 adversus gentes. Appended to *Lactantii opera omnia* (L. C. Firmiani). Paris, 1845.

ATHENAGORAS. Apology. In *Zwei griechische Apologeten*. J. Geffcken. Leipzig, 1907.
       Libellus pro Christianis and Oratio de resurrectione cadaverum in *Texte und Untersuchungen*, IV. E. Schwartz (edit.). Leipzig, 1891.

CLEMENT OF ALEXANDRIA. The Exhortation to the Greeks, etc. G. W. Butterworth (edit.). London, 1919.

EUSEBIUS. The Proof of the Gospel (*Demonstratio Evangelica*). 2 vols. W. J. Ferrar (edit.). London, 1920.

GREGORY OF NYSSA, ST. The Catechetical Oration of St. Gregory of Nyssa. J. H. Srawley (edit.). London, 1917.
       La Création de l'homme. J. Laplace and J. Daniélou. Paris, 1943.

HIPPOLYTUS. Philosophumena. 2 vols. F. Legge (edit.). London, 1921.

IRENAEUS, ST. The Treatise of Irenaeus of Lugdunum against the Heresies. F. R. Montgomery Hitchcock (edit.). London, 1916.

JUSTIN MARTYR, ST. The Dialogue with Trypho. A. L. Williams (edit.). London, 1930.

LACTANTIUS. Opera omnia. L. C. Firmiani. Paris, 1843.

MINUCIUS FELIX. The Octavius of Minucius Felix. J. H. Freese (edit.). London (no date).

ORIGEN. Homélies sur la Genèse. L. Doutreleau (edit.). Paris, 1943.
Origen on First Principles. G. W. Butterworth (edit.). London, 1936.

TATIAN. Oratio ad Graecos. In *Texte und Untersuchungen*, IV. E. Schwartz (edit.). Leipzig, 1888.

TERTULLIAN. Tertullian concerning the Resurrection of the Flesh. A. Souter (edit.). London, 1922.
Tertullian against Praxeas. A. Souter (edit.). London, 1920.
Tertullian's Apology. J. E. B. Mayer (edit.). Cambridge, 1917.

Other Works

ARNOU, R. De 'platonismo' Patrum. Rome, 1935.

BALTHASAR, HANS VON. Présence et pensée. Essai sur la philosophie religieuse de Grégoire de Nysse. Paris, 1943.

BARDY, G. Clément d'Alexandrie. Paris, 1926.

BAYLIS, H. J. Minucius Felix. London, 1928.

DANIÉLOU, J. Platonisme et théologie mystique. Essai sur la doctrine spirituelle de saint Grégoire de Nysse. Paris, 1944.

DIEKAMP, F. Die Gotteslehre des heiligen Gregor von Nyssa. Münster, 1896.

ERMONI, V. Saint Jean Damascène. Paris, 1904.

FAIRWEATHER, W. Origen and the Greek Patristic Philosophy. London, 1901.

FAYE, E. DE. Gnostiques et gnosticisme. Paris, 1925 (2nd edition).

HITCHCOCK, F. R. MONTGOMERY. Irenaeus of Lugdunum. Cambridge, 1914.

LEBRETON, J. Histoire du dogme de la Trinité. Paris, 1910.

MONDÉSERT, C. Clément d'Alexandrie. Lyons, 1944.

MORGAN, J. The Importance of Tertullian in the development of Christian dogma. London, 1928.

PICHON, R. Étude sur les mouvements philosophiques et religieux sous le règne de Constantin. Paris, 1903.

PRESTIGE, G. L. God in Patristic Thought. London, 1936.

PUECH, A. Histoire de la littérature grecque chrétienne depuis les origines jusqu'à la fin du IVe siècle. 3 vols. Paris, 1928-30.

RIVIÈRE, J. Saint Basile, évêque de Césarée. Paris, 1930.

THAMIN, R. Saint Ambroise et la morale chrétienne au IVe siècle. Paris, 1895.

Texts
Chapters III–VIII: St. Augustine
Patrologia Latina (Migne), vols. 32–47.

Corpus scriptorum ecclesiasticorum latinorum, vols. 12, 25, 28, 33, 34, 36, 40, 41–4, 51–3, 57, 58, 60, 63 . . .

City of God. 2 vols. (Everyman Edition). London, 1945.

Confessions. F. J. Sheed. London, 1943.

The Letters of St. Augustine. W. J. Sparrow-Simpson (edit.). London, 1919.

Studies on Augustine
BARDY, G. Saint Augustin. Paris, 1946 (6th edition).

BOURKE, V. J. Augustine's Quest of Wisdom. Milwaukee, 1945.

BOYER, C. Christianisme et néo-platonisme dans la formation de saint Augustin. Paris, 1920.

L'idée de vérité dans la philosophie de saint Augustin. Paris, 1920.

Essais sur la doctrine de saint Augustin. Paris, 1932.

COMBES, G. La doctrine politique de saint Augustin. Paris, 1927.

FIGGIS, J. N. The Political Aspects of St. Augustine's City of God. London, 1921.

GILSON, E. Introduction à l'étude de saint Augustin. Paris, 1943 (2nd edition).

GRABMANN, M. Der göttliche Grund menschlicher Wahrheitserkenntnis nach Augustinus and Thomas von Aquin. Cologne, 1924.

Die Grundgedanken des heiligen Augustinus über Seele und Gott. Cologne, 1929 (2nd edition).

HENRY, P. L'extase d'Ostie. Paris, 1938.

HESSEN, J. Augustins Metaphysik der Erkenntnis. Berlin, 1931.

LE BLOND, J. M. Les conversions de saint Augustin. Paris, 1948.

MARTIN, J. La doctrine sociale de saint Augustin. Paris, 1912.

Saint Augustin. Paris, 1923 (2nd edition).

MAUSBACH, J. Die Ethik des heiligen Augustinus. 2 vols. Freiburg, 1929 (2nd edition).

MESSENGER, E. C. Evolution and Theology. London, 1931. (For Augustine's theory of *rationes seminales*.)

MUÑOZ VEGA, P. Introducción a la síntesis de San Augustin. Rome, 1945.

PORTALIÉ, E. Augustin, saint. Dictionnaire de théologie catholique, vol. 1. Paris, 1902.

SWITALSKI, B. Neoplatonism and the Ethics of St. Augustine. New York, 1946.

Publications for 15th centenary of St. Augustine

A Monument to St. Augustine. London, 1930.

Aurelius Augustinus. Cologne, 1930.

S. Agostino. Milan, 1931.

Études sur S. Augustin. *Archives de Philosophie*, vol. 7, cahier 2. Paris, 1930.

Religion y Cultura. XV Centenario de la Muerte de San Augustin. Madrid, 1931.

Mélanges augustiniens. Paris, 1930.

Miscellanea agostiniana. 2 vols. Rome, 1930–1.

Texts   *Chapter IX: The Pseudo-Dionysius*

Patrologia Graeca, vols. 3–4.

Dionysius the Areopagite on the Divine Names and the Mystical Theology. C. E. Rolt (edit.). London, 1920.

Texts   *Chapter X: Boethius, Cassiodorus, Isidore*

Patrologia Latina (Migne); vols. 63–4 (Boethius), 69–70 (Cassiodorus), 81–4 (Isidore).

BOETHIUS. The Theological Tractates and The Consolation of Philosophy. H. F. Stewart and E. K. Rand (edit.). London, 1926.

       De Consolatione Philosophiae. A. Fortescue (edit.). London, 1925.

Studies

BARRETT, H. M. Boethius: Some Aspects of his Times and Work. Cambridge, 1940.

PATCH, H. R. The Tradition of Boethius, a Study of his Importance in Medieval Culture. New York, 1935.

RAND, E. K. Founders of the Middle Ages; ch. 5, Boethius the Scholastic. Harvard U.P., 1941.

Texts   *Chapter XI: The Carolingian Renaissance*

Patrologia Latina (Migne); vols. 100–1 (Alcuin), 107–12 (Rhabanus Maurus).

Studies

BUXTON, E. M. WILMOT. Alcuin. London, 1922.

LAISTNER, M. L. W. Thought and Letters in Western Europe, A.D. 500–900. London, 1931.

TAYLOR, H. O. The Mediaeval Mind, vol. 1. London, 1911.

TURNAU, D. Rabanus Maurus praeceptor Germaniae. Munich, 1900.

Texts   *Chapters XII–XIII: John Scotus Eriugena*

Patrologia Latina (Migne); vol. 122.
Selections (in English) in *Selections from Mediaeval Philosophers*, vol. I, by R. McKeon. London, 1930.

Studies

BETT, H. Johannes Scotus Eriugena, a Study in Mediaeval Philosophy. Cambridge, 1925.

CAPPUYNS, M. Jean Scot Erigène, sa vie, son œuvre, sa pensée. Paris, 1933.

SCHNEIDER, A. Die Erkenntnislehre des Johannes Eriugena im Rahmen ihrer metaphysischen und anthropologischen Voraussetzungen. 2 vols. Berlin, 1921–3.

SEUL, W. Die Gotteserkenntnis bei Johannes Skotus Eriugena unter Berücksichtigung ihrer neo-platonischen und augustinischen Elemente. Bonn, 1932.

Texts   *Chapter XIV: The Problem of Universals*

Patrologia Latina (Migne); vols. 105 (Fredegisius), 139 (Gerbert of Aurillac), 144–5 (St. Peter Damian), 158–9 (St. Anselm), 160 (Odo of Tournai), 163 (William of Champeaux), 178 (Abelard), 188 (Gilbert de la Porrée), 199 (John of Salisbury), 175–7 (Hugh of St. Victor).

B. GEYER. Die philosophischen Schriften Peter Abelards. 4 vols. Münster, 1919–33.

Selections from Abelard in *Selections from Mediaeval Philosophers*, vol. I, by R. McKeon. London, 1930.

Studies

BERTHAUD, A. Gilbert de la Porrée et sa philosophie. Poitiers, 1892.

CARRÉ, M. H. Realists and Nominalists. Oxford, 1946.

COUSIN, V. Ouvrages inédits d'Abélard. Paris, 1836.

DE WULF, M. Le problème des universaux dans son évolution historique du IXe au XIIIe siècle. Archiv für Geschichte der Philosophie, 1896.

LEFÈVRE, G. Les variations de Guillaume de Champeaux et la question des universaux. Lille, 1898.

OTTAVIANO, C. Pietro Abelardo, La vita, le opere, il pensiero. Rome, 1931.

PICAVET, F. Gerbert ou le pape philosophe. Paris, 1897.
Roscelin philosophe et théologien, d'après la légende et d'après l'histoire. Paris, 1911.

REINERS, J. Der aristotelische Realismus in der Frühscholastik. Bonn, 1907.
Der Nominalismus in der Frühscholastik. Münster, 1910 (Beiträge, 8, 5).

REMUSAT, C. DE. Abaelard. 2 vols. Paris, 1845.
SICKES, J. G. Peter Abaelard. Cambridge, 1932.

Texts   *Chapter XV: St. Anselm of Canterbury*

Patrologia Latina (Migne); vols. 158-9.

Studies

BARTH, K. Fides quaerens intellectum. Anselms Beweis der Existenz Gottes im Zusammenhang seines theologischen Programms. Munich, 1931.
FISCHER, J. Die Erkenntnislehre Anselms von Canterbury. Münster, 1911 (Beiträge, 10, 3).
FILLIÂTRE, C. La philosophie de saint Anselme, ses principes, sa nature, son influence. Paris, 1920.
GILSON, E. Sens et nature de l'argument de saint Anselme, in *Archives d'histoire doctrinale et littéraire du moyen âge*, 1934.
KOYRÉ, A. L'idée de Dieu dans la philosophie de saint Anselme. Paris, 1923.
LEVASTI, A. Sant' Anselmo, Vita e pensiero. Bari, 1929.

Texts   *Chapter XVI: The School of Chartres*

Patrologia Latina (Migne); vols. 199 (John of Salisbury, containing also fragments of Bernard of Chartres, columns 666 and 938), 90 (William of Conches's *Philosophia*, among works of Bede).
JANSSEN, W. Der Kommentar des Clarembaldus von Arras zu Boethius De Trinitate. Breslau, 1926.
BARACH, C. S. & WROBEL, J. Bernardus Silvestris, De mundi universitate libri duo. Innsbruck, 1896.
WEBB, C. C. J. Metalogicon. Oxford, 1929.
       Policraticus. 2 vols. Oxford, 1909.

Studies

CLERVAL, A. Les écoles de Chartres au moyen âge du Ve au XVIe siècle. Paris, 1895.
FLATTEN, H. Die Philosophie des Wilhelm von Conches. Coblenz, 1929.
SCHARSCHMIDT, C. Joannes Saresberiensis nach Leben und Studien, Schriften und Philosophie. Leipzig, 1862.
WEBB, C. C. J. John of Salisbury. London, 1932.

Texts   *Chapter XVII: The School of St. Victor*

Patrologia Latina (Migne); vols. 175-7 (Hugh), 196 (Richard and Godfrey).

Studies

EBNER, J. Die Erkenntnislehre Richards von Sankt Viktor.
Münster, 1917 (Beiträge, 19, 4).

ETHIER, A. M. Le De Trinitate de Richard de Saint-Victor. Paris,
1939.

KILGENSTEIN, J. Die Gotteslehre des Hugo von Sankt Viktor.
Würzburg, 1897.

MIGNON, A. Les origines de la scolastique et Hugues de Saint-Victor.
2 vols. Paris, 1895.

OSTLER, H. Die Psychologie des Hugo von Sankt Viktor. Münster,
1906 (Beiträge, 6, 1).

VERNET, F. Hugues de Saint-Victor. Dictionnaire de théologie
catholique, vol. 7.

Chapter XVIII: Dualists and Pantheists

ALPHANDÉRY, P. Les idées morales chez les hétérodoxes latins au
début du XIIIe siècle. Paris, 1903.

BROEKX, E. Le catharisme. Louvain, 1916.

CAPELLE, G. C. Autour du décret de 1210: III, Amaury de Bène,
Étude sur son panthéisme formel. Paris, 1932 (Bibliothèque
thomiste, 16).

RUNCIMAN, S. The Mediaeval Manichee. Cambridge, 1947.

THÉRY, G. Autour du décret de 1210: I, David de Dinant, Étude
sur son panthéisme matérialiste. Paris, 1925 (Bibliothèque
thomiste, 6).

Chapter XIX: Islamic Philosophy

Texts

ALFARABI. Alpharabius de intelligentiis, philosophia prima.
Venice, 1508.

Alfarabis philosophische Abhandlungen, aus dem arabischen übersetzt. Fr. Dieterici. Leiden, 1892.

Alfarabi über den Ursprung der Wissenschaften.
Cl. Baeumker. Münster, 1933.

Alfarabius de Platonis Philosophia. Edited by F.
Rosenthal and R. Walzer. Plato Arabus, vol. 2.
London, Warburg Institute, 1943.

ALGAZEL. Alagazel's Metaphysics, a Mediaeval Translation.
Toronto, 1933.

AVICENNA. Avicennae Opera. Venice, 1495–1546.

Avicennae Metaphysices Compendium. Rome, 1926
(Latin).

AVERROES. Aristotelis opera omnia, Averrois in ea opera commentaria. 11 vols. Venice.

Die Epitome der Metaphysik des Averroës. S. Van den Bergh. Leiden, 1924.

Accord de la religion et de la philosophie, traité d'Ibn Rochd (Averroes), traduit et annoté. L. Gauthier. Algiers, 1905.

Studies: General

BOER, T. J. DE. History of Philosophy in Islam. Translated by E. R. Jones. London, 1903.

CARRA DE VAUX, B. Les penseurs d'Islam. 5 vols. Paris, 1921-6.

GAUTHIER, L. Introduction à l'étude de la philosophie musulmane. Paris, 1923.

MUNK, S. Mélanges de philosophie juive et arabe. Paris, 1927.

O'LEARY, DE LACY. Arabic Thought and its place in History. London, 1922.

The Legacy of Islam. T. Arnold and A. Guillaume (edit.). Oxford, 1931.

Particular

ALONSO, M. Teologia de Averroes. Madrid-Granada, 1947.

ASÍN Y PALACIOS, M. Algazel: Dogmatica, moral, ascética. Saragossa, 1901.

CARRA DE VAUX, B. Gazali. Paris, 1902.

Avicenne. Paris, 1900.

GAUTHIER, L. La théorie d'Ibn Rochd sur les rapports de la religion et de la philosophie. Paris, 1909.

Ibn Roschd (Averroès). Paris, 1948.

GOICHON, A. M. Introduction à Avicenne. Paris, 1933.

La distinction de l'essence et de l'existence d'après Ibn Sīnā (Avicenna). Paris, 1937.

La philosophie d'Avicenne. Paris, 1944.

HORTEN, M. Die Metaphysik des Averroës. Halle, 1912.

KLEINE, W. Die Substanzlehre Avicennas bei Thomas von Aquin. Fribourg, 1933.

RENAN, E. Averroès et l'averroisme. Paris, 1869 (3rd edition).

SALIBA, D. Étude sur la métaphysique d'Avicenne. Paris, 1927.

SMITH, M. Al-Ghazālī, the Mystic. London, 1944.

SWEETMAN, J. W. Islam and Christian Theology, vol. 1. London 1945.

WENSINCK, A. J. La Pensée de Ghazzālī. Paris, 1940.

Texts   Chapter XX: Jewish Philosophy

Avencebrolis Fons Vitae, ex arabico in latinum translatus ab Johanne Hispano et Dominico Gundissalino. Münster, 1892-5.

MAIMONIDES. Le guide des égarés, traité de théologie et de philosophie. 3 vols. Paris, 1856–66.

Studies

GUTTMANN, J. Die Philosophie des Judentums. Munich, 1933.

HUSIK, I. A History of Mediaeval Jewish Philosophy. New York, 1918.

LEVY, L. G. Maïmonide. Paris, 1932 (2nd edition).

MUNK, S. Mélanges de philosophie juive et arabe. Paris, 1927.

MUNZ, J. Moses ben Maimon, sein Leben und seine Werke. Frankfurt am M., 1912.

ROHNER, A. Das Schöpfungsproblem bei Moses Maimonides, Albertus Magnus und Thomas von Aquin. Münster, 1913 (Beiträge, 11, 5).

ROTH, L. Spinoza, Descartes and Maimonides. Oxford, 1924.

Chapter XXI: The Translations

See the bibliography in M. De Wulf's *Histoire de la philosophie médiévale*, vol. 2, 6th French edition. (In the English translation by Dr. E. C. Messenger the bibliography and the sections by A. Pelzer on the translations have been abridged.) See also B. Geyer's *Die patristische und scholastische Philosophie* (1928), pp. 342–51, with the corresponding bibliography, p. 728.

Chapter XXII: Introduction (to Thirteenth Century)

BONNEROT, J. La Sorbonne, sa vie, son rôle, son œuvre à travers les siècles. Paris, 1927.

DENIFLE, H. and Chartularium Universitatis Parisiensis. 4 vols.
CHATELAIN, A.   Paris, 1889–97.
                  Auctuarium Chartularii Universitatis Parisiensis. 2 vols. Paris, 1894–7.
                  Les universités françaises au moyen âge. Paris, 1892.

GLORIEUX, P. Répertoire des maîtres en théologie de Paris au XIIIe siècle. 2 vols. Paris, 1933–4.

GRABMANN, M. I divieti ecclesiastici di Aristotele sotto Innocenzo e Gregorio IX. Rome, 1941.

LITTLE, A. G. The Grey Friars in Oxford. Oxford, 1892.

RASHDALL, H. The Universities of Europe in the Middle Ages. New edition, edited by F. M. Powicke and A. B. Emden. 3 vols. Oxford, 1936.

SHARP, D. E. Franciscan Philosophy at Oxford in the Thirteenth Century. Oxford, 1936.

Texts   *Chapter XXIII: William of Auvergne*

Opera. 2 vols. Paris, 1674.

Studies

BAUMGARTNER, M. Die Erkenntnislehre des Wilhelm von Auvergne. Münster, 1895 (Beiträge, 2, 1).

MASNOVO, A. Da Guglielmo d'Auvergne a San Tommaso d'Aquino. Milan, vol. 1 (1930 and 1945); vol. 2 (1934 and 1946); vol. 3 (1945).

Texts   *Chapter XXIV: Robert Grosseteste and Alexander of Hales*

Die philosophischen Werke des Robert Grosseteste, Bischof von Lincoln. L. Baur. Münster, 1912 (Beiträge, 9).

THOMSON, S. H. The Writings of Robert Grosseteste, Bishop of Lincoln, 1175–1253. Cambridge, 1940 (Bibliographical).

Doctoris irrefragabilis Alexandri de Hales, O.M. Summa Theologica. 3 vols. Quaracchi, 1924–30.

Studies

BAUR, L. Die Philosophie des Robert Grosseteste. Münster, 1917 (Beiträge, 18, 4–6).

For Alexander of Hales, see introduction to Quaracchi critical edition (*supra*).

Text   *Chapters XXV–XXIX: St. Bonaventure*

Opera omnia. 10 vols. Quaracchi, 1882–1902.

Studies

BISSEN, J. M. L'exemplarisme divin selon saint Bonaventure. Paris, 1929.

DE BENEDICTIS, M. M. The Social Thought of Saint Bonaventure. Washington, 1946.

GILSON, E. The Philosophy of St. Bonaventure. London, 1938.

GRÜNEWALD, S. Franziskanische Mystik. Versuch zu einer Darstellung mit besonderer Berücksichtigung des heiligen Bonaventura. Munich, 1931.

LUTZ, E. Die Psychologie Bonaventuras. Münster, 1909 (Beiträge, 6, 4–5).

LUYCKX, B. A. Die Erkenntnislehre Bonaventuras. Münster, 1923 (Beiträge, 23, 3–4).

O'DONNELL, C. M. The Psychology of St. Bonaventure and St. Thomas Aquinas. Washington, 1937.

ROBERT, P. Hylémorphisme et devenir chez S. Bonaventure. Montreal, 1936.

ROSENMÖLLER, B. Religiöse Erkenntnis nach Bonaventura. Münster, 1925 (Beiträge, 25, 3–4).

Texts   Chapter XXX: St. Albert the Great

Opera Omnia. A Borgnet. 38 vols. Paris, 1890–9. (See also
G. Meersseman. Introductio in opera omnia beati Alberti Magni,
O.P. Bruges, 1931.)
De vegetalibus. C. Jessen. Berlin, 1867.
De animalibus. H. Stradler. Münster, 1916 (Beiträge, 15–16).

Studies

ARENDT, W. Die Staats- und Gesellschaftslehre Alberts des Grossen
nach den Quellen daargestellt. Jena, 1929.

BALES, H. Albertus Magnus als Zoologe. Munich, 1928.

FRONOBER, H. Die Lehre von der Materie und Form nach Albert
dem Grossen. Breslau, 1909.

GRABMANN, M. Der Einfluss Alberts des Grossen auf das mittelal-
terliche Geistesleben, in *Mittelalterliches Geistesleben*, vol. 2.
Munich, 1936.

LIERTZ, R. Der selige Albert der Grosse als Naturforscher und
Lehrer. Munich, 1931.

REILLY, G. C. Psychology of St. Albert the Great compared with
that of St. Thomas. Washington, 1934.

SCHEEBEN, H. C. Albertus Magnus. Bonn, 1932.

SCHMIEDER, K. Alberts des Grossen Lehre von natürlichem Gottes-
wissen. Freiburg im/B., 1932.

SCHNEIDER, A. Die Psychologie Alberts des Grossen. Münster,
1903–6 (Beiträge, 4, 5–6).

Texts   Chapters XXXI–XLI: St. Thomas Aquinas

Opera omnia (Leonine edition). Rome, 1882. So far 15 vols. have
been published.

Opera omnia (Parma edition). 25 vols. Parma, 1852–73. Reprint,
New York, 1948.

Opera omnia (Vivès edition). 34 vols. Paris, 1872–80.

The English Dominican Fathers have published translations of the
Summa theologica, the *Summa contra Gentiles*, and the *Quaestiones
disputatae*. London (B.O.W.) There is a volume of selections (in
English) in the Everyman Library, London.

Basic Writings of St. Thomas Aquinas, edit. A. Pegis. 2 vols. New
York, 1945.

Bibliography

BOURKE, V. J. Thomistic Bibliography, 1920–40. St. Louis Mo,
U.S.A., 1945.

GRABMANN, M. Die echten Schriften des heiligen Thomas von Aquin.
Münster, 1920.
(2nd edition) Die Werke des heiligen Thomas von
Aquin. Münster, 1931.

MANDONNET, P. Des écrits authentiques de St. Thomas. Fribourg (Switzerland), 1910 (2nd edition).

MANDONNET, P. and DESTREZ, J. Bibliographie thomiste. Paris, 1921.

Life

CHESTERTON, G. K. St. Thomas Aquinas. London, 1933, 1947.

DE BRUYNE, E. St. Thomas d'Aquin, Le milieu, l'homme, la vision du monde. Brussels, 1928.

GRABMANN, M. Das Seelenleben des heiligen Thomas von Aquin. Munich, 1924.

General Studies

D'ARCY, M. C. Thomas Aquinas. London, 1931.

DE BRUYNE, E. See above.

GILSON, E. Le Thomisme. Paris, 1944 (5th edition).
    English translation, *The Philosophy of St. Thomas Aquinas.* Cambridge, 1924, 1930, 1937.

LATTEY, C. (editor). St. Thomas Aquinas. London, 1924. (Cambridge Summer School Papers.)

MANSER, G. M. Das Wesen des Thomismus. Fribourg (Switzerland), 1931.

MARITAIN, J. St. Thomas Aquinas. London, 1946 (3rd edition).

OLIGIATI, F. A Key to the Study of St. Thomas. Translated by J. S. Zybura. St. Louis (U.S.A.), 1925.

PEILLAUBE, E. Initiation à la philosophie de S. Thomas. Paris, 1926.

RIMAUD, J. Thomisme et méthode. Paris, 1925.

SERTILLANGES, A. D. Foundations of Thomistic philosophy.
    Translated by G. Anstruther. London, 1931.
    S. Thomas d'Aquin. 2 vols. Paris, 1925. (4th edition).

VANN, G. Saint Thomas Aquinas. London, 1940.

Metaphysics

FINANCE, J. DE. Être et agir dans la philosophie de S. Thomas. Bibliothèque des Archives de philosophie. Paris, 1945.

FOREST, A. La structure métaphysique du concret selon S. Thomas d'Aquin. Paris, 1931.

GILSON, E. L'Être et l'essence. Paris, 1948.

GRABMANN, M. Doctrina S. Thomae de distinctione reali inter essentiam et esse ex documentis ineditis saeculi XIII illustrata. Rome, 1924. (Acta hebdomadae thomisticae.)

HABBEL, J. Die Analogie zwischen Gott und Welt nach Thomas von Aquin und Suarez. Fribourg (Switzerland), 1929.

MARC, A. L'idée de l'être chez S. Thomas et dans la scolastique postérieure. Paris, 1931. (Archives de philosophie, 10, 1.)

PIEPER, J. Die Wirklichkeit und das Gute nach Thomas von Aquin. Münster, 1934.

RÉGNON, T. DE. La métaphysique des causes d'après S. Thomas et Albert le Grand. Paris, 1906.

ROLAND-GOSSELIN, M. D. Le 'De ente et essentia' de S. Thomas d'Aquin. Paris, 1926. (Bibliothèque thomiste, 8.)

SCHULEMANN, G. Das Kausalprinzip in der Philosophie des heiligen Thomas von Aquin. Münster, 1915 (Beiträge, 13, 5).

WÉBERT, J. Essai de métaphysique thomiste. Paris, 1926.

And see General Studies.

Natural Theology

GARRIGOU-LAGRANGE, R. God: His Existence and His Nature. 2 vols. Translated by B. Rose. London, 1934–6.

PATTERSON, R. L. The Concept of God in the Philosophy of Aquinas. London, 1933.

ROLFES, E. Die Gottesbeweise bei Thomas von Aquin und Aristoteles. Limburg a.d. Lahn, 1927 (2nd edition).

And see General Studies.

Cosmology

BEEMELMANNS, F. Zeit und Ewigkeit nach Thomas von Aquin. Münster, 1914 (Beiträge, 17, 1).

CHOISNARD, P. Saint Thomas d'Aquin et l'influence des astres. Paris, 1926.

CORNOLDI, G. M. The Physical System of St. Thomas. Translated by E. H. Dering. London, 1895.

MARLING, J. M. The Order of Nature in the Philosophy of St. Thomas Aquinas. Washington, 1934.

And see General Studies.

Psychology

LOTTIN, O. Psychologie et morale aux XIIe et XIII siècles. Tome 1 Problèmes de Psychologie. Louvain, 1942.

MONAHAN, W. B. The Psychology of St. Thomas Aquinas. London, no date.

O'MAHONY, L. E. The Desire of God in the Philosophy of St. Thomas Aquinas. London, 1929.

PEGIS, A. C. St. Thomas and the Problem of the Soul in the Thirteenth Century. Toronto, 1934.

And see General Studies.

Knowledge

GRABMANN, M. Der göttliche Grund menschlicher Wahrheitserkenntnis nach Augustinus und Thomas von Aquin. Cologne,
1924.

HUFNAGEL, A. Intuition und Erkenntnis nach Thomas von Aquin.
Cologne, 1924.

MARÉCHAL, J. Le point de départ de la métaphysique. Cahier 5;
Le thomisme devant la philosophie critique. Louvain, 1926.

MEYER, H. Die Wissenschaftslehre des Thomas von Aquin. Fulda,
1934.

NOEL, L. Notes d'épistémologie thomiste. Louvain, 1925.

PÉGHAIRE, J. Intellectus et Ratio selon S. Thomas d'Aquin. Paris,
1936.

RAHNER, K. Geist in Welt. Zur Metaphysik der endlichen Erkenntnis bei Thomas von Aquin. Innsbruck, 1939.

ROMEYER, B. S. Thomas et notre connaissance de l'esprit humain.
Paris, 1928 (Archives de philosophie, 6, 2).

ROUSSELOT, P. The Intellectualism of St. Thomas. Translated by
Fr. James, O.S.F.C. London, 1935.

TONQUÉDEC, J. DE. Les principes de la philosophie thomiste. La
critique de la connaissance. Paris, 1929 (Bibliothèque des
Archives de philosophie).

VAN RIET, G. L'épistémologie thomiste. Louvain, 1946.

WILPERT, P. Das Problem der Wahrheitssicherung bei Thomas von
Aquin. Münster, 1931 (Beiträge, 30, 3).

Moral Theory

GILSON, E. S. Thomas d'Aquin. (Les moralistes chrétiens.) Paris,
1941 (6th edition).

LEHU, L. La raison règle de la moralité d'après St. Thomas d'Aquin.
Paris, 1930.

LOTTIN, O. Le droit naturel chez S. Thomas et ses prédécesseurs.
Bruges, 1926.

PIEPER, J. Die ontische Grundlage des Sittlichen nach Thomas von
Aquin. Münster, 1929.

ROUSSELOT, P. Pour l'histoire du problème de l'amour au moyen
âge. Münster, 1908 (Beiträge, 6, 6).

SERTILLANGES, A. D. La Philosophie Morale de S. Thomas d'Aquin.
Paris, 1942 (new edition).

Political Theory

DEMONGEOT, M. Le meilleur régime politique selon S. Thomas.
Paris, 1928.

GRABMANN, M. Die Kulturphilosophie des heiligen Thomas von
Aquin. Augsburg, 1925.

KURZ, E. Individuum und Gemeinschaft beim heiligen Thomas von Aquin. Freiburg im/B., 1932.

MICHEL, G. La notion thomiste du bien commun. Paris, 1932.

ROCCA, G. DELLA. La politica di S. Tommaso. Naples, 1934.

ROLAND-GOSSELIN, B. La doctrine politique de S. Thomas d'Aquin. Paris, 1928.

Aesthetic Theory

DE WULF, M. Études historiques sur l'esthétique de S. Thomas d'Aquin. Louvain, 1896.

DYROFF, A. Über die Entwicklung und den Wert der Aesthetik des Thomas von Aquino. Berlin, 1929 (Festgabe Ludwig Stern).

MARITAIN, J. Art and Scholasticism. London, 1930.

Controversies

EHRLE, F. Der Kampf um die Lehre des heiligen Thomas von Aquin in den ersten fünfzig Jahren nach seinem Tode. In *Zeitschrift für katholische Theologie*, 1913.

Chapter XLII: Latin Averroism: Siger of Brabant

Texts

BAEUMKER, C. Die Impossibilia des Siger von Brabant. Münster, 1898 (Beiträge, 2, 6).

BARSOTTI, R. Sigeri de Brabant. De aeternitate mundi. Münster, 1933 (Opuscula et Textus, 13).

DWYER, W. J. L'Opuscule de Siger de Brabant 'De Aeternitate Mundi'. Louvain, 1937.

GRABMANN, M. Die Opuscula De summo bono sive de vita philosophi und De sompniis des Boetius von Dacien. In *Mittelalterliches Geistesleben*, vol. 2. 1936.

Neuaufgefundene Werke des Siger von Brabant und Boetius von Dacien. (Proceedings of the Academy of Munich, Philosophy.) 1924.

MANDONNET, P. Siger de Brabant et l'averroïsme latin. (Les Philosophes Belges, 6.) Louvain, 1908, 1911.

STEGMÜLLER, F. Neugefundene Quaestionen des Sigers von Brabant. In *Recherches de théologie ancienne et médiévale*, 1931.

VAN STEENBERGHEN, F. Siger de Brabant d'après ses œuvres inédits. (Les Philosophes Belges, 12.) Louvain, 1931.

Studies

BAEUMKER, C. Zur Beurteilung Sigers von Brabant. In *Philosophisches Jahrbuch*, 1911.

MANDONNET, P. See above (Les Philosophes Belges, 6–7).

OTTAVIANO, C. S. Tommaso d'Aquino, Saggio contro la dottrina avveroistica dell'unita dell'intelletto. Lanciano, 1930.

SASSEN, F. Siger de Brabant et la double vérité. *Revue néo-scolastique*, 1931.

VAN STEENBERGHEN, F. Les œuvres et la doctrine de Siger de Brabant. Brussels, 1938.
See above (Les Philosophes Belges, 12–13).
Aristote en Occident. Louvain, 1946.

Chapter XLIII: Franciscan Thinkers

1. *Bacon: Texts*

BREWER, J. S. Fratris Rogeri Baconi opera quaedam hactenus inedita. London, 1859.

BRIDGES, J. H. The Opus Maius of Roger Bacon, 2 vols. Oxford, 1897.
Supplementary volume. Oxford, 1900.

BURKE, R. B. The Opus Maius of Roger Bacon. 2 vols. (English). Philadelphia, 1928.

RASHDALL, H. Fratris Rogeri Baconi Compendium studii theologiae. Aberdeen, 1911.

STEELE, R. Opera hactenus inedita Rogeri Baconi. 16 fascicules so far published. Oxford, 1905–40.

Studies

BAEUMKER, C. Roger Bacons Naturphilosophie. Münster, 1916.

CARTON, R. La synthèse doctrinale de Roger Bacon. Paris, 1929.
L'expérience mystique de l'illumination intérieure chez Roger Bacon. Paris, 1924.
L'expérience physique chez Roger Bacon, contribution à l'étude de la méthode et de la science expérimentale au XIIIe siècle. Paris, 1924.

CHARLES, E. Roger Bacon, sa vie, ses ouvrages, ses doctrines. Paris, 1861.

LITTLE, A. G. Roger Bacon, Essays contributed by various writers. Oxford, 1914.

2. *Matthew of Aquasparta: Texts*

Quaestiones disputatae de fide et de cognitione. Quaracchi, 1903.

A. Daniels (Beiträge, 8, 1–2; Münster, 1909) gives extracts from the Commentary on the *Sentences*.

Studies

LONGPRÉ, E. Matthieu d'Aquasparte. *Dictionnaire de théologie catholique*, vol. 10. 1928.

3. *Peter John Olivi: Texts*

B. Jansen. Petri Johannis Olivi Quaestiones in 2 librum Sententiarum. 3 vols. Quaracchi, 1922–6.

Petri Joannis Provencalis Quodlibeta. Venice, 1509.

Studies

CALLAEY, F. Olieu ou Olivi. *Dictionnaire de théologie catholique*, vol. 11. 1931.

JANSEN, B. Die Erkenntnislehre Olivis. Berlin, 1931.

Die Unsterblichkeitsbeweise bei Olivi und ihre philosophiegeschichtliche Bedeutung. In *Franziskanische Studien*. 1922.

Quonam spectet definitio Concilii Viennensis de anima. In *Gregorianum*, 1920.

4. *Roger Marston: Texts*

Fratris Rogeri Marston, O.F.M., Quaestiones disputatae. Quaracchi, 1932.

Studies

BELMOND, S. La théorie de la connaissance d'après Roger Marston. In *France franciscaine,* 1934.

GILSON, E. Roger Marston, un cas d'augustinisme avicennisant. In *Archives d'histoire doctrinale et littéraire du moyen âge*, 1932.

JARRAUX, L. Pierre Jean Olivi, sa vie, sa doctrine. In *Études franciscaines*, 1933.

PELSTER, F. Roger Marston, ein englischer Vertreter des Augustinismus. In *Scholastik*, 1928.

5. *Richard of Middleton: Texts*

Quodlibeta. Venice, 1509; Brescia, 1591.

Supra quatuor libros Sententiarum. 4 vols. Brescia, 1591.

Study

HOCEDEZ, E. Richard de Middleton, sa vie, ses œuvres, sa doctrine. Paris, 1925.

6. *Raymond Lull: Texts*

Opera omnia, I. Salzinger. 8 vols. Mainz, 1721–42.

Obras de Ramón Lull. Palma, 1745.

O. Keicher (see below) has published the *Declaratio Raymundi* in the Beiträge series.

Studies

BLANES, F. SUREDA. El beato Ramón Lull, su época, su vida, sus obras, sus empresas. Madrid, 1934.

CARRERAS Y ARTAU, T. & J. Historia de la Filosofía Española. Filosofía Christiana de los Siglos XIII al XIV. Vols. 1 and 2. Madrid, 1939–43.

KEICHER, O. Raymundus Lullus und seine Stellung zur arabischen Philosophie. Münster, 1909 (Beiträge, 7, 4–5).

LONGPRÉ, E. Lulle. In *Dictionnaire de théologie catholique*, vol. 9.

OTTAVIANO, C. L'ars compendiosa de Raymond Lulle. Paris, 1930.

PEERS, E. A. Fool of Love; the Life of Ramon Lull. London, 1946.

PROBST, J. H. Caractère et origine des idées du bienheureux Raymond Lulle. Toulouse, 1912.

La mystique de Raymond Lull et l'Art de Contemplation. Münster, 1914 (Beiträge, 13, 2–3).

Chapter XLIV: Giles of Rome and Henry of Ghent

1. Giles of Rome: Texts

Ancient editions. See Ueberweg-Geyer, Die patristische und scholastische Philosophie, pp. 532–3.

HOCEDEZ, E. Aegidii Romani Theoremata de esse et essentia, texte précedé d'une introduction historique et critique. Louvain, 1930.

KOCH, J. Giles of Rome; Errores Philosophorum. Critical Text with Notes and Introduction. Translated by J. O. Riedl. Milwaukee, 1944.

SCHOLZ, R. Aegidius Romanus, de ecclesiastica potestate. Weimar, 1929.

Studies

BRUNI, G. Egidio Romano e la sua polemica antitomista. In *Rivista di filosofia neoscolastica*, 1934.

HOCEDEZ, E. Gilles de Rome et saint Thomas. In *Mélanges Mandonnet*. Paris, 1930.

Gilles de Rome et Henri de Gand. In *Gregorianum*, 1927.

2. Henry of Ghent: Texts

Summa theologica. 2 vols. Paris, 1520; 3 vols. Ferrara, 1646.

Quodlibeta, 2 vols. Paris, 1518; Venice, 1608.

Studies

HOCEDEZ, E. Gilles de Rome et Henri de Gand. In *Gregorianum*, 1927.

PAULUS, J. Henri de Gand. Essai sur les tendances de sa métaphysique. Paris, 1938.

Texts   *Chapters XLV–L: John Duns Scotus*

WADDING, L. Opera Omnia. Lyons, 1639. 12 vols.
> Opera Omnia (2nd edition). Paris (Vivès), 1891–5.
> 26 vols.

B. J. D. Scoti Commentaria Oxoniensia (on the first and second
> books of the *Sentences*). Quaracchi, 1912–14. 2 vols.

Tractatus de Primo Principio. Quaracchi, 1910.

MULLER, P. M., O.F.M. Tractatus de Primo Principio. Editionem
curavit Marianius. Freiburg im/B., 1941.

The critical edition of Scotus's works is yet to come.
> Cf. *Ratio criticae editionis operum omnium J. Duns Scoti Relatio
> a Commissione Scotistica exhibita Capitulo Generali Fratrum
> Minorum Assisii A.D.* 1939 *celebrato.* Rome, 1939.

For a summary of recent controversy and articles on the works of
Scotus, as on his doctrine, cf.:

BETTONI, E., O.F.M. Vent'anni di Studi Scotisti (1920–40). Milan,
1943.

Studies

BELMOND, S., O.F.M. Essai de synthèse philosophique du Scotisme.
> Paris, Bureau de 'la France Franciscaine'.
> 1933.
> Dieu. Existence et Cognoscibilité. Paris,
> 1913.

BETTONI, E., O.F.M. L'ascesa a Dio in Duns Scoto. Milan, 1943.

DE BASLY, D., O.F.M. Scotus Docens ou Duns Scot enseignant la
philosophie, la théologie, la mystique. Paris, 'La France
Franciscaine'. 1934.

GILSON, E. Avicenne et le point de départ de Duns Scot. Archives
> d'histoire doctrinale et littéraire du moyen âge, vol. 1,
> 1927.
> Les seize premiers Theoremata et la pensée de Duns
> Scot. Archives d'histoire doctrinale et littéraire du
> moyen âge. 1937–8.

GRAJEWSKI, M. J., O.F.M. The Formal Distinction of Duns Scotus.
Washington, 1944.

HARRIS, C. Duns Scotus. Oxford, 1927. 2 vols. (Makes copious use
of the unauthentic *De Rerum Principio*.)

HEIDEGGER, M. Die Kategorien — und Bedeutungslehre des Duns
Scotus. Tübingen, 1916.

KRAUS, J. Die Lehre des J. Duns Skotus von der Natura Communis.
Fribourg (Switzerland), 1927.

LANDRY, B. Duns Scot. Paris, 1922.

LONGPRÉ, E., O.F.M. La philosophie du B. Duns Scot. Paris, 1924. (Contains a reply to Landry's work.)

MESSNER, R., O.F.M. Schauendes und begriffliches Erkennen nach Duns Skotus. Freiburg im/B., 1942.

MINGES, P., O.F.M. Der angeblich exzessive Realismus des Duns Skotus. 1908 (Beiträge, 8, 1).

J. Duns Scoti Doctrina Philosophica et Theologica quoad res praecipuas proposita et exposita. Quaracchi. 1930. 2 vols. (Cites spurious writings; but a very useful work.)

PELSTER, F. Handschriftliches zu Skotus mit neuen Angaben über sein Leben. Franzisk. Studien, 1923.

ROHMER, J. La finalité morale chez les théologiens dès saint Augustin à Duns Scot. Paris, 1939.

INDEX OF NAMES

(The principal references are printed in heavy figures. References followed by an asterisk refer to the Appendices)

INDEX OF SUBJECTS

History 85f, 429
History of Philosophy 10ff, 15, 49, 244, 485, 562
Human Acts *see* Acts, Human
Humanism 169, 565
Human Nature *see* Man
Hylomorphism St. Bonaventure 271-4, 278ff, 578*; St. Thomas 325-32, 376, 562; *also* 35, 102, 170f, 183ff, 189, 202, 222ff, 455f, 462f, 513, 579*
  Hylomorphic composition in spirits, *see* Composition
  See also Form, Matter, Soul and Body
Hypostasis *see Suppositum*
Hypostatic Union 29, 102

Idea Abstract 225, 390f *and see* Abstraction
  Analogical 394ff *and see* Analogy
  Composite 137f, 520
  Divine *see* Ideas, Divine
  General 138, 388
  Innate *see* Innate Ideas
  Mathematical 138, 153
  Universal: *Epistemology see* Ideas, Objective Validity of
  Psychology see Idea, Universal (Existence); Ideas, Origin of
  Ontology see Universals
Idea, Universal (Existence of) 138f, 144, 150, 388f, 449f, 490
Idealism, Absolute 124
  Subjective 390
Ideas, Divine St. Bonaventure 259-62; St. Thomas 358ff, 427, 562; also 28, 30, 33, 60, 72f, 126, 131, 170f, 189, 235, 449, 454, 466, 469, 529f, 562
Ideas, Innate *see* Innate Ideas
Ideas, Objective Validity of 137-40, 143f, 151, 225, 390, 484, 494, 512. *See also* Analogy
Ideas, Origin of (*Psychology*) 59, 66, 139, 189f, 224f, 285f, 385, 389f, 449f, 466f, 471, 497, 501, 512f
  See also Abstraction, Psychological conditions of, Illumination, Divine and Innate Ideas
Ideas, Platonic Theory of 16, 28,

30, 33, 57, 59f, 62, 73, 77, 79, 247, 259ff, 287, 327, 390
  See also Prototypes
Identity Theory (Universals) 147f
Idolaters 253
Ignorance of God *see* God, Existence of
  of Natural Law 408
  Causes of 444
Illumination, Divine St. Augustine 61, 62-7, 83; Arabians 189f, 194 and n., 195; St. Bonaventure 256f, 286-9, 291-2, 564; St. Thomas 389, 426, 564; Scotus 483, 497; *also* 31, 165, 200, 225, 231f, 237f, 298, 445, 449ff, 453f, 465ff, 473f, 483
Image, mental and abstract idea 150, 388f, 449f
  Composite 388; Generic 388
  See also Phantasm
Image of God (*Imago Dei*) St. Bonaventure 268f, 278, 281, 285, 290, 554; also 35, 37, 127
Imagination 143, 231, 282ff, 320f, 334, 379, 490f, 520
Immaterial Reality, Knowledge of 392-5, 501
Immortality of Human Soul St. Bonaventure 247, 264ff, 278, 280; St. Thomas 264, 383-7, 425f; Scotus 484f, 528, 541ff; also 24f, 30, 34, 78f, 193, 194n., 198, 204, 223f, 298f, 435, 441, 452n., 585*
Impetus, theory of 451
Incarnation 100, 128, 184, 194
Inclination *see* Appetite
Indetermination 471
Indifference Theory (Universals) 147f
Indifferent Acts *see* Acts, Indifferent
Indirect Power of Church over State 415
Individuality 273, 493, 511ff, 516f, 522
  See also Individuation
Individuals and the Universal 139-44, 147, 150-5, 170, 189, 327, 463, 469, 492f
  The I. and Society 417f, 428, 583*
  See also Singulars, Knowledge of